Forgotten WEAPON

Forgotten

WILLIAM F. ALTHOFF

WEAPON

u.s. navy airships and the u-boat war

NAVAL INSTITUTE PRESS
Annapolis, Maryland

Naval Institute Press
291 Wood Road
Annapolis, Maryland 21402

Library of Congress Cataloging-in-Publication Data
Althoff, William F.
Forgotten weapon : U.S. Navy airships and the U-boat war / William Althoff.
p. cm.
Includes bibliographical references and index.
ISBN 978-1-59114-010-8 (alk. paper)
1. World War, 1939-1945—Aerial operations, American. 2. United States. Navy—Aviation—History—20th century. 3. Military airships—United States—History—20th century. 4. Anti-submarine aircraft—United States—History—20th century. 5. Anti-submarine warfare—United States—History—20th century. 6. Submarines (Ships)—Germany—History—20th century. 7. World War, 1939–1945—Naval operations--Submarine. I. Title.
D790.3.A55 2009
940.54'5160973—dc22

2009009086

Printed in the United States of America

15 14 13 12 11 10 09 10 9 8 7 6 5 4 3 2
First printing

Interior design and composition by Chris Gamboa-Onrubia, Fineline Graphics LLC

To those who serve.

Contents

Preface

IN AN ERA OF COMPUTERS, missiles, and electronic warfare, the naval nonrigid airship (or blimp) seems an anachronism—a twentieth-century platform predestined to obscurity. Indeed, the widespread ignorance of its existence is remarkable. It is easy to dismiss the airship as a military aberration, but this explains nothing. What deserves examination are the naval, political, and technological environments in which the platform had to operate in the decade from 1935 to 1945—until, as the 1960s opened, U.S. Navy lighter-than-air (LTA) was overwhelmed by competing systems that offered more attractive trade-offs.

The writer has tried to insist on the blimp's unique inshore capabilities, to call for a measure of understanding of the problems that afflicted the program before and during the urgent antisubmarine campaign in the North and South Atlantic.

Lighter-than-air was deemed a resource by its proponents, a competitor by many others. Its combat (and Cold War) contributions notwithstanding, scant evidence of the naval airship survives. This work will refresh the public memory regarding a viable though banished military technology.

Acknowledgments

FEW HISTORIES ARE RESEARCHED in isolation; certainly, this project was not. The writer has incurred numerous obligations.

Archival sources were supplemented with oral-history research supported in part by a major grant from the New Jersey Historical Commission. A Ramsey Fellowship in Naval Aviation History (1999–2000) by the National Air and Space Museum (NASM), Smithsonian Institution, supported much of the original research. Here I am indebted to Tom D. Crouch, Senior Curator. At NASM's Garber facility, Marilyn Graskowiak and staff assisted with the George H. Mills and Garland Fulton collections. The finding aid prepared by Mr. Allan Janus, Museum Specialist, was essential for navigating the writer through the Mills and Fulton Collections. The assistance granted by Mr. Phil Edwards, technical information specialist at NASM, improved this work enormously.

Audio-recorded interviews were held with Capt. Maurice M. Bradley, USN (Ret.), Capt. W. E. Delong, USN (Ret.), Capt. M. H. Eppes, USN (Ret.), Cdr. James A. Hotham, USN (Ret.), Capt. John C. Kane, USN (Ret.), Mr. Charles Kauffman, Capt. Frederick N. Klein, USN (Ret.), Cdr. Ben B. Levitt, USN (Ret.), Mr. Roland Mayer, Cdr. Edward R. McMillan, USN (Ret.), Rear Adm. George E. Pierce, USN (Ret.), Cdr. Robert Shannon, USN (Ret.), Lt. Harris F. Smith, USNR (Ret.), Capt. L. Russell Ulrich, USN (Ret.), Lt. J. Gordon Vaeth, USN (Ret.), Cdr. Gerald E. Wheeler, USN (Ret.), and Cdr. Richard W. Widdicombe, USN (Ret.).

Self-recorded reminiscences by Rear Adm. Richard S. Andrews, USN (Ret.), and Cdr. John B. Rieker, USN (Ret.), must be acknowledged.

Correspondence contributed much. Statements, letters, and e-mail support arrived from Mr. Charles M. Bowen, Capt. Douglas Cordiner, USN (Ret.), Capt. J. H. Cruse, USN (Ret.), Captain Eppes [courtesy Evelyn Eppes Azzaretto], Mr. Winfield E. Fromm, Rear Adm. D. Ward Harrigan, USN (Ret.), Lt. (jg) James H. Hughes, USN (Ret.), Cdr. Harold W. Johnston, USN (Ret.), Mr. Charles W. Long, Cdr. Charles A. Mills, USN (Ret.), Mr. Norman Polmar, ACBM, George W. Roberts, USN (Ret.), Lt. Cdr. James W. Spenser, USNR (Ret.), Capt. Emmett J. Sullivan, USN (Ret.), Lieutenant Vaeth, and Commander Wheeler.

Mr. Jeff Noakes made available his superb research at the National Archives of Canada, in Ottawa. Mr. Barry Jan Countryman also provided Canada-related records. Always helpful, Mr. Richard G. Van Treuren loaned materials and outlined his to-date findings from the voluminous records of Tenth Fleet. Research conducted by Mr. James R. Shock also proved helpful. An indispensable compendium, *Statistical Summary of United States Fleet Airship Operations in World War II,* came to the author courtesy of Lt. Cdr. James Punderson, USN (Ret.). Captain Klein offered insights into the wartime LTA organization.

Images for this work come courtesy of Mr. Eric Brothers, Captain Eppes, Captain Kane, Captain Klein, Mr. Eugene P. Moccia, Lt. (jg) H. H. O'Clare, USN (Ret.), Lt. Herbert R. Rowe, USN (Ret.), Lt. Cdr. Leonard E. Schellberg, USN (Ret.), Mr. David Smith, and Commander Widdicombe. Thanks are due particularly to Lieutenant Smith for his support and generosity. Additional images were obtained from the Naval Historical Center, the U.S. Naval Institute, and from collections held by NASM, the University of Texas (Rosendahl Collection), and the still-picture holdings of the National Archives and Records Administration

Thanks to Mr. Langdon H. Fulton, information pertaining to his father, Cdr. Garland Fulton, USN (Ret.), was incorporated.

The late Vice Adm. T. G. W. Settle, USN (Ret.), remains an inspiration, the work of Dr. Richard K. Smith a model of historiography.

Librarians Mary Kearns-Kaplan and Dorothy McLaughlin Alibrando were again invaluable—and a delight to the author.

I am inexpressibly grateful to Penny for her steadfast support, patience, and understanding.

Forgotten WEAPON

We started the war practically from scratch.

—T. G. W. Settle, 1946

The wartime growth of the U.S. Navy was a prodigy, an essential condition of victory; never before in history was a naval war won by a fleet that did not exist when that war began.

—Eric Larrabee, 1987

Introduction: End and Beginning

In the time available to it in the U.S. Navy—which is to say the interwar period of aeronautics—the rigid airship failed to prove its value to naval warfare. Derided as exorbitant and militarily useless—slow, vulnerable, and subject to weather—the big, rigid-type airships (ZR, in naval parlance) met unending criticism, much of it uninformed. As well, the frustration of commercial plans hurt naval lighter-than-air. Merchant airship bills had come within a whisker of congressional approval, only to have passage skitter away in reaction to crashes—and to lobbying from airplane interests fearful that airmail subsidies and the passenger market would not support both airships and their own transoceanic ventures. By 1938, the tide running against it, the airship's reputation was taking on water at an alarming rate.

Carrier aviation and flying boats were the major constituents of U.S. naval aviation in this period. Higher-echelon officers were heavier-than-air (HTA) pilots—men inclined to subordinate the needs and development of "the inflated competition." Accordingly, scant effort was made to find a place for airships in naval aeronautics. In short, the platform performed before an audience predisposed against it. Among pilot-advocates familiar with the type, at least one was obliged to concede, "I think the [rigid] airships had about had their day by 1935. In my opinion, it was the PBYs [multiengine patrol seaplanes] that brought their usefulness to an end. For the $4,000,000 the ships cost one could provide a squadron of 12 PBYs which were certainly less susceptible to destruction and could cover a wider and faster scouting-search curve than the airships. . . . Besides, the enormous ground crews made it difficult to provide landing places other than highly qualified bases."[1]

Properly, the rigid airship was an instrument of very-long-range reconnaissance over ocean wastes. Decades before earth-orbiting satellites, naval scouting was ordinarily performed by cruisers; a ZR carrying airplanes could advance a scouting line at effectively two or three times a cruiser's own speed. Moreover, airships offered a performance unmatched by any airplane in terms of lift, range, and endurance. Still, the strategic possibilities of the lighter-than-air "carrier" were never fully appraised. As historian Richard K. Smith notes, its trials were neither realistic nor exhaustive, nor can they be considered conclusive. But the decision against the type has been final.

[Opposite] USS *Macon* (ZRS 5), Naval Air Station Sunnyvale (Moffett Field), California, 19 June 1934. Macon and sister ship were prototypes for a projected squadron of fleet-type airship-carrier scouts (ZRS) that were never authorized. Following loss of *Macon*, in 1935, the lighter-than-air (LTA) program languished. The 1939–45 war realized a renaissance. (U.S. Navy photograph, courtesy Capt. J. C. Kane, USN [Ret.])

The airship "carrier" was an instrument of very-long-range reconnaissance. This Curtiss F9C-2 was assigned to the HTA Unit of *Macon*. Note the skyhook mounted on the upper wing. (Capt. J.C. Kane, USN [Ret.])

The airship's opponents did not act out of sheer perversity; it was a very expensive machine in its first costs, and its prototype period promised to be long, even for only a few units. There was an honest conviction that the airship was unreliable, its utility marginal, and there were always other needs to which funds could be applied with quicker and more certain results.[2]

The political, military, and technological environments in which the naval airship had to operate were changing. By 1940, the crying need was for thousands of airplanes, not large airships—high-cost platforms with a public record of failure. In consequence, the tiny LTA organization stood isolated, banished operationally to a single naval air base from which to conduct experimentation and development, using the few ships then in inventory.

Rear Adm. Ernest J. King, Chief of the Bureau of Aeronautics (BuAer) from 1933 to 1936, had proven a fair if guarded steward of lighter-than-air.[3] King had little enthusiasm for the rigid airship, but he could not dismiss its potential as the only available instrument of very-long-range reconnaissance. With USS *Akron* (ZRS 4) lost and only USS *Macon* (ZRS 5) operational, the admiral remarked, "I am trying [1934] to keep an open mind on the airship question, but the more I see of airships the more I can visualize a useful field for them in searching operations, especially in conjunction with their airplanes, provided we can get the airships to perform."[4]

Beyond *Akron* and *Macon* (1931–35), King continued to believe that the rigid airship had a place in the navy. As well, events would demonstrate his appreciation for the nonrigid.[5] In broad dimension, the importance of naval aviation was plain to King, and it had been since his Naval Academy days. Yet, as wartime Commander in Chief, U.S. Fleet (Cominch) and Chief of Naval Operations (he "wore two hats"), he resisted the antisubmarine potential of aircraft until 1943—a seeming contradiction that played a crucial role in the first phases of the North Atlantic battle.

USS *Macon* (ZRS 5), the navy's last commissioned rigid, had foundered in February 1935, effectively ending the ZR era. Futility ensued. Flight operations retreated to Naval Air Station (NAS) Lakehurst, New Jersey. Until the 1939 European war and resulting renaissance of the nonrigid type, an extended twilight persisted. Little more than a shell, its strength hollowed out by missed opportunities, crashes, and internal rivalries, naval LTA comprised an odd assortment of increasingly obsolete aircraft. In June 1936, King turned over the affairs of the Bureau of Aeronautics to Rear Adm. Arthur B. Cook. Bureaucratic resistance (or worse) to LTA pervaded the bureau and the Navy Department.[6]

On Constitution Avenue in Washington, D.C., Capt. Garland Fulton, USN, headed BuAer's Lighter-than-Air Design Section. Polite but probing, analytical, calm and deliberate under stress, "Froggy" Fulton had been indispensable to Rear Adm. William A. Moffett during his tenure as Chief of BuAer (1921–33). Moffett's successor, Rear Admiral King (a taskmaster who suffered no fools), relied equally as much upon him.[7] LTA still held great potential, but it also had great problems. "It seems to me," Fulton observed, "that if we are to profit at all by lessons of the last war that lighter-than-air can not be overlooked as a type of craft which has proved itself useful in convoy and anti-submarine patrol work. If we are to need this type of craft in the next war, and I believe we will, then we certainly should develop them in peace and use them in naval operations. The development of blimps has lagged outrageously since the war."[8]

As politics played out, naval opinion—when it considered airships at all—acknowledged that blimps were useful for harbor or coastal patrol, convoying, mine location, antisubmarine work, and for such fleet utility chores as photography and torpedo recovery. Nonetheless, new construction was deemed non-urgent: "The . . . nonrigid type of airship [blimp] will probably have a place in coast defense in future wars as it did in the World War. But this type is not suitable for use with the Fleet. Furthermore, these small blimps have reached approximately the state of development and can be put into quantity production in very short time, and it is therefore not essential to produce this type in any considerable quantities prior to the outbreak of war."[9]

A resuscitated concern for antisubmarine (A/S) measures seeded a wisp of support as early as 1937, when two blimps were projected for the 1938 navy budget—scraps off the table. Prospectively, no extensive building program was yet visualized. Instead, as recommended by the General Board, the long-discussed project of a rigid for training purposes was authorized in the first Vinson Naval Expansion Act.[10] This legislation was named for the chairman of the House Committee on Naval Affairs, Carl Vinson (D-Ga.). Vinson, a frequent spokesman for the administration on naval matters, was an advocate of national preparedness and a friend of the navy. The trainer (the General Board had specified) must be of three million cubic feet and carry at least two airplanes. This was to be the controversial ZRN airship, a replacement for the grounded USS *Los Angeles* (ZR 3).[11] Rear Adm. Cook, chief of the bureau in 1937–38, would make the case for the ZRN, to further explore the large airship's potential as an airborne carrier.

Fulton was assessing retirement from the naval service. In a frank appraisal, meantime, he outlined the status of the nonrigid for Cook: "I wish to call attention to the wide spread between existing blimp activities (facilities, equipment, personnel) and what we would be expected to do in event of war. If the peace time blimp effort is to be something worth while . . . it is going to need more attention than has been given to it in the past few years when nearly all L.T.A. effort went to rigid airships."[12]

At Lakehurst, the sole operating/experimental base for airships, flight time intensified: 2,400 hours in calendar 1937 for the most active trio of training blimps (ZNs), over 3,300 hours during fiscal 1938 with the ships available—an anemic force.[13] These figures implied an average of

[Opposite] Prewar Naval Air Station (NAS) Lakehurst, New Jersey. The syllabus for student Naval Aviators (Airship) called for six months of primary training: ground school plus flight training in free and kite balloons, the nonrigid type (blimp), then rigid airships—"as circumstances permit." (Lt. H. F. Smith, USNR [Ret.])

about eighty hours per ship per month over two years of operations. The portable mast had been introduced, mooring-out techniques improved, mechanical handling applied. To seaward, cooperative exercises (torpedo recovery, visibility and marker-buoy tests, photographic work) were arranged with the submarine base at New London, Connecticut. These services by airship were of inestimable worth: practically (in terms of experience) and politically, as well as fiscally. Replacement torpedoes stood in limited supply: "Every possible precaution must be taken against losses during practice approaches." Also, convoy methods were developed, then practiced with chance merchantmen. "It has seemed to me," Fulton advised, "that the mission of Lakehurst (in addition to training) is to develop and perfect doctrine, or at least the basis of doctrine, for modern uses of blimps in a coastal area such as Lakehurst can serve." Still, distances to the fleet made it impracticable to exercise with surface units or conduct peacetime chores. "Hopefully, the creation of an Atlantic Squadron may offer chances of useful cooperation by blimps."[14]

War plans called for nonrigids to be used as district aircraft, operating with coastal convoys and cooperating with surface escorts for A/S protection. But economy of expenditure had been the cry; years of peace and penury had tolerated no more than "spasmodic" LTA construction. Further, an industrial base was lacking.[15] In certain districts, shoreside facilities—hangars, masts, helium storage—were nonexistent. Nor were clear plans in place for acquiring "even the sketchiest facilities" from which blimps could operate.[16] Lakehurst was a duty station for thirty-five officers and 240 men—roughly the complement of one U.S. destroyer. "In particular," Fulton wrote, "there are no facilities sufficiently near Fleet activities to permit blimps to exercise near the Fleet and to be of service to it." In addition, the personnel situation stood as "critical":

> We have relatively only a handful of trained airship personnel and this is rapidly dwindling through such causes as normal attrition, nonselection for promotion, loss of interest in a project with no apparent future. Many of our trained enlisted men are now going out into the fleet reserve or are irrevocably lost to other more attractive parts of the service, or ordered to such other duties because our present needs do not require them. We have trained no airship enlisted men in the last three years, and only a handful in the last four years.[17]

By law, "naval aviators (airship)" had to log ZR hours; no designation existed for blimp pilots. Also, no reserve status existed for either army or navy airship personnel. In sum, the gap between the status quo and a wartime organization yawned wide. The uncertain situation held "unsatisfactory if we really expect to use blimps in war."[18]

Carl Vinson was favorably disposed toward airships, Admiral Cook somewhat less so. "I foresee two blimps operating at Lakehurst," the admiral told the General Board in February 1937, "two on the Pacific Coast, say from Sunnyvale with some operating facilities near the Fleet; two in Hawaii; and ultimately two in the Canal Zone; a total of eight. This peace-time nucleus ought to permit fairly rapid expansion to the number of blimps that are estimated as necessary in war."[19]

Admiral Cook's "hasty survey" looked to a point between five and seven years off. Construction had been cut from the 1937 naval appropriations bill; in the Naval Expansion Act of 1938, however, modest funds ($275,000) were included for two blimps—a trainer and an improved,

larger ship for coastal work. This was *K-2*—envelope volume 420,000 cubic feet, contract price $238,000. The drought seemed done with. Much more design work, construction, and training would be necessary, however, if airships were to make any substantial two-ocean contribution to World War II. President Franklin D. Roosevelt, a nonbeliever in large airships, had no particular support for their procurement, though he did not take a position against it. Even with a favorable navy recommendation, in the event, Roosevelt was not about to sanction the ZRN; he rejected the proposal peremptorily. The politics relative to commercial rigids had soured: "As to any purely American plan of commercial airships, I am not very hopeful. The job of organizing the necessary political support to get the required financial aid to start these airships will be difficult to obtain

unless the group that does it has plenty of money to spend on propaganda and education. The rigid airship is so closely allied with Germany, in the public minds, that anything German at the present time seems to be taboo with the politicians."[20]

Secretary of the Navy Claude A. Swanson had, for his part, left the development of rigid airships to industry; further, he was reluctant to spend three million dollars on the ZRN—construction of which Vinson had assented to.[21] The Navy Department did not want any such ship, anyway: "The Navy Department does not recommend at the present time the construction of any rigid airships. This decision is based on past experience with these airships, and on the fact that, in the opinion of the Navy Department, their scouting missions can be better accomplished at much less cost with long range flying boats [PBYs]."[22]

Responsibility for procurement and production rests upon the secretary of the navy, as head of the department. In his report for fiscal year 1939, Rear Adm. John Towers, USN (Cook's relief as Chief BuAer), urged upon the secretary "a moderate building program and continue training personnel in non-rigid airships." This recommendation was to resurface unchanged in the bureau's report for fiscal year (FY) 1941, which also held this: "The small group of nonrigid airships at the

NAS Lakehurst have been operated on a more ambitious level than heretofore, with gratifying results. Especially noteworthy have been the simulated patrol services and particularly in various exercises with submarines, where the ability of airships to keep water areas under close scrutiny are proving valuable. Notable improvements in methods of mooring and refueling nonrigid airships, both on shore and on the water, have been effective."[23]

Pursuing an association begun at the Naval Academy, King and Fulton kept in close contact after orders took King to various fleet assignments.[24] Late in 1938, Fulton expressed his professional dismay to the then Commander Aircraft, Battle Force. An undersea warfare platform, Fulton wrote, was hiding in plain sight. Airships were either necessary—or nothing:

> At the moment, the whole lighter-than-air situation looks very dark. . . . This would be too bad as it would mean the temporary end of a branch of aeronautical science that is still capable of useful service. The lessons of the World War and the useful service contributed by blimps seem largely forgotten. I feel it is going to take strong talk and active interest by influential people in aeronautics to avoid having L.T.A. die out. Of course, if this is what considered naval policy demands, then we had better amend war plans and get out of the airship business.

Fulton sought a nudge. "One of the difficulties . . . is there is no spokesman of high rank who is pointing out how and when airships might be usefully employed. Is it too much to solicit your interest to the extent of putting in a word for L.T.A. when opportunity presents?"[25]

A gray eminence in BuAer, Fulton was a lonely (if respected) voice striving to refloat a moribund program.

The Munich conference of September 1938 gave Adolf Hitler the Sudeten districts of Czechoslovakia in return for a paper promise of good behavior. A building sense of dread notwithstanding, America failed to appreciate the growing danger from overseas. When naval needs soared, however, the doubters were to swallow their skepticism. Engineering staffs and industrial plants ramped up to unprecedented rates of war-induced production, in a rapidly changing technological environment. As this pertained to airships, the rigid type proved untenable but the precursor *K-2* nonrigid a windfall—dozens would be built to its design. Through contract orders to Goodyear Aircraft, the navy, its contractors, and civilian scientists would build rapidly on the capabilities of the type, improvising and innovating along the way.

Decisions depend inevitably on the circumstances of the moment. September 1939's first week saw the outbreak of war. President Roosevelt proclaimed the neutrality of the United States and directed the navy to organize a Neutrality Patrol—the first impact of the European war on the U.S. Navy. Three days later, he declared a limited national emergency. To extend sea control over the western Atlantic, the CNO ordered the commander of the Atlantic Squadron to establish combined air and surface reconnaissance—that is, reporting and tracking any air, surface, or submarine units of belligerent powers in the nation's sea approaches. Within weeks, New York and Philadelphia newspapers had added the navy's blimps to active patrol forces.

In the eastern Atlantic and its approaches, the United Kingdom was mounting a spirited defense against U-boats (as German submarines were called). The sea lanes had to be kept open.

[Opposite] Statically "light," *TC-14* is landed high, 19 December 1939. Granted weak support from its command establishment, the U.S. Army Air Service abandoned airships in 1937. LTA officers were reassigned to heavier-than-air (HTA) and army equipment offered to the navy, notably *TC-13* and *TC-14*. Developed for coastal flying, each was superior to any nonrigid then in navy inventory. (Lt. Cdr. L. E. Schellberg, USN [Ret.])

Counteractions were yet weak. Germany's objective: naval strangulation, then invasion, so as to decide the war rapidly in Berlin's favor.

England was dependent in every respect on seaborne supply for food and the import of raw materials. The German navy therefore would interrupt these sea communications. Building a fleet to fight the British navy was impractical. The remaining method, then: to attack sea communications quickly by exploiting the U-boat as the means to penetrate "the main areas of English sea communications in spite of British sea supremacy on the surface."[26]

In light of world conditions, talk of a two-ocean U.S. Navy had grown urgent. Time was ticking down. "We must have an adequate fleet—now," Carl Vinson told newsmen. In terms of shipbuilding, a new $1.3 billion naval expansion program was authorized. In one fiscal year, the "Total, Aviation, Navy" figure swelled from $48 million (FY 1939) to nearly $111.5 million (FY 1940).[27]

A former chairman of the Senate Naval Affairs Committee, Secretary Swanson despised airships. Assistant Secretary Charles Edison, in contrast, thought them a victim of high cost and overreaction to crashes; in his view, the navy had not built, much less operated, a sufficient number to decide their value. In 1939, the long-ailing Swanson died, and Edison was appointed to succeed him. When the acting secretary inquired as to immediate steps, King and Fulton recommended approving and implementing the last General Board policy—a combined ZR and blimp program. Citing Fulton's impending retirement, King urged Edison to commission a special status report on lighter-than-air.

Prepared at Edison's directive, written by Fulton during the winter of 1939–40, the King-Fulton Report was a concise summary of the situation as of 1940.[28] It pointed to the need of a national policy with regard to LTA and observed that ZR development by the navy—custodian of the type—was but partially completed. It urged resumption. It called for keeping the large airplane-carrying airship in the picture but recommended deferring immediate construction in favor of commercial rigids. Lighter-than-air carriers, the report observed, offered "decided possibilities" as strategic scouts immune from mines, torpedoes, submarines. Operating airplanes from airships had been "arrested before its full possibilities could be appraised." This study (as Fulton remarked) "really contains nothing new, but merely rounds up all the conservative, sound, recommendations made in recent years and tries to ask the question—why is nothing being done?"

For that reason, and considering what was to come (and not come), the report bears quoting:

> For the past five years the lighter-than-air situation in the navy has either been static or growing worse due to uncertainties as to the attitude or future policies of the Department with reference to lighter-than-air matters. This indefiniteness in the Navy Department's position has been a handicap not only as it relates to the Department's own program, but has served also to retard or discourage the development and establishment of commercial airship service and the availability of such airships as naval auxiliaries.
>
> The total effort expended on lighter-than-air developments in the past twenty years is infinitesimal in comparison with the effort expended in other aeronautical developments. Definite improvements in lighter-than-air equipment are available, ready for application.

Regarding the nonrigid type, the report recommended additional procurements, bases for airships on both coasts, expeditionary sites in Hawaii and the Canal Zone, and—as opportunity afforded—facilities in the Caribbean and northwestern United States. Lakehurst should continue as the center of Atlantic Coast activities, and Sunnyvale, if and when available, should be made the center for Pacific operations.[29] "Nonrigid airships, or blimps, have demonstrated naval value. They are useful for coastal and harbor patrol work, and for the escort and control of shipping. They are an economical means of meeting certain patrol requirements. Further construction of this type of airship is warranted, as is extension of facilities from which to operate them, until important coastal areas are adequately covered."

The King-Fulton Report anticipated future needs and developments—a prospectus whose essence two years later became strategic as well as operating doctrine. Meantime, a program stalled. Still, "an enormous, pent-up national energy had suddenly been released and aviation in all its aspects fizzed and hollered and kicked in the intensity of rebirth."[30]

The "minimum program" was no more than implementation of the General Board's program of 1937, the report of which—ignored by Swanson—was reaffirmed by the Board in October 1939. This would hold the progress already made, advance the art, and "place airships in a position where they can be of real service as part of the Navy and to our commerce." Projected over the years 1941–45 at an estimated cost of ten million dollars, the program called for by the King-Fulton Report included the three-million-cubic-foot ZRN and fifteen blimps. "Apparently Edison really intends to push through some of his ideas on airships," Fulton observed, "and has passed the word along that he wants more than lip service to airships." The report, Edison hoped, would serve as a holding action and perhaps squeeze "some items" of construction from Congress.[31]

Debate revived as to airships. Rather than shape a policy, however, the formulation was practically ignored.[32]

To remain eligible for promotion, a naval aviator had to alternate sea duty with assignments ashore. Cdr. Charles E. Rosendahl, a former skipper of the rigid airships *Los Angeles* (1926–29) and *Akron* (1931–32), had been ordered to sea duty, after which he was back at Lakehurst as commanding officer of the naval air station (1934–38). In 1940 he was again at sea, this time as executive officer of USS *Milwaukee,* a heavy cruiser.

An officer of towering force and reputation, charismatic and outspoken, "Rosie" enjoyed ready access to Admiral King. Congratulating Mills on his Lakehurst command, Rosendahl speculated as to his own next duty assignment. "If the LTA project blooms sufficiently," he confided, "I most assuredly want to get back into the game and will continue my efforts to put LTA over the top." He was optimistic as to prospects for "a real program," but would a desk job in Washington or Lakehurst be the better? "Froggy [Fulton] feels that I could do more for the cause by being in some billet in Washington but that can not be judged until we see the scope of the resulting program." As it happened, he would deliver a new, ferocious focus. Mills, a superb officer-executive, would handle operational matters throughout the coming war at sea. "You are running the show [Rosendahl continues] and I know you will do an excellent job. I will however from time to time as and if any ideas occur to me, most assuredly pass them on to you. For my heart is still set on getting the American people to take advantage of the great things possible from airships."[33]

This officer soon held new (and highly influential) orders: to the office of the secretary of the navy.

Evangelical in his zeal, blustery, controversial by personality, the man had resounded throughout the ZR project—in the process, provoking resentment as well as admiration. Now, though, the big ships were gone: by 1940, most persons holding responsible positions within the naval establishment or in other organs of the government viewed airships with skepticism if not contempt; some, indeed, were openly vindictive.[34] Secretary Edison was an exception. Remarking on the lean years, when next to nothing could be coaxed free, Fulton later observed, "It was only after the imminence of war caused shelving of any rigid program that a Blimp program got underway."[35]

The onset of the London blitz, the loss of tonnage at sea, and the invasion of Norway, the Low Countries, France—continental conquest had left Berlin holding the western seaboard of Europe from the North Cape in Norway to the Spanish border. The strategic situation had mutated; provoked by the U-boat, the struggle for the life of Britain (the sole remaining defender of western Europe) entered a desperate phase. Key question: the chances for Britain's survival. On 17 August, Hitler declared a total blockade of the British Isles. Save for newly commissioned submarines from German yards, passage to and from Germany now was unnecessary. From western France, boats could cover the whole of the North Atlantic south to the equator, returning to Bay of Biscay ports for repairs and refitting. Immediately the number of boats available in the actual operational area doubled.[36] With Italy's entry into the war, the Mediterranean too became a sphere of interest. Starting in the fall of 1941, U-Boat Command assisted the Italians with a detachment, further threatening Britain's imperial lifelines.

Great Britain stood alone, save for U.S. assistance in an undeclared war in the Atlantic. Its Royal Navy strained to the breaking point, London's ability to carry on the war rested upon ocean communications—keeping sustaining sea lanes open. "The Battle of the Atlantic," writes Samuel Eliot Morison, "was, by and large, a fight for the protection of shipping, supply, and troop transport waged by the U.S. Atlantic Fleet and Allied Navies against Axis submarines, supporting aircraft, and a few surface ships. It was essentially a war of maintaining communications with our own forces in Europe and Africa and with our overseas Allies, including Russia; an offensive development of the original policy of hemispheric defense against an Axis approach to the New World."[37]

The outlook held dark, the threat of invasion real. At sea, the shipping statistics as of June 1940 spoke for themselves. "Total shipping losses of the Allied and neutral nations were about 280,000 gross tons monthly as compared to a building rate of only about 88,000 gross tons monthly, for a total net loss of 1,920,000 gross tons due to all causes during this ten-month period out of a total of about 40,000,000 gross tons of shipping at the start of the war. It appeared that shipping losses were still on the upgrade and the only hope of keeping the rate of loss down was a large increase in shipbuilding."[38]

Desperate for reinforcement, the gravity of the situation was put before Franklin Roosevelt by the new British prime minister, Winston S. Churchill: "It has now become most urgent for you to let us have the destroyers, motor boats, and flying boats for which we have asked. The Germans have the whole French coastline from which to launch U-boats, dive-bomber attacks upon our

Hangar No. 1 at Lakehurst, December 1939. The hull structure is that of USS *Los Angeles* (ZR 3). The dismantling—unique in naval aeronautics—marked the navy's explicit rejection of rigid airships. *TC-14* is berthed at left; the training ship is *G-1*—procured in 1936. (Karl Arnstein Collection/University of Akron Archives, courtesy Eric Brothers)

trade and food, and in addition we must be constantly prepared to repel by sea action threatened invasion. . . . Besides this we have to keep control of the exit from the Mediterranean. . . . Mr. President, with great respect I must tell you that in the long history of the world, this is the thing to do now."[39]

Roosevelt, a master of political intelligence, knew the American public to be reluctant about increasing aid to England and changing the Neutrality Law. However, 1940–41 would chart a progressive change in sentiment in favor of aid. The president announced the transfer (fifty destroyers, from the reserve fleet) that September. A largely one-sided transaction, the aging vessels were in exchange for base sites in Antigua, the Bahamas, British Guiana, Jamaica, St. Lucia, and Trinidad. (Two other sites, in Newfoundland and Bermuda, were granted outright.) With ships swapped for sites, a new line of Allied naval and air facilities was made possible. As 1940 matured, the successful defense of Britain—the outcome of the war, indeed—hung upon Allied grit and American deliveries. The islands' remaining lifeline, the northwestern approaches, continued to suffer the German onslaught: destructive losses from air and U-boat attacks plus the threat of surface raiders. As the Commonwealth carried on, immense American war-production programs were advancing or planned.

His declared neutrality nominal, Roosevelt had committed the nation to the principle of a "common cause" with Great Britain.

As part of its antisubmarine defense, British aircraft were pressing westward; from October 1940, the combination of air and sea-patrol forces pushed Hitler's boats ever farther from the coast west of England. "There was no longer any question of attacks near the coast," Karl Dönitz later remembered; "the disposition of forces had to take place in the open sea." U-Boat Command decided, therefore, on the controlled operation of its at-sea assets against convoys located by systematic search. Tactically, what mattered now was directing as many boats as possible to convoys once found and thus setting concentrations of boats—"packs"—against concentrations of shipping. The difficulty thus lay in the finding, not in the attacking.[40]

Plotting strategy and tactics, Churchill sketched out the Allies' two-ocean prospects that December for the American chief executive: "The control of the Pacific by the United States Navy and of the Atlantic by the British Navy is indispensable to the security of the trade routes of both our countries and the surest means to preventing the war from reaching the shores of the United States. . . . [W]e must try to use the year 1941 to build up such a supply of weapons, particularly aircraft, both by increased output at home in spite of bombardment and through oceanborne supplies, as will lay the foundation of victory."[41]

Naval engineering officers (until 1935 members of the Construction Corps, thereafter Engineering Duty Officers) rarely gained flag rank. Captain Fulton honored the tradition, retiring voluntarily after a naval career of twenty-eight years. At least eighteen of those years had been devoted to lighter-than-air aeronautics in general and to the rigid airship in particular. Late in December 1940, he cleared his BuAer office on Constitution Avenue for civilian employment: chief engineer of the Cramp Shipbuilding Company, of Philadelphia.[42]

Firebrand Rosendahl persisted, shouldering the cause in Washington, inciting senior commanders who, given the choice, preferred to deal with Mills. The ZRN was indefinitely postponed—a seeming artifact of an earlier age. The blimp as platform shifted to center stage.

In this period of rapid expansion in naval defenses, a modification in naval policy as regards airships takes place. The changed policy was first issued by Secretary Edison, and was promulgated in 1940 by Secretary of the Navy Frank Knox.

New policy in place, Congress authorized procurement of forty-eight airships of the *K-2* type.

Accordingly, the navy would establish airship bases at strategic points along the U.S. coastline and assign nonrigids to each new LTA station.

It was only a start. But it was a necessary start.

This war is in many ways a race of scientific developments and devices.

—James B. Conant

The U-boat was finally brought under control in World War II by a dozen or more new devices and methods.

—Vannevar Bush

Technical Decisions of High Consequence 1

World War II did a great deal to—and for—the United States. In the interest of national security, for one, a permanent program of federally funded research was realized. The civilian scientists, engineers, and designers mobilized for this technological chess match were as responsible for eventual Allied triumph as were the soldiers, sailors, airmen. After 1945, moreover, the emerging cold war justified intensive research and development. Physics, again, was the prime beneficiary. It was a time of great ferment in the sciences—and the momentum of those years has carried to the present.

Underwater acoustic technology had its beginnings during 1914–18, when the capabilities of the submarine as an offensive threat to merchant shipping were demonstrated. "The Germans certainly gave the United States all of the indications that submarines could be used [in a commerce war] in World War One. And, of course, the beginning of World War II. The lessons of World War One should have been that you develop a doctrine for merchant-shipping attacks. [But] the U.S. Navy did not. And the Japanese Navy did not."[1]

British vulnerability stood plain: its world-ocean maritime trade. Germany declared unrestricted submarine warfare on 1 February 1917. The German campaign of interdiction "almost proved decisive"—and, as it happened, was a rehearsal. As well, applied science had been integrated into warfare and weaponry, not least antisubmarine (A/S) matters.

One of the most significant points about antisubmarine warfare that became apparent early in World War I was the necessity of having scientific and technical aid in combating the U-boat. The essential problem was that of finding some means of *detecting* a submerged U-boat and then some weapon that would provide a good chance of *destroying* the U-boat.[2]

The fundamental objective, therefore: devising methods of finding the U-boat, then a sure method of attack once located. The first hydrophones were introduced on British naval ships in 1915. This earliest gear (a passive device) depended upon the target to supply the sound signal and "needed both a sensitive ear and much experience to distinguish between various underwater sounds which they picked up and the sound of a submarine's engines."[3] Though imperfect, hydrophones added detection capability—the directional type especially. By the close of

1918, more than three thousand surface ships had been fitted with acoustic listening equipment. For detection from shore-based aircraft, hydrophones fitted to flying boats "achieved little" in operational searches due to limited range and the unwelcome necessity, upon landing, to stop engines before listening. In contrast, during trials in 1917—a time of unrestricted submarine warfare against shipping, the blimp proved effective. An airborne scout, the platform offered longer range, endurance, and loiter time—the ability to hover as well as alight (though the need for shutdown remained). A specially designed hydrophone performed well enough that equipment was ordered for all submarine-searching blimps. The armistice cancelled delivery.[4] "The airship's greatest value to the Allies during the past war lay in convoy work. Indeed, it was common knowledge that a submarine would not attack a convoy escorted by airships. The value depended not so much on their ability to detect a submarine previous to its attack . . . but on the certainty of their locating the submarine after a torpedo attack, with the resultant destruction of the submarine by depth charges from either the airship or the surface escort."[5]

The rigid type too had been at sea: naval Zeppelins scouting for enemy surface vessels, submarines, or mines. Encounters between submarines and Zeppelins hinted at the airship's potential for A/S work. "It is believed that the rigid airship would be best adapted for long distance scouting and outer coast patrol work in general. Against submarines it might be used as auxiliary to a convoy or as a separate hunter."[6]

When the German fleet surrendered, Britain had 103 nonrigid airships in commission. "The blimps proved themselves to be useful, producible, and inexpensive."[7]

For the submerged U-boat as target, the Royal Navy had introduced the depth bomb, or depth charge. It was little more than a barrel-shaped casing filled with an explosive charge detonated by a hydrostatic fuse, or "pistol." Dropped overboard, it was meant to damage or (better) rupture the hull of an escaping submarine. A U-boat could take cruel punishment: its pressure hull was designed to withstand pressure as well as underwater blast. Such was the rate of production, in fact, that the Germans did not realize the bomb was operational until 1917. Moreover, the weapon's lethal range was small. Nonetheless, "it is perhaps not too much to say," one reference holds, "that convoy and depth-charge, taken together, were the two measures primarily responsible for the collapse of the German onslaught on shipping."[8]

The depth charge saw scant innovation; by 1920, Morison tells us, interest had "practically ceased."

The United States had initiated its own research into detection methods during the war. The experimental and development work was conducted through the navy's Anti-Submarine Board. One locus of research: the Naval Experimental Station at New London, Connecticut. Vannevar Bush, a young doctor of engineering in private employ, was working on developing a magnetic submarine detector. The device was effective: "I detected many tame submarines," Bush wrote in a memoir. One hundred sets were built. Courtesy of bureaucratic dithering, none was deployed against German boats. "My efforts did not cause the Kaiser any embarrassment, but they did teach me a bit about how to develop new weapons in time of war, or rather how not to do it."[9]

The Treaty of Versailles outlawed the U-boat, excising the threat. Or so it seemed. American interest in antisubmarine warfare (ASW)—sensors, weaponry, tactics—waned with peace but did not cease. In 1923, for example, the Naval Research Laboratory (NRL) opened at the Naval Air

Station in Anacostia. Echo-ranging sound gear, or sonar, was the NRL's principal interwar innovation; its transducers emitted pulses—"pings"—of ultrasonic energy. (Termed "supersonic" then, frequencies over fifteen thousand cycles per second are in the ultrasonic range.) In a special division of destroyers, practical operation of these devices was studied, and operators were trained.[10] But "there was just too little money, and the Navy was primarily concerned, for most of the interwar period, with the strategic problem of war with Japan."[11] As the thirties drew to close, the U.S. Navy once again had urgent operational needs.

With hostilities in Europe declared, Washington officially was neutral. U.S. military involvement might seem preordained, yet few saw the warnings. Interventionists within the research and educational establishments sought to advance—tentatively at first—the cause of preparedness. Bush was one. Now president of the Carnegie Institution, he was located permanently in Washington. "We were all drawn together early in 1940 by one thing we deeply shared—worry."[12] Unqualified commitment (and national consensus) awaited the Japanese raid on Oahu, but with the invasion of Poland, these like-minded men of science saw war as inevitable *and* highly technical. In the charged atmosphere of 1940–41, anxious academics implored the Navy Department to accelerate rearmament and scientific readiness.

"The days when wars were won by heroism alone are gone. It is generally realized that the next war will be decided by industrial preparedness and applied science. Superior airplanes, warships, tanks, and guns; superior methods for detecting and combating them; superior methods for producing munitions in large quantities, economically—these will be factors that may decide the fate of his nation and of the entire civilization."[13]

War poses intense management challenges. In 1941, experimental and development machinery had to be refashioned, old thinking traded for the original and the audacious. How best to mobilize U.S. science in military and naval research and navigate the transition to war making? How to ensure the best technology was applied rapidly to fleet use? With the leadership of Bush—able and adaptable, a man who understood bureaucracies—a reorganization plan for government science was devised. He intended to elevate science to the presidential level, to make it a new national mission. In June 1940, proposal in hand, Bush touched the requisite bases—the army and navy, Congress, and the National Academy of Sciences—before he met with Roosevelt confidant Harry Hopkins, then the president. His audience: mere minutes. "I came out with my 'OK—FDR' and all the wheels began to turn."[14]

That May–June 1940, the Netherlands and Belgium armies capitulated, then France fell; German troops entered Paris on 14 June. Britain stood alone. On 27 June, a National Defense Research Committee was established in the Executive Office of the President. (NDRC was launched, the order stated, "to correlate and support scientific research on the mechanisms and devices of warfare, except those relating to problems of flight included in the field of activities of the National Advisory Committee of Aeronautics [NACA].") The process of research had been placed under unprecedented central control: the new agency reported directly to Roosevelt rather than through military channels. It had its own funds. James B. Conant, a distinguished chemist and president of Harvard, was promptly recruited. Like Bush, "Conant was a patriot who believed in the application of advanced technology to war."[15] Conant's interventionist credentials were impeccable. "What this country can or will do remains to be seen," he wrote in mid-1940. "There are many who feel as I do, but not enough as yet. We have been sleeping in the warm tropics and now refuse to believe in snow. If England can head off the attempt to storm the island by a frontal attack, we may still awake in time."[16]

Imbued with a sense of urgency, this pair "set a standard of effort which in its combination of soundness and daring left open for such officers as [Secretary of War Henry L.] Stimson no intelligent course but full and hearty collaboration."[17] Entities enlisted into service under contract consisted mainly of educational institutions, such as the Massachusetts Institute of Technology (MIT). Through the NDRC contract process, private scientists from universities, research institutes, and industrial laboratories would craft weapons to assist the army and navy—most famously the atomic bomb. Liaison with the services and their research agencies was vital. The plan was laid before the Chief of Naval Operations, Harold R. Stark, and the Chief of Staff of the Army, Gen. George C. Marshall. (A representative each from the navy and army were among the committee's eight members.) With time, various NDRC elements gathered young army, navy, and air officers familiar with needs in the field, and (later) men of combat experience, as Bush noted. "This system of military members applied all the way at every level," he said. "Scientific men and military men had to learn to work as partners," another wrote.[18]

London, for its part, was giving the U.S. Navy the whole of its "hardly-won war experience and the particulars of virtually all or latest technical developments." Eager for sustained contact, NDRC would open a London office in March 1941, to facilitate interchange of technical knowledge and experience. Also that April, a British Central Scientific Office was established in Washington.[19]

Dangerously isolated, England was engaged to the death with an all-threatening enemy. In the North Atlantic, this was a time of stunning German success in open-ocean trade warfare: so much, so soon. British and American forces found themselves unprepared for A/S defense. Training, material, and tactical deficiencies weakened vital communications. Concerted wolf-pack tactics, for example, overwhelmed defensive forces—with decimating effect on supplies and the British war economy. One homeward-bound convoy that October was twice attacked, losing three ships. Radio control from shore, in effect, rendered the U-boats "mobile surveillance sensors to find the target and then chess-pieces to be manipulated from ashore to kill targets most efficiently."[20] The probable track had been worked out based on reports from a shadowing boat, allowing a patrol line of five U-boats to intercept. The ensuing action proved grimly emblematic of the Atlantic war in 1940.

The scientific aspects of defense against the U-boat as well as the U.S. Navy's own preparations were—given matters at sea—explicit, first-order concerns. The committee therefore assumed broad responsibility in the field of ASW: programs for the development, testing, production, and installation of "special devices" held highest importance and urgency. Still, relations with the navy, Bush concedes, were "often troubled." Retrospectively, Adm. Ernest J. King, the navy's senior uniformed officer during 1941–45, approved the means by which science was applied to the needs of naval warfare: "It was decided to attempt a solution involving maximum flexibility and initiative, in which the fundamental principle would be cooperation between science and the armed forces, rather than to bring the scientists into military and naval laboratories, as was done in England. The principle proved thoroughly sound."[21]

War work demands talent. As Conant's biographer writes, "The first priority, before building weapons, was assembling manpower." (Funds were never a limiting factor.) Aware of the impending demands upon industry, the committee sought mostly academic scientists. NDRC "marked the beginning of a revolution," realizing a "transforming effect on the relation of the universities to the federal government." Scientists were mobilized for the national defense on their home grounds or via large central laboratories created for a specific purpose, such as radar or rockets. "In the latter half of 1940, Conant embarked on a job that would never quite finish until the war ended—recruiting university scientists, securing permissions for leaves of absence and approval for use of facilities and contracts from university presidents, tapping the network he had been building since before World War I. . . . [T]he scientific mobilization dwarfed anything ever previously attempted by the U.S. government."

The NDRC opened a new era in another respect, as well—rather than proposing to draft scientists out of universities and build new laboratories, as the military had done during World War I, the wartime scientific apparatus overseen by Bush broke with the past by carrying out most war-related scientific research under contract to civilian universities and institutes. Later accepted as a norm, this strategy led to thousands of separate research projects being conducted around the country and fostered a transformation of the relationship among American universities, government, and the armed services that would outlast the war for which the NDRC was created.[22]

One linkage had been neatly solved: that between the laboratories (government, industrial, university) and research results. NDRC had at its disposal nationwide contacts with civilian science through the National Academy of Sciences, the National Research Council, and various scientific societies. Empowered to employ people and make contracts, it was able to assemble enthusiastic and capable staffs of (mostly) physicists, engineers, and designers, some with World War I experience in the A/S field.

Girding for war, Washington negotiated the political thickets to assume a more belligerent stance as the government hiked defense spending. Inside the armed services, frenetic preparations masked infirmity: throughout 1940–41, the U.S. military was, so to speak, closed for alterations.

In October 1940, the Navy Department had asked the Naval Research Advisory Committee of the National Academy of Sciences to survey research and development (R&D) in ASW and to report on the adequacy of weapons and techniques.[23] A subcommittee was formed, chaired by Dr. E. H. Colpitts, the recently retired vice president of the Bell Telephone Laboratories. Dated 28 January 1941, its final report on the "submarine problem" went to Rear Adm. Harold G. Bowen, technical aid to Secretary of the Navy Frank Knox. This commended NRL, the principal home of work on undersea warfare, for its accomplishment. The report nonetheless called for overarching change. Now, in a time of emergency, the navy's research requirements—in light of deficiencies—were alarming.

The reliability of A/S weapons on destroyers was a mere few percent. This dismal outcome was a function of the sensors then available and of weaponry, tactics, and training. Navies had bet heavily on depth-charge armament. However, that weapon was hostage to inexact detection, so standard doctrine was to saturate an area with them. The charge itself was a proximity device, fused to explode at a set depth. Too high or too low, the barrage failed. A redesign was in order, to achieve more rapid contact with evading targets. The whole question of depth charges—sizes, fuses, patterns—would be taken up, as would the tactics of attack. Also, wakes and myriad false contacts wasted ordnance. To improve accuracy, instrumentation to convey information on target location, course, and speed awaited development, manufacture, and deployment.

Finding then holding a contact was (and is) hugely complicated. The only known way to push signals through seawater out to several thousand yards was via sound—either direct "listening" or receipt of echoes, that is, either hearing the submarine's propellers or receiving reflections from its hull. The detection gear: sonar ("asdic," in British parlance).[24] This returned a pulse echo to a receiver that indicated both range and bearing to the operator—far superior to the earliest hydrophones. But the signal had to be recognizable against background noise. The acoustical vagaries of water masses limited or even cancelled efficacy. Many of the physical properties of ocean water directly affect the transmission of sound waves. Inhomogeneities of temperature, salinity, density, and convection—as expressed in the layer structure of many oceanic areas—can scatter or attenuate sound, refract or diffract pulses, and create reverberation or false echoes. Seasonal and geographical variations affect performance, as does, in shallow water, the character of the bottom. Even for the shorter-range problem of locating for attack, before 1943 the gear failed to denote target depth, and, further, lost echo contact throughout the final two hundred or so yards of surface approach.[25]

In sum, broader and harder research was needed. To realize a significant and desperately needed improvement, an "intensive study" covering the basic physics of every aspect of the problem was invoked. Oceanographic studies had to continue, into fields including the transmission characteristics of seawater over the entire audible and inaudible frequency range likely to be useful.[26] Improvements both material and human—in personnel, training, tactics, instruments—promised the greatest practical results, fastest. Devices for determining the depth and speed of a submarine, for instance, would improve the accuracy of depth charging. Means for detecting surfaced boats at night or in fog, such as microwave devices (radar) and artificial illumination "should be immediately investigated." Here, as in other aspects of the problem, Admiralty work was to prove vital. In light of British research and experience, liaison would benefit efforts stateside and perhaps make available knowledge of German developments and methods.

As for naval air's contribution to the hunt:

> The direct visual observation of submerged submarines from airplanes is a well established and useful art but it is limited in respect of depth of penetration and to operation during daylight hours; thus visual observation has restricted application. Night searching for submarines on the surface may later be made effective by artificial illumination or by microwave apparatus.

The importance of underwater echo and listening was unquestioned. For the longer term, however, a range of potential remedies was recommended, such as the possibility of using methods to supplement sound with magnetic, microwave, and radio-acoustic devices. No sure and clear answers were predictable. But the risks of not proceeding were potentially disastrous.

> The committee is aware that many of the projects and problems outlined . . . already are recognized and have received some attention. But the committee wishes to emphasize that a much more comprehensive and fundamental research program is needed.
>
> The gravity of the emergency is such that the present research facilities and personnel [of NRL] are wholly inadequate. We need the best talent of the country. In these days of aroused patriotism that talent is available. The effort demands a large staff of the highest competence and a properly located and equipped laboratory, with ample ship facilities.

The report closed insistently, "It is the considered and unanimous opinion of the committee that the importance, magnitude, and difficulty of the problem call for an effort no less than that recommended."[27]

Roosevelt had informed Admiral King of his designation as Commander in Chief, Atlantic Fleet, with the rank of admiral (four stars). In a February 1941 message to the fleet, King enjoined his team, from admiral to seaman, to attend fully to the emergency: "We must all realize that we are no longer in a peacetime status and have no time to lose in preparing our ships and ourselves to be ready in every way for the serious work that is now close aboard. This means hard work—and lots of it!" In March, he again summarized his thoughts in another order to the fleet, ending his message with, "We must all do all that we can with what we have."[28]

The Lend-Lease Act was signed in March 1941. In May, an unlimited national emergency was declared. On 22 June, Germany invaded Russia. Bush asked the president to create an enlarged overall executive agency, with authority for all government science. This was the Office of Scientific Research and Development (OSRD). Bush knew the Washington maze. As director, he would "handshake" the cause of military science in the clubs and corridors of power, reporting personally to Roosevelt. The National Defense Research Committee was folded into OSRD, with Conant taking over its chair. (In practice, NDRC was otherwise little affected.) "Conant retained the NDRC title for the remainder of the war, administering a vast, highly decentralized operation that produced numerous advances in weapons technology."[29]

For the Allies, the German undersea fleet posed a twofold problem. Defensively, the prime objective was protection of seaborne trade, the interruption of which would affect war economies and all fighting plans.[30] Coveted ASW assets therefore concentrated near the intended targets: the merchantmen. Sinking U-boats was *not* the sole gauge of offensive success. The supreme goal was the reduction in their number operating at any one time in the Atlantic. This could be accomplished by "kills" or by damaging the boats—thereby extending their time in repair—or by damaging the repair bases themselves.

Appreciation of *sea denial* had come late. At war's outset, British A/S aircraft lofted no radar, no long-range planes were assigned to A/S patrols, and short-range aircraft carried hundred-pound bombs "quite unsuited to their task."[31] "As in the case of the Royal Navy," another writer notes, "the extent of the German submarine threat proved a considerable shock, to the extent that new laboratories had to be created to devise the means to meet it." Bush agreed: "We nearly lost again in the second war because of the submarine; the margin was critically close."[32] In view of the importance of combating the U-boat, and spurred by British appeals (and direct help), reliable and timely attention to ASW stood imperative—"technical decisions of high consequence."[33] In a 10 April 1941 letter, Adm. S. M. Robinson, Chief of the Bureau of Ships (BuShips), requested that NDRC enter the field of submarine detection and asked what arrangements he should make to cooperate. NDRC approved a plan for the organization of a comprehensive program within days; this in turn went to Robinson, who expressed satisfaction. The necessary arrangements were effected, the plan put into operation.[34]

The program was assigned to Division C (later Division 6) of NDRC, under Dr. Frank B. Jewett, president of the National Academy of Sciences and chairman of the board of Bell Telephone Laboratories. He in turn set up Section 4 under Division C (that is, C-4) and asked Dr. John T. Tate, vice chairman of the division, to assume responsibility for full-time R&D of new ASW devices and material. (Each division built a system of sections to deal with explicit problems, sections that soon became groups of specialists.) Tate, a former professor of physics at the University of Minnesota, would head Division 6—Undersea Warfare—into 1945. Four weeks before Pearl Harbor, a subcommittee was organized to coordinate and direct the NDRC agencies engaged in research on subsurface warfare. Its mandate: the development of detection equipment as well as methods of use. The liaison officer was Cdr. E. W. Sylvester, USN.

Among the immediate decisions, topmost was recruitment. Conferences to choose key men commenced.[35]

In support of A/S programs, two laboratories joined Woods Hole in studies to better understand the submarine's habitat. Set up by Jewett, the San Diego laboratory handled fundamental research; the New London Laboratory was made responsible primarily for bringing promising new devices to a stage satisfactory for operations.

Discoveries tend to be incremental; innovations are seldom brought forth fully realized. Rational, Cartesian methods now would rush a remarkable record. Vision and inventive genius were mobilizing; torrents of analyses, statistics, data, and information were to pour forth. This harvest, in turn, fed the rapidly evolving development, testing, manufacture, support, and deployment of tools for the undersea campaign—in unheard-of quantities—along with analyses of operational results. World War II realized better gadgets and devices and weapons for more platforms in a shorter time than anyone would have dreamed. Technology could not erase the threat, but haltingly, then methodically, the boats would be annihilated. "The muscles and nerves of the division spread all over the globe, wherever our Navy fought."[36]

To assure full integration of OSRD and its NDRC working body with the navy's own science, in July 1941 the navy secretary established a coordinator of research and development. Reporting directly to Knox, the coordinator was just that: a coordinating link, so as to build a robust relationship between NDRC's civilian scientists and the navy.[37] The first man to hold the position was Dr. (and reserve captain) Jerome C. Hunsaker, from MIT. A 1908 graduate of the Naval Academy and pioneer aeronautical engineer, Hunsaker was well respected in technical circles. His assignment proved temporary; when Hunsaker left to chair NACA in December 1941, Rear Adm. Julius A. Furer relieved him. Bush did not have a cordial understanding with the navy, unlike his relations with the secretary of war, Henry L. Stimson. Furer, a friend and classmate of King, "bridged many a chasm and earned the respect of all of us."[38]

The coordinator's office, in sum, was the naval branch of the council—the main interface between NDRC and the navy. Hunsaker at this moment was a man heavily burdened:

> All requests for research originating in the Navy Department are transmitted to these other governmental agencies through the Office of the Coordinator. Similarly he is the channel for transmitting to the various research sections of the Navy Department the work of the other governmental agencies. The Coordinator, therefore, is the central focal point for coordinating the internal research activities of the Navy Department and also for coordinating those internal activities with the work of outside agencies.[39]

In other words, he served as clearinghouse for all of the department's technical and scientific undertakings. Further, his office dovetailed the efforts of researchers between its bureaus, and between the navy and OSRD, thereby maximizing facilities and talent. This officer was in an excellent position to get the right people together promptly and to lay groundwork for practical solutions.

The U.S. Navy was playing catch-up in a high-stakes game of science and technology. Each bureau maintained its own research section, some had research facilities. (NACA supported BuAer, for instance.) As well, each had its own design and engineering sections. The coordinator knit these elements together. Regarding antisubmarine methods, the scientists were given the problem as a whole, encouraged to analyze it themselves and to propose research projects.[40] Conferences were the basic mechanism for initiating new projects, establishing liaison, tracking progress. Two meetings of NDRC's Section C-4 convened in mid-1941. The organizing group approved preliminary steps in executive meeting, on 12 June, and authorized contracts for research. Discussion of the technical program took place on the 30th. Within weeks, extensions and several new contracts were recommended to the OSRD director.[41] That September, a conference was held with BuShips. As well as coordinating the work and controlling duplication, close liaison helped to deliver ideas and suggestions from those charged with, and (soon) fighting, the submarine war. Before the technical program, Dr. Tate articulated some general remarks that, along with his "Statement of Objective," are worth quoting:

> It should be emphasized that NDRC is asked to be of assistance to the Navy in a time of great emergency. Special attention should therefore be given by NDRC to immediate, practical problems and especially to those ways for improving the reliability and effectiveness of present equipment and procedures which will involve a minimum modification of, or addition to, present gear. This does not underestimate the importance of longer-range research and development which is the only sure basis for continued progress. It stresses, however, the necessity for an immediate and thoroughgoing study by the staff of NDRC of the design and performance of the present equipment under operating conditions. It stresses also the need which NDRC has for frequent conferences with Navy personnel and for suggestions and ideas from those who have had operating experience with the present gear and an intimate knowledge of the tactical requirements of submarine detection.

> The objective of this Section of NDRC is to develop for the navy, through cooperation with the Bureau of Ships, improved means for detecting and locating submerged submarines. It has been assumed that this involves not only development of equipment for use on Navy ships but also with the approval of the Bureau of Ships and Bureau of Aeronautics the development of devices for detecting submerged submarines from Navy aircraft.

How to translate science into operational devices of suitable weight, space, sensitivity, performance, and power? Tate outlined an analysis of submarine detection, "presented in the hope that it may serve to show how the details of our program fit into a coordinated attack on the problem." It comprised two facets: long-range detection and the shorter-range means to accurately locate, follow, and attack. As they related to equipment for navy ships, these dual requirements were:

- At maximum range to discover the presence and at least approximate location of the submarine so that proper action might be taken.
- At lesser range to locate with maximum accuracy the position (range, bearing, depth) of the submarine and to determine its course so that a successful attack on it might be carried out.

The two were distinct. For long-distance detection, the emphasis lay on maximum reliable range. Closer in, it was maximum *accuracy* and facility of target location. A wholly satisfactory long-range detector presented, Tate acknowledged, "a complex and difficult technical problem." A solution depended upon "inventive genius backed by a program of fundamental research covering all aspects of the problem." With basic oceanographic data compiled and the most suitable form of underwater signal identified, instrumentation could be adapted. For locating a U-boat at attack ranges, the possibilities were underwater sound, light, and magnetic and electromagnetic effects.

The projects were many—sixteen addressed the detection problem alone. Others included such basics as developing standard instruments (sound projectors and microphones) and methods of measurement; studies of oceanographic conditions and reflection characteristics of submerged submarines; and a survey of underwater noise around ships. A statistical study of attack procedures was yet another. Attack involves intricate coordination among the operations of locating the target, conning the ship, firing the weapon. The more these could be understood and mechanized—to eliminate the human element—the more consistently effective attacks would become. The search problem itself would be described in terms of probabilities of sighting; different plans would be compared, the best found: operations analysis as applied to tactics. The request of then Capt. Wilder D. Baker, Commander, Antisubmarine Warfare Unit, Atlantic Fleet, for NDRC assistance in the study of tactics led to creation (in March 1942) of the Antisubmarine Warfare Operations Research Group.[42] (See chapter 2.)

As yet, surface craft deploying sonar and depth charges were the most potent (if imperfect) A/S tool. Location by aircraft with precision sufficient to permit attack was more daunting still.

But range and speed enable aircraft to sweep large areas. "It is probable," Dr. Tate recorded, "that the initial detection . . . by aircraft will have to be done on surfaced submarines visually or by radio [radar]. If, however, the submarine dives to escape bombing its approximate location is known and the subsequent search may not demand long-range detection devices."[43]

Inherent to attack is acquisition and refinement of target location. As to attack from the air, the operations that pilots and bombardiers had to execute were many and complicated. In cooperation with BuAer, flight tests were exploring the possibilities and limitations of magnetic detection. British researchers had produced a short-ranged magnetic device—it might well be improved. "The ultimate limitations, upon range of detection, which may be secured by instruments of reasonable size (weight 10 to 200 pounds) have not yet been determined, but it is known that the range is necessarily restricted. Probably 600 to 700 feet for a small undegaussed [not demagnetized] submarine represents the best that can be attained in the immediate future."[44]

Six laboratories were striving to secure maximum range of detection. The reliable reach desired was several thousand yards—that is, well beyond the lethal range of U-boat torpedoes. Most of the effort focused on detection, though the problem of maximum probability of *destruction* from a fast-moving airplane was believed "equally important and difficult."

Magnetic Detection from Aircraft

In the sea environment, the most difficult problem facing a commander is *finding* the adversary. If ships or submarines can be found, they become vulnerable. One vital new device for the antisubmarine campaign: magnetic *airborne* detection—in reality, magnetic *anomaly* detection, or MAD. Nonacoustic in nature, MAD exploits the conductive properties of submarines, sensing localized disturbances in the earth's magnetic field. When the 1939 war began, only optical methods existed for detecting surfaced U-boats from aircraft, and no means save visual could detect *submerged* hulls. The navy, in other words, could hardly ignore the *potential* of magnetic methods.

Magnetically, the earth acts as a huge dipole nearly aligned on its north–south axis. The detection problem is one of distinguishing a weak local anomaly from a strong and relatively uniform ambient field. As distance increases (in this case, from the submerged submarine), the target's weak field fades quickly until lost in magnetic signals or noise arising from electrical disturbances in the aircraft, geologic anomalies, and other factors. Winfield Fromm worked for the Aircraft Instruments Laboratory, which operated as part of the Division of War Research of Columbia University under contract to OSRD. AIL was soon asked to assume the major responsibility for MAD development.

> It was not until 1940 that intensive development on magnetic airborne detectors began, first in Great Britain and later the same year in the United States. However, not until the spring of 1942 were the first satisfactory MAD sets . . . being installed in U.S. Navy blimps and U.S. Army Air Force search airplanes. (Surprisingly enough, the first microwave radars for surface search were being installed at the same time.)[45]

MAD was envisaged as an aerial device from the first, although "the added requirement of doing this from an unstable base such as an airplane complicates the problem." Still, "empha-

Prototype coastal-patrol airship (or ZNP), March 1939. Funds for *K-2* (and *L-1*) were appropriated in 1938—when no extensive building program was yet visualized. Loran-assisted navigation would have its first airborne test aboard this aircraft. (U.S. Naval Institute)

sis was placed on detection from aircraft since wide sweeps of the ocean were required."[46] The American approach: adapt and improve the basic detection element developed by Pittsburgh's Gulf Research and Development Company. This was the saturable-core magnetometer, a device readily adapted to the submarine problem—or so it seemed. Tailoring held tangles, however: spurious signals, vibration, deflections induced by the aircraft's maneuvers plus its own magnetic and electrical gremlins. Further, because the fields of submarines are weak, MAD had to be extremely sensitive, with low inherent noise. Also, the matter of size and weight intruded. The project would not have the smoothest path from conception to launch.

Nonetheless, Gulf promptly secured "gratifying results." By October 1941, experimental equipment would show a clear and characteristic response at three and four hundred feet vertically above a target. Still, the platform had to fly low enough to catch a very small signal. Yet Gulf's numbers (which improved as work continued) were "distinctly superior" to those reported from Britain. Dr. L. B. Slichter, professor of geophysics at MIT, was consultant to Division C. "In view of this," he wrote Hunsaker, "would it not be desirable to plan early tests in collaboration with the navy for determining the possible tactical value of the device and the best methods of utilizing it in the tactics of anti-submarine warfare from airplanes?" Progress justified "continued emphasis upon research in the study and development of magnetic detectors with special reference to their behavior aboard warplanes of the type on which they will be used."[47] Among the platforms for field tests: the B-18 and B-24, the PBY *Catalina*—and airships.

Prophet and advocate Charles E. Rosendahl, promoted to captain and placed in charge of development in Naval Operations (the office of CNO), applied his relentless focus to the tasks at hand. A tireless, driven officer, it was he who largely addressed the material inferiority of airships as a defensive shield, orchestrating a renaissance. Less known was his right hand: Cdr. George H. Mills, USN. A graduate of LTA Class VI (1931) at Lakehurst and a steady personality, "Shorty" Mills instilled solid respect in those who served under him. A seasoned airman, he'd held billets aboard *Los Angeles,* then *Macon*, and, as an observer, on both *Graf Zeppelin* (1934) and *Hindenburg*. Orders to command the naval air station at Lakehurst had been cut in January 1940. In a time of staggering responsibility, Mills's service record bespeaks an intuitive grasp of leadership suited to the national emergency.

Professionally, his hope (no less than Rosendahl's) was that LTA would come into its own within naval aviation. Attuned to each other, the two officers established a mutual dialogue that would last the war. That November, Rosie (excitedly) advised Mills as to what he called the "magnetic sweep detection idea." A towed "coil" might detect a submerged submarine from a reasonable distance *above* the surface.

In company with *K-2*, the ex-army *TC-14* and *TC-13* sortie to sea at the New Jersey coast, 1939–40. The image is expressive of an inability to meet war requirements—a prototype, hand-me-down equipment, and tactics unprepared for antisubmarine warfare (ASW). (Arnold Collection, National Air and Space Museum [hereafter NASM], Smithsonian Institution)

[Opposite] The flight deck of *TC-14*, 27 November 1939. A year before Pearl Harbor, Washington had entered into an undeclared war in the North Atlantic. Both the commercial and naval rigid airship stood shelved, an accelerated program of blimp construction begun. As expansion plans were drawn up, experimental projects continued—using the few nonrigids held in inventory. (U.S. Naval Institute)

TABLE 1.1 **Utilization of nonrigid airships, U.S. Naval Air Station, Lakehurst, autumn 1940.** With war in Europe, routine training had become urgent. The station was operating an odd assortment of increasingly obsolete aircraft. *K-3*, the first airship delivered as part of the "10,000-plane" program of procurement, joined the Fourth Naval District's defense forces in September 1941.

Mission	Equipage
Joint Exercises with U.S. Submarines	*K-2, TC-13, TC-14, G-1*
Radio Compass Calibration (from ME to SC)	*K-2, TC-13, TC-14*
Experimental Work[1]	*K-2, G-1, TC-13, TC-14*
Primary Training	*L-1, G-1*
Advanced Training[2]	All ships plus free balloons

1 Bombing, depth charges, mine locations and sweeping
2 Various inshore and offshore exercises, including navigational and simulated patrol flights, convoy exercises, exercises in training for neutrality-patrol duty, and simulated harbor patrol.

> It may turn out to be practicable for each ZNP to carry it as regular equipment and put it out for use in suspected areas. . . . There are, it is true, some incidental aspects requiring solution. For example, it will be necessary to mark the spot where the *coil* is when the *indication* of the sub appears on the instruments, so that the ZNP can *return* there with its greeting for the sub. I believe this can be readily worked out, as can other associated problems. . . . I believe we can sure as hell "hang one on" the patrol planes (or any planes) in so being able to detect a submerged sub, other than by eye.[48]

Within weeks, an NDRC scientist had come to Lakehurst and made his report. The notion bloomed that blimps were an ideal platform for the "New London Project." "Here again," Rosendahl prescribed, "we have a golden opportunity and I sincerely hope you can give the project very high priority for it ranks very high in importance down here."[49] Mills, for his part, pushed a heavy schedule of operations, including ocean neutrality-patrol missions, experimental projects, and training sorties, as well as organizing for antisubmarine patrols, using what few ships he had. (See table 1.1.)

Public Act No. 635 of the Seventy-sixth Congress—the so-called Ten Thousand Plane Program—had included authorization for not more than forty-eight "useful nonrigid lighter-than-air craft." For this procurement, new base-sites would have to be scouted. The dark wilderness years were through. Yet the emotion was far from unalloyed. The rigid type was yesterday's lost battle; only the blimp was operational.[50] A tiny program amid prodigious naval spending, LTA was to prove itself useful if hardly central to the developing drama. Rediscovered as antisubmarine weapon , the blimp would help test and deploy NDRC's newfangled devices.

The myriad projects undertaken by Vannevar Bush's brainchild evolved quickly. In October 1941, trials of a gyroscopically stabilized magnetometer installed in a PBY-1 produced results promising enough to expand the project. On 2 December, the Mark I detector (Gulf

GAS
GAS
AIR
OPERATING
RIGHT
OPEN
CLOSE
AFT
AFT
F'W'D
F'W'D
SLIP
SAFETY
SLIP TANKS
SLIP TANKS
DUMP
CHECK
READ
2
3
4
AIR
MECH

designed) detected the submerged *S-20* off New London four times in nine attempts.[51] The CNO would order the procurement of two hundred sets mere weeks following Pearl Harbor. Of those units falling to NDRC manufacture, ten were slated for delivery to Lakehurst, for preliminary airborne tests.

Though never a marquee player, lighter-than-air was shifting toward center stage. That December, Tate wrote Sylvester:

> Referring to the question of adapting magnetic detection apparatus to use on blimps, we are proceeding energetically to make certain changes in equipment necessary to accommodate its operation to the lower speed of a blimp as compared with an airplane. We expect to have the apparatus necessary to equip one blimp ready by [about New Year's Day], and Dr. Slichter has been in contact with Captain Rosendahl relative to a program of tests. If these tests indicate that the apparatus has promise of being useful, it can be left upon the blimp for use or further trial. . . . Meanwhile we are proceeding to have manufacture started on twelve additional sets, designed to be installed for use on blimps. Continuation of manufacture, of course, is contingent upon the results of the tests to be undertaken, we expect, next week, but in order to save time we are anticipating a successful outcome to these tests.[52]

NDRC had already met with the bureaus "to consider the present [November] position of magnetic detection of submarines by aircraft using the Vacquier detector"—named for Victor V. Vacquier at Gulf Research, first to consider the saturable-core magnetometer. "Its development was begun by Gulf late in 1940 for geophysical prospecting. However, the possibility of using [it] on aircraft for submarine detection was soon recognized."[53] In light of progress, further work focused on its tactical possibilities "and the ordnance problems involved." Questions abounded. In shallow waters, for one, the nature of the bottom could interfere. Due to differences in magnetic characteristics and sizes of submarines, the sensor did not yield target depth. Also, ordnance was critical: What was the most promising weapon for use with the detector?

Minus ordnance adapted expressly for it, airborne MAD was useful only in holding contact until support arrived. Because the first duty of surface units was defense, MAD's value "depends markedly on the chances of success of retrobomb [rocket] installation." A rocket allowed ordnance to be aimed, not just dropped, by neutralizing forward momentum so it fell vertically—crucial because the airplane was practically over the target when MAD-detected. As for tactical use, the limited range of MAD precluded its use as an "effective searching device unaided by other means. The present conception of its tactical employment is the detection of a submarine which has been first picked up by radar or visually," and which then dove to escape the approaching aircraft.[54] Tate held similar views, suggesting to Hunsaker that "special types of bomb barrages" be considered by the navy, based on three factors: anticipated improvements in radar to render air patrols increasingly effective in detecting surfaced submarines; development of magnetic methods for redetection once a U-boat had dived (which was yielding encouraging results); and lightweight bombs for airborne use that would likely yield increased destructive power per unit weight of barrage.[55]

MAD, in sum, was not a weapon or a bombsight but a (limited) *search* then *tracking* sensor. Radar, for its part, extended offensive air operations to night attacks, though on surfaced boats only. (Radar waves cannot penetrate the water and so are reflected off its surface.) But night patrols, let alone offensive operations, would be a rarity throughout 1942.

In this highly technical hide-and-seek, the final answer was convoy with surface and air escorts equipped with search radar and appropriate ordnance packages.

Microwaves and Radar

Radar—*RA*dio *D*etection and *R*anging—is a device for "seeing" distant objects using radio waves instead of light waves. Radar does this by sending out very short but powerful pulses of radio frequency energy spaced widely apart and receiving the weak pulses reflected back from "targets" that the pulses have illuminated. The time required for the signal to travel out and back is measured, the distance indicated by the time of travel.[56]

The need for electronic "eyes" held utmost urgency. On the eve of war, following a June 1939 tour of British east-coast installations, Churchill dispatched his impressions of the new system to his air minister. "The progress in R.D.F. [Radio Direction Finding, the British name for radar], especially applied to range-finding, must surely be of high consequence to the Navy. It would give power to engage an enemy irrespective of visibility. . . . The method of discrimination between friend and foe is also of the highest consequence to the Navy, and should entirely supersede recognition signals with all their peril. I presume the Admiralty knows all about it."[57]

Britain at this moment was well ahead of any other country. By September, indeed, a complete functioning air-defense system was operational.

As evidence of cooperation (and to build relations with American manufacturers), Churchill offered interchange of secret technical information with the United States. A scientific mission headed by Sir Henry Tizard was empowered to exchange in *all* fields of scientific and technical activity pertinent to the war effort. The Americans, London hoped, would respond in kind. Regular and continuous interchange, indeed, was to characterize the Grand Alliance.[58] While in America, August–September 1940, the Tizard mission delivered the resonate cavity magnetron. "It was still so new that it had not yet been incorporated in any operational equipment. Indeed the tube that came to the United States was one of the first twelve to be manufactured."[59] A powerful vacuum tube, the cavity magnetron produced radio energy magnitudes stronger than anything else operating at useful wavelengths and made centimeter or microwave radar practical. The sharpness of a radar beam is dependent on the size of the antenna, measured in wavelengths of the radar frequency. Airborne antennas are necessarily small; hence, great detail requires very short wavelengths.

Though the tube held vast promise, much research lay between it and practical equipment—that is, microwave work needed a new laboratory.[60] The first meeting of what became the Radar Division of NDRC (Division 14) convened in July. Mission: obtain the most effective military application of microwaves in minimum time. The Radiation Laboratory at MIT was organized under NDRC contract that October. The first magnetrons arrived from Bell Telephone Laboratories; by the end of December, the first experimental microwave set was under test.[61]

As the principal scientific and development agency of Division 14, the "Rad Lab" was to develop antisubmarine detectors and ordnance, long-range "pulse navigation" (Loran), and refinements to microwave search radar. During the buildup, and with the Battle of Britain just won (its radar network vital to the outcome), the navy came to regard Cambridge and its outputs as of highest urgency and priority, its civilian scientists as of the highest rank in their specialties in government service.[62]

Still, the lab did not invent radio detection and ranging. The notion of using back-scattered radio-wave energy, so that a return might be detected, was independently and simultaneously developed in England, the United States, and in Germany. The latter (to Dönitz's regret) failed to build aggressively upon its own work: "The significance of shortwaves for locational purposes was recognized [Dönitz wrote], their investigation and exploitation were pushed forward, but we did not succeed, as later experience was to show, in attaining the degree of development reached by our enemies in this sphere. This was a decisive disadvantage to us in our conducting of the war at sea, which we failed to recognize."[63]

NRL and its predecessor had conducted seminal work with high-frequency radio communication and its application to navy problems as well as (somewhat later) the detection of aircraft by radio. Because the army was responsible for protecting cities and military bases, the Signal Corps started its work on pulsed radar. In 1936, NRL demonstrated the capabilities of radar, and in 1937 the Signal Corps held its first demonstration. British radar, for its part, had evolved from meteorology and had subsequently been developed by the Radio Research Board. (The first signals reflected from aircraft were observed near Orfordness in May–June 1935.)[64] Propelled by urgency, ideas flourished. The Air Ministry rushed to construct a chain of coastal stations enabling the detection of aircraft flying above ten thousand feet, with a typical range from about 120 to 150 miles. Britain, in other words, had woven radar into its air-defense system. "[I]t was the operational efficiency rather than the novelty of equipment that was the British achievement."[65]

For the Americans, liaison with the British government—prompt exchange of vital information—proved indispensable.

> The OSRD, through its Office in London, receives a large number of reports and memoranda containing scientific and technical information on many subjects of Military or Naval importance. In the field of Radar, it receives regularly reports from British Government research establishments and many papers and reports issued by industrial research establishments working in cooperation with the British Government. These reports contain valuable information concerning the latest British developments in these many fields.[66]

The Rad Lab set to work combining British microwave designs—including the new magnetron—while working with industry to develop and produce airborne radar.[67] Within a year, the microwave (AI-10) radar had had its initial airborne test in an XJO-3 at Boston Airport. These trials continued through mid-October, with scientists operating the gear and naval personnel piloting. Surface vessels could be detected out to forty miles and radar-guided approaches/intercepts achieved at ranges up to three and a half miles. Operational equipment developed from this apparatus was to include the ASG-type (air-surface-ground) radar for non-rigid airships. "Recently," Rosendahl wrote in August 1941, "it has been realized that the carrying and use of the 'Radar' equipment by airships is a natural and logical adaptation. The advantages accruing are entirely evident. Steps are underway to develop this function in airships."[68]

Rear Adm. John H. Towers, Chief, BuAer, issued a preliminary plan for installing radar in naval aircraft. By December, private contractors were enlisted into detection from aircraft as well as shipboard radar. Assisting NRL and MIT were Bell Telephone Laboratories, Western Electric, and the Raytheon Manufacturing Company. Time and work, then practice, would integrate airborne radar into a superbly effective ASW system.

> The aircraft is the most efficient vessel for searching out surfaced submarines. Radar ASV [air to surface vessel] gear is an essential adjunct to this function. Even in the day time the newer radar gear gives an increased range of detection over visual methods.
>
> It is to be noted that the night attack is the place where radar is likely to be of the greatest value. Here the usefulness of radar is at present seriously handicapped by the lack of means of illumination of the attack (in order to provide recognition of the target). Until some means of illumination for night attack is installed on planes, an important part of the usefulness of radar can not be realized.[69]

Here (as in many particulars) the Anglo-Canadians were ahead of the Americans, by virtue of belligerent status. (The major commitment of at-sea partner Royal Canadian Navy was to maintain escort forces for the protection of shipping in Canadian coastal waters and in the North Atlantic.) "One of the most potent weapons for hunting the U-boat and protecting our convoys," Churchill writes, "is the long-range aircraft fitted with ASV equipment." The seesaw of measure, countermeasure, and counter-countermeasure was accelerating. Radar is illustrative. For Britain's Coastal Command, the Bay of Biscay was action central; there U-boats sortied from French bases and returned on their patrols. By mid-1942, ASV Mark II–equipped Wellingtons were able to harass boats making the bay passage. On approach, the locating plane's radar returns were lost at about a half-mile (because of surface clutter). To enhance nighttime odds and for target classification, a powerful searchlight was mounted.[70] Taking passage at night, surface running, the boat's first knowledge of peril was a sudden, blinding light trained on its lookouts from close astern as the plane made its visual run-in.[71] U-Boat Command countered: by autumn, boats were fitted with Metox, a device able to detect Allied meter-wave radar transmissions. (Meter-wave radar transmissions, like any other radio transmissions, are picked up by receivers tuned to the proper frequency.) Granted warning, Dönitz's commanders had time to dive. Sightings declined accordingly.[72]

When hostilities broke out, U-boats had attacked almost exclusively during daylight, at periscope depth. As the months added, the percentage of nighttime attacks rose; by October 1940, save for occasional daylight attacks on stragglers and independents, Dönitz had adopted night surface attacks almost exclusively. In frustrating this tactic, radar proved decisive.

The Loran System (Introduction)

The value of navigating precisely far out to sea is plain. On hunt for a located enemy or for convoys, stragglers, or lifeboats, ships, and aircraft sped to predetermined points in a vacant blank.

Loran helped them reach the desired coordinates with precision, hence confidence.

A scheme *for directing* hunters to the hunted was most urgent. The British preceded NDRC with just such a scheme. "They developed a system by which a ship or aircraft by precisely timing the arrival of radio pulses from a number of shore stations could determine its own location with truly remarkable precision. This system is of such great importance in their bombing program, as well as in antisubmarine activities, and is so vulnerable to enemy jamming that extraordinary measures were taken to keep it secret. The British told me [Bush] about it, and also Conant, but asked us to let it go no further."[73]

For the western Atlantic, the Rad Lab's Microwave Committee devised Loran—essentially the same idea, independently derived (see also chapter 2). The "long-range pulse navigational system" or LRN, project was under the direction of Melville Eastham. When operational, Loran was intended to provide—by radio—an aid to aerial and surface navigation over longer distances and with greater precision than hitherto possible. As well, pinpointing one's position without transmitting a signal eliminated audio clues for enemy ears.

The science was practicable: pulsed (and consistent) radio energy from a chain of shore-based transmitting stations to special receivers at sea. Operating in pairs, the stations would transmit in precise synchronism. Receivers would measure the time differences in receipt of the pulses to great precision, allowing placement of position on a hyperbolic locus of constant time difference plotted onto a chart of that sector. The system, in other words, compared the signals from two widely spaced transmitters. Referring to tables or special charts, the shipboard or airborne operator could fix his position along a *line*. To fix position at a *point*, a repeat measurement exploited pulses broadcast by another pair of transmitters.

Tests of pulsing equipment at different wavelengths offered, by early 1942, a good indication of what might be expected. (Experimental stations had been sited in Delaware and on Long Island; more followed.) Further tests established the accuracy and range of the system under all conditions. "As was typically the case," the navy and army were "only mildly interested in this gadget at first. . . . Then, suddenly, everybody wanted the new equipment at once."[74] The strategic naval emphasis: the heavily traveled North Atlantic run to the British Isles.

That spring, the application of Loran to the navigation of airships underwent testing.

War at Sea, 1941

Statesmen must react to problems thrust upon them. For Franklin Roosevelt, the darkening European war of 1940–41 proved awkward. At sea, it was a time of staggering German success. Trusting his instincts, pursuing his hunches, calibrating his public statements, Roosevelt pressed the limits of constitutional constraint. The nation was struggling to form a national policy in light of sweeping global events. The anti-mercantile campaign posed a dilemma: Churchill and the president both knew what had to be done to secure strategic control on transatlantic shipping cycles—an absolute necessity. Yet Churchill lacked the means to forestall strangulation, Roosevelt lacked the domestic political support necessary to respond boldly—and with full disclosure. The stance, then: all aid "short of war."

As yet, U-boat commanders were forbidden to steam west of Newfoundland. The intent: to foreclose the possibility of an incident that might provoke Washington. Hence, the boats had to await outward-bound convoys east of their dispersal points instead of attacking concentrated shipping near ports of departure. As sinkings mounted through the fall and winter of 1940–41, discussion in the United States intensified on the question of whether the nation should take steps to "deliver the goods" to Britain. Concluding months of exasperation for Adm. Harold R. Stark, CNO, during which forces were reorganized and plans set in motion for an Atlantic-first strategy, presidential decisions placed the navy squarely in the Battle of the Atlantic.

Addressing a suspenseful nation on 11 September, Roosevelt unambiguously revealed his orders to the navy. His words mark a triumph of pose and politics over naval reality: "Upon our naval and air patrol—now operating in large numbers over a vast expanse of the Atlantic—falls the duty of maintaining the American policy of freedom of the seas—now. That means very simply and clearly, that our patrolling vessels and planes will protect all merchant ships—not only American ships but ships of any flag—engaged in commerce in our defensive waters. . . . [L]et this warning be clear. From now on, if German or Italian vessels of war enter the waters the protection of which is necessary for American defense, they do so at their own peril."

Two days later, Stark translated the speech into an operational directive, ordering the Atlantic Fleet to assume responsibility for transatlantic merchant convoys of all flags in the western Atlantic. This was the "Defensive Sea Zone." A limited number of patrol planes were assigned to the Support Force, and operations commenced to cover the movements of merchantmen from the United States and Canada between fifty degrees west longitude and Iceland. "From this point on, the United States was engaged in a de facto war at sea with Germany."[75]

In mid-October, an American destroyer, USS *Kearny,* was torpedoed during a melee with several U-boats southwest of Iceland. On the 31st, USS *Reuben James* was blown in two by a "fish" from *U-562* that set off her forward magazine; 115 sailors perished. *Reuben James* had been escorting an eastbound convoy to a mid-ocean rendezvous, at which point British warships would take over. That November, the Neutrality Act of 1939, which had prohibited the arming of American merchantmen, was revised.

Raider operations underscored the realities of unsecured sea control. In darkness, the first evidence of attack was invariably a torpedoing. (Convoy formations demand sea room: as a result, cases occurred in which time elapsed before any escort unit was aware that a merchantman had been hit.) Compounding matters, vessels of every type were insufficient in number, naval escorts particularly. The forces assigned each convoy were inadequate for maximum protection—a function of too few ships and too many convoys. Too few escort vessels left none to detach to attack the raider. For the winter of 1941–42, escort strength would be cut further due to operating conditions. Sea commanders and all concerned had to make do.

In the air and afloat, "special devices" for detection were as yet experimental (hence unreliable). Or they were too few—fast-sinking A/S ordnance, radars, radio sonobuoys, marker floats. Inexperience would further delay *effective* deployment. For example, operators trained for underwater sound (using sonar) could not possibly be available to all vessels. Nor were facilities available to quickly augment their number. A shortage even of TNT delayed filling of the depth-charge cases in production. Lack of uniformity in the collection of operational data impeded statistical analyses of attacks by, as well as on, the U-boat enemy.

The British and Canadians, profiting from two years' war experience, were priceless partners for U.S. initiatives, making available a tremendous amount of antisubmarine information.

> [London] had learned that the ocean convoy system did more than anything else to reduce shipping losses. They knew that the convoy system works best in open water where evasion can be employed and that its success depends upon efficient escorts armed with effective offensive weapons. They were also aware of the fact that an efficient U-boat tracking system is necessary to practice effective evasion, and daily U-boat plot based on contacts, DF [direction finding] fixes, and intelligence was used throughout the war.[76]

A month before Pearl Harbor, the CNO issued a study of British reports of ASW for the period September 1939 to June 1941. The document received wide service distribution.[77] In the Atlantic, a dozen American destroyers had British-type AVS radar installed; aloft, no more than fifty radar-equipped patrol planes were available to hunt. German tactics, particularly surface attacks at night or in poor weather, had demonstrated the incalculable value of radar.

The U.S. Navy was ill equipped for an emphatic defense—according to Samuel Eliot Morison, its foremost historian, it was a state of unpreparedness that was "largely the Navy's own fault." Still, King held few options. In a perfect world, evidence trumps opinion. For months, Cominch would oppose an offensive search-and-attack strategy, conceding to tremendous pressure only in April–May 1943. Meantime, "surrounded by all sorts of interservice recriminations," the army and navy disagreed over the tactics and control of A/S aircraft.

For the War Department, the lessons and *the* model of air operations were British. Autonomously organized, "Coastal Command had developed and applied with striking success the theory of the antisubmarine offensive. Granting the essential function of the convoy, this theory assigned to aircraft the primary mission of searching out and killing submarines *wherever* they might be, and although it regularly responded to Admiralty requests for convoy cover in critical areas, Coastal Command devoted the weight of its effort to a direct offensive on U-boats."[78]

Stimson and Bush became convinced that aggressive action was not only logical but inevitable: convoys must be boldly protected. Strategic planning, Bush held, "needs to be carried on with a full grasp of the implications of new weapons, and also the probable future trends of development." The navy proved slow in making full offensive use of new devices and weapons for the undersea war. Exasperated, the pair took the issue to Roosevelt. General Marshall and the British also pressed King. Until the antisubmarine effort was reorganized into the Tenth Fleet command, in May 1943, the impasse endured—Cominch holding stubbornly to his concept that defense of convoys promised the most effective means of blunting the menace. Ironically, then, while the model was British, any blending of Anglo-American operations into a coordinated performance stood deferred. "Our long delay in really getting down to the job of fighting the submarine," Bush records, "was due partly to Navy-Air Force [Army Air Corps] relations, which were none too good at times, but principally to the conservatism of the Navy, if we can call it that, which was evident in Admiral King's insistence that the only way to carry on the war against the submarine was by use of the convoy system."[79]

U.S. air- and surface-defense forces would adapt. Sensor-fitted aircraft soon proved potent, the airplane decisive.[80] Meantime, King held to his decision not to introduce convoys. As for individual blame, a proper assessment demands appreciation of context. And nuance. Though liable, King-as-villain is a facile explanation. Military planners must weigh options. The decision was "not simply a thoughtless blunder but an agonizing decision made with full awareness of the possible cost."[81]

The U-Boat attack was our worst evil. It would have been wise for the Germans to stake all upon it.

—Winston S. Churchill

Only by destroying Allied tonnage could we deal Britain a decisive blow.

—Karl Dönitz

Preparations 2

In January 1942, Germany pushed its war on commerce to distant battlefields: U-boat attacks off the eastern seaboard of the United States. The impact was seismic. Sinkings escalated alarmingly, in the sector south of Chesapeake Capes particularly—"an unparalleled massacre." One returning U-boat commander reported that the opportunities for attack in the area south of New York to Cape Hatteras were so abundant that he could not possibly exploit them all.[1] "You could fly out there in an airship—if you had one in '42—and you could see the masts (just the masts sticking up) of all these ships that had been sunk along our coast."[2]

U-boats slipped inshore for night attack, then ran back out to wait out daylight, only to steal back in. In the era of the diesel boat, submarines were *surface* raiders that could submerge. As an operating area, the continental shelf of the western Atlantic favored air-breathers: a low, sandy shore sloping gradually out to sea. Bottomed, a boat could conserve its batteries—essential for underwater propulsion.

Its forces unskilled and in short supply, the U.S. Navy responded defensively. Few if any surface or air units were so proficient as to be dangerous to a U-boat. Thus was the enemy enabled to approach, his probabilities for success excellent. In a time of complete disruption, the naval leadership changed the Defensive Coastal Frontier to a Sea Frontier organization. Inshore, the need for "Navy Air" held urgent: air coverage for naval forces is essentially a *naval* problem. Though unused to the ways of the sea, the U.S. Army Air Forces contributed bomber units to patrol work. Aloft and by sea, U.S. forces could barely retaliate: few U-boats were brought to action.

For this contest, twenty-four pilots and four patrol airships (ZNPs) were assigned to the operational environment. Main base: NAS Lakehurst supported by a mast at Cape May, in South Jersey. Orders: to deploy to best advantage consistent with facilities. Goodyear Aircraft—the sole prime contractor—would deliver three ships through June (ZNPs *K-7, K-8, K-9*).[3] Still, hangar construction would not keep pace, thus requiring mast-based ships to meet requirements.[4] Indeed, slow progress in every phase of the program would, by September, make only nine aircraft operational. In brief, lighter-than-air was wholly unprepared: materially, operationally, doctrinally, and in terms of trained personnel. Amid the carnage, a tiny LTA force helped defend the inner sea-lanes of merchantmen traffic.

Sea Frontier commanders were among the first to recognize the worth of LTA and to exploit its potentials. Much harried, these major commands consistently urged the filling of blimp squadrons up to allowances. They "accepted us gratefully; they thought we were doing a great job. And they saw the *need* for the job." Reported the chief of staff of the Eastern Sea Frontier, "Blimps are doing excellent work. The magnetic detector shows excellent possibilities. The blimps have also been handicapped by poor action of depth bombs. There was one report where a depth bomb was almost bounced off the conning tower and failed to explode."[5]

The U-boats struck quickly and hard. Off the Canadian and American coast, surface and air forces could neither apply adequate coverage nor overbear the opposition.[6] As well, tactics and communications for *combined* A/S measures had yet to be adopted, let alone adapted to. So a punishing attrition persisted. Training, doctrine, methods, sensors, equipment, weapons: all were wanting. U-boat "kills" did not begin to outweigh the damage. In sum, LTA was but one element of a patched-together defense against a skilled adversary dominating the inshore convoy routes—that is, when a coastal-convoy system *was* established. Until that decision, "merchant ships are being routed Boston to Norfolk so that they are underway only during daylight. They are held in port during darkness. This is not possible south of Hatteras, but ships leave Hampton Roads as early as possible (about 3 A.M.) so as to clear Hatteras during daylight. Southbound traffic is directed to hug the line of lights and buoys and Northbound keeps two miles out."[7]

Lakehurst's assignment: to patrol off New Jersey and the megaport of New York—the best natural deepwater harbor on that coast. *Any* aerial presence tended to discourage U-boat operations in the approaches to port complexes, where shipping was densest. Its ZNP handful sought to cover vast sectors traversed by independent shipping. Other defending forces, few in number and overworked, were so meager as to be nearly nonexistent: scant surface forces and spasmodic coverage by airplanes. And so the enemy evaded its would-be killers. Only following hurried preparations would the decision to require coastal vessels to steam in convoy (in May) cut a sensational loss rate.

A frightful year had opened. With good news a rarity, weeks evolved into ever more bloody months. Augmenting surface and HTA forces, LTA represented the sole striking force in the Third and Fourth naval districts. Actual operations commenced on 2 January, with commissioning of Squadron Twelve. Strength: four ZNPs of the *K-2* class. A fifth reached New Jersey late in April. Thereafter, deliveries were one per month until August (two), then September (four). Total for 1942: fifteen K-type through Lakehurst, eight to Sunnyvale. As more units became available and definite patrol areas established, airships furnished daily and, at times nightly, coverage to their plodding charges. In addition to patrol and escort duties, searches were assigned: for survivors of sunken merchantmen and to investigate reports (or rumors) of sinkings, sightings, explosions.

Air facilities for blimps would extend first to a main coastal base in North Carolina; another followed in Massachusetts, then others Georgia and in Florida. The Fleet Airships Atlantic command would regenerate from a single squadron into ten—newly commissioned units assigned ever-improving platforms, each equipped (then reequipped) with new sensors. For antisubmarine forces, the target opportunities were limitless: the cargo corridors of the world ocean. Airships would find missions well away from the Eastern Sea Frontier—ultimately, forty-one main and auxiliary facilities in the Canadian maritimes, the gulf, in the Panama area and Caribbean Sea, in the British West Indies, Brazil, North Africa, and in southern Europe.

Meantime, LTA logged sea-lane patrol and (increasingly) escort services. It would assist the service trials for secret devices, and it would be first to deploy operational MAD and the radio sonobuoy. Still, it ranked low among competing priorities. And with few powerful friends—influential congressmen to shepherd appropriations or Navy Department advocates, procurement of aircraft, sensors, and assorted essentials (notably spare parts) proved to be painfully slow.

The late thirties had been dark years, a period of rhetorical flying during which the ZR vanished altogether. Naval LTA waned to an impotent operating force, with all activities concentrated at Lakehurst. Now, as 1940 opened, proponents—a tiny cadre—would savor a grudging recognition for their blimps as a useful naval instrument.

> Small airships are used for flight training and experimental development work connected with airships. In naval warfare, the non-rigid airship is used to escort merchant and naval vessels through waters in which submarine attack may be expected. During the World War, no convoy guarded by airships was successfully attacked by submarine; small airships were effective in spotting and trailing submarines and either bombing them or reporting them to anti-submarine surface forces; they were used also for coastal patrol and observation purposes to spot submarines and mines off coasts and harbors.[8]

Cdr. Jesse L. Kenworthy Jr., USN, station skipper (1938–40), pleaded for blimps as one element of the national defense organization. "The forces afloat," he wrote, "have been frank and forceful in their repudiation of the non-rigid as a useful type." Yet nothing since the First World War had lessened the "unique merit" of the platform for coastal escort, observation, mine search. "Moreover, increased building of submarines by other powers demands that no defense weapon for anti-submarine warfare be neglected." Permanent and adjunct bases on the West Coast were urged as well, from which experience could be gained operating with the fleet. "It is further recommended that non-rigid operating bases be established in the vitally important Hawaiian area and that semi-permanent and expeditionary bases be established on the Atlantic Coast to permit the extension of operations now conducted at Lakehurst to Fleet operating areas."[9] Rosendahl would prove prescient: "The importance of anti-submarine measures cannot be overestimated when we note that just about the only way—and certainly the most likely—in which any prospective enemy of today could get near our shores is by submarine."[10]

Hawaii never hosted an airship—nor, until February 1942, did the West Coast. Along the eastern seaboard, even rudimentary facilities for LTA basing and operations were lacking within reasonable operating distances from homeport. Every sortie was thus circumscribed by the need to put back to Lakehurst. Still, LTA bases for inner coastal patrol were in the offing, for both continental margins and for overseas.

G-1 operates with a friendly or "tame" boat off Long Island, 30 April 1940. Anti-submarine patrol training was obtained by working with units attached to Submarine Squadron Two, New London, Connecticut. Convoy escort was practiced by picking up and remaining with merchant vessels in the approaches to New York and off New Jersey. (U.S. Navy photograph)

In December 1939, the commander of Submarine Squadron Two, based in New London, Connecticut, had requested Lakehurst aircraft for training. The returns proved double-edged: experience for both submariners and naval airmen. "During the past seven months," Mills wrote the CNO in mid-June 1940,

> frequent exercises have been carried out by non-rigid airships operating from this station with various units attached to Submarine Squadron TWO.
>
> This work has afforded an excellent opportunity to prove the feasibility of non-rigid airships for various utility missions. The exercises have been divided into four general classifications (1) search and rescue exercises (2) marker buoy tests (3) torpedo practices in which the participating airship has been effectively used in the prompt recovery of all torpedoes fired and (4) aerial photographic and observation exercises.

This work with tame boats assessed effectiveness for sighting surfaced as well as submerged submarines. Pronouncing the results gratifying, Mills continued, "The exercises have afforded very valuable experience to non-rigid pilots in sighting submarines in their various altitudes. All pilots attached to Lakehurst have been used in submarine exercises."[11] New London was high in its praises: during a May visit, the station command heard, "Much better in every way than planes," and, "Your smoke bombs are always so near the torpedo that we never have to search for it."[12]

These exercises were held off New London and Provincetown, Massachusetts. Typically, a combat air crew (CAC) commander was aboard the boat, working as a liaison officer with its skipper. "The majority of blimp pilots have no earthly idea as to what goes on aboard a submarine." Armed with the experience, pilots (many from ZP-12) believed they could fly a "much better" attack.[13]

At Lakehurst, the outlook in 1940 was expectant yet anxious, the fiscal lid not quite off. Still, the wilderness years lay astern. The objective now: to procure the equipment, erect the facilities. LTA tendered a unique, long-endurance capability that HTA could not provide. "We had a freedom of action," one officer remembers, "that was almost giddy." Rosendahl was then at sea, as executive officer of the cruiser USS *Milwaukee*—sea duty required for promotion. The influence of this one officer must be emphasized: his contacts, his charisma with members of Congress and with persons in the naval establishment. A strong personality and advocate, "he elicited either intense like or intense dislike, depending upon your attitude towards him and the attitude he had towards you." "Every pilot looking for favors came into Rosendahl's office," an aide would recall. "And some of the brass in Washington. Looking back on it, his main role was politics."[14]

"If the LTA project blooms sufficiently," Rosie wrote Mills as the year opened, "I most assuredly want to get back into the game and will continue my efforts to put LTA over the top. At this time it is, of course, impossible to predict what the out come will be but I nevertheless continue optimistic over prospects of getting a real program. No doubt you are better posted than I on this prospect since you are near Washington."[15] Ordered ashore in May 1940, he reported for duty in the Office of the Secretary of the Navy;[16] that February, Rosendahl transferred to the Office of the Chief of Naval Operations.

Mills saw in war an end to the program's fiscal strangulation.

> I am inclined to think that we should soft pedal every claim which has not already been demonstrated. We should concentrate on claims for rigids as plane carriers remembering that a "non-vulnerable" surface airplane carrier is never sent on a mission without a heavy supporting and guarding force. Airship carriers might go as a striking unit unsupported. And blimps for convoy, mine and submarine search, patrol and utility work can't be surpassed![17]

Base facilities were indispensably necessary for support of the airship portion of the "10,000 Plane Program" authorization of naval air strength. Facing obstacles, it awaited execution. That same month, Mills received word to begin daily inshore patrols.

Mills primed his command. The Neutrality Act of 1939 prohibited American ships from sailing in proclaimed combat zones and forbade the arming of American merchantmen.[18] Lakehurst had scratched together a contribution—training for neutrality patrol. By April 1940, Mills was ready to take active part in patrol. Also, he'd gotten Submarine Squadron Two to ask for airships to recover torpedoes, take part in search operations, and conduct photographic exercises. Collaborating with defense forces in the Third and Fourth districts, Lakehurst's prime mission was to cover the approaches to the port of New York—*the* squeeze point for shipping on the eastern

littoral.[19] For patrol-type training, blimps were assigned to surveil specific sectors: making a record of intercepts, developing the contacts, and communicating results to base.[20]

Operations Officer at Lakehurst: Lt. Cdr. Raymond F. "Ty" Tyler, among the most experienced LTA officers in naval aviation. "Each pilot is cautioned," Tyler advised, "to be particularly alert for vessels of foreign registry acting in a suspicious manner, or for any details which in his opinion should be relayed to NEL [Lakehurst]. Do not report sighting any vessels by radio unless considered in a suspicious category or an armed merchantman. Such reports must be encoded."[21]

By midyear 1941, Lakehurst was operating its ships almost daily. Some patrols sortied as early as 0400 or 0500; on other days, missions would begin with training flights at 0800. Patrols might last from eight to fourteen hours, training flights from one to four hours.

Flying Fundamentals

A blimp is a balloon plus engines. The basic airframe: the envelope, or "bag, streamlined in form, together with various fabric and mechanical accessories, the empennage or control surfaces, and control car. Hung beneath, the car—simple and rugged—in the war years hosted crew, useful load, accessories, ordnance. Fastened to its sides were outriggers that support the engine nacelles and propellers. The K-car structure was composed of a welded chrome/molybdenum-steel tubu-

[Opposite] L-ship envelope is unrolled by a work party in the inspection room of the Fabric Shop at Lakehurst, 26 March 1943. The inspection, repair, maintenance, and storage of airship-related fabrics was centered here. The flooring is polished maple, to prevent abrasion. (Lt. [jg] H. H. O'Clare, USN [Ret.])

A K-ship envelope air-inflated for internal inspection. Airship "bags" were constructed of three-ply rubberized fabric. Four fabric catenary curtains were woven into the inside-top of the bag for attachment of the suspension cables for the control car. (Lt. H. F. Smith, USNR [Ret.])

lar framework, its covering light-gauge aluminum alloy and fabric. Ample windows conferred a nearly full-horizon view.

The envelope (three-ply fabric impregnated with rubber) carries a blimp's various flight stresses; it is a primary structure for the type—but functions only under tension produced by internal gas pressure. Most of the car weight is carried by internal suspensions, the balance by an external system. The bag also supports bow stiffening, air and gas valves as well as patches for various attachments. A blimp's shape is maintained by internal (helium) pressure. To compensate for expansion and contraction due to altitude and temperature changes, blimps are equipped with ballonets—air chambers within the envelope. Air is valved when the helium expands (freeing internal volume), air is pumped in when the lifting gas contracts.[22] Two scoops, located aft of the props in the slipstream, conduct air into the ballonets, the flow regulated by a "butterfly" valve fitted inside each. Managing these scoops is vital: if they are opened too wide, excessive pressure can cause a loss of helium. Not opened enough, and pressure can drop dangerously low, perhaps buckling the bag. Properly manipulated, this pressure-control system maintains a near-constant internal pressure and is exploited to adjust flying trim.

Maintaining the proper pressure differential between helium and atmosphere was (and remains) a basic operational requirement. The pressure-control system maintains this differen-

[Top] Envelopes were aluminum painted on the outside and paraffin treated on the interior surface. Here Fabric Shop work parties apply heated paraffin (blended with carbon tetrachloride), to decrease permeability. Escape of helium "overboard" and inward intrusion of air through fabric and valves degraded purity, realizing unwanted loss of lift. (Lt. [jg] H. H. O'Clare, USN [Ret.])

[Bottom] Head of the Fabric Shop, "Harry" O'Clare, helps inspect an air-inflated envelope. Interior and exterior surfaces will be examined for damage or deterioration, then repaired and cleaned as needed. (Lt. [jg] H. H. O'Clare, USN [Ret.])

Fabric Shop personnel secure an envelope with flannel tie-offs, 26 March 1943. Note the canvas carrier; later, articulated carts were introduced to move the heavy fabric. If slated for storage, the bag will be shunted to a nearby "finger," where it will be stretched out on a long shelf. If needed elsewhere, it will be packed for shipment to another LTA station or, instead, shunted to a nearby hangar for mating with a car, control surfaces, and accessories. (Lt. [jg] H. H. O'Clare, USN [Ret.])

tial within a prescribed range—and, with skill, a minimum loss of helium overboard. Airships comply with Archimedes' Principle—that is, the buoyant force acting on a body immersed in a fluid (the atmosphere is a fluid) is equal to the weight of fluid displaced. Airships are thus analogous to submarines; the fundamentals of operation are very similar, as both are submerged—afloat—in a fluid. Each type reacts to conditions that intrude upon control. For example, the raider *U-432* recorded to its logbook that June: "In periscope airship came into sight which shortly afterwards passed right overhead and forced us to dive, deep. Boat sank slowly on account of heavy density layer."[23]

Gross lift, or buoyancy, of an airship is its *static* lift (buoyancy of the helium) plus *dynamic* lift—the airfoil effect of the aircraft itself. Buoyancy is variable, depending on atmospheric con-

"Weighed off" at a safe altitude to define static condition—the interaction between weight and buoyancy, a K-ship drops to a landing party. Ideally, speed was at a minimum when a ship reached the car party. (Capt. J. C. Kane, USN [Ret.])

ditions and the purity of the helium.[24] A blimp is said to be "light" when the gross *lift* exceeds the gross *weight,* "heavy" when the gross weight exceeds total lift. By ballasting, a blimp can be brought to a state of *equilibrium*—the point at which weight is literally zero. In an emergency, this condition was met by droppable "slip" tanks and by jettisoning ordnance. (Release of fuel and water ballast sufficed only in non-emergency conditions.) The fuel system of the K-type airship was designed to dump from the two overhead tanks and, as well, by the release of two slip tanks (180 gallons, 1,080 pounds) located aft, below the cabin deck.[25]

Payload weight for war had pilots exploiting dynamic lift via rolling takeoffs, so as to loft full fuel, ordnance, sensors, and equipment.[26] Loads at takeoff were not to exceed 1,800 pounds flight heaviness—and never to exceed an overload of 10 percent of gross static lift (about 2,600 pounds).

The ZNP pilot held responsibilities comparable to the commanding officer of a surface vessel: he operated at sea and had to know wind, weather, and seagoing practices. Learning the art, mystery, and feel of ship handling, pilots became practical meteorologists—just as surface ship officers are practical seamen. Emerging from beneath a cloud (for instance) quickly warms the helium, thus lightening the ship.[27] A vital element of ship handling, then, is static condition and trim. Prior to takeoff and in flight, pilots ensured the best distribution of disposable ballast, according to static condition. The pilot was, in short, aware of his approximate static condition at all

The G-ships were exploited for advanced student training and for various utility services—notably, "chasing" practice torpedoes fired by friendly submarines. (Lt. Cdr. L. E. Schellberg, USN [Ret.])

times. As in HTA, the better pilots rehearsed in their minds the steps to be taken in the event of emergency, so as to be ready to react instinctively, without thinking. The real test of a LTA pilot's skill is an ability to fly in turbulence and gusts yet maintain altitude within reasonable limits, and with minimal pitching.

Blimps tend to diverge from prescribed courses, rather than fly straight and level. This complicates navigation, so drift sights are essential. The slightest wind tugs insistently. The wind, static condition, altitude at the instant of contact, experience and judgment, and the mission itself were factors confronting pilots given the demands and sudden emergencies of LTA flying, weather, and wartime.

Ship-handling skills are honed through practice, training, and long experience.

Designers had yet to exploit the limits of engineering for the nonrigid type—a specialty now urgent. A lack of navy orders during the disarmament years left Goodyear's design, engineering, and production departments for airships inadequate for war expansion. The *K-2* (an advance, to be sure) was a mere prototype. Under utmost urgency, military demand was translated into operating production lines. Ever-improving innovation would realize a formidable weapons system. "When I returned to lighter-than-air in January 1942 after my departure in June 1938 [Class X]," retired Admiral "Dick" Andrews recalled, "it was hard to believe that this highly developed submarine hunter was the same 'K' ship I knew in 1938, and that instead of one 'K' ship there were many that were fully operative and already engaged in ASW operations in the Atlantic and Pacific."[28]

Early in 1940, neither metal nor fabric had yet been cut for construction. "Once the ships got started," Maurice Bradley remembers, "then everybody wanted to add new equipment to 'em.

About the time radar came out, auxiliary generators were required for the new equipment—and the ships got heavier and heavier. So we were forced to put a couple additional sections in the envelope, to give it more lift to carry the additional load."[29] As well, limitations inherent to the K type would drive development of a better-performance platform: the M-type (see chapter 5).[30] Meantime, defects were addressed, refinements added.

The L and G types had the characteristics of the larger K-ships. Simple in design, these smaller craft were excellent for qualifying pilots and aircrews in the basic principles of aerostatics and aerodynamics.

[Opposite] *L-1* is walked to a mobile mast. All nonrigid airships are handled with mooring masts. Primary flight training using L-ships proved ideal for practicing "heavy" takeoffs on the taxi wheel—standard procedure given combat payloads of fuel, ordnance, armament, sensors, and personnel. (Capt. J. C. Kane, USN [Ret.])

Helium

Infrastructure would necessarily attend airship production: shore stations, masts, flight and support personnel, and helium production. The logistic situation with respect to helium, indeed, had to be handled before operations from new bases could start.

A natural resource, helium is an important commodity: its unique physical properties and its complete inertness render it useful in industry as well as in national defense. Helium occurs as a tiny component of natural gas in the mid-continent and Rocky Mountain areas. In 1918, the first helium-extraction plant had been constructed near Hamilton, Ontario. The U.S. Navy asked the Interior Department's Bureau of Mines to consider the matter of helium *purification* in 1922. Lakehurst's was the first successful plant designed for that purpose, forming the basis for design of subsequent liquefaction plants built by the Bureau of Mines.[31] It was not until 1922 that any airship was inflated with helium. Thereafter, demand rose and fell as interest in airships flared and waned.

World War II delivered a transformation. As the number of airships and support bases multiplied, helium demand soared. Three plants were built to augment the (enlarged) government-owned plant near Amarillo, Texas, exploiting helium-bearing natural gas from the Cliffside field. The first high-pressure helium pipeline, completed in 1944, was built to help meet requirements.

Demand would peak in 1943. For the duration, meantime, the brunt of the navy's helium-related requirements fell to its plant at Lakehurst, and to the civilian employees who operated it. Charles Kauffman led this group. "As business picked up," he remembered, "we added more people, we got more storage. They started to ship [helium] overseas: we shipped (mostly small cylinders) overseas to South America—all those expeditionary bases, and we set up a building to fill and service cylinders. And we were *extremely* busy filling cylinders. Course, they were practically new [air]ships; by that time [1944], they had developed a pretty good fabric so they didn't require purging [repurification] too often, unless they got a hole."[32] This was the busiest phase. "We really had plenty to do at that time," a fellow employee agreed, "because they were asking for cylinders in a lot of remote places where they couldn't get . . . railcars." Lakehurst was supporting its own squadron and, as well, servicing other "ziprons" (blimp squadrons) when purity dropped below specified minimums in *their* ships. Further, hydrostatic testing of *all* the navy's cylinders was conducted on station.[33]

Military requirements eased in October 1944. Even before the defeat of Germany, surplus production was being piped back into Cliffside, below ground.

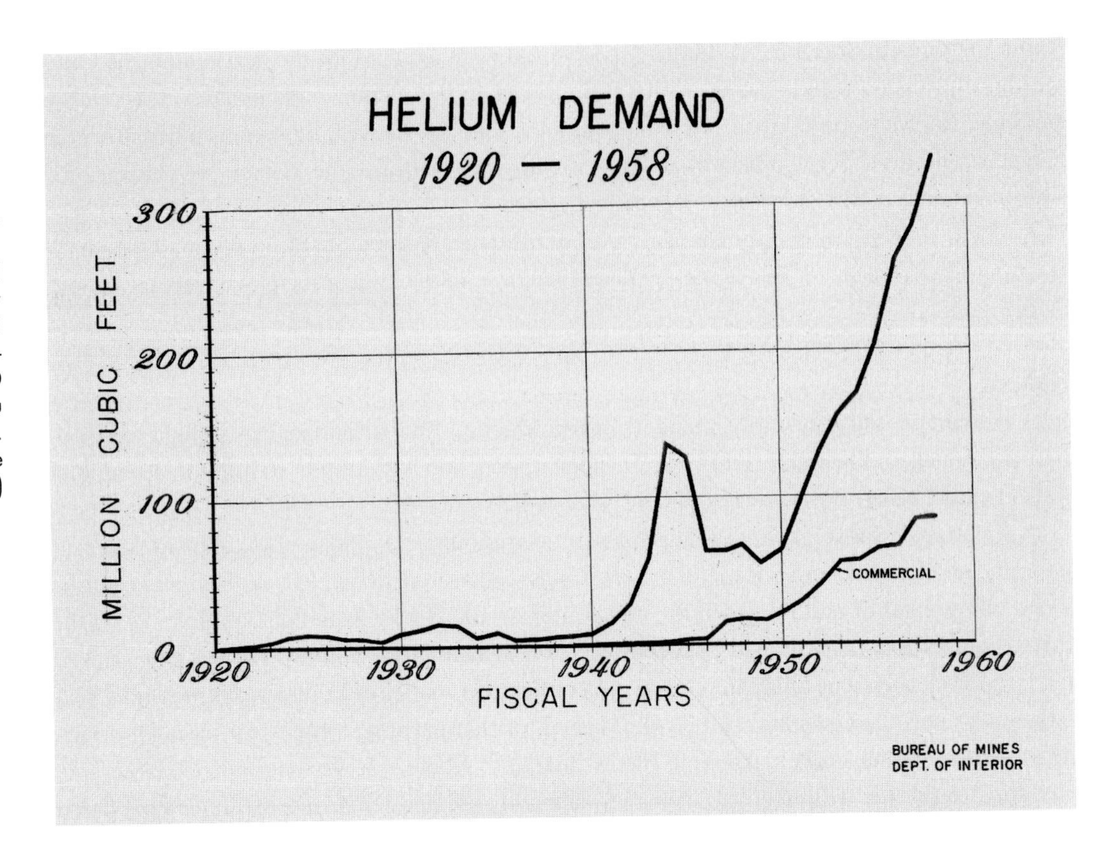

U.S. demand for helium, 1920–1958. Note wartime requirements. Heaviest demand came in 1943, when 108 airships (92 K-type) were delivered to the U.S. Navy operator. Total wartime production: 370,787,000 cubic feet. (Bureau of Mines, U.S. Department of the Interior)

Total wartime production: 370,787,000 cubic feet. Meanwhile, multicylinder semitrailers were procured to service ships assigned to continental bases and at scattered expeditionary sites. As well, the navy's fleet of helium railcars—less troublesome and economical for shipping—increased from twelve to seventy-eight.[34] To help sustain envelope purity in the field, portable helium-purification units were procured for advance bases.

Expanding Programs

Representative Carl Vinson, chairman of the House Committee on Naval Affairs and bold on preparedness, had introduced a new naval expansion bill for fiscal 1941 that included total strength of six thousand naval aircraft and thirty-six nonrigid airships. On 24 January 1940, Admiral Towers, Chief, BuAer, testified before Vinson's committee. The admiral and his planners called for lesser totals; the committee agreed. "Towers could not support the need for three dozen blimps in peacetime either, although he thought them 'extremely useful in time of war for patrol of the sea lanes, outside the harbors and along the coast.'" He therefore compromised: the bill should include an authorization of four blimps per year."[35]

Congress not only provided for thousands of planes (together with shore facilities) but committed itself to a program for naval lighter-than-air. Though some higher-ranking officers did not see much purpose in it, Congress had endorsed what had become a majority position—if not in naval opinion at least in legislative fact. The so-called 10,000 Plane Program legislation, passed in June 1940, authorized forty-eight non-rigid airships. Since Lakehurst was the only applicable station, support facilities would be required to carry out the obligation, spaced along shore points for access to coastwise commerce and vital ports. Of the authorized forty-eight, six were in production at midyear. The new U.S. program for the air "was soaking up every bit of aeronautical equipment that you can imagine. We had a hard time even equipping those first six airships, *K-3* to *K-8*. But after 4–5 months everything came along very well. I don't think there was any holdup after the middle of '42 on government furnished equipment [GFE]—unless there was something special, of course."[36]

On 30 October, Secretary Knox announced a $1,324,000 order for six blimps. Sole bidder: Goodyear Aircraft. The contracts called for four patrol types (ZNPs, in naval parlance) and two L-type trainers. Delivered from the contractor on 1 February 1941, *L-2* was immediately pressed into service. On 7 April, the department authorized three more ships. Of the first four K-types on order, erections were expected to start in late summer, test flights and deliveries about July 1941, at a rate of one airship per month. Expectations were denied: buildup proved slow. Awaiting the initial increment, Rosendahl would find his patience strained.

> What we need more than additional personnel at this time is additional ships and I sincerely hope that no more obstacles will arise in the way of getting production on a proper basis. After all, it is no fun fighting for the project here in Washington and then finding that we are not getting the production due to miscellaneous matters that *can* be cleared up. I cannot emphasize too strongly the importance of getting production going at a more rapid rate.[37]

Meantime, authorization reached Lakehurst for construction of two hangars and other expansion. "The amount of $2,000,000 was allotted and construction that had been long planned, started immediately." *L-3* arrived on 9 June.[38]

During House debate on the blimp-base appropriation, Representative Carl Vinson parried the doubters. Airships, one member had sneered, were "a useless weapon." "It is panzer divisions now, not balloons," another opined.

> By this time [Vinson argued] it should be apparent to anyone who wishes to see that once we become engaged in actual hostilities we shall most probably be seriously confronted, from the very opening moment, with actual danger from enemy submarines and mines, both highly developed and modernized, and both in vastly greater numbers than some 25 years ago. I trust that the public as well as we in the Congress have not forgotten the enemy submarine attacks against us in the summer of 1918. . . . We know also, only too well, the terrible plight of British shipping wherein terrific losses, largely due to modern enemy mines and submarines, threaten Britain's very life line of supply. . . . We shall use our 48 nonrigid airships as members of the inshore patrol to guard our densely packed coastal shipping lines and the approaches to our numerous important harbors from attack by lurking enemy submarines and planted enemy mines.[39]

FDR note to secretary of the navy, 22 April 1941. (National Archives)

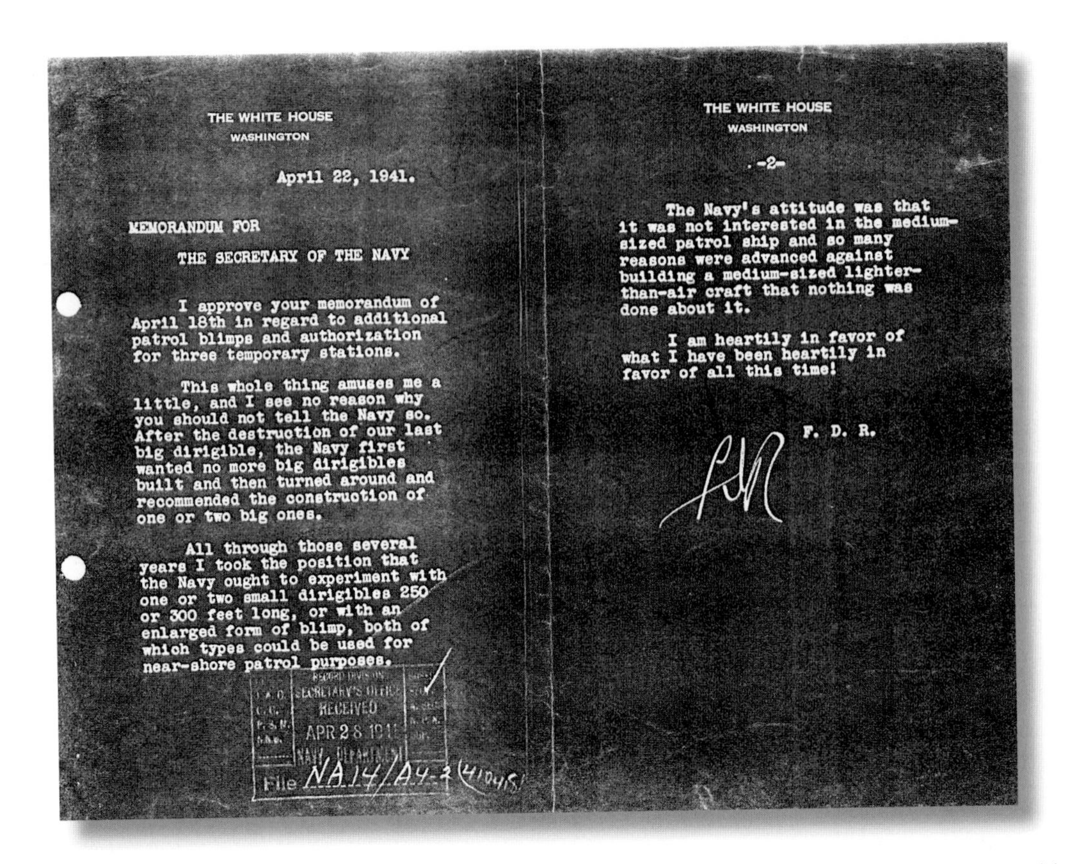

THE WHITE HOUSE
WASHINGTON

April 22, 1941.

MEMORANDUM FOR

THE SECRETARY OF THE NAVY

I approve your memorandum of April 18th in regard to additional patrol blimps and authorization for three temporary stations.

This whole thing amuses me a little, and I see no reason why you should not tell the Navy so. After the destruction of our last big dirigible, the Navy first wanted no more big dirigibles built and then turned around and recommended the construction of one or two big ones.

All through those several years I took the position that the Navy ought to experiment with one or two small dirigibles 250 or 300 feet long, or with an enlarged form of blimp, both of which types could be used for near-shore patrol purposes.

SECRETARY'S OFFICE
RECEIVED
APR 28 1941
File NA14/A4-3

THE WHITE HOUSE
WASHINGTON

-2-

The Navy's attitude was that it was not interested in the medium-sized patrol ship and so many reasons were advanced against building a medium-sized lighter-than-air craft that nothing was done about it.

I am heartily in favor of what I have been heartily in favor of all this time!

F. D. R.

FDR

Without sufficient numbers of "aerial observation posts," Vinson added, the navy would need "enormous numbers" of surface vessels, such as destroyers. These were less effective for observation, and far more expensive than airships. Further, "With the aid of modern science, it is not unreasonable to expect new additional uses for modern blimps."

The Navy Department had laid down its LTA prospectus in two increments—a two-year program. Initially, President Roosevelt opposed any expansion beyond what was already flying and on order. No friend of big dirigibles, FDR favored a small ZR trainer or an enlarged nonrigid. Another factor intruded. In the art of political war, Charles Rosendahl was no artist: intolerant of opponents, brusque and obsessive, this hard-charging officer had seeded enemies within the chain of command. One outcome was influential factions bitterly opposed to airships—more appropriations represented further publicity for Rosendahl. This was personal grudge as policy. Still, he persuaded Knox and CNO Stark that, perhaps, Roosevelt had the rigid type in mind. Knox agreed to intercede. FDR's playful endorsement resulted, approving additional patrol blimps and three air stations.[40]

The second-year program had no imprimatur, however; to maintain headway in the face of House debate, it was decided to abandon that part of the bill that the budget had not yet recommended and the administration had yet to approve. Still, provision for needful facilities outside the continental limits had been included, at the express wish of the CNO.

Public Law 210 of the 77th Congress, approved 16 August 1941, authorized the navy secretary "to establish, develop, or increase naval aviation facilities, designed primarily for lighter-than-air purposes," at or near Norfolk–Cape Hatteras and at Boston. The legislation further authorized auxiliary LTA facilities and, for the West Coast, transferred custody and control of the former naval air station at Sunnyvale from the secretary of war (army) to secretary of the navy. Sunnyvale would serve as an operating base in the San Francisco area. Research was encouraged as well: "The Secretary of the Navy is hereby authorized to conduct aeronautical experiments in the field of other than standard heavier-than-air craft, such as, but limited to, rotary-wing type aircraft, gliders, metal-hulled and other than conventionally propelled lighter-than-air craft and the like at a cost not to exceed $100,000."

In terms of aircraft, the initial procurement comprised twenty-seven ZNPs. Supporting shore establishment: a new air station at South Weymouth, Massachusetts, and at Elizabeth City (Weeksville) in North Carolina. Authorized strength: six K-ships at each station. In May 1942, the CNO issued a shore-establishment directive that included LTA. To help accommodate a growing air arm, a number of auxiliary servicing facilities were to begin as well. Sited between the main stations, these bases provided emergency refueling and reservicing, thereby extending patrol capabilities. When complete, each would hold an anchored mast centered in a mooring-out circle—a prepared path or concrete circle to receive ship's taxi wheel as the blimp weather vaned about its mast-tether. Servicing facilities—supplies of fuel, helium, water, power, lighting, telephone, lubricating oil—would be in place at each.

A second increment would, upon execution, consist of twenty-one units—total forty-eight (to *K-50*). The additional bases, advanced in priority, were sited in the Puget Sound region, another in southern California, and a third in southeastern Florida to cover the Florida Straits and the eastern Florida littoral. The latter location could also support operations within the Gulf Sea Frontier and the sea area surrounding Panama, a zone increasingly threatened by marauding boats.[41] They would be constructed by different contractors but at the same time.[42] As well, the desirability of as many as five stations *outside* the continental limits was noted by CNO—locations (as of August) not yet specified. Hangar space would remain scarce, obliging operational aircrews to moor at expeditionary sites pending completions.

Sited five miles inland and south of Miami, NAS Richmond was to be second only to Lakehurst as a primary overhaul base for ZNP units assigned to the Atlantic Fleet. Completion: fall 1942. Richmond's fleet squadron, ZP-21, would log its commissioning on 1 November.

In New Jersey, facilities were hurriedly installed.[43] The center of training and experimentation, NAS Lakehurst was to function as "navy yard" for major overhaul of East Coast–based airships. Further, when ZP-12 was placed in commission, Lakehurst served as homeport for a squadron assigned to the Atlantic Fleet. Until ships were available and hangars complete at South Weymouth and at Elizabeth City, Mills elected to dispatch one or two from ZP-12 to ZP-11 (Weymouth) and to ZP-14 (Elizabeth City), relieving a ship at intervals to ensure its 120-check inspection and engine changes.

In California, Sunnyvale would serve an overhaul function for Pacific Coast LTA commands and operations (see chapter 7). Retrospectively, Fulton was to remark, "The planning and setting up of the crop of new blimp bases was a project of first magnitude—and I got the impression that it was pretty well handled all things considered."[44]

How would these forces and personnel be organized?

LTA training had required seven free-balloon flights for student officers, three for enlisted personnel. The national emergency de-emphasized the requirement. Note the control cars for *TC-13* and *TC-14*—deflated, dismantled, and packed for rail shipment to Moffett Field, California. The nucleus for Blimp Squadron Thirty-two (ZP-32), each took part in the first antisubmarine patrols off the West Coast. (Lt. Cdr. L. E. Schellberg, USN [Ret.])

K-car interior, from the aft door looking forward. Portside, the mechanic's instrument panel is visible, the radar station beyond it. The magnetic anomaly detector or MAD gear is not apparent. In summer 1942, a mock-up called for the Type IV MAD to be mounted above the radar thereby allowing one operator to work both sets. (Lt. H. F. Smith, USNR [Ret.])

> It seems probable however that the basic tactical and administrative unit will be a "ZP Squadron" paralleling the existing "VP" [HTA patrol squadron] organization. It may also prove necessary to organize ZP squadrons into the next higher unit or "Group." ZNPs are intended for utilization in the "inshore patrol" in the coastal shipping lanes and the approaches to important harbors. Just where the ZP units will fit into the existing naval organization is now in the process of determination.[45]

Training for LTA Duty

The matter of inexperience haunts all military ventures. Planning for war is tied to personnel as well as material considerations. The human factor is vital: poorly trained personnel are invitations to failure. In the war between aircraft and U-boat, professionalism was to prove decisive. Naval-air assets held scant value unless they could execute the mission: "We hear so much about radar and camouflage and secret new gadgets that we finally come to think that the gadgets can fight by themselves. Actually there is not an experienced squadron commander who would not gladly swap radar and all the other tricks in the bag for a crew that know their business thoroughly and went at it with intelligence and conscience."[46]

In its aviation organizations, the Navy in 1941–42 faced a shortage of flight status and non-flying personnel to man its squadrons *and* the prospective air stations supporting them. For LTA,

[Top Right] Early in 1942, the Bureau of Navigation issued a letter to various recruiting stations asking for cadets for LTA training. Seasoned airmen few in number, the demand for both officer-pilots and enlisted LTA personnel would persist into 1944.

[Bottom Right] Class XIX, 8 October 1942. An accelerated flow of personnel for squadrons, air stations and auxiliary commands deemed urgent, officer training was reduced to about six months and fewer flight hours required. One graduate here had logged 123 hours, including one balloon flight. Intended to balance the increasing numbers of inexperienced junior officers, Class XIX (sixty officers selected from volunteers) promptly assumed command responsibilities throughout the LTA organization. (Capt. F. N. Klein, USN [Ret.])

TABLE 2.1 **Courses, Officers Training School at Naval Air Station Lakehurst, New Jersey (1941).** Class XV—the first accelerated, expanded class of twenty-four students—convened on 1 July; graduates were designated the last day of 1941.

First Term	Second Term
Balloons	Navigation
Lifting and Fuel Gases	Aerology
Non-Rigid Airmanship	Strategy, Tactics, and Mission
Ground Handling and Mooring	Photography
Dock Routine and Ship Maintenance	Instruments
Engines	Aerodynamics
Aerostatics	Materials Design and Construction
Parachutes	Communications
Miscellaneous (preliminary work)	
Reports Submitted	
Book Reports (3)	
Pamphlet Reports (3)	
Thesis	

Courtesy Cdr. L. R. Ulrich, USN (Ret.)

this particular issue had festered since the loss of *Macon*. As Garland Fulton observed in 1937, "Personnel shortage is acute. There is no designation for a blimp pilot (Naval aviators airship must, by law, have had rigid airship experience). There is no well recognized reserve status (either Navy or Army) for L.T.A. personnel. The Goodyear blimp fleet is the only commercial blimp activity. A few of their personnel hold reserve status, but there is no plan for building up a reserve of qualified L.T.A. personnel."[47]

Experience had dwindled through attrition, nonselection for promotion, and (not least) loss of interest in a project offering no apparent future. Moreover, the potential pool of seagoing officers and enlisted personnel had scattered throughout the service. Of the ninety-two officers still on active duty in 1940, twenty-eight (17 percent) were assigned to Lakehurst.

Getting them back now stood urgent. Among the officers so ordered: each member of LTA Class X (1936–37), as well as Class XI. In 1942, Lt. Cdr. George E. Pierce was a gunnery officer aboard a destroyer. "I was just about to beat these characters [green crew] into a damn good fightin' destroyer when I got these orders. . . . I have no objection to that," he continues. "That's why they trained us. When the need arose, they fingered us."[48] Then Lt. W. E. Delong also got new orders. "I was standing on watch on the subchaser [*SC 515*] one night when an 'All Nav' came through and they were requesting officer candidates for lighter-than-air training. And I sent in the application." On 1 February 1942, he received orders to Lakehurst.[49]

To spur infusion of regular officers and reservists (cadets), the officers' school at Lakehurst enrolled large classes. Class XIV inaugurated the practice of combining officer-students with aviation cadets ("AvCads"). Its number-one graduate would be Lt. (jg) Douglas L. Cordiner, USN; his designation as Naval Aviator (Airship) was conferred on 8 July 1941.[50] (See Table 2.1.)

Class XIII had graduated five officers in 1940. Five cadets were designated from the next class—the last to receive their commissions before the raid on Oahu. In July 1941, meantime, the first accelerated, expanded class convened. Class L-15 (two dozen men) was trained in six months, after which Class L-16 assembled on 6 October: forty student-pilots were sworn in as aviation cadets. Following an introduction to the station, each man settled down to ground-school routine.[51] By 1943, classes of officers, cadets, and enlisted men (no less vital) were convening regularly. In light of the emergency, officer indoctrination was shortened from twelve to about six and one-half months, from six to three months for enlisted men. "Personnel is still a problem with us," Mills was to report as 1942 ended, "and will continue to be for at least another year."[52]

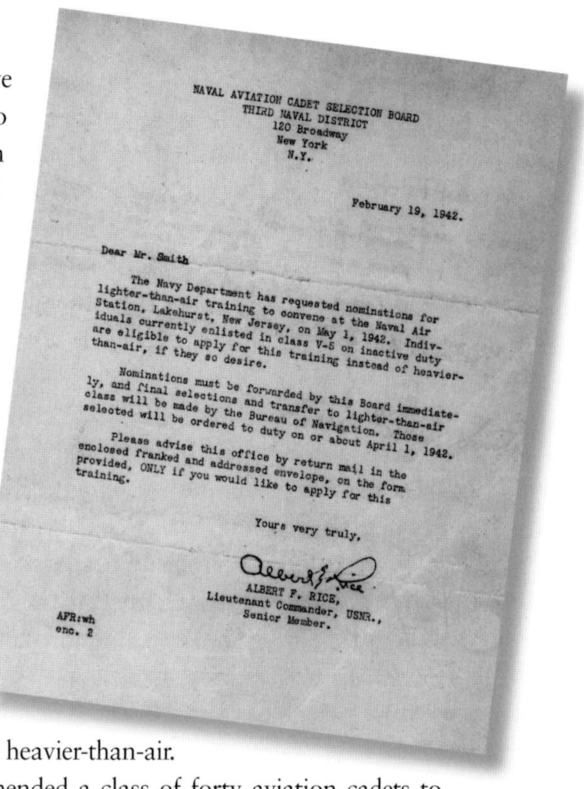

NAVAL AVIATION CADET SELECTION BOARD
THIRD NAVAL DISTRICT
120 Broadway
New York
N.Y.

February 19, 1942.

Dear Mr. Smith

The Navy Department has requested nominations for lighter-than-air training to convene at the Naval Air Station, Lakehurst, New Jersey, on May 1, 1942. Individuals currently enlisted in class V-5 on inactive duty are eligible to apply for this training instead of heavier-than-air, if they so desire.

Nominations must be forwarded by this Board immediately, and final selections and transfer to lighter-than-air class will be made by the Bureau of Navigation. Those selected will be ordered to duty on or about April 1, 1942.

Please advise this office by return mail in the enclosed franked and addressed envelope, on the form provided, ONLY if you would like to apply for this training.

Yours very truly,

ALBERT F. RICE,
Lieutenant Commander, USNR.,
Senior Member.

AFR:wh
enc. 2

As the war worn on, moreover, the program would lose seasoned officers to the surface navy and to heavier-than-air.

Looking forward through 1942, BuAer recommended a class of forty aviation cadets to convene about March, about fifty cadets around 1 August, another fifty on or about 1 Febru-

ary 1943. In late April 1942, meantime, the commander of ZP Group One (Mills) had fifty-five regular and thirty-nine reserve qualified officers available, as well as 314 enlisted men, to man all ZP squadrons and LTA stations. Squadron Twelve, for its part, had twenty-six officers and 108 qualified enlisted men assigned; within weeks, this nucleus of experience would be divided to man Squadrons Eleven, Thirteen, and Fourteen.[53]

The then LTA program: seventy-two (from forty-eight) nonrigid airships.

The importance of enlisted personnel tends to be overlooked. Yet the navy is dependent on more than its commissioned ranks: every hand contributes. When asked about preparations for wartime patrol, one pilot remarked, "The pilot could only have a broad view of the situation. You had guys that were technicians that were your right and left arm. The pilot—you were there to make decisions. But as far as the nitty-gritty, they were the ones that really took care of their specific requirements. It was the enlisted personnel who specialized in their equipment [who] were key to the operation."[54]

The school for enlisted LTA ratings had closed in 1934. Richard "Dick" Widdicombe, QM3c, reported in June 1940. "From the beginning [he recalls], Class Nine received excellent theoretical classroom instruction, hands on practical training and continuous ground-handling experience. Indeed, because of the heavy flight operations schedule, we were essential for G.H. [ground handling] duty with regular experienced Flight Division personnel. We also were sent aloft as students for training as air crewmen in the training and patrol airships."[55]

As experience was acquired, training included inshore operations: convoy-escort hours and detection exercises. No tactical manual for patrols was yet available, so as an expedient escort time was gained by meeting up with merchantmen, then holding station. Working with U.S. boats in torpedo practices, airships held position on targets and on fired "fish."[56] Antisubmarine training was obtained by working with friendly boats in New London waters, practicing sighting surfaced boats and hunting them submerged. As well, ZNPs were assigned to cover proscribed inshore sectors.

Without training honed through practice, the instruments of war are but gadgets. The best pilots attain a proficiency that gets their commands to the battle ready to fight on arrival—and that allows them, at the scene of action, to act instantly, instinctively, effectively. For the A/S war, immense exertions introduced new systems and gadgets and sensors that, too often, would be poorly exploited. Why? Well-trained personnel can extract satisfactory results with the equipment available, whereas unqualified personnel will not produce with the best of gear.

Aloft and afloat, locating submerged diesel boats posed a challenge. In 1940, the Naval Research Advisory Committee had pronounced the navy's detecting apparatus "far ahead of the trained personnel which operates the [sonar] equipment." Yet detection/destruction depended more upon the skill and judgment of the operator. Thoroughly able officers and instructors were therefore recommended for the navy's sound schools, and the "highest possible standards" applied to the selection of trainees.

Technology-assisted, navies were becoming increasingly electronic:

> The U.S. Navy continued to increase its reliance on electronics at a furious pace partly at least because of the influx of recruits with few sea skills who needed all possible tech-

> nical assistance. . . . This was particularly true in the campaign against German U-boats which became more and more technology oriented during the course of the war. The navy's ability to cope with this expansion was always a case of running to keep up.[57]

As 1941 ebbed, a committee of psychologists and physicists was appointed, in the hope that tests could be devised so as to select men of the greatest aptitude. NDRC also would study training methods at the Key West and San Diego sound schools to realize a more effective program. As the problem festered, the importance of simplification would be stressed—a difficult course to steer, inasmuch as equipment usually gets more complicated as it becomes more automated.

Though scientists warned of the importance of training in allowing ships to get the most out of new equipment, senior officers at Admiral King's headquarters failed early in the war to heed the advice. Ironically, academics had to remind senior admirals of the importance of training.[58]

For forces both afloat and ashore, the matter of personnel persisted "To summarize, while efforts should continue to improve the quality and effectiveness of our detection devices and ASW ordnance, our principal aim should be to provide an adequate number of properly trained units to provide effective protection in all areas."[59]

The merchant marine, for its part, was no less afflicted. According to a 1943 bulletin, Vice Adm. Adolphus Andrews acknowledged "the difficulty and danger of navigation in convoy and sailing under all conditions without lights. He is well aware also of the risk involved in operating coastwise without so many of the customary aids to navigation. . . . The expansion of shipping obviously has required and will continue to necessitate the addition of personnel, whose sea training actually begins after they have reported on board."[60]

Expectation suffused airship circles. Below the most senior officers, would the right ones *stay* in what was still a lean, disparaged program? And would officers and enlisted men elect to *return* to LTA? Unofficial word came via Rosendahl—on duty in Washington. Having outlined the projected wartime organization, Rosie offered his appreciation of the situation: "It would appear that before many more months we shall have to be calling back a considerable number of both officers and enlisted personnel. . . . Suffice it to say, we all have you in mind and hope to get most of you back as the LTA organization expands. There is lots to be done and if you do get ordered back to LTA we hope it will be with enthusiasm for hard work and long hours in what we feel is a very interesting and promising activity."

On 27 November, Lakehurst was notified that relations between the United States and Japan were strained. Extra security precautions were ordered.

Mills knew that the directive placing Squadron Twelve in commission was in preparation. The CNO request to the Commander, North Atlantic Naval Coastal Frontier, is dated 10 December.[61]

At approximately 1500 on 7 December, broadcasts were heard announcing the raid upon Oahu. Abruptly, fears of sabotage and enemy attack were rife. At Lakehurst, such concerns were addressed via armed watches posted in the hangars, a doubling of the guard, and security inspections of all departments. "All possible precautions," the station log records, "were taken to prevent sabotage upon orders of the Commanding Officer, after receipt of the information that Pearl Harbor, T.H. had been attacked by Japan." Confirmation was soon received from Washington.

NAS Lakehurst, 1941–42. Taxiways connect new circles; moored out, three ships swing to their masts. Mat 1 is not yet paved; the abandoned circles for *Los Angeles*, *Macon*, and *Hindenburg* have yet to be pulled up and their roadbeds leveled. On 7 December, the air station had ten airships on hand. Two airplanes rounded out the inventory. (National Archives, courtesy PAO, NAEC, Lakehurst)

"The events of yesterday," Mills observed, "have changed a good many of the pleasant peacetime conditions around here. . . . Three ships are out on patrol today and that will be about our normal patrol for the time being."[62]

Next day, Rosendahl wrote Mills. One up on the future, Rosie now held the authority to shape it. Acting as liaison between Hunsaker's office and the Lakehurst command, he had conferred with NDRC about the so-called Quonset–New London equipment (magnetic detection). Dr. D. G. C. Hare, field scientist on the project, was "very enthusiastic over the prospects of its successful application and use by blimps. . . . In fact, everyone connected with the project is most anxious to give it a test in a blimp at the earliest practical moment. Particularly as a result of the startling events of yesterday, this project ranks high in priority."[63]

Following further testing aboard a Quonset plane, "this only set" was slated for Lakehurst. Once it was ZNP-installed, the next phase would be flight analyses—maneuvering in the vicinity of surface vessels, followed by tests with U.S. submarines. "If this Mark I equipment shows promise, then these scientists will rush to completion the dual coil installation for the earliest possible installation in a ZNP. . . . I expect to be engaged in starting the second increment of the ZNP program within a day or so. As a matter of fact Senator Andrews of Florida is today introducing in the Senate a bill for the shore facilities required by the second increment plus five stations outside the continental limits."[64]

A fresh program for the naval airship was gratifying. Still, in truth, Rosendahl cared little for blimps; his faith in the large rigids was consuming. "Needless to say," he cued Mills, "I am also taking every opportunity to plug the ZRCV as a result of this horrible mess in Oahu."

Contrary to misconception, rigid airship development in the U.S. had not halted with the loss of *Macon*. A series of proposals for both military and commercial rigid airships had ensued.[65] The ZRCV studies of 1936–38 described a very large airborne "carrier" of 9,550,000-cubic-foot volume. Calculated useful lift: 297,000 pounds. It would have carried a striking force of nine hook-on airplanes—fifty-four thousand pounds of combat-loaded scout dive-bombers similar to the Northrop BT-1, direct ancestor of the SBD *Dauntless*. Maximum speed was seventy-five knots; cruising at fifty knots, the ZRCV had an endurance of 175 hours, or an out-and-back range of 4,375 miles. Exploiting ZRs as strategic "carriers" had been—in the naval environment of the 1930s—the raison d'être of the type. But funds for development had not been forthcoming. Rosendahl reintroduced the matter. When, in January 1942, Admiral King hoisted his flag as Commander in Chief, U.S. Fleet, King (and Vinson also) sought to revive and implement the ZRVC idea. The possibility of construction created months of excitement in the LTA organization, prompting further studies by C. P. Burgess, BuAer's enduring authority on airship design.[66] Estimated cost for one unit: ten million dollars. By way of comparison, the PBY-1 flying boat cost the navy approximately $100,000.

But the Navy Department did not want a rigid airship wished on it. In reply to Admiral Harold R. Stark, CNO, the Bureau of Aeronautics estimated a year for detail design and two additional years to build. BuAer opposed construction, given shortages in facilities, raw materials, engineering talent, trained personnel, helium. Instead, if there was to be a ZR program, it recommended first building the three-million-cubic-foot rigid for training purposes. King agreed to defer the ZRVC "for the present" but pressed for the training rigid. "So the fat is in the fire on that also—whoopee!!" Rosie exalted. But Admiral Towers could not agree, citing the time required to realize even one ZRCV and diversion of essential materials. Goodyear's engineering staff was limited; besides blimps, the company was also producing vital subassemblies for airplanes. Also, industrial dislocation would result if the new project were built at Akron. Erection at Lakehurst or Moffett Field would interfere with operations. Further, Towers opposed long-range scouting airships on the grounds of vulnerability to planes. Indeed, most persons holding a responsible position in the naval establishment or in other organs of the government could not imagine where a single rigid airship fit into an urgent wartime picture.[67]

The ZRCV never left paper. A certain futility marks the final years for the naval rigid. Sputterings for airplane- and (or) cargo-carrying airships were to persist into the postwar period. Early in 1944, for example, Rosendahl submitted a paper to the navy secretary urging construction of ZRs for naval transport purposes. Indefinitely postponed, the issue of the next ZR would expire, finally, to nothing.[68]

Mills, meantime, held weekly conferences with his core staff. On Monday, 8 December, he set the tone. "Last week when I indicated that this country was near war and told you to start our security measures," he reminded, "it was unexpected that I would say at this conference that the Japanese had started war against us and from some radio reports we have been in rather severe difficulties." For Mills, a host of urgencies awaited, from major to marginal—forming squadrons, finishing hangars, and getting enough steel for mooring masts to an insufficiency of lockers for the next LTA class.

Berlin, on the ninth, lifted its restrictions on attacks against U.S. warships and merchantmen under the U.S. flag. Germany and Italy joined the enemy list two days later. Abruptly, millions of additional tons of Atlantic shipping were targets. Within weeks, U.S. forces would be fighting to hold their own along the East Coast.

The week's operations included routine patrols and training, plus an additional patrol. Project Sail got a mention, obliquely: "I have a letter from Captain Rosendahl concerning the project now being worked on out at Quonset. I think some of you are familiar with that. It is a confidential project and I can't discuss it here, but that is to be worked out for lighter-than-air."[69] The "project": magnetic detection of submarines.

On 10 December, at the Underwater Sound Laboratory (USL), the navy and the NDRC group at New London convened to discuss various developments. In his opening remarks to the forty-odd officers and civilians (Section C-4) duly assembled, Admiral Van Keuren was near-desperate in tone: "Now that war has been forced upon us, research and development on the detection and destroying of submarines is of utmost importance and should be carried forward with dispatch. If additional ships and submarines are needed for experimental work," he felt sure that in spite of the great needs elsewhere they could be provided."[70]

Innovations would be realized for hyper-urgent projects—for example, increasing the descent rate of depth charges. Helpfully, information from recent conferences with Royal Navy officers in England was shared. Dr. L. B. Slichter reviewed recent developments on magnetic detection from planes, and he mentioned tests in planning in which the detector (with small alterations) would be towed from a blimp. "It seemed to be the opinion," notes record, "that the range of magnetic detection which has now been obtained . . . was sufficient to indicate that it would make an extremely useful method of detecting submarines from aircraft."[71]

At sea, British and Canadian naval and air forces were strained to near breaking point. Concentrating Coastal Command aircraft in the Western Approaches to give absolute protection was impracticable. Therefore, deciding *where* to deploy assets was an art requiring a professional gambler's ability to outguess an opponent. No less vital were good intelligence, ever-improving tactics and doctrine—and the equipment and weapons to detect, track, then sink the submerged foe. Essential ingredients: training, aircrew vigilance, constant practice.

Airborne attack on submarines is exemplary of the challenge:

> Accurate anti-submarine bombing is by far the most difficult task that is given to any pilot in the R.A.F. to perform. The problem which is presented to him is to get [by eye] a straddle with a fairly close spaced stick of depth charges on an unseen and moving target, using as his aiming mark the fixed and visible swirl. To add to his difficulties he must get down from operational height to 50 feet and deliver his attack within a matter of one or two minutes if he is to be successful, and the lethal range of underwater weapons is so small that an error of only a couple of feet may make all the difference.[72]

Sharing a sense of combined fates, Churchill greeted America's formal declaration "with relief and an uprising spirit. Henceforth our load would be shared by a partner of almost unlimited resources and we might hope that in the war at sea the U-boats would soon be brought under control."[73]

Managing matters in Washington, immersed in planning, Rosendahl coordinated with Mills. Few in number within the naval air bureaucracy and low in budgetary and programmatic priorities, Lakehurst's most senior officers (and experienced junior officers) were probably the best team the program could have wished for. Combative and sardonic, Rosendahl applied his infighter skills, churning the waters with tireless work.[74] Lent crucial support from Admiral King, his voice carried. Dynamic, driving, and unyielding, the soul of the project, Rosie nurtured the revival.

The raid on Oahu triggered defense of an exposed coast. The threat embraced not only U-boats but, as well, attack by surface-raiders or enemy aircraft, spies, raiding parties, and saboteurs. Atlantic beaches were a restricted area, under army control. (Arnold Collection, NASM, Smithsonian Institution)

A supremely able leader and officer-manager, Cdr. George H. Mills, USN, was Rosendahl's polar opposite in personality: quiet, calm, noncombative. Devoted to airships, "Shorty" Mills shared little of the quest for renown (and sense of aggrievement) so central to the Rosendahl persona. Excellent in judgment, long on experience, Mills enjoyed the trust, respect, and complete confidence of his subordinates, as well as that of the top naval commands.

Six days after Pearl Harbor, Rosendahl (a polemical correspondent) wrote a very busy Mills. It was lecture by CER: "I feel that it may possibly be our Lakehurst blimps who make the first contact around the Atlantic Coast in this new phase of the war. My guess is that just as in the last war the Axis will make some kind of a splurge around New York or the same general vicinity operated in by German submarines in 1918. . . . After all the years of tough sledding, it would only be justice for some lighter-than-air crew to draw first blood on the enemy."

As it pertained to German intentions, the instinct proved sound. An idiosyncratic warning added: "We should not exclude the slight possibility" that German rigid airships might yet exist and be used for a surprise attack! And (more sensibly) this, "I hope you stress in all our ships and crews complete familiarity with their own life saving devices, rubber boats, emergency rations, etc."[75]

Mills echoed preparedness, though any concern on his part as to threatening Zeppelins has gone unrecorded. "We must make sure," he cautioned, "that every pilot who goes on a mission understands what he is going for, how he is going to attack, how he is going to signal, and how he is going to answer recognition signals. We took a good deal of this up at a conference of watch officers the other day but I am afraid that not all of them yet understand just what they are supposed to do. We have a good chance of really making contact with a German submarine and we have got to know exactly what to do."[76]

A U.S. coast-defense battery. Ground defenses along the West Coast included antiaircraft as well as fixed guns, antisubmarine nets and minefields, beach patrols, guarding troops, blackouts, searchlights, barrage balloons, and camouflaged war industries. (Arnold Collection, NASM, Smithsonian Institution)

On 20 December, by executive order, President Roosevelt elevated Ernie King as Commander in Chief, U.S. Fleet (abbreviated Cominch), with headquarters in the Navy Department, Washington. A few months later, as well, he became Chief of Naval Operations. Wielding singular authority, King was to wear both hats throughout the war. In overall command of naval operating forces, King was subject only to the authority vested in the president by the Constitution and in the secretary of the navy by law. Thus devolved onto one officer the bureaus in the administrative chain of command as well as operational command of all fleet units.

> Without question, King was a brilliant naval officer and an exceptionally capable seaman. But he had a willful, mean, and brittle side to his nature that limited his effectiveness as a leader charged with bringing new people and new ideas to bear on problems of developing untraditional and unanticipated ways of waging warfare. . . . In his new position as COMINCH, his institutional power buttressed the instinct of a brilliant though eccentrically stubborn mind. This flaw had an unfortunate effect on the campaign against the U-boat.[77]

Along with daily patrols and training out of Lakehurst, flight "ops" for 1941 ended with a photographic mission, the testing of propellers (exploiting *K-3*), and two "blackout flights" using

TC-14. Word was received that two ships might be ordered to California. A list of equipment intended for NAS Sunnyvale was ordered, including all gear necessary for erecting an airship. L. Russell Ulrich was an aviation cadet in LTA Class 15 (July 1941–January 1942). "We were *terribly* short of airships," he reminds. "The early K-ships with the Wright engines were *just starting* to be delivered. The requirements for escorts were tremendous because of all the shipping. . . . I remember there was a lot of press to get as much possible out of the airships that we had—which were not many."[78]

Capt. Lyman K. Swenson, USN, [left] receives congratulations from Rear Adm. Adolphus Andrews, USN, at the New York Navy Yard, 14 February 1942.

As Commander of the Eastern Sea Frontier, Andrews shouldered a fateful responsibility: control of U.S. escort and naval air operations for the whole of the Eastern Seaboard, from Maine to Florida. (NavSource/U.S. Navy photo)

Officers holding orders to Lakehurst's prospective squadron (ZP-12) were relieved of station duties to allow them to apply full attention to the commissioning. In terms of security, extra holiday precautions were installed to guard against sabotage.

In Washington, Churchill was a guest of the President and Mrs. Roosevelt; the crown prince and princess of Norway, now refugees from their occupied nation, were also in residence. At the traditional lighting of the District of Columbia's Christmas tree, the prime minister exercised his oratory. "This is a strange Christmas eve. Almost the whole world is locked in a deadly struggle, and with the most terrible weapons which science can devise, the nations advance upon each other. Ill would it be for us this Christmastide if we were not sure that no greed for the land or wealth of any other people, no vulgar ambition, no morbid lust for material gain at the expense of others has led us to the field."[79]

Invitations to the commissioning included Admirals Stark and King, Rear Admiral Towers, Rear Adm. Randall Jacobs (Chief of the Bureau of Navigation), and Vice Adm. Adolphus Andrews (Commander, North Atlantic Naval Coastal Frontier, soon to be renamed Eastern Sea Frontier). Just now, these officers shouldered an immense burden—responsibility for the conduct of East Coast antisubmarine warfare.[80]

Stark had ordered sea frontiers established in July. By virtue of their control of coastal convoys and defense of inshore waters (out to roughly two hundred miles), a singular responsibility fell to these commanders. Until his retirement in November 1943, Andrews exercised operational control over all forces allocated to the eastern seaboard of the United States.[81] Headquarters: the Federal Building at 90 Church Street, in lower Manhattan. From this nerve center, Andrews exercised responsibility for a shipping supply chain and sea space arcing from the ports of Maine through New York, Norfolk, and the Atlantic littoral fully to Key West. (See chart on next page.)

Via CNO confidential letter dated 1 December, Airship Squadron Twelve was established—the first ever in the U.S. Navy. "It was organized," squadron history records, "to add to the antisubmarine forces present or being formed to operate as part of the Eastern Sea Frontier, and contributed toward filling an urgent need for such forces." Created under the same authority: Airship

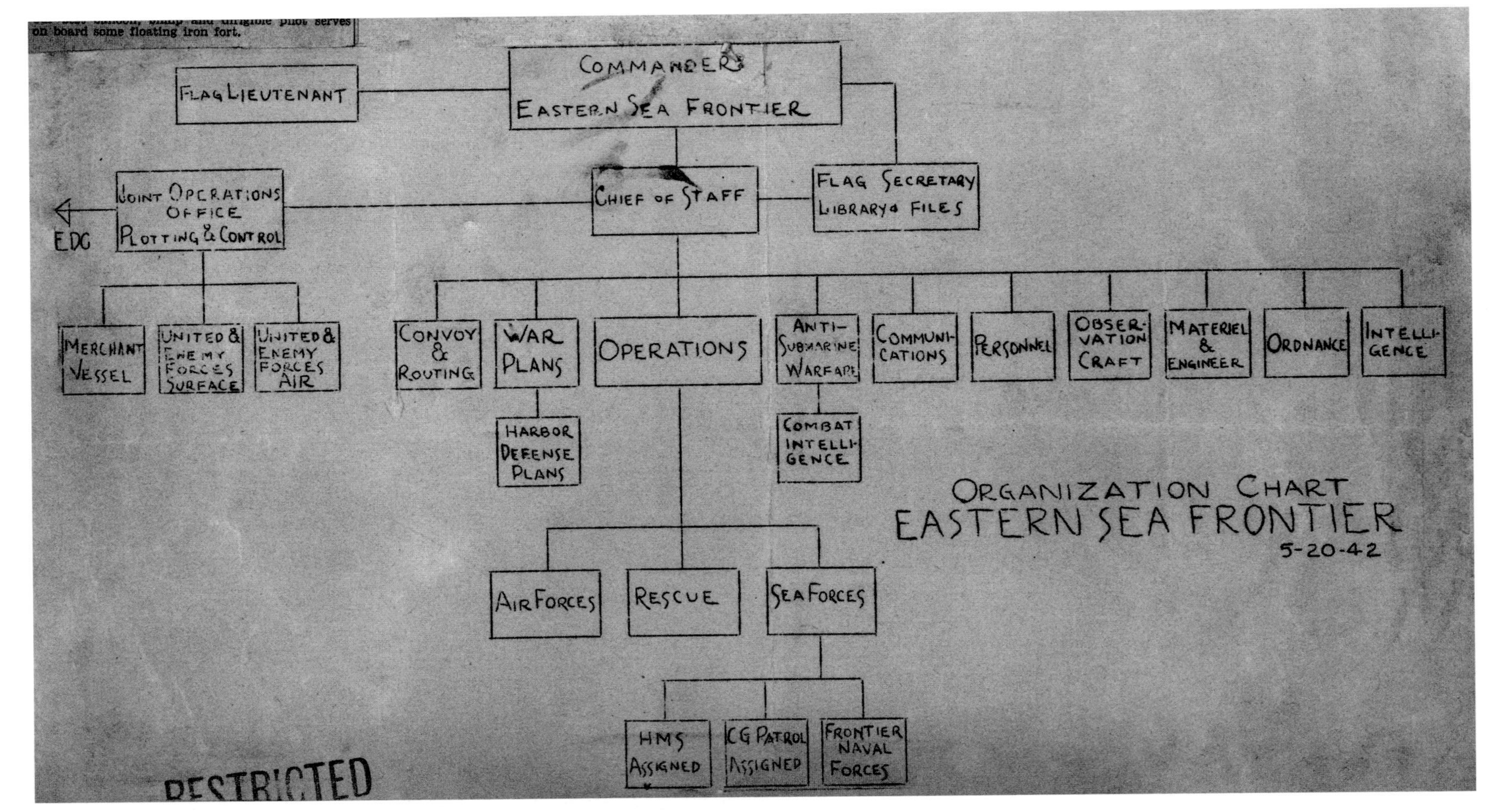

Organization chart, Eastern Sea Frontier, May 1942. (National Archives)

Patrol Group One, Cdr. George H. Mills, USN, commander. In the echelon of command, ZP-12 would report to Mills; in turn, Group One would operate under Andrews's direct authority.[82]

A triple ceremony was laid on at Lakehurst. Command of the station devolved from Mills to his executive officer, Cdr. F. C. Sachse. Next, Andrews read his orders from the navy secretary: "In accordance with the authority, etc., I hereby place ZP Group 1 in commission and place it under the command of Comdr. G. H. Mills, USN." The colors were hoisted, commission pennants and the admiral's flag (one star) broken. Thus was conferred upon Mills direct supervision of and responsibility for all LTA defending forces. The new group commander read his orders, after which his subordinate commander—the new squadron skipper, Tyler—read his. Tyler then ordered his second in command to set the watch. Brief speeches followed.

> We are several years late with this commissioning [Andrews told his audience]. Rather than relaxing in the achievement of the formation of this squadron—we must bend every effort to bring these ships up to maximum efficiency as quickly as possible—and add more units as fast as we can. . . . This is the first lighter-than-air squadron to be commissioned in the United States Navy. Today, after discouraging years, airships have an opportunity to prove their effectiveness and earn the place they deserve in our navy. . . . With so much accent on airplanes, the airship has been almost overlooked by the Nation. By your performance, you can achieve the recognition that lighter-than-air warrants.[83]

Ceremonies closed, Andrews and his party enjoyed luncheon, then a tour of the air station. Andrews at this moment faced appalling defense headaches. His thankless assignment: to execute American A/S strategy and protect all coastwise shipping in a poorly defended littoral arcing, as we have seen, from Maine all the way to Key West. Everything stood in short supply: destroyers and other escorts, A/S aircraft, support gear—and the experienced sailors to man them. In all, twenty surface ships were available to protect more than three thousand miles of sea-lanes, along with slightly more than a hundred planes. Of these latter, a mere four (navy PBYs) were equipped and their aircrews trained in ASW.[84]

Fleet airship operations were now under way, with one squadron of four ships, ZNP *K-3* through ZNP *K-6*. The available list for the *station*: *K-2*, *G-1*, and three L-ship trainers, plus two airplanes. At this moment, the ex-army *TC-13* and *TC-14* were being packed for shipment west—nucleus for a Pacific Coast squadron (see chapter 7). This inventory represented a welcome if meager addition to Andrews's pitiful array of A/S resources.

Experimental work on depth charging, bombing, and mine spotting had begun at Lakehurst in 1940. Soon, the station was saturated with respect to space and workload. By summer 1943, the high-priority projects alone embraced the testing of bomb racks, ZNP camouflage, studies to improve gun armament, the installation of improved MAD gear, a system for blimp-towed hydrophones, the expendable radio sonobuoy, as well as various ground handling projects.[85]

Planning, training, and operations accelerated. Two fleet airship wings would be operational by mid-December, with 200 blimps authorized (120 contracted for). By 1944, indeed, ten ZP

squadrons would be operational. These assets were exploiting main and auxiliary air facilities along the Canadian and U.S. eastern seaboards and the gulf coast, in Panamanian waters, in the Caribbean Sea, British West Indies, Brazil, Africa, and in Europe. As well, a utility squadron was conducting various services, notably torpedo recovery and photographic missions.

LTA assumed the following organization: Fleet ASW squadrons were commissioned as fleet units and reported to the C-in-C of the Atlantic Fleet through the administrative *and* operational chains of command. Administratively, this took place through Commander, Naval Air Force. Operationally, squadrons were under the Sea Frontier commanders or, for overseas units, directly under a numbered-fleet commander (e.g., Commander, Fourth Fleet). Logistic support to the squadrons—berthing, messing, fuel, ammunition, and so on—was provided by a series of continental as well as overseas air stations devoted primarily to LTA, plus mast bases at HTA stations.

Among the positive developments were encouraging reports pulsing through the bureaus concerned with magnetic detection: BuAer, BuShips, BuOrd (the Bureau of Ordnance).[86] The navy had wanted a practical assessment; NDRC pressed to deliver one, exploiting ships and planes and airships made available for MAD development work (mainly) at Quonset and at Key West.[87] Equipment slated for Lakehurst was expedited; barring a supply upset, two additional instruments would be furnished by midmonth—then two per week thereafter until a dozen were in hand. Still, tests were preliminary only, to determine if the equipment would function as expected when ZNP-installed.

Tate wrote NDRC, "After their completion, we hope to be able to advise you more definitely concerning the matter of supplying additional models; at present the conditions of operation on Blimps seem too little explored to warrant predictions, and we ought, I think, to continue to regard the matter as in the experimental stage until some practical operation has been accomplished on Blimps."[88]

NDRC stood in an advisory capacity to the Airborne Instruments Laboratory (AIL) on improvements incorporated into the equipment, without delaying the procurement program for the Mark VI—a much-improved version of MAD.

When truly operational for both HTA and airships,

> The blimp MAD detector was mounted in a towed, streamlined capsule at the end of several hundred feet of cable. This was occasionally done with airplanes also in order to remove the detector from magnetic effects associated with engines, struts, and control cables, as well as eddy currents in metal wing surfaces as the airplane maneuvered in the earth's magnetic field. Most MAD installations however were internally mounted in aircraft, with the detector unit mounted at the wing tips or tail so as to be as distant from unwanted sources of the aircraft as possible. Permanent and induced magnetic fields and eddy current fields at the detector from aircraft sources were then compensated by compensating magnetic sources mounted appropriately in the aircraft, usually controlled by rather intricate electronic equipment.[89]

Field researchers attended each NDRC project. Their inputs were analyzed to assess the relative efficiency of different equipment, weapons, and tactics coming into service use and to deduce changes in enemy tactics—in short, operations research. A flood tide of data and information had to be scrutinized, sorted variously, then digested. Information from, say, the fleet or ONI as to the performance of new enemy weapons tended to bog down rather than speed to the commands able to exploit the results to best effect. However clumsily collected and distributed, however, early statistical work held a grim implication: Germany dominated the war at sea.

Inside the Navy Department, "machine computing" assisted a myriad of such analyses. Modified IBM electromechanical machines processed data, enabling analyses once thought

[Opposite] NAS Lakehurst, 21 March 1942. By directive from the CNO, Airship (later Blimp) Squadron Twelve was commissioned on 2 January, reporting to Commander, North Atlantic Coastal Frontier. Assets: *K-3* through *K-6*. ZP-12 was the first LTA squadron placed in commission and the first such organization formed in the U.S. Navy. That May, the squadron logged 1,616.5 flight hours—mostly escort duty. (Capt. J. C. Kane, USN [Ret.])

impracticable. These devices were precursors to the modern computer; different plug-board wiring (programming) was necessary to perform each special task. The military had been given top priority for the acquisition and use of all available IBM machines, under rental agreements.[90]

This activity was centered in the ASWORG Machine Room—set up for serving both Cominch and the *A*nti*S*ubmarine *W*arfare *O*perations *R*esearch *G*roup. ASWORG's early studies stressed A/S operations and planning, air search, and attack efficacy. Data were transcribed to punched cards—meticulously prepared for statistical analysis, employing codes representing various classifications. Soon, the machines were analyzing data on army and navy A/S flying in the Eastern and Caribbean sea frontiers. Improvements in procedure further sped data reduction, thus helping to analyze errors in tactics or reveal inadequacies of materiel. "The machines have also been of considerable help in preparing speedily reports and lists of data."[91] Rosendahl, for one, would request a theoretical study of the probabilities of success in attacking U-boats from airships, using data on various types of ZNP ordnance. This statistical analysis, in turn, was used to judge their tactical value.

High-Frequency Direction Finding (HF/DF)

Evasive routing of convoys and shipping lessened the probability of attack. Still, evasion often proved hopeless once targets had been located, then shadowed. Why? The slow speed of merchantmen—6.5 to 9 knots for Atlantic convoys.[92] Upon sighting, U-boats transmitted reports to shore stations in Europe. This intelligence in turn was rebroadcast to all boats in a position to intercept; headquarters organized mass attacks, instructing as to course and speed. But this persistent use of H/F transmissions plus Allied code breaking left U-boats vulnerable to D/F (taking bearings on signals) from shore as well as escorts. This radio traffic, indeed, made Allied code breaking (and timely interdiction) practicable —a primary intelligence tool as to composition and position of enemy forces. An example: "The U-boat which operated so aggressively off Panama during Nov was located and severely attacked off Aruba after sinking his 6th victim. Currently he is well fixed about 900 miles NE of Trinidad homebound."[93]

Was Germany aware of listening Allied ears? Given its fixation on radar, probably not. "The fear of radar was so much in the forefront of all German thinking then, and almost until the end of the war, that nobody took note of the possibility of HF/DF sets aboard the escorts."[94] Still, Dönitz should have appreciated this vulnerability. Tenth Fleet messages suggest so: "Enemy radio traffic continues very light with majority of transmissions by short signal indicating growing appreciation of the effectiveness of our HF/DF net." And this: "When operating in coastal waters U-boats show marked reluctance to transmit by radio apparently restricting their reports to first periodic summary reports of some length generally made upon departure from operating area and second distress reports when under attack or badly damaged."[95] HF/DF assisted mightily in winning the U-boat war in the Atlantic. "Passage routes can be deduced from D/F plots and actual sightings noting their times and the course of U-boat so that in a short time the high probability sighting areas can be plotted and appropriate A/S patrols laid on them."[96]

In summary, then: "As a tactical device for the location of U-boats, shipborne HF/DF was constantly in use in the Atlantic from mid-1942 onward, picking out U-boats for attack every time they went on the air. Even more than radar or sonar, HF/DF deprived the U-boats of their stealth."[97]

As well, the U-boat deployed radio direction-finding (RDF) equipment for detecting convoys and independents. Its accuracy, the Allies worried, seemed excellent even for short transmissions. Hence, save for the gravest at-sea emergencies, strict radio silence was deemed vital.

HF/DF antennas were too large for aircraft, so this particular electronic assist departs our story.

Long-Range Position Finding (Loran, Continued)

MIT's Radiation Laboratory was the center for wartime research on microwave radar. One project of its Microwave Committee: to develop and test the use of pulses at several different wavelengths as an aid to navigation, for both surface ships and aircraft. Because it depended upon the consistency of radio-wave propagation, stringent testing was essential to establish the system's accuracy and range under all conditions. Nearly two months into the war, such tests were most encouraging.

> The results indicate a fair probability that an airplane or ship using receiving equipment only can locate itself within five or ten miles at distances up to one thousand miles. One objective has been to provide an accurate navigational framework for distances within five hundred miles, and a second objective has been to provide a less accurate but useful navigational framework for distances to the order of one thousand miles. Tests have now gone far enough to give at least a good indication of what may be expected from these systems.

The Loran system in effect measured the times of travel of radio waves from two or more ground stations to the reception point, and deduced distances from these times. But first, two additional shore stations (total four) were needed to give the two coordinates required for navigation in the western Atlantic—accurate position finding across the North Atlantic convoy route required the help of the U.S. Navy. "As a next step an informal conference between three or four members of N.D.R.C. and a few Naval officers who would represent both operational requirements and technical knowledge would seem to be advisable."[98]

Compton called a February meeting to discuss the system in light of possible use by the Navy Department and to suggest steps to put it into operation. The conferees agreed (among other items) that the first tests would be with receiving equipment on shipboard rather than aircraft and that the possible application of Loran to blimps would be explored.[99] By April, NDRC had ordered ten transmitters and about twenty receivers for use in the Newfoundland–Greenland–Iceland area, and hoped to have part of the northern convoy route covered in July.[100] Certain critical items might bring delay, so a double-A preference rating (priority) for "special items needed on the long-range navigation project" was requested for the Rad Lab.[101]

The project acquired express endorsement: a Cominch directive dated 26 April. Long-range pulse navigation would be established for the North Atlantic. During April–May, NDRC had contracts for the production of five additional transmitting stations and twenty shipboard-type receivers. Further, RCA was designing several airplane receivers, and the Hydrographic Office had been asked to develop transparent overlays for charts. "It is proposed that two ships in each convoy in the North Atlantic be equipped with the receiving sets."[102] The project was leaving the laboratory, entering the installation stage. Still, there could be no adequate operational test until four stations were transmitting—a condition achieved at midyear.

That May, meanwhile, the possibility of using long-range pulse navigation "for position-finding of blimps" was examined. The conferees included Rosendahl. NDRC's own investigation complete, operational tests followed. With the addition of three more transmitting stations (two in Florida, one off Cape Hatteras), operated in conjunction with the North Atlantic system, the entire eastern seaboard could be covered. A fourth system could cover Lakehurst and the New York Harbor region.

"The Bureau of Aeronautics will request the NDRC to supply one receiving equipment to Lakehurst to enable a blimp to test homing on one coordinate from the two stations now in existence."[103] On 22 May, BuAer advised Capt. W. E. Zimmerman, Lakehurst skipper, as to upcoming experimental tests. On or about 1 June, NDRC would have available "a special receiving equipment." When suitable, Lakehurst was to conduct field trials in cooperation with NDRC and BuAer.[104]

> While the proposed tests will be mainly confined to seaborne equipment, it seems desirable also to utilize the same equipment and principles for navigation of lighter-than-air units. Owing to their circuitous patrol paths and susceptibility to windage drift, it is considered highly desirable to provide lighter-than-air patrol craft operating along the East Coast with this precise additional means of navigation. . . . It is requested that the Chief of Naval Operations give consideration to immediate application of this type of navigation by lighter-than-air units.[105]

Geography and also production and manpower considerations brought delay. (The system was limited as to the distance between stations, due to the need for synchronization.) A four-station element—to provide two sets of coordinate lines, or "fixes"—was achieved on 11 June. Following preliminary tests in the hangar, a laboratory model of the LRN receiver and indicator was installed aboard *K-2*—not part of any squadron but, instead, attached to the station as a training and experimental ship. Weight of the equipment: approximately seventy-five pounds.

Exploiting *K-2,* Loran would be well and properly tested. On the 15th, the gear was lofted to sea, coastwise, as far south as Ocean City, Maryland. Loran operator: NDRC's J. A. Pierce, a particularly good experimenter. Two transmitting stations only were in operation, precluding a complete fix. Still, the "line of position" derived was generally perpendicular to the coastline. In order to test the system's accuracy, *K-2* flew over as many precisely defined points as possible—Coast Guard stations, lighthouses, canals. The indicator reading was then compared with the value computed from geographical positions from the transmitting stations. Some measurements agreed exactly with calculated values; half had an error less than a thousand feet. Largest observed error: one mile.

The high-frequency D/F potential of Loran had been underestimated. Using the system as a homing device, the first-ever Loran homing was conducted. This involved bearings taken on the two stations then transmitting, using an improvised loop added to the airship's indicator-receiver. Reaching the hyperbola that passed through Lakehurst, and with Pierce instructing the pilots, that particular line was flown. From fifty to seventy-five miles offshore, the civilian operator brought *K-2* across the beach on a course for home so precisely that the air station skipper remarked, "We weren't [just] headed for the hangar. We were headed for the middle of the hangar."[106]

It was possible, Pierce pointed out, to home on any point within the system's range. Though the extreme range of the complete system had not been tested, signals were "still excellent" with this laboratory-type gear at a distance of 250 miles. The navigational results of field trials with *K-2* (and surface-ship observations) seeded immediate action to procure operational equipment. Mobile trials continued, these included airplane observations up to five to six hundred miles, long-range trials of loop direction finding, and continuation of surface-ship work at long range.

Further performance tests were conducted by Rad Lab engineers that June–July, aboard the Coast Guard cutter *Manasquan*. Results: satisfactory. There now seemed "little doubt that the system actually can provide long range navigation facilities at distances up to about 1100–1200 miles from ground stations under ordinary conditions."[107]

Installation of receivers for the Atlantic Fleet commenced at the Norfolk Navy Yard in mid-October, though full sea trials awaited four stations operational sixteen hours a day. The navy shouldered this trial system, furnishing personnel and materials. By 20 January, the VCNO could report shipboard receiver-indicators in service aboard twenty-two destroyers and ten other vessels of the Atlantic Fleet, including three battleships and two Coast Guard vessels, with further installations hurriedly under way.[108]

Exploiting a PBY platform, navy trials of the airborne receiver persisted. The receiver was made by Philco under army contract, one of the first models of which had been turned over to BuAer for flight tests. But the airborne receivers under development by General Electric proved better. (The Rad Lab was acting as consultant to both developments.) Preliminary tests proved "sufficiently favorable to warrant further action at this time in expectation of further extensions of the system." By December, BuAer was procuring receivers to determine their utility in navigation of naval aircraft.

The U.S. Army Air Forces held keen interest in the airborne potential of Loran; the scheme, in effect, had had dual-service sponsorship. The army wanted it initially for its bombers deployed off the Atlantic seaboard. As field trials began to confirm the system's accuracy and value, army pressure would be applied to have Loran extended to cover other at-sea regions, Alaska and Panama in particular.

Army-navy sparring as to cognizance of the scheme was, by this time, "getting a little tense."[109] Still, at sea, Loran was taking hold. The North Atlantic chain was operating essentially on a twenty-four-hour schedule by mid-1943, providing day coverage out to approximately seven hundred miles and night coverage to about 1,400 miles along the North American coast from Delaware to Greenland. The predicted claims by NDRC for Loran—range, accuracy, performance—were being met. Effective 1 July 1943, the system was transferred from an experimental to an operational status.[110]

Antisubmarine Ordnance

Finding and then sinking submarines is complex, a process that integrates both material and human factors. In the antisubmarine war, devising new weapons to meet service requirements (or modifying standard equipment) persisted into 1945. Still, ASW ordnance failed to keep pace with advances in detection. Afloat, for example, Mousetrap (a forward thrower) proved much better suited to sonar (Asdic) than depth-charge attacks. As well, a large number of small charges—released in a pattern—was found to confer a higher kill probability per unit weight of explosive than a single large charge.

Unlike projectiles, undersea *weapons* rely almost entirely on the force of explosion for effect. The matter of determining the minimum charge required to sink a U-boat—to rupture the thick plating of its pressure hull—proved vexing, as did the effective range for noncontact charges. The probability of reestablishing contact after a first attack using conventional depth charges was only about 50 percent—due largely to the effect of the explosion on sound conditions. As well, a faster-sinking charge was desired, to reduce vertical travel time. "We are still depending on the depth charge type of weapon," Admiral Furer would lament, even in 1944. "Power-driven weapons of some kind like the torpedo or rocket look as though they would eventually be the answer to the submarine." Hence the acoustic torpedo—a weapon exploiting echo-ranging rather than sound. It would find particular application against the newer, deep-diving (to eight hundred feet) U-boats introduced late in the war (see chapter 7).[111]

The depth charge had long needed refinement. Given sonar's acoustic shadow within two or three hundred yards of the target, the ratio of "kills" to attacks had proven dismal. The keen interest in new A/S weapons flowed from this poor performance. Among those showing greatest promise: the Hedgehog. An Admiralty priority, this system involved ahead-thrown multiple projectiles fired while the attacking ship was still in Asdic contact. Though complete descriptions and drawings had been forwarded to the United States, at midyear operational information on the weapon was "negligible and very few conclusions can be drawn." Nonetheless, its virtues were clear. The projectile employed a contact fuse, thereby covering all depths—an advantage over preset hydrostatic-fused ordnance. Further, absent any hits, no explosions occurred, thus leaving the water near the target undisturbed for follow-up Asdic runs.[112] Though Hedgehog was prone to misfires, further experiments realized a superb operational weapon.

ZNP-specific ordnance was nonexistent: blimps had lofted none since 1918. Practicable and available, the standard 325-pound depth charge or bomb was adopted as an expedient. Still, it was realized, "pattern" ordnance offered greater probabilities.

In the early months, patrol airships deployed four Mark 17 depth bombs, their fuses set to fifty feet—twice that used by A/S airplanes. (Blimps are slow-speed craft: a diving boat was expected to be deeper than twenty-five feet when its LTA attacker reached the point of submergence.) Experimental work was under way at Lakehurst, however, using the eighty-pound, fast-sinking bomb.[113] Why? The probability of success, studies had shown, was related to the speed with which charges penetrated the water column. Rapid fall conferred advantage. Fitted with the proper rack, K ships could deploy sixteen to twenty fast-sinking bombs or, instead, eight along with two of the Mark 17s.

For airships, ordnance as well as bomb racks would prove slow in becoming operational. In

The K-class ZNP carried a military load of four Mark 17 depth bombs: two in the bomb bay, two on outboard racks. The bomb was mere expedient; low in priority, effective ordnance for patrol airships came late in the war. Here a 325-pounder is secured to an outboard rack, starboard side. (National Archives)

1943 USL was engaged—still—with the design of quick-sinking bombs and magnetic fuses and the racks to deploy and optimally release. That August, Fleet Airships Atlantic noted unhappily, "The ordnance aspect of lighter-than-air appears to have been rather sadly neglected, at least from the creative standpoint. Nothing is so perfect that it cannot be improved upon, and while that truism is somewhat superlative in this connection, nevertheless it is desired to remind Blimprons that any ideas or suggestions along the line of improving airships' armament may be certain of an enthusiastic reception and proper consideration."[114]

In 1943, a dispenser for ZNPs was under development, designed to carry eight fast-sinking projectiles with magnetic or contact fuses. The following year, improvement in ZNP ordnance was still under active investigation—the Mark 52 bomb rack to replace predecessor versions.

Meantime, a six-inch-diameter, forty-pound, contact-fired projectile had been developed; in spring 1942, a hundred were requisitioned for Lakehurst for low-speed, low-level use, adapted for low-velocity release. Work on a fast-sinking, lightweight (100-pound) influence bomb for ZNP use was initiated—the Mark 52. In July 1943, following development work at New London, all information and drawings on existing and proposed designs of fast-sinking contact charges were turned over to BuOrd, which had agreed to design and furnish the Mark 52 for ZNP deployment.

The untested Mark 52—problematical yet promising—would not see production until July 1944. Also, though the Mark 53 bomb rack had proven satisfactory, only twenty had been manufactured. "The new Mk. 53 bomb rack was tested recently [spring 1944] at Lakehurst. The new rack is capable of carrying as many as 16 underwater contact bombs of the 100-lb. class. Tests were satisfactory, but no recommendations have as yet been received."[115] "Airship ordnance equipment [had] a nebulous start," Rosendahl lamented, "and is still [1944] in the state of flux."[116]

Primary to delivery is release. The lethal range of the available weapons was so small, and the hull of the U-boat so strong, that only a proximate explosion could realize lethal damage. As late as March 1943, however, pilots were dropping usually by eye, the accuracy of which was "not good enough. Consequently, it is of the utmost importance that a single, satisfactory, low-elevation bomb-sight be developed and gotten into use as soon as possible."[117]

The maximum magnetic signal occurred when an aircraft had just passed over its target—the obvious release point. But if the operator did so, forward speed would carry an ordinary charge beyond it. Cancellation of forward motion allows the charge to fall vertically. Cal Tech produced the so-called retrobomb, a smallish device fitted with a solid-fuel rocket that propelled it backward, off its rails, to a midair stop. As applied to undersea attack, these retrobombs enabled aircraft to release on MAD signal.

Although overtaxed, the thrust of government R&D was realizing ever-quickening innovations, as devices from NRL of NDRC and other agencies were developed, installed, tested, and refined for deployment. All-out development into 1945 was to characterize the "anti-submarine material program" (antisubmarine warfare equipment), a label for dozens of individual programs pertaining to air and surface craft, many assigned triple-A status.[118]

Airship Armament

Armament aboard ZNPs comprised small arms and, as well, defense of the platform. For patrol operations over the open sea, the Bureau of Ordnance authorized two .38-caliber Smith & Wesson double-action revolvers, belt, and holster, plus a hundred rounds of ammunition. Two five-inch sheath knives also were aboard.

Experiments had begun in 1940 to select the armament for the TC and K types and its location on board. Based on early trials, it was decided to adapt Browning aircraft machine guns (BAMs). That winter of 1940–41, drawings for an experimental machine-gun installation for *K-2* were prepared. "Until we get the *K-2* fitted with the new gun mounting and actually try it out," Mills advised, "there can be no real assurance that this type of mount will completely solve our problems." Drawings were dispatched to BuAer. "In transmitting this data it is suggested that the point be emphasized that the machine gun installation is experimental and that some difficulties with it are anticipated."[119]

Initially, armament included two .30-caliber BAM guns, one mounted at each end of the K-class car. (*K-3* was the first airship delivered since the Great War to be armed.) Gradually, these were replaced by a forward-mounted .50-caliber BAM gun equipped with a telescopic sight. Its firing rate was 1,200 rounds per minute. As late as 1944, however, the gun was regarded as an expedient, pending production of a .50-caliber turret with an arc of fire of 360 degrees.

Gunner and .50-caliber Browning aircraft machine gun. The BAM gun was loaded over water and in areas of likely attack, unloaded when returning to base. Here the gun is test-fired. (George H, Mills Collection [hereafter GHMC], NASM, Smithsonian Institution)

"It is not considered the ideal weapon for an airship. However, of all the weapons that were considered, the BAM was chosen because of its light weight, ease of procurement, ease of controlling fire, and flexibility. It did not require that a special mount be developed before it could be used. When used from an airship with a window ledge for support, it provides an easily controlled effective fire." The BAM gun was a flexible weapon, but all crews were advised to exercise caution in its handling. That said, the need for firepower was appreciated. Indeed, certain detachments exercised "commendable initiative" in developing their own mounts, pending development and

[Opposite] Escort duty for a coastwise convoy. Proficiency and experience would be acquired on the job, including tactical use of progressively improved electronic, navigational and tracking "special devices": MAD, radar, Loran, radio sonobuoys, surface markers. This image is expressive of the tedious, plodding—sometimes furious—antisubmarine campaign. The great goal of the Allied naval war: to get ships to their destinations. (Cdr. R. W. Widdicombe, USN [Ret.])

issue of a standard version. Still, its use remained optional, with wing commanders empowered to determine the necessity for carrying the BAM gun.[120] "Our only use of a gun . . . occurs when we get in close enough to make an attack; if a submarine were caught on the surface, it might keep the crew from manning their guns, and perhaps would penetrate the outer hull of an oil tank with resultant seepage and slick formation."[121] The matter never fully resolved. In January 1944, the Glenn L. Martin Company completed proposal drawings for a manually operated .50-caliber turret for the K-type ZNP.

Meantime, when a machine gun had to be fired from a ZNP, Rosendahl remarked, "the situation will undoubtedly arise very suddenly." He was correct.

Radar (Continued)

The first U.S. airborne radar was NRL's workhorse Model ASB. The use of frequencies higher than the ASB promised increased capability. For lighter-than-air, the inaugural unit had been installed on *K-3*. That April, the next set—though too heavy still—went aboard *K-4*.

In the series, the Model ASG (aircraft-ship-ground) S-band radar (Philco) was of particular significance and the first to become available in quantity. When the Army Air Forces became interested in this radar, it was redesignated the Model AN/APS-2 (Philco). During late 1942 the navy installed this radar on K-type airships to track down submarines. It was also installed on navy PB4Y-2 patrol aircraft.[122]

Stimson, an early believer, lectured the president and Secretary Knox on the potential of radar for the submarine contest; after having himself flown offshore to observe the new set in action, he ordered Marshall and Arnold (in April 1942) to follow his example.[123]

Much was expected from this new sensor. With more ZNPs assigned (and assuming ample and reliable sets), radar-equipped blimps could provide *nighttime* patrol and escort, hence better coverage. By December, radar would be aboard ten of Mills's ZNPs. Two installations were the MIT experimental model, the other eight the Philco ASG type. The ASG was slated for *all* patrol airships: its use in conjunction with MAD and with surface forces held great promise. Radar could engage surfaced U-boats at night. Also, as a navigational aid and for rendezvous in grim weather, the sensor held inestimable merit. At 600 to 700 feet, airships were logging ranges on coastlines to 92 statute miles, on large convoys 17 to 35, on large vessels to 11, and on spars and buoys 1.7 to 2.3 miles.[124]

Whatever the sensor, instilling teamwork fell to the operating squadrons and to individual pilots. ("A good radar operator may be defined as an ordinary operator who has flown with good pilots.") Efficiency fell off after thirty minutes at the screen. Pilots therefore rotated aft, to secondary roles: "George" (radar) and MAD had to be *continuously* manned when at sea. The earliest detectors were experimental, so malfunctions were frequent. Subject to ghost outlines as well as disappearing (but genuine) echos, plus "sea return," radar bred inaccurate interpretations from fatigued navigator-operators. Positive identification had to be established visually. As well, the MAD was subject to false signals; the deflections it recorded (onto a scrolling chart) needed alert, thoughtful interpretation.

The enormous weight of American industrial production and civilian research was being brought to bear. One result: a host of instruments, devices, sensors, and weapons indispensable

in blunting the U-boat threat—delivering success to a protracted at-sea campaign fought from ashore, aloft, and afloat.

Still, for most of war, the tactical application of "special equipment" (a locution that avoided disclosure of confidential information) was to remain a work in progress. Rosendahl believed that the *combined* tactics of radar, MAD, and sonobuoy conferred a singular airborne capability. He was correct. But would—or could—LTA exploit the potential of the sensor-equipped antisubmarine ZNP?

The Atlantic battle held the answer.

The battle in the Atlantic is becoming harder, but it is the decisive factor in this war.

—Admiral Karl Dönitz

The planning and setting up of the crop of new blimp bases was a project of first magnitude.

—Capt. Garland Fulton, USN (Ret.)

Bitter Spring 3

Exploiting their bigger boats, Berlin's submarine forces applied near-crippling pressure to the western Atlantic—the locus now for shipbuilding as well as merchant-fleet imports and resupply to Europe. The cascading effects proved immeasurable. "Every ship sunk there is not merely just one more ship lost," the U-Boat Command war diary records, "but a blow which hits both shipping and armament production at the same time and at their origin."[1]

Washington marshaled resources as the war's most grueling months were logged. An epochal year, 1942 would witness bumbling by U.S. naval surface and air forces—as well as a quickening innovation. Driven by urgency, American defenses sought their bearings. The price was dear: thousands knew the hard consequences of war, many dying horribly amid the pitiless expanse of the grim Atlantic pipeline. American merchant seamen, indeed, would die in record numbers that year. "The submarine was the only weapon with which the Germans could take aggressive advantage of American weakness," the War Department secretary observed, "and they used it energetically."[2]

An almost uncontrolled offensive had invaded American and Canadian home waters—the first wave of a sweeping westward assault. For all its intensity, the remarkable thing is how poorly the naval service was prepared to fight it. "My Navy," Roosevelt conceded, "has been definitely slack in preparing for this submarine war off our coast. . . . I have begged, borrowed, and stolen every vessel of every description over eighty feet long—and I have made this a separate command with the responsibility in Admiral Andrews."[3] The U.S. Navy had not ignored submarine warfare, but yet unready, its surface and air defenses were thoroughly overwhelmed. The U-boats prevailed. Still, the Americans held on. The North Atlantic convoy cycles as well as independent inshore traffic persisted; that May, coastwise convoys were introduced between Norfolk and Key West, Florida. (See table 3-1.)

At sea, the combatants veered and tacked in a contest of action and counteraction—each reaction stimulating the U-boat to new tactics or to opportunities in less dangerous waters. Projects to enhance effectiveness for Allied antisubmarine surface-defense and air-defense forces escalated. Years were compressed into months.

A U.S. destroyer escort from the flight deck of a patrol airship, "somewhere in the Atlantic." Torpedo attacks in 1942–43 were concentrated in sectors where individually routed ships (not proceeding by convoy) were plentiful and convoys poorly protected. Attacks on single ships were especially high at focal points of routings. Often, a search mission became a rescue mission. (Wide World)

Evasive routing along the transatlantic sea-lanes, growth in escort strength (plus experience), improved air coverage/coordination, and the advent of new sensors and weapons were to multiply opportunities for sighting, tracking, and attacking the U-boat day and night.[4]

A review of ASW research was held in mid-January at the Navy Department. Commitment to the problem of detection is signaled by the attending bureaus: five officers from the office of the Coordinator of Research and Development, five from the office of the CNO. BuAer dispatched four, BuOrd two plus one civilian, and BuShips six and two, respectively.[5] NRL sent an officer plus one civilian, David Taylor, Model Basin one, Radio and Sound Lab (San Diego) one, Underwater Sound Lab one, Naval Ordnance Lab one and one, and NDRC a dozen.

The conferees took briefings on such projects as depth-charge redesigns (including rocket-propelled versions), tests on proximity fuses, hydrophones for harbor protection, and deeper-running torpedoes. Studies of the hydrodynamic characteristics of domes on destroyers were under way; in a related development, the tilted-beam dual projector for installation in dome-fitted destroyers awaited field testing.[6] Gyrostabilized narrow-beam echo-ranging gear (for depth determination of targets) showed promise, as did the small expendable radio sonobuoy. Shipborne magnetic detection units had reached production, though development work continued. In a report on Gulf's magnetic device for aircraft, field tests on S-class submarines had shown a useable range of from four to five hundred feet.[7] Tests continued. An analysis of possible attack methods utilizing the device was, Slichter advised, in preparation.[8] A confidential report of the conference was forwarded to the CNO. (See table 3.2.)

Cognizance for MAD shifted. Sponsored by BuShips, "This equipment," Admiral Van Keuren wrote BuAer, "was developed primarily for use by aircraft, both lighter than air and heavier than

TABLE 3.1 **Losses along the U.S. Atlantic coast,** March–May 1942.

February	73 ships	423,300 tons	
March	74 ships	455,251 tons	
April	62 ships	363,229 tons	
May	120 ships	583,500 tons	[44 in Gulf Sea Frontier and 37 in Caribbean Sea Frontier]

TABLE 3.2 **Conference personnel,** United States Navy and Section C-4, National Defense Research Committee at the U.S. Navy Underwater Sound Laboratory, New London, 12 March 1942. Meeting was chaired by Rear Admiral J. A. Furer, USNR, coordinator of research and development—"who emphasized the urgency of the need for improvement in anti-submarine weapons."[1]

Office, Agency or Company	No. of Representatives
For the Navy	
Office of the Coordinator	4
Atlantic Fleet, Anti-Submarine Warfare	2
Bureau of Ships	8
Naval Operations	2
Royal Navy Reserve	1
Bureau of Ordnance	1
Naval Air Station, Lakehurst	3
Headquarters, Commander-in-Chief, U.S. Fleet	3
Commander Experimental Division One	1
USS *Sardonyx*	1
Bureau of Aeronautics	1
Navy Underwater Sound Laboratory	5
Staff, Submarines Atlantic Fleet	1
Inshore Patrol, 1st Naval District Headquarters	1
Naval Research Laboratory	1
For the NDRC	
Vice Chairman, Division C, NDRC New York	1
Liaison Office, NDRC, Washington	2
Harvard University	2
New London Laboratory	12
Rice Institute	1
Consultant, Division C, NDRC, New York	1
Consultant, Division C, NDRC, Bell Telephone Labs	1
General Electric Company	3
San Diego Laboratory	3
University of Pennsylvania	1
Columbia University	2
New York Office, NDRC	4
Technical Aide, Division C, New York	1
Technical Aide, NDRC, New York	2
Bell Telephone Laboratory	1
Worchester Polytechnic Institute	1

1 Among the agenda items: attack predictors, anti-submarine ordnance, personnel selection and training, British report on Hedgehog, magnetic detection from aircraft, harbor-defense systems, and aircraft radio sonobuoys.

air, and is designed specifically for installation in lighter-than- air craft and patrol planes."[9] Admiral Furer, for his part, requested NDRC at this time to develop an expendable radio sonobuoy for nonrigids.

On the 10th, action was taken to coordinate research and design more completely within the Navy Department and outside the navy on hydrophones (BuAer rep: Lt. Cdr. Maurice M. "Mike" Bradley). It was agreed that a Hydrophone Advisory Committee be organized, comprising army and navy, NDRC, and the principal industrial and manufacturing laboratories concerned.[10] Within weeks, on 7 March, in an exercise off New London, *K-5* had demonstrated the practicability of "airborne hydrophone devices." The buoy detected the propellers of the submerged *S-20* at distances up to three miles, with reception aboard *K-5* satisfactory up to five miles. (See page 101.)

Inexperienced and reactive, the defenders of the waters of American responsibility were in their apprenticeship.[11] Escort and air cover tendered intermittent protection. Surface units were neither strong, persistent, nor accurate in their attacks. Vessels charged with screening a convoy—fleet destroyers, destroyer escorts, cutters—dropped charges at random then resumed escort station. The value of patrol aircraft stood underappreciated, as were the problems of hunting and then "killing" from the air. (British Coastal Command had had similar views in 1939.)[12] Platforms and weapons were few, anti-U-boat devices unreliable (and unfamiliar), manuals and spares nonexistent, the aircrews callow, tactics unperfected, weapons' potentialities yet to be tested in active service.

The merchant marine was no more prepared. Single-ship traffic held plentiful. Clumsily handled against possible attack (steaming on steady courses rather than zigzagging), merchantmen steamed fully lit and transmitted routing information in plain English over frequencies monitored by the raiders. The glow from seaside cities and resorts silhouetted hapless targets. "So strong was the business-as-usual sentiment and so remote were the implications of war that people steadfastly resisted the modest and half-hearted requests of the authorities to dim their seaward lights, at a time when most Europeans spent their nights in total blackouts."[13]

Under operational control of the sea frontier, airships flew patrols, submarine searches, rescues, and torpedo-recovery missions. The army assisted with coastal test firing, the navy with calibration of direction-finder (D/F) equipment. And the enemy was sighted. Development of *suspected* contacts, a few of which doubtless were U-boats, was mostly *magnetic*, however. Whatever the mission, an aerial presence helped hold the raiders down, forestalling attacks on shipping.[14]

January 1942 saw the first MAD contact by airship. Was it a submarine? Airmen mistook bubbles and oil slicks for the enemy, especially in the early, manic months. The Mark I MAD was itself experimental. Also, MAD detected wrecks as well U-boats—when it worked at all. Pilots were unfamiliar with its "range"—that is, the height of magnetic disturbances. Deployed too high, MAD recorded nothing. Operators, for their part, did not know the magnetic characteristics and depths of suspected submarines. How then to recognize "noise" and false signals from true ones, even with equipment calibrated and in proper mechanical and electrical condition?

LTA doctrine was not to attack if no immediate threat to shipping was present but, instead, to hold the contact—maintaining station (beyond range) while calling in air or surface support.

ZNP *K-4* flew the first operational patrol on 3 January. Pilot: Lt. W. H. Keen Jr., USN, flying in company with *K-5*, Lt. (jg) R. J. Antrim, USN, command pilot. Mission: to escort a convoy consisting of the USS *Palmer,* six transports, and six attack transports (APDs) during daylight hours from the Barnegat Lightship to the Five Fathom Bank Lightship. Neither ZNP lofted MAD; in mid-January, only *K-3* was deploying a detector—the Mark I.[15] The gear was experimental; it lacked the refinements of later models. "King-3" logged the first magnetic contact on 14 January. A flare was dropped. The convoy maneuvered clear while a destroyer depth-charged the area. No sighting was logged. The merchantmen passed unmolested.

The seaborne adversary *was* present—sea power projected into far distant waters. An attack force of five U-boats (under exceptional commanders) had been deployed to the western Atlantic for commerce raiding, distributed between the St. Lawrence and Cape Hatteras.[16] Delivering war nearly to the beach, the first-blow offensive against the northeastern seaboard was code-named *Paukenschlag,* Operation Drumbeat. The long approach route notwithstanding,

> the attack was a complete success [Dönitz wrote]. The U-boats found that conditions there were almost exactly those of normal peace-time. The coast was not blacked-out, and the towns were a blaze of bright lights. . . . Shipping followed the normal peace-time routes and carried the normal lights. Although five weeks had passed since the declaration of war, very few anti-submarine measures appeared to have been introduced. There were, admittedly, anti-submarine patrols, but they were wholly lacking in experience.[17]

For the next half-year Drumbeat successes "took the Atlantic coast away from the United States."[18] Lakehurst had foreseen the assault. "If they [nonrigids] are ever to be of use," Cdr. Jesse L. Kenworthy had advised, "certainly it will be in the early stages of war when the full force of enemy submarine strength will doubtless be exerted against our shipping and naval movements in coastal waters."[19] The force and scope of the assault surprised the defenders.

Shortages ensued. Certain materials, such as aluminum, copper, iron, steel, and nylon, became strategic commodities. Production requiring them became increasingly difficult; finally, the manufacture of a long list of consumer items was stopped altogether. In May, gasoline rationing would be introduced, and that June, sugar and coffee rationing, due to losses in the Caribbean.[20] (See chapter 5.)

Sinkings bred survivor searches, the dropping of emergency rations, standing by until rescue. *K-3* logged the first on 15 January. On patrol near the Nantucket Lightship, she was approached by a plane, which circled, then made off. Lt. L. P. Furcolow, USNR, command pilot, changed course to follow. Southeast of Montauk Point, the forward lookout had an object in his glasses dead ahead. *K-3* closed on a large oil slick and the bow of a ship, its stern on the bottom. A search found one raft. Nose-on to the wind, copilot Lt. C. A. Bolam let down his window and, via megaphone, queried four shivering survivors. The words "*Norness,*" "submarine" and "Norwegian" were heard. Lakehurst was appraised, Furcolow ordered to stand by until surface craft arrived. Hot soup, coffee, and sandwiches, together with matches and smokes, were lowered. A further search realized an overturned lifeboat.

The assist heralded what was to come. On 17 April, *K-5* located a lifeboat with twenty-seven survivors; on 7 May, *K-3* (again) stood by a lifeboat until surface craft arrived. That June, a ZP-12 blimp found two boats with survivors from a torpedoed vessel and dropped food and cigarettes. In July, the squadron assisted the rescue of three boats more—and located the survivors of a destroyed German U-boat.

Norness, a motor tanker built in 1939 by a German yard, was Norwegian-owned with a crew of forty. Its attacker, *U-123,* had expended five "fish" to sink her. Undetected and unopposed, the boat—a Type IXB—would deliver further harm in the approaches to New York. The *New York Times* headlined the assault: "TANKER TORPEDOED 60 MILES OFF LONG ISLAND: The Battle of the Atlantic flared within 150 miles of New York City yesterday."[21]

Next day, LTA sighted the enemy. At sunset of 16 January, *K-6* had a surfaced U-boat close aboard the Barnegat lightship buoy. Distance to target: about three thousand yards. Tactical doctrine called for blimps to maneuver if the target lay in position to use its guns. A sighting realized a contact report, after which the ZNP maneuvered upwind, then stood by outside the range of fire, bringing surface ships into contact. The instant a dive began, attack was to ensue. On escort missions, the prime objective was protection: ZNP pilots immediately attacked regardless of distance, with the convoy itself alerted on a warning frequency.

Eight vessels were within view this day along the inner sea-lanes of coastal traffic.

Lt. Douglas Cordiner, USN, command pilot, ordered battle stations, after which, at best speed he steered to intercept. The target crash-dived, vanished.[22] The probability of an effective attack on a long-submerged U-boat was small; a strong *first attack* on a visible target was therefore preferable. (A visual sighting, as it happened, proved to be far more valuable than a disappearing radar blip.) Boats dived deep—two hundred to three hundred feet—if caught on the surface, gaining relative safety in about sixty seconds. At depth, "slow" on electric motors would be ordered, to conserve battery power. If water depth was 150 feet or less, *Herr Kapitan* would probably make for the bottom. Steep-angle dives on the main motors at "full" left telltale foam, disturbed water, and air bubbles. A trail of oil might be emitted. Hence, airmen investigated any streak.

Blimps were to enjoy few opportunities to attack a surfaced boat. In this action, the target vanished before *K-6* reached the point of interception. Neither MAD nor a bombsight were aboard, and sea conditions were ideal for evasion. At the estimated aim point, swells and whitecaps had erased all trace of slick, wake, and swirl.

The scene of action was circled, one bomb dropped from six hundred feet on the boat's estimated position (fifty-foot setting), with one held in reserve. A direct or near hit was required to hole the pressure hull of a submarine. Absent a lethal hit, attackers hoped for damage sufficient to surface the boat. Also, the concussion itself might shatter glass in gauges, electric lights, or dials. A severe shaking could rupture external (oil fuel) tanks or distort ship's structure, causing hydroplanes or rudder to jam or leak. This particular attack fell short of noticeable damage: no traces of oil or debris resulted.[23]

The commander of ZP-12 was requested to dispatch *K-3* (and MAD) to locate the target—assumed to be bottomed. The area was searched for further signs of the enemy, and shipping was warned by signal light.

The gyrostabilized MAD developed by Gulf had shown under field tests a useable range of four hundred feet, with good signals obtained from "somewhat more than" five hundred feet.

> Installations have been made in both heavier- and lighter-than-air craft. Four units have been installed in navy patrol blimps based at Lakehurst and three of these units have been on routine patrol operations since the 1st of February, one having been installed and operated continuously since January 6. Several contacts with submerged moving objects have been reported. There is strong evidence to indicate that in some instances the results of these contacts have been highly satisfactory.[24]

The gear had a possible contact less than four hours after the sighting by *K-6*. It was tracked on an apparent north-northwest course at slow speed—until a merchantman cancelled further tracking and the power supply for MAD failed. Ship's radar also proved temperamental. Search through the night realized no contacts.

Undependable yet, the "special equipment" inspired scant confidence. "The MAD didn't work very well at the outset," a Twelve pilot recalls. As well, "we had practically no instruction on it." Or radar.[25] On 30 May, for instance, thirty minutes after meeting its convoy, "King-7" observed a coast guard cutter making a depth-charge attack. The blimp sped to the scene.

> Prior to arriving at spot, was informed that M.A.D. was not working. Informed M.A.D. operator that recommendation should be made to remove the M.A.D. from the ship as it always broke down when needed. At 0615 the M.A.D. operator reported the M.A.D. in working order, but received no contact. The much harried M.A.D. operator in his excitement dropped a bronze powder bomb inside the ship filling hair, coffee, chow, teeth, and lungs with the bronze stuff. Informed M.A.D. individual that any more such antics and he would be offered the use of the ship's parachute.[26]

Properly adjusted, thoughtfully operated, MAD plus radar tendered a potent search-and-tracking tool—again, when it worked. In 1943, operating out of Guantánamo (for example), a ZNP was cheated of a damaged U-boat, perhaps a "kill": "Made distinct radar contact 4 miles ahead. Pip maintained 3 minutes before disappearing. Blimp arrived over spot 5 minutes later searched area results negative. Visibility 1 mile. Mad out of order. Pilots evaluate pip as submarine. Gambit tactics during day unsuccessful. Our evaluation probable."[27]

Low in priority, and with few experienced officers and men, lighter-than-air was a work in progress. To seaward, combat aircrews were learning on the battlefield. Inevitably, opportunities were missed, poorly exploited, or squandered.

K-3 trailed a contact, then attacked, on 18 January.[28] Orders: convoy coverage and antisubmarine patrol. At 0653, the blimp three miles from rendezvous with her convoy, the MAD needle roused. The cue was confirmed—a surfacing boat clearing part of its conning tower before crash-diving. This chase too failed, due to a dud depth charge and inadequate markers. Over seven hours later, at 1410, a second magnetic contact was made. An hour later, the trail was lost because of inadequate markers. Two charges were dropped (one a dud): no evidence of damage.[29] Another (less definite) contact was logged at 1730, having been indicated by *K-4* earlier. Continued after-dark tracking proved impossible, due to lack of flares.

It was a baptismal time, and the enemy dominated these months. Press blurbs originating at Lakehurst brought a rebuke to the desk of Cdr. Fred Sachse, USN, air station skipper. "Here the country is engaged in a life-and-death struggle," BuAer's Scotty Peck scolded, "and lighter-than-air finds time for 'circus-riding' in the approved Hollywood fashion. . . . You can search the papers from stem to stern during the same period and find no publicity for HTA, which has a far more important role in this war than our rather small and limited function." The best long-range interests of LTA, the commander advised, called for the system to "hold this publicity business within reasonable limits."[30]

While investigating a large oil slick on the 22nd, ZNP *K-5* sighted foaming water to port from which *two* submarines emerged. "They were on a course that would take them ahead and across our bow," according to the pilot. "I ordered the ship headed towards them and went ahead at full throttle maintaining an altitude of six hundred feet. Our bombs were armed and a man stood by the release. The submarines were clearly seen and could not be mistaken for anything else." The pair crashed-dived. Crossing their course, *K-5* released three charges, to straddle about two hundred yards ahead of the submerge-point. Nothing conclusive emerged, though oil spots seemed to issue a hundred yards or so from the detonations on the course the targets had held in diving. The fourth bomb was dropped an hour later on suspicious bubbles, flares let go. *K-5* then cleared the area for an army bomber. It and another plane realized no definite result.

Called to the scene, *K-3* surveyed the suspect area. There it recorded, lost, and regained strong signals on an apparently moving object. For about two hours a series of attacks totaling eleven bombs was carried out—by *K-3*, two navy OS-2 airplanes, and by *K-4* (at the direction of *K-3*). Persistent air bubbles and considerable oil surfaced, as well as a life ring and wood. *K-3* was attempting to retrieve the former when two destroyer escorts arrived. One DE put an eight-charge pattern (the pilot reported) "squarely over the spot. The two columns of air bubbles were still strongly in evidence prior to and at the time of this attack." The second DE delivered two more attacks.

Group commander's assessment: a "probable." The lack of photographs precluded confirmation, however. At headquarters, Cominch's (later Tenth Fleet's) criteria tended to under-reckon action successes. "Both the Admiralty and the Tenth Fleet had hardheaded, incorruptible and exasperatingly skeptical evaluation committees at work to check up on every single action report claiming the destruction of a U-boat. The committees had orders to give the benefit of every doubt to the U-boats and confirmed sinking claims only when they were accompanied by the most conclusive evidence."[31] Evaluation assigned: "Insufficient evidence of presence of U-boat."

"Daily we are having brushes with subs," Mills wrote of these weeks. "So far we cannot claim any kills but we have been close and no doubt have prevented the sinking of many ships. Tankers appear be No. 1 bait right now." With MAD working "wonderfully," Quonset, he said, had promised three more sets within the week.[32]

In the western Atlantic, LTA did its utmost to help counter the threat at the doorstep of North America. As yet, the Navy Department had no *offensive* strategy. The tools of offensive undersea war (and doctrine) were being shaped at the laboratories and by contractors. However poorly equipped or handled, the mere presence of aircraft tended to hold down the enemy, denying him the surface—a contribution beyond estimation. Submerged, a U-boat's high-speed endurance

TABLE 3.3 **Reports prepared from immediate sources[1] of information available to Headquarters.** Eastern Sea Frontier (ESF), August 1942. (National Archives)

A. A weekly report of ship losses in ESF, broken down
   a. Number and tonnage of tankers lost
   b. Number and tonnage of cargo ships lost
   c. Losses in specified zones offshore

B. Wreck chart data—specialized for ASW users

C. Submarine movements
   a. Plotting of sub positions (from sightings, attacks, RFD's, etc.)
   b. Daily estimate of probable positions, based on previous known positions

D. Chart indicating geographic distribution of attacks made by submarines
   a. Divided by critical dates (e.g., beginnings of convoys, etc.)

E. Record of action taken as a result of sightings

F. Monthly report—Enemy Contact Summary

1. Dispatches to Commander ESF, mission reports (air and surface), action reports (air and surface), and survivor reports. "Air" is both U.S. Army and U.S. Navy.

was limited. Forced to dive, it could not track or maintain station on independent shipping and convoys. "Plane crews must not be discouraged by an unsuccessful attack," a manual advised, "for just keeping the U-boat down and constantly harassed is a large part of the game."[33] The need for Navy Air held urgent—airplanes as well as airships.

The U.S. Army was cooperating in the hunt, but was unused to the ways of the sea.[34] (See table 3.3.)

German archives document U-boat sightings of America's lighter-than-air forces. On 11 March 1942, for example, *U-94* dived to escape aerial surveillance, then suffered attack:

1916 Alarm! Medium sized airship to port, also patrol vessels in the same direction.
1920 To periscope depth, airship bearing towards us at 0 degrees
1940 3 depth charges set at 10 minute intervals set for depth A-50. Shock but no damage. Made off at high speed to get into deeper water.

In mid-April, *U-571* was obliged to abort an attack: "2033 While scanning the horizon, I discovered an airship on the port beam (south) flying a zig-zag course. It was apparently looking for U-boats between the 20 and 200 metre line. Since I could not fire at the steamer again and since, because of the clear blue water, I did not like the airship which would soon be over me, I turned tail and went to deeper water to lie on the bottom."

And from the logbook of *U-402*, 30 April: "1842 An opportunity for further firing was not likely so on account of airship approaching the vicinity and the smooth sea, we dived to 30 metres. At 1900 went to periscope depth and patrolled along observed traffic lane."[35]

These were defensive successes. Still, *offensive* actions by LTA forces were to realize no confirmed, unassisted U-boat "kill."

Too few land-based aircraft, quirky devices, plus inexperience beset the defenders. Prototypes seldom perform well. The inaugural MAD units (Mk I and Mk II) were preproduction sets scarcely advanced beyond novelty.[36] Attendant equipment, such as flares and float lights, awaited refinement—or had yet to be devised. Afloat as well as aloft, new ordnance was needed, along with improved tactics for detection: faster-sinking charges, contact fuses, ahead-thrown "pattern" ordnance, and rocket-propelled versions of the same. Practice may not make perfect, but well-drilled airmen are bound to get better. "Naturally," Mills was to write, "experience is the great factor in this work. The inexperienced pilot is liable to drop his bombs before he has definitely found his mark."

When sighted, the target usually escaped by crash-diving, then maneuvering evasively before ship-borne sound gear could be brought to bear. The need for equipment for undersurface tracking was urgent. The navy had to increase the number of contacts *and* the percentage of encounters ending successfully. British experience was comparable:

> At present [March 1942] it is clear that depth charge attacks are not being carried out to the best advantage. There is considerable waste of material, and in view of the rationing of so many strategic materials, it is wasteful not to use depth charges more effectively. This is particularly significant now since information on the submarine building program in Germany indicates that there may be many more submarines to deal with within the next two months. . . . The British are especially concerned regarding

[Bottom Left] Patrol airship ZNP *K-7*. Delivered in April 1942, "King-7" was the fifth of its type to reach the operator, the first after Pearl Harbor. Note the gunner's perch above the flight deck. (Lt. H. F. Smith, USNR [Ret.])

[Opposite] SS *Persephone*, 25 May 1942. Bound for New York, the tanker took two "fish" from *U-593*—probably the only vessel torpedoed while under LTA escort in two world wars. The majority of attacks in the North Atlantic during 1942 were delivered from U-boats either submerged during daylight or on the surface at night. (U.S. Navy photograph)

attacks from air. These attacks have little chance of success if they are carried through after the submarine submerges.[37]

Air coverage, the British had found, was most effective in combating the menace within range of shore-based aircraft. Additional fleet aircraft were therefore recommended. The U-boat's runaway success in the western Atlantic aroused "the gravest anxiety" at the Admiralty. "It was . . . natural that the Naval Staff should have been astonished to hear about the procession of unescorted merchantmen which was proceeding up and down a well-known and narrow offshore route, still showing lights and still using their wireless freely; for they knew that such practices played straight into the enemy's hands."[38]

On 10 April, Knox wrote Roosevelt. The number of naval planes authorized in the 10,000 Plane Program had been upped almost immediately (July 1940) to 15,000. A proviso in this subsequent act allowed the secretary—with presidential approval—to increase the procurement "as the situation may demand." The authorized number of ZNPs (forty-eight) had not been changed. "At this time," Knox advised, "it is impracticable to state the exact number of non-rigid airships which may prove necessary but it is desired to order an additional 24 of the patrol type now." The department therefore planned to ask for legislation paralleling for airships the flexibility pertaining to planes: "Presidential approval of this plan and procedure is requested." Roosevelt penned his "OK FDR."[39]

The lid off (as with naval HTA), the forty-eight-ZNP program became seventy-two aircraft. Naval air bases, equipment, personnel—all related components would have to be stepped up in proportion. Deliveries from Goodyear, as it happened, were to outpace hangar space. LTA sta-

[Top Left] Hangars No. 5 and No. 6 were authorized for Lakehurst on 31 July 1942. Preliminary site work commenced immediately. Both were completed and occupied in July–August 1943. The station was headquarters for Fleet Airships Atlantic and for Fleet Airship Wing One—commands responsible for ZNPs assigned to the U.S. Atlantic Fleet. (Capt. J. C. Kane, USN [Ret.])

[Opposite] By mid-1942, expanding naval-air strength included a forty-eight-ship authorization. Facilities for LTA basing, flight personnel, and operations were therefore urgent. Here the steel-arch, semi-parabolic hangar at NAS South Weymouth, Massachusetts nears completion, 10 October 1942. (Lt. H. F. Smith, USN [Ret.])

tions were large-scale engineering projects. Via memorandum to CNO, Rosendahl recommended that the hangar design at the three prospective bases—southern California, Florida, and the Puget Sound areas—conform in cross-section to those in Massachusetts and North Carolina. A modification was requested from length of six hundred feet to a thousand. "This extended hangar should be provided at each of the new stations including South Weymouth and Elizabeth City." Money was available in April, the sites selected, contracts for construction let. The Bureau of Yards and Docks, standardizing its design, exploited wood and concrete construction instead of (rationed) steel; during 1942–43, seventeen of these extended arched-truss hangars were erected.[40]

At Lakehurst, the outlook held mixed. "Right now it is impossible to give proper training in K-ships to all students. This condition will grow worse with the proposed increases in officer, cadet and enlisted classes." Sluggish production in Ohio was to persist; on 31 December, *K-25* concluded the year's deliveries to both Moffett and Lakehurst—twenty-four K-types. Spare parts were "almost impossible" to get, engineering talent scarce. On the other hand, "Our getting into the Fleet has already raised our stock some with the Fleet boys, and I am confident that we will be able to get more recognition of our work."[41]

Naval Air Stations Weeksville and South Weymouth

ZP-12 operated alone until midyear. Ordered back to Lakehurst that spring and checked out in K-ships, Class XI's George Pierce received orders to the prospective air station at Weeksville, North Carolina. The demands during these months on unit commanders' time was staggering. "Well, the station down there was nothing but pine woods and bulldozers running around knocking down trees, so we operated out of a coast guard air station at Elizabeth City. During the build-up at Elizabeth City, we only had three qualified pilots—four counting the skipper. But he was so damned busy trying to build a squadron he didn't get as much flying time as the rest of us." Pierce himself logged 168 hours during one month.[42]

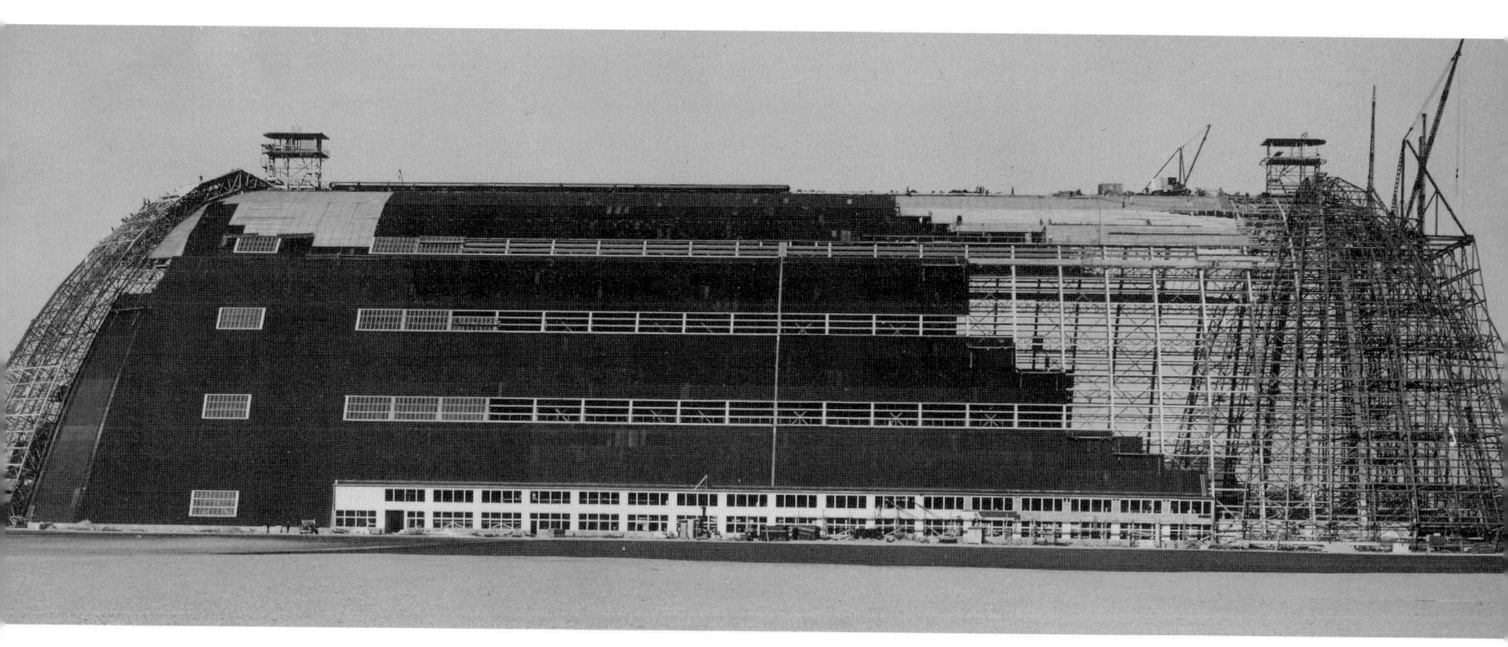

On 1 April, Naval Air Station Weeksville (near Elizabeth City) was placed in commission.[43] Rationale: it was near to Norfolk and the threatened focal point of shipping off Cape Hatteras. The first months of 1942, indeed, recorded over sixty ships sunk between Cape Lookout and the Virginia border. In his remarks, the commandant of the Fifth Naval District sketched the lurking danger:

> The Lighter than Air Base at Elizabeth City is a tremendous asset in the defense program of the Fifth Naval District. As we have found out, the worse menace of the Atlantic seaboard lies in the axis submarine. Axis submarines, as we all know, have concentrated principally on oil tankers on this coast, and as a consequence our gasoline rationing will increase unless we can stop this menace. Tankers are vital to the prosecution of this war.[44]

ZP-14 was placed into commission the first day of June—the second airship squadron, or "zipron," to be commissioned within the Eastern Sea Frontier.

The landing mat at Weeksville was not yet ready for mast operations, so expeditionary operations helped meet a desperate need. Commencing in mid-April, a ship from ZP-12 was put on loan to Elizabeth City. Daily patrols ended each Sunday when that ZNP was returned—conducting patrol or escort en route to Lakehurst. Each Monday morning, a replacement was dispatched to the coast guard station; from there, it repeated the cycle. "That continued until they completed the hangar . . . and had enough mat so we could operate. Soon as we got more ships of our own we could then have a ship go on a navigational flight training for the young AvCads that we had there. But until that time, when we're operatin' *one* ship, it was just-before daylight and long-after-dark flight *every day.* So there wasn't a hell of a lot of sleeping going on. People worked pretty hard . . . a pretty busy time. But enjoyable."[45]

Commissioning day, Naval Air Station, South Weymouth, 1 March 1942. When the Massachusetts station and one at Weeksville, North Carolina, were nearly complete, their respective squadrons—ZP-11 and ZP-14—were commissioned as units of the U.S. Atlantic Fleet. (Lt. H. F. Smith, USNR [Ret.])

[Insert] Squadron insignia, ZP-11. (GHMC, NASM, Smithsonian Institution)

"We did a lot of patrols off the Cape," another remarked of ZP-14, "and we were assigned to various sectors to patrol. And almost every other day or so, we would go up to the swept channel out of Norfolk and help form up the convoys. We'd protect the area while the convoys were being formed to go overseas."[46]

Near Boston, a third unit joined the hunt. On 3 June, Airship Squadron Eleven logged its first operational patrol. (The ship: *K-3*, on loan from Lakehurst.) NAS South Weymouth lies twelve miles southwest of Boston. There a marshy expanse succumbed to fill. Soon, arches were climbing skyward—ribs for a steel hangar enclosing eight acres, ample room for six K-ships. Facilities to support an airship squadron—shops, office and classroom spaces, a landing mat, fuel and helium storage, a power plant, housing—were erected. Before this work concluded, facilities for a *second* blimpron were established across the mat—a timber hangar with corresponding increases in helium, fuel, and housing. At a cost of six million dollars, the air station was the largest wartime project on Massachusetts's south shore (First Naval District).

Local, state, and national representatives attending, NAS South Weymouth was commissioned—"an event of utmost importance to lighter-than-air and we believe to our country." This station, Mills continued, "is part of the expanding chain of similar bases being built to the end that our coastal areas may be provided with airships—the type of aircraft that through the years have so eminently demonstrated their ability in patrol and observation work. . . . South Weymouth is

Atlantic Fleet ASW assets, South Weymouth, 28 October 1942. When operating from masts, a flight crew had to be in or nearby the ship, ready for call. (Lt. H. F. Smith, USNR [Ret.])

of particular importance because of its location, and because of the area to be covered by ships from this base."[47]

K-14 was first to moor in the (steel) hangar. New England weather dictated shelter. Moor-outs on the mat conferred operational flexibility, but exposed ships deteriorated faster. This translated into more frequent deflations for major overhaul. Another consideration: the wear on crews. Moored three hundred pounds heavy (then the method), ships tended to "kite" and required constant attention by watch standers. The K-type, moreover, was a work in progress: as yet, no one knew if the nose mooring could withstand wind shifts and temperature changes.[48] Nor had the matter of snow and ice loads been resolved.[49]

Squadron Eleven patrolled a vital focal point of shipping. ZP-11 that year would log a dozen incidents in which a supposed magnetic contact was investigated. All but two, later study proved, were due to geologic anomalies. This typified the early months of MAD in airships. To seaward, a potent defense was unachievable. Surface and air forces could not hope to deny targets to the enemy, let alone easily sink him. Still, forcing a dive slowed the boats, causing them to lose track of plodding convoys. So it was not necessary to destroy or even sight U-boats to harry them. Surface escorts and aircraft denied full freedom of action; submerged, the process inherent to tracking, coupled with slack speed, might make impossible an ahead-position for an attack—or mean loss of contact altogether. Further, loitering on a contact (hold-down tactics) kept a boat from resurfacing until surface support arrived or until friendly shipping had steamed clear. "The aircraft compelled the boats to dive more frequently," Dönitz acknowledged, "thus rendering them immobile for the time being."[50]

By day, the enemy rested on shelving bottom (150 to 450 feet) then pushed inshore. With dark, commanders made high surface speed to assail merchantmen with torpedo or gun. By autumn, position weakened inshore, the main weight of Dönitz's war on shipping would be withdrawn—redeployed to the more hospitable convoy lanes of the central Atlantic, beyond the combat reach of land-based air cover. There his commanders reverted to submerged attack by day. In the meanwhile, havoc reigned just off the beach.[51] Targets were many and poorly handled. Radar-assisted night attack by suitably armed aircraft might have blunted night operations and capitalized on the boats' vulnerability in light. But surface units, aircraft, weapons, and crews were neither ample nor seasoned. "The U-boat had without question proved that it was more than a match for the defence in American waters," Dönitz was to record. "The same thing could not, unfortunately, be said with certainty as regards the British defensive system in the eastern Atlantic."[52] Unknown to U-Boat Command, however, a long-range and highly accurate locating device was now operational.

[Opposite] Aerial of NAS South Weymouth, headquarters for Blimp Squadron Eleven (ZP-11). One steel and one standard wood hangar (right) stand complete. (Lt. H. F. Smith, USNR [Ret.])

Magnetic Detection (Continued)

"I am confident, just as you are, that we must quickly evolve the standard technique and tactics to be followed in the use of this magnetic device," Rosendahl wrote Mills as January ended. "The more I see this thing, the more I believe we have something extremely useful as soon as we can put it on an every day basis."[53]

Of four in service at Lakehurst, three of the devices had flown on patrols since 1 February; installed aboard *K-3*, a Mark I unit had been operated continuously since 6 January. Contacts with submerged moving objects were promptly logged. It was, as yet, unreasonable for a MAD-equipped aircraft to confirm a "kill." Aircrews were groping, learning; as well, tactics were still experimental.[54]

Not only the detector but the necessary training, markers, launchers, and weapons were as yet unready—offensively, a technological disadvantage.

Topside, Rosendahl—a proponent of MAD—was speaking his mind:

> While it is true that impressive results have already been obtained with this device installed in a ZNP, it should be remembered that this installation is still a laboratory product and that the technique of its use is still in the process of development. By pure coincidence, its first practical tests in an airship were against an enemy, since of course the device had not been tried at all in an airship until the enemy submarine threat had already appeared on our coasts.
>
> The success of M.A.D. in detection and tracking of a submerged submarine as well as successful ensuing attack by bombing both depend upon the ability of the airship to mark with a high degree of accuracy, the points on the surface over which magnetic contacts are made. For such marking and tracking there are required smoke and light floats which will burn longer than any successful type now available.
>
> An element of prime importance in this whole project is the training of personnel qualified to operate and interpret the magnetic detector and its indications.[55]

Early airborne MAD *could* pinpoint a moving submerged object and hold the contact. However, the procedure called for practiced airmanship, as well as patience and experienced eyes. Upon receipt of a signal not known to be false (e.g., a wreck), a marker had to be dropped, then successive passes flown, each contact defined with a marker to confirm motion and define course—in short, a *tracking* procedure.[56] Together with surface support, the aircraft might then initiate a bombing run with decent odds of success. Still, a weapon that could be dropped on maximum signal *over* the target was called for. Eventual solution: the retrobomb, or retrorocket, with a rocket charge that cancelled the platform's forward motion.

Early in 1942, a reliable model suitable for large-quantity production demanded further months of development. Ancillary gear also was wanting: reliable surface markers together with

TABLE 3.4 **Operational Record for the MAD Equipment** out of NAS Lakehurst, January–August 1942, as reported by the Airborne Instruments Laboratory of Columbia University. Transition from the Mark II to Mark IV-B design occurred in June. (National Archives)

	Total Flight Hours	Hours Breakdown in Flight	% Time Outage[1]	Scientific Staff Hours Operation[2]	Navy Man Hours Operation
January	172	87	50	172	0
February	283	98	35	283	0
March	615	151	25	615	0
April	1,001.3	200	25	1,001.3	0
May	1,237.4	211	25	1,237.4	0
June	1,081.1	102	10	1,018.1	0
July	809.3	46	8	595.1	214.2
August	890.6	45	5	119.4	771.2

1 Note the improvement in operation of the equipment deployed.
2 Rosendahl was to remark, "For many months, civilian scientists . . . operated the MAD gear on actual ASW missions while working the bugs out of it." Operation with army and navy aircraft totaled 11,380 set-hours by 30 September, 8,317 of which were by Laboratory personnel.

a satisfactory launching device. Smoke floats were the most satisfactory marker for day work, flares, for night. At midyear, no satisfactory device was yet operational. The Mark V float light had proven a satisfactory marker when it ignited—on average, about half the drops. (See table 3.4.)

The human factor is as vital as technology. Adm. Sir Maxwell Horton, entrusted by Churchill (November 1942) to conduct the Battle of the Atlantic, deemed training and experience more important than "mere numbers." Tex Settle, a universally admired officer, held that the personnel factor always dominated the material. "In the last analysis," S. E. Morison writes, "the problem was human. All these devices and methods and gadgets would have been so much junk without proper knowledge of how to use them; and that is what doctrine, training and experience accomplished."[57] Settle's standard: excellence. In a time of high national urgency, the slackness the (then) captain saw vexed him.

> With our very green personnel, with the numerous material bugs still in the ships, and with the numerous operational and tactical problems remaining to be solved, we should keep every ship we have at sea the maximum proportion of the time, regardless of the submarine situation. Only in this way will we be able to cope with subs when they show up.
>
> We have got to instill into our young pilots and enlisted men the fact that we are in a tough war and that the prime objective is to whip our squadrons into a rugged, competent, seagoing outfit. . . . We need "taut-ship" squadrons.[58]

This was a time of hapless air attacks, due to false magnetic signals—operator failure to distinguish sunken wrecks from live targets. Near New York, derelicts were so numerous that operators were squandering ordnance on them. When U-boats *were* present, the confusion and detonations enhanced the probability of escape. (The British did not hesitate to drop at least one charge on any doubtful contact.) "Unfortunately," Mills fretted, "the instrument re-acts to wrecks as well as to submarines and many contacts which have been investigated and even attacked, have turned out to be wrecks. The trace made by the instrument on the electro magnetic graphic recorder does give some evidence of the type of contact by the shape of the trace, but cannot be relied upon definitely, as this trace is somewhat affected by ground speed."[59]

And so depth charges were wasted on wakes, false contacts, wrecks. Shipboard, echo-ranging and listening techniques were yet poor. Inexperience and hurried training explain the reflex. Ashore, training programs could not yet turn out ample manpower. Also, technical staff was at a premium. Before creation of the Office of Field Service (in 1943), the laboratories fielded too few instructors to properly introduce new devices into the hands of green personnel or to maintain them in top condition.[60] "It cannot be hoped," NDRC conceded, "that trained people can be introduced at a very rapid rate; that means [squadrons] will be able to have only a small nucleus at each place."[61]

At the laboratories, disdain greeted these feckless attacks. Early on, Admiralty forces too had wasted many charges. The United Kingdom now held an edge: having fought longer, its anti-U-boat forces were more discriminating. Asdic operators, moreover, received between three and nine months' training, compared to the American six-week course.

The Expendable Radio Sonobuoy

Enter the expendable sonobuoy—a British notion and one consequence of MAD. A listening device for aircraft, the sonobuoy combines a hydrophone and frequency-modulated radio transmitter that may be dropped from aircraft in flight. Deployed, it relays underwater sounds to be heard by a special receiver installed in aircraft. Airborne hunters use them for target classification and to pinpoint location. Sonobuoys are today's principal airborne submarine detector, "the principal means by which ASW aircraft can overcome the opacity of the sea surface. Without them, aircraft are limited to a very short-range detector (MAD) and to whatever signatures a submarine may choose to project above the surface."[62]

A "sono-radio buoy" project was undertaken by NDRC at the request of the British, whose manufacturing establishment stood stretched beyond limit. The work was contracted to the Radio Corporation of America, which developed a light, inexpensive buoy. By December 1941, the RCA unit had been tested at the navy's Underwater Sound Laboratory (USL) and at Key West. The concept was confirmed—but, inexplicably, the project languished until war came.[63] By fall 1943, however, these buoys would be effective, invaluable, and famed, their production pushed to supply the demand. Also important: providing an automatic launching device.

New London had proposed either a towed hydrophone or a passive buoy. As yet, the sensor's inherent range was unappreciated. On 26 February, USL had been authorized to "conduct preliminary tests and develop an expendable sono-radio buoy for tactical use by lighter-than-air craft in attacking submarines." Deploying a prototype installation, it held a series of tests on Long Island Sound on 7 March: *K-5* with the submarine *S-20*. Results: eye-opening. In the left seat, Lt. J. H. Cruse was at the wheel. On earphone aft (with an aviation helmet to help quiet noise) sat USL's V. V. Graf, maintaining a listening watch on an RCA FM receiver. Afloat, NDRC personnel supervised handling of the RCA buoys, operated monitoring gear aboard the USS *Semmes* (AG 24), and directed buoy placement by ship's launch.[64] *Semmes*, an experimental sonar vessel, was fitted with its own receiver, phones, and radiophone.[65]

A schedule between *K-5* and *S-20* had been worked out in advance. It was not consistently followed; nevertheless, test of a two-buoy array "was successful without interruption from start to finish," Cruse reported. "Both buoys functioned and the underwater sound from each could be clearly received in the ship." As *K-5* acquired, a freighter hove into view. "The sound from the freighter's propellers was very distinct although [it] was never closer than one mile to the buoy," a USL report notes. "The propeller sounds from the freighter were so intelligible and loud that the loud-speaker was usable above the *K-5*'s own ship noises." Further, "during the time of submergence of the *S-20,* communication carried on between the *Semmes* and *S-20* was heard quite distinctly from the receiver in the *K-5*." Even the conversation of the men placing the buoys proved audible. When, prior to surfacing, *S-20* steamed a course dead-on to the floaters, her propellers grew steadily louder. "This told us the course the *S-20* was following."

Aboard *Semmes,* results proved no less astounding. Despite having been poorly positioned for the tests (rough sea and misunderstandings), causing the crude antennas to be blocked at intervals by the AG, the buoys were received "perfectly at all times."[66] The maximum radio and sonic range used: five miles. In one instance, the bridge was notified of sonic signaling that could not be explained. A few minutes later another friendly submarine surfaced.

NDRC repeated field trials, air-dropping buoys from a K-ship, then fast-dropping them from a Douglas B-18. The decisions that grew from these tests realized a wholly new sensor.[67] "Generally speaking," USL concluded, "it seems safe to summarize that the buoys furnished adequate proof that sonic listening is thoroughly practical and of real help in a search." They were LTA-deployable. "The tests proved quite definitely that the propeller sounds can be received on a Blimp and can be heard above the motor and propeller noises of the Blimp itself."

The microphones were not (yet) directional—that is, they yielded no accurate bearing. Demonstration tests on a directional sonobuoy, begun in 1942, realized a primary search sensor. Meantime, having consulted Columbia representatives as well as pilots from ZP-12, Lakehurst's Lt. Cdr. Clinton Rounds offered recommendations. If weight were reduced, sonobuoys could be carried—and released—when a MAD signal was registered "and the object thus identified as a submarine underway."

> More useful information could be made available if the Sono-Radio Buoy was directional. Still more useful information could be obtained if a fix could be obtained by the use of two or more buoys. . . . If microphones can be developed which will register direction of sound when towed at 10 knots or more it is believed a marked increase in the effectiveness of anti-submarine warfare is possible. Considerable experience has been gained in towing a stream lined shape from airships, and it is possible to submerge shapes weighing from 25 to 150 pounds almost any depth below the surface at speeds from 0 to 35 knots, and a towing winch is available.

"If modified, the sonobuoy," Rounds concluded, "will provide means of greatly increasing the percentage of successful attacks."[68] Indeed, redesign focused upon *directional* listening (1943), a radio range of ten miles, and an acoustic range limited only by water noise and by the acoustic output of the target. Weight and size appeared more or less irreducible. Of primary importance, as before: providing an automatic launch to deploy the device.[69] (See pages 285–86.)

Test day off Long Island saw MAD and bomb experiments as well. *K-5*'s Mark II instrument proved irksome (most of its defects well known to the scientists). The test event to determine "hitting probability" of quick-diving dummy bombs—using MAD to track the *S-20*—realized full failure. This was

> due to improper functioning of MAD and MK V aircraft smoke floats. At intervals the MAD would cease operation. At other times, the necessary variation in engine speeds while maneuvering would cause excess variation in MAD input voltage giving "stoppages" or erratic operation. At other times, the MAD, although in proper operation would become so erratic upon the slightest turning of the ship that no "true" signals could be recognized. The above faults, coupled with frequent failures of the smoke floats rendered the trial runs so unreliable that no dummy bombs were dropped.[70]

When its MAD performed well, *K-5* achieved perfect straddles on the (bottomed) *S-20*—its position buoy-marked. Salvos released by eye proved disappointing, however.

From the operator's point of view, the MAD defects (in order of importance) were:

1. Turns realized signals closely resembling that caused by a metal object.
2. A ground speed of not less than forty knots was required for best results, though speeds as low as sixteen knots were wanted.
3. The instrument was yet unreliable, "dying" several times while operating against S-*20*.

In April, RCA was awarded a contract for a small expendable sonobuoy. Though not adopted, it was the basis for an air-launched device, a notion advocated by Rosendahl. Design refinement soon was under way, to adapt the sensor for "blimp use." Further, there was a towed listening device. Lakehurst would apply many a research hour to the towing of streamlined shapes adaptable either to hydrophones or magnetic detection.[71] Most immediately, the Brush Development Company of Cleveland was designing hydrophone listening gear to be mounted in a housing for towing at Lakehurst and by NDRC at New London.

The expendable sonobuoy was designed for use from aircraft. Ejected, the buoy's rate of fall was controlled by parachute. The hydrophone was released upon striking the water and dropped to a depth of about twenty-five feet on the end of a cord. That autumn, experimental installations were made in K-ships and in the PBY-5A, with buoys launched satisfactorily from each platform.[72] On 28 October, procurement was initiated by Commander in Chief, U.S. Fleet, directing BuShips to procure a thousand of them, and a hundred associated receivers. The original device for service use, the AN/CRT-1, weighed fifteen pounds. By fall of 1944, the original transmitter had been redesigned and manufactured as the AN/CRT-1A. It was lighter, the replacement of batteries easier. As lis-

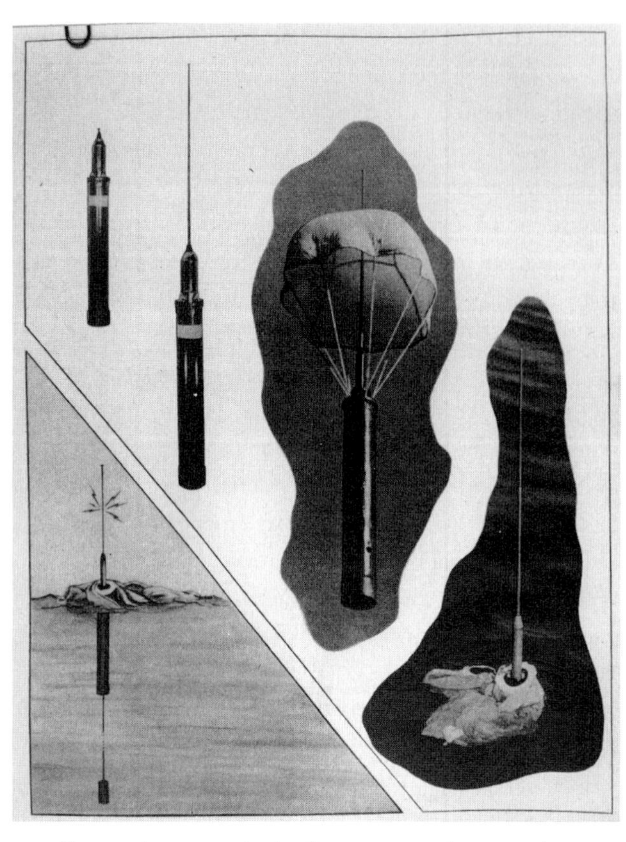

Two models of the expendable radio sonobuoy, 1945. Experimental installations of sonobuoy receivers were aboard K-type airships and PBY-5A airplanes by November 1942, with buoys launched satisfactorily from each. Like Loran and MAD, sonobuoy research and development exploited urgent coordination with lighter-than-air. (U.S. Naval Institute)

tening equipment, the sonobuoy soon proved its worth tactically. "A number of successful applications have been reported in which submerged submarines were heard, and in some cases tracked. Through the use of this gear, planes have been able to vector destroyers to the spot which in turn have established sound contact and delivered effective attacks."[73]

MAD-equipped ZNPs (and antisubmarine HTA) profited enormously from the device; it enhanced the probability of locating, then tracking, submerged targets. Still, as of April 1944, no fleet ZNP was yet regularly equipped with sonobuoys. Hence, there had been no opportunity to service-test proposed MAD doctrine for sonobuoys in ZNPs.[74] This was a function of distribution: procurement was slow because LTA usually was low on priority lists. Late in the war, the gear aboard, sonobuoys attended an apparently effective—and singular—ZNP attack on a submerged U-boat (chapter 7).

Shipping losses were rising alarmingly; in June 1942, sinkings crested. During this period U-boats exacted a heavy toll of independently routed coastwise shipping. The first coastal convoy sailed in May, its escort vessels a heterogeneous group strengthened by a few destroyers of the Atlantic Fleet. Delivery of merchant and naval vessels accelerated in 1942–43, increasing the proportion of escorts to merchant tonnage.[75] With the increase of U.S. patrol and escort craft (notably destroyer escorts), ever more independents could be routed in convoy. By May 1943,

> UNTIL DIRECTED TO CONTRARY ALL INDEPENDENT MERCHANT SHIPPING BEYOND KEY WEST NORTH BOUND ATLANTIC EAST COAST CANCELLED EXCEPT MERSHIPS OF 14.5 KNOTS OR ABOVE NOT LADEN WITH AVIATION GAS. ALL OTHER MERSHIPS WITH DESTINATIONS ATLANTIC EAST COAST PORTS WILL SAIL IN TRADE CONVOYS OR ADEQUATELY ESCORTED.[76]

Berlin countered early U.S. defenses by adding operational areas: the Caribbean Sea and Gulf of Mexico. Thus, May saw continuation of a robust offensive in western Atlantic as well as the Caribbean and its approaches. Until ample escorts were available to extend convoy routes to Trinidad, Panama, and to gulf ports, losses would persist unacceptably high. In eastern Canadian waters, one U-boat operating in the Gulf of St. Lawrence sank two ships. "Happily, the Canadian authorities had anticipated just such a development and had organized A/S air patrols and convoy escorts in readiness. This organization was put into effect and this particular development of the U-boat campaign has, so far been short-lived."[77]

Hardly. Lulls ended with renewed torpedoings inside the Gulf of St. Lawrence. That September, for one, convoys in St. Lawrence waters were consistently attacked. On the 5th, two ships at anchor were sunk while their masters attended a convoy conference at St. John's—a vital convoy port. Two days later, three ships were lost within ten minutes, on the 16th four vessels.[78] The Canadian Coastal Zone held target-rich—the outbound convoys floating in their bottoms (and decks) cargo imports into the United Kingdom, including oil requirements. Naval messages attest to the stubborn persistence—and unquestionable perils—of the transatlantic lifeline:

> U-BOATS WHICH REMAIN UNLOCATED IN CANADIAN COASTAL AREA MAY BE EXPECTED TO OPERATE AT CONVOY FOCAL POINTS WITH POSSIBLE ATTACKS ON SHIPPING OFF ST JOHNS OR HALIFAX.[79]

Eight months later:

> IN THE WESTERN ATLANTIC THE ENEMY CONTINUES TO CONCENTRATE IN THE CANADIAN AREA. PRESENTLY 3 U-BOATS ARE ESTIMATED MOVING INTO CANADIAN WATERS WITH A FOURTH PROBABLY NOW RETURNING FROM THE ST LAWRENCE.[80]

U.S. airships never operated under Canadian authority. ZNPs *did* patrol Canada's eastern littoral. Deploying blimps from Canadian bases had been considered by the department as early as January 1942 if not before. "The outlook for work in the far North is becoming more promising," Mills would write. "I am advocating the establishment of four bases, each to operate three ships from hangars."[81] Unofficial communications as well as intermittent talks at the highest levels in the Ottawa government and its military examined, then reexamined, the use of blimps for ASW—that is, a *Canadian* airship program. Still, this largely internal debate would come to nothing.[82] (See also chapter 6.)

Communications

Training alone could not deliver a kill, nor could sensors or weaponry. Unified and clear-cut *command* and rapid, secure *intercommunication* were paramount to offensive warfare. In this campaign, central coordination was the sole means by which A/S aircraft, or aircraft and A/S surface forces, could effectively operate—and they could not coordinate without efficient communication.[83]

Canada's most important naval contribution to the war effort was protection of North Atlantic convoys. Collaborating with the Admiralty and U.S. authorities, its U-boat Tracking Room at Naval Service Headquarters was "able to compile information on the movements of enemy U-boats, of the most vital importance to the Commands and ships at sea. To promulgate this information with the utmost dispatch, *efficient and speedy communications are essential.*"[84]

In 1942, common frequencies for U.S. forces—navy, coast guard, army, surface, and air—were yet few. Radio *discipline* was lacking, codes and systems wanted improvement. Already, facilities at many stations were insufficient to handle the volume of coded traffic. Ten months into belligerent operations, Commander, Caribbean Sea Frontier, deplored the deficit: "Failure

[Opposite] Control tower duty atop Hangar No. 5, Lakehurst. Waves arrived on board in 1942. (Lt. H. F. Smith, USNR [Ret.])

in communications has been one of the glaring deficiencies which has cropped up more than any other," robbing antisubmarine forces of opportunities to deliver effective attacks. "Communication between surface ships and planes has and continues to be either almost totally nonexistent or a form of 'sign language.'"[85]

Communications continued to hamper antisubmarine operations even more than other branches of warfare. Ship-to-ship and ship-to-shore communications improved. But as aircraft took on an increasing role, trouble persisted with plane-to-ship exchanges.[86]

On what was to have been a tryout of MAD in Lakehurst's maritime front yard, Dr. Edward L. Bowles with two NDRC civilians witnessed the state of intercommunications at sea. Bowles had kindled Stimson's interest in radar. Now special consultant to the war secretary, he proved adept at coordinating electronics with tactics. This day, an army B-18 fitted with a LaGuardia-built MAD unit was performing. (Its tail had had an eight-foot appendage added, to house the detector's sensitive elements.) Following successive passes across a known wreck at three to eight hundred feet, off Barnegat, black smoke erupted above a tanker six miles distant, part of a New York–bound coastwise convoy. Two runs were flown over the torpedoed ship, during which a life raft was dropped. Within minutes, as patrol vessels approached, there ensued "a tragically hectic mix-up of planes, blimps and surface vessels in which there was no coordination whatsoever," NDRC's W. B. Lodge reported. "It developed that our plane could not communicate with either the surface vessels or the blimps. There was no organized or systematic search. . . . The confusion in the plane, dud depth charges, lack of coordination in the submarine hunt, failure of communications and lack of adequate surface markers plus release mechanisms painted a poor picture of our present ability to destroy a submarine."

Bowles (an MIT colleague of Bush) was appalled. Surface and shore-based support had proven impotent: a ship had been lost under ideal daylight conditions, with no air-surface teamwork to reply. For about an hour "there was a mixture of airplanes, blimps (three) and surface craft which gave me, as a layman, the impression of confusion, lack of any command control on the spot, lack of systematization of individual search and coordination of joint effort—each craft for himself so to speak and no leadership."[87] The experience doubtless reached Stimson, whose opinion of the navy at the strategic level of command was already low. More conferences with Bush convinced him that "the Navy's resistance to the role of aircraft in antisubmarine warfare, its emphasis on a defensive strategy, and a lack of unity of command over the antisubmarine campaign leave me with a rather stiff problem of how to get another Department pushed along into the right channels on what is probably the most critical problem that now threatens the war effort."[88]

As part of the navywide buildup in forces, the expansion program for 1940 was enlarged. On 16 June, the Seventy-seventh Congress authorized an increase in airship strength to two hundred aircraft. The Bureau of Aeronautics recommended, and SecNav approved, a 120-ship program that month. Also in June, a contract was awarded to Goodyear Aircraft for a new prototype antisubmarine ZNP, the *M-1* (see chapter 5). The necessary planning for the additional coastal bases was promptly realized, including the selection of sites and the letting of contracts. Construction commenced that summer. "One hell of a lot of airships are going to be on our hands quick," Peck observed.

U.S.NAVY

The central issue remained shipping. For Britain, mid-1942 was a time of disasters. Its chairman of the Chiefs of Staff, Alan Brooke, had to give priority in shipping to the Indian Ocean rather than the English Channel. In Washington, midyear found General Marshall troubled. "The losses by submarine off our Atlantic seaboard and in the Caribbean," he wrote King on 19 June, in an exchange of memoranda, "now threaten our entire war effort. . . . We are all aware of the limited number of escort craft available, but has every conceivable improvised means been brought to bear on this situation?" King replied on the 21st, "I have employed—and will continue to employ—not only our regular forces but also such improvised means as give any promise of usefulness. However, it is obvious that the German effort is expanding more rapidly than our defense, and if we are to avoid a disaster not only the Navy itself but also all other agencies concerned must continue to intensify the antisubmarine effort."[89]

In July the concentration of enemy boats in the western Atlantic reached its highest since start of the war. Still, this assault realized but five sinkings and a "marked decrease" in that sector as a whole. "Convoying of merchant ships was the main reason for the decrease in sinkings, but secondarily, particularly in the Eastern Sea Frontier, support and offensive action by aircraft played an important role."[90]

Toward the end of July enemy forces shifted away from North America, concentrating instead on the transatlantic convoy route and near to the shipping bottleneck at Trinidad, the southeastern extremity of the convoy system as it was then. (See chapter 5.)

Air assets controlled by the Eastern Sea Frontier totaled 178 naval and 141 Army Air Forces aircraft, plus seven blimps. This force was allocated among twenty-six fields along the coast from Argentia, Newfoundland, south to Jacksonville.[91] Lakehurst was operating two patrol ships per day. With delivery of *K-9* (on 29 June) and *K-10* (12 July), one ZNP would sortie daily from Cape May, two out of Lakehurst. Squadron Twelve had its hands full.

[Opposite] A patrol ship lands at Lakehurst. Long lines in hand, the ground crew has just grabbed the ship's short lines. Note the radar "hat" beneath the control car. (Mrs. F. J. Tobin)

> The movement of ships from New York and Cape May in many cases have included vessels ranging in speeds from 8 to 14 knots, and by the time the ships have arrived at destination they are spread out over an area from 4 to 14 miles in length. With such dispersion it has been impracticable to provide adequate coverage of these vessels. . . . When one blimp is assigned to a group of ships it patrols on the seaward side and gives most of its time to the greatest concentration of ships, unless orders have been issued directing the coverage of some special ship or ships.[92]

Early orders from the New York office of the sea frontier read thus: "Three vessels will depart Delaware Bay at about 0600, destination Hampton Roads. ZNP *K-6* will escort as far as Winter Quarter Shoals Buoy, there will be relieved by the ZNP *K-4*." The ZNP would take up station on the van or seaward flank of its charges, and provide coverage to convoy destination, to "chop line," or until relieved, the returning ship's logbook often noting "nothing unusual sighted" or "no submarine indications"—mission accomplished without incident.

Though embattled, the Allies were asserting some offensive control. "In spite of their successes, the Germans found adapting to the ability of the Allies to develop new antisubmarine capabilities increasingly difficult. This indicated the trend of future events."[93] During May, three Atlantic convoys were assailed, ten ships lost. Nonetheless, escort groups heavily attacked and drove off the pursuers. Ocean escorts responsible for screening the convoy could not yet detach to range widely—and hunter groups were not yet to sea.

Toward midyear, Admiral Andrews could report favorably concerning support from LTA coastal air operations:

> Airships have been found especially useful in escort of surface craft and in anti-submarine patrols along the eastern seaboard. These non-rigid airships have been able to operate under conditions of reduced visibility when heavier-than-air craft have not been able to fly. The airships have good offensive power, are able to observe surface areas effectively, can search areas for submerged submarines by the use of MAD gear, and can remain on station for protracted periods. For these reasons it is recommended that the number of non-rigid airships in the Eastern Sea Frontier be increased as rapidly as possible to the maximum number which can be operated from the available ground facilities.[94]

In their respective sea areas, the sea frontier commanders *controlled* their aircraft and surface forces. Each had direct contact with the bases within their districts and coordinated ever-changing demands for air coverage with surface activities. During 1941–45, these commanders were exceedingly busy officers—responsible for assembling convoys, monitoring shipping, plotting sightings and the enemy's apparent movements, and assessing his intentions as well as coordinating air and surface escorts, and providing air-sea rescue. Each operational office set the patrol and escort requirements for its sector and defined the area of sweep. Naval air bases were informed and, in their turn, were responsible for assigning missions and allocating aircraft and personnel. Mission execution was left to the individual stations.

The A/S airship, then, was responsible to its base, which, in turn, had sea sectors for which it was responsible. Escort-of-convoy instructions might be assigned or, instead, orders given to sweep an area in which a sighting had been reported. ZNPs rarely conducted independent operations. Frontier aircraft were told what to do—their crews executing as best they could under the conditions prevailing. From the New York, Norfolk, and Miami headquarters, frontier commanders "gave the blimps a lot of support. We often were requested to do many things that we weren't sure we could manage—limited supply of ships we had. But we were always glad to have more requests than we had equipment."[95]

U-Boat Command, for its part, had every reason to be pleased. In all theaters, 585 merchantmen totaling 3,080,934 gross tons had been sunk. More than a hundred boats had been commissioned, against twenty-one losses—seven in the Mediterranean and six in the western Atlantic. It had taken longer than Dönitz had expected to organize defenses and the routing of shipping. The record by a small number of boats for January–June: staggering. To the Admiralty, such an "exchange rate" would soon augur disaster.[96]

The U-boat campaign was a teetering contest of measure and countermeasure, gadget and countergadget. Accordingly, U-Boat Command interrogated its captains "very closely." "We followed with particular interest the operations against convoys in May and June [1942], in an effort to ascertain whether there was any evidence to show that the British had evolved any new methods of defence or were in possession of any new detection device, particularly any device for locating a boat on the surface." Also, "with a series of suggestions and requests U-Boat Command set urgently about the task of accelerating improvements in the multifarious devices which constitute the armament and equipment of a submarine." Of primary importance: a counter to British meter-wave radar.[97]

Eastern Atlantic, Arctic Waters, Mediterranean

In the crucial Northwestern Approaches to the British Isles, Coastal Command maintained vigorous air-watch and attack routines. The number of attacks was found (tellingly) to bear a close relation to the number of hours flown in areas necessarily traversed by the U-boat.[98] Further, an accurate locating device was operational in escort vessels and aircraft: short-wave radar. The enemy's invisibility had been cancelled, the advantage of surprise stolen. "Aircraft had suddenly become a very dangerous opponent—dangerous not only to the isolated U-boat surprised and attacked, but also to our whole method of conducting submarine warfare, which was based on mobility and operations on the surface, and which reached its culmination in the wolf-pack tactics we had evolved." The absolute need for a U-boat capable of high submerged speed "became once again very insistent" for the Germans.[99]

Thus was applied a further strain unto the morale of Donitz's undersea crews.

> Our horizon has the diameter of a thimble as compared to the circle an RAF reconnaissance plane can survey. In the early days, the weather did at least give us an occasional advantage. But no longer. The enemy is unaffected by poor weather conditions now. Radar works in all weather. Indeed, the situation is reversed: bad weather now give the airplanes an added advantage. When they are navigating by radar our bridge guards spot them ever later than otherwise. The planes take our boats even more easily by surprise.[100]

Seeking a constant offensive patrol, long-range A/S squadrons assigned to the Bay of Biscay were reinforced. The number of surprise day attacks climbed; in June, for the first time, transiting boats were attacked from the air in moonless dark. "A searchlight had suddenly been flashed on at a range of 1,000 or 2,000 yards and had at once picked up the U-boat. The bombs followed immediately." On the 24th, Dönitz gave orders that boats proceed submerged both by day and night and surface only to recharge batteries. Antiaircraft armament was strengthened.[101] Despite the campaign off France and British counters elsewhere, U-boat warfare in the western Atlantic emphasized defense. Admiral King persisted in the view that air-search operations in open sea were unavailing.[102]

Expanding its own defense capabilities, the United States accelerated Lend-Lease. Great Britain would receive thirty-two billion dollars' worth of assistance and the other principal recipient, the Soviet Union, eleven billion. The first convoy to Russia had sailed for Archangel—through Arctic waters—in August 1941. The transporting of supplies to Russia entailed titanic effort in lethal cold, with both USSR-bound (PQ) and outgoing (QP) convoys meeting air and destroyer and U-boat assaults.[103] ("American material is aiding the Red Army in its victorious drive.") In the Mediterranean, one German boat was sunk by destroyers. In two instances of air attack, however, an apparently disabled target could not be found by surface units. During one, a U-boat was blown to the surface by a Hudson aircraft as it dived. The superstructure filled with men in life belts, hands up. Short on fuel, the plane withdrew. Destroyers dispatched from Gibraltar to effect capture or kill were unable to locate the boat—which, in the end, made a Spanish port.

For shipmasters, convoying conferred a commitment to both the security and the constriction of united, preplanned performance. For slow-speed vessels, detection gear—even if available—was undesirable, given maintenance and training demands. Multiples of the equipment in one convoy would realize confusion anyway. Hence, for the masters and seamen of the merchant marine, survival demanded passive protection:

> The principal methods which are available to the master of a ship for thwarting his attacker are those of concealment and evasion. Thus, strict adherence to sailing instructions with regard to darkening ship, zigzagging, and similar precautions is clearly indicated. While these are negative means of defense they have positive and concrete

results. Too often does the testimony of the survivors of a merchant ship state categorically that the lights were burning brightly or that the ship was not zigzagging.[104]

MAD *Plus* Radar

As yet, U.S. Navy ships and aircraft held scant odds of sinking a well-handled submarine. Commander in Chief, U-Boats, took satisfaction as to springtime conditions in American waters:

> Before U/B attack on Amer. was begun, it was suspected that Amer. A/S activity would be weak and inexperienced; this conjecture has been fully confirmed. A/S vessels have no asdic, some are equipped with hydrophones. Crews are careless, inexperienced, and little persevering in a hunt. In several cases escort vessels—C.G. [coast guard] ships and destroyers—having established presence of a U-boat, made off instead of attacking her.[105]

The MAD project was transferred to NAS Quonset Point that June. This was Project Sail—whose purpose was to thoroughly test, under flight conditions, MAD and similar submarine detection gear. Sail would coordinate efforts by the army and navy and NDRC, by creating a group with which the latter could deal directly.[106] Broadly, "this group is set up to fill the gap between an accomplished apparatus and the accomplished use of the apparatus." Sail would have its own aircraft for field tests, to shake down the equipment and work with NDRC groups with respect to training and maintenance.[107]

At its facilities, Sail began to develop detectors under contracts administered for NDRC by the Division of War Research of Columbia University. Various alternative magnetic-detection methods had been suggested and, in some cases, worked on. "Although several solutions to the MAD problem were developed by other groups in the U.S. (including Bell Telephone Laboratories) the most successful MAD," Fromm adds, "was the equipment developed by the group at Quonset Point," the main part of which had moved to a TWA hangar at LaGuardia Field. That September, labeled officially the Airborne Instruments Laboratory, the group occupied buildings in Mineola, Long Island. The greatest portion of MAD development by far—fundamental research, design of equipment, interim production—would be carried on by AIL.

On 1 July, a meeting was held at Goodyear. The Inspector of Naval Aircraft (INA), Akron, was Cdr. C. V. S. "Connie" Knox. As its representative at the manufacturer, Knox reported directly to the Bureau of Aeronautics. An NDRC rep had brought a complete mock-up of the MAD equipment. The conferees tentatively decided to place the panel rack just above the radar control box of the navigator's table, portside. This assumed that one operator could handle *both* the radar and MAD; consultation between the MAD, radar, and Lakehurst groups would be required, though, to verify this.[108]

Conference with Lakehurst's operations group brought agreement: joint operation of MAD and radar equipment was "entirely feasible." During daylight, patrol ships usually held at about eight hundred feet. Between six and eight hundred feet the horizon is normally at the limit of visibility, objects down on the water are readily identifiable, and the immediate circle of sea near enough for close inspection. But eight hundred feet exceeded the range of MAD. Contacts there-

Early-morning sortie to seaward. Note the "hat" for the ASG radar below the car. Although defeat of the U-boat would not of itself win the war, the Allies could not win without first blunting the U-boat campaign against merchant shipping. (Lt. H. F. Smith, USNR [Ret.])

fore had to be established either visually or by radar before MAD came into play. "It is, therefore, possible for one operator to handle the radar equipment until the blimp drops down to lower elevations in order to investigate the contact more thoroughly with MAD after the submarine has submerged."

> In regard to night operations, it was generally agreed that blimps could under most circumstances operate at elevations of 200 or 300 feet above the water surface provided it was necessary to do so to develop a Radar or a MAD contact. This means that for the present it will be necessary to depend almost entirely on blimps as far as the use of MAD is concerned during instrument flying conditions, since airplanes definitely require considerably more altitude to maneuver when flying on instruments.[109]

That July, an escort commander commended the skipper of *K-7,* from ZP-14. Two days of escort services with convoy KN114, the destroyer skipper wrote ComFive, "was the most effective air coverage this escort commander has experienced."[110]

In August, Project Sail was asked to forward six Mark IV-B1 MAD units to Lakehurst. These came from Quonset, where NDRC was testing production units for acceptance. "Changes are being made in the frequency discrimination circuits to adopt them to airship use. In addition, the replacement of certain vacuum tubes by less microphonic types will reduce noise in flight."[111]

On station, security concerns held strong. "With the increasingly important part that Lighter-than-Air is playing in the prosecution of the war, it is natural to assume that our enemies will be more and more interested in our activities and more than ever desirous of knowing just what we have done, are doing, and propose to do. Therefore all hands must be extra diligent to see that any information which might be of aid to our enemies is denied them."[112]

In addition to LaGuardia, satellite laboratories engaged in flight testing were set up at Mitchell, Moffett, and Langley fields, at Lakehurst, and in Alhambra, California. As for platforms, the B-18 and B-24, PBY *Catalinas*, and K-type ZNPs were exploited. Courtesy of promising results of early trials with blimps and B-18s, the navy elected to procure two hundred airborne sets, of which fifty were to be available for army use.

> In these two years, the AIL group produced an amazing record. Several versions of sophisticated MADs were developed and produced. In addition, trainers, flare and bomb release devices, and techniques of magnetic compensation of aircraft were developed and in use. By late 1943, operational squadrons of MAD aircraft were active in Europe, South America, and the South Pacific, as well as along the east and west coasts of the United States.[113]

Still, the Goodyear factory proved slow on rack construction and miscellaneous wiring for MAD units; accessories (racks, cables, "blister") did not reach the station until November. That September, meantime, Lakehurst became the point of installation: OSRD staff, assisted by enlisted personnel, installed IV-B-1 equipment aboard *K-13, -14, -15,* and *-16*. The IV-B-2 soon replaced the older model, however.

> The first installation pf Mark IV-B-2 equipment in a blimp was completed in *K-19* [October]. This installation followed several conferences at [Goodyear Aircraft], where final details were agreed upon. It is understood that starting with *K-30,* all blimps will leave the factory completely equipped with wired racks and all necessary cables for Mark IV-B-2 MAD equipment. Goodyear is committed to furnish a sufficient number of racks and associated equipment [except MAD units] to completely equip, by the end of December, all ships of earlier manufacture which now carry IV-B-1 MAD. IV-B-2 MAD equipment [of RCA manufacture] will be shipped to Lakehurst and Moffett Field as required for these replacement installations as well as for new installations.[114] [See table 3.5.]

December saw MAD fleet-fitted into all patrol airships, radar in ten, and the Philco ASG type in eight ZNPs. Flight crews relied on sightings or reports of U-boats in their sectors or, increasingly, upon radar contact. (The elevatorman would then shed altitude, to develop the contact.) As well, ZNPs could now night-hunt for *surfaced* enemies. But release-on-suspicion was demonstrably ineffective; an automatic scheme was needed. Under intensive development, pilot models for detecting magnetically had been completed by five of the six contractors; by mid-June, all had performed satisfactorily in flight tests.[115] Under NDRC supervision, MAD had been authorized for limited production. A set of specifications was in preparation, as were operation and maintenance manuals. And working models adapted to use in towed "birds" were slated for production.[116]

Design stood far from ideal or final. As well, tactics to exploit magnetic detection as preface to attack were tenuous, still. "Recent tests of magnetic airborne detection equipment indicate that

TABLE 3.5 **Geographical distribution of scientific staff,** Airborne Instruments Laboratory, LaGuardia Field, New York City, 29 August 1942.[1]

Location	No. of Staff
Office of the Coordinator	4
LaGuardia Laboratory, New York	46
Quonset Point Naval Air Station, Rhode Island	8
Lakehurst Naval Air Station, New Jersey	4
Langley Field, Virginia	5
Jacksonville, Florida	3
Elizabeth City Naval Air Station, North Carolina	2
South Weymouth Naval Air Station, Massachusetts	2
Moffett Field, California	2
San Diego–Goldstone (C.I.T.), California	1
Sperry Gyroscope Co., Garden City, Long Island, New York	3
New men not yet report or en route	2
Total	82

	No. of Men Trained	No. of Men in Training
Langley Field	37	14
Quonset	12	10
Lakehurst	83	24
South Weymouth	7	14
Elizabeth City	18	17
LaGuardia Field	14	9
Jacksonville	0	37

1 Scope of NDRC-sponsored (Airborne Instruments) MAD training program. Objective: to provide a pool of operators and maintenance men at operating stations. (National Archives)

this apparatus may be effective as an attack directing weapon. Airships and army bombers have reported a number of successful operations in which MAD units were used. Indicated ranges are from 400 to 500 feet. Tactics for the most effective use of the gear are still being developed."

So as to improve MAD and its tactical use, NDRC set itself to developing engineering based on performance of the equipment under known conditions of operation.[117] Radar (along with the human eye) was to be the *search* tool, magnetic detection a *tracking* device upon sighting a target.

Surface Markers

To be useful, floating markers had to easily visible for at least ten minutes from a distance of two to five miles. The slicks belched from aluminum or bronze-powder types sufficed if sea-surface conditions were congenial but were hard to see in chop. The most satisfactory type for day work was a smoke float, for night work a flare. None of either type was yet operational.

Also under development: a flare rocket motor and chute for ZNP use. A U.S. retrorocket had been fired successfully in July 1942, from a PBY-5A. To assist acquisition, radio sonobuoys had tested fairly satisfactorily. Cost: less than one hundred dollars, with two firms contracted to turn out five dozen. Towed hydrophones also were slated for ZNP use—a platform particularly well-adapted to the technique. Further, a rack for contact and magnetic antisubmarine projectiles was under construction.

Two chutes were proposed for float lights or other markers, each activated by either the radar-MAD operator or the pilot. Lakehurst had agreed to develop a flare chute and control mechanism; details complete, plans were forwarded to Akron.

Throughout 1942, the patrol airship, with its quirky sensors and unseasoned crews, was a work in progress. Further months would hone platform, sensors, and their operators into a formidable A/S weapon system. For example, on 25 April 1943, aboard ZNP *K-45* (ZP-15), "at 1019 another strong MAD contact was received followed by several others. In the series of contacts, additional flares and slicks were dropped. When three of the slicks were in a straight line, a bombing run was made and three Mark 17 bombs dropped using a strong MAD contact to decide the point of release."[118]

Still, engineering headaches refused to vanish. An inspection of the radar installation in *K-9* showed that the lower part of the supporting frame for the central control box wanted redesign, since it did not allow ample knee room. Insertion of a medium-sized airman in winter gear was precluded. On the matter of interphones, seven stations were thought adequate: pilot, copilot, gunner, radioman, radar-MAD operator, mechanic, after lookout. A study of the two direct-current generators driven by the engines was recommended, with a view to adapting them to parallel operation. Already, the demand for power was escalating—courtesy of radar-MAD, IFF, Loran navigation gear, ship's radio, cooking facilities, lighting. "The whole problem has been brought to the attention of the Radio and Electrical section, Bureau of Aeronautics and an effort is being made to reach an early and satisfactory solution."[119]

Strengthened patrols and the introduction of the convoy system obliged Dönitz to suspend operations off the American coast. "There seemed to be no justification for keeping boats there any longer, and so I withdrew them." The "happy time" inshore had ended. The German command was collecting strength for a renewed attack on the convoy routes in midocean, beyond the range of land-based aircraft. Strategy, counterstrategy. Whenever Allied counters began to be felt, Dönitz shifted his boats. "With the oceans to play in he could always gain a short period of immunity in a new area before we overtook him there," Churchill was to write.[120] As this pertained to airships, by midsummer the time of greatest danger was largely done. Events had outrun the ability of LTA to properly train, equip, and deploy for *offensive* success.

Project Sail's first assigned aircraft had been a PBY-1. One of three PBY-5As would reach Quonset that August for installation of MAD—a Mark IV-B2 unit from LaGuardia Field. Meantime, the necessary changes in the first aircraft "were immediately started."[121] As well, changes were being made in the frequency-discrimination circuits in Mark IV-B1s, to adapt them to ZNP use. In Ohio, an additional radar-MAD mock-up meeting was held. In terms of leg room, the new radar control unit mount was found satisfactory. "Space above this setup is still sufficient for the M.A.D. rack."[122]

Naval Intelligence

Knowledge of an opponent's strategy, operations, methods, and his intent—or its absence—can move events. The appetite for raw intelligence is voracious. From the British, the Tenth Fleet had unrestricted access to the Admiralty's U-Boat Tracking Room and its various research and intelligence agencies. Inside the Navy Department, the Office of Naval Intelligence (ONI) was one link—especially a division of Cominch headquarters organization, Combat Intelligence.[123]

Communications eavesdropping holds particular value. For this marine drama, what the enemy was saying to himself was decisive. The Allies held a priceless advantage: decrypted German radio traffic to its U-boats, transmitted as information to operational commanders. This was the top-secret Ultra intelligence—the reading of the German Enigma codes.[124] The British, at Bletchley Park, had broken the Enigma ciphers.[125]

Timely intelligence is always preferred—that is, during experimental development of new devices—well before production, installation, deployment by the enemy. Allied and Axis concern as to the others' gadgets never eased. In August 1941, south of Iceland, *U-570* was captured by Coastal Command. Washington soon had the particulars. Analyses of the boat's technical installations were conducted, after which classified summaries were distributed to senior officials in interested commands and bureaus. Purveyor: ONI. Because of Bell Telephone Laboratories' A/S work, Section C-4 sought authorization for loan of the report to Bell.[126]

Routing of intelligence to high-level service and civilian managers had become routine. Highly desired product was enemy state-of-the-art—the status and use of German radar, guided missiles, rockets, mines, and other devices held utmost importance. Such knowledge would guide development of similar devices and countermeasures—and signal which projects on similar devices were over- or underclassified. Why this emphasis? Devices were being withheld from combat because of high security; if in fact Berlin knew of a specific development, the weapon could debut immediately. "On the other hand, the dangers of unnecessary exposure to the enemy of devices of which he has no previous knowledge are obvious."

So as to keep scientists informed of weapon and equipment performance in combat, the coordinator's office requested that it be placed on the list to receive battle-action reports.

> [The office] is vitally interested in various Operational Reports, War Diaries, Reports of British Admiralty Experiments and Trials of a technical or scientific nature, Reports of the British Air Commission, British Central Scientific Committee, the RAF Delegation, Enemy Prisoner statements, Boarding Party Reports, Reports on Captured Enemy Material, and any and all observations pertaining to devices and equipment which present unusual tactical problems calling for immediate or ultimate solution.[127]

Disapproved: such reports contained tactical information and hence were restricted to very limited circulation. Nonetheless, vital information reached the office by indirect means, such as naval intelligence channels.[128]

For Berlin and U-Boat Command, the strategic objective held incontrovertible and abiding: disruption of Allied sea communications. "However the Battle of the Atlantic may develop, we shall always be able to adjust ourselves to the constantly changing situation. . . . The tactics of submarine warfare frequently change, the major objective, however, remains the same; to destroy more enemy tonnage than can be replaced by all our enemies put together! The day will come when the lack of tonnage will be so serious, that our adversaries will no longer be free in their strategic decisions."

When queried as to America's "dwarf dirigibles," Dönitz replied: "In contradiction to a wide-spread belief, I should like to emphasize that operations in American waters are by no means a simple matter. It cannot be denied that even the 'blimps' have a certain effectiveness, in defense, and the Americans have known how to organize very rapidly a defense which commands respect."[129]

U-boat sailors were having to brave escalating odds. By September, "the enemy's improvements in locating devices and the increasing air cover he was providing filled me with the gravest misgivings for the future."

> I had repeatedly warned my captains that the dangers of attack from the air could not be exaggerated. But time and again we had found that they were inclined to underestimate the dangers of an attack, the essence of which was surprise and sudden onslaught. They were far too inclined to believe that, as long as there was no aircraft in sight, their boats were perfectly safe, only to realize in the very next instant, when an aircraft appeared, that their position was already hopeless.[130]

That July, while sweeping ahead of a southbound convoy, an airplane was seen to circle. Soon after, the escorting blimp (ZNP *K-12*) dropped a smoke float. Increasing speed to full, HMS *St. Loman,* one of the surface escorts, made for the position. A sonar echo at about two thousand yards developed into a "very firm contact" at one thousand. A pattern of five charges was let go, set to detonate at one hundred feet. During the run-in *K-12* had dropped more floats as it made contact, thus defining the escort's maneuvers. An excited action ensued: two coast guard cutters and a patrol boat proceeded to drop charges on every float, the ships twisting and turning to avoid the charges released by each other. *St. Loman* dropped a second pattern. Minutes after, the sea over the target again smooth and calm, a large eruption of escaping air and oil boiled up, lifting the surface. *St. Loman* pressed further attacks on the contact, as did "King-12" (four bombs) and airplanes, after which the position—bleeding bubbles—was buoyed.

The commanding officer, HMS *St. Loman,* hailed the action as an "excellent practical example" of the effectiveness of combined air and surface work. "Within 13 minutes of the U-boat being sighted by the plane, and contact made by the Blimp, we had also obtained contact and the U-boat was being hammered. Within a half hour after sighting, the latter's hull had been ripped open." Blimps, the officer continued, were "most useful" on convoy escort. "They can give long coverage, and can hover over and pin down a U-boat until a surface ship can get on the spot," he reported. They "can attack by themselves with considerable accuracy," and, further, "should be invaluable for night patrols, and in low visibility."[131]

Research persisted hard at the laboratories. Yet a fundamental was absent. Transferring laboratory results to service operation requires field trials under controlled conditions. Submarines, for one, were integral to tactical studies involving magnetic detectors. Development in the absence of field tests (Jewett had lamented) was not engineering but "sheer gambling." For antisubmarine and subsurface warfare R&D, at least one boat as well as surface craft was "inescapably vital." The matter festered. By August, the need remained "intolerably unsatisfactory"—the test delays likely costing both shipping and lives. If tactics were to be developed and devices improved, Jewett implored, data had to be gleaned under service conditions approximating those of actual attack.

While "extremely promising," MAD (for one) urgently required a PBY-5 to bring the apparatus to full development for reliable service. "I realize that the demand on the Navy for vessels of every description is enormous. In comparison with these demands the need at New London and San Diego for combat craft is extremely small. If we have faith in the ultimate effectiveness of some of these new and promising tools as a means for increasing successful attack on submarines, we must, I think, be prepared to pay a small price in their early introduction."[132]

Furer brought this concern to Admirals Edwards and Purnell, and to Admiral King.

First Casualties

Lighter-than-air suffered its first casualties at midyear: during an experimental mission off New Jersey, a midair collision took twelve lives.

L-2, then *G-1,* had departed Lakehurst, after which both trainers secured for sea. Five Columbia scientists accompanied, as technical aides. Among them: Drs. F. M. Varney and Harold Rack of the antisubmarine group, OSRD. The use of high-intensity underwater flares was under study—a possible means of detecting submarines from aircraft. Designed to ignite beneath a target, they might reveal a U-boat as a nighttime silhouette as it moved between flare and hunters.

Visual contact with coast guard cutter *4344* was made at about 2130 about five miles off Manasquan Inlet. Awaiting the test, the pair of airships commenced maneuvering at about the same altitude, the navigation lights of one switched off. At four hundred feet, *G-1* turned in front of its smaller sister. The nose of *L-2* impacted just forward of the *G-1* gondola, ripping both envelopes. Badly entangled, the pair splashed in about three hundred yards from the cutter. The cars sank almost immediately but hung, submerged, beneath floating fabric buoyed by entrained helium and air. Diving efforts proved futile: no water-contact lights were fitted to guide divers in or entrapped men out. For its part, the cutter had no flashlights capable of underwater use, and its after-range light (used for blinker signaling) had balked. This led to repeated attempts by *L-1* to communicate, thereby distracting the pilots. Possibly no one in either airship saw the other for some seconds prior to impact.

All aboard save one had perished—the first fatal nonrigid accident since 1933. Only Ens. Howard S. Fahey Jr. survived, having escaped through the pilot's window of *L-2*. That ship was towed ashore, the bodies removed. The derelict *G-1* broke free of its tow.

Underscoring the need for safety upgrades, another blimp slapped the sea under ceiling-zero conditions the following day, taking water into the car. Letting go depth charges—lightening ship—conferred escape. (Once immersed in saltwater the car generally required a major overhaul, to thwart corrosion.) That same day, two K-ships on convoy duty nearly collided. "With the current fitting of blimps with Radar equipment, it is likely that more and more blimps will be put into night convoy duty, in that they have with Radar some measure of protection against submarines. It is clear that this protection is not complete, and that blimp casualties by gun fire can be expected."[133]

The Office of Scientific Research and Development, having lost five staff, issued a statement: "These men lost their lives in an accident encountered in an experimental flight in connection with important scientific war research and gave their lives for their country as truly as any soldier or sailor killed in battle."

As well, OSRD's Bush dispatched a letter to Admiral Furer, who, in turn, forwarded them to the Chief, BuAer. OSRD/NDRC urged expedited development of a prototype waterproof light for ZNP use. Meantime, the accident and unsuitable weather upset progress on the flare project; given poor test results, the research was dropped.

Rosendahl wrote from Washington. "Amazed" that neither the pilot nor copilot of *G-1* had previously logged a night flight, he wrote Mills, "It is simply impossible to give these new officer pilots and cadets too much experience in the air. . . . As soon as I get caught up with some of the details of the new program, I am coming to Lakehurst to discuss a number of matters. Meanwhile, I hope you continue to fly at every possible moment and keep all hands so busy that they do not have time to think of their troubles."[134]

The year's second half saw, in addition to the commissioning of NAS Weeksville, North Carolina (June), the start of construction for a naval air station at Glynco, Georgia (September). NAS Glynco would support ZP-15 when commissioned. On 13 February 1943, delivered via the acceptance center at Lakehurst, *K-34* landed at the Glynco station. Concurrent with these initiatives, however, U-boat activity declined in the patrol and escort sectors of ZP-11, 12, and 14. U-Boat Command had shifted its emphasis into the gulf, the Caribbean, and to the South Atlantic off Brazil. Unlike the Eastern Sea Frontier, where defenses were tightening, tanker traffic in those waters were comparatively unprotected, as well as plentiful. (See chapter 5.)

It was becoming increasingly apparent that, although the defeat of the U-boats would not, of itself, win the war, the Allies could not possibly win the war without first defeating the U-boats.[135]

That October, ZNPs *K-18* and *-19* were delivered through Lakehurst, then ferried to NAS Richmond, Florida. Located inland, southwest of Miami, Richmond became second only to Lakehurst as an overhaul facility for airships assigned to the Atlantic Fleet. Its location, moreover, permitted coverage of the Florida Straits—a major transit route between the Atlantic and the gulf and Caribbean basins. Further, missions from there could reach the gulf as well as the sea area surrounding Panama—a zone increasingly under threat in late 1942. Accordingly, many a ferry crew bound for the Caribbean or Southern Hemisphere passed through Richmond. The station's assembly and repair (A&R) officer was a key man at Richmond.[136] (See page 187.)

Meantime, *K-18* and *-19* constituted the nucleus for what became the largest LTA squadron, ZP-21. Commissioned on 1 November 1942, this unit operated as a part of the Gulf Sea Frontier but reported administratively to the Commander Airship Patrol Group One, Lakehurst.

As a vexing year neared its close, intelligence intimated renewed activity in East Coast waters. Via naval message, Andrews advised his supporting commands:

> CESF considers there are strong indications enemy is resuming submarine operations this frontier. Task groups commanders will be guided accordingly. Ships making less

than 14-1/2 knots will not proceed along coast unless escorted. Ships over 14-1/2 knots proceeding singly will zigzag. Contacts will be followed up and maintained to fullest extent forces permit. Planes, patrol vessels, including coastal pickets intensify efforts to attack and keep subs down and to prevent enemy mining operations.[137]

BuAer made report as to the status of the Mark IV-B2 installations for October–November.

Final details of a satisfactory mock-up of an MAD installation in K-type airships has been completed in cooperation with Lakehurst and Akron. Racks, mounts, and all plugs and cabling (Group A parts) are being installed by the aircraft contractor. Group B parts will be installed at Lakehurst and other suitable lighter-than-air bases. All ships from *K-30,* including *K-24* and *K-28,* will come through with Group A parts installed by the contractor. Airships already delivered will be changed over by 1 January, 1943, with some racks coming from bases, and others from Goodyear Aircraft Corporation.

In mid-November, BuAer could tally production and allotment as follows: 60 units to army bases, 31 to the navy, 56 on hand—149 in all. In a related development, maintenance training courses had been established at Corpus Christi, Texas, and at Lakehurst.

Sonobuoys soon became indispensable to magnetic detection. Why? The device enhanced effectiveness by conferring the capability to *track* a submerged boat. (A search with MAD alone was like hunting the proverbial needle.) In the meantime, the lack of buoys continued to undercut kill ratios for ASW air operations.

Acting on a directive from C-in-C, BuShips was handling procurement of a thousand buoys and a hundred receivers. As specified by the president, initial deliveries were being apportioned among the Atlantic Fleet, to Project Sail, and to the Commander, Caribbean Sea Frontier. Not content with the existing device, NDRC was working on a "more suitable production model," including the addition of suitable slick markers and float lights.[138]

Captain Mills (promoted in June) was appointed Commander, Fleet Airship Wing Thirty, effective 1 December. As well, east and gulf coast lighter-than-air was subordinated to the Atlantic Fleet—administered by Commander, Fleet Air Wings, though still assigned to the sea frontiers for operations. "I find I will have four bosses, namely: Cinclantflt, Comairwingslant, CESF, and CGSF. Already all four of them are issuing directives, so I anticipate a very merry season in this new job of Wing Commander. . . . I believe the arrangement of assigning us to Fleets will tend to put blimps on a more solid foundation, and should bring us into closer contact and relationship with the rest of the navy."[139]

Squadron Twelve had begun operations deploying *K-3* through *K-6*—and had held to four ships through April. The number of ZNPs operational rose to six during May–July; to nine in September; fourteen in October, fifteen that November. ZP-11 had been commissioned at South Weymouth, ZP-14 at Elizabeth City, ZP-21 at Richmond. In total, Wing Thirty was deploying eighteen patrol-type airships early that December, assigned thus:

A parade of celebrities entertained service personnel. Here Judy Garland chats with a student from Lakehurst's Parachute Materiel School about to embark for his graduation jump. (Capt. J. C. Kane, USN [Ret.])

Four—at NAS South Weymouth (Squadron Eleven)
Seven—at NAS Lakehurst (Squadron Twelve)
Five—at NAS Elizabeth City (Squadron Fourteen)
Two—at NAS Richmond, Florida (Squadron Twenty-one).

From auxiliary sites, ZNPs had operated in expeditionary status, awaiting completion of hangar facilities. Auxiliary bases stood ready at Cape May and at Charleston, South Carolina. Another two had been authorized with further sites desired.[140] When first authorized, 48 airships had been projected, then 120. Two hundred now were authorized, 120 contracted for. Five patrol ships *(K-13* through *K-17)* were delivered that September, 3 during December—a total of 24 ZNPs in navy hands.[141] Three blimps had been ferried west, another 6 rail-shipped to the Pacific coast.

ZP-12 had logged 1,249 flights, for 18,615 hours under way. Nearly seven hundred escorts stood logged, 361 patrol sorties. Average duration: 14.7 hours, the longest 27.5 hours. During January–December, airships had averaged about 225 hours per month. Night sorties were yet few. "Of course," Mills explained at conference, "night aviation operations, do have the advantage of keeping submarines down. We undoubtedly will all go to night operations as soon as we get RADAR on all the ships. The big problem . . . appears to be the positive identification, at night, of radar targets."

TABLE 3.7 **Antisubmarine operations by patrol airships** (ZNPs) in the Eastern Sea Frontier for 1942. Operational duties assigned: escort flights, patrol flights, and combined escort-patrol sorties. That calendar year, Airship Squadron Twelve (ZP-12) flew 331 days, for a percentage of 90.7. (George H. Mills Collection, Smithsonian)

	J	F	M	A	M	J	J	A	S	O	N	D
Squadron												
ZP-12												
Total Flights	51	42	53	75	106	51	53	59	73	97	104	88
Total Hours	599	513	635	1,075	1,571	827	873.7	907	1,067	1,350.5	1,349	760.6
ZP-11												
Total Flights	—	—	—	—	—	28	35	38	36	32	18	12
Total Hours	—	—	—	—	—	417.8	345	411.5	381.4	372.3	216.7	104.7
ZP-14	—	—	—	—	—	28	31	30	36	47	61	62
	—	—	—	—	—	433.9	468.2	414.7	440.3	581.4	739.4	704.8
Combined Totals, Flights						107	119	127	145	176	183	162
Combined Totals, Flight Hours						1,678.7	1,686.9	1,733.2	1,888.7	2,304	2,305.1	1,570.1

As for contacts, airships of the Atlantic Fleet had logged twenty-one on submarines, twenty on submarines or wrecks, and about fifty on wrecks. Officially, ZNPs had delivered eighteen attacks on U-boats, thirteen on wrecks or submarines, and twelve on confirmed wrecks. ZP-12, for its part, had logged thirty attacks on sighted or indicated contacts during 1942. "It is difficult for an aircraft to determine when a submarine is definitely destroyed," Mills reported, "and no claims have been made of total destruction. We feel that at least two submarines, from evidence or air and oil, were badly, if not totally, damaged, and that on several other occasions some damage was done."[142] Starting in May, attack appraisals—based on contact and attack information from war diaries and reports—went before a submarine damage assessment committee for final judgment as to probable damage to the enemy. (See table 3.7.)

That December, meanwhile, the Commander in Chief, U.S. Fleet expressed concern as to the lack of tangible success obtained by pilots reporting apparently excellent attacks on German submarines. To some degree, this was attributable to over-optimistic assessments of what, in fact, were bombing errors and to unsuitable ASW ordnance.[143]

On 1 January 1943, the number of U-boats operational in the Atlantic totaled 164. (Many were in passage to/from operational areas.) Adverse weather is the great leveler of ambitions and technologies. Tactical, scientific, and operational headway notwithstanding, January 1943—weeks of extreme storm at sea—had the Allies losing the submarine war. Britain faced a fuel crisis and, as well, a shortage of ships and naval escorts. At Casablanca, Churchill and Roosevelt agreed that the campaign against the U-boat in the Atlantic would hold first priority. The rate of sinkings, unless eased, held potential to disrupt Allied strategic planning. Dönitz summarized the year from

[Opposite] Twenty-two percent of all the depth charges dropped by Lakehurst's ZP-12 the first year of war failed to explode. A slow-speed platform, blimps found few opportunities to attack a surfaced submarine. The ability to track a submerged target and drop ordnance by instrument—on MAD signal—was realized only in 1944. (U.S. Naval Institute)

[Above] A depth charge fired from a "Y" gun, January 1943. The U-boat war against merchant shipping would be blunted by coordinated air and surface forces deploying progressively improved antisubmarine sensors, weapons, and tactics. (U.S. Naval Institute)

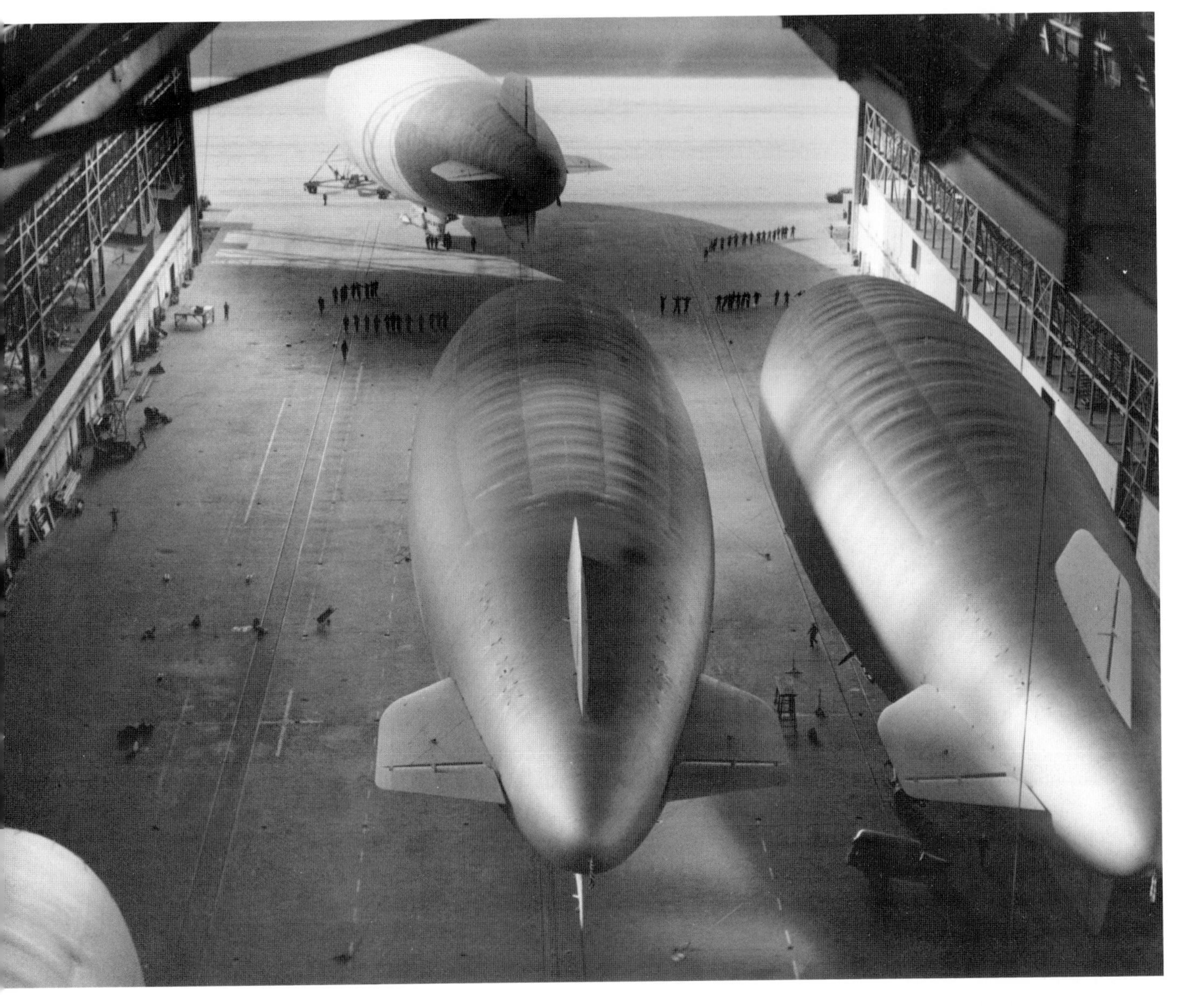

the perspective of Berlin and its Axis allies: "Generally speaking . . . the U-boat attack in 1942 was superior to the defense. The finding of convoys was facilitated by the large number of boats. The U-boats' greatest possession, the element of surprise, was still effective. The U-boats, when on the surface, were not spotted soon enough for the enemy to be able to avoid them and, when attacking, they could not be detected early enough by surface or submerged means of location."[144]

Within months, the balance was to tip unmistakably. The convoy lanes were yet vulnerable in the central Atlantic, beyond land-based air coverage. When training, devices, weapons, and the number of ASW escort vessels became ample to accompany all convoys, "hunter-killer" groups began to operate *offensively* against the undersea foe. (See table 3.8.)

[Opposite] The main hangar at Lakehurst, 13 January 1943. Ships in berth, a watch officer was on duty at all times to supervise the hangar watch. Blimps depend on internal pressure (air scoops and blowers) to maintain tension in the envelope—necessary for structural integrity. (U.S. Naval Institute)

[Top Right] A wartime afternoon, NAS Lakehurst. (U.S. Navy photograph, courtesy Mrs. E. P. Moccia)

TABLE 3.8 **Merchant-Vessel Losses and Construction**, 1942. (National Archives)

Completions	Number	Gross Tons
United States	721	5,350,695
United Kingdom	183	1,267,885
Canada	81	578,280
Total	985	7,196,860

Losses	No.	Gross Tons
By Submarine	1,161	6,249,577
By Aircraft	147	721,924
By Surface Craft	70	326,354
By Enemy Mine	54	114,307
By Other Enemy Action	94	184,831
By Unknown Enemy Action	45	103,981
By Enemy Action	1,571	7,700,974
By Marine Casualty	222	546,643
Total	1,793	8,247,617

Shipping was at once the stranglehold
and sole foundation of our war strategy.

—Winston S. Churchill

Turning Tide 4

The United States with its maritime partners sustained continued heavy losses on shipping, crews, tonnage, cargoes. The anti-U-boat campaign was a world-ocean contest for the sea-lanes of resupply and reinforcement. Of primary importance: the lifeline of materiel and food to Britain.[1] The transatlantic flow persisted, pressed to the limit of available merchantmen. "The battle must be won on the supply line," the Vice Chief of Naval Operations advised, "before we can smash the enemy on the firing line."

As it happened, 1943 saw a favorable trend against the seaborne adversary, but only after midyear. Improvements in the efficiency and numbers of escorts accounted for much of this; in the North Atlantic, indeed, the number of ships sunk per month related closely to the number of U-boats at sea divided by the number of escorts available. Also contributory: increased air coverage from shore *and* carrier-based task groups, a decline in the training of German crews, and a remarkable array of new Allied weapons and equipment—products of the action/reaction technology cycle between U-boats and the forces hunting them.[2] (See table 4.1.)

The not-yet-learned lesson of patrol and escort forces (surface and air) was coordination of effort: locate the enemy, then attack, repeatedly—to either sink or force him to the surface by damage or exhaustion. In the meantime, the learning period came at a very high cost.

A persistent zone of danger was that part of the North Atlantic more than six hundred miles from land-based aircraft. There transiting convoys—sixteen a month—were heavily attacked. The midocean area, known as "the Gap," had to be closed. Escort carrier support groups ("killer groups") would push the U-boat into more southerly waters, leaving the great-circle convoys more or less unmolested.[3] "Eventually, the killer group, comprised of surface vessels and aircraft working together as a coordinated whole, will probably be the ideal method for hunting down submarines. Due to the scarcity of surface vessels and the needs for convoy escort, such groups are not likely to be available in the near future. Consequently the burden of offensive warfare must rest on the aircraft."[4]

TABLE 4.1 **Total worldwide losses**—United or neutral merchant vessels known to have been sunk, all causes, February 1943. (National Archives)

Cause	Number	Tons
Submarine	52[1]	328,494
Surface Craft	1	4,858
Enemy Mine	5	14,064
Unknown Enemy Action	1	?
Marine Casualty	8	18,896
Total	67	366,312 plus
Location of Losses		
North Atlantic Convoy Area	28	178,312
Caribbean Sea Frontier—East	1	7,957
Mid-Atlantic Area	1	4,312
Northeast Atlantic Area	8	58,225
Mediterranean Area	5	30,257
Southeast Atlantic Area	5	27,915
Southwest Pacific Area	2	11,988
Total	50	318,966

1 Of the 52 vessels sunk by submarine, 33 were in convoy, 7 were stragglers. Several other vessels were known to be torpedoed or were overdue, hence not yet classified as sunk. The bulk of the losses were cargo vessels torpedoed at night.

Until then, long-range air support was seldom available at the moment and place needed—and, necessarily, wasted operational hours in transit. Under unified command, planes from escort carriers (CVEs) could be launched almost instantly.

Shore-based U.S. Atlantic Fleet LTA—one element of sea/air cooperation—began the year with eighteen K-ships operational in four squadrons. In convoy work, LTA helped conserve scarce escorts by forcing the enemy down. The year would close with operating strength at seventy-one ZNPs distributed among ten "blimprons," including overseas deployments. U.S. fleet airships would be operating over waters arcing from New England's Bar Harbor south through the Caribbean fully to Santa Cruz (Rio de Janeiro).

Germany held large submarine reserves, completed and under construction. One major development: the ordered withdrawal of boats from the western Atlantic into safer waters and adoption of a stay-surfaced-and-fight-it-out tactic against aircraft. And so the inner coastal zone was largely vacated by the undersea enemy—the operational sector assigned to LTA. One outcome: fewer contacts and attacks during 1943 than in the year prior, this despite a several-fold boost in the number of airships operational.

As 1943 opened, Lakehurst's ZP-12 comprised *K-3* through *K-5, K-8, K-15,* and *K-16*—six aircraft. Further deliveries from Ohio were arriving for transfer into sister squadrons or to the air station's own command. *K-42,* for example, delivered 1 March, was transferred to ZP-21 on the 28th. The delivery rate from the contractor in April 1943: six ships per month,

[Top] Capt. George H. Mills, USN. A graduate of Lakehurst Class VIII, Mills had trained aboard USS *Los Angeles* (ZR 3), was billeted to USS *Macon* and, in January 1940, read his orders as commanding officer of the Lakehurst station. He received command of the first airship group in 1942; from July 1943 to July 1945, Mills held the rank of commodore—Commander, Fleet Airships Atlantic. (GHMC, NASM, Smithsonian Institution)

[Bottom] Capt. Mills and Paul W. Litchfield, chairman of the board of Goodyear Aircraft Corporation—the navy's prime contractor for airships, May 1943. Mills would receive the Legion of Merit for distinguished service, including his "unusual executive ability." (GHMC, NASM, Smithsonian Institution)

and this rate may be doubled within the next six months. We now have on hand or on order, for operating ships and spares, practically the whole of the two hundred authorized by Congress, but it will be a year from now before we can expect to have built up to that figure. Fundamentally, this is the old story of our civilian leaders reducing the armed services to the vanishing point in the fat days of peace. . . . This is the story of the blimp service except it took a rather aggravated form with us as compared to the older branches of the Navy.[5]

During January–February, more than a thousand hours were flown by ZP-12 for escort and patrol missions. In addition, thirty-five training, test, and experimental flights were logged during January, thirty-two in February. By June, the total hours flown had nearly tripled. Pilots logged an average of 100.5 hours per month that April–June, with 6.3 airships flown each flying day during June.[6]

For the western Atlantic—that is, the East Coast of North America—the threat embraced not only U-boats but also surface raiders and enemy aircraft, raiding parties, spies, saboteurs, suspicious persons. Along coastal New Jersey, "training and experimental flights over land—especially those over the New Jersey Pine Area should serve to keep watch over areas adaptable to the uses of spies and saboteurs. Officers and men must be constantly on the watch for unusual activity on the ground, suspicious looking buildings or structures, and other evidences of possible subversive or enemy action."

And this: "Personnel visiting communities on the Atlantic Ocean are reminded that this is a restricted area under Army control. Regulations forbid anyone on the open beach during the hours of darkness either on foot or in cars; use of cameras, field glasses or telescopes on beach or boardwalk at any time. . . . Service personnel apprehended violating these restrictions will be returned under guard to their station."[7]

"Special Devices"

No single panacea won the Atlantic campaign for the Allies. It was the combined weight of multiple elements—platforms, sensors, ordnance, training, coordinated experience—that would defeat Dönitz and his determined commanders.

NDRC/NRL projects had included a variety of sensors applicable to aerial ASW. One investigation applicable to ZNPs involved dispensers for launching small bombs. Another was a "towed sound device" for listening and echoing. As well, development of an underwater flare was under way, as were tests of float lights—both out of Lakehurst. Bomb racks were under study, this in connection with development work on a fast-sinking, streamlined projectile. (That January, this particular ordnance lacked a suitable fuse.) Installed on *K-2,* a rack developed by NDRC at New London appeared to offer satisfactory performance. The function of *spacing* several bombs in a "stick"—to realize an effective straddle—was performed by an intervalometer. An automatic release mechanism developed to operate with this device "has just been completed and is now ready for test at Lakehurst."

In the realm of magnetic detection, test results were under analysis, further studies and flight development either under way or proposed. Model types were the Mark IVB-2, Mark VI, and

Mark X. Each held the same basic components: an assembly of three mutually perpendicular coils mounted on a double gimbel device belted to two servomotors, electronic detectors and amplifiers, a recorder, and miscellaneous electronic gear, including an oscillator and a power unit. Various advantages as well as drawbacks attended each type: weight, performance, adaptability. The IVB-2 had gone into production in June 1942. Its tactical value, BuAer advised, "will manifest itself as more crews [HTA and LTA] become familiar with its use." Satisfactory performance exploiting a towed "bird" was anticipated. Still, the Mark IV was not readily adaptable to *directional* MAD. Also, given the improvements incorporated into Types VI and X, already the Mark IV was deemed obsolescent.

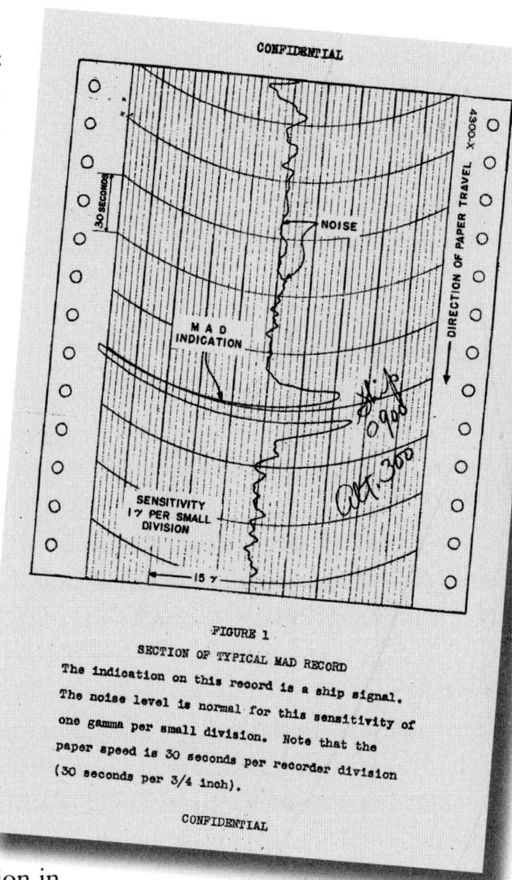

A typical MAD graphic trace. Effective use depended upon the operator's ability to recognize and properly interpret swings of the recording pen, so as to distinguish valid signals from spurious—the latter caused by faulty operation, surges in the electrical system, sunken wrecks, or geologic anomalies. (National Archives)

For the national emergency, "limited quantities" had reached the services; the Type VI, for one, entered production only in March 1943; no maintenance manuals had been distributed. As yet, most intensive operational deployment of magnetic detection in the navy was by LTA. First to be fitted, *K-3* had flown MAD equipped since January 1942. On both coasts, ZNPs now were receiving the outmoded Mark IV-B2 gear. That April, the navy had sixty sets, about forty of which were installed. LTA schools held another eight, naval HTA thirty.

"Sono-radio buoys" (essentially hydrophone radio transmitters installed in small buoys) also were under development (as we have seen), primarily by the NDRC group at New London, with support from NRL and other agencies. In March 1943, production buoys and receivers were being built for both the army and navy. Though not yet fully service tested (let alone in service use), reports showed promise; soon, both operation and weight improved markedly. Still, the navy had on order ten thousand expendable buoys and one hundred receivers—all assigned to CincLant. Limited operational use of the equipment had been reported by LTA at Lakehurst, by Project Sail, and by VP-63 (an HTA patrol squadron), in addition to army tests.[8] One unsolved problem pursued by New London: adequate surface markers (float lights, slicks). A primary hurdle at this phase was interpretation by operators of the audio received. "It is anticipated that the expendable sono-radio buoy will find its greatest practical use as adjunct to MAD, as far as ASW applications are concerned."[9] A *directional* buoy was to render the comment prescient.

When 1943 began, Lakehurst held thirty-two transmitters and one receiver, mounted in a Squadron Twelve airship. The underwater range was about two miles, and the transmitter could be heard aloft about five or six miles away. That April, Lakehurst tested AN/CRT-1A sonobuoys and MAD together against a fleet submarine, USS *Harder*. Its skipper, Cdr. Samuel D. Dealey, was no novice; quite the contrary. Still, "Dealey discovered that *K-49* . . . had located his new, state-of-the-art submarine by listening to her main motors and reduction gears and the operation of her trim pump as she cruised between 130 and 1250 feet at speeds of 2 to 4 ½ knots. The tests led to an order for full-scale production of the sonobuoys."[10] The latest type gained "limited production" in September.

Radar Maturing

The sensor commanding highest priority was microwave radar. "Radar was now the favored instrument for which an almost insatiable appetite grew."[11] By 1943, airborne radar was proving its mettle at both ends of the transatlantic convoy circuit. "The radar was very effective, very handy," a ZP-32 officer recalls, "even with the small antenna that the K-ships had . . . because it was easy to present to both the pilot and the operator—very useful in making a landfall, for example, in bad weather. And useful sometimes in landing: finding your way home. . . . All in all, I thought it was a very effective piece of equipment." The early MAD equipment, though, "wasn't impressive."[12]

In most cases, the number of contacts per hundred hours of U.S. flying at night was four to five times that obtained by day, using visual means only. The reason, in part, was radar's larger range; much of the difference, however, was due to U-boats being more often on the surface at night. Nonetheless, relatively few contacts were attacked or even slightly damaged. Why? Pilots withheld attack unless the target was confirmed as enemy. This doctrine required a fly-by; by the time the pilot had circled back, his target-to-be had dived. Radar-equipped patrol airships were likewise deterred.

Night operations had been tried, particularly in the South Weymouth sector. That August, Cdr. Daniel J. Weintraub, USN, a skipper within ZP-14, inquired of his group commander, "Has any policy been formulated, or doctrine, with regard to night operations? Any information would be greatly appreciated as to the correct procedure. I believe surface support is absolutely necessary in order to do any good with night patrolling for submarines with radar."[13]

The importance of waging twenty-four-hour warfare against the U-boat was plain. By night, however, the precondition to radar attack was adequate illumination, so as to identify targets well away. (Indeed, the success of the A/S war would force the enemy to surface *only* at night, except for especially compelling reasons.) In the meanwhile, for the first six months of 1943, not a single known successful night attack was made by U.S. planes. For airships, "The identification of small objects on surface at night is going to be most difficult for us," Mills noted. "With so many picket boats working in close to the shore and with unscheduled craft entering the area, it becomes necessary to identify the craft before dropping bombs."[14] A lumbering platform, hence slow to close, LTA would get very few chances to release upon U-boats caught on the surface.

The first production installation of the ASG type was aboard a K-ship in the summer of 1942. Within eighteen months the navy had upward of a thousand operational, the British some 350. The ASG provided all-around search, courtesy of a rotating antenna dish in a "hat" projecting beneath the car. Accordingly, all radar-equipped K-types were equipped with retractable landing gear—essential because the radome (also retractable) was located just aft of the wheel; it housed a twenty-nine-inch spinner that would have been obstructed when scanning forward, blocking out a pie-shaped segment of over thirty degrees. Flight procedure then: retract the landing wheel (by hand crank), then lower the radome.[15]

The ASG type was the first airborne radar displaying a maplike picture: its business end, the plan position indicator (PPI). The center of this PPI cathode-ray tube represented the spot directly beneath the aircraft, targets at various azimuths from the aircraft being plotted along corresponding radii of the circular display. Land targets could be seen well to sea. "The PPI picture of shorelines, harbors and rivers is remarkably similar to their appearance on charts. Experiences with ASG radar have been highly satisfactory with respect to reliability. Lighter-than-air ships have in many instances accumulated more than 1,300 hours of service in the course of their long coastal patrols. They report 95–100% satisfactory radar operation regularly. The PPI type of search and indication probably reaches its greatest usefulness in the convoy protection operations of these K-ships."[16]

Still, radar was no miracle gadget. Nor did it replace the human eye. Until introduction of centimeter-wavelength radar, such as the ASG, the meter type gave away its presence before the aircraft had gained detection range. As the battle matured, radar-equipped craft continued to log most of their sightings by eye alone. "The radar is a new and marvelous instrument, but its novelty must not blind us to the fact that it is in its infancy and still has many imperfections."[17]

The year 1943 held frenetic—and, for U-Boat Command, ominous. "Assuming as we did, that the British and Americans were building more ships than we were sinking, we had already become quite sure, in February 1943, that victory over the two maritime powers in this war on tonnage could not be achieved." Though a severing of Allied sea communications lay beyond hope, "the war on his shipping had to continue," to destroy as well as tie down enemy air and surface forces engaged in combating the U-boat.[18]

Indeed, "I am extremely anxious about shipping situation," Churchill wrote Roosevelt in March, lamenting the heavy losses. Crippled for lack of shipping, the requirements of military operations—including for crossing the English Channel—stood unmet. "In order to sustain the [offensive] operations in North Africa, the Pacific, and India, and to carry supplies to Russia, the import programme into the United Kingdom has been cut to the bone, and we have eaten, and are eating, deeply into reserves."[19]

February proved the bellwether for ZNP support within the Eastern Sea Frontier. ZP-15 was commissioned on the 1st, Cdr. J. D. Reppy, USN, commanding. It was the newest "zipron" in the Eastern Sea Frontier, and its southernmost. (The next down-coast was ZP-21, assigned to the Gulf Sea Frontier.) Authorized strength when Fifteen took delivery: eight ZNPs. The squadron was directly subordinate to Fleet Airship Group One. The ceremonies were held at NAS Glynco, Georgia—Fifteen's operating base. Constructed six miles north of Brunswick, the station had been commissioned (unfinished) on 25 January. Glynco boasted two wooden hangars, a two-thousand-foot asphalt mat, six mast circles, and a pair of four-thousand-foot runways. Station complement that March: 184 officers, 1,132 enlisted, and 269 civilians.[20]

October found the squadron's operations hangar still not yet complete, obliging ZP-15's intelligence office to occupy a temporary office. Nonetheless,

The intelligence duty officer briefs about forty-five minutes prior to takeoff and interrogates as soon as the crews report to the Intelligence office. During interrogation, he executes the form mike, secures the track chart from the pilot, and fills out the monthly operational summary. . . . It is the responsibility of the duty intelligence officer to submit before 0800 to the Squadron Commander a report on the condition of the radar, MAD, and radio during operations of the previous day. He also prepares a submarine summary for the 1300 "Captain's Conference" of pilots.[21]

In blue water (that is, far to sea), thirty-eight U-boats threw themselves against two conjoined convoys over three days (16–19 March), the first night that the convoys had had no air cover. Twenty-one ships were lost, a total of 141,000 tons, along with one escort. One U-boat was sunk by aircraft, nearly all the others taking damage from depth charges or bombs.

In March, 1943, conditions on the main battleground, the North Atlantic, were again very favorable. Many convoys were met and attacked with very great success. The most successful convoy battles of the whole war were fought. The U-boat leadership in these battles, and also the attacks on the convoys by the Commanding Officers reached their peak. . . . The number of U-boats was continually increasing, losses were slight, and reinforcements by boats from home considerable.[22]

This group U-boat assault was the biggest success to that date. No one admitted it, Roskill writes, but defeat confronted the Admiralty. No one could know that this was the last staggering German victory in the battle of the convoys. Along with support groups and long-range aircraft, a third factor (as Dönitz records) was foreclosing the U-boat being decisive: "On March 26 an aircraft carrier was observed inside the screen of a west-bound convoy. Its aircraft foiled the attempts of the U-boats to close the convoy. . . . Their advent finally closed the air gap in the North Atlantic, and from then onwards convoys enjoyed the protection of continuous air cover throughout their voyage."[23]

That March 1943, 400 U-boats were in service, of which 222 were frontline boats. Of these, in turn, 18 were prowling the Arctic, 19 the Mediterranean, and 3 the Black Sea. In all, 182 were available for Atlantic operations.[24]

Under examination this same month: a reorganization of U.S. Navy lighter-than-air. In BuAer, the relative priorities strongly favored airplanes; the ASW airship was secondary. Mills wrote Rear Adm. John S. McCain, proposing a "director of airships," to both carry out the program and give it proper recognition. If created, the billet would require a senior officer in charge of the LTA section within BuAer comparable in rank to the heads of divisions in the bureau, with additional orders requiring him to report to Cominch for duty on his staff.

LTA is such a small unit in the Aeronautical organization that it cannot receive the proper consideration essential to success in the development of a separate weapon. LTA has been the "poor country cousin" for so long that an unfavorable attitude regarding its value had developed among many officers in the navy. To make itself effective, it like all other undeveloped weapons, (for example the submarine and the airplane in the lean years of their early development) must have a guiding hand in the Department, otherwise it is lost in the maze of work incidental to the carrying on of the whole show.[25]

Blimp Squadron Twenty-two (ZP-22) and Twenty-Three (ZP-23)

On 20 April 1943, the secretary of the navy approved a 126-operational-ship program plus 21 spares. This action reduced the two projected Gulf of Mexico squadrons from 12 to 6 ships each, and their bases from two hangars to one. The 12 withheld were diverted to Brazil, where operations commenced that September. The U-boat threat had eased in the gulf and escalated off the Brazilian littoral. (See chapter 5.) In total, 137 K-type and 21 M-type fleet ZNPs were on order. In service in the sea frontiers were 24 of the K-type: 8 in the Pacific, 36 in the Atlantic theater. Rate of delivery: 6 to 7 airships per month.[26] That May, 11 ZNP-Ks reached the operator: 7 to Lakehurst, 4 to Moffett Field. One L-type trainer, *L-15,* also was delivered.[27] "The prospects are that [the builder] will work up to a peak of ten K-ships per month in October; the first fleet M-ship will not be delivered before October and we expect to be getting 3 M-ships per month one year from now."[28]

Program reductions would slash the M-type procurement to four "Mike" ships, the rest cancelled.

As for trainers and experimental ships, thirty-four were projected, thirteen of which were on hand that month, the remainder expected within one year. Both the May and July 1943 deliveries represented the largest monthly totals of the war. And the May–July period witnessed a near-frantic rate of delivery: thirty-two ZNP-Ks, of which ten were assigned to Moffett Field.

To augment coverage in the Gulf of Mexico near the debouchment of the Mississippi River, Airship Squadron Twenty-two (ZP-22) was ordered established. On 1 May, Naval Air Station, Houma, Louisiana, was placed in commission by the acting commandant of the Eighth Naval District. The site, thirty-six miles inland, was flat former sugar land in Terrebonne Parish. The air station's complement was thirty officers, a hundred enlisted men, and thirty-five marines. Certain base elements were not yet complete: landing mat, HTA runways, mobile masts (unassembled), office equipment—and the thousand-foot wooden hangar. An unusual door design, however, threatened delay. "The hurricane season starts in that area about August 15, and the need for the rapid completion of the dock is obvious."[29]

ZP-22 was placed in commission on 15 May, Lt. Cdr. J. J. McCormick, commanding. Aircraft complement (upon delivery): six "King" ships.

Houma was one of two gulf-area LTA stations under construction. A second squadron for Group Two was commissioned on 1 June. During ceremonies at Lakehurst, Commander, Fleet Airship Wing Thirty placed Airship Squadron Twenty-three in commission, Lt. Cdr. Michael F. D. Flaherty, commanding. Before delivering the squadron to its CO, Captain Mills addressed its officers and men:

> Most of you were trained at Lakehurst and should be well versed in flying and maintaining airships. Most of you have served in squadrons of this Wing and have learned to carry out missions. . . . Our blimp squadrons have developed fine traditions of service

and have built up a reputation for carrying out missions under all kinds of weather conditions. We do not have to feel that our work is secondary. Our missions are important and blimps have taken their place in the team of forces protecting our shores. Some of our ships have located submarines and have been bold and forthright in attacking them.[30]

The wing commander then directed Flaherty to take command. Having read his orders and accepted command, Flaherty turned the microphone over to Rosendahl, who extended congratulations. Rosie's new training command (see page 140), the admiral added, would foster the development of new devices and improve ZNPs to afford crews the best types of weapons. Airships had given fine war service; the new squadron, he was confident, would contribute splendidly. When he had wished the unit good luck and good hunting, the watch was set, retreat sounded.

Immediately upon commissioning, the unit was transferred to the Naval Air Station, Hitchcock, Texas.

When Texas was ready, *K-60* and *K-62* (assigned to ZP-23) departed Lakehurst; on 19 June the squadron took delivery when *K-62* (Flaherty, command pilot) landed.[31] Operational area: the western gulf area, under direct operational control by the Commander, Gulf Sea Frontier. Located about ten miles from Galveston, Hitchcock was the last link in the chain of main LTA bases planned for the continental United States. It had been placed in service on 22 May, when Capt. Arthur D. Ayrault, representing the Eighth Naval District, read orders authorizing commissioning. Cdr. Charles W. Roland then read his orders making him station skipper. The national ensign was hoisted. Although no arches had been raised, hangar completion was projected for September.

Meantime, in baking heat amid clouds of mosquitoes, the contractor attacked the hangar, mooring-out sites, servicing facilities. "Right now it is pretty torn up, and disorganized," squadron skipper Lt. Cdr. M. H. Eppes confided, "but it is taking shape rapidly." But, "waiting for the airships out on the mat at nights is real agony for the men unless they are well protected with nets and gloves."[32]

November saw Hitchcock's wood-and-concrete hangar just shy of completion. Absent the dock-smarts of experience, ground-handling parties received "concentrated instructions" in dock routine. Though the contractor had not formally released the hangar, the big day came. On 30 November, a ship was shunted under roof. "The operation was a success in that all went safely and fairly smoothly. There was a turn out of all hands for the momentous occasion, Station, Hedron, and Squadron."[33]

[Opposite] Naval Air Station Houma, Louisiana—headquarters ZP-22. Note the clamshell doors, opened on tracks to one side. (Lt. H. F. Smith, USN [Ret.])

Tenth Fleet

Bending to pressure from the British, the president, Stimson, and his own staff, Adm. E. J. King established the Tenth Fleet on 20 May 1943. "Seventeen months after the onset of hostilities, more for political than operational reasons, the US Navy finally formed an organization with responsibility for formulation and execution of the operational strategy for the antisubmarine campaign. Admiral Low soon found that the weapons for a decisive counterattack lay at hand."[34] Adm. Francis S. Low was charged with its administration. Under Low, backed by King, the Tenth Fleet organization "was broad in scope, sweeping in power and virtually absolute in influence, yet it was astonishingly small and tight."[35]

In the interests of centralized control, operating with about fifty officers and enlisted personnel, Tenth Fleet included a hundred or so civilian scientists of the Antisubmarine Warfare Operations Research Group. Responsible to King, ASWORG collected all relevant data on ASW, then analyzed it, recording an enormous amount of statistical data on punched cards.[36] A systematic study was under way of all attacks made on U-boats in the U.S. strategic area in the Atlantic. As well, "Effective June twenty-third Cominch will analyze all contact and action reports against enemy submarines made by United States air and surface forces world wide."[37]

"We begin to be useful when we can combine with our scientific training a practical background gained from contact with operating personnel. . . . Our position as liaison men between the operating officers of the Navy and Army and the research and development laboratories of NDRC is a delicate one."[38] King now exercised direct control over all the Atlantic sea frontiers;

[Opposite] Chief of Naval Airship Training and Experimentation, Rear Adm. Charles E. Rosendahl, USN (center, front) with CNATE personnel, 1943. That April, the secretary of the navy approved a "126 operating ship" program plus twenty-one spares. (Lt. H. F. Smith, USNR [Ret.])

using their commanders as task force commanders, Cominch directed the allocation of antisubmarine forces to all Atlantic commands.

The navy had developed the analysis of communications intelligence into "a fine art," the fruits of which yielded an in-depth picture of U-boat operations. An effective counteroffensive was thus made possible: at sea this May, locating devices, killing weapons, and tactics were applied with renewed operational discipline. Results were immediate, as Dönitz was to lament:

> By May it was quite clear that the enemy's air strength in the Atlantic, consisting of long distance machines and of carrier-borne aircraft, had increased enormously. Of even greater consequence, however was the fact that the U-boats could be located at a great distance by the enemy's radar, apparently on short wave, without previous warning on their own receivers, and were then heavily attacked by destroyers and aircraft carriers without ever seeing the convoy, which was obviously diverted. . . . From this new situation it was evident that the enemy's aircraft and destroyers must be fitted with new radar.[39]

In one operation, eleven boats in contact with a convoy were detected with "astonishing certainty" (Dönitz would record) and driven off while it was still light. "There was no part of the Atlantic where the boats were safe from being located day and night by aircraft," he noted, ruefully. "The U-boat packs were kept underwater and harried continually," Churchill would write, "while air and surface escort of the convoys coped with the attackers. . . . In anti-U-boat warfare the air weapon was now an equal partner with the surface ship."[40] Dönitz was obliged to concur: "Radar, and particularly radar location by aircraft, had to all practical purposes robbed the U-boats of their power to fight on the surface. Wolf-pack operations against convoys in the North Atlantic, the main theatre of operations and at the same time the theatre in which air cover was strongest, were no longer possible. They could only be resumed if we succeeded in radically increasing the fighting power of the U-boats."[41]

On 24 May, the grand admiral, commander in chief of the Kriegsmarine, signaled all boats to withdraw to the area southwest of the Azores. The assault had been blunted, the balance turned. Still, the battle was not done; the U-boat war, which had begun the first day of hostilities, was to persist to the last.

Naval Airship Training (and Experimental) Command

ZNP material and sensors remained the subject of urgent experimentation, as did the platform itself. Indeed, on 15 May 1943 a separate command was established expressly for such work. From a distinguished tour in command of the heavy cruiser USS *Minneapolis,* in the South Pacific, Capt. Charles E. Rosendahl was ordered stateside, promoted to rear admiral, and assigned a new billet: Chief of Naval Airship Training (that October, Chief of Naval Airship Training and Experimentation, CNATE), with headquarters at NAS Lakehurst. The admiral's arrival set in motion a program to combine all LTA training under a single unit, thereby placing the program on an equal footing with commands in heavier-than-air. As well as training on both coasts, the command had cognizance—under the Vice Chief of Naval Operations—over flight testing, experimentation, and

development work.[42] All were to be conducted in the Lakehurst–Quonset locale.[43] "The Command is testimony of the airship's usefulness and importance as a war weapon," the base newspaper boasted.

His two-star flag broken out, Rosendahl was the first flag officer to hold headquarters on the base. That November, Capt. George Mills, Commander, Fleet Airships Atlantic, officially assumed the rank of commodore. "After Commodore Mills read his orders, the Commodore's flag was broken out at the peak and the broad command pennant hauled down. Rosendahl, after officially being welcomed by the Commodore, inspected the Marine detachment which formed the guard of honor, while the assembled company stood at attention."[44] The ceremony marked the arrival of the second flag officer on station.

Among the projects for the new command: improving magnetic detection; refining the sonobuoy for ZNP use; blimp-towed hydrophones; float and rocket flares; a bombsight; fast-sinking depth charges; bomb racks (e.g., the Mk 53), and automatic releases. Ideas flowed in for prosecution under Lt. Cdr. George Crompton, USN, the station's experimental officer. Service tests would exploit *K-2* or (depending on the project) *K-3, -5, -7,* or *M-1*.[45] Collaborating with

New Jersey governor Charles Edison at Lakehurst, 13 September 1943. Edison is escorted by Rear Admiral Rosendahl; following are Commodore Mills and Capt. Maurice M. Pierce, station commanding officer. (GHMC, NASM, Smithsonian Institution)

[Opposite] *L-7* at NAS Lakehurst. Sensitive to the controls, the L-type was an excellent primary trainer. Student-pilots practiced the arts of aerostatics and aerodynamics, and developed a "feel" for the condition of their ship. (Lt. H. F. Smith, USNR [Ret.])

Commander, Fleet Airships Atlantic, and his counterpart on the West Coast, CNATE maintained liaison with NDRC and with BuAer's Experiments and Development Branch, Engineering Division. "The Naval Airship Training Command will arrange with the Coordinator of Research and Development for necessary collaboration by basic research agencies, such as the National Development and Research Council."[46]

Still, priceless assets though they were, the latest antisubmarine gadgets were no panacea. The human eye tendered a most effective tool against the undersea enemy.

> Let us not forget that in the last war airships did excellent work without the special equipment we now enjoy. The present LTA program was conceived before the installa-

tion of special equipment in our first airship. Airships proved their value in the current war before special equipment was installed. The special equipment should be used in a manner which will *add to* our capabilities and should not be used *in lieu* of fundamental airship practices of careful navigation and diligent performance of duty on the part of lookouts. Do not expect the special equipment to ring a bell to wake up the crew.[47]

The training command faced another insistent concern: combat personnel. Reactions in combat must be instinctive—the fruit of exacting training plus operational seasoning. "The training command," Mills had written, "must evolve methods for improving the course and at the *same* time impregnate each student with a high sense of duty, a keenness for airships, and a love of the Navy. A hell of a big job."[48]

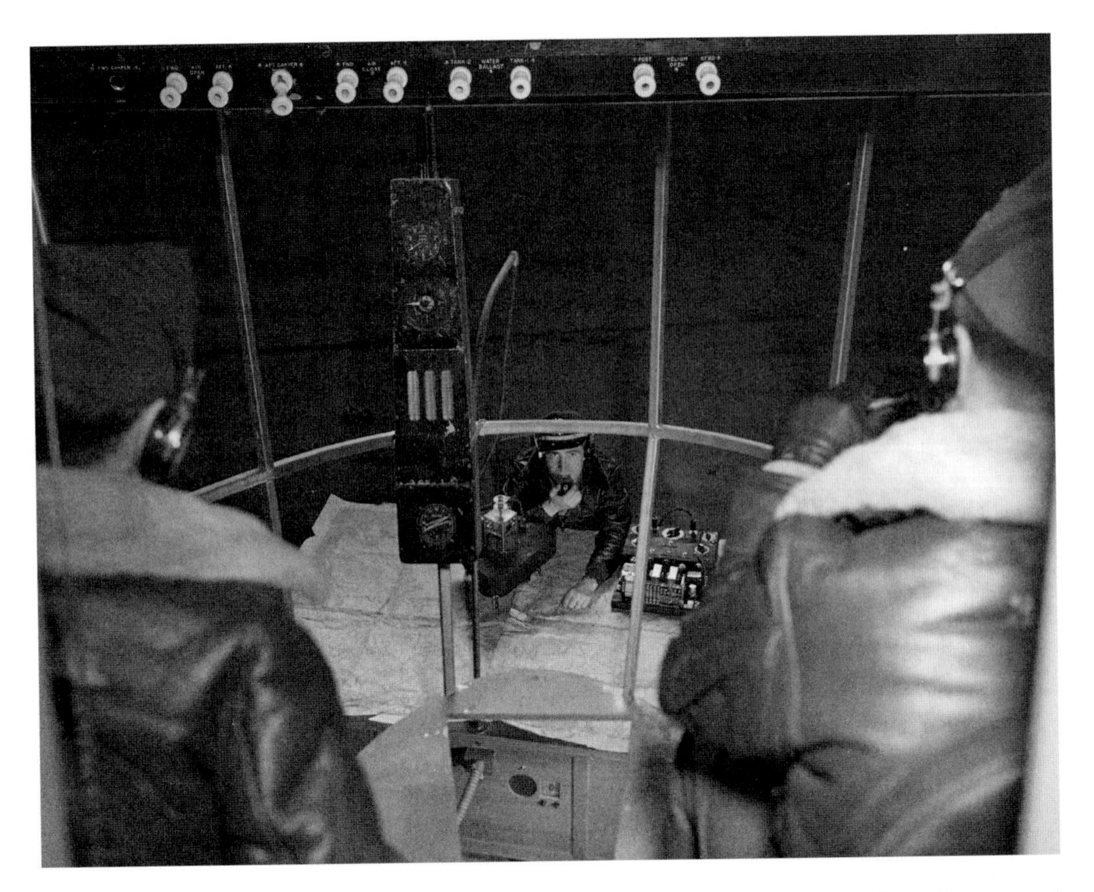

Instructor at the recording table below them, aviation cadets work a flight simulator or trainer, 13 April 1943. "By purely mechanical devices, the instructor can create the effect of gusts, crosswinds and other actual flight conditions to train crews for blimp operations." (U.S. Naval Institute)

[Opposite] LTA-qualified enlisted personnel, indispensable to operations, supplemented the program's commissioned ranks. Exploiting California con-ditions, Moffett Field became a primary-training base and Lakehurst the advanced school—thus allowing each air station to specialize. The chief boatswain's mate is Leonard E. Schellberg. (Lt. Cdr L. E. Schellberg, USN [Ret.])

What *was* the most effective training for officer and enlisted personnel? CNATE proposed to the Chief of Naval Personnel that the LTA course be extended to six months. Moreover, it proposed a division of emphasis, assigning Moffett Field for primary training and leaving Lakehurst to handle advanced instruction. This would exploit the flying weather in California for balloon and L-ship flying and enable each base to specialize. This program became effective 1 August, with students training under the plan until 30 June 1944, when LTA training ceased for the war.

As for *qualified* personnel: some officers and men were experienced and capable, certainly; most, though, were newly trained in the art of LTA flying. That December, for example, ZP-15 did not have enough naval aviators assigned to form three sections per ZNP. Further, an "extreme shortage" of "Qualified LTA" enlisted men persisted: "The acute personnel situation in the airship branch makes it essential that the Airship Training Center intensify its instruction to the maximum. Peacetime standards of working and flying hours must be discarded to the end that the maximum ground school and flight instruction be given the student officers, cadets, and enlisted men in the specified period."[49]

Training record for 1943: ten graduating classes of officers at Lakehurst, six at Moffett. The average number of flight personnel had swelled in 1942 from 200 to 700; it jumped to 2,300 the following year, then peaked at about 4,000 in 1944. Reductions in pilot training for all the services ensued; in 1945, about 2,500 flight personnel held LTA orders. Lakehurst's

officer school reached its maximum enrollment in November 1943: 534 officers, aviation cadets, and aviation pilots.[50]

That October–November, as has been seen, contract terminations ended airship production. The K series closed at *K-135*—the four additional ships cancelled and their envelopes delivered as spares. It was now that Goodyear's wartime contract for the M type was reduced to four, thereby canceling eighteen aircraft. The ten G-ships on order were reduced by three, their envelopes delivered as spares. The small trainers *L-13* through *L-22* were delivered between April and September. Thus, in November 1943, the approved program comprised 122 airships, including spares. Still, other LTA contracts continued: a series of overhaul and erection contracts, deliveries of spare envelopes, and also overhaul, to relieve the strain at Richmond and Moffett. "A reasonable flow of structural spare parts for all models was maintained."[51]

Magnetic Detection from Aircraft (Continued)

For A/S air forces, the contribution tendered by the airborne detector was yet problematic. Though MAD development had been pushed, service tests had yet to examine the limitations of magnetic detection.[52] What, for one, was the sensitivity or range. Or the magnetic moment of a submerged Type XX boat? Airborne carriers could not *track* with the equipment, maintaining contact, marking the exact spot of each received signal. For airplanes, an automatic (as opposed to manual) release was crucial, that is, retrobombing. But the navy had *no* MAD-equipped planes in service.

[Opposite] At Lakehurst, the CNATE command drove a MAD-related program of continued development. (National Archives)

(Two at Jacksonville assigned to Project Sail could not be spared, operationally.) The exact number procured and installed by the army was unknown.[53]

By November 1943, all ZNP-Ks were flying MAD-equipped, though some had the older units installed. Still, performance was deemed satisfactory for a slow-speed platform.

> The blimp MAD detector was mounted in a towed, streamlined capsule at the end of several hundred feet of cable. This was occasionally done with airplanes also, in order to remove the detector from magnetic effects associated with engines, struts, and control cables, as well as eddy currents in metal wing surfaces as the airplane maneuvered in the earth's magnetic field. Most MAD installations however were internally mounted in aircraft, with the detector unit mounted at the wing tips or tail so as to be as distant from unwanted magnetic sources of the aircraft as possible.[54]

The newest equipment was effective—if deployed with skill and confidence. Was MAD doctrine as applied to airships informed, practiced, sound? Eager for LTA to perform, Cdr. George Watson—in 1943, assigned to Tenth Fleet—found himself an unabashed skeptic on this matter. The program had yet to put it all together: equipment, tactics, and experience.

> We are enunciating doctrines and using operational plans and procedures based on an assumed M.A.D. performance which no one knows whether can be achieved or not. This is a horrible state of affairs. Until we can get a tame submarine and make at least 200 runs simulating action conditions and find out whether or not our average pilot can in fact and practice actually establish, develop and maintain MAD contacts with reasonability probability of success under most conditions—then all our plans based on the use of MAD are just so many words and lead us only to self-delusion.[55]

The new dual-head Mark VI, Watson hoped, would help simplify the tactical problem of magnetic detection. Still, why deploy it if ZNPs did not deftly exploit its singular A/S capabilities? "The proficiency [he continued] required to make even a passable MAD run requires long, tedious and continuous practice which our pilots have not had and must have if the instrument is to justify even one pound of weight."

The Mark I and II MAD had pioneered the equipment. Improvements realized the Mark IV-B, the transition to which occurred in June 1942. Of the half-dozen units, one was at Lakehurst, another at NAS Quonset Point, the remaining four under test at LaGuardia Field (where one was installed in a B-18.) Production rate had reached one hundred units per month, with two assigned to the Brits. Also, a rocket depth charge had been suggested for the equipment—"and is being worked on." In sum, intensive experimentation persisted at each test location.

Refinements incorporated, NDRC produced a lighter, more effective design—the Mark VI. As 1943 ended, development work pertaining to magnetic detection stood "substantially complete." On the operational side, NDRC had furnished observers and instructors to assist with trials until navy personnel could assume routine operation and maintenance of the gear. In bases shoreside, particularly LTA, engineering talent was yet scarce, obliging one man to assist at several commands.[56] In November 1943 (for instance), the support staff assigned to LTA numbered two for Lakehurst (Messrs. Blake and Humm), one for Moffett Field, and two at Richmond, with one assisting at South Weymouth.

Seafaring will always be dangerous. That October, for example, *K-66* went into the water at Key West: the manila beckets on the top fin-bracewires had been carried away, weakened by tropical conditions. (See chapter 5.) Aloft, a miscalculation can bring two ships into each other's path. On 16 October, off New Jersey, a midair collision took eight lives when *K-64* collided with *K-7*. The trainer *K-7* had been circling off Barnegat Lighthouse. Due to a misunderstanding of orders, *K-64* (ZP-12) proceeded to sea, then south along the beach. In near-zero visibility, *K-64* went under the lower fin of *K-7*, the latter's wire projection striking the top of the former's bag, ripping it open. *K-64* plunged into the ocean; only one of its crew of nine was saved. Damaged but navigable, *K-7* returned to Lakehurst.

OFFICE FOR EMERGENCY MANAGEMENT
NATIONAL DEFENSE RESEARCH COMMITTEE
OF THE
OFFICE OF SCIENTIFIC RESEARCH AND DEVELOPMENT
1530 P STREET NW.
WASHINGTON, D. C.

JAMES B. CONANT, Chairman
RICHARD C. TOLMAN, Vice Chairman
ROGER ADAMS
CONWAY P. COE
KARL T. COMPTON
FRANK B. JEWETT
CAPT. LYBRAND P. SMITH
MAJ. GEN. CLARENCE C. WILLIAMS
IRVIN STEWART, Executive Secretary

REFER: PC:MM

January 6, 1944

CONFIDENTIAL

Coordinator of Research and Development
Office of the Secretary
Navy Department
Washington 25, D. C.

Re: Project NA-120

Dear Sir:

This is in further reference to your letter of December 4, 1943, requesting that the Naval Airship Training and Experimental Command be provided with a MAD "bird" to be carried in a suspended head below an airship at speeds between 10 and 65 knots.

The above work has been accepted by the NDRC and assigned to Division 6. You will be notified at a later date of the OSRD appointee in Division 6 who will be responsible for the direction of this work.

Very truly yours,

Irvin Stewart
Executive Secretary

FOR VICTORY BUY UNITED STATES WAR BONDS AND STAMPS

In May 1943, forty-three U-boats were sent to the bottom. Except for April 1945, when their comparatively inexperienced crews were near exhaustion, this was the highest monthly kill of the battle: "The Battle of Atlantic has taken a definite turn in our favour during the past two months and returns show an ever increasing toll of U-boats and decreasing losses in convoys."[57] By spring 1943, "the U-boats had acquired just too many adversaries, who were equipped with a remarkable array of new weapons. Of these adversaries the airplane and the convoy were foremost. When nearly all shipping could move in convoys with air cover, the submarine's day was over. . . . A sighting led to an attack, more often than not frustrated by a crash dive, but often followed by surface vessels and more aircraft."[58]

In July, seven U-boats were destroyed within thirty-six hours in the Mediterranean and Atlantic areas by naval air forces. In contrast, the fearful loss in shipping had peaked (though the Allies could not know this) at 7.6 million tons. Losses now declined. Less than one-half this tonnage was sunk in 1943—with the totals continuing to drop for the rest of the war. However, the Deputy Chief of Naval Operations (Air), noting Allied successes, remained wary of the enemy's undersea capabilities:

The current subsidence of submarine activity off the coasts of the United States undoubtedly is caused by the effectiveness of the anti-submarine measures now being operated. Were these measures to be weakened we might logically expect a return of the submarine to these waters. Furthermore, the effective patrolling of the waters adjacent to the United States has resulted in the re-appearance of submarines in the Caribbean. It appears probable that our anti-submarine activity in those areas must be expanded. Certainly on the Pacific coast we should not complacently accept the inactivity of Japanese submarines.[59]

The submarine war had turned: Dönitz had lost the advantage. A resurgent campaign could now deny the enemy command of the sea; indeed, the Allies had captured that command. One historian phrases the transition thus: the U-boats could now be "Discounted from the stature of menace to that of problem."[60]

Shoreside, declining interest in MAD led to AIL's formalizing its concern for keeping its staff intact, noting that MAD was "our only means of detecting submerged submarines." The pace at AIL held feverish. The main task now: electronics countermeasures, including equipment for use against Berlin's guided missiles and "flying bombs." (See chapter 7.) About three-quarters of the staff took on the countermeasures job; the balance continued on the final stages of MAD. Work pertaining to training equipment and the training of naval personnel continued, as did experiments to apply MAD for army use.[61]

The Underwater Sound Laboratory was no less engaged. Founded in July 1941, USL was operating directly under the commandant of the Third Naval District for its military administration, its technical administration being handled by BuShips. The civilian scientific staff—125 scientists—was employed by Columbia University Division of War under its contract with NDRC, of the Office of Scientific Research and Development. USL's projects were many and varied—some developed especially for lighter-than-air. "The laboratory is of particular interest to airship personnel because it has been instrumental in the development of such devices as sonic buoys, underwater flares, airship hydrophones and airship bomb 'dispensers.' Much work has been carried out at the request of Lakehurst and K-ships have frequently participated in laboratory experiments."[62]

In-Flight Vigilance: The Search

Patience was the essence of this antisubmarine war. The Atlantic seems infinite: most patrols found little or nothing save for blank sea and curving horizon. The endless hours required a conscious attempt to subdue boredom and fatigue—and maintain interest. Thousands of operational hours would be logged for every opportunity to attack. Visual lookouts were posted throughout the car, watches maintained and rotated in order to sustain efficiency: "Success on almost all LTA missions depends upon the ability of lookouts to sight and report contacts correctly. Despite the use of special equipment, there is no substitute for the good lookout, and the ability to sight objects during daytime and at night depends not only upon good vision, but upon good training."[63]

The submarine-searching ZNP had been reconfigured. Whereas cramped spaces typified HTA, a blimp's crew occupied a veritable solarium, granting full-horizon visibility—with no obstructing wings.[64] "The dispersion of eyes around the car was good," a naval aviator recalls;

Seated between pilot and copilot, the forward lookout occupies the bombardier's seat or "well" fitted with the releases. The radar-MAD operator is nearest the camera portside, the on-duty navigator forward. The radioman is seated to starboard. Note the recording chart for the magnetic detector. (GHMC, NASM, Smithsonian Institution)

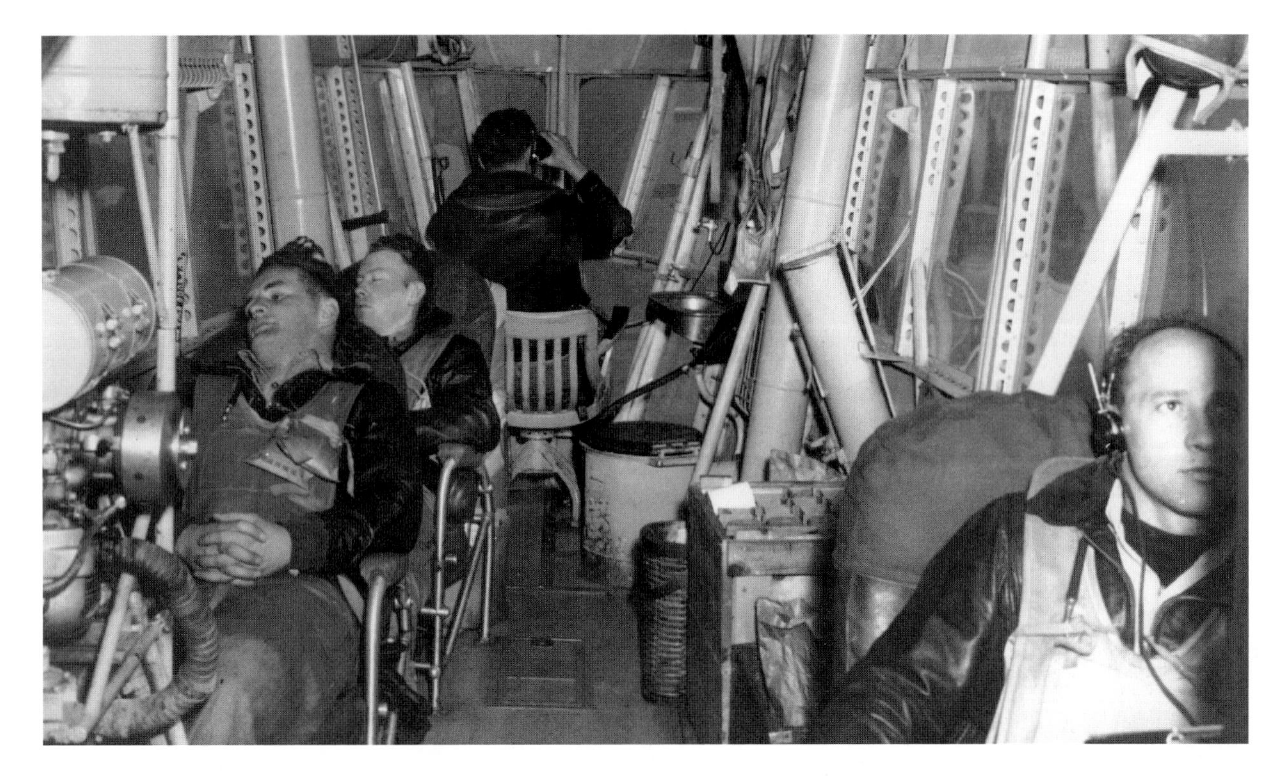

"visibility was excellent." The commandant of the Fifth Naval District, sampling the bombardier's seat in *K-81* during an inspection, agreed. "You certainly have a wonderful view from here," the admiral remarked. A stable platform, the K-type ZNP brought sonobuoys, the magnetic gear, and radar, *plus* the visual, to the campaign. "We always had a bunch of our crew—as many as possible—with binoculars searching the sea when we were out on patrol." And the blimp had the power, the speed—"it did the job."[65] Still, blimps are fairly rough riding: subjected to motion in three axes, even experienced sailors got ill.

Missions demanded from twelve to eighteen hours, though exceptional circumstances held combat aircrews aloft for more. Qualified pilots occupied the elevator and rudder positions. A March 1944 graduate (hence junior pilot) assigned to ZP-12 (CAC 17) recounts the somewhat tame Atlantic war of 1944:

> We usually flew with three officers and a crew of eight enlisted. As the junior pilot, I usually had to do the navigating, with occasional relief by one of the other pilots. In attack drills (we never attacked anything) I would sit in the bombardier position between the two pilots. The command/senior pilot usually made the take-offs and landings from the left-hand seat (elevator control wheel) and the number two pilot took the right hand seat (rudder wheel) for take-offs and landings. From time to time, as the junior pilot, I was allowed to man the rudder during take-off or landing; and on rare occasions, usually during training flights, I was allowed to sit in the left-hand seat and do a take-off or landing. For training flights, the airship was usually just a bit heavy, for patrol flights we normally had a long take-off run on the ground because we were very

[Opposite] The aft lookout scans the sea while shipmates rest between watches. Note the mechanic. The command pilot saw to it that both "mech" and radioman also were lookouts. (GHMC, NASM, Smithsonian Institution)

[Top] Aircrew officers are briefed by an aerological officer prior to liftoff, ZP-14, NAS Weeksville. Ideally, combat crews consisted of four pilots (three if a fourth was not available) and six enlisted men. Pilot shortages would persist into 1944. (GHMC, NASM, Smithsonian Institution)

[Center] Conference done, directives and any special instructions were obtained and navigation gear signed for. Confidential folders held a copy of operations orders; confidential chart; calls and recognition signals; and a listing of ships within the assigned sector—call signs, type, speed, vessel destinations. The folder, weighted, was intended to go down with the ship. (GHMC, NASM, Smithsonian Institution)

[Bottom] Life jackets are distributed prior to reaching the coastline. Note the radio equipment. (GHMC, NASM, Smithsonian Institution)

Photographs were taken of sightings, including suspicious oil slicks and floating debris. Photographic evidence was deemed crucial to confirmation of a U-boat "kill." (GHMC, NASM, Smithsonian Institution)

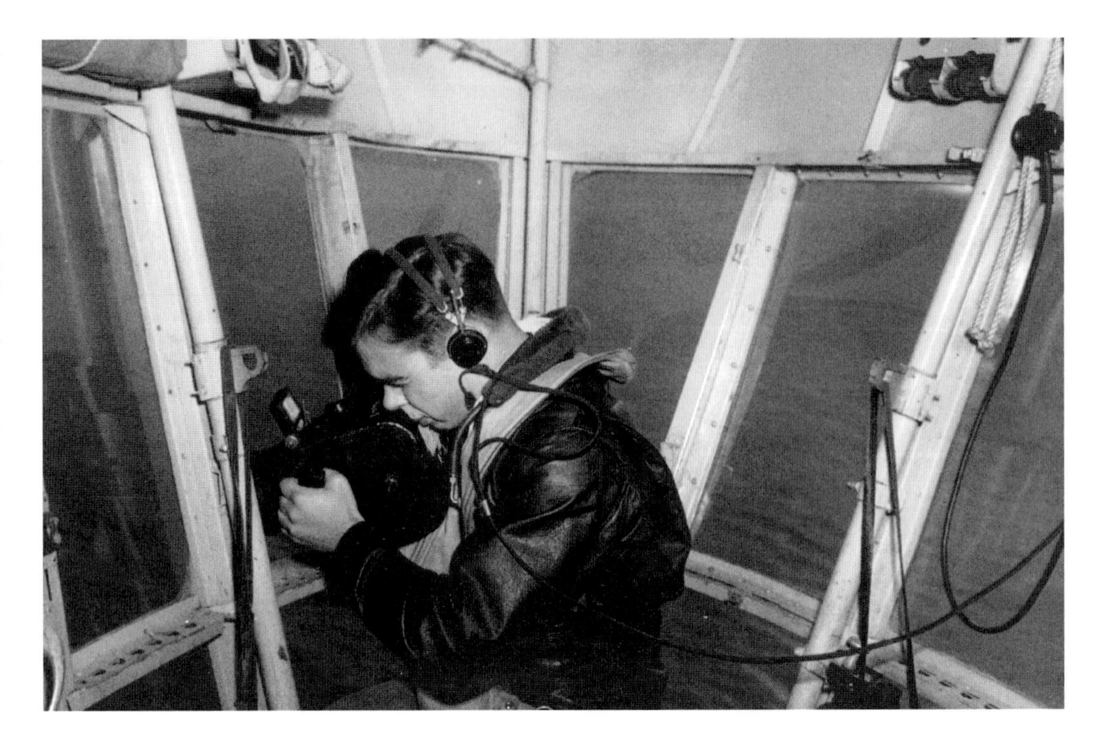

> heavy. Later, when officers junior to me were added to the crew, I split the navigation chores with them. During regular patrol flights, besides navigating, I would occasionally man the rudder or man the bombardier position and use binoculars to look for anything interesting. Because of doing the navigating, I was also tasked with tossing out the two pigeons at some point in the flight. When investigating shipping, I took photos of the ships encountered.[66]

Lookout stations were manned throughout, as were ship's radio, radar, the MAD. A watch on the radar was maintained at all times (when the equipment proved capable). If qualified, the radar-MAD operators were relieved by the radio operator for rest periods; all "mad-rad" qualified mechanics or riggers also were exploited. (See table 4.2.)

Suspicious objects were checked, every sighting reported. Time and coordinates for rafts, oil slicks, bubbles—all were dutifully logged. Few missions saw action (attacks numbered nineteen in all of 1943). Seldom was the enemy seen—adrenaline shots of hyperarousal. Sightings of periscopes, let alone surfaced boats, were exceedingly rare: the experienced enemy commander showed himself for mere seconds as he stalked. Accordingly, exhaustive search surrounding convoys and thorough investigation of all suspicious objects or sea conditions were vital if an attacker was to be detected before he struck. As it happened, false MAD contacts proved frequent—and each had to be painstakingly developed. Tracking called for teamwork. For flight crews, then, the work, strain, tedium, and fatigue seemed unavailing—endless vigilance, scant action, no victories.

In convoy, success meant nothing happened—antidramatic displays of force.

Effective patrol is a function of vigilance. Patrols were a monotonous, apparently fruitless vigil—endless hours of draining duty. (U-boats, for their part, kept a very good lookout when on

TABLE 4.2 **Standard ZNP Combat Crew and Watch Bill.** (National Archives)

Combat Air Crew (CAC)	Crew, Watch Bill[1]
1. Command Pilot	1. Elevator
2. Senior Pilot	2. Rudder
3. Junior Pilot (Navigator)	3. Forward Lookout
4. Junior Pilot	4. After Lookout
5. Rigger	5. Navigator
6. Mechanic	6. Mechanic
7. Radioman	7. Radio
8. Gunner	8. Radar and MAD
9. Assistant Mechanic	
10. Special Equipment Operator	

1 These stations were to be manned at all times. On a normal flight, a) watches were changed every hour, and b) each member of the CAC had at least one hour of rest in five.

TABLE 4.3 **ZNP Contacts and Attacks on U-Boats**, 7 December 1941 to 26 August 1943.[1] (National Archives)

Contacts (sightings, radar, MAD)	
Positive	2
Probable	4
Possible	26
Doubtful	51
Not Evaluated (or definitely not a U-Boat)	29
Total	112
Attacks	
Probable Slight Damage	2
Insufficient Evidence of Damage	4
No Damage	6
Insufficient Evidence of a Sub	42
Target not a Sub	9
Insufficient Information to Assess	3
Total	66

1 Statistics compiled in connection with a study of the lighter-than-air organization, mid-1943.

the surface, generally three men with backs together and each sweeping a 120-degree arc.) "Blimp patrol is not glamorous by a damn sight," Mills observed. "It is just tedious, hard work and keeping up the interest to ensure efficiency is a tough job." Writes Morison: "It could not be otherwise when by far the greater part of anti-submarine warfare consisted in searching and waiting for a fight that very rarely took place; yet every escort or patrol ship was supposed to be completely alert from the time she passed the sea buoy until she returned to harbor." Mike Bradley, wing commander at Richmond, recalled the drill: "You're out there looking for something, and don't expect it to show up—and generally it doesn't. It means your [*sic*] out there looking around all day and never seeing what you want to see. It's quite tedious and tiresome—it's a boring thing."[67] (See table 4.3.)

"The galley was super." (GHMC, NASM, Smithsonian Institution)

Except for emergency ops, the maximum sustained monthly flight time for LTA pilots was 125 hours. Squadrons had operating allowances of combat aircrews, based on two CACs per airship for squadrons based within the continental United States and three CACs for units based outside. In May 1944, ZP-11, for example, was stabilized at twelve CACs, ZP-15 at nineteen, ZP-21 at thirty-six, ZP-42 at twenty, ZP-51 at twenty-three. Ample personnel, qualified and effectively distributed, proved to be a chronic concern never fully resolved. *Balance* among enlisted personnel, as well as too few experienced aviators, added to the strain. That spring, Lt. Cecil A. Bolam, commanding ZP-11, wrote the commodore: "I hope you can bring us up to 16 crews again before too long. With transfers, Blimp AstraLant [see page 213], detached duty (we sent 2 ships and 4 crews to Weeksville for CESF), and relief crews not arriving, we have been down fairly low. For a few days we had 5 ships and 7 crews. Just now we have 6 ships and 10 crews."[68]

Properly staffed, each CAC consisted of ten men; at sea, at least eight were on watch most of the time and acting as lookouts. Theirs was an unglamorous, low-drama world of vacant sea and unrolling sameness. Given the limits of human biology, lookouts found it difficult to keep at least part of the mind focused; tedium tended to lessen effectiveness, thus reducing the possibility of sightings. Respites from this heavy diet of watchfulness: meals, seat rest, or a bunk. "The efficiency of the crew falls off very rapidly after about 15–18 hours," Mills reported, "and I prefer to keep the flights, except for very special missions, within this duration. I would prefer to relieve ships on station rather than keep them out too long." The cabin had no soundproofing or automatic pilot—a further strain.[69]

The "special equipment" tendered its own frustrations. ZNPs were dependent upon MAD for locating submerged targets. Markers dropped on signal might reveal no pattern—that is, no large *moving* metallic body. On 29 August 1942, for instance, the daily war diary for ZP-12 records this entry for ZNP *K-12:* "At 1130 a M.A.D. contact was made just south of Barnegat. A bronze flare was dropped and the area searched. Several more contacts, not in a pattern, were made and more flares were dropped. No wrecks were shown on our chart where the water was estimated to be between 9 to 15 fathoms deep. Continuous false contacts by the M.A.D. caused us to secure the gear and we proceeded on our [convoy escort] mission."[70]

The radar, for its part, bred vanishing "blips"—unconfirmed targets that apparently had dived. The onus of identification was upon the pilot. A disappearing or suspicious radar contact was reported immediately (the radioman given a contact report). The would-be attacker made best speed toward the point of submergence, thereafter developing the area with MAD. If (as seldom happened) the radar contact materialized into a U-boat, attack procedure was followed. Squadron war diaries record the result of such inconclusive contacts. The log for *K-82* (ZP-12) offers an example: "While the airship was proceeding on a course towards the blip, the contact was lost at 5 miles after being held on the scope about two minutes. The contact was strong and clear and the airship made a search of the area for three hours before it resumed patrol; no more contacts were received."[71]

On 22 October 1943, on patrol at dusk at five hundred feet, ZNP *K-52* (ZP-15) recorded an ASG contact. "Turned immediately to object at 10 miles distance. Power failure. Went to scene and saw slight oil slick which appeared as small wake. Made visual search for 45 minutes with negative results."[72]

Night operations were confounding: How to identify blips? On 25 April 1943 (for instance), Squadron Fifteen's *K-45*, out of Glynco, was on patrol using its radar and MAD. On receipt of a strong magnetic signal, a slick was dropped and the position circled to develop the contact. The wreck chart held no candidates. "At 1019 another strong MAD contact was received followed by several others. In the series of contacts, additional flares and slicks were dropped. When three of the slicks were in a straight line, a bombing run was made and three Mark 17 bombs dropped using a strong MAD contact to decide the point of release."[73]

No apparent result. Three bombs more on another contact in good alignment with the slicks realized nothing. The pilot elected to enlarge the search. He carried no more bombs, but should he locate a target, air and surface support could be brought to bear. Suddenly, radar contact was made astern, then a sighting—a conning tower about five miles from the depth-charging. Corroboration. A systematic MAD search for the boat ceded five swings of the recorder needle, then a pair of oil slicks.[74] *K-45* was joined by surface craft. No further contacts were logged. Command was turned over to "King-34" at 1600, four hours after *K-45* had resumed its MAD search. Position and equipment were checked on a known wreck, after which "King-45" set course for home.[75]

The Radio Sonobuoy (Continued)

The expendable "sono-radio buoy" had been under development for months, though largely in the laboratory. (The expendable part was the transmitter; the receiver was platform installed.) Late that year, the device was distributed to the fleet for service tests. The army—the procuring agency for the device—ordered five thousand, of which the navy was to receive one thousand. By mid-January the navy had nearly a hundred in hand, distributed to Project Sail, Lakehurst, and the Caribbean Sea Frontier—waters in which tests under combat conditions were likely. "Reports have been favorable enough so that we [Cominch] are now proceeding with a program to equip patrol planes with the buoys." Accordingly, it was planned to order forty-five qualified aircraft radio operators to receive training in underwater sound detection.

In the meantime, BuAer was asked to develop a broad plan of training operators.[76]

The device held immense potential. Before 1943, when a sighted U-boat submerged the aircraft arrived too late for attack, one alternative was to apply hold-down tactics, waiting for the boat either to reappear or for surface forces to reach the scene. Sonobuoy equipped, the aircraft now could *track* its target: "The use of sono-buoys to investigate oil slicks, disappearing radar blips and MAD contacts must therefore be obvious. It might easily be said that in the very near future there should be no need to question whether an oil slick is a wreck or a submarine. Drop a sono-buoy and you will soon know."[77]

Installation was soon widespread, with emphasis on equipping fleet CVEs operating in the Atlantic.[78] As of December 1943, the total contract called for approximately 15,750 transmitters and 915 buoys. In the Atlantic, 2,274 buoys and 247 transmitters had been received.[79] Still, supply of the equipment did not meet demand—for one program, certainly. At Lakehurst, pleas by Commodore Mills for sonobuoys brought scant result, his requests seemingly lost in department back channels. "In regard to your sono-buoys," BuAer's Bradley advised, "I am informed that COMINCH has turned over the available supply to ComAirLant [Commander, Air Force, Atlantic Fleet] for distribution and that you will have to make your request to him for your desired supply. Situation normal."[80]

On 12–13 July 1943, seven U-boats were destroyed by British and U.S. naval and air forces within thirty-six hours. Pleased, Churchill suggested a special joint press release. Roosevelt demurred: "The wave of optimism that has followed recent successes," the president responded,

HMS *Queen Elizabeth* enjoys inshore escort, 1943. Steaming "Ahead, Full" so as to frustrate torpedo attack, the two British "Queens" made their transits of the North Atlantic unescorted. (Lt. H. F. Smith, USNR [Ret.])

"and our latest release on the antisubmarine situation is definitely slowing down production. We cannot afford to further inflate this costly public disregard of the realities of the situation, and therefore I doubt the wisdom at this time of giving the cat another canary to swallow."[81]

Airship Reorganization, U.S. Fleet

On 15 July, the airship organization of the U.S. Fleet was modified. Fleet Airship wings Thirty and Thirty-one were redesignated Fleet Airships Atlantic and Fleet Airships Pacific, respectively. Airship patrol groups became airship wings; wings administered the squadrons. Airship patrol squadrons, in their turn, were renamed "blimp squadrons"—fleet units with a mission to hunt and destroy the enemy. As well, the commissioning of two additional wings was directed: FairShipWing 4 and FairShipWing 5.

Mills had recommended the formation of a *headquarters squadron* ("hedron") in each proposed LTA wing, along with a *hedron detachment* assigned to each fleet LTA squadron—the setup used in heavier-than-air fleets. Hedrons were maintenance and utility organizations formed to relieve squadron skippers of time-stealing duties incidental to maintenance and ground support, thus freeing him to concentrate on operational matters—that is, fighting the enemy. An arrangement duly authorized, each wing commissioned a hedron under a commanding officer reporting to the wing commander; in turn, hedron detachments were formed to support each squadron in the wing under an officer in charge. The O-in-Cs reported to the hedron COs.

> In brief, blimprons were operating units and blimphedrons maintenance units. Blimphedrons will assume responsibility for the safety of an airship upon completion of mooring an airship in a hangar until it is next accepted for flight by the pilot in preparation for undocking, when responsibility shall shift to the cognizant blimpron. In the case of an airship moored out, the responsibility for the airship's safety shall remain with the cognizant blimpron, although necessary servicing and maintenance will be performed by the blimphedron.[82]

All field repairs other than major overhauls now were conducted under this setup, the hedrons furnishing detachments to accompany ZNPs operating from forward bases and auxiliary sites. Mission: to conduct operational maintenance and minor repairs and to check all accessories. The major overhaul bases—Lakehurst, Richmond, and Moffett Field—retained that status, and each hosted a civilian assembly and repair organization. All other LTA stations were designated as operating air stations, with no A&R departments.

As for command structure, the hierarchy now was headed by Fleet Airships Atlantic (Mills). Next in order were fleet airship wings; these controlled the various blimprons and hedrons. The hedrons, in turn, maintained a detachment for each operating unit (blimpron). The detachment was commanded by a naval aviator (airship) assigned to that unit; organized along fleet lines, a hedron had (on paper) sufficient personnel assigned to care for all services of its squadron.

A station commanding officer (an officer of relatively long service) held a shore-duty billet under a naval district commandant. A squadron commanding officer, in contrast, was under a fleet commander; he held responsibility for the ships and was senior officer for decisions regarding flying. "We have come a long way in earning a good reputation with Fleet personnel," Mills noted, "and this includes HTA aviators. I firmly believe we should follow Fleet practices and stay in the Fleet as long as possible."[83]

U-boats in Caribbean and South Atlantic waters had realized additional LTA units of the U.S. Fleet. Airship Wing Four was commissioned in August 1943, with headquarters at Maceió, Brazil. Comprising squadrons ZP-41 and ZP-42 plus Hedron Four, it reported to Commander, Fourth Fleet. Wing Five—commissioned that same month—was headquartered on Trinidad, British West Indies. Its operating unit: ZP-51, supported by Hedron Five. Fleet commander: Commander Caribbean Sea Frontier (see chapter 5 and table 5.1).

Notes on Operational Procedure

Lakehurst was locus for the fleet airship organization. Raymond "Ty" Tyler, in command of Airship Wing One, presided in its operations room. There, on four large maps depicting the entire Atlantic, the movements of enemy boats were plotted daily. Movements were taken from submarine estimates made by Cominch, CESF, and the naval districts. (On occasion, the intelligence officer would make his own estimate from the data at hand.) Also plotted were submarine-related activities, such as attacks upon the enemy and U-boat assaults on vessels, submarine sightings, U-boats sunk as well as radar, MAD, and sound contacts. These came from Cominch's *Daily Submarine Sighting and Attack Summary,* the Eastern Sea Frontier's "Zebra" radio intercepts, naval district "operational intelligence bulletins," and submarine estimates for ESF. These were written up in the form of a daily "enemy action summary," which in turn was distributed to CNATE, ComFairShipsLant, ComFairShipWing 1, ComBlimpRon 12, and the CO of the station as well as his executive officer.

Whenever enemy boats were estimated in Twelve's operating area, the Intelligence Officer kept in constant phone communication with the plotters in New York City (Eastern Sea Frontier) and kept the squadron advised as to late-breaking developments. And when any action between squadron units and enemy boats was taking place, the Intelligence Officer kept CNATE and the Commodore advised by phone.

The intelligence officer for the wing had further responsibilities. He plotted the courses and hourly positions (or operating areas) of all friendly submarines in Twelve's own operating area. Moreover, he plotted the courses and hourly positions of all convoy and naval movements, as well as all independent movements under ZNP escort. And all other shipping movements in Twelve's operating area for which the wing received information were plotted as of 0600 daily.[84]

For Dönitz, the tide was ebbing. "In the last months of 1943 and through June 1944," one historian summarized, "the U-boats struggled merely to keep from being killed."[85] Operating policy for the Allies: aggressive, continuous operations within each sea frontier, keeping as many planes and ZNPs in the air as possible—limited only by maintenance and foul weather.

At Lakehurst and in ZP-14 and ZP-15, three combat air crews were assigned each fleet ZNP—altogether, nine officers and twenty-one men per ship. Three crews translated into one day of flying in three.

ZNP combat air crews consisted of four pilots (ideally) and six enlisted men. Naval aviators were yet too few to meet an expanding program. Moreover, the shortage of LTA-qualified enlisted

[Top] Operations room, nerve center of Fleet Airship Wing One, NAS Lakehurst, 18 September 1944. Capt. Raymond F. "Ty" Tyler, USN, wing commander, is at right (bending). (C. E. Rosendahl Collection/History of Aviation Collection [hereafter HOAC], University of Texas)

[Bottom] A ZP squadron ready room, May 1944. The chart depicts inshore sectors within the operational area assigned to this operating unit of the Atlantic Fleet. As well, all LTA squadrons had certain training requirements to fulfill. (C.E. Rosendahl Collection/HOAC, University of Texas)

Patrol Area chart for Airship Squadron Twelve (ZP-12). Areas Able and Baker, for example, were divided by latitude 40° north.
(C. E. Rosendahl Collection/HOAC, University of Texas)

Detached from ZP-11 for southern duty, this combat aircrew is about to embark ZNP *K-117* for the forward base at Ipatanga (Bahia), in southern Brazil, January 1943. Standing: Lt. Harris F. Smith (CAC commander) and Lt. Robert S. Morton, USNR. Detachment 42-4 at Ipatanga was one of four supporting ZP-42. Squadron headquarters: Maceió, Brazil. (Lt. H. F. Smith, USNR [Ret.])

men persisted. Compounding the matter of personnel, some commandants of naval districts were assigning LTA enlisted men to other duties. Where pilot shortages existed ("right now that means everywhere"), there were vacancies in the crews.

Each combat crew was to fly as a *team.* Its officers consisted of a command, or senior, pilot, two copilots, and one navigator (also a pilot). The enlisted personnel comprised one rigger, one ordnance man, two mechanics, and two radiomen. "Cope is having quite a struggle with combat crews," Bradley observed that August of ZP-21, the largest squadron. "The enlisted crews work out pretty well but the officers not too good as yet as there aren't enough to go around. He has thirty-three (33) crews and the officers in these are scant; twenty-four (24) with three (3) officers and nine (9) with two (2) officers and one (1) Aviation Pilot. With only a three (3) officer crew, the binnacle [sick] list can raise the duce with a combat crew."[86]

Training within combat squadrons was therefore limited due to the maximum effort directed to combat missions. So team-welded aircrews, fully trained and ready, tended to be few.

Ideally, each ZNP would have three CACs assigned. To maintain the watch and despite inexperienced officers, reduction to two CACs was proposed. Protests ensued. Daytime operations began well before dawn and ended late. A ship assigned to escort an outbound convoy took off in early-morning dark, searched the harbor approaches, contacted its charges, and covered their sortie. Typically, the blimp provided escort until dark, at which time it departed its mission and returned to base. "Flying one day in two over extended periods and with the type of flights that we run out of Lakehurst (14 to 18 hours)," Tyler opined, "it would allow the pilot very little time to study, attend lectures, indulge in some form of exercise (and this is all important on this type of schedule) or having brief periods of personal relaxation." Lt. Cdr. Franklin S. Rixey was chief staff officer, Fleet Airship Wing One. "If night flying is to continue," Rixey advised, "and it is to be assumed it will, three crews are necessary to permit each ship to operate continuously day and night (except for maintenance periods) and yet permit time for training, physical education, and personal relaxation. . . . During summer months with reveille at 0230 in some cases and 0330 in others, the crews have a good long day of at least 20 hours and naturally require a relaxation period the following day."[87]

The two-crew option was deferred.

Midyear found ZP-11 (for example) operating seven "King" ships: *K-11* and *-12, K-14, K-37* and *-38, K-42,* and *K-50.* At Weeksville, headquarters for ZP-24, two ships had hit the hangar doors. The culprit: lack of men, plus insufficient experience among ground-handling officers.

> There no longer is a ground handling party. All hands, except special details . . . are required to handle ships. For every landing, takeoff, docking, or undocking, all maintenance work must stop. With one third of this group on liberty, the maximum number of men available is about 65 men. With the few in sick bay, on emergency leave, etc., that number has fallen below the minimum of 60 men to be used for docking in the minimum weather conditions. . . . Where do we get the men to dock when the wind is 25 knots or more? The ships must be docked, or the Hedron Detachment cannot prepare them for flight on the field, having been stripped of every single engine work platform. As a result the ships are being docked continually with too few men. . . . Flight crews are being debarked to help dock the ships, but sooner or later, it is not going to be enough.

Upkeep was arranged to permit routine overhaul and inspection in minimum time between flights, thus keeping units in the air the maximum possible. Mission duration: from fourteen to eighteen hours. Combined with about an hour and a half of preflight and postflights of one to two hours for securing ship, plus interrogation by the air combat intelligence officer, the elapsed time approached twenty hours.[88]

Accidents, Casualties

Inexperience haunted the combat record for navy lighter-than-air. Losses climbed concomitant with operating hours. In May 1943, for instance, a thirty-five-thousand-cubic-foot free balloon was one of five logging intermediate landings for training. Preparatory to final landing, its pilot pulled the rip panel open, to quickly deflate the balloon. Within seconds an explosion occurred, followed by hydrogen fire. The burning balloon settled onto the basket, trapping its three officer-passengers.

The following May, again at Lakehurst, with ceiling and visibility unlimited, the training ship *K-5* completed a practice ("bounce") landing on the mat. The pilot then failed to clear the west end of No. 1 Hangar. *K-5* struck ten feet from the top; the car hung momentarily, then dropped 250 feet to the apron. Only one man survived—in critical condition; ten crewmen died instantly. The crash alarm sounded, rescue efforts began. "Ambulances shuttled between the scene of the accident and the hospital with bodies of the officers and men as they were taken from the wreckage." The ship was scrapped, following removal of the few remaining salvageable parts.

[Top] ZNP *K-11* in the trees, Scituate, Massachusetts. On 31 July, while on inshore patrol with *K-14*, the two were ordered back to South Weymouth "with all possible speed." Departing the patrol area with course laid for base, conditions deteriorated. A line squall put "King-11" on the deck—hitting trees and a barn. (Lt. H. F. Smith, USNR [Ret.])

[Center] All hands ordered to the mat, NAS South Weymouth helps fight a disabled K-ship to landing, summer 1943. A blimp is a large mass, lacking fine control under most conditions. Rudder controls out, ordnance jettisoned, and steered by engines only, this ZNP was brought down on the fifth attempt. Command pilot: Ensign Harris F. Smith, USNR. (Lt. H. F. Smith, USNR [Ret.])

[Bottom] Wind was a primary factor when docking or undocking—wind direction relative to the hangar axis as well as gusts, eddies, and hangar spillovers. Here *K-69* lies deflated, having struck the steel hangar at South Weymouth, 13 August 1943. (U.S. Navy photograph, courtesy Lt. H. F. Smith, USNR [Ret.])

TABLE 4.4 **Airship losses**, NAS Lakehurst, 1942 to September 1945. There were also at least five ground handling accidents at Lakehurst during the war not involving the loss of a ship. Airship and personnel causalities throughout the LTA organization multiplied these losses, the result of ground handling accidents, material failure, pilot error, weather, and other causes. One ship, possibly two, was lost to enemy action.

Date	Ship	Location	Casualty	Lives Lost
8 June 1942	*G-1*, *L-2*	Off the N.J. coast	Night mid-air collision during research flight	12
10 May 1943	Free balloon #04421	Ellisberg, N.J.	Exploded and burned on landing	3
16 October 1943	*K-64*, *K-7*	Off the N.J. coast	Midair collision in low visibility; *K-7* returned to Lakehurst	8
16 May 1944	*K-5*	NAS Lakehurst	Ship hit Hangar No. 1 during training flight	10

Squadron ships broke free from masts or suffered material failures, such as engine fires. Pilot errors realized forced landings—ships hitting masts, hangars, trees, the landing mat. In July 1943, due to stoppage of both engines, *K-30* flew into trees on approach at Richmond; that year, indeed, three ZNP-Ks more met trees. That August, off Venezuela, *K-68* exceeded its prudent limit of endurance and made an emergency landing due to lack of fuel. Salvage operations were the first to be effected in the Caribbean area. (See page 203.) In October, *K-64*, on patrol in low visibility, collided with *K-7*. The patrol ship fell into the water, killing eight. Also in October at sea, *K-94* mysteriously burned and crashed while on routine ferry flight from Guantánamo Bay, Cuba, to San Juan. Nine men were lost. Poor navigation exhausted the fuel aboard *K-13* that November, obliging a forced landing and deflation a few miles from NAS Charleston.

The year 1944 would record a grim total: thirty-seven accidents, with twenty-six men lost. Investigations ascribed most of these casualties to pilot error, a half-dozen to ground-handling lapses. The 1942–45 air-surface campaign saw eleven airships *flying* into the water, killing sixteen airmen. On the mat, errors in judgment damaged ships during ground-handling operations, some resulting in full or partial deflations. (See table 4.4.)

The Commander, Fleet Airship Wing One (Ty Tyler), found himself exasperated about the combat proficiency at Lakehurst:

> Repeated airship accidents within this command, involving loss of personnel, and major damage to material, indicate a definite lack of knowledge, or the application thereof, of basic principals of airmanship and of proper operating technique. The majority of these accidents could, and should, have been avoided had the situation been more intelligently handled by the person, or persons, concerned. Failure to properly analyze a particular situation, a mental lapse though only momentary,

A cardinal procedure for blimpron pilots: "Do not take off with a nose-heavy ship." (GHMC, NASM, Smithsonian Institution)

failure to take prompt and decisive action when necessary, and failure to be forceful, alert and quick witted, have been contributing factors to these recent losses.[89]

Loss of *K-74* by U-Boat Action

On the night of 18 July 1943, a ZNP was lost to enemy action while pressing an attack upon a surfaced U-boat. *K-74,* hit by AA gunfire, made a forced landing and sank. A singular engagement, its reverberations proved to be outsized.

Delivered through Lakehurst and assigned to ZP-21, *K-74* had departed Richmond at 1909 for a patrol of the Florida Straits. In command of a ten-man CAC: Lt. Nelson G. Grills, USNR. Mission: a routine night patrol off southeast Florida. Visibility: over twenty miles, with unlimited ceiling and a bright moon through three-tenths cloud cover.

At 2340, the blimp floated at five hundred feet on a track of 189 degrees true. Ground speed: forty-seven knots. The preflight (that is, briefing) had held that no enemy or friendly boats were in its assigned patrol area. Then came a radar blip, eight miles away on a bearing of 240 degrees true. This contact was in fact *U-134,* a Type VIIC boat en route to its intended patrol station off Havana, Kapitänleutnant Hans-Günther Brosin commanding. His position lay approximately halfway between the tip of Florida and the coast of Cuba. An incorrect position was radioed to base and battle stations were manned as the ZNP pressed in. Abruptly, a half-mile to port, a U-boat was seen "perfectly silhouetted" in bright moonlight. At this instant Grills was serving as navigator; Ensign Eversley was on the elevators, A/P Janrowitz on ship's rudder. ARM3c R. H. Bourne, USNR, had the radioman's seat, AMM2/c Isadore Stessel the bomb releases.

The interval between sighting and delivery of an attack is dependent on speed and maneuverability. Conning from the flight-deck doorway, Grills ordered a circle to starboard, to hold the target, making fifteen to eighteen knots, under observation. A "King" ship in still air at sixty-five knots could turn in sixty-eight seconds—a circle about two thousand feet in diameter. The sighting was lost, though a second, larger circle reacquired the boat by its wake. At 2350, *K-74* commenced an attack run. Altitude: 250 feet, target angle thirty degrees (that is, the blimp on the target's starboard bow).

Abruptly, everything was on the line.

One quality of command is initiative. No doctrine can foresee every contingency; the field commander retains the prerogative, to seize opportunity. LTA doctrine was *not* to attack but, instead, for pilots to hold the sighting, keeping station upwind and beyond range, meantime calling in air and surface support. A ZNP was to attack only if the boat began to dive or posed an immediate threat to shipping. This night, two merchantmen were steaming the straits, about twenty miles distant. If he gained position just after submergence but too late to bomb, the pilot was to track and attack.

A kill by air attack required surprise, speed, accuracy, persistence. A single misstep could easily cancel success; the details have to cohere. Pilot self-control coupled to aircrew coordination were determining. As yet, the U-boat gave no indication of having seen its attacker until, abruptly, it turned hard to port. The maneuver presented the boat's stern, thus bringing its deck guns to bear. Standing behind the pilots, conning, Grills ordered course altered. (When targets crash-dove, making fifteen to eighteen knots, the navigator clocked the run-in and called out the elapsed time from submergence to drop.) At 250 yards—some estimates are as high as 500 to 600 yards—the German opened fire from the after part of his conning tower. Eckert, manning the blimp's gun turret, immediately returned fire. (Fire had been withheld, in the belief that the airship was unseen as it closed.)

Bourne immediately sent a special squadron distress signal indicating his being fired upon. This transmission would prove indirectly responsible for saving nine lives.[90] The .50-caliber seemed to halt the boat's fire for five to ten seconds. A flash and loud report announced the boat's deck gun going into action: one round as *K-74* pressed in at best speed, two more once it had crossed the U-boat at a fifteen-degree angle—a beam attack. "The fire from the machine gun [20-mms] came up towards the *K-74* in a 'V' shaped fan which bracketed the car. The crew could hear the bullets thudding into the bag on either side of the car but none saw the car itself being hit except for one bullet hole in the plexiglas of the gun turret. . . . Enemy tracer track indicated that additional bullets probably hit the turret."

Eckert got off sixty rounds (one can), reloaded , and had fired forty more before his gun could no longer be brought to bear—all in an estimated twenty to thirty seconds. Depth charges were let go in a stick, that is, dropped singly but as rapidly as possible. Grills had ordered his bombs—two rack-mounted Mark 17s, now armed—dropped as he crossed his target 250 feet off the water.

Preparing for takeoff, the bomb-release-lever safety locking collar would be moved to "ready" position, a man in the bombardier's seat alert for orders to drop them if the engines failed. The lever was reset to "safe" until over water, then back again to "ready" for possible contact with the enemy. This night, the bombardier pulled the releases, but the ordnance stayed aboard. Stessel, apparently, had pulled the handles to the selective notch, where they locked. He had failed to keep pressure on the release knobs, which would have permitted movement to "salvo" position.

For Stessel and his ship, it was a fatal misjudgment.

From below, enemy return fire hit the attacker's engines just after the blimp had passed over. Its starboard Wasp caught fire. The mechanic activated the fire-suppression system. The elevatorman, for his part, throttled back the port engine to regain control; the port Wasp fell off in RPMs. Stern down, controls unresponsive, *K-74* began a steep, uncontrolled climb: the elevator had no effect in reducing climb angle, and the rudder was inoperative. Antiaircraft fire ceased when the distance opened to about a half-mile. Now the U-boat's further actions were blocked by the airship's tail-down attitude.[91]

Blimps are *pressure* craft: the heavy car (no armor) pulls down on the suspension curtains within the bag. Holed , *K-74*'s envelope had rapidly lost gas pressure. With low pressure, the envelope sagged, its deformation forcing the elevators hard up and the rudder-control lines to slacken.

AIRSHIP FLIGHT EMERGENCY BILL

2. *PREPARE for FORCED LANDING*

A. COMMAND PILOT

IF BLIMP IS EXCEEDINGLY HEAVY: DROP SLIP TANKS IF BLIMP CAN CLEAR AREA WHERE TANKS WILL LAND SO THAT NO FIRE HAZARD WILL RESULT FROM COMBINATION OF FUEL AND FLARES OR HOT ENGINE.

B. ELEVATOR MAN

HOLD SHIP OFF THE WATER AS LONG AS POSSIBLE. OPEN FORWARD WINDOW AND REMOVE THE POST.

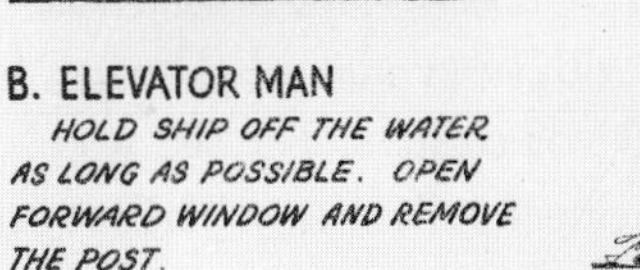

AIRSHIP FLIGHT EMERGENCY BILL

Part 2. PREPARE FOR FORCED LANDING

F. RADIOMAN

SEND IN ON OPERATIONAL FREQUENCY IN PLAIN LANGUAGE BT KING__FORCED LANDING POSITION__N__W. CONTINUE REPORTING DEVELOPEMENTS. IF POWER FAILS SWITCH TO GF TRANSMITTER AND CONTINUE REPORTS ON SCENE OF ACTION FREQ. USING BATTERY POWER. *Important:* TURN IFF TO "EMERGENCY" POSITION.

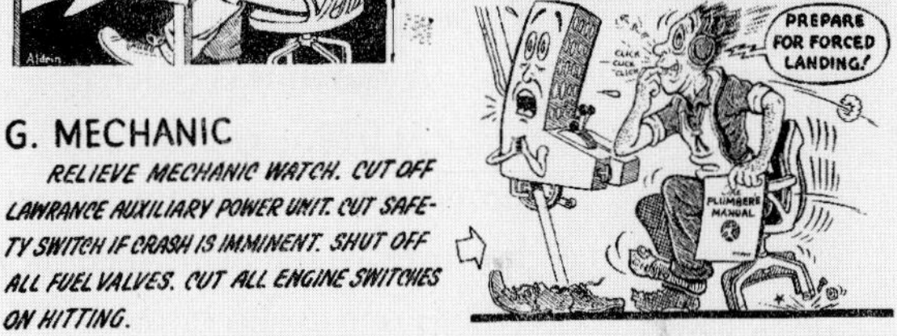

G. MECHANIC

RELIEVE MECHANIC WATCH. CUT OFF LAWRANCE AUXILIARY POWER UNIT. CUT SAFETY SWITCH IF CRASH IS IMMINENT. SHUT OFF ALL FUEL VALVES. CUT ALL ENGINE SWITCHES ON HITTING.

AIRSHIP FLIGHT EMERGENCY BILL

Part 2. PREPARE FOR FORCED LANDING

C. NAVIGATOR

QUICKLY GIVE THE RADIOMAN MOST ACCURATE POSITION OF BLIMP. PUT ALL CONFIDENTIAL DATA IN METAL FOLDER AND KEEP FOLDER IN HAND. OPEN NAVIGATOR'S DOOR AND NAVIGATOR'S WINDOW.

D. RUDDERMAN

TURN SHIP INTO WIND. OPEN FORW'D WINDOW AND REMOVE POST.

E. RADARMAN

PREPARE TO DESTROY ALL SPECIAL EQUIPMENT. TURN RADAR OFF.

AIRSHIP FLIGHT EMERGENCY BILL

Part 2. PREPARE FOR FORCED LANDING

H. ASS'T. MECHANIC

STAND BY AT MECH'S STATION TO TAKE ORDERS FROM MECHANIC.

I. RIGGER

TIE RAFT AND EMERGENCY KIT TO SELF BY WHITE LINE IF OVER WATER.

J. ASS'T. RIGGER

MAKE SURE BOMB RELEASE BARRELS ARE SET ON "UNARMED." STANDBY FOR ORDERS FROM THE COMMAND PILOT TO RELEASE BOMBS.

Loss of lift soon ended the rise; a descent began. The pilot advanced the port throttle to ease impact and dumped about 1,400 pounds of fuel. The port engine was running as the car struck the water, the starboard prop windmilling. Estimated time of impact: 2353. The car settled stern first, its after spaces flooding. The crew evacuated—via the aft door (three men), via the rudderman's window (four), one each over the starboard outrigger and starboard bunk. Grills escaped via the elevatorman's window, having first dumped the ship's confidential folder. The life raft was tossed out—only to vanish. All personnel managed to get clear.

No time had been found, presumably, to secure the helium valves (before abandoning). The weight of the sinking car would build up gas pressure, popping the valves until finally the ship sank. Meanwhile, the car hung afloat; this allowed the crew to collect astern of the wreck. Seeing that it was not about to plunge, Grills swam back aboard for a look round. (Added positive buoyancy was conferred if one or more gasoline tanks were empty or nearly so.) Aft of the mechanic's panel, the cabin was fully submerged. Re-exiting, he swam around the derelict to rejoin his men. Failing that, Grills decided to remain at the fins of his foundered command, after which, believing that his crew had shoved off on the raft, he struck out for the Florida Keys.

His crew, fearing the U-boat's return, had cleared the immediate vicinity; during the night, four of the nine returned to exploit the ship's buoyancy as the others floated as a group, within sight.

ZP-21 learned of the action from Bourne, radioman of *K-74*. On his own initiative, he had sent off a series of "OFUs"—an unofficial code unique to the squadron. This signal was heard up by shipmate Turek, in *K-32,* who deduced *K-74* as its source. Exercising initiative, the radioman relayed the "Urgent, fired on" message to home base. At Richmond, squadron skipper Lt. Cdr. Al Cope was awakened.

A search was ordered.

At 0745, a Grumman J4F amphibian reached the scene with Cope aboard. The bag's stern tip was all that remained above water. Nearby were two survivor clusters. The sea was rough, however, so the plane sped off to buzz the destroyer *Dahlgren* fifteen miles away. The J4F led the DD to one group of men. *K-74* sank at 0815, after eight hours afloat. Four hundred yards off, the survivors, save for Grills, watched it go under, then heard its bombs detonate—proof of their having been armed.

A second, five-man group had hung together. At light, the J4F overhead, the men formed a circle and kicked and splashed to attract notice. This separated them; as the plane moved off the five strained to re-form. Stessel, a weak swimmer, was vomiting—and about fifty or sixty feet from the others. A fin was seen to cut toward the lone man. Stessel was taken down, reappeared with blood covering his face and shoulders, then pulled under again. The surviving four, knives drawn, got back to back for protection and swam away from the bloodied water. Though more sharks were seen, no further attack came. The four were picked up by *Dahlgren* at 0945, the second group at 1000.

Only Grills awaited rescue. He had made six miles in his swim toward land, during which two sharks had come near but left him unmolested. Adrift for more than eighteen hours, sunburned and near exhaustion, Grills was sighted late in the afternoon—from a distance of about four thousand yards—by AM3c M. E. May, USNR, after lookout aboard the dutiful *K-32,* which then led a subchaser to Grills.[92] Recovery was logged at 1930.

Navy Response to Loss of *K-74*

K-74 was the first of its type to exchange gunfire with the enemy. Demonstrably, a ZNP could attack a surfaced U-boat and, in the face of fire, gain position from which to bomb. Further, its .50-caliber proved useful when trained on target.[93] Still, an analysis by Fleet Airships Atlantic concluded that the attack was not consistent with navy doctrine:

> The procedure followed by the *K-74* was not in accordance with doctrine which, under the conditions which existed, required the immediate transmission of a contact report. . . . The doctrine also called for the use of trailing tactics until the submarine began to submerge. An immediate attack was not indicated in as much as no friendly shipping was in the immediate vicinity. Airships are not presently sufficiently armed normally to justify an attack on a surfaced submarine, and should not attempt one unless the submarine is in a position to attack shipping or discovery of a submarine in a position which permits attack as the enemy surfaces. By guiding a killer group to a U-boat, an airship is performing valuable service and is showing good team work as an individual member of the antisubmarine team.

Had its bombs left as ordered, the result might, just might, have had far-reaching effects. Some disagree. "Naturally, it would have been nice that he'd got it. I don't think it would have had any [long-term] effect; there were much deeper forces at work on doing away with the airship program."[94] But opportunity was lost, the prize forfeited—a failure that pointed to deficiencies. "Now, more than ever before, squadrons must, by intensive and extensive training, prepare their personnel to face the problems which the *K-74* was called upon to meet. The chance to attack comes but seldom and behooves all hands to be so trained as to react properly on sighting and then to act instinctively from that point."[95]

Equipment had aided failure. The bomb release was antiquated, its action awkward. Improvements were not yet operational. (That April–May, indeed, a better intervalometer—for dropping a pattern—had been mounted and tested on *K-2.)* To activate the *K-74* release, one had to depress the knob at the end of the release handle, then, keeping it down, pull the handle back to a *detent*, or middle notch, to arm the bombs, then *fully* back to free the ordnance. "The incident," Rosendahl writes, "did bear fruit in modification of the questionable release device to make it suitable for airship use. Definite steps are being taken to simplify the operation of the bomb releases from a mechanical standpoint. However, in the final analysis this problem resolves itself to one of training. Bombardiers must be so thoroughly schooled in the handling of bomb releases that the act becomes automatic with them."[96]

Research also was initiated into the design problem of increasing the effectiveness of the machine guns.

Commander, Gulf Sea Frontier, cabled the commander of FairWing 2 on the 22nd: "The unfortunate loss of K74 by enemy action has not reduced the high regard I hold for the value of blimps in antisubmarine operations. The failure to release depth charges when ordered probably contributed directly to the loss of the ship and must not be permitted to recur. The action of Lieutenant Grills in pressing home his attack in the face of enemy fire is in keeping with naval tradition."[97]

Grills faced possible court-martial. A central dogma of command: the commanding officer of any unit is totally, ultimately, and finally responsible for the safety of his craft and crew. Further, decision to attack had not been in accordance with doctrine, which, in the prevailing conditions, required an immediate contact report followed by trailing tactics until the boat commenced a dive. "An immediate attack was not indicated in as much as no friendly shipping was in the immediate vicinity," Fleet Airships opined in its analysis.

The only way to master all the details of an operation is to perform it. Thus a further culprit: inadequate *training* of combat crews. This included the operation of ship's equipment, communication instructions, proper use of lifesaving gear. "The failure of the bombs to release appears to have been due to the lack of training of the bombardier who failed to pull the releases more than half-way. Combat crews must be highly trained units to be effective. . . . Research is being conducted into the design problems of increasing the effectiveness of machine guns now carried on airships and in providing a less complicated bomb release gear. Intensive training will serve to get the best out of the equipment now installed."

As it happened, ZNP *K-74* proved to be not only the first but the sole ZNP to exchange gunfire with the enemy. The felling underscored the platform's ability to press an attack in the face of enemy fire. Still, vulnerability to antiaircraft was patent: "Airship pilots must realize that U-boat tactics against them may change. Now, more than ever before, squadrons must, by intensive and extensive training, prepare their personnel to face the problems which the *K-74* was called upon to meet. The chance to attack comes but seldom and behooves all hands to be so trained as to react properly on sighting and then to act instinctively from that point."[98]

The merits of this engagement have been debated since 1943—most arguments focusing on aircrew preparedness to effectively attack a submarine. Some have thought Grills a hero, others that a court-martial was warranted for ignoring doctrine—that is, not keeping his target under surveillance while homing in air and surface support.[99] "Grills really violated what was an *unspoken* rule around there [ZP-21]: that you didn't attack a fully surfaced submarine day or night, although it was particularly pertinent during the day. Later, it became a written rule."[100]

Before the officers and men of Fleet Airships Atlantic, Mills awarded Grills the Purple Heart for wounds received as a result of the action. The lieutenant received orders to the commodore's staff at Lakehurst, to help develop ASW doctrine and tactics for airships. Following the war, Grills received the Distinguished Flying Cross.

His intended target, *U-134,* was sunk off Spain by the Royal Air Force—captain and crew perished returning from the same mission. Unknown until later was that *K-74* had damaged the U-boat's ballast tanks, causing Brosin to abort his mission to maraud the Caribbean. His logbook was lost with the boat—one of 739 submarines lost to Germany during the war. The sole account of the engagement is *U-134*'s radio message of the action against *K-74:* "19.7 DM 5216 Attacked at night by a Navy airship with 5 bombs and cannon fire. Main ballast tank 5, quick diving tank on starboard side and no. 4 on starboard damaged. Airship shot down. Many 2 cm. misfires."[101]

The action held lessons. Grills therefore made the circuit, meeting with Rosendahl and briefing the officers of ZP-12. Mills then sent the young lieutenant to Washington, to confer with Tex Settle and George Watson (the latter in Tenth Fleet), thence to South Weymouth and Weeksville. At ZP-11, Grills narrated his singular experience and answered questions: "The conference was limited to pilots and intelligence officers only. . . . Lieutenant Grills proved most interesting and instructive; was extremely obliging and anxious to accommodate in every way. His visit was greatly appreciated by all hands."[102]

"I believe most officers who have talked to Grills," the commodore told Mike Bradley, "have gained confidence in the ability of the blimp to withstand heavy gunfire and to get into a position where the ship can effectively drop its bombs."[103] He also noted, ruefully, "It is imperative that we eliminate any further possibility of having such an important situation fouled up and completely lost through the failure of any individual or any ZNP crew."[104]

Canadian Reaction to *K-74* Loss

The engagement rippled well away from the Gulf Sea Frontier. In April 1943, the Permanent Joint Board on Defence had recommended that a joint Canadian-American board of officers "investigate and report on the possibility of using non-rigid airships as an anti-submarine measure in Eastern Canadian waters." This Joint Board of specialists—four U.S. officers (headed by Mills), two from the Royal Canadian Air Force, and one RCN—met in Ottawa on 6 July. They then proceeded to Halifax, Yarmouth, Sydney, and the Gaspé Peninsula to assess possible sites and conditions. Further meetings ensued. The board's conclusions: avoiding the winter of the Maritimes, it was feasible to operate for escort and patrol from 1 June to 1 October using expeditionary equipment—but installing full hangar and overhaul facilities in a central location, such as Halifax. First, though, it recommended a trial operation, to provide verification:

> a) That an American expeditionary unit of one patrol type airship be established as early as possible in the summer of 1943, at the R.C.A.F. Station at Yarmouth to operate as a demonstrational unit for study by Canadian officials.
> b) That determination of whether or not to utilize airships in the Eastern Canadian area be made by joint R.C.A.F.-R.C.N. Boards after a study of the airship operations mentioned above.[105]

This report was adopted on 13 July.

When word of the casualty reached Ottawa, particulars were requested; in a naval message, details were "Urgently required by Friday A.M. View negotiations now under way respecting operation of blimps in Canadian waters." The Naval Member Canadian Staff in Washington consulted with U.S. naval authorities, noting in reply that "US Navy state that this loss has not repetition not reduced the high regard held for the value of blimps as an anti-submarine weapon."[106]

Devoting "careful consideration" to the Joint Board report, the Chiefs of Staff Committee did not recommend approval for consideration by the Canadian government, in view of the following:

> 1. The recent change in U-boat tactics [read K-74] whereby U-boats had adopted a policy of fighting it out with attacking air forces.
> 2. The improved coverage by airplanes then available in the St. Lawrence and Atlantic Coast area.

3. The weather and technical limitations to the operation of non-rigid airships.
4. The very high cost of establishing permanent lighter-than-air stations.

The submission to this effect was approved by the Cabinet War Committee, Department of National Defence, on 20 August.[107]

Cutback

In August 1943, the projected expansion of lighter-than-air stood more than half executed. At full strength, 108 airships were projected to be operational (with twelve spares), dispersed among thirteen squadrons assigned to air forces of the Atlantic and Pacific fleets. As it happened, however, authorized strength would not climb higher than the low three figures.

The Vice Chief of Naval Operations linked strategy to production. That month, the VCNO directed that a survey of the program be made and a report submitted with recommendations as to the advisability of *reductions*. A rollback in both ships and shore establishment threatened. The apparent motive: to reduce expenditures. (See tables 4.5, 4.6.)

This 1943 survey by the Deputy Chief of Naval Operations for Air included recommendations subsequently approved by King. Among them: the matters of as-yet-undelivered airships on order and reductions in personnel. Many ships were so far along in construction (or material ordered for them) that the navy would be obliged to take them off Goodyear's hands even if contracts were cancelled. Also, funds for much of the LTA shore establishment had been obligated. No change was therefore made in the authorized program of 126 operating fleet airships and 21 spares—but no further orders would be made to cancel attrition.

Carried through "King-135" and the "Mikes" to *M-4,* production contracts for both types were terminated that November. Despite these stoppages, a series of overhaul and erection contracts were let. In fall 1944, upon completion of a contract for spares, Goodyear began dismantling its LTA manufacturing machinery and shifting to other types of production.

As for personnel: "[LTA] personnel shall be restricted to the number necessary for the administration, maintenance and operation of the approved; the pilot training program shall be based on 2 crews for each airship operating with squadrons based in the continental United States and 3 crews for each airship operating with squadrons based outside the continental United States."[108]

Within the Navy Department and in the realm of naval aviation, LTA was a stepchild. It was a well-protected stepchild under Admiral King. But not even King could erase contempt for airships—and for Rosendahl—among certain prominent officers. In this instance, the motivation was the army-navy struggle to protect and advance interests—concerning, specifically, the involvement of the Army Air Forces in ASW and, at the highest level, a dispute over air command. The army objected to assigning air forces to sea frontier commanders and wanted, instead, *all* shore-based air forces integrated into a separate, independent command. King, for his part, wanted army forces withdrawn from ASW. As the issue festered and the army's George Marshall (allied with Stimson) exchanged memoranda, the survey was submitted. The then DCNO(Air) was Rear Admiral John S. McCain. His report to the VCNO is a measured judgment, calling for certain "possible" reductions. Still, "the many considerations involved and the uncertainty as to future enemy strategical and tactical measures makes me reluctant to recommend an appreciable curtailment of the Lighter-

TABLE 4.5 **Anti-Submarine Aircraft** assigned to North and South Atlantic sectors, September 1943. Figures include very long-range (VLR) as well as long-, medium-, and short-range Navy and Army Air Force aircraft. Number of sorties that September: 10,768—of which 972 were flown by lighter-than-air forces. (National Archives)

Sector	Average Number Aircraft Assigned	
Iceland	11	
Greenland	6	
Eastern Sea Frontier	262	(includes 28 ZNP)
Gulf Sea Frontier	180	(15 ZNP)
Guantánamo (Caribbean Sea Frontier)	47	(2 ZNP)
Trinidad (CSF)	91	(4 ZNP)
Aruba-Curacao (CSF)	34	
Puerto Rico (CSF)	43	
Bermuda	28	
Fourth Fleet (excluding Brazilian)	64	
Ascension Island	6	
Moroccan Sea Frontier	57	
United Kingdom	24	
Panamanian Sea Frontier (Atlantic)	38	
CVE (two escort carriers)	48	

TABLE 4.6 **Monthly Antisubmarine (A/S) Report** for the Eastern Sea Frontier (Navy Aircraft), September 1943. (National Archives)[1]

Average number long-range (LR) aircraft assigned	26
Average number medium-range (MR) aircraft assigned	26
Average number short-range (SR) aircraft assigned	152
Average number of blimps assigned	28

Type Aircraft	Escort Sorties	Escort Flying Hours
LR	169	1,658:08
MR	153	636:26
SR	900	2,830:20
Blimps	205	2,768:33
Total	1,427	7,893:27
	Other A/S Sorties	Other A/S Flying Hours
VLR	1	6:03
LR	37	372:49
MR	30	128:55
SR	1,602	4,041:20
Blimps	288	3,961:14
Total	1,958	8,510:21
Total Sorties	3,385	16,403:48

1 The Anti-Submarine Command, Army Air Force (25th Wing) contributed 207 sorties, for an additional total of 1,203:10 flying hours.

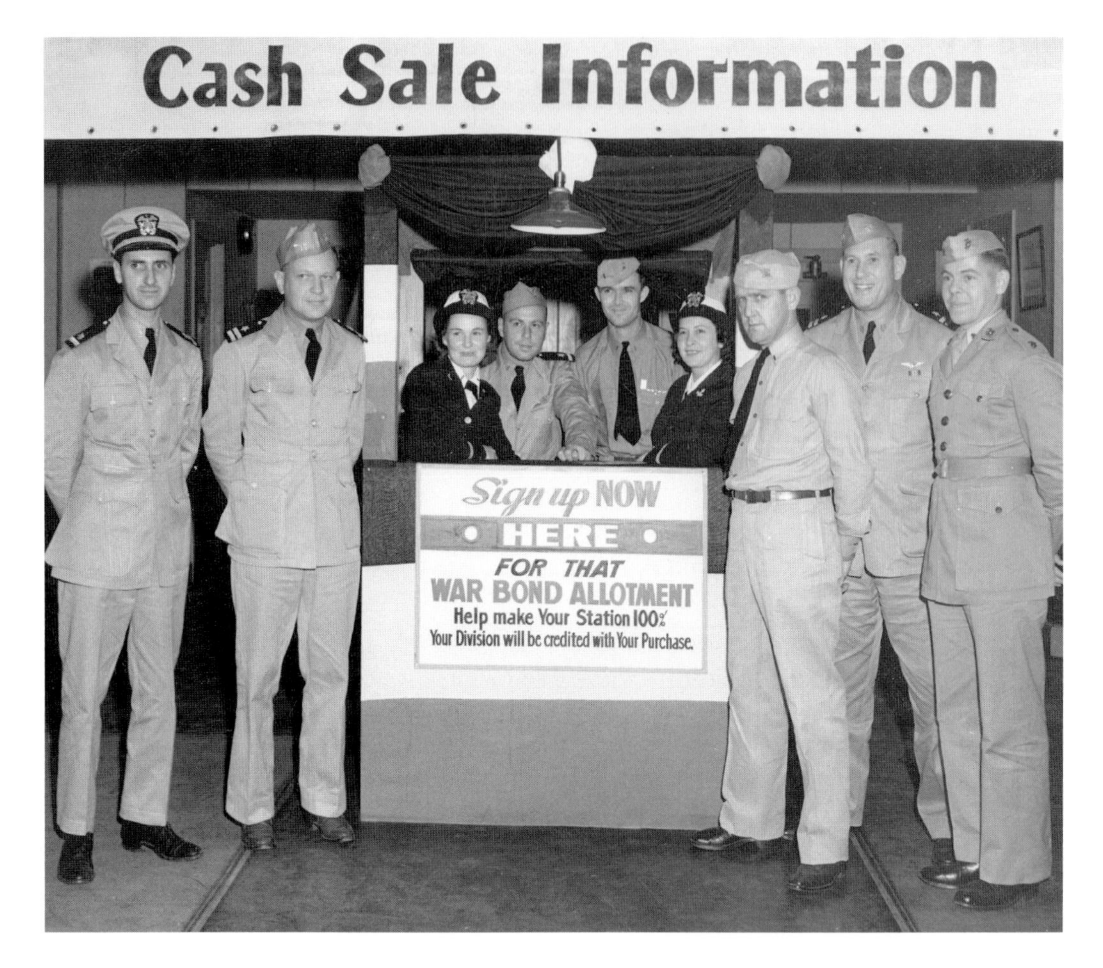

War bond campaign, NAS Lakehurst, September 1943. Pressure on air station personnel—military and civilian—was sufficient to make each onboard drive a success. (Lt. H. R. Rowe, USN [Ret.])

than-Air Program, particularly when I remember the speed and urgency with which the Lighter-than-Air Program was started in the face of tremendous losses from submarines."

November concluded the transfer: antisubmarine operations, both sea and air, would remain a Tenth Fleet responsibility.[109] Admiral McCain had helped broker the agreement. However, some of those surveyed had assumed that King wanted recommendations on the minimum number of airships each operating unit needed. The replies in most cases were prepared by HTA officers. "There is right now," Mills warned, "a campaign to reduce expenditures in the Department, and many eyes are cast upon us looking for an easy out by having us provide a big slice of the total cut. It is up to the Commands for which we work to see that their honest requirements and desires are transmitted to the Department."[110]

Commendatory remarks from higher command were welcome, certainly, particularly if such reached the Tenth Fleet. "We sorely need favorable comment during this critical period," Mills had noted.[111]

In contrast to the Anglo-American effort, Germany had been slow to use its excellent universities and technical institutes; these were little exploited for war-related research until relatively late. Still, given the turn of events at sea, Dönitz was obliged to react. On 14 December, he charged a leading German scientist with the formation of a new thrust in the submarine field.

> For some months past, the enemy has rendered the U-Boat war ineffective. He has achieved this object, not through superior tactics or strategy, but through his superiority in the field of science; this finds its expression in the modern battle weapon—detection. By this means he has torn our sole offensive weapon in the war against the Anglo-Saxons from our hands. It is essential to victory that we make good our scientific disparity and thereby restore to the U-Boat its fighting qualities. . . . I have therefore ordered the creation of a Naval Scientific Directional Staff, with its headquarters in Berlin, in addition to other measures already taken. I have nominated Professor Kuepfmueller as head of this staff and directly subordinate to myself.[112]

The year 1943 ended with a total of seventy-one K-types operational under Fleet Airships Atlantic. The ships were distributed among ten squadrons: Eleven, Twelve, Fourteen, Fifteen, Twenty-one, Twenty-two, Twenty-three, Forty-one, Forty-two, and Fifty-one—the last three operating outside the continental United States. Lighter-than-air was logging ASW and convoy escort patrols from the Canadian border to southern Brazil, covering both U.S. coasts and the entire Caribbean basin.

Nineteen antisubmarine attacks had been logged by airships of the Atlantic Fleet—most on the basis of MAD contacts. The equipment's (and operator's) inability to distinguish true targets from wrecks and geological anomalies had, doubtless, realized fruitless calls to General Quarters.

The war in the Atlantic is still a long way from being won . . .

—Commodore George H. Mills, USN, Commander Fleet Airships, Atlantic, May 1944

5 Southern Squadrons

Seaward of East Coast ports, the combat environment had calmed. Pushed from the continental shelf of the western Atlantic, forced to range south—to hunting grounds in the Gulf of Mexico, off Panama, and coastal Brazil, Dönitz's raiders gathered a rich new harvest of hapless, unescorted shipping.

The first U-boat known to enter the Gulf Sea Frontier was *U-186,* in February 1942. Tonnage losses began—though, according to naval historian Morison, that boat's presence was "a mere scouting mission, fortunately for the ill-prepared frontier. Estimates of the situation varied all the way from the comfortable belief that no submarine would venture within the gulf, to the expectation of a commando raid by ten to twenty submarines to land saboteurs in some Gulf port."[1]

The weight of enemy attacks did not shift to the Florida area, including the Caribbean and gulf focal areas (mouth of the Mississippi, Yucatan Channel) until escorted convoys and improved air cover were organized for the eastern seaboard. That May, losses jumped to forty-one ships in gulf waters—nearly double those of April in the Eastern Sea Frontier. "Of this loss, 53 per cent was tanker tonnage, which made it all the worse." On 6 May, Cominch declared the Gulf of Mexico and Florida Straits a danger zone in which no merchantman could steam unescorted. Geography now defined the value of NAS Richmond: the Florida Straits were the transit route for U-boats between the Atlantic and the gulf. "Unescorted merchant shipping received the full weight of this U-boat blitz, which gave the Gulf Sea Frontier the melancholy distinction of having the most sinkings in May (41 ships, 219,867 gross tons) of any area in any month during this war. All this was wrought by not more than six submarines operating at one time; not more than two, most of the time."[2]

Fleet Airship Group Two was commissioned on 1 March 1943, Capt. Walter E. Zimmerman, USN, commanding. "Heinz" Zimmerman (Lakehurst LTA Class V, 1928–29) was a veteran, with ZR time in his flight logbook. FairShipWing 2 held responsibility for all LTA operations within the Gulf Sea Frontier. Its component units: Blimprons 21, 22, 23, and (in 1944) 24. Within weeks of his assuming command, Zimmerman would be relieved by Capt. Maurice M. "Mike"

Flight deck view from a K-type ZNP, 13 January 1943. The pilot (left) controls the elevator wheel, the co-pilot the ship's rudder. The magnetic anomaly detector or MAD was limited in range—that is, the vertical distance from detector to submerged target. On antisubmarine patrol, pilots were to operate as low as possible so as to enhance the probability of establishing contact. Such close-in flying demands precise airmanship. (U.S. Naval Institute)

Bradley, USN, naval aviator from the big-ship era (also Class V). Zimmerman had orders to South America; as Commander, Fleet Airship Wing Four. There he would establish bases, then inaugurate LTA operations in the South Atlantic, off Brazil. (See page 192.)

Blimpron 21 was commissioned at Richmond on 1 November, Cdr. G. D. Zurmuehlen, USN, commanding. ZP-21 would operate solely within the Gulf Sea Frontier until December 1944 (nearly thirty-two thousand total hours/3,022 flights), when it established a detachment in Panama. The submarine threat to the Gulf of Mexico—particularly off the Louisiana coast—stimulated the commissioning of two ZP squadrons more. Based at NAS Houma, Louisiana, ZP-22 was put in commission on 15 May 1943, Lt. Cdr. J. J. McCormick, USN, commanding. Two weeks later, on 1 June, ZP-23 was in commission at Lakehurst for transfer to NAS Hitchcock, Texas. Commanding officer: Cdr. M. F. D. Flaherty, USN. First ZNP to base (through Lakehurst) at Hitchcock: *K-60* (on 19 June), accompanying *K-62*.

But the threat in gulf focal areas had eased—and become critical along the Brazilian coast. That is, by the time Twenty-two and Twenty-three were operational, the raiders had largely vacated. Each ZP would be disestablished in fall 1944. The record for ZP-22 (15 May 1943 to 12 September 1944): 16,766 hours aloft on 1,443 flights, having escorted 2,339 ships. Operating from NAS Hitchcock, ZP-23 logged (1 June 1943 to 1 March 1944) 6,972 hours on 628 flights. In all, 759 vessels had seen escort.[3] In March 1944, headquarters for Twenty-three would be shifted to Vernam Field on Jamaica, in the British West Indies. From the island, Twenty-three would help cover traffic navigating interconnecting Caribbean waters.

Following SecNav approval (on 5 March 1943) of recommendations by Cominch, work ceased on the second hangars at both Hitchcock and Houma; instead, together with necessary ancillary facilities, the two structures were diverted to coastal sites in Brazil. The twelve diverted ZNPs were to establish overseas operations. A board was appointed to inspect the Brazilian coast and, via the Commander, Fourth Fleet, to submit recommendations as to base sites, facilities, and organization.

The board's report was forwarded in April. Main base selection: a site northwest of Maceió, a city south of the Brazilian "bulge." One of the diverted docks would be erected there—operational, overhaul, and maintenance facilities for six operating ZNPs and one spare. Four mast sites would be set up, along with high-pressure helium storage, shops, housing, messing, and so on, for ninety-six officers and 420 men. When commissioned, squadron ZP-42 would have its headquarters at Maceió.[4] (See page 197.)

Further site selections included intermediate and advance mast facilities in the (from north to south) Amapa, Igarape Assu, São Luiz, Fortaleza, Fernando do Noronha, Recife, and Ipitanga (Bahia) areas—a string of coastwise sites fully to Rio. The terrain and transportation north of São Luiz, where headquarters for ZP-41 would be, were to bedevil logistical support and flight operations at Amapa and Igarape Assu, both of which proved to be hardship bases. Save for Ferando de Noronha, each mast base was slated to receive two mooring circles, takeoff mats, water supply, helium storage, facilities for personnel, and other required services. Fleet strength for each LTA detachment: two ZNPs.

As well, developments were under way to support a six-ship squadron out of Trinidad. The second dock diverted from the Gulf Sea Frontier would be erected at Edinburgh Field—chosen headquarters for Blimpron 51. (See page 184.) In addition, in the northeastern reach of the Brazilian coast, "airships requiring docking should then be sent to Trinidad for maintenance, overhaul and repair."[5] (See map on page 212.)

The Caribbean represented a vital sector. Here shipping lanes were heavily trafficked—interconnecting East Coast convoy ports with the gulf, Mexico, Central and South America, Africa, and the Pacific—a major drawing card for concentrated offensive. Hence Tenth Fleet's urging to deploy into the northeastern reach of the Brazilian coast—and promptly: "In order to expedite the commencement of blimp operations, work should be taken in hand immediately at all of the [recommended] bases with a view to obtaining partial facilities for one airship on an expeditionary basis at each base at the earliest practicable date. This work should be particularly pushed at the Amapa, Igarapa Assu and São Luiz mast bases."[6]

Tanker traffic from the oil ports of Mexico and Venezuela presented a strategic target. "We were a *very busy* subchaser," Capt. (then Lt.) W. E. Delong (Lakehurst Class L2-43) would recall. "We spent most of our time in the Mona Passage [between the Dominican Republic and Puerto Rico] and the Windward Passage [Cuba and Haiti]. All the oil coming up from Venezuela had to go through those two passes. And there was a *lot* of submarine warfare in that area. So we were a busy ship: most of the time not detecting and sinking submarines but picking up survivors."[7]

Bauxite is the principal ore for aluminum, a metal vital to aircraft production. The mines were in British and Dutch Guiana—neighbors to Venezuela. (The U.S. imports 100 percent of this strategic mineral, still.) As well, numerous United Fruit Company vessels were operating between Honduras and the gulf and East Coast ports. The maritime traffic steaming Caribbean waters and the West Indies was life-supporting to England, hence indispensable to Allied war planning. That July, the Commander, Panamanian Sea Frontier, was obliged to "stop all sailings United Nations Ships of less than 15 knots unless escorted between Aruba-Curaçao-Trinidad area [north coast of Venezuela] and Panama except local coastal traffic."[8]

United Fruit vessels were instructed to follow inshore courses—the Yucatán Peninsula close in, crossing the Yucatán Channel during daylight (with air coverage), then the north coast of Cuba. Shipping enjoyed protection from Havana to Key West. From the Gulf Sea Frontier to Belize, however, the return flow was vulnerable: escorts were not available for that leg.

The weight of the offensive had shifted, from the Hatteras area to the Florida sector, including the gulf—and to the Caribbean and its approaches. Fewer U-boats seemed to be operating, but in fact German undersea forces had simply *dispersed*—there were two sinkings well away from tropical waters, in Canada's Gulf of St. Lawrence.[9]

Exploiting the straits of Florida via the Yucatán Channel, U-boats could "drift noiselessly with the Gulf Stream, making the area a profitable hunting ground."[10] Farther south, fatal danger seeped into Panamanian waters, the Caribbean, and the South Atlantic. The center of attack: the waters contiguous to Trinidad—an island in the West Indies off the northeast coast of Venezuela.

Ordered to the Caribbean, a five-boat force struck hard. "The U-boats met very considerable tanker traffic and achieved immediate success." At the beginning of March a sixth boat reached the area. It sank nine ships within two weeks. "Like the first," Dönitz recorded, "this second attack on shipping in American waters was a complete success."[11]

In a bold move, additional boats were transferred to that theater, many of them sustained by the Type XIV tanker submarine, or "milch cow." During April–June, thirty-seven U-boats were successively engaged in the Caribbean Sea. The convoy system was only gradually being introduced. "There has been little change in the general U-boat policy of the enemy during the month of May," an intelligence report intoned. "For the majority of the month the enemy has conducted a vigorous U-boat offensive off the Atlantic coast and in the Caribbean and its approaches."

> With the introduction of coastal convoy between Norfolk and Key West we may confidently expect a pronounced change in the situation on the Atlantic coast. The first such convoy was run on 14 May and this has now become a regular schedule. As far as is known, no ship has yet been attacked in one of those coastal convoys, and it seems clear that the U-boat occupant of the Cape Hatteras area is no longer finding it such a happy hunting ground.[12]

Not enough, soon enough. Because of independent traffic sailing regularly on predictable courses, the equatorial Atlantic held fruitful for Berlin, especially the approaches to Trinidad—a focal area through which all shipping had to steam bound for the Caribbean from the east (notably

Freeport, on Africa's western coast) and from the south. Within days that August, a concentration of six boats, working together, bagged ten vessels. That fall, forces withdrawn to the Caribbean's eastern fringe, toward Trinidad, the estuary of the Orocono, and the coast of Guiana, realized further sinkings.

Among the aftershocks: shortages (e.g., bananas), then rationing for the civilian economy. Materials such as steel, aluminum, copper, and nylon reached the U.S. critical list: production of goods requiring them became increasingly difficult, then stopped altogether. Ration books appeared. When Congress declared a state of war, the Office of Production Management issued a curtailment order on automobile production that very day. In an awful half-year, Puerto Rico could not export its crops: more than one-fifth of its merchant tonnage had been sunk by June. That May, gasoline rationing was announced for eastern states;[13] in June, sugar (from Cuba and the West Indies) joined the list, as did coffee—every pound of which came in by sea. That December, its supplier of ice cream notified Lakehurst that rationing was necessary: "Members [of the Officer's Club] are requested not to ask for ice cream as a desert unless it is on the regular menue [*sic*] for that meal." As late as July 1945, reflecting the nationwide shortage, the Navy Department would restrict all commissary stores within the continental limits to 75 percent of sugar-contained foods procured during the prior quarter.

> Oil for domestic consumption was cut, because of staggering tanker losses. Britain alone needed four tankers from Venezuelan, West Indian, and U.S. gulf ports per day to sustain its merchant fleet and navy. "Week by week, the scale of this massacre grew." Single boats prowled the Caribbean and the Gulf of Mexico "with a freedom and insolence," Churchill growled, "which was hard to bear." Tanker construction (in tons) was not to overtake tanker sinkings until December—a result of increased building and fewer losses to torpedoes. Meantime, "it was a fairly desperate situation. The British were beginning to lose confidence in the ability of the United States Navy to protect merchant ships in home waters, and the South American republics began to wonder whether their big neighbor was strong enough to beat Hitler. So large a proportion of the sunken ships were tankers that severe rationing of domestic fuel had to be imposed, and the supply of military fuel oil to Europe and the Pacific was threatened."[14]

Drastic action was prescribed—most immediately, convoys with escort forces. During April–May, a coastal system had been inaugurated off the eastern seaboard, but not (yet) in tropical waters. Independently routed traffic persisted—vessels sailing irregularly but on defined courses. Bauxite ships repeatedly disobeyed orders to steam close in, worsening losses. From U.S. entry into the war through October 1942, twenty-two ships were lost in the Trinidad area. Alarmingly, the bauxite trade had been deftly interdicted. "The [September] attack on all bauxite carriers but one occurred in waters in the vicinity of Trinidad, or between Trinidad and Paramaribo. In all, seven bauxite-carrying ships were sunk; 3 of these 7 ships were operated by Alcoa; but 5 ships in the bauxite trade returning to pick up bauxite cargoes were also torpedoed and sunk; 4 of these last 5 vessels were operated by Alcoa. This makes a total of 12 vessels lost, 7 of which were operated by Alcoa."[15]

[Opposite] *M-3* at Akron, 15 January 1944. Intended for operations in the tropics, the M-type was a formidable ASW platform. Four were delivered in 1943–44, but eighteen were cancelled (along with four K-types) when the antisubmarine campaign brightened. The "Mike" ships arrived too late to make a convincing contribution to the Atlantic campaign. (Goodyear photograph)

Depredations held fast for U-Boat Command, obliging a countereffort. By October, "escorts, and especially air cover, were notably strengthened [Dönitz wrote], but the enemy lacked experience in location work and night attacks."[16] A reorganization of the Atlantic coastal convoys had been instituted; not until year's end, however, did the Interlocking System threading the Maritime provinces of Canada to the Caribbean Sea become fully effective.[17]

The M-type Airship

Airships operate best at midlatitudes, wherein lay the focal points for most international shipping. The tropics, in contrast, are not their natural domain.

Gross lift (buoyancy) is a variable, depending upon atmospheric density and, consequently, upon changes in pressure, temperature, and superheating of the helium, as well as its purity. (Humidity has scant effect.) With pressure constant, the volume of a gas varies directly as the absolute temperature—that is, if its temperature is increased, the volume increases. This reduces lift—because lift per unit volume declines in proportion to the temperature of the surrounding air.[18] A larger volume was therefore desirable for operations in the tropics, where the warm and less dense air generates less lift per cubic foot. With orders to warmer latitudes, greater lift and speed were operationally desirable.

Already, the *K-2* type was deploying an ever-increasing weight of equipment.

BuAer assessed a design intended expressly for such operations. In seventy-degree air, armed with four Mark-17 bombs, the *K-2* type had a twenty-eight-hour capability at fifty knots. Armed with *eight* bombs, the projected ZNP-M offered an endurance of forty-two hours.

On 27 February, Capt. Walter E. Zimmerman, station skipper, received a phone directive from Scott E. "Scotty" Peck, at the LTA desk in BuAer. Adm. John H. Towers, bureau chief, wanted letters answering the question: "Do you favor the construction of a prototype nonrigid of 600,000 cubic feet with a view to its use either to replace the K-type or as an additional type?"[19]

Few technologies appear with their potential fully realized. Thrown into mass production, the K-type was no ideal design. Upgrades, moreover, would devour uncountable hours of consultation. Still, no one recommended an outright replacement; indeed, five of the six replies urged go-ahead. Downside: a new construction initiative would divert resources—perhaps hindering procurement of the forty-two K-ships on order. As well, development would be protracted: the design, construction, test, and corrections for a prototype would burn twelve to eighteen months or more, followed by ground-handling, spare parts, training, and facilities complications.

Cdr. George V. Whittle, USN, outlined his concerns:

> To abandon this type now in favor of the 600,000 cu. ft. size would be to nullify in large measure our intensive work of preparation and set us back for a long and uncertain period of time. For instance our K type mooring masts cannot handle a 600,000 cu. ft. airship and we have on order all material and equipment for 45 masts. . . . Much of this material and equipment is now being delivered and most of it required six to twelve months to get. This is just one item of the situation. . . . I consider it would be a serious mistake with the war situation as it is to interfere with the current K class airship program.[20]

Contracts for the prototype from Goodyear Aircraft Corporation, the shipbuilder, are dated 17 June 1942—a killing time for Dönitz's boats in both the gulf and Caribbean. Contracts were followed by directives until, on 16 August 1943, a planning directive specified a total of twenty-two M-types. The contract was signed on 11 September.

The prototype ZPM class was christened by Jean Rosendahl on 27 October 1943 in Akron —part of the city's observance of Navy Day. Commissioning was followed by contractor's trials. As these neared, *G-2,* first of the Model ZNN-G training ships then under contract, was ferried cross-country. At Lakehurst, *G-2* was put through acceptance trials by a subboard appointed by the Board of Inspection and Survey.

M-1 was air-delivered to Lakehurst for trials and for service tests on 27 November. Envelope volume was 625,500 cubic feet—smaller than its M-ship sisters. Useful load: ten thousand pounds (excluding dynamic lift). *M-2, M-3,* and *M-4* were ferried that January–April. As well, amendments to the contracts for spare envelopes were negotiated, increasing volume from 425,000 to 456,000 cubic feet for the model K and from 647,468 cubic feet (for *M-4,* a useful load 11,900 pounds) to 725,000 cubic feet for the M-type. The change increased gross static lift for the latter 12 percent.[21]

A long, articulated car (117 feet) minimized shear loads in the envelope—a headache in the Ks. The only gun (.50-caliber) was mounted in the forward end of the "blister" below the car. The M-type was equipped with four ballonets. The two at midsection were used to compensate for small changes in altitude and temperature. Interconnected, the forward and aft ballonets allowed the pilot to shift air to maintain a desired trim angle. Fuel and ballast were distributed throughout

[Opposite] A Piper Cub fuselage beneath *XM-1*, 3 March 1944. A radio control and guidance experiment, no hook-ons were attempted. Assigned to Lakehurst's CNATE command for experimental projects, "Mike-1" was deemed unsuitable for antisubmarine operations. (Capt. J. C. Kane, USN [Ret.])

the car, the disposable loads being arranged so that the overall center of gravity was approximately at the center of buoyancy. Electrically powered auxiliary blowers offered push-button control for the pilot. The propellers were controllable in pitch and reversible—"so you could have a prayer of making a decent landing without jerking the [ground] crew off their feet or mowing them down with the props." Radar, exit ladder, landing gear, and escape doors were hydraulically actuated.

The M-type embodied engineering innovation—and BuAer was looking to a larger-still prototype.

> The Bureau of Aeronautics is arranging for Goodyear to conduct an engineering study of an O-type ship of about 1,500,000 cu. ft. volume (over twice the volume of the M-class). Should the engineering study indicate the advisability of constructing airships of the O-type, it will be two and one-half years at the earliest before the first O-ship can be completed under present conditions. Such a ship would be useful for convoy escort on routes such as Bahia to Dakar, and Hawaii to Samoa.[22]

Contract was let on 29 May 1943; that October, drawings and fabric specifications for the design study were received from Goodyear. The Model O proposal—a conventional if large nonrigid having an M-type car with four engines—never left paper. The initiative, presumably, was too costly and would have deployed too late to warrant construction.

Meantime, Mills concerned himself with assigning *M-2, M-3,* and *M-4.* (*XM-1* was deemed unsuitable for A/S work.) One each had been planned for Lakehurst, Weymouth, and Weeksville; however, lack of spare parts cancelled this. Cdr. Alfred L. Cope, USN, ZP-21 CO, would exploit them in Florida until M-type masts reached outlying bases.[23] "It was desirable to have all M ships at one base" Mills wrote, "to prevent having to spread the few available spares among 3 stations. . . . I also could not keep all three ships at any one [station] due to the fact that all might become hangar bound at one time, thus throwing the smaller squadrons into an undesirable position."[24]

The M-type made its debut in Atlantic Fleet ASW operations in August 1944. A formidable weapon (and pilot favorite), it arrived too late to contribute much to the antisubmarine war.[25]

Trinidad and ZP-51

For much of 1942, shipping in the waters contiguous to Trinidad steamed poorly protected. The potential harvest was immense: a monthly average of three hundred vessels cleared at Trinidad—riches not lost on the enemy, who made Trinidad a center of attack. As well, Port of Spain (the island's convoy port) was a center for enemy agents seeking information as to merchant ship movement. In December 1942, Cominch directed that six ZNPs deploy in the Trinidad–Guiana area. This set in motion a process that Mills, through his officers, had to complete.

The first LTA squadron to operate wholly outside the continental limits of the United States was placed in commission on 10 February 1943, preparatory to transfer overseas. This was Airship Squadron Fifty-one (ZP-51), Cdr. C. D. Zurmuehlen, USN, commanding. Headquarters: Edinburgh Field—home, as well, of Fleet Airship Wing Five. Operational sector: the Trinidad area south to the Dutch Guiana–Brazil border. FairShipWing 5 was under the operational control of Commander, Caribbean Sea Frontier.

Formalities astern, the transfer began. Six days later, the squadron's first ZNP, *K-17,* reached its operating area. LTA was overspreading the map. ZP-21 based a ship at Key West for the first time. *K-25* (ZP-51) reached Guantánamo, to initiate operations in Cuba, and *K-19* (ZP-21) was delivered to Isle of Pines, to begin operations from a stick mast. In April, upon delivery of *K-48,* ZP-21 took over Guantánamo operations. That December, the first ZNP landed at San Julian, in western Cuba: stick mast, native ground crews. Every A/S sensor, every platform was wanted:

> ABOUT 5 U-BOATS EXPECTED TO CONTINUE RECONNAISSANCE CARIBBEAN AND GULF AND PROBABLY PANAMA SEA FRONTIERS IN EFFORT TO FIND WEAK SPOTS IN DEFENSES. . . . TOTAL [NUMBER OF U-BOATS] ATLANTIC 105 WITH PROBABILITY OF CONSIDERABLE INCREASE NEXT 90 DAYS.[26]

Trinidad, by virtue of its geographic location, guards the southern approaches to the Caribbean. A major trade choke point, the island holds immense importance with respect to traffic plying routes interconnecting South America, the West Indies, and the United States, as well Europe and Africa. "Already important at the opening of the war in Europe," Morison reminds, "Trinidad gradually built up until in 1943 it was one of the world's greatest centers of sea traffic."

The U.S. Army facility at Edinburgh (after November 1943, Carlson Field) was headquarters not only for ZP-51 but its hedron detachments of Blimp Headquarters Squadron Five. Augmenting the main operating base, ZP-51 would operate three squadron and hedron detachments: two in the Guianas and one on Cuba, at NAS Guantánamo (Detachment One). Collectively, the wing's operational area embraced an immense sea sector off northeastern South America between coastal Venezuela and Brazil. Atkinson Field (Det 2) was home to a British Guiana detachment and (a mile away) navy HTA. The site boasted single-story wooden quarters, plus mooring circles, masts, and a two-thousand-foot runway. ZP-51's other South American detachment was installed at Paramaribo (Det 3) in Dutch Guiana—by no coincidence a departure port for vessels transporting bauxite from a local mine north to Trinidad. As at Atkinson, the base held standard equipment to support ZNP operations, including a two-thousand-foot "asphalt strip recently laid across a scrubby patch of mango brush and semi-jungle."[27] (See map on page 212.)

The run's southern leg (known as "Lower Bauxite") arced from Paramaribo north to Georgetown, in British Guiana; the upper run ("Upper Bauxite") delivered the ore to Trinidad. There, at Port of Spain, loads were transshipped onto ore carriers for further passage. Standard mission for Detachment Two: patrol the Upper Bauxite. When Paramaribo was closed (in 1944), Atkinson-based ZNPs took over coverage of the lower run, those at Carlson defending the upper one.[28] NAS San Juan lent support, serving as a refueling point for Richmond–Trinidad ferry flights.

Day to day, missions assigned ZP-51 were directed to Carlsen Field via dispatches from Naval Operating Base (NOB) Trinidad. On the basis of these (sources: shipping movements, U-boat plots, and other operational information), the squadron assigned the day's mission(s).

South of Fifty-one's operating areas (that is, beyond German-controlled French Guiana) lay the immensity that is Brazil—a 4,250-mile coastline arcing from French Guiana to Uruguay. Its threatened waters would soon see another fleet airship wing, operating two squadrons.

Late in February, the Commander, Task Force Three (U.S. Atlantic Fleet), pressed the CNO as to matters in those threatened sunlit waters. He provides a vivid snapshot:

> Recently a strong enemy submarine thrust in the Caribbean Area found our own, as well as British forces stationed there, so lacking in adequate facilities that neither proper offensive nor defensive action could be taken. Our counter-measures against this thrust can best be described as pitifully impotent and futile. Only the lack of ability on the part of the enemy prevented wide scale destruction at Aruba and in the Gulf of Paris. . . . Positive and immediate action is necessary to successfully combat submarine warfare.[29]

Integrated units were proposed. Inshore, "striking groups" would comprise fast seagoing vessels equipped with the "latest detection apparatus," using both rack and stern throw-guns for depth charges, two planes equipped with bombs, charges, and flares—and "one or more blimps." In blue water, free-roving CVE groups would operate as "hunter-killers" under the Commander in Chief, Atlantic Fleet. Mission: to hunt contacts to exhaustion and destruction.[30]

By opening up the transatlantic cycle, enough forces were diverted to the Caribbean to introduce a convoy between Aruba and Trinidad. ONI could not know, but whether by coincidence or as a direct result of the Caribbean convoys, the U-boat offensive seeped into the Gulf of Mexico. To ONI, this illustrated "the well-known trend of the U-boats into increasingly distant waters as counter-measures tend to make an old area of operations unhealthy for them. Another example on these lines has been a series of attacks off the Brazilian coast as far south as the equator."[31]

Tentative losses that May in the Caribbean: 129,500 tons, with another 141,500 tons in the Gulf of Mexico. Yet a foundation for optimism was being laid: "There has been a splendid increase in the number of attacks made on U-boats in the waters west of 40° west and, during the month, 49 attacks have been reported by surface forces and aircraft. Little is yet known of the results."[32]

Blimpron 51 entered active operating status when, on 16 February 1943, *K-17* landed, refueled, and loaded 350-pound Mark 44 torpex-loaded charges. The ship was reported ready for duty to NOB Trinidad, the local operational commander. Its commandant, unlike the commander of the Caribbean Sea Frontier, was a supporter of LTA and fully exploited his ZNP assets.

Coordinated with Edinburgh, daily missions included A/S patrols, convoy escort, and in-close investigation of reported sightings. Prior to takeoff, pilots and crews were briefed by army personnel who explained the general tactical situation before a large wall map that held a complete picture of the area's surface and air operations. Upon landing, the flight crew was taken to Operations, for interrogation by an army intelligence officer.

Except for sticking exhaust valves, local squalls, and in-flight turbulence, most missions proved uneventful. Still, no unit found itself trouble free.[33] The MAD gear serving Fifty-one proved to be, well, maddening: "Numerous wrecks and geological disturbances make special equipment work most unsatisfactory, in fact so many 'contacts' were made in the first three days, even in depths of water up to 1100 fathoms, that all available bronze and green markers were expended. In this area, a visual contact of some sort seems necessary before attempting to work with the special equipment."[34]

Attacks mounted that August in the area around Trinidad and northern Brazil. Bauxite freighters shuttled constantly from the Guianas to Port of Spain—a point of shipping concentration and, as well, a center of subversive activities. An average of seventy-seven bauxite freighters cleared monthly between March and September 1943. "The Navy blimps based on Edinburgh Field, Trinidad, were useful escorts for the bauxite route, and for covering other convoys while forming up in the Gulf of Paria [Venezuela]. There is nothing like a blimp to make a convoy feel easy at that critical moment."[35]

Naval Air Station Richmond, Florida

In Ohio, Goodyear had revved up ZNP deliveries to six or seven per month. "The prospects are that [Goodyear] will work up to a peak of 10 K-ships per month in October; the first fleet-type M-ship will not be delivered before October and we expect to be getting 3 M-ships per month one year from now."[36]

Richmond supported operations beyond Florida coastal waters. Atlantic Fleet ZNPs from Wing Two (three squadrons) were assigned to *both* the Gulf and Caribbean sea frontiers. (In truth, gulf-related demands bruised training—"and there have been numerous occasions when the avail-

Naval Air Station Richmond, Florida. Headquarters for Fleet Airship Wing Two (three squadrons), Richmond was homeport for its own fifteen-ship unit, ZP-21. Richmond was a vital command and maintenance center, supporting coverage for both Atlantic and gulf shipping. As well, Richmond served as transit stop for all airships ferried to/from commands in the Caribbean, eastern Central America, and in South America. (Lt. [jg] H. H. O'Clare, USN [Ret.])

ability of airships could not meet the requirements for operations.")[37] ZP-21 operated as well from outlying bases at Santa Fe; Isle of Pines, San Julian, and Guantánamo; and at NAS Banana River, Florida. A major overhaul, repair, and maintenance station, Richmond a nexus through which ZNPs were ferried to the squadrons (and back), including units in South America. Transients were frequent, aggravating the congestion.

> No ferry flight shall be made unless the commanding pilot has secured complete weather information, recognition signals, and other communication material. Naval Air Station, Richmond is not equipped to issue Registered Publications such as Aircraft Codes to visiting or transient airships. Pilots ferrying airships to Richmond will, therefore, obtain sufficient copies of Aircraft codes to cover (1) the flight to Richmond, (2) the period of duty, and (3) the return to home base.[38]

In sum, operational, overhaul, and training requirements proved heavy; NAS Richmond felt the strain. One headache: helium repurification. "This was a problem: we were so busy at Richmond that we didn't have a chance to keep our bags at the purity level we wanted. We were down around 92%—that meant instead of carrying four torpex depth charges we could carry one. We were never lighter-than-air. Never."[39]

Still, Richmond was pivotal, located so as to help protect the gulf as well as the southern end of the East Coast. And the station was repair base (hedron) for units deployed southward. The largest squadron (in 1944, thirty-three CACs), ZP-21 was flying more night missions than any other zipron—in all, 661 nights out of 664. Twenty-one would operate every day of its existence between commissioning and 15 May 1945. "We had tremendous hours compared to guys up north or south of us," one pilot remarked. "We were busy at Richmond—an awful lot of patrols," another recalled. "We were patrolling all the time." For October 1943, prior to his transfer to Brazil's ZP-41, "Bud" Delong flew a dozen missions out of Richmond. Average length: about twelve hours.

[Top] An envelope or "bag" from the supply officer at Lakehurst is unpacked at NAS Richmond, 21 February 1945. Note the ground cloth. Overhead falls support successive bights of fabric as the box is pulled forward and the bag laid out. The envelope will be unfolded, inflated with air for inspection and installation of internal suspensions and accessories, and made ready for helium inflation. Weight: about 9,350 pounds. (Lt. [jg] H. H. O'Clare, USN [Ret.])

[Bottom] Sailors repair a leaky helium valve prior to air or helium inflation of a K-ship envelope. (Author)

As well, a lot of rum flew into Miami.

Winter operations stood in marked contrast to that of, say, ZP-11. In New England, the autumn of 1943 bred prewinter gremlins: September saw temperatures swing from thirty degrees to eighty in a single week at South Weymouth. For one ship, a pressure height of 3,500 feet was recorded at predawn takeoff; that afternoon on the mat, it floated *at* pressure height.

October attested to Richmond's merit as a nexus for the LTA shore establishment—that is, getting Atlantic Fleet squadrons up to their allowances, then keeping the units operational. An already congested roster listed twenty-one ships assigned: four on operational sorties, four at advance bases, plus seven in the barn (for patch repairs and other work). Another half-dozen ZNPs were to hand for 120-hour checks, interim overhauls, repairs.

Florida was no operational ideal. Stagnant and moving fronts beset patrols. *Several* fronts at once were not unusual—the radar indispensable for picking the lightest spots to punch through. "Florida was a nasty place to fly for part of the year, because the clouds would often go off the mainland at night. We'd get some terrific storms out there, mostly line squalls. Under one of those darn things you took a ride up and down whether you wanted to or not. I've been going full down-elevator and full down throttle and going *up* at 500 feet a minute under some."[40] Crew at dampers and valves (air and helium), auxiliary blower on, loose gear secured, ship in trim and flying by instrument, airmen navigated through fronts and thunderstorms. Often, though, bombs or fuel were shed—emergency lightening—just above the water, before engines and elevators took effect.[41] On night mission in October 1943, a flight crew was obliged to maintain a continuous standby on the bomb releases and slip tanks (quickly disposable fuel ballast), the throttles nursed constantly. (More power boosted turbulence, yet sufficient power was crucial to maintaining course and headway.) Almost uncontrollable, the ship was thrown from 1,200 to 100 feet and spun in three complete circles amid heavy rain and lightning.

Blockade Runners

Germany's need for strategic commodities from overseas (tin, rubber, hemp, wolfram [tungsten], quinine, opium, fuel oils) was such that blockade-running operations came to assume paramount logistic importance. By 1943, risk had become subordinate to need, thus mandating an all-out effort by sea. Fast German merchantmen instituted traffic between western France and Japan. "This blockade running worked very well to begin with," Dönitz noted, "and provided us with an important quantity of supplies." The Italians assisted by developing a fleet of cargo-carrying submarines.

[Opposite] Winter operations, NAS South Weymouth. (Lt. H. F. Smith, USNR [Ret.])

Only two routes were practicable for Axis vessels plying between Japanese ports and occupied Europe: the Pacific and Cape Horn or, instead, the Indian Ocean around Africa—approximately sixteen thousand miles.[42] The latter was shorter and, as well, intersected Allied shipping lanes only in the Atlantic. The narrowest waters through which (disguised) enemy runners had to steam: the equatorial mid-Atlantic between South America and Africa. "The range of modern bombers, submarines, and fast surface raiders has reduced the Atlantic narrows, between Dakar [Africa] and Natal [Brazil], to practically the status of a strait."[43]

LTA assisted Fourth Fleet barrier patrols in Brazilian waters. Blimps are not strategic scouts. Rigid airships could have extended coverage in sea areas beyond coastal waters, fully across. "If we could have had two or three rigid airships to use in the Atlantic Narrows between Brazil and the African coast," Captain Spicer (ZP-21) remarked, "I feel certain that not one of the many surface blockade runners would have got through, and that we would have used far less combatant aircraft and surface ships, while at the same time doing a much better and more complete job."[44] (An airplane can search a much larger area in a shorter time; however, it cannot follow a convoy across or loiter long, because of its speed.) But the naval rigid had been deferred. One notes here that in June 1943, the Zeppelin works in Friedrichshafen was bombed as a suspected radar factory. Luftschiffbau-Zeppelin, indeed, was much engaged in weapons production—radar equipment, jet fighters, and V-2 rocket parts.[45]

Working to isolate Germany from all sea communication, German merchant shipping and contraband in neutral bottoms were subject to interception. Since U.S. entry into the war, fifteen blockade runners were known to have run the gauntlet from eastern to European ports—successful breakthroughs. In December 1942, eight vessels were reported en route from the Bay of Biscay to Japanese ports; a half-dozen were believed sailing the homeward passage.[46] Interceptions and scuttlings cut this trade; still, this traffic was not fully stopped.

> LACK OF SUCCESS WITH SURFACE BLOCKADE RUNNERS ANTICIPATE ENEMY WILL UTILIZE LARGE CARGO TYPE U-BOATS PROBABLY EX-ITALIAN FOR THIS PURPOSE. ONE OR MORE OF THESE MAY ALREADY BE OUTBOUND FROM BISCAY PORTS. AN INBOUND SUB PROBABLY JAP RUNNER CURRENTLY IS FIXED ABOUT 300 MILES WEST OF ASCENSION.[47]

Germany's war on Allied commerce increasingly unavailing, runner traffic bearing strategic materials—surface vessels as well as submarines—were vital to a shattered industrial production. During February 1945:

ABOUT FOUR U-BOATS ARE NOW ESTIMATED ENROUTE TO NORTH ATLANTIC FROM THE FAR EAST. ONE OF THESE IS ESTIMATED TO HAVE ENTERED THE SOUTH ATLANTIC. THE REMAINDER ARE STILL IN THE INDIAN OCEAN PROBABLY SOUTHEAST OF MADAGASCAR. ANTICIPATE OTHER CARGO BOATS WILL DEPART GERMANY FOR FAR EAST WITHIN NEXT MONTH.[48]

And that March,

UP TO THREE MORE CARGO U-BOATS PROBABLY ENROUTE TO GERMANY FROM THE FAR EAST ARE CURRENTLY ESTIMATED WEST OF CAPETOWN. THERE ARE NO RECENT INDICATIONS OF ANY U-BOATS ACTIVE IN THE INDIAN OCEAN.[49]

Many runners failed to evade interdiction. Blimps, for their part, were one element of the enforcers—and rescuers. Early in January 1944, for example, ships from ZP-42 supported U.S. forces in the rescue of German and Italian sailors from a pair of blockade runners sunk by surface gunfire.

More than 250 sailors had taken to the boats from *Rio Grande* and *Burgenland*—nine lifeboats at sea for days. (The possibility of U-boat escort for the merchantmen had foreclosed immediate rescue.)[50] Operations for Detachment Two (Ferando de Noronha), of ZP-42, were inaugurated that month by *K-36*. Mission: search for enemy survivors. After nearly twenty-three hours, "King-36" landed; the blimp was serviced, aircrews changed, the search resumed. Next day, it assisted the rescue by rounding up three lifeboats (by blinker), then homing in surface craft to retrieve 73 survivors. Five days later, on escort, Detachment One's ZNP *K-98* happened upon a boatload. The escort commander was advised, after which "98" held station until another 34 men were taken aboard.[51]

It should not be imagined that searches were routinely successful. Survivors faced a low probability of rescue; crews often disappeared without trace despite intensive hunts. In July 1942, *K-8* (ZP-14) located oily, sun-baked survivors of a destroyed U-boat about forty-eight hours after a fruitless search by HTA and surface craft. The Germans stated that planes had frequently overflown them while they were in the water. Off Brazil, one U.S. aircrew in a rubber lifeboat came ashore after eight days adrift. They had sighted sixteen searching planes (one flew directly over them), one blimp, two subchasers, and one merchant vessel—which almost ran them down.[52]

Still, rescues were logged. In July 1943, for instance, *K-52* (ZP-15) searched for ship survivors—and found fifty.

When Italy surrendered in September 1943, six Italian cargo-carrying boats were reportedly operating. On 10 May 1945, following surrender orders to all German U-boats at sea, *U-532* surfaced near the Faeroe Islands and was sent to Scotland for formal surrender. Its cargo, courtesy of Japan: 110 tons of tin, 601 tons of rubber, 5 tons of wolfram, 5 tons of molybdenum, and a half-ton of quinine.[53]

Blimps to Brazil

In January 1942, Brazil had broken off diplomatic and commercial relations with the Axis. No Brazilian vessel had yet been attacked. That February–April, seven were torpedoed. (In Dönitz's view, these targets had neither been recognizable as neutrals nor behaved as such.) More Brazilian ships mounted guns. In mid-May, the German naval high command issued orders that ships of all South American states were to be attacked without warning, except those of Argentina and Chile. "Without any formal declaration, we thus found ourselves in a state of war with Brazil, and on July 4 the U-boats were given permission by our political leadership to attack all Brazilian vessels."[54]

> Brazil's entry into the war on 22 August 1942 was an event of great importance in naval history. Brazil was the largest and most populous of the South American Republics. Her territorial waters extended from lat. 5° N to lat. 32° S, and had an excellent small Navy, including several modern minelayers and planes which only needed modern equipment and training to be suitable for escorts. . . . Although Brazil was a valuable ally, she was also highly vulnerable. . . . The dependence of Brazil on coastwise shipping recalled that of the United States before 1850.[55]

That August, Dönitz's boats turned their attentions to shipping near Trinidad and the north coast of Brazil, where bauxite carriers and outbound ships with supplies for the Middle East proffered attractive targets. "For a time," Churchill records in his memoirs, "the South Atlantic caused us anxiety." One outcome: additional units of the airship organization of the U.S. Fleet.

Cominch had introduced (in September 1942) its biweekly *U-Boat Trends,* a forecast intended for commands in the U.S. Atlantic Strategic Area. Though an "estimate" only, the reports represented a well-digested appreciation of the best available intelligence from every possible source.[56] Attacks on convoys, the first biweekly advised, were expected to continue in the Caribbean area, with an average of twelve boats active, particularly east of Trinidad. There one boat maintained a close patrol, reporting convoys outbound from Port of Spain harbor to an outer patrol, which then rendezvoused with the convoys, trailed them, and attacked upon dispersal. (This same tactic prevailed off Newfoundland east of St. Johns, in the North Atlantic: there boats sought initial sightings of eastbound convoys close in, so as to form up wolf-packs just beyond effective air coverage.) The Gulf and Eastern frontiers, meantime, held "little activity," save for the occasional boat passing to assess air and surface patrols or to lay mines. As well,

> AN INCREASED NUMBER OF SUBMARINES WILL SOON BE OPERATING ALONG BRAZILIAN COAST X SINCE THEIR OUTBOUND AND HOMEBOUND ROUTES CUT ACROSS SHIPS LANES FROM TRINIDAD TO FREETOWN AND CAPETOWN INCREASED SHIPPING LOSSES FROM INDEPENDENT SAILINGS MAY BE EXPECTED IN THESE AREAS.[57]

The next two weeks realized little change in Cominch's estimate of the situation:

> EXPECT THAT CONVOYS CARIBBEAN GUANTÁNAMO RUN WILL CONTINUE TO BE TRAILED REGULARLY SINCE HIGH PERCENTAGE OF STRAGGLERS ARE GETTING SUNK X SWEEPS ASTERN MAY PROVE FRUITFUL X LOOKOUT SUBMARINE AT TRINIDAD CONTINUES ACTIVE REPORTING ARRIVALS DEPARTURES AND ROUTES USED.[58]

[Opposite, top] The forward base at Amapa (Detachment 41-1), on the coastal plain of northeastern Brazil north of the "bulge." A string of coastal auxiliary facilities for ferrying and refueling stops were constructed to augment logistical support by the main LTA stations and, as well, to confer operational flexibility (Author)

[Opposite, bottom] The Naval Air Facility at São Luiz, in northeastern Brazil—headquarters for Airship Squadron Forty-One (ZP-41). (GHMC, NASM, Smithsonian Institution)

To help counter this threat, additional units of the airship organization of the U.S. Fleet were commissioned. Shore facilities for LTA authorized to operate from South America is outlined on page 179. First squadron to navigate Brazilian airspace did so when ZP-41 was commissioned on 15 June 1943, for transfer to, and operations in, the Fourth Fleet (Brazilian area).

Two weeks thereafter:

> INCREASED ACTIVITY ANTICIPATED CARIBBEAN AND BETWEEN TRINIDAD AND AMAZON. AT LEAST 3 U-BOATS EXPECTED TO CONTINUE ATTACKS ON INDEPENDENT SHIPPING OFF SOUTHERN BRAZIL WITH FOCAL POINT AT RIO DE JANEIRO. 33 U-BOATS NOW ESTIMATED WEST OF 26W. TOTAL OPERATING ATLANTIC 90.[59]

Fleet LTA operations commenced in September. Outfitted at Lakehurst, the ships had been air-delivered via intermediate mast facilities to bases on the Brazilian coast. (All material for these units was crated for shipment to their respective activities.) Permanent headquarters: at São Luiz, in northeastern Brazil. Organized under Fleet Airship Wing Four, a sister squadron, ZP-42, was commissioned on 1 September for transfer to its Maceió headquarters. Its operations were inaugurated in November 1943.

For sixteen months, U.S. forces had more survived the campaign than mastered it. May–June 1943 saw the tide turned from defensive to offensive ASW: in a strong performance, alert, better-equipped defenses had blunted wolf-pack tactics. For the first time in this sea battle, the escort held the initiative. Attacks on U-boats had gained—then sustained—a "gratifying level." In the Eastern Sea Frontier, U-boat activity subsided noticeably: a function of A/S measures ashore, afloat, aloft. Increasingly effective measures along the U.S. littoral, however, spurred a reappearance in the Caribbean as well as continued depredations in the South Atlantic.

> ANTICIPATE EARLY SHIFTS IN U-BOAT DISPOSITIONS FOLLOWING RECENT ALLIED SUCCESSES IN NORTH ATLANTIC A/S WARFARE AS ENEMY CANNOT AFFORD CURRENT U-BOAT LOSSES WITHOUT PROPORTIONATE SINKINGS OF MERCHANT SHIPS X U-BOAT WITHDRAWALS FROM NORTH ATLANTIC ALREADY APPARENT WITH PRESENT AVERAGE OF 40 U-BOATS IN THIS AREA AS COMPARED WITH TWICE THIS NUMBER EARLY MAY.[60]

That July, at least fifteen U-boats were operating off South America. "This was by several times the largest number ever to appear in this area in any previous month," the Fourth Fleet commander reported. Off Brazil, the focal areas of activity were Rio de Janeiro, the Amazon River north to the Guianas, and the shipping crossroads off the Brazilian "bulge." (Regularly scheduled convoys had been established between Trinidad and Bahia, south of the bulge, that January.) "The great increase in submarine activity off the South American coast was a result of the enemy shifting forces to West Atlantic and South Atlantic coastal shipping lanes to attack [unprotected] independently routed ships and less well protected convoys after having been forced to pay a heavier and heavier price for sinkings of United Nations ships in the North Atlantic convoy lanes."[61]

Dönitz's commanders in far-southern waters took U.S. *Luftschiffe* into account. The logbook for *U-193*, for example, holds this notation for 27 November 1943: "Coast of Cuba, Havana in

sight. A Zeppelin off starboard bow approaching at 400 metres height; it turns and has undoubtedly detected us but not seen us; it sends a recognition signal which we do not understand. We need our 3.7 gun very much right now. Radar decoy balloon (Aphrodite) is set up."[62]

Fleet Airship Wing Four and ZP-41 (Northern Coastal Brazil)

Headquartered at Recife, Fleet Airship Wing Four had two squadrons attached. Airship Squadron Forty-one (designated Fifty-two while in planning) was commissioned on 15 June 1943 for subsequent transfer to, and operation in, the Fourth Fleet. Commander, Fleet Airship Wing Thirty (Mills), read the commissioning directive during ceremonies at Lakehurst. Complement: twenty-three officers and twelve enlisted men. Mills directed a few remarks to Lt. Cdr. Daniel M. Entler, Jr., and staff. Mills emphasized the importance of the new fleet unit and assured the squadron skipper that every assistance would be rendered. ZP-41 and detachments would provide air coverage for more than 1,800 miles of geography from coastal bases at Amapa, Igarape Assu, São Luiz, and Fortaleza. Given the conditions to be met and problems to be solved, the ZP-41 command would surely prove "most interesting." Congratulating Entler, Mills wished him and his squadron good luck.[63]

The program would need it. Captain Zimmerman, commander of Fleet Airship Wing Four, visited his prospective bases that August. Forceful and quick to decision, Zimmerman held a good service reputation and was well liked by contemporaries occupying well-placed billets within the department. At Fortaleza, inspection found the site "complete in all respects."[64] Lonely Amapa, on the coastal flats of the Amapa district, in far-northern Brazil, was poorly laid out—quarters and buildings well away from the proposed mat. For flight ops as well as subsistence, soggy Amapa would prove a hardship. Igarape Assu was pronounced "all right," save that the circles and buildings were separated by nearly a mile. Moreover, the buildings were set in botanical mesh; the field could not be seen. Rather than incur delay, Zimmerman "compromised by arranging for the engineers to cut down the woods between the buildings and the field and mooring circles to permit the squadron commander to see what is going on." The main base at São Luiz, was what "it should be and could have been in every one, particularly in view of the fact that we started from scratch in each case." Meanwhile, operations now depended "entirely" on receipt of mooring masts, equipment, personnel. Deficiencies ensued—supplies, tools and spares, masts. The transport system struggled. Early commencement of operations had been ordered, with one ship at each Brazilian base on an expeditionary basis. Vital, therefore: mobile mooring masts. Zimmerman knew that ground handling was as important as mission flying. "We have been following your dispatches with regard to shipment of material from [Supply Depot] Bayonne [New Jersey]," Zimmerman wrote the commodore. "It is extremely disappointing to us that operations could not begin sooner and that there will be this delay because of failure to ship the masts." (Shipping had been diverted for Torch, the invasion of North Africa.) Further, HTA was easing into facilities intended for LTA. "We are anxious," he concluded, "to begin our operating and justify the expenditures, funds, thought and planning, and hope our material will get to us without interruption from now on."[65]

Authorized strength for ZP-41: six ZNP-Ks. *K-84* was first to sortie for South America. In anticipation of lowered lift from high temperatures plus decline in helium purity, excess gear had been removed prior to liftoff on 10 September.[66] The flight to Fortaleza marked the beginning of operations in Brazil. For this, the longest ferry to date, "King-84" transited NAS Glynco and Richmond, thence Guantánamo and San Juan en route Trinidad. Paramaribo was the pilots' next touchdown. Amapa marked penetration of Brazilian airspace—and of the equator; the first by a nonrigid. Igarape-Assu then São Luiz were astern before "84" settled to waiting handlers at Fortaleza, where temporary headquarters were established—the base nearest to completion. Passage had been uneventful until Fernando de Noronha. The island (a rugged shaft of bedrock) is a hazard to night-fog flying. Coordinates established, *K-84* "hove to" on one engine awaiting daylight.

Ferry distance: 4,430 nautical miles through four countries. Actual flight time: ninety-eight hours. *K-84* logged the unit's first ASW patrol of the South Atlantic the next morning, on 28 September, "returning to base in the late afternoon. Flight crews then changed and the airship took off again, late in the evening, for her first night patrol. It was a vigorous beginning."[67]

Two ships more departed promptly for Brazilian airspace. ZNP *K-88* had Fortaleza below on 11 October. ZNP *K-90* put Lakehurst astern on 29 September, arriving over Igarape Assu on 13 October.[68]

ZP-42 (Southern Coastal Brazil)

ZP-42 was commissioned at Lakehurst on 1 September for further transfer to, and operations in, the Fourth Fleet. Skipper: Cdr. Charles L. Werts, USN. The action enlarged to ten the number of squadrons attached to Fleet Airships Atlantic. Squadron Forty-one was assigned the inshore waters of the South Atlantic off northeast Brazil; the operational area for Forty-two arced south from the bulge fully to Rio de Janeiro. A string of detachment sites supported Forty-two: Ipitanga Field (Det 42-4), near the city of São Salvador; at Caravelas (Det 42-5), a mast site midway between Recife and Rio; and at Vitoria (Det 42-7), a refueling site. Outside of Rio, the naval air facility (NAF) at Santa Cruz (Det 42-6) completed the chain. There the Brazilian government had erected a facility to support the South Atlantic crossings of *Graf Zeppelin* and *Hindenburg*—that continent's only hangar. When the Americans arrived, elements of the Brazilian air force were in occupation.

ZP-42 was slated to receive the new "Mike" ships until it had reached authorized strength: "The Ms have been designed for tropical service and will be assigned to South American squadrons as soon as possible. Unfortunately, the first M-ship for the use of any squadron will not be available until November at the earliest."[69]

BuAer's original program for the "Mikes" grew to twenty-two airships, though production was cut later to four. Unsuitable for fleet work due to serious deficiencies plus minor (but annoying) defects, *M-2, M-3,* and *M-4* were consigned to training and indoctrination. Corrective action granted the M-model operational status in 1944, after which it conducted combat patrols and special missions. Still, no ZNP-M ever operated outside the continental limits of the United States. In mid-September 1943, the LTA organization of the Atlantic Fleet extended from Maine to Rio: "Fourth Fleet air arm was powerfully reinforced by lighter-than-air in the fall and winter of 1943–44 [Morison wrote]. Fleet Airship Wings Four and Five were commissioned, with bases at Maceió and Trinidad; and in September the blimps began to arrive . . . and by 1 January 1944 blimps were operating south of Rio [ZP-42]. . . . These were the first advanced operations conducted by lighter-than-air in World War II."[70]

[Top] Located south of the "bulge" of coastal Brazil, Ipitanga (Bahia) was a forward base for Detachment 42-4—one of seven detachments supporting ZP-42 headquarters, at Maceió. Note the HTA runway in the foreground. (Lt. H. F. Smith, USNR [Ret])

[Bottom] Main overhaul base at Santa Cruz, Brazil. The hangar had been erected for *Graf Zeppelin* and *Hindenburg*; improvements installed ("We built the base around the hangar"), the facility was taken over by a detachment of ZP-42. Anti-submarine operations in the Caribbean commenced in February 1943, in the South Atlantic from Brazilian bases that September. (U.S. Navy photograph, courtesy Capt. F. N. Klein, USN [Ret.])

[Opposite] A K-ship on landing approach, NAS Guantánamo, Cuba—site of a detachment supporting Airship Squadron Twenty-One (ZP-21), headquartered at NAS Richmond, Florida. (Author)

Familiarization flights acquainted officers with the topography and coastlines (and confidential publications) of their new operating areas. Forty-one and Forty-two and their detachments (save for Amapa and Fernando do Noronha) had identical operational setups. ZNP missions in most cases were either convoy escort or special sweeps. Daily patrols—routine in continental squadrons—were not undertaken. If LTA was the only naval aviation activity, escort missions were drawn up by the detachment's O-in-C at the relevant base. (HTA worked out of certain bases.) Escort missions were prepared based on position reports of shipping movements approaching a detachment's assigned area; when a convoy crossed its "chop line," a ZNP from that detachment immediately took up coverage. "When there is no convoy within the detachment's area, and when no instructions have been received to make special sweeps, the detachment utilizes the available time for training flights."[71]

Caribbean and South Atlantic operations sustained three losses and major casualties during 1943. (At least nine incidents would mar the following year.) An unexplained casualty off Puerto Rico killed a full flight crew when, in October 1943, *K-94* (ZP-51), on a ferry flight from Guantánamo to NAS San Juan, took fire in midair the night of the 30th—and self-destructed in sight of surface craft. "Suddenly, a small flaming object was seen to drop from the *K-94*. Then the blimp became illuminated in a bright glow, yellowish orange or red. The airship fell toward the water, a large burst of flame enshrouding it as it neared or struck the surface. The flames died out, and black smoke followed."[72]

Arriving on scene, vessels found bits of wreckage but no aircraft, no survivors, no bodies. Enemy action was possible, though a fire-related cause is more likely. It behooved flight personnel to exercise extreme care to eliminate that particular danger—securing electronic gear when shifting fuel, for example.[73]

Fleet Airship Wing Four conducted flight operations to spring 1945: ZP-41 concluded its flying at the end of European hostilities, on 15 May 1945; ZP-42 and its wing that April. (See chapter 7.)

Operating in Forward Areas

Forward deployed, antisubmarine aviation was to be ready for defensive/offensive sea control at all times. Still, various hassles afflicted both maintenance and flight personnel. Communications and the transport pipeline proved especially vexing. Distance from major and supporting supply points spawned shortages, among these tools, spark plugs, and the specialized fittings and attachments peculiar to LTA. Result: eroded operational proficiency and readiness.[74] As well, "getting the word" throughout a squadron could be difficult thanks to isolation, night flights, and the attendant difficulties of getting scattered pilots together.

Supply inefficiencies confounded unit commanders—officers-in-charge as well as squadron COs. Patrol ships were *sensor* platforms. The radar, for one, was complex by its very nature—hundreds of parts, many of which (e.g., tubes and resistors) might have a life of less than a hundred hours. Keeping critical equipment operational required an inventory of replacement parts. As for the MAD equipment, the conventional head-assembly required conversion for use in the vicinity of the magnetic equator, where the dip angle is comparatively small. Field-related frustrations fed laments up the chain of command. "Troubles consist mainly of those attributable to lack of equipment," ZP-41 reported. "It is unfortunate that an airship base becomes ineffective for several days because some part has to travel 2500 miles to reach us. Some sort of centralized pool of equipment would cut the time lost down considerably."

[Opposite]
A ZNP lifts clear at NAF Santa Cruz, Brazil—home for Detachment 42-6. (Capt. F. N. Klein, USN [Ret.])

Shortfalls bred annoyances. The Mark 15, for example—a water-fillable practice bomb. It became so scarce that ZP-42 investigated having molds made for concrete miniatures. (Sand-filled beer-bottle empties substituted.) Ordnance held more serious. The Mark 44 or Mark 47 depth charges (and their respective fuses) were carried on all operational missions. Nonetheless, "we have found [ZP-51 reported] that two Mark 47s cannot be carried in the bomb bay. One Mark 44 and one Mark 47 can be squeezed in due to the fuses being somewhat offset. When the supply of Mark 44 depth charges here has been exhausted, there can be no alternative but to carry two (2) Mark 47s on the outside racks and one (1) in the bomb bay."[75]

Conditions for construction had proven "simply awful" at advance bases, Rosendahl was to record. "The situation demanded great ingenuity, skill and great guts on the part of the construction engineers." Now they harassed operations: high humidity, steam-bath heat, thunderstorms, wind, gustiness, downpours. Rainfall was truly tropical—fourteen inches in one week at Amapia.[76] The heat expanded helium: on the mat, valving might be needed simply to remain masted. So streams of water were played over the ships in order to conserve the precious gas. (Cylinders exposed to the pounding sun also benefited from cooling spray.) "The hot temperatures and the humidity were no help," one airman summarized. Under way, envelope fullness kept working ceilings close to the water. On night missions, landings took place before the sun got high: superheat added unwanted lift. Ground crews had orders to hustle.

Local fuel supplies hosted contaminants, due in part to accelerated corrosion: scale, foreign matter, water. Drum-storage of leaded gasoline oxidized the drums; this iron oxide residue was inimical to aircraft fuel systems. Smoke from jungle fires cut visibility. Mosquitoes, scorpions—uncounted insects infested the coastal swamps and jungles. Tropical diseases threatened, especially malaria. ("It can attack without notice and may be more serious and devastating than bullets.") The lush, rotting green hosted vampire bats. Units operating in Central and South America reported serious problems with snakes.

Billeted in temporary wooden buildings in frontier conditions, knowing isolation, discomfort and empty patrols, duty hard by the equator held its satisfactions: the exotic new worlds of the tropics, gaudy sunrises, the "violently beautiful and terrifying jungle." Liberty excursions were understandably popular, to Rio especially. USO shows conferred distractions. At Fortaleza, field staff purchased horses, saddles, and bridles, "complete with corral and stable boys." The waters enclosing Ferando de Noronha abounded with barracuda, red snapper, tuna. As with all organizations, at any outpost, individuals make things happen. Caravales was a "real jungle area; we were away from everything. And there's one man that kept the whole thing together. He was a baker. . . . Every evening, after our movie (which we'd seen about twenty times) why, we had some mighty good cookies and sweet rolls. This guy kept the morale going, just that one guy. The baker did it."[77]

[Top] A K-ship assigned to Detachment 42-4 from the flight deck of a sister ship off Bahia, Brazil. (Lt. H. F. Smith, USNR [Ret.])

[Bottom] Lt. Robert S. Morton, USNR, at the rudder wheel of ZNP *K-116* or *117* somewhere above the South Atlantic. (Lt. H. F. Smith, USNR [Ret.])

The first amphibious salvage operation for LTA, August 1944. Out of fuel, ZNP *K-68* made an emergency night landing on an island off Venezuela. Next morning, the envelope was "ripped" to save the car. Shunted to the beach by jeep, it is being held upright as men work two skiffs into position to float it to a waiting net tender. Car, fins, and vital parts salvaged, the ship was re-erected and returned to service. (U.S. Naval Institute)

Operational satisfactions compensated. The combat air crew of *K-68* (ZP-51), for instance, savored surprising a convoy SOPA (senior officer present afloat) when, emerging from the overcast, the ZNP dutifully took up station. None of the ships arrayed below had had any notion that blimps were operating so far from U.S. waters.[78]

Emergencies bred operational losses, with some crash sites defying access: no roads, trail, or river.

A forced landing by ZNP *K-68* on 6 August 1943 realized the first amphibious salvage for lighter-than-air. Exceeding its prudent limit of endurance, the pilot made an emergency night landing onto an island off (neutral) Venezuela.[79] Undamaged, *K-68* was lashed down, base informed. Next day, an army plane dispatched to refuel the ZNP did not find it—the island had been misidentified. Meanwhile, unable to counteract a fresh morning breeze and fearful confidential gear would be carried away, the bag was ordered ripped. *K-68* settled on its port side. Equipment, personnel and transportation organized, a salvage crew (two officers, fourteen enlisted men, and a jeep) took six days to move the derelict out. The best route to shore, a mile distant, had been surveyed by a sister ZNP, which then helped sustain the party. Parts grouped pending shuttle, the jeep shunted everything to the beach.[80] The most delicate maneuver: floating the car through surf to a waiting net tender.

K-68 was re-erected following major overhaul and returned to active duty.

An engines-out in 1944 put *K-90* into trees on Fernando de Noronha, a remote rock three hundred miles off Brazil. (The island hosted a tiny detachment, for emergency refueling. When a U-boat approached, Maceió was ordered to dispatch a ZNP and prescribe the mission—

usually a barrier patrol.) Using trails slashed to the wreck, a salvage crew worked 4 ½ days in dense jungle. Though major assemblies such as engines were not retrievable, native carriers brought out all removable parts to an inlet from whence these reached the mainland via sailboat and dug-out canoe.

Heat and humidity attack electronics. One mischief: erratic MAD operation. "Our forward special equipment has proved most unsatisfactory so far. The set will not orient or balance. The Hedron people here have done all they know how to do, but without instruction books or drawings, they are at a loss as to what to do next. If there is any instruction material available on this gear it would be greatly appreciated here."[81] Experts were dispatched.

Stick or expeditionary masts (single shafts anchored by guy wires) were widely used beyond the continental limits, particularly at advance bases in Brazil. When used exclusively, it was essential to exploit weather lulls (before sunrise and the sunset period) for masting and unmasting. *Mobile* masts, in contrast, added to ground-handling safety. Still, the stick-type was easy to erect and required little room. The penalty for operating without hangar protection: all maintenance, repair work, and inspections had to be conducted in the open as the ships swung, bounced, and kited about the mast.

As with all complicated machines, ZNPs required increasing maintenance the longer their service. Upkeep called for periodic inspections. Ideally, flight and maintenance planning were coordinated; often, though, this proved impracticable—or was simply not done. For mast-based ships, as much as possible was done at the circle.[82] *How much* could be done in the open? Routine inspections, maintenance, and repairs were thought to be impractical. Further, with no hangar protection, the loading of bombs proved onerous given their weight combined with the motion of the ship. (*K-125* from ZP-42, caught in an extreme wind shift, kited to an estimated angle of eighty degrees.) Rather than sacrificing routine maintenance to operations, it was realized that more operational time was lost trying to make up for lack of upkeep than was gained by prompt correction of minor discrepancies.

Nearly everything rots in heat and humidity. Envelopes deteriorated. Topside, especially, the aluminum paint became dry or powdery or the fabric itself cracked. Though gradual, the process was unrelenting. Mildew caused oxidation of rubber and coatings: "It is realized that operating conditions will often preclude a topside inspection during the 120-hour check, but such an inspection should be conducted if at all possible, and in any case during each interim overhaul."[83]

Using ladders, hedron riggers checked for deteriorated fabric as well as thin-wearing paint, blistering seam-tapes, tears, snags, holes. The aluminized finish broke down quite rapidly, exposing the underlying fabric. Officers and riggers at one detachment concluded that one year of operation in the tropics represented an envelope's maximum.

Control surfaces, patches, and bracings were checked as well. Handling lines and brace cables (for the empennage, notably) were attached to the bag by finger patches; their size and number depended on load. South of North Carolina, the manila element degraded where the ropes entered the fingers. This was unknown—until an in-flight announced failure. On 11 October 1943, ZNP *K-66* (ZP-15) lost its topside fin while exercising with a tame submarine. One or more brace-wire patches had failed. Envelope holed, "King-66" fell off wind and

K-ship empennage. Note the brace cables for the horizontal fin. Unknown to southern-based squadrons, tropical heat and humidity had deteriorated the manila element of the "finger-patch" attachments for the cables. A fin failure in 1943 put *K-66* into the sea, prompting inspection of all similarly assigned ZNPs—and a hurried patch redesign. (GHMC, NASM, Smithsonian Institution)

circled, then went in. The ship was lost, its crew rescued. The consequent inspections and tests, a Goodyear rep remarked, prompted one of the largest conferences ever held in Akron.

All similar-duty ships were ordered to Richmond, for inspection. Findings proved worrisome. Accordingly, emergency rules mandated reduced max airspeed and allowable rudder throw. Meantime, a new design evolved—hurriedly. A fan-shaped patch of fabric strips replaced the rope beckets, the strips looped around metal D-rings. These were shipped to the operator as quickly as Goodyear could manufacture them.

> The inspection of the airship in service must be a periodic and routine affair, especially in the southern operating fields where climatic conditions have a very deteriorating effect on envelope fabric and outer protective coatings. For mast based ships, routine inspection presents somewhat of a problem; nevertheless, it is this field inspection that may be the deciding factor, as to the need for flying the ship to a hangar equipped base for an interim or major overhaul.[84]

Selected Operational Totals

Airships on line in July 1943: seventy-two—forty-four assigned to the Atlantic Fleet, thirteen the Pacific. Fifteen more were attached to shore commands. The Atlantic Fleet total would climb to fifty-seven blimps in January, then peak at seventy-seven in September 1944. At his Lakehurst headquarters—now a central element in a sprawling organization—Captain George H. Mills, ComFairShipsLant, assumed the rank of commodore on 17 November 1943. That same month, Mills was flown south (via R50), to inspect his LTA commands dotting coastal Brazil. "I have just returned from an inspection trip of our units in South America and I have seen K-ships carrying out missions and performing work which even the most enthusiastic LTA proponent could not have visualized a year ago."[5]

Fleet Airship, Atlantic operations for 1943 ended with fifty-three ships on line, distributed among ten fleet squadrons: Eleven, Twelve, Fourteen, Fifteen, Twenty-one, Twenty-two, Twenty-three, Forty-one, Forty-two, and Fifty-one. Number of hours flown that year: 136,459 during 12,331 flights—eight times the total logged during 1942.[86]

The year 1944 was to prove equally demanding for the LTA Administrative Command, Atlantic Fleet. From six aircraft in January 1942, total Fleet airship strength would peak at ninety-three that March—its Atlantic Fleet complement (seventy-one) operating from squadrons assigned to the eastern and gulf seaboards *and*, as well, in Central America, South America, Africa, and Europe. (See chapter 6.) The navy had deployed the largest lighter-than-air force ever.

Atlantic Fleet LTA—1942 through 1944—would log more than 32,000 flights totaling 337,000 hours, its ships deploying progressively improved electronic, navigational, ordnance, and communication equipment. The intensity of operations is evident in the figures for Squadron Twelve: 1,755 flights totaling 706,539 miles. Flight hours: 19,197, of which 15,898 were over water. An example of its other services: out of 279 fired, 272 practice torpedoes would be recovered.[87]

That February, meanwhile, operations in the Panamanian Sea Frontier commenced with the transfer of ZP-23 to Jamaica. (See page 217). And Richmond's ZP-21 established a detachment in Panama. Still, a decline in U-boat activity in the Caribbean reduced operations; when discontinuance of air coverage was authorized, Fleet Airship Wing Five (ZP-51) was decommissioned as an operating unit late that year—the first such action of the war.[88] Two wings more were to vanish officially in 1945.

More Problems

An acute personnel shortage was to persist. Then, hard on the expansion, cutbacks beset the program, as did requests of regular officers for sea duty—to qualify for promotion or, having given up on airships, out of concern for their service careers. (Officers holding the future of LTA above their personal careers were an ardent minority.) The unqualified are ineffective with the best equipment. Poorly qualified and indifferent personnel fed performances below expectations—as did the priorities, prejudices, and jealousies afflicting the Navy Department. Its contributions notwithstanding, LTA placed low on priority lists; procurement proved painfully slow. ZP-42 had a higher percentage of command pilots assigned than the average zipron: in 1944, its personnel roster held thirty-eight radiomen and mechanics with nineteen combat crews assigned.

> We have received advance orders for more combat crews and note the usual discrepancies as far as balance is concerned. We are short on radiomen and long on mechs, and yet crews continue to come through with three mechs. Several crews do not even fill ComFairShipsLant minimum ferry requirements and yet they are detailed to fly much longer and more difficult ferry hops than they would ever encounter in the United States. We have shifted some personnel about in an effort to balance our crews, but our pay accounts are in three different places, transportation is scarce and we feel that this matter should be taken care of before crews are ordered away from the continental limits.[89]

The initial lot of hedron personnel assigned to Wing Four (ZP-41 and ZP-42) had been intended to operate/service twelve ships at six bases, with an advance base at Fernando de Noronha plus Recife (headquarters) and Caravelas as refueling sites. April 1944 found the Wing operating sixteen ZNP-Ks from eight sites, having added Caravelas and Santa Cruz (overhaul base) plus one advance base more, at Vitoria. On 30 April 1944, foreign duty in the Brazilian theater comprised

Men	854 [90]
Operating Bases	8
Advance Bases	2
Refueling Bases	1

A directive issued at midyear had called for Rosendahl to visit all LTA facilities. Object: to ascertain what *reductions* in deployed strength were possible from each unit or, instead, to justify to high commands the increased use of airships in their respective operating areas.

A few weeks earlier, the Administrative Command (Mills) had written his wing and squadron commanders. One up on the future, "I am sure that we all realize that in the post-war times blimps must of necessity become utility type aircraft, and it is up to us to develop means and methods for such use of blimps."

> It is not our job to promote work for the blimps which will take them from their presently assigned operational duties; however, it is well for all of us to think of possible utility uses and to work out in our own minds the probable methods for these uses. The war in the Atlantic is still a long way from being won and we must continue to keep our minds set on training combat crews to be proficient in handling the presently assigned missions.[91]

On 10 June, he advised his commanders: "Admiral Rosendahl's visit should afford each of you a good opportunity to express your views on present uses of airships and to outline any proposed uses you may have for postwar times."[92]

Capt. Jules James, Commandant, Naval Operating Base and Naval Air Station Bermuda, a plain-speaker, was making himself "somewhat unpopular" in the department by vigorous reiteration of his needs. In October 1943, he opined as to the value of ZNPs as convoy escorts within his operational command:

Rear Admiral Rosendahl, Commodore Mills, and staff of the U.S. Navy's Air Transport Command, city of Belem, Brazil—a hundred miles up the Amazon, 14 July 1944. The LTA officers are on inspection tour of expeditionary sites. (GHMC, NASM, Smithsonian Institution)

> Non-rigid airships assigned to the Commandant Southern Group have provided, by far, the greater percentage of offshore coverage assigned to surface vessels in these waters. Without airships, missions at times would have been unescorted due to the inability of other craft to meet the necessary requirements of the mission. . . . Also they are considered an essential unit for air escort operations in an area such as the waters of the Sixth Naval District where they have proved advantageous over the shipping lanes up to 130 miles offshore and on routine patrols with extreme offshore units of 250 miles. . . . The Commander Southern Group is entirely satisfied with the performance of duty of non-rigid airships as assigned him, and hopes that his present number of ships (8) may soon be increased to the assigned complement of twelve.[93]

A rear admiral in late 1944, James became Commandant, Sixth Naval District.

Action Reports

Paperwork attends every flight operation. Incomplete record-keeping and the want of standardization had characterized the war's earliest months. In January 1943, a uniform system for grading attacks was approved; thereafter, assessments were decided by an Anti-Submarine Warfare

Capt. Walter Zimmerman, USN (Commander, Fleet Airship Wing Four), Adm. Jonas H. Ingram (Commander, Fourth Fleet), Admiral Rosendahl, and Commodore Mills about to depart Recife for the advance LTA base at Maceió, Brazil, 16 July 1944. An outstanding officer, "Heinz" Zimmerman served a tour of duty in South America that proved challenging: August 1943 to mid-June 1945. (GHMC, NASM, Smithsonian Institution)

Assessment Board established in headquarters, Tenth Fleet. Only compelling evidence—particularly photographs—could secure a "Probably Sunk" or "Probably Damaged" award from the evaluating authorities.

A special form, the ASW-6 (Report of Antisubmarine Action by Aircraft) was used when an attack with live bombs had been run on an estimated target. (A MAD or radar contact without subsequent action did not require the form.) Each attack was unique. So that every possible lesson could be extracted from each incident, full and accurate reports were vital. Pilots therefore were to return with a clear play-by-play filed, preferably, within twenty-four hours. Still, incomplete, contradictory, and inconclusive "action forms" proved chronic. Outcome: insufficient evidence to assess attacks. Nearly two thirds of all LTA *attacks* for the period 7 December 1941 to late August 1943—twenty-one months of operations—indeed lacked evidence even of the enemy's *presence*. And nearly half of all *contacts* (sightings, radar, MAD) had been assigned a "Doubtful" rating.[94] Mills and his staff and commanders could only speculate as to the number of negative assessments due to hurried, sketchy records and, after 1942, poorly prepared action reports—or none at all. One skipper instituted a training exercise to cut these "snafus." "Information received from reliable sources," warned Lt. Cdr. John Nahigian, USNR, "indicates that increased submarine activity may be expected in areas under the jurisdiction of this [ZP-51] command." Accurate, clear, and timely reports were therefore ordered:

> It is recognized that, during an attack, it is not the easiest thing for the pilot and other responsible parties to make . . . accurate notations. Each attack, however, will have certain peculiarities about it, and, though it is much to ask, a pilot must return with a play-by-play description.

Admiral Rosendahl and his party inspect Squadron Forty-two at Maceió. Fleet Airship Wing Four (ZP-41 and ZP-42) were headquartered at Maceió, on the "bulge" of central Brazil. (Cdr. R. W. Widdicombe, USN [Ret.])

Much has been accomplished through these ASW-6 reports, and not a little of our highly developed intelligence as to the tactics, habits and developments of the Axis submarine stems from them [statistical analysis of operational reports by ASWORG]. But, to repeat, the form must be filed promptly so it may be correlated with other significant material.

LTA has comparatively few opportunities to attack. When such an attack has been made, it would be indeed unhappy were a negative evaluation to result because of an inadequate report. LTA is not alone interested in the kudos of such an attack; a poor report inevitably reflects on the efficiency and value of the entire organization.[95]

Airship Utility Squadron One (ZJ-1)

Developed as an antisubmarine weapon, blimps presented a versatile platform for utility work, particularly torpedo "chasing" as well as aerial observation and photography, RDF calibration flights, and incidental services. Utility missions by LTA were receiving emphasis—insurance against the close of the Atlantic campaign. In April 1944 already, a reduction plan for airships of the U.S. Atlantic fleet stood prepared.

During 1943 alone, blimps in fifty incidents had located downed aircraft, disabled vessels, drifting survivors. Not all rescues were at sea. On 2 July 1944, in extreme heat, ZNP *K-95* (ZP-31) effected a controlled crash-landing into the California desert; despite damage, an ingenious takeoff plucked three exhausted airmen to safety. The evacuation brought the Distinguished Flying Cross to Lt. Peter I. Culbertson—the first ever awarded a lighter-than-air pilot for rescue work. (In May, Culbertson had earned the Air Medal for the rescue of a Marine Corp flier from a life raft off Santa Barbara.) As well, two officers and five enlisted men of his July combat crew received commendations from Adm. Chester W. Nimitz, CincPac, at ceremonies at NAS Santa Ana.[96] That October, off New Jersey, the navy conducted a demonstration on how it rescued men forced down at sea. Following a hangar exhibit at Lakehurst of air-sea rescue gear and parachutes, the Assistant Secretary of the Navy for Air, Adm. DeWitt Ramsey, Chief BuAer, Adm. Rosendahl along with various officers, manufacturers, and the press were shunted to the Coast Guard Station at Manasquan, thence offshore: "The demonstration was conducted at a point two miles off shore from Manasquan Inlet. The military and civilian guests watched parachute jumps, the dropping of various types of life rafts and rescue gear, and a dramatic pick-up from the sea by a Navy airship."[97]

Commander in Chief, Atlantic Fleet, was directed to form and commission Airship Utility Squadron One (ZJ-1) on or about 1 February 1944. Commissioned on the 10th at Lakehurst, ZJ-1 thus relieved Fleet squadrons of utility assignments. "The functions of the utility squadron, really, were concentrated *at that point* in supporting [observer] services to the torpedo test station up in Newport, Rhode Island," using an advance base established on Fisher Island in Long Island Sound. The function: to stay with fired torpedoes until the weapon, spent, was recovered by surface craft.[98]

Assets assigned: two K-ships and six G-types. The ZNN-G was deemed superior for hovering and handling characteristics; as well, aircrews were fewer and the car offered more ports for still and motion cameras.[99] Squadron headquarters: Meacham Field, Key West. The unit operated under the Commander, Fleet Airships Atlantic—Commodore Mills.

Atlantic Fleet lighter-than-air forces in support of the U.S. Fourth Fleet, 1944–45. Headquarters: Recife, Brazil.

In March, a detachment (Det1) was established at South Weymouth. It would render general utility services—especially torpedo recovery—for fleet and shore units from subordinate detachments in New York, Maryland, and Virginia. Attracting escalating attention, the number and variety of utility requests soared—from individual unit commanders and from bureaus of the Navy Department. Within months, ZJ-1 was receiving more requests than it could accommodate. Missions: aerial photography; ship camouflage and submarine operations; observation of torpedo track and impulse bubbles; shell bursts and underwater explosions; and various incidental one-day services. Scientists or technicians aboard, Detachment One aided scientific experiments (one for the Rad Lab). As well, the unit was called upon to make radar and RDF calibration flights for surface craft and shore stations.[100] "All of these requests no doubt reach favorably to the lighter-than-air situation and I am glad to see our being asked by outside units. Some day the Navy Department is going to realize that blimps have a great value both as fleet operational units and as utility craft."[101]

Assignments ballooned on the West Coast as well, ensuring cooperative utility services during the Pacific war's closing months *and* following Japan's surrender. Almost all available airships were continuously operational for sonobuoy training, the training of radar operators, or for air/sea rescue work at the scene of crashes. Sold on LTA, the Commander Fleet Air, West Coast (for one) recommended continued deployment: "Should blimps continue to operate in this area during the post-war period, it is desired that their services be made available to fleet aviation units. At the present time [August 1945] the services of two (2) to four (4) blimps are employed on training missions with this command."[102]

ZJ-1 compiled 4,502 hours (989 flights) in 1944: torpedo-recovery hours (69 percent of all missions), photographic missions, calibration, training, ferry, and other flights. At Guantánamo, one blimp assisted the join-up of convoys and delivery of sailing instructions to merchant vessels not entering the bay. The year 1945 added 2,495 hours. Grand total to decommissioning, on 15 May 1945: 1,547 sorties, totaling nearly 7,000 hours in the air—time saved from fleet units relieved of utility obligations. Seventy percent of flight time had been devoted to the recovery of exhausted torpedoes.

The scope of utility services—search-and-rescue, photographic and other surveys, fleet training missions—promised fertile fields for postwar employment of airships. Or so it seemed.

Airship Anti-Submarine Training Detachment (BlimpASTraLant)

Accidents imply a want of training and practice. As well, wartime deficiencies in technical knowledge persisted. What tactics, for example, might extract maximum performance from ZNP-installed equipment and sensors? What *were* its particular capabilities—and operational limitations? Only intensive training could tease out answers and hone proficiencies, enabling aircrews to act immediately, instinctively, correctly.

Not every man shared a dedication to LTA. In ZP-41, for instance, indifferent personnel vexed Detachment One (Amapa). Lt. R. A. Powers, USNR, resented receipt of flight crews whose caliber he deemed wanting:

TABLE 5.1 **Airship organization of the United States Fleet,** effective 1 February 1944. (National Archives)[1]

Fleet Airships, Atlantic			
Commander, Fleet Airships, Atlantic			
Airship Utility Squadron 1 (ZJ-1) – 2 ZNP, 6 ZNJ[1]			
Fleet Airship Wing 1	Fleet Airship Wing 2	Fleet Airship Wing 4	Fleet Airship Wing 5
Blimp Hedron 1	Blimp Hedron 2	Blimp Hedron 4	Blimp Hedron 5
ZP-11 – 8 ZNP	ZP-21 – 12 ZNP	ZP-41 – 8 ZNP	ZP-51 – 9 ZNP
ZP-12 – 8 ZNP	ZP-22 – 4 ZNP	ZP-42 – 8 ZNP	
ZP-14 – 8 ZNP	ZP-23 – 4 ZNP		
ZP-15 – 8 ZNP	ZP-24 – 4 ZNP		

Fleet Airships, Pacific
Commander, Fleet Airships, Pacific
Fleet Airship Wing 3
Blimp Hedron 3
ZP-31 – 8 ZNP
ZP-32 – 8 ZNP
ZP-33 – 8 ZNP

1 When commissioned.

> We are sent crews of this nature to do credit to Lighter-than-Air in its farthest and most active front. Here much more is expected of a Combat-Air-Crew than mere piling up of 18 hours flight time each day. Cooperation with heavier-than-air and every other unit of the Fourth Fleet is a primary requisite to the safety of all concerned. We must have first class personnel to do a first class job. We can train them ourselves—but that takes time and the job has to be done now. Furthermore we do not have the facilities or the time for an extensive training program.[103]

Training exercises for men holding orders to "duty involving flying" attended all fleet squadrons. Inevitably, violations of flight rules, an inability to conform to military standards, fatigue, and other factors realized suspensions from flight orders.

> Speaking of training [Bradley wrote Mills], our squadrons are not getting enough but are progressing. What with interim overhauls and helium purifications, squadrons 22 and 23 generally have only two (2) ships each with as many missions. In reporting ships available to Commander Gulf Sea Frontier, these squadrons frequently report all available but request one for training in assigned patrol area. In Blimp Squadron Twenty One it is a bit different. All the expeditionary ships, at present four (4), get nothing but operations. Ferry flights to and from these expeditionary bases also tie up ships. Here at Richmond, Florida we generally get 5 or 6 operational flights daily, about half at night. Generally though there is at least one ship, sometimes two available for training.[104]

A reemphasis on training and doctrine had improved the quality of attacks by Atlantic Fleet forces. Inside lighter-than-air, save for senior flight officers, service experience was wanting. Rushed through the course, young pilots and enlisted men were learning seagoing duties as they flew. "We didn't know what we were doing as well as we should have. It was not deliberate ignorance—it was a lack of preparation."[105]

When, in October 1943, Commander Fleet Airships Atlantic was directed to establish under his command "a program of A/S experiment, development and training," an ASW school was slated for Key West. Along with congenial weather, fleet submarines were berthed there, with a Fleet Sound School nearby. As well, the Florida platform is geologically quiet relative to Quonset–Long Island Sound for working out tactical problems of magnetic detection.

That December, Airship AntiSubmarine Training Detachment, Atlantic Fleet (BlimpASTraLant) was established at Meacham Field.

Tame, or target, submarines were essential to provide practical training. ZP-11 exercised with New London–based units in the sanctuaries off Block Island and Long Island. These drills had combat crews observe their quarry under operating conditions. At Key West, on orders, one submarine (an R boat) was to be "always available" to local air commands. But target-sub time proved elusive. "*Rarely* during the war could you get a tame submarine—submarines were too busy fighten' the war to be playing around. But we needed 'em *badly*. They needed some old training submarines—lots of training submarines, but we didn't *have* 'em."[106]

Key West required a senior O-in-C, plus a strong force of instructors. A shake-up ensued. Why? Given very tight allowances, the squadrons could spare few officers. Lt. Cdr. M. H. Eppes, USN, was selected. Reporting directly to Rosendahl, at Lakehurst, Eppes was transferred to Richmond to set up logistic support for the new detachment. Henry Eppes had qualified as a naval aviator (airship) as part of LTA Class XI (1937–38). Following a tour of sea duty, he had served with Airship Patrol Group Three and, in July 1943, had reported for duty as Commanding Officer, ZP-23.

Captain T. G. W. Settle had assumed command of Fleet Airships Pacific and Fleet Airship Wing Three en route to a distinguished surface command. "Tex" had long advocated advanced LTA training, noting "a deplorable state of peacetime softness and lack of a proper fundamental Navy viewpoint and discipline." (Mills concurred.) Pressing for taut squadrons, Settle put his concerns before wing, group, and squadron commanders.[107]

The expansion had had to rely on "very green personnel." Compounding matters, material deficiencies remained in the ships. And various operational and tactical problems had yet to be solved. The entire burden of these necessary developments fell upon the Administrative Command—Mills plus a handful of senior ranking officers. "In addition to the great value of the actual training at Key West, I think the school will turn out to be most valuable as a meeting place of combat crews from all over the LTA organization, affording a clearing house for exchange of ideas, operating technique, etc. I think that the West Coast squadrons have much to throw into such a pool, as well as much to learn from other units."[108]

The inaugural group reported to Key West in January 1944. (Aircrews dispatched to "Mecham Tech" trained as a unit.) The launch had proved slow—instructors, library, space, equipment, ships, tame submarines.[110] Instead of three or four airships assigned, the command realized two: ZNPs *K-120* and *-122*. Meantime, it flew one. With limited targets made available for practice, the school could accommodate but two combat air crews per week. "About the end of the month we expect to assign another airship to the school, however, the providing of submarines and other aircraft targets in the Key West area is very undecided. . . . At present we are using one submarine between HTA and LTA and in addition are working with some of the submarines engaged in Sound School practices."[110]

That March, the school enjoyed the use of a target boat *one hour* per day ("Naturally, we are not getting much out of the submarine training"), with one boat in prospect mostly for LTA work.

How best to organize the fleet school? What definite policies and doctrines to indoctrinate? Modern electronic ASW was emphasized as it pertained to LTA operations and sensors for searching, tracking, destroying. The principles of MAD and its tactical use exploiting sonobuoys were basic to the curriculum, along with radar, navigation, search and patrol routine, survival, and related topics. The "attack training" was intensive, Gerry Wheeler (ZP-12) recalled. "They wanted us to learn how to handle MAD more effectively"—that is, flying low, so as to *track* a sighting (visual or radar) when the boat had gone under. "After you've flown a blimp for a few hours at fifty feet above the water—a [K-type] blimp is 250 feet long—it gets to be a little weary. But that's what we did down there."[111]

> The course of a/s instruction is two weeks in length, and each class consists of combat air crews from various squadrons. Lectures are given on U-boat characteristics bombs, MAD and its use, photography, bombing technique, search and patrol, convoy escort, developments in a/s/w, blimps in a/s/w, radar identification, and the like. Classes are given flights to practice MAD and radar tactics, bombing, and .50 caliber strafing. In addition, personnel attending classes are given cruises aboard either submarine or surface craft. Commander Fleet Air Wing Five coordinates the activities of BlimpASTraLant with those of other Air Force, Atlantic training units in the Key West area.[112]

Constructed by the Airborne Instruments Lab, the school's "magnetic attack trainer" was a Rosendahl initiative. In fall 1943, the Training Command had written NDRC requesting the device. Similar to one at Mineola, the trainer had been adapted to ZNP characteristics.[113] All officers worked it; radiomen also got time on the trainer. A civilian technician from AIL supported it technically for lectures, advice, repairs.

Instruction went to three weeks late in 1944. New courses were added, including a special one-week course set up for all squadron commanding and executive officers. "The course has been considerably altered. Much of the material in the course which was repetitious . . . has been summarized briefly for review purposes, and considerable new material added. It is our aim that the courses will represent the latest developments in Airship Anti-Submarine Warfare, together with significant advances in airship operations."[114]

Early in 1945, a lecture on air/sea/jungle rescue was added; this included a flight to learn the special gear required. As well, the school produced training films; the first concerned the "special equipment" adapted to ZNPs.

Unquestionably useful as it was, the detachment at Key West achieved less than it might have. For LTA it was already nearly too late. "After we formed these training units—the tactical training units—we began to get something down on paper, began to act like we knew what we were doing," Klein continued. "But the war was essentially over by that time."[115]

As well, its objectives were undercut by a second-tier priority assigned LTA, by unaspiring students, and by war-sponsored shortages. For example, sonobuoys and the Mark V float light/flare were vital to checking out crews on tactics. Each was powered by two types of batteries, eight in all; these required replacement about every second use, and securing spares proved onerous.

> Our experience [Eppes wrote Mills] with sono-buoys to date has not been very conclusive, either as to whether they are the answer to all our prayers as a submarine detector or whether they are over-rated for that job. One reason . . . has been the absolute necessity of conserving the sono-buoys. This has become so critical that I think we have been prone to emphasize this conservation angle at the expense of actually giving the crews any real experience in the proper use of these devices.[116]

Among those holding temporary-duty orders to Key West, Eppes added, certain officers had failed to exercise initiative. Mills's response is illustrative: he insisted on "quick and drastic action" for every arriving officer who failed to act responsibly. "All senior officers" in each fleet unit, the commodore scolded, "can help in this matter by constant attention to the proper training of young officers. It is our job and all must help if the proper morale is to be obtained and maintained in the airship organization."[117]

Squadrons had orders to form combat aircrews consisting of four pilots (three, if a fourth was not available) and six enlisted men. In selecting Key West–trained personnel for South America, Mills specified crews with one hundred combat hours and that had trained together as a unit. "I hope that this will produce a good flying team for the squadrons which are operating under very primitive conditions in South America."[118]

ZP-23, Republic of Panama

The enemy was throwing considerable strength against North Atlantic convoys. In adjoining operating areas that winter of 1943–44:

> THREE MERCHANT SHIPS HAVE BEEN SUNK IN US SEA FRONTIERS DURING DECEMBER BY THREE U-BOATS OPERATING NORTH OF HATTERAS, IN GULF OF MEXICO, AND OFF PANAMA RESPECTIVELY. THE LATTER, WHICH PROBABLY ALSO ACCOUNTED FOR FOUR MERCHANT SHIPS IN THE PANAMA AREA DURING NOVEMBER, IS NOW ESTIMATED HOMEBOUND AFTER THE MOST AGGRESSIVE CRUISE OFF OUR COASTS IN RECENT MONTHS. A FOURTH U-BOAT UNLOCATED IN THE WESTERN CARIBBEAN IS LIKELY TO MOVE INTO THE PANAMA SEA FRONTIER.[119]

Talk circulated of forming a zipron to operate from Panama, to help blunt an aggressive enemy prowling the western Caribbean. "It seems to me," Mills wrote, "that it would be a good idea to send a squadron down that is already formed and has been operating together." ZP-23 had been commissioned on 1 June 1943 at Lakehurst for transfer to NAS Hitchcock, Texas, where it operated within the Gulf Sea Frontier. In February 1944, orders arrived for transfer to Vernam Field, Jamaica, for operations in the Pacific Sea Frontier. Geography had ZP-23 operating in *two* sea frontiers: the only LTA unit based in one sea frontier but operating wholly in another. Its ships did not give coverage to convoys within the Caribbean Sea Frontier; instead, Vernam-based ships were obliged to fly at least a hundred miles to their operational sector, to pick up missions for the command in Panama.

The squadron had logged 628 flights out of Hitchcock, totaling almost seven thousand hours—62 percent devoted to patrol. Also, 759 ships had received escort. Concluding three weeks of no flying, its first overseas ZNP touched down at a new operational headquarters in March.

The Panamanian sector (an important defensive area) represented a sensitive command. "In sending a squadron to Panama," Mills reflected, "I think it is absolutely essential that a man of considerable tact and ability to get along with HTA, Navy and Army be the squadron commander."[120] The commodore selected Lt. Cdr. James H. Cruse, USN, then on the staff of Commandant, NOB Trinidad.

ZP-24 was commissioned at Hitchcock on 9 February 1944; it operated in the Gulf Sea Frontier into May, filling empty bunks left by ZP-23 when it decamped for Jamaica. On the 23rd, Twenty-four established a detachment, then headquarters, at NAS Weeksville, North Carolina, to assume the responsibilities of ZP-14 in the Eastern Sea Frontier, which was that same month transferred to North Africa for operations in the Moroccan Sea Frontier. (See chapter 6.)

ZP-24's commissioning had been somewhat farcical. Lt. Cdr. Louis M. Ayers had assumed command on the orders of "Mike" Bradley, Commander, Fleet Airship Wing Two; no orders were yet in hand from Bureau of Personnel.[121] Ayers at that moment had only his executive officer and one enlisted man in his "command." By day's end ZP-24 had swelled to one full combat crew of three officers and six enlisted men; within a week Ayers had three crews assigned: two at Hitchcock and a third waiting at Richmond, assigned to ferry *K-46* to Jamaica. Its delay was a function of a faraway casualty: on 27 January, while landing, *K-118* (ZP-41) had caressed the jungle. Field repairs by maintenance personnel allowed the ship to reach Florida "on the wing" instead of in a box.[122]

Commanded by Lt. (jg) Gordon Burke, USNR, "King-60" gained Vernam Field on 8 March. "The entire base turned out to watch the landing which was made under fairly gusty conditions. Everyone held his breath while the ship was masted—the big question being, was the mast assembled correctly. All went well, however, and the Navy lost no face in front of the assembled Army."[123]

So as to cover the whole of its assigned sector, ZP-23 (like each overseas squadron) deployed from supporting detachments. In Panama, Mandinga was on the north-facing (Caribbean) flank of the isthmus, La Chorrera on its Pacific side. Barranquilla, a seaport in Columbia to the northwest, hosted a detachment. Missions (assigned by Fleet Air Wing Three) typically were patrols; few escort missions were assigned. (Shipping through the Barranquilla area consisted primarily of high-speed tankers routed as independents.)

Squadron operations for June 1944—the month of the Normandy invasion—totaled 759 flying hours. (Paris would be liberated in August.) The Eastern Sea Frontier compiled 4,582 LTA hours that same month, the Fourth Fleet 887, the Moroccan Sea Frontier (chapter 6) 617.

ZP-23 operated entirely from auxiliary sites; it depended upon Richmond as its main hangar and overhaul base. Amid the mangrove thickets of north-coastal Panama, ZNP *K-60* initiated operations at Mandinga—the most wretched of the advance bases: a mélange of heat, downpours, humidity, malaria, isolation, mosquitoes, crocodiles, land crabs, and snakes.

> After tiring days of unloading and helping to clear the jungle, Detachment 23-1 is now in operation. . . . The men are availing themselves of the opportunities for splendid hunting in the vicinity on their off days. Several have bought a cayuca (dugout) from the Indians, and have taken several lessons in sailing. . . . [M]orale is high and the boys make the most of it by going banana hunting and buying coconuts from the natives. Usually these expeditions end with crocodile or two shot and several snakes killed. . . . [T]here appear to be more snakes here than anyplace in the world.[124]

The men made the best of it—without electricity. "It was a *miserable* place." Then-Ens. Robert Shannon endured three months at Mandinga until orders to "Bag School" at Lakehurst brought rescue. "We had no lights, so, consequently, all of our patrols had to be flown during the day—daylight takeoffs and daylight landings. There were no night operations because of the lack of facilities."[125]

LTA had arrived too late. Deployed for convoy coverage and A/S work, ZP-23 logged no direct contacts. Still, augmenting its primary mission, the two-ship La Chorrera detachment provided torpedo recovery services for Submarines Atlantic. (The latter sent an officer-observer on each flight, as liaison.) Headquartered in the British West Indies, the squadron logged 759 flights totaling 8,291 hours, 53 percent of which were devoted patrol and escort missions, including night escort and survivor rescues. Nearly 1,500 vessels enjoyed its escort services.

ZP-23 was officially closed as an operating unit on 2 December 1944.

I note with marked satisfaction the expeditious delivery of the first two airships to Eighth Fleet.

—Cominch and CNO to Commander Fleet Airships, Atlantic, 2 June 1944

6 Mediterranean Squadron

Antisubmarine operations now comprised a huge force of Allied sea and naval air units.[1] Still, the array of escort forces was too small, defenses in the Canadian and American coastal zones no more than adequate. Berlin, for its part, had introduced new U-boat tactics and weapons, obliging ASW forces to react. And merchant-ship tonnage held crucial to U.S.–United Kingdom supply lines—not only to sustain that island nation but, as well, to supply the buildup in Britain and the campaigns in Africa and southern Europe.

The high maritime drama continued in full vigor.

Fortress and seaport, Gibraltar is a bulwark, a focal area. It guards the straits—a constricted (eight to twenty-three miles wide) sea passage between Europe and Africa at the Atlantic entrance to the Mediterranean. German land forces in North Africa had sharpened the importance of the Strait of Gibraltar. "The occupation by Germany of both sides of the straits would be a grievous addition to our naval strain, already severe," Churchill cabled Roosevelt late in 1940, framing his concern. "The Germans would soon have batteries working by radio direction finding, which would close the straits both by night and day. . . . The Rock of Gibraltar will stand a long siege but what is the good of that if we cannot use the harbor or pass the straits? Once in Morocco the Germans will work south, and U-boats and aircraft will soon be operating from Casablanca and Dakar."[2]

Early in August 1942, ONI had estimated that 16 enemy boats were in the Mediterranean; Germany had about 13 operating as the year ended. Another 75 were in port along the Atlantic coast of France, another 105 at sea in the Atlantic.[3] Expulsion of Axis troops from North Africa in May 1943 left Allied naval and air installations dotting the western and central Mediterranean. Still, with Sicily and Sardinia occupied and the Anglo-American advance in Italy, the straits' primacy persisted. "Fortress Europe" was being menaced from the south. "In a crisis as acute as this," Dönitz observed, "it was the plain duty of the Navy to do all it could to assist in the defence of Italy." He therefore sought to reinforce his units east of the slot, to engage the Allied sea lines of communication with ports in North Africa, Sicily, and southern Italy.[4] (Italy capitulated that September—with immediate effect in the Mediterranean operational zone.) More boats working

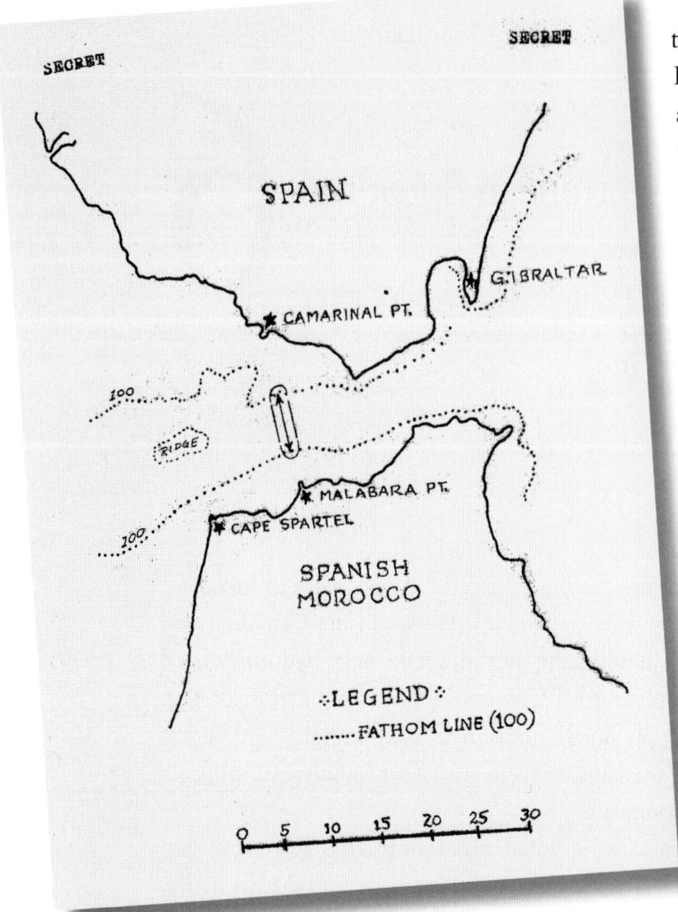

the entrance would accentuate convoy escort—a British commitment. For the Allies, then, denying access to the basin had by autumn assumed "special importance" to the Admiralty.

Heretofore, U-boats attempting eastward passage had traversed on the surface, at night. By November 1942, thirty-five boats had run the straits, practically all of them exploiting "dimouts"—nights with no moon, or heavy cloud cover. "Obviously," a navy report observed, "MAD equipped planes used for ordinary search would have no advantage over ordinary A.S.V. planes, under these conditions."[5] Offensive A/S operations, night air patrols with Mark II radar, had realized numerous sightings inside the slot—a threat apparently too feeble to warrant submerged runs.[6] That November, the introduction of searchlight-equipped Wellingtons raised the risk. A radio war ensued: strategy and counterstrategy, a levering of advantage. German boats compromised the ASV II (meter radar) with special receivers for detecting its signals, enabling them to listen to British airborne equipment and thus dive before danger arrived. ASV III (centimeter or shortwave radar) offset this counter, which, in its turn, was compromised by GSR, a search receiver (radar detection device) designed to detect microwave signals.

Surfaced U-boat runs were abandoned; the policy was no longer speed but, rather, silent *submerged* passage on the straits. Making enough speed only to maintain trim, their helmsmen keeping (presumably) near the channel's center, commanding officers now would let the current carry their boats. Heretofore, magnetic detection had seemed inapplicable. Assuming Dönitz's boats had in fact adopted submerged entry, interception within the straits appeared impracticable—save for the application of MAD.

Natural geographic conditions and the bathymetry of the hundred-fathom line elucidate the situation. Thirty-five miles in length, the straits narrow to about eight miles near its eastern terminus. There the channel meets the Mediterranean basin at abyssal depths (about 3,600 feet); here also stand the steepest subaqueous walls. In contrast, the western, or Atlantic, end widens to twenty-three miles and is shallow. The deep channel, though, was key. It does not conform to the general shape of the waterway; rather, it maintains roughly the same width throughout—a narrow slot within the slot. This bathymetry produces a conduit, defining the complex of inflowing shallow currents into, as well as currents debouching (westward) from, the basin. For a furtive U-boat, the fact of *submerged* passage constricted the sea room for full transit. As well, reasonable center keeping—avoiding the channel walls—discouraged rapid course changes or other evasive maneuvers when traversing the inner notch.

For purposes of detection by air, the narrowest portion of the deep channel is at the straits' western end and lies more than five miles from either shore—outside neutrality zones. Any air barrier would be most profitable there. Submerged U-boat transits had been made at depths between 200 and about 250 feet. An airplane at 100 altitude—its MAD gear in proper mechanical and electrical condition, properly adjusted—would thus find its quarry within range.[7] MAD, in other words, circumscribes freedom of altitude. Its "range" is the height of the magnetic change, or disturbance, above the target; hence, the distance between aircraft and *target* is defining, not altitude over the *water*. Accordingly, reduction of altitude increases the amplitude of signal—other factors constant.

In short, pilots would have to operate as low as practicable to maximize the probabilities of establishing contact.

Surface A/S forces, for their part, faced dismal sound conditions within the straits due to density variations within the water column. Sonar therefore was unreliable. As well, listening held little promise, given the enemy's slow motor speed and creeping headway. All in all, conditions—both physical and military—seemed ideal for the application of MAD. As one report concluded, "Since passage is now apparently made submerged, detection of the U/B by means of aircraft under these conditions is impossible unless by MAD."[8]

Except for the Gibraltar Peninsula, all shore boundaries to the straits comprised neutral territory, with an accompanying three-mile neutral zone. Planes kept to international airspace, attacking enemy boats only when openly violating territorial waters.[9] At its narrowest, then, the nonneutral, deep-water channel was squeezed into a two-mile band. Thus, enemy boats were limited to a predictable tube of water. "It would be very difficult [the report continues] to detect by MAD a U/B passing through if the entire width of the straits had to be patrolled. Besides obstacles such as neutrality zones, the sheer width (eight miles at the narrowest) would make tight coverage difficult. The fact, however, that passage is made submerged greatly reduces the possible area that may be traversed."

Inside the western approaches, a logical area of submergence was known: the center of the channel between Cape Spartel (the northwestern corner of Spanish Morocco) and a shoal area about eight miles off, called "the Ridge." Test trials had conveyed friendly submarines roughly parallel to the hundred-fathom line.

> It would seem reasonable . . . to place the MAD barrier across the narrowest portion of the deep channel. This occurs at about one-third the distance from the western end of the straits, the distance to neutral territory on either side is sufficient to avoid territorial waters. If passage is begun sometime before daylight, the barrier should be placed during daylight hours depending upon the currents.
>
> The coordinated air-sea barrier calls for saturated surface-craft patrols which may be used in the narrower portions of the channel further to the east. Thus the MAD barrier should be encountered first, before presence of surface craft is detected. Fast transits have been made at depths between 200 and about 250 feet,

[Opposite] The Strait of Gibraltar—entrance to the Mediterranean basin. Note the "race track" across the narrowest portion of the deep channel. MAD-equipped, a *low-level* barrier was flown by U.S. aircraft to detect submerged U-boats attempting the strait. A pair of PBYs flew the barrier in daylight; at dusk, the "MadCats" were relieved by two airships. (National Archives) and unless the technique is altered the MAD should thus be capable of detecting the U/B.[10]

As for *time* of passage, prisoner-of-war intelligence as well as the predictable choices of U-boat commanders signaled daylight dashes. Both the start and end of any transit would profit by darkness; hence, batteries having been charged during the approach, a submerged run commencing just before daylight seemed most probable.

The MAD detector indicated *changes* in the magnitude of the total field; for MAD to signal its presence, the target itself had to produce a sufficiently large change. Hence, as noted, distance from target to detector was a critical variable. MAD-equipped planes and ZNPs delivered a magnetic detection "range" (total vertical separation) somewhat greater than four hundred feet. Accordingly, the aircraft had to be low if it was to identify tiny signals. Inversely, a moderate increase in depth of submergence caused a large reduction in the MAD signal—a potential evasion tactic. Germany, however, was never aware of the magnetic sensor deployed against it.

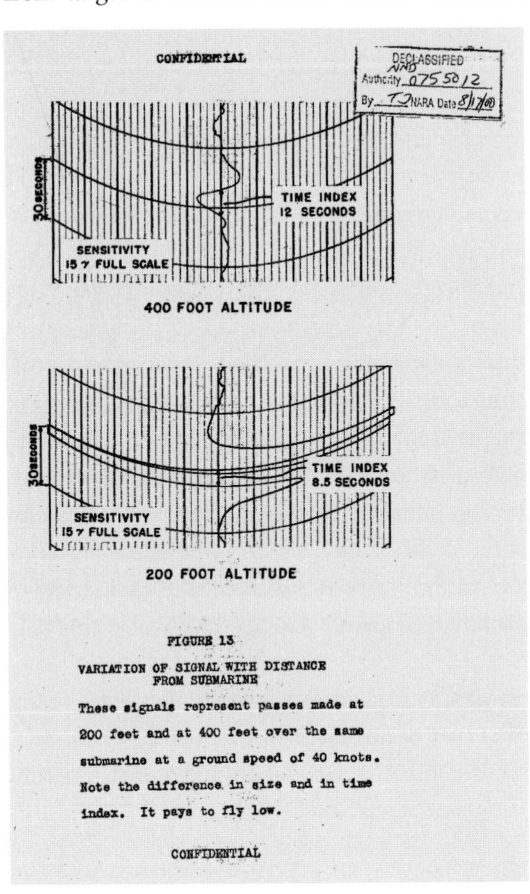
CONFIDENTIAL

DECLASSIFIED
Authority NND 075512
By TJ NARA Date 8/17/00

FIGURE 13

VARIATION OF SIGNAL WITH DISTANCE FROM SUBMARINE

These signals represent passes made at 200 feet and at 400 feet over the same submarine at a ground speed of 40 knots. Note the difference in size and in time index. It pays to fly low.

CONFIDENTIAL

[Opposite] MAD indicates *changes* in the magnitude of the total magnetic field. Hence, vertical separation from a submerged target is a critical variable. Note the variation in trace of a magnetic signal with distance. The *lower* the aircraft, the *larger* a signal. (National Archives)

[Left] Magnetic detection was a poor search tool. Instead, the sensor enabled aircraft to *redetect* and attack a U-boat whose position had been estimated via contact: visual, radar, or sound (sonobuoy). ZNP aircrews flew prescribed "trapping circles" to *locate then track* a target's course while calling in air and surface support. (National Archives)

Properly, MAD searches were made at the lowest safe altitude for the conditions prevailing, but not below 100 feet. The preferred search altitude: about 150 feet off, or lower. Close-in flying called for precise airmanship; the effort was both physically and mentally taxing. Darkness compounded the strain. A blimp was a large mass; the directional instability of the K-type necessitated continuous close control. Pilots had to know their approximate static condition at all times. In sum, low-level night patrols required utmost exactness: "Dope off for a second, you're in the water." Application of rudder caused a loss of airspeed and hence dynamic lift, allowing the ship to settle—at low altitudes, a dangerous error. Intelligent naval aviators and aviation pilots used rudder cautiously at low altitudes.

> A pilot [of an airship] inspecting a surface vessel or suspicious object, or making a MAD search at low altitudes, shall not let himself be distracted from his primary duty of flying the airship. When descending from a higher to a lower altitude with a heavy ship, it shall be standard practice to open the after damper and pump air aft in sufficient quantity to keep the ship properly tail heavy.[11]

planes in view of the low altitude at which they must fly while searching; thus the planes may be operated *only during daylight hours*. If however, passages continue to be made during the daytime this should be no obstacle."[12]

For any *multiplane* barrier, therefore, only daylight operations were deemed prudent.

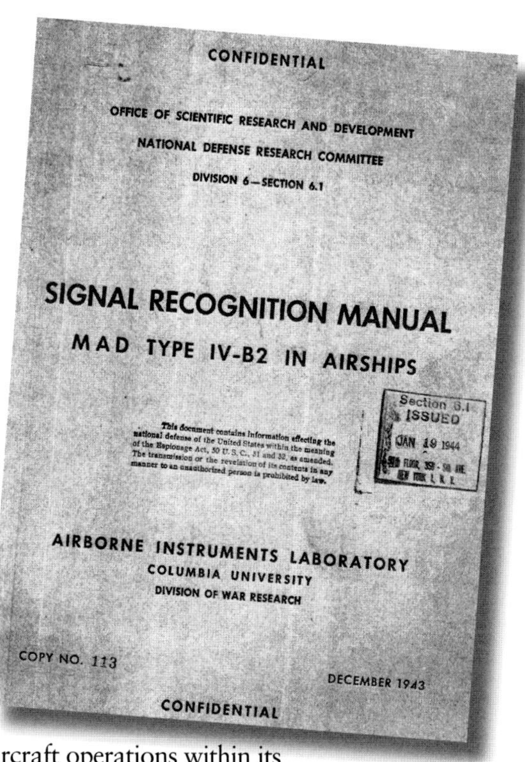

CONFIDENTIAL

OFFICE OF SCIENTIFIC RESEARCH AND DEVELOPMENT
NATIONAL DEFENSE RESEARCH COMMITTEE
DIVISION 6—SECTION 6.1

SIGNAL RECOGNITION MANUAL
MAD TYPE IV-B2 IN AIRSHIPS

This document contains information affecting the national defense of the United States within the meaning of the Espionage Act, 50 U.S.C., 31 and 32, as amended. The transmission or the revelation of its contents in any manner to an unauthorized person is prohibited by law.

Section 6.1
ISSUED
JAN 19 1944

AIRBORNE INSTRUMENTS LABORATORY
COLUMBIA UNIVERSITY
DIVISION OF WAR RESEARCH

COPY NO. 113

DECEMBER 1943

CONFIDENTIAL

The naval air station at Port Lyautey, French Morocco, in northwest Africa, reflected U.S. naval interests in the place. Local working and operating conditions were congenial, with climate and conditions over adjacent waters similar to that of California south of San Francisco. Living conditions were reasonable: personnel could be comfortably established with small acts of adaptation—tents. The field was home to Commander, Fleet Air Wing Fifteen, and the wing staff.

The Moroccan Sea Frontier (headquarters in Casablanca) exercised control of all surface and aircraft operations within its area of responsibility (35° N to 26° 10′ N). Directives from higher Mediterranean authorities for air operations were transmitted to the sea frontier commander, who in turn assigned missions to his Lyautey-based squadrons. The field's strategic location and its facilities (e.g., two six-thousand-foot runways) made Port Lyautey the most important air base for A/S operations covering shipping into the Med.

HTA Patrol Squadron Sixty-three was no stranger to ASW; in July 1942, VP-63 had received the first service installation of the retrorocket weapon as a complement to MAD. Its platform: the PBY-5A. As well, the unit was thoroughly trained in the use of sonobuoys. Having helped develop operational techniques to make best use of ASW equipment, VP-63 had been the first navy squadron to operate from Great Britain, assisting A/S patrol over the Bay of Biscay. On 18 January 1944, VP-63, by then based in northwest Africa, flew its first barrier patrol of the strait and its approaches. Thanks to Project Sail and laboratory R&D, this HTA squadron was lofting the very latest A/S devices, tactics, and weaponry.

At Lakehurst, the first graduating class of 1944 (LTA Class 2-44) comprised 123 officers, cadets and enlisted men, all of whom held orders to the squadrons for duty. Introduced by Rear Admiral Rosendahl, the principal speaker was Rear Adm. Dewitt Ramsey, chief of the Bureau of Aeronautics. Naval aviator No. 45 (1916) with a decorated service record, Ramsey congratulated the graduates, then outlined the mission of LTA and their own forthcoming assignments, orders for which might take them to either coast or to duty stations outside the continental limits.

> I consider these assignments among the most exacting, the most demanding, upon vigilance, patience, and endurance in the whole field of our operations against the enemy. Day in and day out, week in week out, you may be engaged in a long, lonely overwater patrols or convoy escort with, perhaps, no tangible evidence of return for effort expended. Such experience may be discouraging to you, you may get tired and feel that you are not making a real and substantial contribution to the war effort. . . . I would like to state, without fear of contradiction, that the submarine is still the greatest threat to our successful prosecution of the war in Europe. The waters that you will cover will be used by transporting vessels either in direct or indirect support of the invasion effort.

Even if no definite contacts were logged, the airmen would never know how many U-boats had been kept down by their presence. "You can find satisfaction too," the admiral added, "in the boost to morale the sight of the good old Navy Blimp gives to crews of the ten-knot merchantmen. Those boys need all the help, the encouragement, and the support we can give them."[13] (See table 6-1.)

In Gibraltarian–Moroccan waters, a pair of MAD-equipped PBYs orbited each morning opposite each other on a prescribed oblong; in relief, a second two-plane unit flew the afternoon.[14] The air barrier: a race-track-shaped circuit between Point Camarinal, in Spain, and Point Malabara, part of Spanish Morocco. The VP-63 search plan represented the latest operational technique in the MAD field; still, it held limitations. Its pilots (specially trained) had to fly as low as was deemed safe: MAD gear in good working order, suspended at one hundred feet, was unlikely to "see" below three hundred feet of water. (Again, had Dönitz known, the most effective method of evasion would have been simply to dive deeper.)[15] Squadron doctrine prescribed an altitude at one hundred feet and assumed a target depth of no more than a hundred feet—a vertical separation of two hundred feet. This conferred a search *width* of eight hundred to a thousand feet. Most runs on the straits had been made by U-boats of the five-hundred-ton class, a type whose signal intensities offered a difficult target. Further, the change measured at the detector was dependent in part on target orientation with respect to the total field; within the strait, target hulls floated east/west, thus minimizing their induced magnetic moment. Favoring MAD, however, were the distances to background geological anomalies, which reduced magnetic noise. And unlike sonar, MAD could not be detected by the enemy.

At the operator's station, when the chart pen registered a contact complementary devices assisted the detector. The Mark V propulsive float light and a retrobomb weapon would fire on maximum signal—that is, when the plane passed over the object. Marker drops on successive passes defined whether or not the target was moving and, if so, its course. Then, "Briefly, the procedure is to fly up the track of the submarine over the line of float lights at approximately 100 feet altitude and 105 knots ground speed. Small discrepancies in altitude and speed will cause negligible errors in the fall of the bombs [retrorockets]. The bombs are fired on the peak of the first swing of the magnetic indication and are not fired unless a good magnetic indication is received."[16]

TABLE 6.1 **Fleet Airships,** Atlantic antisubmarine instructions with respect to submerging submarines, March 1944. (National Archives)

Upon contacting a submerging submarine the following procedure will be followed:

a) Make contact report immediately to base.
b) Close range at full speed.
c) If bombing position is not reached within 30 seconds after submergence of submarine an attack will ordinarily not be executed. However, these instructions do not forbid an attack after 30 seconds if in the opinion of the pilot the existing tactical situation warrants such an attack.
d) If attack is not made upon first approach, establish MAD contact and attack in accordance with the current instructions when the contact in sufficiently developed.[1]
e) Continue effort to assemble striking force.
f) Do not leave the scene until authorized or until PLE [prudent limit of endurance] is reached.

The point of aim was forward of the swirl. The full stick (all bombs) was dropped in train in one attack. "The possibility of causing damage with less than four is too remote to warrant dropping in any other matter."

With a 50-foot setting, the ahead distance was determined in accordance with the following table:

Time After Submergence (seconds)	Distance Ahead of Swirl (feet)
5	165
10	215
15	265
20	315
25	365
30	415

1 The "lowest safe altitude" given conditions was specified when developing a contact using MAD, but not below 100 feet. Fuses for the external depth charges were at 50-foot depth settings for day missions. This deviation from the standard 25-foot setting was specified because, typically, airships did not reach a diving submarine until it was submerged.

That February, Cominch estimated one U-boat patrolling the Moroccan Sea Frontier, with "several others" believed to have gained the basin during January:

> ESTIMATE SEVERAL U-BOATS HAVE ATTEMPTED MEDITERRANEAN PASSAGE DURING PAST MONTH OF WHICH 1 WAS SUNK IN GIBRALTAR STRAITS RECENTLY. UP TO 3 MORE CURRENTLY FIXED WEST OF PORTUGAL MAY ALSO BE HEADING FOR MEDITERRANEAN.[17]

The "Mad Cats" of VP-63 had scored this "sunk" after little more than a month. On 24 February, two weeks out of Brest, *U-761* crossed the air barrier. At 1559, magnetic contact was established, then rapidly developed, exploiting MAD tracking. A search plan and attack method against a moving target must be suited to the speed and maneuverability of the hunter. For the "Mad Cats," the tactic was spiral search and tracking, so as to realize a series of successive contacts. That day, serial passes were flown over the U-boat and, on signal, propulsive float lights fired from the MAD operator's station.[18] This marked the U-boat's track: the line between the floats *was* its track. Lost thanks to interfering British destroyers, contact was regained via a cloverleaf tracking pattern, after which course and speed were established for the submerged target . Hits reasonably assured, each PBY executed a bombing run by flying the line of float lights, a pair of destroyers supporting.

The retrobombs were fired on the peak of the first swing of the magnetic indication. At 1702, a bow and conning tower broached directly in line with the string of floating lights. The boat lost all way and, at 1703, submerged. Surfacing after seven minutes and before its final involuntary dive, the crew abandoned ship without manning guns. Among the forty-eight survivors was a "greatly perplexed" U-boat commander. Interrogation revealed that he was at "a loss to understand the extreme accuracy and devastating effect of [the] initial explosions."[19]

The efficacy of MAD had been verified. Increased air and surface patrols notwithstanding, the air barrier across the straits was to prove porous: nine of twelve boats transited successfully during January–March. That April–May, with seventeen U-boats estimated in the Mediterranean, the Admiralty reaffirmed its opinion that large reinforcement of U-boat strength in the basin was unlikely; still, it expected that the normal flow of replacements and small reinforcements would "probably continue." The theater's top naval commander (CincMed), suitably concerned, deemed additional A/S measures, such as blimps, as most essential:

> CONSIDER EVEN SMALL REINFORCEMENT OF U-BOATS IN MEDITERRANEAN JUSTIFIES EMPLOYMENT OF BLIMPS IF THIS CAN BE DONE WITHOUT EMBARASSMENT TO OVERLORD.[20]

One more boat got through, in May. Of the sixty-two U-boats ordered into the Med from 1941 onward, forty-eight were lost.[21] The price too dear, Dönitz cancelled further undersea reinforcements into the basin; runs on the straits ceased.[22] Tenth Fleet and the Admiralty, unaware of this decision, persisted in a joint campaign to deny passage.

Airships for Gibraltar

The notion of blimps for the eastern Atlantic dates as early as February 1943: a British request for a squadron in Africa.[23] The notion languished, only to be resurrected. In March 1944, Commander, Naval Forces North African Waters (ComNavNAW) requested consideration of ZNP assets to augment the MAD air fence at the straits. The probability, in his view, of U-boats attempting eastward passage continued high. Looking to April, when sonar conditions within the slot would deteriorate, "reliance to prevent passage must fall on MAD."

> REQUEST CONSIDERATION BE GIVEN POSSIBILITY EMPLOYING MAD EQUIPPED BLIMPS IN SUFFICIENT NUMBERS MAINTAIN DAY AND NIGHT FENCE ACROSS STRAITS. CONSIDERED FEASIBLE ESTABLISH BASE WITH HANGAR AND 2 MASTS AT NAS LYAUTEY, 1 MAST AT AGADIR [SOUTHWEST MOROCCO] AND 2 MASTS AT GIBRALTAR. LATTER WILL REQUIRE BRITISH CONCURRENCE. THIS PROCEDURE WILL REDUCE FLYING HOURS PBY SQUADRON NOW BASED LYAUTEY AND DUE TO SLOW SPEED OF BLIMPS WILL GIVE BETTER AS COVERAGE.[24]

Tenth Fleet concurred. "It is considered practicable and desirable," Admiral Low summarized, "to furnish the blimp services requested." But to be useful, LTA would have to be made operationally ready, and promptly. Delivery by flight was therefore essential; shipment, then erection, at Lyautey would necessarily await a hangar—delaying in-theater operations. As for personnel, there were eleven blimprons in the Atlantic. An existing squadron could be transferred. "Consideration has been given," Low continues, "to the use of additional MAD equipped airplanes to furnish required services. This is not considered desirable due to unsuitability of MAD airplanes for night operations."[25]

ZNPs *would* be ordered to northwest Africa—though not quite yet. Deployment awaited control of the air at the straits, King's (changing) assessment of the tactical situation, and arrangements to exploit the Azores as an expeditionary mast site—essential for transatlantic flight delivery. "I am prepared," King advised the Admiralty, "to furnish six blimps and operating facilities in Gibraltar area as proposed. It will be necessary to transmit these blimps via Nova Scotia, Argentia and Azores which will require two 25 foot demountable refueling masts and 25 relief personnel."

Not until 1 June, however, would the first ZNP *(K-130)* gain the mat in French Morocco.

In Tenth Fleet's operations group, meanwhile, Cdr. George F. Watson worked up an estimate for inserting blimps into the Gibraltar theater. Watson had served aboard the rigid airship USS *Los Angeles;* in 1942, he had commanded the West Coast's first blimpron, ZP-32. (See chapter 7.) On temporary duty on the staff of Commander, Fourth Fleet, in 1943, he had helped select bases for ZNPs in Brazil. Assuming immediate availability of a tender to deliver masts, personnel, helium, and equipment, Watson calculated a total elapsed time of ten weeks to "ready to operate." A hangar would consume twelve weeks—completion about 1 July. "Airships could be expected to operate until 1 Aug. without hangar, if necessary."[26]

At Lakehurst, Commodore Mills was away on inspection tour. Back at his headquarters, his chief staff officer, Lt. Cdr. Douglas L. Cordiner, took an urgent call from Lt. Cdr. Charles H. Becker, Mills's liaison in Norfolk, at Fleet Air Atlantic. Tenth Fleet, Cordiner was told, wanted a ZNP squadron in the Med. Cordiner took the necessary initiative:

> With the authority vested in me by Commodore Mills I ordered helium, masts, special equipment etc. shipped overseas to an intermediate base in the Azores and the final base in North Africa. I ordered John Shannon, CO of the squadron at Weymouth to give intensive training to six USNA graduates for navigation training. . . . I picked nucleus crews and airships from several squadrons and designated myself as squadron commander. When Commodore Mills returned from his inspection, I presented him with my plan, which he instantly approved.[27]

But Admiral King changed his mind. One result: both Becker and Cordiner found themselves in "real trouble" for commandeering critical shipping space.

What had changed? On 3 April, ComNavNAW had advised as to "certain complications" in his command. An experienced LTA officer now was requested to report for temporary duty, "to investigate and make full report before further action is taken." The man selected: Cdr. Emmett J. Sullivan, USN. An informal board was designated, its senior member, Capt. G. T. Owen, who was Commander, Fleet Air Wing Fifteen. Days before, Owen had requested additional MAD aircraft (sonobuoy-equipped PBY-5As) be assigned the wing—assets to help mount a *double* barrier during daylight. Owen apparently was reconsidering. His boss, ComNavNAW, held a further concern: enemy mines. Could MAD-equipped planes detect and locate all types? ComFairWing 15 had advised in the affirmative.

Within twelve days, the board made its (unanimous) report: the blimp proposal was feasible and should be approved. ComNavNAW and the theater commander concurred. On 15 April, a top-secret signal was dispatched to King from ComNavNAW: "Strongly recommend approval blimp program" and, further, that Sullivan continue with the project as officer-in-charge of initial operations. Low nonetheless recommended that a decision as to sending ZNPs be delayed "pending determination as to whether the desired results may be accomplished in a simpler and more economical way, and that if this proves to be the case, the blimp project be cancelled and we inform the Admiralty and others concerned what we are prepared to do so in substitution."

On the 19th, King advised the Admiralty that he was "withholding action" on the matter of ZNPs or additional MAD-equipped planes to Fleet Air Wing Fifteen, pending "further developments."

This hesitation worried the commands affected. Repeated intelligence information on German U-boat activity in the Moroccan Sea Frontier compelled aggressive patrols. In a top-secret message on 6 May, ComNavNAW advised King of his desire for additional A/S assets to help guard the straits from further reinforcement:

> ENEMY SUBMARINES CONTINUE TO ENTER MEDITERRANEAN. . . . IN ORDER TO PROSECUTE AGGRESSIVE OFFENSIVE AGAINST ENEMY SUBMARINES IT IS STRONGLY RECOMMENDED THAT FAW [FairWing] 15 BE EQUIPPED WITH TOTAL OF 24 MAD PLANES AND AT LEAST 6 BLIMPS SIMILARLY EQUIPPED. BLIMPS SHOULD BE EXCEEDINGLY EFFECTIVE AS CLOSE SEARCH CAN BE CONDUCTED BY THEM NIGHT AND DAY. FURTHER POSSIBILITY OF COUNTER ATTACK IS NEGLIGIBLE DUE TO SURFACE PATROLS IN AREA. THESE FORCES WOULD INSURE ANTI-SUBMARINE BARRIER OVER STRAITS OF GIBRALTAR DAY AND NIGHT.[28]

In preparation for Overlord—the code name for the cross-channel invasion—British and American commanders pulled naval and air forces from the Mediterranean, not least from Vice Adm. H. K. Hewitt, Commander, Eighth Fleet. Army Air Forces (Mediterranean) advised the Air Ministry at Whitehall of its distress:

> Admiral Hewitt has just told me that he is having to send a number of trained Liberator crews from Moroccan Sea Frontier to UK. This coming on top of Cominch's decision not to send the blimps is a serious blow. I hope it is realized that this means as far as air is concerned there is virtually no stop on the straits. There is no doubt U-boats are still trickling in and we have had some serious losses recently. We have not enough aircraft to afford adequate protection to shipping inside the Mediterranean particularly at night against either submarine or air attack and CincMed and I are seriously concerned at this situation which allows the Hun to build-up his U-boat strength through the straits

practically without let or hindrance. I hope you will do what you can to persuade Cominch to review his decision about the blimps.[29]

Advocate Watson now put forward his most artfully cogent recommendations for deployment of ZNPs—making speed the paramount consideration—to help put a stop on the transits of the Strait of Gibraltar.

(a) ComNavNaw has reiterated and reaffirmed his request for blimps in addition to MAD CATS, after having opportunity to thoroughly evaluate the ferrying, logistic support and operational requirements against the expected usefulness. All cognizant British authorities have supported the recommendation.
(b) The blimps are desired primarily to supplement CATS at night and in low visibility on barrier patrol. Even with the double barrier in daylight and good weather, the barrier cannot be kept closed without this supplemental help.
(c) Blimp Mark 6 MAD gives an excellent performance, possibly better than CAT Mark 4 MAD.

Summarizing, Watson noted that ComNavNAW was "insistent in his request for blimps. Blimpron can be made available, delivery can be effected with a very moderate expenditure of effort. It is earnestly recommended that CinCLant be directed to furnish the blimps as expeditiously as practicable."[30]

Admiral King settled his mind: he *did* want lighter-than-air for night patrol of the straits, where, already, VP-63 was running MAD patrols. On 9 May, Commander in Chief, U.S. Atlantic Fleet, was directed to order a blimpron to NAS Port Lyautey. Authorized strength: six airships.

FURNISH AS SOON AS POSSIBLE SIX BLIMPS, PESONNEL AND EQUIPMENT FOR SERVICES REQUESTED USING AIRSHIP SQUADRON NOW ASSIGNED EASTSEAFRON [ZP-14] X WHEN READY THIS SQUADRON PROCEED AND REPORT TO COMMANDER EIGHTH FLEET FOR DUTY IN FAIRWING 15 X REMAINING SHIPS THIS SQUADRON CONTINUE AS DETACHMENT [ZP-24, DET 1] UNDER CONTROL COMEASTSEAFRON.[31]

Two years' operations from Weeksville by ZP-14 (33,099 hours; 2,821 flights; 6,410 ships escorted) ended. Fourteen's newly assigned mission: increase effectiveness of the MAD air fence across the Strait of Gibraltar. Authorized strength for overseas duty: six ZNP-Ks.

ZP squadrons Fourteen and Twenty-four were transferred to new headquarters. Organizationally, ZP-14 was under the operational control of the Commander, Eastern Sea Frontier, and Commander, Fleet Airship Wing One. On 22 May, however, it and specially designated personnel were detached from both commands. At the time of transfer, Commander Sullivan relieved Lt. Cdr. Harold B. Van Gorder, USNR, as squadron commander. His executive officer: Lt. Cdr. Gordon H. Winton Jr., USNR. Ships and personnel detached from Fleet Airship Wing One (and from the control of Commander, Eastern Sea Frontier) now reported administratively to Commander, Fleet Airships Atlantic (Mills), for orders to duty under the operational control of Commander, Eighth Fleet.

Effective 31 May, the homeport of ZP-24 was thus changed from NAS Hitchcock to NAS Weeksville. ZP-22, for its part, took over operations at Hitchcock, by opening a detachment.

The Movement

Transfer of ZP-14 entailed ferrying six ships to the operating area. Exploiting a great circle, three independent flights (in pairs) would depart Lakehurst for South Weymouth; from the United States, each would track a Canadian Atlantic route to Newfoundland, there to await flawless weather for the transoceanic runs: Argentia to the Azores, thence to Morocco. LTA had wide experience in expeditionary operations—now crucial.[32] Mast sites were set up in eastern Canada (Yarmouth or Sydney as alternates) and in the Azores; on 24 May, two masts with emergency supplies of helium reached the refueling stop at Lagens, on the island of Terceira. (Two at Argentia were already up.) As well, a stick-type had been trucked to the RCAF station at Sydney, Nova Scotia: with two enlisted ratings attending (and, if needed, forty to fifty ground handlers), it would serve as alternate if weather ruled out Argentia.

Operations Officer for the transfer: Cdr. Alfred L. Cope, USN. Former skipper of ZP-21, in 1944 Cope was now chief staff officer to Commodore Mills. Another man of the hour: Lt. John Dungan, USN, aerology officer for Fleet Airships Atlantic. Dungan had to predict a "go" correctly. And he did.

The first detachment of officers and men, together with masts and other gear, had sailed from Norfolk on 17 May to set up a new base. Further personnel (other than ferry crews) followed aboard escort carrier USS *Mission Bay* (CVE 59).[33] The initial shipment comprised six mobile masts, two stick masts, and eight hundred cylinders of helium. Portable purification units would come after,[34] as would extra engines and related equipment.[35] En route to northwest Africa, two masts and cylinders had been offloaded and ten men disembarked at Lagens, to set up an expeditionary site to support the transit. From dockside at Casablanca, the bulk of the shipment would be trucked north to Port Lyautey.

Commander, Eastern Sea Frontier, notified Eastern Air Command, RCAF Headquarters, in Halifax, Nova Scotia, as to the impending movement of six blimps via Nova Scotia to the Azores. "Will advise 24 hours prior to movement." On the 25th, at Lakehurst, the first pair stood ready to fly, on notice of favorable weather at Argentia. A two-day wait ensued.

How to navigate across? Dead reckoning with drift sights at fifteen-minute intervals was reasonably accurate in fair weather. But at night, and with frequent course changes, navigators were hard pressed for a *precise* fix. What were needed, then, were airmen adept at celestial navigation. Reserve officers lacked such training; accordingly, each pilot selected for the transit was Naval Academy trained. Still, bubble octants—used by navigators to measure angles—were not good enough. How to ensure exact fixes?

"Sully" Sullivan sought volunteers for an unspecified mission. He selected five from the academy class of 1943, among them Ensigns Ben B. Levitt and John C. Kane, USN. "At the time," Kane remembers, "all I knew was it was a chance to get into aviation without waiting two years of sea duty before you could even apply. Those were the rules in those days." Ordered to NAS

A pilot-navigator at the "nav" table, portside. (GHMC, NASM, Smithsonian Institution)

Moffett Field for primary training, both arrived that September. As yet, the why of their selection and the mission were unknown.

Following advance training at Lakehurst, graduation realized orders to ZP-11. Shortly after, "we were told that we were selected to be navigators on transatlantic flights to take airships over to Port Lyautey, North Africa, to establish a squadron over there for a barrier patrol across the strait of Gibraltar to deter or to detect German submarines in transit."[36]

"There was a lot of worrying about it [navigating across]," Levitt later remembered. "Within a few days, though, Sullivan told me to go to MIT . . . and take a look at some new navigation equipment they were coming up with, there, and see if it could be adapted to airship use." Loran in 1944 was a "black box" of vacuum tubes. "That's the way to go," he reported. Ordered up to Cambridge, officers were trained on it—"particularly, how to do the maintenance on it. And that, indeed, is the way we got the airships across."[37] (See pages 33 and 73.)

Modified for transoceanic flight, *K-123* and *K-130* would be first to try. Depth charges (for example) had been eliminated, additional fuel tanks improvised—1,100 gallons in total. From New Jersey, the two airships advanced to Massachusetts. Briefings ensued, a wait upon the weather begun. Conditions had to be perfect: a high-pressure system in midocean whose clockwise flow would confer tail winds. Attending the transfer: weather ships along the flight-plan route, augmenting land-based broadcast reports.[38]

[Above] En route Africa, *K-123* (ZP-14) is about to moor to an expeditionary mast installed at Naval Air Station Argentia, Newfoundland, 29 May 1944. (GHMC, NASM, Smithsonian Institution)

[Opposite] Flight personnel—each specially designated—assigned to ferry *K-123* and *K-130* to Argentia, Newfoundland, from NAS South Weymouth—the first leg of the transatlantic transfer of ZP-14 to Northwest Africa for operations in the Mediterranean theater. (GHMC, NASM, Smithsonian Institution)

Near Boston, in the morning dark and fog of 29 May 1944, two blimps were pulled via masts into position for takeoff. Both were airborne at 0306, and the first transoceanic flight by nonrigid airships was under way. Inaugural leg: a 782-nautical-mile run seaward of New England to Nova Scotia thence to Argentia, Newfoundland, near the port of St. John's, on the southeast part of the island. Takeoff weight: approximately 3,500 pounds "heavy." At altitude, both ships were trimmed eight to ten degrees down-elevator; each would not ride evenly until the weight of extra fuel had burned off.

On board, an atmosphere of absorption obtained, broken by occasional orders and responses. At "nav" tables, the pilot navigators, immersed in procedure, worked their particular magic. Takeoff time logged, the ZNP pair departed the control area. Given the course and heading to cross the coast, the ruddermen came up to it. At the designated place, wind was checked. At sea, the duty navigators would keep their skippers informed of progress, expected checkpoints, estimated arrival times. Flight track would be maintained throughout, each navigator exploiting every means to fix position. Drift was checked, position reports prepared for the radiomen, hourly entries recorded in the log. The radarmen, for their part, reported bearing and distance of all land returns and of all contacts.

During each transatlantic transfer, each member of the ZNP pair was to check the position of its companion throughout each leg.

In company, *K-123* and *-130* pushed northeastward. Concluding a sixteen-hour run, their first touchdowns, at Argentia, were flown in near-zero air. John Kane commented. "What we did, we got down to about 50 to 100 feet off the water, put our radar on expanded range—which gave us five miles out to the end so you could really measure a mile or a half-mile on the scope. The windows were open; we watched the scope and we listened for breakers on the shore. . . . We dove the ship in to where we thought the airfield and the runways would be. The first thing we saw was the shoreline (which was rocky), the end of a runway and a man standing at the runway and he's doing this [gesturing that they should turn left, ninety degrees]. We turned left (still don't see anybody), got the runway, put the wheel down on the runway and closed up in the fog to the landing party. Fantastic! An airplane would *never* have gotten into Argentia under those conditions."[39]

Arrival, Argentia: 1922, 29 May. Total time in the air: sixteen hours, sixteen minutes—an average ground speed of 48.4 knots. Landing party: experienced men augmented by enlisted personnel gathered locally. (Ground parties could be nonskilled personnel given a one-hour instruction in handling the lines.) The K-ships were masted and secured.

> After the airships were secured at the masts, measures were immediately instituted to conduct a thorough engineering, electrical, and rigging inspection. A regular 30-hour check was made. The front banks of plugs were changed in all engines. All electrical, radio, and electrical equipment was tested and found to be in proper operating condition. Flight crews were secured at an early hour in order to afford a generous allowance of rest.
>
> Final briefing and weather analysis were made during the ensuing morning, and loading completed. The airships were loaded to maximum capacity of fuel, 1180 gallons, and 36 gallons of oil. With provisions and a flight crew of nine (9) persons on board, the static condition was in the neighborhood of 3100 pounds heavy. At 1045 [30 May] the *K-123* took off followed shortly thereafter by the *K-130*.[40]

Stand-by time at the mast: fifteen hours, twenty-three minutes. Taking departure of NAS Argentia, the duty navigators set course to seaward. Next refueling stop: Legens, the island of Terceira in the Azores. More than thirteen hundred miles of ocean waste interposed between jump-off and the next expeditionary masts. Under way, the radiomen transmitted and received on 6,563 kilocycles. Position reports: every two hours on the even hour (Greenwich Civil Time, or "Zed" time). Loran, dead reckoning, celestial navigation, radar as well as radio aids to navigation would be exploited in piloting across.

Ens. William K. Kaiser, USNR, was aboard *K-89* in 1945 (in company with *K-114*) over longest leg of the *southern* route to North Africa, via Bermuda. "We used dead reckoning and some radio navigation," he recalls. Courses were altered as necessary to avoid visual contact with targets on radar screens. "It was a first, but I don't recall any thoughts about difficulties other than being concerned about the weather. The squadron, except for crews, had left by ships months [in fact, weeks] before."[41]

Secured at 0839, 31 May, in the Azores, the duty aircrews rested. As the flight-crew reliefs readied, the ships were checked and refueled. The second leg had advanced at an average ground speed of 60.4 knots, elapsed time six minutes short of twenty-one hours. Forecast congenial, the transit resumed after six hours, thirty-one minutes.

Checking drift at sea. Navigators maintained the flight track—exploiting every available means to fix position. When a MAD signal was received, its operator dropped a slick and the navigator checked water depth and position of known wrecks on the chart. Wrecks in shallow water—often used by pilots for checking the detector—usually gave a very large magnetic signal. (GHMC, NASM, Smithsonian Institution)

Destination North Africa, takeoff was logged at 1510, 31 May. The remaining 1,510 nautical miles would be covered in just short of twenty hours—a ground-speed average of 53.3 knots. Aboard *K-130,* "Sully" Sullivan occupied the portside seat for this leg. Command pilot of *K-123:* Lt. (jg) Homer B. Bly, USN. The Portuguese island group astern, altitude three to four hundred feet,

> The *K-130* assumed the lead position at cruising altitude on the prescribed course. Engines were synchronized and leaned out at 1420 RPM, giving an indicated airspeed of 54 knots. This speed was maintained through the flight, with the exception of a brief interval of time when it was deemed desirable to slow to 1275 RPM in order to reduce the effect of turbulence while passing through a series of squalls. . . . Through breaks in the clouds, the navigators were able to obtain good results from celestial observations Positions were periodically checked by RDF bearings obtained from Lagens.[42]

The radio range at Port Lyautey was heard well away. *K-130* landed at 1105, 1 June, into the hands of an advance ground crew. *K-123* was secured at 1123. Flight distance from South Weymouth: 3,145 nautical miles. Air time for the transatlantic run: fifty-eight hours, five minutes, for an average ground speed of 54.33 knots.[43]

The squadron had moved its area of operations to a new command. Two blimps stood delivered in twenty-two days (9 May–1 June) following the directive to transfer. By virtue of the crossing, *K-123* and *K-130* became the first of their type to log transoceanic flights. For the first time, as well, an operating (instead of new) ZP squadron had shifted overseas *as a unit.*

Still, a full transfer totaled *six* ships. Three separate crossings were therefore flown to northwest Africa—three individual pairs. The second group, *K-109* and *K-134,* put Massachusetts

astern on 12 June. Retracing the Argentia–through–Lagens route, arrival at the new base of operations concluded three days' flying. On 28 June, *K-101* and *K-112* lifted clear of the mat near Boston:

> BLIMPS K 101 AND K 112 DEPARTED NAS SOUTH WEYMOUTH FOR NAS ARGENTIA 0235Z [I.E., GREENWICH TIME] ENROUTE LAGENS AND PORT LYAUTEY. ETA ARGENTIA 16 HOURS.[44]

The flight track was the same as that flown by the preceding two pairs, the third transit concluded its transatlantic run on 1 July.

Congratulatory messages from Cominch and from the Commander, Air Force, Atlantic Fleet, reached ZP-14, as did a mention by "Axis Sally" in her regular broadcast. ComNavNAW, for its part, dispatched a "well planned and executed—well done." When word reached Mills, the commodore offered his own congratulations. Then he added: "In your [Sullivan] new job, I shall assume that you will let us know when you need logistic support. My staff and I stand ready to provide you with whatever support you may need and which it is practicable for us to obtain. I shall expect to receive such requests."[45]

Operations, Overseas Mediterranean

Now under the operational control of Commander, Eighth Fleet, Squadron Fourteen was an element of Fleet Air Wing Fifteen. Sullivan reported ready for operations on 2 June. Still, local commands required briefing. "A certain amount of orientation . . . was clearly called for. Few of the South African, French, British, and other Allied servicemen in the area had ever seen a blimp before. Some did not know what it was when they saw it."[46] The first flight in the European theater occurred on the 3rd, by *K-123;* the inaugural operational flight was logged on 6 June, D-Day in France. "Invasion Begins! Allies Attack French Coast," Lakehurst headlined the day after. "Lakehurst personnel awoke Tuesday morning to learn that the Allies had begun the long-awaited invasion of the coast of France. Buglers, after playing reveille, announced that 'the invasion has started.'"

The week before, at graduation exercises on the Lakehurst station, five officers and six cadets from the Flight Training School Class 6-44 had earned their wings, receiving designation as naval airship aviators.

Two ZNPs would fly the fence jointly. Operations commenced in the evening hours of 10 June 1944. Clearing the mat at French Morocco, "King-123" and "130" logged a 15.5-hour barrier mission. Submarine detection gear: the Mark VI MAD. New when 1942 ended, improved Mark VI equipment had been promptly engineered into production to meet procurement commitments. The design had an enhanced signal-to-noise ratio; further, dual heads enabled its use as a bombsight, allowing release automatically when the signal from both heads swung equal on the graphic tracer.

[Opposite] The British liner SS *Aquitania*, here serving as a troop transport, 6 June 1944—D-Day in Western Europe. Fleet airships became a symbol of safety and protection. (U.S. Naval Institute)

> The scheduled time of departure for mission flights is 1800 daily. Depending upon prevailing conditions of wind, the arrival on station has been made between the hours of 2000 and evening twilight. While on station, airships fly at 1300 RPM and maintain altitude between 100 and 125 feet. Watches are brief in duration to guard against fatigue. Strict adherence to a prescribed watch bill is imperative. Departure for the base is regulated by conditions of visibility and unless otherwise directed by competent authority, remain on the magnetic fence until relieved. The average duration of such a flight is in the neighborhood of 15 hours.[47]

K-134 flew 31 hours or more that month—at least two nighttime patrols on the straits, *K-130* at least one. That June, ZP-14 made forty night-patrol flights, logging 589 hours. Totals for June: altogether, 1,021 hours in the air for ninety-four flights (170 hours per ship). As well, sixty-five vessels had been escorted. In July, 966 night patrol hours (sixty-six flights) were flown for the Moroccan Sea Frontier; another 1,072 (seventy-five) would be logged in August.[48]

On 18 July, *K-112* tested the mast facilities installed at the Royal Air Force base at Gibraltar, the war's first LTA installation established on the continent of Europe. (Additional, if temporary, sites were to come.) That first arrival, four experienced men constituted the nucleus of a ground handling party, augmented by fifty ratings drawn from local British aviation. None had ever seen a blimp. The flight-path approach to the field was limited to a narrow slot between the Spanish border and "the Rock." Geography as well as severe eddies challenged. "Careful steering" realized two landings, after which "112" was moored and refueled for the return leg. This was the first landing of an American airship in Europe since World War I and the first ever by a U.S.-built airship.

Basing at Cuers, in the south of France, "112" would make the first minesweeping operation in that theater.

Cdr. James Hotham, USN (Ret.), flew for ZP-14 overseas. "We knew by experience," he recalled, "that to get the most out of the MAD gear you had to fly as close to the surface as reasonably safe." "Our mission," Kaiser adds, "was primarily anti-submarine work at the straits of Gibraltar. A twenty-four hour Magnetic Airborne Detector air cover was maintained for several months. The two PBYs flew dawn to dusk, hanging on station until relieved. All M.A.D. work was flying an elliptic circle in the straits at 75 to 100 feet." Takeoff: just before sunset. "In the straits," Hotham, continued, "it was quite windy almost all the time, so that on our headings back and forth we always had to crab—you never could head straight north or straight south; it was always quite a drift. . . . The currents were tricky too." All navigating was by radar—already an indispensable aid. The two K-ships crossed the slot alternately. Such low-level, close-proximity flying demanded that pilots not only keep clear of each other and not ditch the ship but, as well, dodge the masts of the British surface-patrol ships.[49]

Nightly operational patrols would be maintained from D-Day to 2 October 1944—119 days, until weather interposed a hiatus.

Canadian Interest Revives

Success at Gibraltar revived Canadian consideration of airships. A study by a joint American-Canadian board (Capt. George H. Mills, a member) had concluded that operations were feasible in the Gulf of St. Lawrence and eastern Nova Scotia from mast sites—no hangar facilities—from 1 May to 1 October. Recommended trial operations in summer 1943 were deferred, however: too few ZNPs. Admiral King held concern as to "possible bottlenecks in blimps, masts and helium affecting requirements for U.S. coasts."[50] As 1944 ebbed to autumn, the Canadian military worried about a new German offensive. Indeed, the 1944 campaign by *schnorkel*-fitted boats in the gulf was to match the 1942 assault.[51] In the eastern Atlantic, the enemy was again returning to the English Channel. Exploiting the snorkel (which allowed the diesel to be operated submerged, extending underwater endurance) and difficult sonar conditions, boats were operating much closer inshore in waters previously untenable because of air coverage (see chapter 7). "The enhanced capabilities of U-boats fitted with the Schnorkel device, and the probability of a new offensive with improved types of U-boat, suggest that the threat to our shipping will increase rather than diminish before the end of the war with Germany."[52]

Tenth Fleet had renewed concern as to the Canadian littoral:

> ANTICIPATE CONTINUED ENEMY ACTIVITY IN CANADIAN AREA WHERE 4 U-BOATS CURRENTLY ARE ESTIMATED OF WHICH 1 IS PROBABLY HOMEBOUND. FOR THE FIRST TIME IN 2 YEARS U-BOATS AGAIN APPEAR TO BE OPERATING IN THE GULF OF ST. LAWRENCE.[53]

So the matter of blimps at Canadian bases was again raised—this flare of concern resuscitating on-and-off-again discussions. Three days after Christmas, at the 37th meeting of the Joint RCN-RCAF Anti-Submarine Warfare Committee, the senior service representatives agreed to investigate the possibilities of having the U.S. Navy operate MAD-equipped blimps in Canadian waters from Canadian bases.

Admiral Rosendahl inspects the tent city ("Helium Acres") for enlisted personnel assigned to Squadron Fourteen at Port Lyautey, Northwest Africa. (GHMC, NASM, Smithsonian Institution)

Among the considerations: using ZNPs to create a MAD barrier against snorkeling boats in Cabot Strait—a heavy-traffic approach to the Gulf of St. Lawrence. Such a barrier, or "fence," might be deployed when the enemy was known to be making for the gulf. A series of tests had considered a sonar fence, then a flown barrier. Sonar required an undue number of ships, tests revealed. Why? Conditions within the gulf were nightmarish: pack ice, icebergs, low visibility, density layers. Upward refraction frustrated sonar performance, thereby favoring the raider over ASW surface forces. Outcome: "U-boats had the run of the Gulf."[54] Aircraft conferred a plus: by forcing submergence, they could drive a boat's air and battery charge to exhaustion once MAD had located, then tracked its target, obliging surfacing—and probable destruction.[55]

With four nonrigids deployed plus two in reserve, "two M.A.D. fences were established, one patrolled by Catalina aircraft and the other by blimps. One of our submarines made passages at depths of 50, 100, 150 feet and speeds varying 2–5 knots and 5–8 knots. Of 12 passages at lower speeds the Catalina detected 11, but they were not so successful during 7 more runs when submarine was proceeding between 5–8 knots. The Blimps were extremely effective as they detected 13 out of 14 crossings of their fence."[56]

That March, nonetheless, upon further discussion (fortieth meeting), it was decided *not* to ask the U.S. Navy to operate its airships in Canadian waters.[57]

Rollbacks again threatened. "The word was brought from Washington," Mills wrote Bradley, the latter nearing the end of his cruise as wing commander, "that we must be prepared to lose some pilots immediately from LTA, perhaps up to a total of 200 from Airships Atlantic within a very short time. . . . [W]ith anti-submarine units being reduced in the Atlantic, there apparently is not much hope for maintaining our units at full strength." Alive to naval politics, Mills shuffled his more seasoned officers. George Watson and John D. Reppy, for instance, saw changes of duty—Watson went to Moffett Field and Reppy to sea, as did Cordiner. A survivor of the foundering of the rigid *Macon,* Reppy had been the first commanding officer of ZP-51. Mills had to furnish reliefs. Among his selections, Cdr. Charles L. Werts—under whom ZP-42 had been commissioned (in 1943) preparatory to South American duties—was ordered from Squadron Forty-two to ZP-21; Spicer (from Zimmerman's staff) received orders as his relief.

Mills had to plan beyond the contest with Berlin. "From the entire outlook of economy, limitations, and politics," Lt. Cecil A. Bolam, ZP-11 skipper, observed, "it appears that all East Coast installations will take a severe if not a complete cut-back after the European war is finished. LTA will probably receive more than its share." At midyear, the Under Secretary of the Navy for Air, Artemas L. Gates, ordered a detailed breakdown of all personnel associated with LTA. "He certainly is no friend of ours," Bradley commented, "and turns down flatly almost any request which has to do with LTA stations." A directive was issued for Rosendahl to visit all facilities to ascertain what reductions were possible at each—or to justify to high commands the increased use of ZNPs in their respective operational areas.[58]

Cutbacks ensued—the first loss, 171 men. With further reductions ordered later that year, "We are having a hell of a time," the admiral fumed, "with these personnel reductions. Obviously, we want to save as many experienced personnel of wide adaptability as possible." In particular, Rosendahl sought to retain the ex-Goodyear pilots who'd been released for active duty before Pearl Harbor and during the war's earliest months "and gave us important help." But the CNO and BuPers, for their part, were to insist upon a rapid cutting down on officers, "causing a lot of confusion."[59]

No new continental stations were started in 1944. Cutbacks of the shore establishment commenced that fall, including conversion of LTA bases to serve other commands and functions.[60] As it happened, three blimprons were decommissioned, their ships ferried to storage: Houma's ZP-22 in September and, that December, ZP-23 at Jamaica and ZP-51 out of Trinidad. As well, Fleet Airship Wing Five at Trinidad was decommissioned. The decline in U-boat activity in the Caribbean explains the reduction.

In the Gibraltar–Moroccan theater, ZP-14 had logged three months (June–August 1944) of flight operations.[61] Primary mission: MAD barrier night patrol across the straits. Daylight escort missions also were assigned, as were survivor searches, utility missions, and other services. While on escort, on 4 July, *K-109* made an attack—the only known airship attack in that theater. A MAD contact was recorded at 1700, a smoke float dropped. A standard tracking procedure ended with the release of two depth charges. The surface reportedly "boiled with mountain of water and waves." No corresponding Tenth Fleet action report has been found to confirm the incident, nor confirmation that U-boats were then operating in the basin.[62]

Ferry flights and training added further hours. No one knew when the European war would fold; still, by mid-August, the prospect was plain. Sullivan's appraisal: the overseas mission had proven effective—and gratifying: "Commodore Owen has been an excellent boss.

Actively interested in anything that pertains to blimp operations, he has made us feel very much at home as an integral part of an H.T.A. wing. Conclusively has it been demonstrated here that blimps and airplanes and associated personnel can jointly use the same facilities and harmoniously work together in carrying out their separate assignments toward the fulfillment of a common mission."[63]

Expulsion of German forces from the Atlantic coast of France ended the U-boat threat to the Med by exploitation of French ports. For ZP-14, then, tactical considerations dictated redeployment. Should its personnel, ships, and equipage be deflated for shipment back to the States or, instead, be assigned to another disposition—perhaps to continental Europe for mine spotting? Indeed, the mine-locating mission was to expand squadron operations fully to the Italian Peninsula in the European war theater. Meantime, "Relative to evacuation of your area," Mills wrote, "I too have been studying this problem and will soon have some preliminary data worked out. I hope we can fly the ships to their next duty, however, that will depend on many factors of which you will have to be the judge of some."[64]

ZP-14 had compiled an admirable record of overseas operations in 1944: 7,473 hours (745 sorties), 4,956 of which were devoted to night patrol flights. As well, 1,332 ships had been escorted. And, as an adjunct to local minesweeping forces, 718 hours (95 flights) had been devoted to mine-spotting missions, the first of which was logged that September.

In mid-March 1945, Tenth Fleet held insufficient evidence to confirm the presence of any U-boat in the Gibraltar area; still, previous successes pointed to early resumption of enemy activity. "No report recent activity off Gibraltar although enemy is not likely to leave this area unattended for long."[65]

In fact, an exhausted foe had relinquished the Mediterranean.

Mine Spotting

The notion of blimps as adjunct to mine-related services was, in 1942, hardly novel. Doctrine had been crafted as early as 1920: "Their characteristics obviously render them extremely well-fitted for the work of locating floating or surface mines. Due . . . to the airship's ability to hover over one spot, she can carefully reexamine and buoy a mine if necessary, but can not well destroy one. . . . The customary procedure, therefore, is to call some surface craft to the vicinity by radio and let them sink the mine by gun fire."[66]

British forces had found the nonrigid ideal, "able as they were to pass safely over the fields, to hover and inspect, and to report their findings at once by W/T."[67] As in 1918, U-boats loitered off the entrances to eastern Canadian and U.S. ports vital to the transatlantic convoys, some laying mines: off St. John's and Halifax, Boston, New York, Delaware and Chesapeake bays, and southward.

> AT 930 Q TODAY AMC 67 EXPLODED MINE 1/2 MILE EAST ST JOHNS BUOY. DUE POSSIBLE PRESENCE OF OTHER MINES ENTRANCE TO ST JOHNS RIVER CONSIDERED UNSAFE AND CLOSED TO SHIPPING UNTIL ENTRANCE CHANNELS THOROUGHLY SWEPT. ESTIMATED TIME OF REOPENING TO SHIPPING AFTERNOON 12 AUGUST.[68]

[Opposite] ZNP *K-53* founders off Jamaica, 7 July 1944. The ship was flown into the water, killing one crewman. For naval LTA, 1944 proved costly: thirty-five fatalities, twelve patrol ships lost. The wartime program would lose seventy-seven officers and men altogether, plus six fatal accidents to ground handlers. (C. E. Rosendahl Collection/ HOAC, University of Texas)

And so again, as in 1918, LTA was assigned mine-related missions: leading sweeper groups to (and through) fields and clearing traffic through marked channels.[69] A slow, low-altitude platform, the blimp had an ability to search, detect, and hold station. Blimps, in sum, offered an ideal perch from which to spot mines, particularly in clear waters like the Mediterranean and South Pacific.

Rosendahl had pressed for mine-related work: "If we can do that *one* job better than anyone else (and I am convinced we can), then we have a great toe-hold and a talking point for our planned expansion. I can't impress on you too strongly the need for the most serious concentration on this anti-mine business."[70]

At Lakehurst, the commodore welcomed utility assignments for his unit commanders. Now the Mediterranean theater tendered opportunity: "The necessity for immediate action on this is of the utmost urgency," Mills advised, "if blimps are to get in on mine work. I therefore urge that you use all speed in determining the attitude of Eighth Fleet in this matter. Of course, you will have to have Commodore Owen's approval and blessing on this. I understood from conversation with him that he thought blimps could be used profitably in mine work."[71]

Indeed he did. That November, over a field in waters near Key West, Richmond's ZP-21 flew special missions to assess the merit of MAD applied to both submerged and floating mines, for which the airship was judged "extremely valuable." Overseas, ZP-14 operations bloomed to include two ZNPs deployed for mine spotting in French, Tunisian, and Italian home waters.

U.S. Operational Accidents, Casualties

On the U.S. side of operations, accidents claimed lives and aircraft, inflicting political as well as operational bruises. Fleet Airship Wing Two (Richmond) was especially hard hit. On 19 April, *K-133* (ZP-22) was forced into the Gulf of Mexico by a thunderstorm, becoming the first ZNP to founder from severe weather. Turbulence had pushed the ship to eleven thousand feet during one rise, the rate of ascent exceeding two thousand feet per minute. (Envelope pressure dropped to zero—"and we never did get it up after that.") Accelerated up and down for nearly an hour, the hapless craft, swept backward, met a roiled sea surface, filling the car.[72] The severity of the crash and state of the sea took nine men. Impeded by weather, an intensive air and surface search retrieved one man. Assignment of cause by the evaluating board: pilot error.

Less than two days later, *K-56*, *-57*, and *-62* were blown out of the hangar at NAS Houma, Louisiana—further losses for Wing Two. On the morning of 21 April, a gust pushed the huge northwest door (which had been fully closed) fully open, creating a venturi effect as the wind funneled through. The three ships (crewless) began to kite and roll, after which each broke free of its moorings. *K-57* charged down the deck and was blown clear; it went out sideways. Then *K-56*, which had been moored abreast, skidded out tail first. Both crashed outside the air station perimeter, causing no injuries. Surging and bouncing violently, its slip tanks afire, *K-62* was swept onto the field and was destroyed—again, no injury to personnel, naval or civilian.

On 16 May, ceiling and visibility unlimited, pilots were practicing wheel landings and takeoffs using *K-5*. An instructor-pilot and class were aboard. In climbing, the ship apparently got off the wind; it veered to port, then failed to clear the west end of Hangar One. The car struck its upper ledge, hung momentarily, then tore loose, crashing to the mat. One man only—in critical

condition—survived; six officers and four enlisted men died instantly. Crash alarm sounding, equipment and salvage crews were on the scene at once. "Ambulances shuttled between the scene of the accident and the hospital with bodies of the officers and men as they were taken from the wreckage." The ship was scrapped following removal of salvageable parts.

Intelligent pilots developed their sense of judgment for low altitudes. When a ship encountered trouble in dynamic flight, it might free-balloon clear (static control). During 1943, *L-10* and three

"King" ships had *flown* into the water. Minimal outcome: damage, though not always outright crashes and fatalities. For instance, on 3 October, returning from sixteen hours of patrol, the senior pilot of *K-53* (ZP-21) allowed his ship to impact the sea on approach. He gunned the belly-damaged ship clear to a normal landing.[73]

Operations for 1944 saw more of this peculiar casualty. That May, at sea, two ships hit the water; no airmen were lost. ZNP *K-46* (ZP-24) struck in a nose-down attitude; recovery was instant, damage minor. The pilot of *K-24* (ZP-21) had turned a heavy ship *downwind* at an altitude of seventy-five feet. Immediate response: a rapid settling. Emergency ballast (including the jettisoning of two Mk 47 bombs) allowed his command to free balloon clear. During July, two more blimps met salt water. On the night of 2 July, *K-14* struck while on MAD search of a square of sea in which a submarine had been reported. The car immediately filled, taking five men. Five survivors were retrieved; one succumbed to exhaustion, shock, and exposure. (The wreck was towed ashore, the bodies recovered.) Evidence of enemy action to the contrary, a court of inquiry ruled pilot error.[74] *K-53* was on night submarine search when it went in.

The West Coast was hardly immune. On 18 August 1943, the training airship *L-10* settled into San Francisco Bay: the ship had been weighed off in a heavy condition with engines idling at five hundred feet. And in August 1944, on approach in Oregon, *K-119* flew into Tillamook Bay.

Off faraway Brazil, in an attempt to check his altimeter from an altitude of twenty-five feet, the pilot of *K-84* (ZP-41) hit the water lightly at an air speed of forty-three knots, completely sheering off the radar "hat" (protective covering) and spinner (antenna). The mission was completed, the ship returned to base.[75] On 6 November 1944, *K-34* (ZP-11) flew into the water, killing one. Together, these casualties claimed sixteen lives. Boards of investigation concluded that, save for one, each incident had resulted from pilot error.

Losses for 1943 from all causes (material failure, personnel, pilot, weather, enemy action, and unknown) had been high: three dozen incidents involving airship losses and major casualties. Three had attended overseas operations. Twenty-four men were killed. As well, a dozen major casualties not involving ship losses took five more lives; ten of these accidents were ascribed to personnel error.

Thirty-seven incidents of ship loss and major casualties sullied 1944, killing twenty-six. Most were ascribed to pilot error, a half-dozen to ground handling lapses.[76] Nine incidents had occurred overseas. Another fourteen major casualties not involving ship losses killed one man; five resulted from overseas operations. Cause of all but one of these accidents: personnel failure.

Mine Spotting in Mediterranean Waters (Continued)

Overlord *and* the invasion of the south of France (a supporting operation) transformed the strategic picture in the western Mediterranean. Still, the capture of Toulon and Marseilles, major French

[Opposite] Salvage operations for ZNP *K-14*, Bar Harbor, Maine, 7 July 1944. Assigned to ZP-11, officially the ship had flown into the water while conducting a MAD search. Evidence suggests an encounter with a surfaced U-boat. Six crewmen were lost, their bodies recovered. (Lt. H. F. Smith, USNR [Ret.])

[Bottom Right] French civilians line the streets of Paris with "shouts, signs, and smiles" to welcome General Charles DeGaulle as he enters the city at the head of Allied liberation forces, 26 August 1944. (U.S. Naval Institute)

[Opposite] ZNP *K-109* unmoors from an expeditionary mast at Cuers, near Toulon, in southern France. Note the twin hangars—re-erected as spoils from Germany following World War I. The Cuers facility had been to the French Navy what Lakehurst was to the U.S. Navy: the center of airship operations. (U.S. Naval Institute)

ports, left a lingering menace: German-laid mines. Indeed, French harbors and their approaches were fraught with mines. (The Axis had lain an estimated five thousand mines in the Mediterranean alone.) Commands under ComNavNAW had requested information as to the practicability of using MAD-equipped planes in detecting and locating these underwater hazards.

Vice Admiral Hewitt held substantial LTA assets—a half-dozen K-type airships. Conferring that September with Commander, Fleet Air Wing Fifteen (under which ZP-14 operated), Hewitt issued verbal authority to dispatch a blimp to the Toulon area to assess its adjunct value to local minesweeping forces. At ZP-14, Cdr. Edward R. McMillan, USNR, was then squadron navigator: "Several days after the allied invasion of southern France, following the sinking of a number of LSTs and support ships by coastal mines placed off the beaches by the Germans, Admiral Hewitt asked our skipper Capt. E. J. Sullivan for help. 'Sully' ordered a senior crew with himself and me . . . to fly a blimp up to Cuers, France, and begin mine spotting operations."[77]

And so, a detachment set up operations in the European war theater, at the reopened naval air base for airships at Cuers. Located northeast of Toulon, its twin hangars offered the only inside shelter for LTA on the continent. Ahead of *K-112,* an R4D deployed eight officers and fourteen men, together with a stick mast and equipage.

On 16 September, "112" sortied for France. Ferried northwest, the ship was masted that afternoon to a hurriedly erected intermediate base at Oran (La Senia Field), Algeria. After an early unmooring (0426), the trans-Med leg from Oran found the ZNP in the air off southern France next day. "While some two hours out of Cuers, the *K-112* picked up the mountains near Toulon on the radar screen. At 1830 ABLE [time zone], 17 September, the airship was landed at Cuers and moored. Its arrival marked the first time in a quarter century that a U.S. Navy airship had been based in Europe."[78]

German air units had evacuated the site mere days before. Now, instead, an Australian unit flying Spitfires was exploiting its grass strip. The Aussies helped land the airship.

Ending a three-day wait on weather, *K-112* inspected known fields on 20 September. Purpose: to familiarize personnel with moored mines as seen from the air. Next day, a demonstration flight yielded superb results—visiting officers were gratified with the accuracy with which mines could be plotted. Radar bearings and distances, together with pelorus bearings [for relative bearings], proved satisfactory in fixing their positions. *K-112* had not *swept* any mines; instead, slow, low-level flying had sighted the silent menaces then (accurately) plotted them for later clearance.

ZNP installed, the MAD proved especially useful in such restricted waters, where wrecks were known or readily charted. So it was that the LTA brand of air spotting facilitated a mammoth maritime cleanup. Prescribed sectors were assigned: a special search, a photographic flight, working with minesweepers—searching ahead, pinpointing mines, and directing sweepers to them. Operating personnel from Squadron Fourteen flew nine mine-related missions that September—forty-five hours.

On the first day of October, "*K-112,* in company with three minesweepers, investigated an area in which there were believed to be undiscovered mines. It sighted two, marked them with smoke floats, and, using a loudspeaker, directed the surface vessels to them. This was the beginning of active airship cooperation with surface minesweeping craft. The blimp communicated with the ships by loud hailer or radio, carrying a French officer on board to handle linguistics."[79]

By 27 October, "the Cuers detachment of BlimpRon 14 had spotted 400 mines and had directed sweepers to them by loud speaker, voice radio, and smoke floats. On one occasion, the airship saved a sweeper by directing it to make an emergency turn to avoid hitting a mine close aboard and along its projected track."[80]

Performance fed further orders. "Tunisian War Channel" was a swept approach to the Bay of Bizerte. Following approval by Admiral Hewitt, flight crews and a stick mast were dispatched to Bizerte, a seaport in northern Tunisia. On 3 November, *K-109* (Lt. Cdr. F. S. Rixey, pilot) landed at Sidi Ahmen Field. The first operational mission was logged the next morning. Later, mine spotting done, the British Flag Officer, Tunisian Area, would send a commendatory dispatch to the squadron. And Hewitt, in a dispatch to CNO, would remark that "blimps prove better suited to this mission than airplanes in areas beyond enemy fighter range."

In mid-November, ZP-14 was basing four ZNPs at Port Lyautey, primarily for all-night patrol on the straits, one at the semipermanent detachment at Cuers for mine spotting along the French coast, and one at Bizerte (three combat aircrews): "Minesweepers, used to waiting for thundering explosions to announce the presence of mines, liked having the blimps tell them mines lay ahead. They liked it even better when the blimps told them there were no mines ahead."[81]

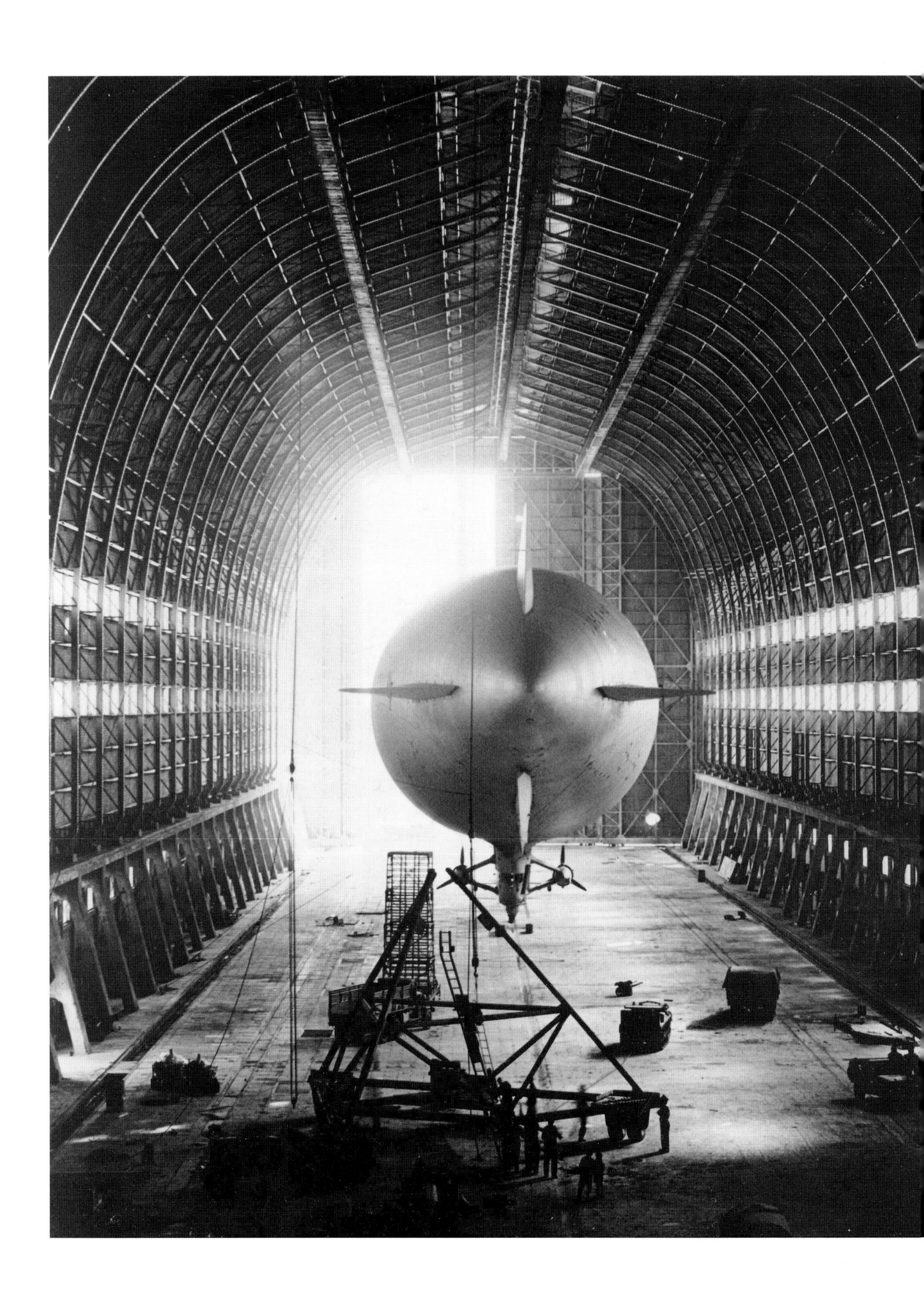

Temporary operations at Bizerte concluded on 21 November, when ZNP *K-109* was ferried to Cagliari, on the island of Sardinia. "Upon arrival, the *K-109* made a preliminary survey of the outer harbor. Mine-spotting operations . . . began the following day (22 November) during which 61 mines were sighted and plotted under unfavorable weather conditions of high winds and overcast sky. The *K-109,* on its first three flights from Cagliari spotted 268 mines!"[82]

[Opposite] Rare view: an American airship berthed at Cuers, France. (U.S. Naval Institute)

Operations for the Moroccan Sea Frontier totaled 511 flying hours by April 1945, including sorties out of Sardinia. In all, 384 ships enjoyed escort.[83] Until termination, the island's detachment would depend on British communications and aerological support.[84] In addition to spotting mines, coordinated air and sea operations exploited its airship for guiding surface sweepers in, then assisting "sink boats" in finding, then destroying, cut-free mines.

Hostilities in Europe ended on 8 May 1945—VE Day. (The unfinished war in the Pacific would persist into August.) And so the Mediterranean was freed from the need for combat air coverage. Still, coastal segments had yet to be swept and cleared. For ZP-14, spotting and related mine missions continued to enlarge its operating area.

March 1945 had inaugurated operations from Italy. A minesweeper squadron commander had recommended that the Cagliari-based ZNP assist in sweeping near the wreck of the minesweeper USS *Swerve*—sunk northwest of Anzio. The Cagliari detachment dismantled the stick mast at Bizerte; as part of advance preparations, this was re-erected at Littorie Field, Rome.

On 3 March, *K-101* cleared Cagliari; five hours later she floated above the sunken sweeper. Wreck position was established by magnetic detection; *K-101* then began plotting moored contact mines in the vicinity. Next day, the assistant air operations officer of the Eighth Fleet, aboard "101," directed sweepers (via voice radio) as they sought a clear channel in. On the 5th, the MAD gear (and smoke flares) was again used; wreck located, a marker buoy was dropped. "Upon completion of this day's flight, the task group commander disembarked at Anzio; this was accomplished by the *K-101* making a wheel landing on a fighter strip without the aid of a landing party."[85]

The Sardinian detachment closed officially in April after which, in response to a British request, *K-101* based briefly at Pisa. Mission: to provide assistance in clearing waters near Genoa, fifty miles northwest of Pisa. (That August, at Pisa, *K-89* hit the mast and deflated—a ground-handling failure.) As well, detachments operated temporarily from Malta and from Venice, the latter for work over the adjoining Adriatic.

Altogether, some four thousand mines were plotted by airships in the Mediterranean. ZP-14 was ordered deactivated on 15 November 1945; at Cuers, squadron ships were deflated that November–December.

Operational war record for ZP-14, overseas (6 June 1944 to 15 May 1945): 5,898 hours on 435 night patrol missions, 1,332 hours devoted spotting mines (177 flights). Daylight escort (85 sorties) totaled another 947 hours, with 850 flight hours recorded for training. Grand total, overseas: 1,061 flights, 9,027 hours aloft, 2,760 vessels escorted.[86] The unit had rendered escort assistance in both the Atlantic and Mediterranean, and had conducted air-sea rescues as well as utility work.

ZP-14 was decommissioned on 22 January 1946. Commander in Chief, U.S. Atlantic Fleet, in recognition, made awards to twenty-six officers who had participated in the transoceanic flights. The Bronze Star went to Cdr. Emmett Sullivan, squadron commander when it flew the transit.

[Opposite] The Allied invasion of France transformed the strategic situation in the Western Mediterranean. A lingering menace: German-laid mines. Slow, low-flying, and able to hold station, airships offered an ideal perch for spotting mines, particularly in clear water. Detachments from ZP-14 were set up in the European theater—France, Sardinia, Tunisia, Italy. Searching ahead, pinpointing mines and directing sweepers to them, some four thousand mines were spotted by Squadron Fourteen—the sole American contribution to the international program to clear the Mediterranean. (Kevin Pace)

Air Medals were awarded to Ernest W. Steffen Jr., squadron operations officer (he had flown in command of the first section during the flight's most difficult leg) and to six flight captains. Letters of commendation went to the twelve copilots and the six navigators.

In November 1945, the Mediterranean Zone Mine Clearing Board—composed of Allied naval representatives—recommended that Squadron Fourteen be allowed to carry on: "Their [blimps'] continuance in the Mediterranean is strongly advocated by the Zone Board," noted the Commander in Chief, Mediterranean. "The Admiralty and ComNavNAW were advised via naval message, which feels that this would be an appropriate contribution by the United States to the work of mine clearance in these waters where they have considerable shipping interest."[87]

ZP-14 represented the sole American contribution to the international program to clear the Mediterranean. As well, squadron ships diverted ten sweepers from mines or shoal water. Commander, North West African Waters, supported the board's proposal; to Commander, U.S. Naval Forces, Europe he "strongly recommended" the squadron's retention until August 1946. As he outlined:

> (1) extensive mine clearance operations remain and with the smaller forces likely to be available air spotting expedites the task by accurately locating the lines of mines. (2) In areas of considerable minefields such as between Sicily and Tunisia, the greater endurance, slower speed and better arc of vision of the blimps compared to aircraft ensure continuous cover to the minesweeping forces. (3) Blimps greatly reduce the hazards to minesweepers during extended searches in suspected waters. (4) The blimps are a contribution that cannot be replaced by any other nation.[88]

In 1947, the Airship Advisor to DCNO (Air), Adm. "Tex" Settle, would write: "All operations were carried on with outstanding efficiency, effectiveness and zeal, in furtherance of the war effort, and with great credit to the Navy." He therefore recommended that ZP-14 be awarded the Navy Unit Commendation for its services overseas.

Vice Admiral Hewitt concurred. "I consider the services of this squadron to have been outstanding," he wrote the navy secretary. "It was instrumental in forming a very tight block of the straits of Gibraltar which effectively prevented the enemy from introducing additional submarines in the Mediterranean. The later services of this squadron in mine searching . . . was most effective. It resulted in expediting minesweeping work and in saving lives and property."[89]

Determined and imaginative, Cdr. Emmett J. Sullivan, USN, was awarded the Legion of Merit for his services. "He was," a pilot from his squadron summarized, "the right guy at the right time for the job."

If we could have a pair of them [blimps] operating off this port daily, I would feel that shipping would be much more secure.

—Rear Adm. J. W. Greenslade, USN,
Twelfth Naval District (San Francisco),
December 1941

7 Pacific Coast Operations and Atlantic Finale

The German U-boat dominated the Axis undersea campaign in World War II. Yet the first strikes against U.S. shipping were inflicted by the Imperial Japanese Navy.

After the raid on Pearl Harbor, nine boats of the *I-15* class took up station in the eastern Pacific off the American coast—from Puget Sound south to the Los Angeles area. Four tankers were torpedoed (three sunk) that uneasy December, six vessels shelled. The SS *Medio*, for example, was torpedoed off Eureka, California, on 20 December. Late that month, this Japanese force withdrew—untouched.[1]

The West Coast had braced itself for a strike, including submarine attack on the U.S. merchant fleet. "Enemy submarine attacks on shipping in the coastal waters of the Northwest Sea Frontier are highly probable. Enemy air attacks from carriers may be made upon military objectives and important industrial areas. Attempts at sabotage and subversive activities may be expected."[2]

For fifteen minutes on 23 February, in an extraordinary action, *I-17*, having "slunk close inshore," shelled oil derricks at Ellwood, north of Santa Barbara. Damage: minor. (A newly formed squadron, ZP-32, dispatched the tired *TC-14* to search for the intruder and escort any merchantmen in that sector.) During March, two tankers were shelled, one by *I-17* before departing the West Coast. In June, a second deployment *(I-25* and *I-26)* took up stations off Washington; both boats attacked shipping (two sinkings) and shelled shore installations—a lighthouse on Vancouver Island, a fort on the Columbia River. *I-25* returned in September–October and sank two tankers, after which the Western Sea Frontier was left unmolested. "Japanese submarine operations," Rosendahl writes, "were over in most areas before we ever got an airship near the localities involved."[3]

Between its opening raid and the Battle of Midway, in June 1942, the Japanese carrier fleet rampaged throughout the Pacific. In terms of submarine warfare, U.S. forces were urgently engaged in *two* maritime campaigns, one in the Atlantic and one in the Pacific. Quarry in the Pacific strategic zone: the Japanese merchant marine. This was an *antishipping campaign.* "The United States was in the unusual position of participating in antisubmarine warfare in two oceans while actively prosecuting an all-out offensive submarine campaign in one of them."[4] The decimation of its freighters and transports by a tight U.S. blockade of its home islands would deliver Japan to eventual strangulation.

In the broad Atlantic, Germany was prosecuting—for a second time—an aggressive, forward war on commerce. Japanese naval thinking, less flexible or adaptive, deployed submarines as adjuncts to its fleet and for supply to bases when (later in the war) these were cut off or threatened by the American transpacific advance.

Japan's submarine force had begun the war with 64 boats, including elements assigned to the raid at Pearl Harbor; Tokyo added 125 during 1943–44. Maximum force in commission: 77. But in May 1942, U.S. intelligence was obliged to admit: "Our knowledge of the activities of Japanese U-boats continues to be extremely scanty."[5] That year would to end with Admiral King's headquarters estimating Japanese strength at 75 boats.

Tokyo deployed its submarines mainly to attack warships or act as scouts for the imperial fleet. Gerald E. Wheeler—naval aviator, scholar, professor—was a student of the Pacific war. He writes, "Americans were always puzzled that the Japanese never used their submarines at the chokepoints. They should have."

> That was because the Japanese doctrine was to use their submarines with their fleets, as scouts—to be ahead. Their Grand Plan was to intercept the American Fleet—any American fleet—en route to engage the Japanese Fleet, and to cause attrition with their submarines, and then to pick 'em off after the battle (the wounded ones). . . . The thought of using them for merchant-shipping attacks or choke-point attacks just was not in their naval thinking. And never was.[6]

The Japanese navy was a good one. But it had made a fundamental error in tying its boats to the fleet instead of missions as commerce raiders, as the United States and Germany did. Tanker and other traffic from the West Coast to Hawaii sustained the U.S. Pacific Fleet. "If they'd put submarines between Pearl Harbor and San Francisco, they would have made a big difference. We would have had to *heavily* escort everything."[7] The full weight of that further burden never materialized.

> Although the protection of our task forces against submarines remained a problem requiring destroyer escort and combat air patrols, and affording an opportunity of using some of the advanced techniques developed in the Atlantic, the protection of merchant ships from underwater attack was not a major task for us in the Pacific. Small, special convoys operated between San Francisco and Pearl Harbor, San Francisco and the South Sea Islands, Seattle and Alaska, and Seattle and the Aleutians, but practically all of our shipping in the Pacific was able to operate independently.[8]

As the threat eased in the Atlantic, the subsurface warfare division of NDRC shifted its emphasis to enhancing the effectiveness (and safety) of fleet submarine operations in the western Pacific. As well, the impending defeat of Germany realized a redistribution of naval strength, including LTA forces. The November 1943 directive from Tenth Fleet decommissioning ZP-51 and ZP-23 in the Atlantic Fleet (chapter 5) had ordered—"at the earliest practicable date"—the transfer of eleven K-type airships to the U.S. West Coast. "It is essential that there be no disclosure . . . as to the tactics, methods and new weapons employed in warfare against the U-boats, because any information the Japanese may get will cost us many submarines and the lives of many men of our submarine crews. . . . Caution all officers and men to maintain absolute secrecy as to new developments in anti-submarine warfare."[9]

The Japanese did have MAD, the development of which they had begun in mid-1942. Though its detection range was low, "the need for such a device was regarded as urgent enough to justify its production."[10] By 1945, the use of magnetic detectors as part of Japanese antisubmarine aircraft doctrine stood confirmed. Accordingly, methods of evasion were recommended if American skippers suspected MAD tracking: go deep, turn to within thirty degrees of an east or west heading, then, "Go fast for 4000 yards or more."[11]

Sensor deficiencies (including poor sonar) notwithstanding, the Japanese submarine was a potent platform. Still, "When the Germans urged Japan to use her undersea fleet against Allied supply ships, the Japanese invariably replied that they would risk their submarines only against warships."[12] Unlike the Atlantic sea battle, then, Allied supply lines threading the vast western Pacific basin were left comparatively unmolested.

When Japan struck the United States, American LTA had no official organization to conduct fleet operations, or forces for defensive sea control of the inshore Pacific, or air-base facilities devoted to its requirements. "Our only blimp activity," Rosendahl had testified, "is a meager one at Lakehurst; we have none at all with the Fleet or on the Pacific coast." Urgent action was needed to protect West Coast maritime traffic. Similar to senior command for the Atlantic, the applied organization was headed by Commander, Fleet Airships Pacific; in 1943, this would be Capt. Howard N. Coulter, USN, with additional duty as Commander, Fleet Airship Wing Three (an intermediate command), with its component squadron and headron organization.

Mere months after USS *Macon* (ZRS 5) had foundered, the army had taken over the Sunnyvale station; by 1941, this was the West Coast training center for the Army Air Corps. When the navy, hungry for facilities, maneuvered to get it back, the army resisted. The final decision belonged to the president. A barter agreement had the army vacating in April 1942, thus ending the hemming and hawing. "I drew the job of clearing this latest deal with Army Headquarters," Rosendahl would record. The Air Corps, "Mike" Bradley remembered, "didn't even leave us a light bulb. They took off all the fixtures and everything else, so we had almost to start from scratch out there."[13] That October, the first cadets arrived on station for flight training. And in November, construction commenced on Hangars No. 2 and No. 3.

Rear Adm. J. W. Greenslade, Twelfth Naval District, headquarters San Francisco, was unambiguous: he wanted airships augmenting his patrol forces. "If we could have a pair of them operating off this port daily," he remarked, "I would feel that shipping would be much more secure." But its car precluded rail shipment of the K type. The answer: dismantle *TC-13* and *TC-14* for fast freight to Sunnyvale. "I learned that both ships are equipped to carry depth bombs and machine guns," Rosendahl advised. "While they are not quite as fast as the K-type, they are nevertheless entirely serviceable ships and can give a good account of themselves. . . . I wish we had more blimps to give you at this time but this is undoubtedly the best that can be done at the moment."

The day after Christmas, in a memo for Admiral King, Captain Rosendahl recommended that orders be issued to transfer the ex-army *TC-13* and *-14,* along with necessary gear and personnel. The pair (with later ships) represented a nascent LTA squadron for the Western Sea Frontier. "To supply Comtwelve's urgent need for ZNPs, it is recommended that orders be issued to transfer the *TC-13* and *TC-14,* together with all necessary equipment, operating items, etc., as well as necessary personnel from Lakehurst to Sunnyvale as quickly as possible. It is further recommended that if the Army cannot evacuate Moffett Field before the arrival of the above shipments and personnel, arrangements be made with the Army for joint occupancy until final evacuation."[14]

To this King scribbled "OK EJK."[15] Accordingly, "The Bureau of Aeronautics is requested to accomplish immediate shipment by fast freight, to Moffett Field, of the airships *TC-13* and *TC-14* together with all equipment, spares and material for re-assembling and placing these ships in service at Moffett Field as expeditiously as possible."[16]

As well, the commissioning of ZP-32 was directed, with both TCs assigned as the inaugural ships for that first Pacific Coast LTA squadron.

As per orders, the pair were deflated and disassembled, packed for transcontinental shipment (eleven freight cars), then hauled west on 12 January. Assigned to Moffett Field, this secondhand force represented the first operational patrol types. "They were serviceable enough and efficient enough and they worked okay," a pilot recalls, chuckling. "But they weren't very modern in a lot of ways. We started anti-submarine patrols soon as we got the airships set up and ready to go." Remarked another, "The old *TC-14* scared most of us [students], when [we] first got in the thing."[17] That May–September, *K-8, -11, -12,* and *-16* were rail-shipped west, after which *K-20, K-21,* and *K-22* exploited a planned cross-country air-ferry route to California. Subsequent deliveries were rail-shipped for erection at Moffett.[18]

Meanwhile, urgency had the navy raiding Goodyear assets, impressing its publicity blimps into antisubmarine defense. (Los Angeles–based *Resolute* was that coast's only airship on 7 December.) "U.S. Navy" replaced the Goodyear logo; redesignated *L-4,* the former *Resolute,* along with *L-5* through *L-7,* joined U.S. naval aviation. Still, reinforcements were in order, so as to establish a squadron. ZP-32 was commissioned on 31 January; nine days later, *TC-14* logged the unit's inaugural sortie, Lt. W. W. Boyd, pilot. Squadron skipper: Lt. Cdr. George F. Watson, USN—a father figure to Lakehurst's cadets and ensigns.

That winter, Watson had fifteen pilots (including him) and six airships under his command—the sole LTA assets assigned the Pacific Fleet. And these were ill equipped for ASW: installation of MAD was not completed in the *TC-14,* for example, until August. The Western Sea Frontier was never to have more than four ZNPs on line in all of 1942. That November, as well, *TC-13* and *-14* were relegated to training duties; each were deflated in 1943. As units of ZP-32, *TC-13* was to log 153 flights; *TC-14* would compile 1,543 hours during 201 sorties.

On 26 April, meanwhile, ZP-32 and the Western Sea Frontier suffered its first casualty. Landing that day, *TC-13* was light. Instead of letting go his line, an apprentice seaman in the ground crew hung on until about a hundred feet up, then fell clear.

The *K-3* through *K-8* series was underpowered, granting a performance unsuitable for Moffett-area operations and its offshore winds. "We must have a 55–60 knot ship to operate effectively," Watson advised. The Pratt and Whitney R-1340-AN-2 Wasp, operating down-rated at 425 horsepower, would propel *K-9* through *K-135.* In August 1943, the region's weather history would "propel" primary training westward, to relieve the pressure on Lakehurst. "Moffett, of course, was a wonderful place to train. The weather was usually pretty good, they had that huge hangar there. . . . That [however] wasn't where the action was at the time. The sooner you got to the East Coast, the faster you got into the war."[19]

First of the production-model K-type to reach the Western Sea Frontier was *K-20,* on 10 October, Lt. Cdr. Emmett J. Sullivan, command pilot. *K-21* gained the mat on the 31st. Delivered through Moffett, ZNP *K-22* was the first assigned to NAS Santa Ana, *L-8* the first to *land* there.[20] *K-23* was the first K-type *erected* at Moffett. That year, nine K-types were dispatched west from Akron, eleven air-delivered from the contractor to Lakehurst. Deliveries for 1943 were to dwarf these totals: twenty-seven K-ships reaching Moffett, sixty-five to Lakehurst.

A morale booster to surface sailors, not least the merchant marine, the lumbering, loitering blimp tendered reassurance: "In 1943 as a Navy pilot, my squadron left San Francisco on a Navy transport for the South Pacific. Since we were not in convoy it was most reassuring to have a Navy blimp covering us all the way down the coast until we headed west off the coast of Los Angeles."[21]

[Opposite] *L-9* on the mat at NAS Moffett Field, California, 2 November 1942. The base served as headquarters for Commander Fleet Airships Pacific and, as well, Fleet Airship Wing Three (*ZP-31, -32,* and *-33*). Moffett was the primary overhaul base for all Pacific Coast lighter-than-air. ZP-32, its home squadron, was commissioned on 31 January 1942. (U.S. Naval Institute)

[Opposite] L-ships in formation near Moffett Field, February 1944. Under the new CNATE command at Lakehurst, Moffett was assigned primary training in 1943, leaving Lakehurst to specialize in advanced flight indoctrination for naval aviators (airship) and aviation pilots. (U.S. Naval Institute)

Thirty-two flights were logged during February 1942: twenty-seven for patrol and escort, three for training, and two for experimental missions. The national emergency soon eclipsed these modest totals: by June, indeed, sorties had tripled in number, and hours per month had roughly doubled. ZP-32 was to log more than a thousand flights during 1942—6,410 hours in the air.

LTA was asserting itself. At headquarters of the Twelfth Naval District (in San Francisco), Vice Admiral Greenslade seemed satisfied as to the contributions of LTA assets under his command: "Our blimps out here seem to be doing very fine patrol work, but Watson appears a bit concerned over the prospective delay in receiving the new K-type ships. I imagine new production of this type of ship is being diverted to the East Coast, where they seem to need them more than we, at least for the present."[22]

The scale and pace of construction in the Western Sea Frontier approximated that along the East Coast and the Gulf of Mexico—the two other continental sea frontiers. In July, a program to better adapt Moffett Field for LTA operations was under way. Moffett became headquarters for the Commander, Fleet Airships Pacific, the primary base for ZP-32, and the main overhaul base for all West Coast lighter-than-air. In 1943, the Airship Training Center would be established, to help ease the burdens at Lakehurst. "I was impressed with the topography, and the beautiful buildings, and, of course, the hangar—the steel hangar there," an arriving student recalled. "Beautiful, absolutely beautiful. And all the streets were named after the old pioneers, and everything was *clean*, close to San Jose. The BOQ was a great place to live. . . . The atmosphere at Moffett, I thought, was California."[23]

Outlying or expeditionary facilities augmented the main headquarters stations, conferring operational flexibility and refuge alternates. Naval Air Auxiliary Facility (NAAF) Watsonville, California, for one, offered three circles. The station hosted a one- or two-ship detachment from ZP-32 for routine antisubmarine patrols of the Monterey area.

As erection advanced at Moffett, two timber hangars were authorized for a site at Santa Ana; the first was begun in April 1942. As well, work started on a standard LTA station at Tillamook, Oregon, to help with air cover over the Puget Sound sector. Weather-related reservations attending this site proved fully justified: "In the Northwest, it is felt that the blimp patrol should be one covering, primarily, approaches to the Strait of Juan de Fuca and the Strait itself. Tillamook is 225 miles airline from this extremely important area. The time involved would often be 8 to 10 hours one way assuming that the ships operated from the main base."[24]

NAS Tillamook was commissioned on 1 December 1942. Ten days later, wing commander Scott E. "Scotty" Peck—up from Moffett—officiated at a brief ceremony (in the rain). Patrol Squadron Thirty-three was placed in commission to operate as a fleet unit of the Western Sea Frontier. Commanding Officer (December 1942–March 1944): Cdr. Emmett J. "Sully" Sullivan, USN, now a commander. The squadron had yet to be fitted out; a full complement of officers and enlisted ratings did not report for duty until January. The first patrol ship, ZNP *K-31,* reached the station on 15 February.

Northwestern operations dared awful weather. Frequent fogs, rain, and mud had vexed erection timetables and construction costs. Inshore patrol along the Washington–Oregon coast met frequently hazy, gray, and cloudy skies. ZPs were rarely down for repairs, and few of their missions were cancelled or aborted due to adverse weather. Still, losses occurred. On 27 March 1943,

riding out shifting, gusty winds and rain squalls, *K-31* was wrenched from its mast, badly damaging the car. A three-man pressure watch got clear, uninjured. A November incident ended somewhat better, as command pilot Harold W. Johnson, USNR, relates:

> On November 19, 1943 while piloting *K-71,* I was caught some 150 miles at sea with the onset of a storm not forecast by Aerology. . . . The severity of the storm and the direction of the wind dictated flying low to the water and making a track toward Tillamook of approximately 90 degrees to the heading of the aircraft. Our problems were aggravated by a stuck exhaust valve in the starboard engine which greatly reduced the power and constituted a future hazard. By watching the whitecaps and bringing . . . the ship almost into the wind and then letting it fall off toward the coast, we were able to make good 25–30 knots toward base.
>
> Unfortunately, we lost daylight when we were about ten miles from home and could no longer see the ocean. The only compass in those days was a floating magnetic one which was useless in the type of turbulence we were encountering. Low fuel state

[Opposte] Ships assigned to Airship Squadron Thirty-One (ZP-31), NAS Santa Ana, 7 November 1943. Note the blowers and inflation sleeves connected to each ship, to maintain envelope pressure. The need to "fly" airships on the ground is an inherent weakness of LTA logistics. (U.S. Naval Historical Center photograph)

was now a problem also as we had been airborne some eleven hours. Our first contact with the coast was the Columbia River Lightship, some 30 miles north of Tillamook Bay. Unable to make headway toward the south and with conditions worsening (pre-frontal fog), we held over Long Beach, Washington.

Skipper Sullivan had been able to get manpower from a nearby army base to help provide a semblance of ground control in the gusty 40-knot winds. A little after midnight, we received a heavy gust . . . which rolled the ship to starboard and the starboard prop anchored itself in the sand up to the cowling. We evacuated the ship after turning off all power and ripping the envelope. Total flight time: seventeen hours. No injuries. Maintenance later confirmed that there was less than ten gallons of fuel remaining in the tanks. Except for the deflated envelope and sudden stoppage on the engine, only minor damage was incurred and *K-71* was flying again after being fitted with a new envelope.[25]

Less weather-afflicted, ZP-31, the Santa Ana squadron, was commissioned on 1 October 1942 and commenced flight operations that December.

Neither station contributed significantly the first twelve months following Washington's declaration: neither had had ZNPs immediately assigned. Santa Ana logged less than forty sorties once two K-ships were assigned; ZP-33 was unable to fly at all until 1943. Thus, LTA support to forces within the frontier fell to patrol ships assigned to Moffett. Operational experience held scarce: night patrols, for example, were risky—one was logged by LTA in all of 1942 along that seaboard. Inexperience was plain in every element of the A/S mission. Evaluation of early contacts was slow in being standardized (on either coast), because aircrews were new to ASW. Moreover, the machinery for collecting, much less evaluating information and intelligence was slow in being devised.

"There was always," an airman remembers , "the report of submarines and the occasional sighting of one off our West Coast." Sweeps of assigned areas or suspicious sightings realized an occasional depth charging; still, genuine targets proved scarce. ("Report received of suspicious partly submerged object one mile off Point No Point. Investigation by plane and surface vessels reveals another log.") ZP-31, for its part, attacked its first definite MAD contact in March 1943—not a submarine. Allied intelligence did not yet know, but Japanese offensive operations had ended in most eastern Pacific areas before proficient A/S units had been deployed against them.

Unlike the Atlantic campaign, with its escalating destruction, the war in and along Pacific coastal waters proved tame. Howard W. Johnston, commissioned and ensign, USNR, in 1941, was designated a Naval Aviator (Airship) in February 1943. Assigned to Squadron Thirty-one, he received his Command Pilot rating at Santa Ana, after which, in October, he was transferred to Tillamook, along with five pilots, to help staff ZP-33. "A couple of 'kills' would have greatly enhanced our standing in the ongoing and post war aviation hierarchy. Although I was occasionally assigned to participate on a 'hot' ASW search, I cannot truthfully say I ever flew in the vicinity of an active enemy submarine. Post war reports from Japanese sources indicate their submarine operations in our west coast theater were severely limited after 1942."[26]

In California, civil defense classes had become mandatory as schoolchildren readied for submarine or air attack. "Teenage students learned how to douse the lights and take cover when the air-raid sirens sounded." Many schools had armories and shooting ranges where students practiced firing .22-caliber rifles.[27] Assigned to the 122nd Battalion, U.S. Army, Phil Robinson recalled the anxieties afflicting coastal California. "We had guns to set up around defense plants, guns to set up around shipbuilding docks—anything like that that was important to the government. And be prepared to defend it. . . . We went on many alerts."[28]

The more modern "King" ships (ZNPs *K-13* and *-14*) slated for the Western Sea Frontier reached Lakehurst on 11 September; within weeks, all had been rail-shipped west. Meanwhile, rack installations for MAD equipment—the Mark IV-B—were effected, with final installation slated for California. The research labs continued to pursue redesign: though provisional, the operational record for MAD had verified the latest redesign *and* its in-flight potential by naval—as opposed to laboratory—personnel. (See table 3-4.)

Skipper Watson had queried Lakehurst as to its experience with the MAD sensor in Group One. Mills's reply:

> The new MAD model is about 30 lbs. lighter than the Mark II; is just as rugged in construction and more so as concerns operation. It is simpler to operate in that there are fewer controls (basic controls are the same). It stays in adjustment longer during flight. Its effective range is about the same. That is 400 to 600 feet. Its mounting is as one unit at the controls. The compactness of all units mounted in one group make for a neat installation and simplicity of the support stand. New mock-up calls for it being mounted above the RADAR so one operator can work both sets. On recent ships it is mounted aft of the mechanic on port side.[29]

December 1942 saw Mark IV-B-2 sets delivered to *all* LTA stations, thereby replacing the Mark IV-B-1 equipment; on the West Coast, MAD operations were under way from the new station at Santa Ana. Modeled on South Weymouth/Weeksville, construction had begun in April 1942. Cost: $11 million, half of which went for two timber hangars. Six months following groundbreaking, the air station and ZP-31 were commissioned. Twelve days later, *L-8* (an element of ZP-32) settled into the hands of a ground handling party. Squadron Thirty-one saw its first ZNP on 11 November, with the arrival of *K-20*—the first *assembled* on that coast.[30]

At Columbia's Airborne Instruments Laboratory (AIL), on Long Island, New York, further design work soon outmoded the Mark IV-B.[31]

On 1 October 1942, Scotty Peck assumed command of Airship Patrol Group Three. His senior: Commander, Western Sea Frontier. Upon the commissioning of the new group and his assuming command of it, he said,

> I would like to remark . . . that the commissioning today of Airship Patrol Group Three has a special significance. We are dedicating an enlarged and more comprehensive lighter-than-air organization for the West Coast of the United States to the task of assisting

in the protection of that coast. By this dedication we are notifying the enemy that any future raids on this coast will be made at increasingly greater risks to his own raiding forces. The commissioning of this Group indicates that the determination of our highest naval authority to bring the full force of lighter-than-air power to bear against the enemy's submarine fleet. . . . It is our job to sink every submarine that the enemy sends to these waters.[32]

At sea, the presence of an iron or steel object (if large enough) produced a recognizable magnetic signal—an oscillating sweep trace on a clock-driven recording tape. The ZNP would maneuver to develop such a contact. (LTA enjoyed few opportunities to attack a surfaced U-boat.) On escort with vessels in sight, a blimp would drop a flare to mark the position for surface ships and supporting planes. Its pilot then circled, trying to approach upwind on each pass over the object. On patrol, LTA marked the contact point—graphic traces of MAD signals—with bronze slicks or flares as the ZNP maneuvered to define the course of its target. (Sonobuoys simplified this tracking.) Still, training, practice, and experienced piloting were crucial to any real chance of success.

The MAD operator was crucial. The equipment had to be properly adjusted, thoughtfully operated. Unfortunately, the instrument itself reacted to wrecks (as we have seen), geologic anomalies and other noise, fluctuations in power supply or ground speed—even to extreme maneuvers of the platform. Effective use thus depended upon ability to interpret its signals—traces on the electromagnetic graphic recorder—and to reject spurious swings of the pen. Peak size (in gammas—a unit of magnetic field strength), number and shape, the time taken to record them, and the smoothness of the trace were fundamental to deciding whether an indication was spurious or, in fact, a true signal.

Fleet Airships Pacific Tactical Unit (FAPTU)

Counterpart of that at Key West, an antisubmarine school for LTA was established for the West Coast. This was Fleet Airships Pacific Tactical Unit. Installed at NAAF Del Mar in March 1944, FAPTU was an auxiliary of Santa Ana. Facilities: an asphalt mat with two mooring circles and barracks. Similar to the Atlantic Fleet detachment, the school provided operational training for combat-crew personnel assigned to the three ZP squadrons of the Pacific Fleet. First officer in charge: Commander Sullivan, who in May was ordered to command ZP-14 (see chapter 6). "The mission of FAPTU was to train combat air crews for overseas deployment."[33] Further, "It [FAPTU] was geared to training combat crews in airship ASW techniques, particularly in the use of MAD gear, as well as navigation, tactical doctrine and carrier landing procedures. The unit operated under the control of Commander, Fleet Airships Pacific. After training 64 combat air crews, the unit was disestablished on June 27, 1945."[34]

Del Mar developed a number of flight-training exercises. Designed to sharpen aircrew skills, a FAPTU manual specified exercises on the application of the Mark VI MAD for the trapping, tracking, and bombing of a submerged submarine. (See appendix G.) Drills on the use of sonobuoys were outlined, as was the use of radar as an aid in night or low-visibility bombing. It is to be regretted that such were unavailable when war came.

A bizarre casualty marred that first wartime summer. At 0600, 16 August, *L-8* departed for patrol. Five hours later, she drifted inshore and floated clumsily onto the streets of Daly City, California. Its crew of two officers was not aboard.

> The most logical theory—and it is only a theory—is that the crew's disappearance was entirely accidental and unintentional. Both officers knew that, because of prevailing winds, they could free balloon back to the mainland if in trouble. If they had experienced difficulty with the airship, it is inconceivable that they would immediately abandon it especially without radioing their intention to do so. Furthermore, no evidence of trouble, except the dead motors, were found when the ship was salvaged.
>
> The usual explanation is that at some time during the flight, one of the officers may have leaned out of the car, lost his balance, and fallen part way out. The other then rushed to his aid and that during the struggle to get back in . . . , both fell from the ship. The open door is regarded as fairly good proof that they left the ship by means of it.[35]

Another factor heightened the mystery. Both men were wearing life belts, yet their bodies were never recovered. Could the men have been picked up? And if so, by whom?

Joint Operations with Escort Carriers (CVEs)

Extending the range of sea-based aircraft had intrigued experimenters since the birth of naval aviation. Test moors to a British carrier were conducted during World War I, after which the notion languished. In 1939, the Commander, Battle Force, U.S. Fleet, had opined that airships were valuable adjuncts to defense forces afloat. Hence, expanding their employment seemed "beyond question." But, he added, the use of ship-based blimps was "not favored."[36]

When, late in 1943, the U-boat menace in the North and South Atlantic had been blunted (though not subdued), Lakehurst pondered disposition of its East Coast forces "when the European submarine picture folds up." The Pacific war had shifted half an ocean away: the threat of serious attack on the American continent by Japan had vanished. "Troops guarding the waterfronts and other vital installations and manning emergency defenses had been withdrawn along with their guns, barrage balloons, radars and searchlights. Gates in the anti-submarine nets were left open and unattended. All lights ashore and on the water burned without interruption."[37]

A major supply point, the West Coast (and Pearl Harbor) now lay far behind the lines. To contribute further to the defeat of Japan, LTA would have to deploy *beyond* Hawaii—into the southern and western Pacific. The mission of FAPTU, after all, had been to train combat air crews *for overseas deployment.* Also, the abortive O-ship had been proposed for blue-water missions, "for convoy escort on routes such as Bahia to Dakar, and Hawaii to Somoa." The DCNO (Air), however, had pointedly excluded discussion of "the possible future use of blimps in the Hawaiian or mandated island areas" in his 1943 recommendations. Still, "If we are ever to expand LTA into the Pacific, it seems to me we should be making such plans right now so that we should be prepared to move at once if the signal were given. . . . The basic question is how to bring the issue up for decision without getting it knocked cold without a chance to discuss it. Obviously, if a request came from the Pacific itself the whole business would be much simpler."[38]

No "signal" came. As fleet carrier forces advanced naval airpower toward the Japanese home islands, had senior commands considered airships for antisubmarine operations or for mine spotting in the clear waters of the South Pacific?[39] Given command resistance to LTA (and to Rosendahl), a serious-minded assessment at the time seems improbable. Retrospectively, one historian of the aircraft carrier is "doubtful":

> The situation in the Pacific did not lend itself to large-scale airship use: (1) Japanese submarine threat was very small compared to U-boats, (2) airship bases—a major consideration—were practical in the U.S., UK, and North Africa (although very expensive) but they were not practical on Pacific islands where the distances to ASW areas were considerable, (3) there were no set trade routes in the Pacific as they changed with every island conquest, and (4) there were plenty of CVEs for ASW in the Pacific and multiengine aircraft suitable for ASW were being produced in large numbers—PB4Y-2, PB4Y-1, and PBM *Mariner,* with P5M *Marlin* and P2V *Neptune* planned.[40]

When FAPTU was established for schooling officers in ASW developments and methods, tactics had been reassessed, exercises prepared, innovations explored. Among the latter: trial joint operations with carriers.

The first touchdown occurred on 4 February 1944, when *K-29* (ZP-31) landed on *Altamaha* (CVHE 18), an escort carrier. Objective: a test of refueling operations. Six months later, 20–23 August, a 72.5-hour, six-landing exercise demonstrated the feasibility of refueling and replenishment. Operating off San Diego with *Makassar Strait* (CVU 91), the crew of ZNP *K-111,* Lt. Cdr. Frederick N. Klein, USN, command pilot, was relieved every twelve hours, the blimp's engines operating continuously. In one evolution, "111" was held to the deck for thirty-two minutes. This demonstration implied the feasibility of extended operations and, as well, of ferry flights to distant overseas bases. In April, ZJ-1 introduced a training exercise: the simulation of refueling at sea (by picking up floating cans). And that fall, *Instructions for Carrier Landing Operations 1944* was released by Fleet Airships Pacific. "You may need that postage stamp landing field someday," pilots were advised.

Joint operations in the Atlantic and Caribbean would, later, build upon these incipient trials—one element in the postwar evolution of hunter-killer groups. The first inflight refueling would be logged in 1949 *(M-4),* the first night carrier qualifications in 1950 *(K-124).* These exercises would refine methods to extend the airship's time with surface forces—refueling, replenishing, and rearming as well as remanning with fresh aircrews. "Carrier qualifications for ZP pilots were routinely required in the late 1940s and early 1950s. . . . Airship-carrier landings, refueling and replenishment from carriers and night operations with carriers became commonplace for the airship squadrons."[41] The postwar N-type, however, was too large for shipboard handling. The last carrier-deck touchdown was logged in 1956.

In November 1943, Rear Adm. Herbert Leary, USN, commandant of the Fifth Naval District, assumed command of the Eastern Sea Frontier from the retiring Adolphus Andrews. A believer in LTA, he had queried Rosendahl as to why ZNPs were still being sent to the West Coast instead

ZNP *K-29* on approach to the escort carrier *Altamaha* (CVE 18) off San Diego, 4 February 1944. A test of joint operations, to open the door to deployment into the western Pacific, this was the first carrier landing by a U.S. Navy blimp. Feasibility notwithstanding, no ZNPs accompanied U.S. naval forces toward Japan for mine spotting or for ASW against the Japanese. (U.S. Naval Institute)

of deploying, practically all of them, along the Atlantic, "where the real submarine threat exists." In fact, one out of each three patrol ships out of Akron was being assigned to Pacific squadrons.[42] Indeed, in August, an *increased* allocation to the Western Sea Frontier stood approved. The intense air traffic off California mandated enhanced air-sea rescue capabilities for downed airmen; hence, the augmented strength assigned to Fleet Airship Wing Three. A November directive called for transfer of eleven ZNP-Ks to the Pacific coast, five of which were to be used as spares.[43] The operational allowances for Fleet Airships Pacific thus climbed from twenty-four to thirty-four, with six retained as spares to support the deployment.

This action realized the following LTA organization under the Commander, Fleet Airships Pacific. For Fleet Airship Wing Three:

- ZP-31, with twelve ZNPs based at NAS Santa Ana supported by NAAFs at Del Mar and Lompoc
- ZP-32, with fifteen ZNPs based at NAS Moffett Field with NAAFs at Watsonville and Eureka
- ZP-33, with six ZNPs based at NAS Tillamook

Fleet Airships Atlantic comprised eighty-three ZNP aircraft in October 1944 (four wings, eleven squadrons). Directives that fall called for new deployments, however: the Atlantic Fleet's authorized allowance was *reduced* to two blimprons, with fourteen ZNPs assigned: Lakehurst the operating base for six, another eight assigned to the Panama Sea Frontier. (Rosendahl had recommended one wing and four squadrons: twenty-eight total.) In addition, four ships would be retained as spares and replacements.[44]

One measure of the perceived Japanese submarine threat in the Pacific : mission allocation for destroyers and destroyer escorts. In September 1943, 10 percent were assigned to ASW; Atlantic-based destroyers and DEs, in contrast, devoted 100 percent to ASW. As well, dissemination of

information relative to antisubmarine work (such as advising on attack technique) was slow to reach Pacific Fleet destroyers. By 1944, indeed, "Our training program in the Pacific is facing several difficulties; first the Japanese sub menace is not sufficiently serious to maintain enthusiasm without artificial stimulation. Whether right or wrong the Japanese sub menace is held in very low repute. Many of our commanders are very reluctant to sacrifice tactical flexibility and convenience for security."[45]

[Opposite] A postwar squadron flies carrier qualifications off the Virginia Capes, 1951. Postwar exercises refined methods to extend the airship's time with "hunter-killer" groups—refueling, replenishing, rearming, remanning. Soon a routine—if precise—operation, LTA antisubmarine services were never integrated into U.S. fleet forces. (Capt. F. N. Klein, USN [Ret.])

[Right] Adm. Herbert F. Leary, USN, inspects *M-1*, 28 January 1944. Leary had relieved the superbly able Vice Adm. Adolphus Andrews as Commander, Eastern Sea Frontier. (GHMC, NASM, Smithsonian Institution)

The war in the western Pacific seemed well in hand late that year. Midway had stopped Japanese expansion. To be sure, the Japanese navy still posed a blue-water threat, with its submarine force deployed to help stop the American advance through the Solomons and subsequent Allied island taking. Still, its undersea fleet presented a diminished force; after October 1942, none of its units had again penetrated the Western Sea Frontier. Still, Japanese boats were yet potent—Cominch noting, for example, "appreciable enemy activity during January in Indian Ocean where about 6 German and several Jap U-boats are estimated operating."[46]

As 1944 progressed, scientists of Division Six began to wind up their work on ASW and concentrate on the Pacific, where the campaign was expected to be protracted. American submariners needed assistance in countering A/S techniques of the Japanese navy. Although the emphasis on equipment waned, work on operational analysis continued apace.[47]

The submarine war in the Pacific persisted, with sea-lane attacks into 1945 until the demise of the Imperial Japanese Navy *and* Japan's merchant shipping.

> A USS [*SIC*] LIBERTY SHIP WAS TORPEDOED ABOUT 800 MILES WEST OF AUSTRALIA ON 6 FEBRUARY PROBABLY BY A GERMAN U-BOAT RETURNING FROM OPERATIONS OFF SYDNEY WHERE A SHIP WAS SUNK IN DECEMBER. THERE APPEARS TO BE NO OTHER U-BOATS AT SEA IN INDIAN OCEAN AT PRESENT. PACIFIC ACTIVITY DURING THE MONTH INCLUDES AN LST TORPEDOED BY JAP U-BOAT WEST OF PALAU AND THE OUTSTANDING PERFORMANCE OF 2 US SUBS IN SINKING 4 ENEMY BOATS OFF THE CHINA COAST IN A 5 DAY PERIOD.[48]

The Admiralty's appraisal of the Japanese threat: a spent naval force. "It is unlikely that the Japanese will have sufficient U-boats and aircraft to exert in the Combat Areas torpedo attacks comparable to those which we have had to meet in the North Atlantic and Western Approaches. Moreover, anti-U-boat forces for the protection of shipping in those areas will then be augmented by those released from the European theater."[49]

A half-world away, the war in Europe—and along its North Atlantic lifelines—was approaching climax. The Allies had come ashore at Normandy in June 1944; pushing inland, (growing) Allied armies were advancing across France toward the German frontier. Having failed to disrupt the invasion forces, the U-boat now proved unable to interdict its necessary supply: "Thousands of Allied ships have been moved across the Channel to Normandy and coastwise to build up the Military Forces engaged in the liberation of Europe. No merchant vessel of this vast concourse has been sunk by U-boat. . . . This despite attempts by a substantial force of U-boats to pass up-channel from their bases in Norway and France."[50]

The *Schnorkel*

In waters patrolled by aircraft, a U-boat's crew endured constant tension. According to Coastal Command, "An aircraft has the power, if the Captain [pilot] uses his imagination, to cause more heart fluttering among a U-boat crew than any other craft used in A/S warfare." Still, boat commanders preferred the surface, keeping storage batteries (which fed the electric motors) fully charged for submerged attacks—or escape.[51] Driven underwater, mobility was compromised. In January 1944, Dönitz boasted of a "new submarine weapon"; fresh technology, indeed, was about to be leveraged in the war on shipping.

Recurrent prisoner-of-war reports had attested to development of a new high-submerged-speed type. The Type XXI U-boat was expected to appear in operating areas, but no evidence signaled its deployment. Instead, as we have seen, a new device appeared. This was the extensible diesel air vent, or *schnorkel.* At periscope depth, the vent, or breather, extended a short distance above the surface, offering only a tiny radar target. Fresh air was vital to submariners; despite purifiers, the supply inside the boat could become very foul. And the diesels required a continual supply, hence were useless submerged. *Schnorkel*-trunk equipped, sufficient air to ventilate the boat and to operate its diesels was drawn inside—and the exhaust smoke discharged. The device's small size effectively canceled radar contacts. (During tests, the Model ASG radar had been known to pick up periscopes. But in actual practice, a periscope gave an indication similar to that of spurious echoes.) Introduced in 1944, the *schnorkel,* or snorkel, was intended for deployment where frequent patrols and air coverage were probable. The breather (as noted in chapter 6) conferred near-immunity—producing, combined with the new high-speed-type U-boat, a nightmare for A/S commanders. Further, radar-absorbent or -deflecting coatings reduced its already small signal—"the only success of the Kriegsmarine in the electronic war."[52] The first boats so equipped had sailed in October 1944. Accordingly, Tenth Fleet gave snorkel detection A-1 priority.

By enabling the charging of batteries at periscope depth *and* ventilation of the boat, *schnorkel* conferred continuous submergence. Operational that autumn, it made fitted U-boats largely immune from airborne radar. By default, detection reverted chiefly to visual sightings—but the breather was difficult to sight even in daylight. Meantime, the enemy operated close inshore (and more profitably) in waters previously untenable because of coverage. Dönitz concentrated his assets around the United Kingdom, all ports of which (as in the western Atlantic) were congested with freight.

For the first time since 1939, U-boats returned to British inshore waters. Operating singly, free of the surface and wireless silent, the raiders dropped to the bottom when hunted; there, numerous wrecks and difficult sound conditions frustrated sonar. The rate of killing dropped. Snorkel "significance was appreciated only in the urgent circumstances of 1943, and the development of the snorkel submarine was not possible before the summer of 1944. The units equipped with snorkel acquitted themselves admirably and were able to penetrate into the most heavily patrolled areas and there operate successfully, cruising submerged for weeks at a time."[53]

On the first day of October, a worried Commander in Chief, U.S. Fleet, advised his commanders,

> MERSHIP LOSSES AND U-BOAT KILLS WERE MODERATE DURING SEPTEMBER REFLECTING BOTH LACK OF ENEMY OFFENSIVE OPERATIONS AS WELL AS DIFFICULTY OF LOCATING AND ATTACKING SCHNORCHEL [*SIC*] EQUIPPED U-BOATS.[54]

The efficacy of the device was immediate:

> INSHORE SCHNORCHEL OPERATIONS FINALLY BEGAN TO PAY DIVIDENDS DURING DECEMBER WITH 6 MERSHIPS AND 1 ESCORT SUNK AND 3 SHIPS TORPEDOED IN THE SW APPROACHES AND ENGLISH CHANNEL AREA AND 1 ESCORT SUNK AND 1 MERSHIP TORPEDOED OFF HALIFAX. DIFFICULTY CONTINUES TO BE EXPERIENCED IN LOCATING AND EFFECTIVELY ATTACKING SCHNORCHEL AS A RESULT OF WHICH FEW U-BOATS WERE SUNK DURING THE MONTH.[55]

Still, the diesel-breather did not confer an unvarnished gift to the men it served. "For the crews snorkeling was an agony: whenever a wave made the valve at the tip of the snorkel shut off the air supply to the diesels, the engines satisfied their considerable need for oxygen by draining the air directly from the boat's interior. At times the men were writhing on the floor in torment as their eardrums burst. Officially, such mishaps were attributed to 'incorrect application' of the gadget's directions for use."[56]

Germany, after 1942, had rarely operated inshore of the United Kingdom, a zone rich in merchant traffic—and risk. Now the raiders need not surface at all. Visual A/S search was not crippled, as puffs of snorkel exhaust could be sighted at a considerable range. Still, "the fitting of U-boats with *schnorkel* has largely removed this [radar detection] hazard," an Admiralty message advised. "Indeed," the British Air Commission in Washington moaned, "there is grave doubt whether [radar] is effective at all against a determined enemy using submarines so equipped."

In the play of measure/countermeasure, the British were pushed to respond. Norwegian-based *schnorkel*-equipped boats now could loiter in principal channels or zones of approach without surfacing. (The implications for the coming Allied invasion were soon evident.) As well, by lying on seabeds where wrecks abounded, a U-boat could effectively negate itself as a sonar target. On the approach of hunting forces, boats "bottomed," drifted with the tide, or exploited a dense water layer.[57]

At Tenth Fleet that February–April 1945, the list of triple-A-priority projects included "Radar Detection of Schnorchel" and, as well, "Deep Sonar Target"—a reference to the deep-diving Type XXI U-boat.[58]

The development of radar had rendered convoy escort by airship practicable at night or in poor visibility. Further, ZNP-deployed radar could pick up a periscope or *schnorkel* trail; its detection of *small objects,* indeed, had proven superior to that from airplanes—with adoption of *schnorkel,* a cardinal capability. Coatings notwithstanding, the breather head remained detectable, particularly from slow-speed aircraft. Likewise, wake was discernable visually (though not in rough or choppy seas), as was the diesel smoke.

U.S. Airships in England

In March 1945, conferences examined the utility of airships in British coastal waters. Early in April, initial discussions completed between interested authorities, facilities at the former rigid-airship base near Bedford were inspected. All overhaul work and repurification, it was decided, would be accomplished at Cardington, line maintenance at the main and subsidiary operating base or bases.

In the Western Approaches, a major chokepoint, the U-boat remained a naval and air preoccupation. A naval message from the Commander in Chief, Western Approaches (CincWA), dated 17 September 1944, is plain,

> At this particular stage in the anti-U-boat (German) war when it is more important than ever before to make certain the unimpaired arrival of our convoys I wish to make one general observation. When the presence of a U-boat is revealed by any means the greatest chance of killing it is in the first few hours. During this time ships should be at their most alert at action stations and with their best operators on duty. Every second lost in closing the datum point reduces the chances of a kill and to do this involves rapidity and clarity of communications as well as the efficiency of weapons instruments and their operators.[59]

As for the western Atlantic sea-lanes, "CNO considers effective schnorkel detection a part of general program of developing more effective radars and is not sanguine about early satisfactory tactical solution schnorkel problem. Modifications current airbourne [*sic*] radar expected to provide minor improvement only."[60]

This same month, Tenth Fleet, in a message to Commander, Eastern Sea Frontier, requested air and surface ASW exercises employing a *schnorkel*-equipped submarine, blimps, and surface units. Why? General deployment of the snorkel was forecast:

> IN VIEW OF INCREASING EVIDENCE OF U-BOATS IN BISCAY AND CHANNEL BEING EQUIPPED WITH EXTENSIBLE DIESEL AIR VENT (SCHNORKEL) ANTICIPATE ITS EARLY USE BY OTHER BOATS OPERATING OFF COASTAL AREAS THROUGHOUT ATLANTIC.[61]

Tonnage losses as well as kills had held moderate that September, reflecting on one hand lack of German offensive operations and, on the other, the difficulty of locating the snorkel-equipped U-boat. In October, activity reached its lowest since U.S. entry into the war, including scant evidence in the British approaches. The fall of French ports and the necessity of transferring boats to Norwegian and Baltic bases had dislocated German naval operations, realizing relatively light at-sea forces. Once completed, however, a renewed offensive was foreseen.

> IN VIEW OF THE DESPERATE STRAITS IN WHICH THE ENEMY NOW FINDS HIMSELF TOGETHER WITH THE LARGE NUMBER OF U-BOATS HE NOW HAS AVAILABLE IT IS ANTICIPATED THAT THE INITIAL PHASE OF THE U-BOAT OFFENSIVE WILL BE OF CONSIDERABLE MAGNITUDE. YET TO BE DETERMINED IS THE EFFICACY OF THE NEW HIGH SUBMERGED SPEED TYPE 21 WHICH MAY BE EXPECTED TO APPEAR SHORTLY IN OPERATING AREAS.[62]

Had it been operational and in numbers, the new boat would have revolutionized the campaign. The necessary drawings had been finished in November 1943, contracts assigned. "Dönitz had made it clear that only the production of a new type of U-boat could save our submarine warfare. The navy wanted to abandon the previous type of 'surface ship' which occasionally moved under water. It wanted to give its U-boats the best possible streamlining and attain a higher underwater speed and a greater underwater range."[63]

Eight of the 1,600-ton Type XXI boats were delivered in August 1944. Forty XXIs a month had been promised by early 1945, but air raids by RAF Bomber Command had slowed production, destroying a third of the boats at the dockyards.[64] Still, construction was to persist until the yards themselves were captured.

Following sea trials, each new boat logged workups in the Baltic before it was released for operations. However, no experimental models had preceded series production of the Type XXI. And without experience with prototypes, testing of early units as well as crew training proved protracted: one boat only *(U-2511)* gained operational status prior to VE Day. Still, performance was remarkable: a maximum surface speed of 15.6 knots, a maximum submerged speed of 17.5 knots. "The snorkel enabled the Type XXI to cruise almost indefinitely below the surface and was virtually undetectable by the contemporary airborne radars, especially in anything over Sea State 2."[65]

Confident with *schnorkel,* U-boat patrols had shifted close inshore, into operating areas previously untenable; indeed, from mid-1944 to campaign's end, U-boats made increasing use of the breather. The most vexing areas for A/S forces: concentrations in the Southwest Approaches (a trade focal point), around the Orkneys, and the inshore waters of the United Kingdom, including the English Channel.

> THERE APPEARS TO BE A GRADUAL INCREASE IN THE NUMBER OF U-BOATS IN THE ATLANTIC WHICH TREND WILL PROBABLY CONTINUE FOR THE DURATION OF THE EUROPEAN WAR. WHEN THE TYPE XXI BECOMES OPERATIONAL A MARKED INCREASE IS ANTICIPATED SINCE IT IS LIKELY THAT A LARGE NUMBER OF THEM WILL COME OUT TOGETHER.[66]

To help counter this exertion, LTA was ordered to dispatch a second squadron to Europe. In April 1945, ZP-42 received orders to transfer operations from Brazil to southwestern England.

The notion of U.S. airships in England may date from fall 1944, when the U-boat returned to the Channel—a sea-lane posing extremely poor conditions for asdic (sonar) contact. (In Canadian waters as well, the issue of ZNPs had revived, in response to renewed U-boat operations inshore.) Adm. Harold R. Stark, commander of U.S. naval forces in European waters, had suggested to Churchill and to the War Cabinet that blimps be brought over to help deal with enemy concentrations. The offensive continued to escalate in the United Kingdom area, particularly in the Southwest Approaches and the Channel, where at mid-March 1945 about fifteen boats were estimated. Early April found Commander Sullivan in England, on temporary duty from Fleet Air Wing Fifteen. Lending his experience, he conferred at Headquarters Coastal Command, with Admiral Stark, and with Fleet Air Wing Seven—a unit of Coastal Command. Questions of feasibility and logistics settled, facilities had been suggested, then inspected. Flight operations would center on the RAF Coastal Command base at Chevinor, in southwest England.

LTA, all agreed, could tender a useful contribution to inshore convoy escort—a mission assigned mostly to long-range planes designed primarily for *ocean* work. Coastal Command's shore-based aircraft were realizing no kills, "though their continual presence over all our coastal waters had an enormous influence in restricting the enemy's activity."[67] As well, minefields were being laid to help counter the snorkel-fitted boats. On 6 April, Air Chief Marshal Sir Shelte Douglas, Commander in Chief, Coastal Command, requested—through the Admiralty—that blimps be sent to England:

> I have considered that a very great saving in the flying effort of these long range aircraft could be effected by employing "Blimps" on close escort work. If this can be done, the flying hours thus saved by my aircraft [mostly B-24 *Liberators*] could be devoted to offensive as well as defensive patrols further from these shores. The development of the present situation makes it more than ever desirable that long range aircraft shall be utilized effectively in the area from the South Western Approaches toward the Azores.[68]

The Admiralty endorsed the proposal: incorporated into Coastal Command, blimps would be under the operational control of the Admiralty, exercised through Douglas's own command. The formal consent of Admiral King would initiate the transfer for duty in Fleet Air Wing Seven—the unit of U.S. Navy airplanes in England.

Four ZNPs assigned to ZP-42 were ordered to Richmond, then on to Weeksville for overseas deployment: *K-93, K-100, K-126,* and *K-127*. Midmonth had Sullivan at Lakehurst, in conference at Fleet Airships Atlantic. Agenda: the ferrying of two ships to Port Lyautey and setting up a squadron immediately in England.[69]

The directive from Commander, Air Force, Atlantic Fleet, came on 15 April: air-ferry four ZNPs to England. (In March, for its part, the Joint RCN-RCAF Anti-Submarine Warfare Committee had decided *not* to ask the U.S. Navy to operate MAD-equipped airships in Canadian territorial waters.)[70] Squadron Forty-two was to be reorganized and outfitted, preparatory to transfer to Commander, Fleet Air Wing Seven, for duty. The setting up of a new squadron found

Crewmen board ZNP *K-89* for the Weeksville-to-Bermuda leg to Northwest Africa, 29 April 1945. Exploiting the southern route, the two-ship transatlantic transit (with *K-114*) of 3,532 nautical miles was made in sixty-two flight hours, sixteen minutes, an average ground speed of 56.7 knots. (GHMC, NASM, Smithsonian Institution)

Mills short on aviators: sending four blimps to Europe, with three crews per, hit Fleet Airships Atlantic hard. As it happened, those assigned to ZP-42 were in need of overhauls; further, its personnel had been serving out of country for months. So the squadron would go over in name only, the men (including an advance contingent) to be drawn from Squadrons Eleven, Twelve, and Twenty-four. Orders were requested for key officers and enlisted ratings. Selected to command the reconstituted unit: Lt. Cdr. Harold B. Van Gorder, skipper of ZP-24.

Defeat for Germany seemed certain. "If we are to be of value," Mills wrote Zimmerman, commander ZP-42, "there is great necessity for haste, therefore, things are going at a great rate around here."[71] Outfitted for the transit, the movement would take place on or about 1 May. "I certainly could use some of the excess personnel I was forced to give up so recently," Mills added dryly. And further cutbacks loomed.[72] That spring, meantime, prospective LTA assets over the inshore waters of the United Kingdom seemed inarguably useful: "The enemy continues to send U-boats to sea and there is no assurance that when the German armies are finally beaten that the U-boats will all stop their operations. The possibility that they will continue operations (some of them at least) is considered not beyond the realm of possibility. Consequently our returning troop convoys may need escort against U-boats long after land hostilities have largely ceased."[73]

No hyperbole, that. "Even in April 1945," Morison wrote, "the scale of U-boat operations around the British Isles gave no indication that the end of the war was near." On 5 May, the Admiralty advised home forces afloat that U.S. Navy blimps "may be seen in this country anywhere West of 2 degrees East and South of 56 degrees North" on antisubmarine patrols. VE Day, 8 May, found the first pair en route; in the Azores, two flight crews awaited the arrival. (A maintenance detachment had already been dispatched to England.) Victory in Europe cancelled the movement.

In the western Atlantic, an increase in independent U-boat operations suggested a spring offensive aimed at key terminal points of the North Atlantic convoy system and its feeder lines. The anticipated campaign, Tenth Fleet warned, might well be augmented by the laying of mines off principal harbors. But merchant sinkings proved light that April, with U-boat kills "continuing at a satisfactory level." The situation at sea persisted well in hand into July (see tables 7.1 and 7.2):

> WHILE ENEMY STILL APPEARS TO HAVE CONSIDERABLE U-BOAT CONCENTRATION IN NORTHERN WATERS APPRECIATE SITUATION HAS REACHED AN IMPASSE DUE TO HIS PRESENT INABILITY TO COPE WITH ALLIED A/S MEASURES.[74]

Late 1944 to VE Day saw an upswing in ASW operations, one result of increased enemy activity in the Eastern Sea Frontier to its highest pitch since 1942. One pilot's logbook for March of that year documents many a flight hour at the controls of *K-26, K-58, K-101, K-123,* and *K-130.* "And there was a difference among them, especially in terms of the quality of equipment."[75] Average patrol length: about fifteen hours.

To seaward, a novel threat haunted the eastern seacoast: the prospect of terror attacks by U-boats launching "robot bombs" against such population concentrations as New York City. Alarming reports had earlier reached the Allies concerning German long-range rockets. Now so-called robot, or flying, bombs were falling on London and had been since June 1944.[76] This was

TABLE 7.1 **Monthly antisubmarine statistics for Navy aircraft,** June 1944, Eastern Sea Frontier. Average number airships assigned: 28. Average number total aircraft assigned: 211. (National Archives)

Type Aircraft	Escort Sorties	Escort Flying Hours/Minutes
Long-range	335	2,659:45
Medium-range	4	18:49
Short-range	287	911:23
Blimps	146	1,853:55
Total	772	5,443:52

Type Aircraft	Other A/S Sorties	Other A/S Flying Hours/Minutes
Long-range	93	551:59
Medium-range	2	10:36
Short-rage	329	946:51
Blimps	227	2,727:40
Total	651	4,237:06
Total Sorties	1,423	Total hours 9,680:58

TABLE 7.2 **A typical month's operations** (August 1944), Fleet Airships Atlantic. Ten lighter-than-air squadrons (blimprons) were the operational units engaged in antisubmarine work. Platforms: about 80 K-type and three M-type airships. Main and auxiliary bases were located along the U.S. continental littoral as well as overseas: the Caribbean and Panamanian Sea Frontiers, Brazil (Fourth Fleet), North Africa, and in southern Europe. An Airship Utility Squadron and an Anti-Submarine Training Detachment also were operating. (GHMC, Smithsonian)

Number of Flights	1,711
Flight Hours	16,015.4
Miles Flown	685,795
Surface Ships Escorted	3,265

the V-1—a low-winged, jet-driven rocket. Although the threat to the eastern seaboards of Canada and the United States was in fact without foundation, official apprehension was understandable. When Adm. John H. Ingram, Commander, U.S. Atlantic Fleet, announced this dire possibility of a V-weaponry attack at a press conference in January 1945, he "created a sensation."

Rocket-propelled weapons *were* operational. ME-109s of the German air force, for example, were deploying rockets against B-17 *Flying Fortress* formations. And radio-controlled bombs, equipped with wings, threatened convoys and surface ships. Dropped from a launch plane, the weapon was then guided to its target. "A real menace to shipping is believed possible of development in this weapon and it may, because of its possibilities, take the place of a submarine as ship-destroyer number one."[77] Winfield Fromm, at the Aircraft Instruments Laboratory (AIL), recalled that time and the rocket-related threat:

> As the submarine menace began to disappear in 1943 because of the use of convoys, radar-equipped aircraft, MAD, and sonobuoys, a new threat began to develop in

Europe. This was the threat of radio command, guided bombs launched by the Germans against our ships. An urgent need existed for electronic counter-measures against guided missiles, to be developed and produced quickly, and so on January 1, 1944 AIL was transferred to Division 15 of NDRC, which had the responsibility for developing such countermeasures.[78]

Late in 1943, the Peenemünde Rocket Research Institute—the locus for German rocket work—had been urged to examine the possibility of launching V-2s from floats towed by U-boat. If practicable, Germany would be able to bomb objectives across hundreds of miles of water. A U-boat, it was calculated, could tow three seaborne launch platforms weighing about five hundred tons at an average speed of twelve knots—their submerging and surfacing controlled from the boat: "On arrival at the launching point the floats could be partially flooded so that they stood up right in the water. The top hatch could then be opened and the A-4 [V-2] erect upon its gyro-stabilized platform, after being fueled, prepared for launching, and adjusted, could be discharged."[79] Temporarily suspended, work had resumed at the end of 1944. The notion had advanced no further than the first design sketches when Allied bombing forced evacuation of Peenemünde in February 1945. Thus ended "a not unpromising project."[80]

Dönitz indeed had planned a final blitz: six snorkelers from Norwegian bases. The boats conveyed no secret or unconventional weapons—Dönitz had none. To counter, Allied operational plans were devised for the western Atlantic: Operation Teardrop. As Tenth Fleet plotted progress of the oncoming group, two fleet barrier forces took up station—CVEs and DEs—concentrations of force to deny the entire seaboard of Canada and the United States to the incoming attackers. In the New York sector, surface units initiated special patrols as, aloft, airplanes and blimps patrolled inshore against this singular threat. Naval planners were convinced that unrestricted warfare against shipping, including the use of mines, would continue in the Eastern Sea Frontier. The services of an airship task group to the frontier commander are plain from the record.

There was no mistaking the mission: all forces were to search for, discover, attack, and sink the enemy. "Well, they really stepped up the patrols," Gerry Wheeler (ZP-12) recalls. "The blimps started going 'round the clock"—flying at fifty feet, to fully (and properly) exploit the MAD gear. Equipped with a first-generation radio-altimeter, "We just kept our eye glued on that damned thing, to stay at fifty feet and not lower."[81] The task group commander instructed, "Stress training of personnel for war including instructions and qualifications for advancement in rating. Emphasize training and development of depth bomb attack methods, including radar search and MAD development of search and attack. Positive contact with an enemy submarine must be seized upon as an opportunity to dog him persistently and destroy him."[82]

The first months of 1945 had seen no successful attacks in the Eastern Sea Frontier—not one merchantman lost or U-boat sunk. A final defiant gesture from U-Boat Command commenced late in March, climaxing during April, when it met coordinated air and surface patrols. Recognizing that submarines would now probably operate submerged both day and night, Coast Guard sailing pickets equipped with sensitive underwater listening gear were deployed aggressively and coordinated directly with blimps to fully investigate all contact reports. Local defense craft patrolled swept channels day and night to attack any U-boat which might evade the offshore forces.

Already, the employment of ZNPs "after defeat of Germany" was generating memoranda, letters and directives as to reassessments, redeployments, and force reductions. Rosendahl parried, offering recommendations so as to minimize the damage to operating forces when European operations ended and to continue training and R&D. Object: to install LTA as a permanent element in the naval service. Every avenue of argument was offered. "There will be continued need for an Airship Utility Squadron on the Atlantic coast," he wrote, "whether the United States is at war or not."

> In view of the late start in airship experimental work, numerous important development and improvement projects are only now reaching the trial stage. The ZNP can be made a much more effective type against submerged submarines by improved ordnance and equipment just now becoming available. Since it is inconceivable that the improvement and development of any useful A/S type will ever be allowed to lapse, such ZNP development should be continued until the optimum value of the type for this work can be achieved and evaluated.[83]

Fleet Airships Atlantic boasted a far-flung organization. Four wings reported to the commodore (Wings One, Two, Four, and Five). This embraced ten squadrons in all (ZP-11, ZP-12, ZP-24, ZP-15, ZP-21, ZP-23, ZP-41, ZP-42, ZP-51, and ZP-14). Four hedrons supported these commands (1, 2, 4, and 5). One utility squadron was operational. Operating strength: eighty-three ZNPs and six ships consigned to utility work (ZNJs.) The Pacific coast organization comprised three squadrons totaling twenty-four aircraft. (See table 7.3.)

The Mark XXIV "Mine" (FIDO)

Concocted at R&D laboratories, scores of ASW devices were developed for service use, then placed into production. One was the air-dropped torpedo. A normal torpedo was not favored for attacking submarines: the target was too small, the projectile too expensive. The German acoustic homing torpedo steered for the sound of an enemy's propellers. Deployed by *U-270,* the device scored its debut successes in September 1943, realizing immediate effect: "U-boats in North Atlantic have adopted the policy of attacking A/S escort vessels. There is a strong probability than an acoustic homing torpedo is being used which is probably electric and may be inaudible on asdics."[84]

Countertactics were analyzed, then recommended by NDRC. Towed astern, a noisemaker decoy largely cancelled this latest undersea threat.

American ingenuity had worked to produce its own version of a target-seeking torpedo—an air-dropped antisubmarine acoustic homing weapon. Three days after the raid on Oahu, the notion was suggested by Dr. Tate at a conference of navy and NDRC representatives. Feasibility agreed upon, Project FIDO (later PROCTOR) was promptly set up and "actively pursued."[85] Performance tests for the Mark XXIV "mine" (so named to mask its nature) were under way in summer 1942.[86] Progress satisfactory, the design was frozen in October 1942 and two hundred on order from the Bureau of Ordnance. The first production model was delivered to the navy in March 1943.[87]

TABLE 7.3 **LTA-Related Activities** at naval air stations for lighter-than-air, continental United States, December 1944.[1]

East Coast	West Coast
South Weymouth, Massachusetts Main base for Blimp Squadron 11 (ZP-11) *Lakehurst, New Jersey* Airship Training Center, Officers and Enlisted Airship Training Center, Brazilian Air Force Headquarters, Commander Fleet Airships Atlantic Headquarters, Commander Fleet Airship Wing One Headquarters, Blimp Headquarters Squadron One Main base for Blimp Squadron 12 (ZP-12) Center of LTA Experimentation Major LTA overhaul and outfitting base—East Coast Parachute Riggers School Parachute Experimental Unit Aerographers School Base for various experimental projects *Weeksville (Elizabeth City), North Carolina* Main base for Blimp Squadron 24 (ZP-24) *Glynco, Georgia* Main base for Blimp Squadron 15 (ZP-15) *Richmond, Florida* Headquarters, Commander Fleet Airship Wing Two Main base for Blimp Squadron 21 (ZP-21) Main LTA overhaul base Headquarters, Blimp Headquarters (Hedron) Squadron Two	*Tillamook, Oregon* Main base for Blimp Squadron 33 (ZP-33) *Moffett Field, California* Headquarters, Commander Fleet Airships Pacific Main base for Blimp Squadron 32 (ZP-32) Blimp Headquarters Squadron Three Main overall base for Pacific coast LTA Airship Training Center *Santa Ana, California* Main base for Blimp Squadron 31 (ZP-31)

1 Each East Coast station also served as hurricane refuge for airplanes. Various heavier-than-air utilization—particularly at Moffett Field—are not included.

The Mark XXIV homed on the sound of a target's cavitation—the partial vacuum created by high-speed marine propellers. Combat debut of the FIDO weapon: May 1943 near the Azores, when a Liberator from the RAF Coastal Command holed *U-456*.

That October, Tenth Fleet's George Watson briefed Rosendahl on developments relating to the project. Not yet in "real production," eventually about four thousand of the FIDO weapons would be produced during the war.

> For your info the super secret security job is subject to great many restrictions as to areas, depths, proximity to own ships, etc., which may preclude our use except in spe-

cial circumstances. . . . The gadgets themselves and the special personnel which accompanies will soon be available in reasonable quantity but in order to get we must be able to give a logical proposal of when and how we are going to use it including how we are going to find a submarine to use it on.[88]

In May 1943, *K-2* had tested the effectiveness of "train bombing" on a MAD signal. ("Train," or time-interval, release spaces the bombs.) Auxiliary equipment actuated an experimental bomb rack, exploiting MAD as bombsight. Target: a U-boat shape (cleared brush) near Lakehurst's HTA runways.

Months passed, LTA standing by. In March 1944, Commodore Mills requested additional Mark 53 bomb racks to equip Fleet Airships Atlantic, among other recommendations. This rack could carry a larger number of smaller bombs, realizing better patterns. (Although satisfactory, only twenty of the Mark 53s had yet seen manufacture.) That May, ZNP *K-91* flew the run to South Weymouth for experiments involving the FIDO weapon (NDRC at New London). And in July, referencing Mills, the issue of airship ordnance was ventilated by CNATE to CNO. For the ZNP type, Rosendahl wanted the Mark 53 rack installed in the interior bomb bay, plus two Mark 51s on the outside. For the Mark 51s, he wanted scatter bombs (pattern ordnance) and the FIDO (PROCTOR) torpedo: "Since [March], there has been considerable development in the use of the dual head, Mark 6 MAD by ZNPs, notably development of the ability to track a submerged target and drop ordnance instrumentally. Also, under cognizance of Tenth Fleet, certain ZNP tests have been carried on with Proctor equipment clearly indicating the suitability of that type ordnance for ZNP use. The Mark 51 bomb rack is readily usable for carrying the Proctor item on the outside of the car."[89]

Fleet Airships Atlantic deployed the FIDO operationally late in 1944. Not all squadrons received the weapon. Those units that did saw the highest order of security applied. At Squadron Twelve (ZP-12),

The only time I ever saw Marines actively engaged in what you'd call high-level security. . . . Back in 1944, we started to get a weapon, which was really a killer. The Mark 24 was called a mine, because they didn't want anybody to know it was a torpedo. . . . It was probably the most secret thing we had. . . . Because of the security of the thing, it was very hush-hush and, as I remember when it was trucked out to and put on the ship—they were quite a lot bigger than depth charges—they came under a Marine guard.[90]

Assigned convoy duty, ZNP *K-72* (ZP-24) cleared Weeksville on 18 April 1945. Senior officer taking the flight out: Lt. (jg) George Nichols, USNR. Ens. James Hughes, junior pilot, was at the "nav" table, George Roberts manning the circuit. This CAC had not even *seen* the weapon it was deploying: the "mine" hung concealed in a breakaway cover. Larger and heavier than any ZNP depth charge, the Mark XXIV measured seven feet in length, nineteen inches in diameter, and weighed 683 pounds—92 of them accounted for by a warhead of torpex high explosive. Maximum underwater speed: twelve knots.[91] "We had been told very little about this torpedo

A Mark XXIV acoustic antisubmarine homing torpedo is secured to an external bomb rack, 12 April 1949. (Images of the wartime Mark XXIV are rare.) The ship is a modernized K-type, the aircraft carrier USS *Sicily* (CVE 118). Note the "hat" for the radar scanner projecting below the car. (Mrs. E. P. Moccia)

except what was necessary to use it," Roberts recalls. "It was much smaller than a conventional torpedo."

All weapons impose limitations. A superb product of civilian science, FIDO was subject to tight operational restrictions based on strict official secrecy. It was not to be released, for example, unless the target was diving, so that the weapon would not be observed. The proximity of Allied ships also precluded use: their propeller sounds might deflect the torpedo and, again, no observers were wanted. Deployment via airship held no practicable concern, however, assuming the weapon was made available: "Do not anticipate any mechanical difficulties in mounting and launching from ZNP," Watson had advised.

The Mark XXIV sank sixty-eight submarines and damaged another thirty-three for 340 releases against U-boats—a commendable kill rate.[92] Two months following its introduction, *K-74* had had its fateful engagement (see chapter 4) off Florida. The way one sees facts is shaped by the outcome one desires. In his memoir-polemic, Rosendahl laments the war's having been "almost over before blimps got to carry this valuable asset." Had Nelson Grills been FIDO equipped, "the blimp very probably would have sunk the *U-134* without its German crew ever knowing what had hit them or what had happened. But, since blimps got delayed decision and support in almost every aspect including armament in particular, whoever was responsible for arming blimps apparently gave no thought to the added value the target-seeking missile would give blimps."[93]

April 1945 saw the Atlantic war nearly won. East of Norfolk, Virginia, a sea battle was unfolding—its *n*th iteration: an unescorted tanker had been torpedoed and sunk. Unlocated at first, Tenth Fleet estimated the raider to be patrolling the general area south of Hatteras. At 1608, on escort duty, the patrol frigate USS *Annapolis* (PF 15) logged a sound contact. General Quarters sounded, the frigate attacked at 1620 and again six minutes later on a second contact—twenty-four hedgehogs. A search at various courses and speeds realized no indication of damage. A third run was secured before firing: 1659 found the frigate lying to, all engines stopped. "King-72," vectored to the scene, had requested a listening watch.

Crew at battle stations, the blimp maneuvered to establish sound contact—that is, to verify contact. The first buoy immediately found screw noises. Hence the voice request to *Annapolis*. "We dropped a sonobuoy and could clearly hear the sub's screw and could count the RPMs. ['As distinct as a classroom exercise.'] We then asked the frigate to pull off about ten miles or shut down its engine, which they did. We dropped four more sonobuoys [original buoy at the center], each on a different frequency to form a large square."[94]

Tactical use of sonobuoys was now integral to improved MAD, with standard doctrine prepared for HTA and LTA both. Operational experience (by 1944, the AN/CRT-1A, weighing fourteen pounds) had verified indispensability of the device.

Transmitter sets comprised six expendable buoys, each of a different color—the signals identified with the hydrophone transmitting them. These sea markers, in other words, were deployed in *patterns*—thus providing *directional* capability. A feature of frequency-modulated receivers is that they can listen to any *one* buoy without interference from the others. Listening to each in turn, an operator could identify the buoy nearest the target by the loudest signal. As the boat transited the zone, now under monitor, an estimate of its course was made by checking relative sound intensities. "The senior pilot continued the pattern for dropping the last sonobuoys," Hughes relates. "Propeller noise still heard with direction of movement quite apparent, [we] lined our ship with the direction of movement and dropped the homing torpedo." Roberts elaborates, "Tuning from one to the other . . . we were able to determine on which one we heard the loudest return. We then armed and dropped the torpedo. It was, we were later told [incorrectly], the first combat use of this weapon."

"King-72" released over its best estimated position. Target: probably *U-879*, soon to be missing off the U.S. coast. Upon penetration, the weapon dived to a preset depth; there, via electric propulsion, it commenced an acoustic search, a circular pattern it could maintain for twelve to fifteen minutes. After about four minutes, sound source acquired, controls activated, the torpedo homed in on the only propeller noise audible. At 1830, a remote concussion was felt throughout *Annapolis*, origin unknown.[95] Then nothing on her sonar, her ASW officer testified—"No, nothing." The sound of the sub screw immediately stopped, Roberts recalled, and was not heard again although it was kept under observation for two days.[96]

The classification assigned action reports depended largely on the weapon used or the report's contents. Comparatively few ASW-6 "action forms" were deemed secret. This weapon, however, commanded utmost security. For the few cleared to know, the drop by *K-72* (one can speculate) was hypersecret and therefore not disclosable.

> When we returned to base, a team of two officers and an enlisted man who had developed the weapon had flown down from Washington to debrief us. They were confident it was a confirmed sinking. By the time it got to the next level of review it was rated "possible." By the time it got to the next level of review it was rated "doubtful" because there was no presence of debris. There was no reason to expect debris from a weapon this small.[97]

Up-chain from the interrogators, plausibly, reviewers had no knowledge whatever as to a guided acoustic weapon designed to inflict damage at the shaft—a casualty leaving little or no observable lethal result for the attacker to report.

The last attack in the western Atlantic occurred on 5–6 May off Point Judith, Rhode Island—sixty miles from the site of the first torpedoing in 1942. A U.S. collier was sunk. An immediate search found a stationary (bottomed) sonar target off Block Island. A DE task group made successive hedgehog attacks, assisted by *K-82* (ZP-11) and *K-16* (ZP-12) with sonobuoys, MAD runs, and depth charging. *U-853* died with all hands—the last U-boat sunk by U.S. forces.[98]

South America Closeout

At ZP-42, "we find ourselves at the lowest ebb in the squadron's history. Four of our pilots are hospitalized locally, three with malaria, and eighteen are in the States. This leaves us with but six crews on board, spread out over three detachments, with one ship in each location. With mast watches, duties, and flights, this is certainly the bare minimum, and practically obviates any possibility of liberty, such as it is. We therefore offer a slight prayer that no contingencies will arise to further decimate our little flock before reinforcements arrive."[99]

Germany capitulated on the 8th. A signal from Dönitz was sent on all frequencies to all U-boats at sea to cease hostilities: surrender to the nearest Allied port or naval vessel. Following acknowledgment, five boats effected rendezvous with Atlantic Fleet forces. On 14 May, *U-858* berthed at Cape May. Off the Maine coast, from 16 to 19 May, four boats were boarded and searched, their officers disembarked. Escorted by ships of the Northern Group, Eastern Sea Frontier, and manned by U.S. Navy crews, *U-805, U-873, U-1228,* and *U-234* steamed in turn into Portsmouth, New Hampshire, amid intense excitement and full media coverage. Ashore, the German crewmen were shunted by bus to a naval prison.[100]

The battle over, merchant shipping again steamed unconcerned. As the Admiralty announced,

Surrendered to U.S. naval forces, *U-858* proceeds into Lewes, Delaware, May 1945. Five U-boats surrendered off the American coast; under escort, each made for an East Coast port. With victory in Europe, fleet antisubmarine commands would await orders to decommission. (Lt. H. F. Smith, USNR [Ret.])

THE U-BOAT WAR IN THE NON-COMBAT AREA IS TO BE CONSIDERED ENDED AT 0001/4TH JUNE. H.M. SHIPS, TROOP CONVOYS AND MONSTERS IN THIS AREA MAY THEN RELAX WAR-TIME PRECAUTIONS AND ARE TO BURN NAVIGATION LIGHTS AT FULL BRILLIANCY BY NIGHT.[101]

For Atlantic Fleet antisubmarine squadrons, force reductions and decommissioning orders now awaited. Some ZP units would be assigned new missions: air-sea rescue and utility operations. On 15 June, Fleet Airship Wing Two was decommissioned at NAS Richmond. Two weeks later, in South America, Fleet Air Wing Sixteen was decommissioned at Recife, Brazil. Its ZP component stayed on until Fleet Airship Wing Four also was decommissioned, on 15 July.

ZNPs for the Brazilian Air Force

In August 1944, at Lakehurst, a class of officers and enlisted men from the Brazilian air force reported aboard, preparatory to a Lend-Lease transfer of ZNPs and equipment to Brazil's air ministry. The Brazilian training program was the first class for non-American personnel. As well, training for a hedron outfit got under way at Santa Cruz. In addition to fifteen ratings there, sixteen each would be required for Ipitanga and Fortaleza, plus two men at each of the other bases to care for equipment and make preparations for receiving a ship.[102] Ultimately, these personnel would conduct their own operations, making Brazil the first nation other than the United States to operate modern blimps.

[Opposite] Lakehurst, 8 May 1945—VE-Day. Cessation of hostilities in Europe realized a change in mission: transition from the antisubmarine warfare phase of Atlantic Fleet operations to utility and air-sea rescue missions. LTA wings, squadrons, and hedrons were soon decommissioned as operating units. (Lt. H. F. Smith, USNR [Ret.])

[Right] Airships were ideal platforms for lifesaving rescue—slow, low-altitude approaches to targets at sea and in inaccessible areas. Indeed, a utility squadron (ZJ-1) had been commissioned in February 1944. The scope of utility missions—photographic, torpedo recovery, calibration, and other services—implied active operations following demobilization. Nonetheless, by September 1945 most of the wartime program stood dismantled. (U.S. Naval Institute)

Although wing commander "Heinz" Zimmerman was keen for an early decision, CNATE declined to predict when the Lakehurst group would return south, to receive (paralleling navy practice) field training in an operating squadron. "I wish it were possible to give you a worthwhile estimate as to when the Brazilians will be ready to return to their country and begin their operational training. . . . After all, we simply cannot let them leave here without a thorough basic knowledge of the subject and some proficiency in airship operation."[103]

ZP-41 had been retained, for air-sea and jungle rescue and for transfer under Lend-Lease. May 1945 found Squadron Forty-one, the last Brazil-based unit in commission, logging search and jungle rescues of combat air personnel—Air Transport Command ferry traffic from Europe. Return of Brazil's trainees from Lakehurst would signal closeout of squadron operations. But in truth, that class was progressing poorly.

U-boat resurgence in the sea areas under control of the Eastern Sea Frontier—Operation Teardrop—had necessitated beefed-up ZNPs and combat aircrews. The repercussions hit Wing Four hard. Deployed strength for ZP-41: one ship at Amapa, two based at São Luiz, one at Fortaleza: "With regard to Brazilian training in the field I hope that some of the Brazilians can come down here [from Lakehurst] to fly with our people out of Fortaleza, São Luiz and Amapa in these searches and possible jungle rescue, as this is one of the reasons for which the Brazilians asked for blimps."[104]

Keen for surface command, Mills had intended Zimmerman as his relief. Rosendahl, however, deemed it best that Heinz remain in situ: a new admiral for Fourth Fleet was en route. Further, training of the Brazilians continued "unsettled." And when war ended in Europe, the Atlantic LTA organization would shrivel, leaving a commodore billet improbable.[105] So captain and wing staff

[Opposite] Communications class practices receiving coded messages. These are Brazilian air force officers at Lakehurst's Airship Training School. Along with enlisted men, this group had reported on board in August 1944 for flight training preparatory to Lend-Lease transfer of a ZNP squadron to Brazil. (Lt. H. F. Smith, USNR [Ret.])

[Right] Brazilian air force graduates, Airship Training School, NAS Lakehurst, 23 June 1945. This was the navy's first non-American LTA class. Material transfer to the Brazilian Air Ministry—four latest-equipped K-types and equipment—was not made. (Lt. H. F. Smith, USNR [Ret.])

dutifully carried on—"trying to give the Brazilian LTA outfit a good start." Among Zimmerman's arrangements: a list of material and equipment for one year's operations for each base. When Admiral Ingram was relieved, decorations were awarded—among them, the Legion of Merit for Zimmerman.[106]

At Lakehurst, four ZNP-Ks were being outfitted. "We were putting new MAD, large bags, radio altimeters and everything good we could think of on the ships." As of 1 December, however, no directive had been received for sending them south.[107] Late March came, and still no word. "I think it very important that we get their ships here as early as possible," Zimmerman urged, "because the way the war is going in Germany, we will be out of here by 1 June."

The Brazilian graduates completed their Lakehurst phase on 23 June. Within weeks, Admiral Ingram was back in Rio, to talk to the Air Ministry. Reportedly, he was blunt. "You can have the blimps if you want them," he advised, more or less, "but I am going to recommend that the U.S. Navy give them up entirely." The Brazilian effort promptly folded. "From the implication of where would the Brazzies be with blimps given up by our own Navy," Zimmerman remarked, ruefully, "there was no course left to them but to give up too. . . . I don't understand Ad. Ingram's hostility." Replying, Mills wrote, "So far I have had no exact information on the reason the Brazilians turned down the use of blimps. I know that it followed Admiral Ingram's visit to Rio and your information from Sullivan is as good as any. Admiral Ingram and Admiral Rosendahl have not gotten along too well and were not in agreement at any time on the methods used in training the Brazilians."[108]

ZP-41 "came north" on 31 January 1946—decommissioned. The squadron had logged (October 1943–15 May 1945) 2,274 flights for 17,535 hours. Ships escorted: 5,608.

Loss of NAS Richmond

On 12 September 1945, the San Juan weather bureau had issued a preliminary hurricane alert advisory. The storm's track implied a potential threat within forty-eight hours to the Richmond area. On station, a conference was called of key personnel. An alert condition was decreed, all liberty cancelled, a Command Control Center established, and steps taken to secure against hurricane damage. That afternoon, the commanding officer granted permission for privately owned planes to seek shelter at the station. When, at 2205, the station and all activities were reported secure for hurricane weather, NAS Richmond's hangar spaces were sheltering twenty-five airships (twelve in long-term storage), 212 navy airplanes, 31 other government aircraft, and 124 private planes.

During the morning of the 15th, the wind averaged between six and ten knots, with gusts to twenty-five. The barometer began to fall rapidly at 1100. The velocity average rose to eighteen knots and the first high gust (forty-one knots) was recorded. After 1500, both gusts and velocity averages climbed rapidly. At 1515, hangar personnel were instructed to evacuate to the lean-to sections in the event of structural failure. By 1600, the southeast doors to Hangar No. 1 were bending inward a foot to a foot and a half with each gust. Water was streaming into the shops; in the berthing space, two to four inches covered the deck. The hangars began to fail—tar paper, ventilators, and timbers airborne as roof sections lifted clear from the pylons. At 1720, at No. 3, "a fifty-foot hole appeared in the northeast corner of the roof; then the west roof . . . was blown outward and immediately the east roof crashed inward. At this time, Lt. Robinson observed a large beam falling upon an F6F located approximately 200 feet from the hangar door. The plane immediately exploded spreading fire over a large area."

At No. 2, the roof pulled away at one corner, split down the center, rose slightly, then collapsed. Smoke filled the air. The general collapse continued, various failures deflating airships, crushing planes, igniting fires. Falling timbers set fire to a TBF; the flames spread rapidly "with explosions occurring frequently." Outside, the air was alive with debris. At 1730, the emergency power ceased. And at 1800, an urgent message: "Send all available fire fighting equipment to Richmond—all hangars afire."

Search parties were dispatched at 2145; not long after, state police reported on board. Station skipper Cdr. Frank Worden, USN, contacted Seventh Naval District Headquarters. A marine watch was established near the hangars. All personnel were mustered. The body of one civilian—a fire chief—was found in No. 1.

NAS Richmond vanished from the inventory of naval air stations, as did twenty-five airships.

Hurricane protection, NAS South Weymouth, Massachusetts, 14 September 1944. Altogether, 326 airplanes landed on station and were shunted inside. In Florida, a hurricane in September 1945 ignited hangar fires at NAS Richmond that killed one, destroyed dozens of aircraft, and effectively demolished the naval air station. It was the worst fire in the United States in 1945. (Lt. H. F. Smith, USNR [Ret.])

Well done.

—Commander, Eastern Sea Frontier,
16 May 1945

The Performance 8

Exercising inexhaustible invention, Allied cooperation in combating a few hundred submarines had been prodigious. For the war, total Allied losses amounted to a punishing 23,351,000 tons. The counterweight: construction of 42,485,000 tons. (Shipbuilders turned out more than 2,700 ships, on a mass-production basis.) Prior to 1943, the Allies had sustained an annual net *loss* of available merchant tonnage. Further, the lives lost by submarine action reached the tens of thousands. Admiral Ingram himself predicted, "When the history of this war is written, the navy will undoubtedly be required to answer the charges of being dilatory in the study of antisubmarine measures during the post World War I period, and of being negligent in providing means to combat a submarine menace such as faces the nation today."[1]

Operational readiness implies high standards of performance: trained personnel, material support, advanced sensors, effective weapons, capable and reliable platforms. No single panacea had defeated the U-boat; rather, the *combined, integrated weight* of elements had rescued the tonnage war from catastrophic losses. Although unready at the outset, antisubmarine commands established brilliant combat records. A U.S. destroyer commander outlined why, from his vantage, ASW had proven potent in the Atlantic: "The effectiveness of the destroyer escort (DE) in World War II was the result of skilled crews, simple weapons, over-the-water air coverage that paralyzed U-boat surface mobility, tremendous shore-based intelligence, a busy anti-submarine warfare scene, and a long war."[2]

Between the two world wars (and to Rosendahl's lasting distress), U.S. Navy lighter-than-air had been reduced to impotency. A force tiny in size and outmoded, operating from a single base, its budget in chronic crisis, LTA stood marginal as war neared—a time of frantic expansion in naval air forces. "The core of lighter-than-air experienced people was rather slender at that time," one officer was to recall.

The pernicious effects of naval politics must be appreciated. Stingy appropriations had bred rivalries, spawning intense personal enmities. Strong personalities, by force of circumstance, were compelled to collide, to oppose each other—thus shaping attitudes toward competing officer-advocates. "To some extent," Captain Eppes observed, retrospectively, "I think that much of the attitude of the naval aviation establishment toward lighter-than-air was a reflection of individual personal feelings toward Rosendahl—particularly as time went on and he became more senior and the people with whom he dealt earlier had themselves become more senior in the other parts of the organization." A fellow airman agreed. "The biggest problem that airships had was during the lean years [thirties], when the military . . . everybody was fighting for every dollar."[3]

A rigid airship and its auxiliaries represented a substantial procurement: *Akron* and *Macon* had "cost eight million dollars. During the interwar years this would buy two or three hundred carrier planes or four dozen twin-engine flying boats. So the heavier-than-air men could never resist dividing airships by airplanes—and turning purple over the result."[4]

John Kane mused, "When I think back on my career and those times, I can understand the heavier-than-air wing of the navy fighting for what they wanted and seeing the monies going into this thing [naval LTA] that they could use for their carriers and their planes. It would be the same battle that the aviators in the past had fought with the battleship elements—to get a share of the dough."[5]

The budgetary process, even in war, is an expression of the political system. Lighter-than-air vied directly with other program priorities and agendas; in turn, these "others" secured favorable fiscal health and grew faster. LTA could not hope for parity, let alone a proportionate share. A tiny element of the naval aeronautical organization, the program did not receive the consideration essential to success in the development of a separate weapon system.

The value of manned platforms stands in direct proportion to the knowledge and experience of operating crews. Fitted with the latest gadgets, the expansion program for LTA realized the largest such fleet ever manufactured, organized, and flown—a dimension of the Atlantic campaign seldom mentioned. "I think it was pretty well handled, as a matter of fact, going from nothing to as big as it was so fast. Somebody had to be doing something right."[6] But too often, this revival had realized inconsistent application. Early air and surface patrols had been weak: in tactics, experience, sensors, weaponry. Note Dönitz's headquarters log of 12 April 1942: "Crews are careless, inexperienced, and little persevering in a hunt." Effective tactical use of magnetic detection by LTA came only late in the war. "We just didn't have as much training as we needed. We didn't know what we needed training in until toward the end of the war."[7]

As well, priorities, accidents, misconduct, and indifference extracted their toll. "The airship project," Admiral Rosendahl had said, "needs zealous enthusiasts who are willing to risk their service careers with it." As with any clique or cause, the program hosted all shades. "There were some people that were just gung ho on lighter-than-air—[it] was the absolute answer to everything. And then there were others that were more realistic about what the airship could do. And there were some who were just in it because it was just a good ride."

The aviation cadets, for their part, had performed admirably: fleshing out flight crews, easing the strain for the older hands, assuming collateral duties and responsible billets. "There are many examples of young officers," "Ty" Tyler observed, "who have come in as aviation cadets, who would be a credit to this organization and to the regular Navy." Indeed, most "of the officers in the navy during the war were reservists, so," Admiral Pierce insisted, "who the hell won the war?

They did. Damn good job." And, as a third confided, "We often overlook the importance of enlisted personnel."[8]

Confidential reports to Mills from unit commanders lament the officer situation. Training commands reported mediocre or below-average performance; the advanced school at Key West provides a troubling example.[9] The sea-duty qualification for general-service Naval Reserve officers had not functioned as hoped in filling billets: "Probably due to the reluctance of commanding officers at sea to forward the requests of officers useful to them, the type of individual received for training was not always of the desired standards. Most squadron commanders did not consider that the added maturity and experience of these officers offset their lack of airship experience."[10]

Failing to accept responsibility upon assignment to a fleet squadron, some officers proved incapable of carrying out independent missions. Lacking initiative, the less qualified sought desk jobs and flew infrequently. As one commander put it to the commodore, "Their attitude mirrors their lack of interest in our major objective, the finding and destruction of the enemy."

Mills himself was to lament the quality of decision making within *his* far-flung organization. "God only knows how we got along in this war!" he wrote, retrospectively. "I have seen so few cases of the use of any initiative that I could count them on one hand and still have enough fingers to measure off a real drink."[11]

And there is George Watson's anguished near-rebuke from Tenth Fleet to Rosendahl in October 1943—well into the campaign:

> I hope very much that the Mark 6 will help to simplify the tactical problems involved but even if it proves to be the absolute ultimate of all best possible MADS it will be of little use if the airship cannot be handled tactically to employ its abilities. The proficiency required to make even a passable MAD run requires long-tedious and continuous practice which our pilots have not had and must have if the instrument is to justify even one pound of weight.[12]

Only time in the air—training, practice, operations—could grant that kind of proficiency, to cancel errors in judgment, poor technique, carelessness.

Personnel, discipline, and commitment are crucial, as "Tex" Settle had always insisted. Pressing for first-class naval officers, material factors (he said) stood secondary: "The preponderance of losses and major casualties caused by design and personal failures is striking, 94.4%. This was the price of our pre-war negligence in not building up design and manufacturing resources, pools of personnel and ships—we started the war practically from scratch."[13]

One may ask: Was there ever a time for the combatant airship as a naval platform? Assignment to the Atlantic Fleet had brought LTA into close association with fleet commands and units. Yet Admiral Ingram's blistering indictment (see also the Epilogue) as to its undemonstrated value is illustrative of institutional biases. And it initiates the question as to whether the program—tangled in adverse opinion and institutional self-interest—was ever able to do enough to integrate itself into naval aviation as a permanent adjunct of the U.S. Navy.

A deterrent to German boldness (in closing range on the target), the antisubmarine airplane and airship had suppressed the undersea threat—by obliging submergence *and* by disrupting the process for torpedo attack. At periscope depth, U-boat captains needed mere glimpses to keep on the target. Patrol and escort forces, watching for periscopes, cancelled (as well as hurried) the attack procedure: determination of range, bearing, and target angle.

German opinion as to American "dwarf Zeppelins" versus submarines? Karl Dönitz has tendered an appraisal: "Each air patrol was disturbing to the operation of U-boats because they were forced underwater, making it no longer possible for them to reach their attack positions. As a consequence, the American 'blimps' were very disturbing to German U-boat activity. Naturally airplanes, compared with 'blimps,' had the advantage of higher speed. Thus they represented for U-boats a greater danger than 'blimps.'"[14]

If the Atlantic war has receded from view, its LTA component has persisted unseen. And unexamined. Histories of the campaign tend to offer bare sentences, as if the contributions merit a mere nod of acknowledgment. Yet,

> COMMANDER EASTERN SEA FRONTIER DESIRES TO EXPRESS TO THE PERSONNEL OF THE BLIMPRONS HIS GREAT APPRECIATION OF THE SERVICES THEY HAVE SO EFFICIENTLY RENDERED PARTICULARLY UNDER TRYING CONDITIONS OF THE NORTH ATLANTIC X HE WISHES YOU SUCCESS AND GOOD LUCK X WELL DONE.[15]

According to historian Morison, most naval officers regarded blimps as inferior to planes for patrol and were "worse than useless in convoy coverage, because they could be sighted by a U-boat even further away than the most smoke-careless freighter."[16] Dönitz's judgment was less damning: "It is possible that a U-boat commander, at the sight of a 'blimp' might conclude that a convoy was nearby. On the other hand, there was also the possibility that the sighted 'blimp' was only on patrol. But even if their commander, upon seeing the 'blimp,' surmised a convoy, that would only be a slight disadvantage to the use of a 'blimp' since it would hinder the U-boat's approach, at the very least severely."[17] The tanker *Peresephone*—torpedoed on 25 May 1942 en route New York—is probably the only vessel lost while under LTA protection in two world wars.

The aim of antisubmarine warfare is *destruction.* Yet *damage* predominated. On *joint* attacks, each hunter's contribution was impossible to discern. Whose weapon had inflicted harm or a crippling, fatal blow? Offensively, LTA apparently had achieved little: as per Tenth Fleet, it had sunk no submarines. The rest is interpretation—of a now declassified yet highly fallible Tenth Fleet archive.[18] As well, the only certain *proof* of destruction was a large mass of debris, bodies, or prisoners. (Usually, oil streaks were a deception.) Debris was rare: a U-boat's pressure hull was remarkably stout. Concussions within lethal range did not necessarily open up the hull but could, instead, cause serious internal flooding or otherwise foreclose ability to regain the surface—realizing (as with "King-72's" attack) no external evidence of the death of a crew.

The military airship had again proven itself for convoy escort of merchantmen, especially in coordination with air and surface forces. As well, countless survivors owed their eventual rescue to the watchful eyes of LTA aircrews and to the airmanship attending retrievals from the sea, lifeboats, rafts, beaches, jungle, and desert.

The official *offensive* record: an assist on one sinking and possible damage to three other enemy submarines (see table 8.3). Was this of sufficient value to offset the expenditure in industrial

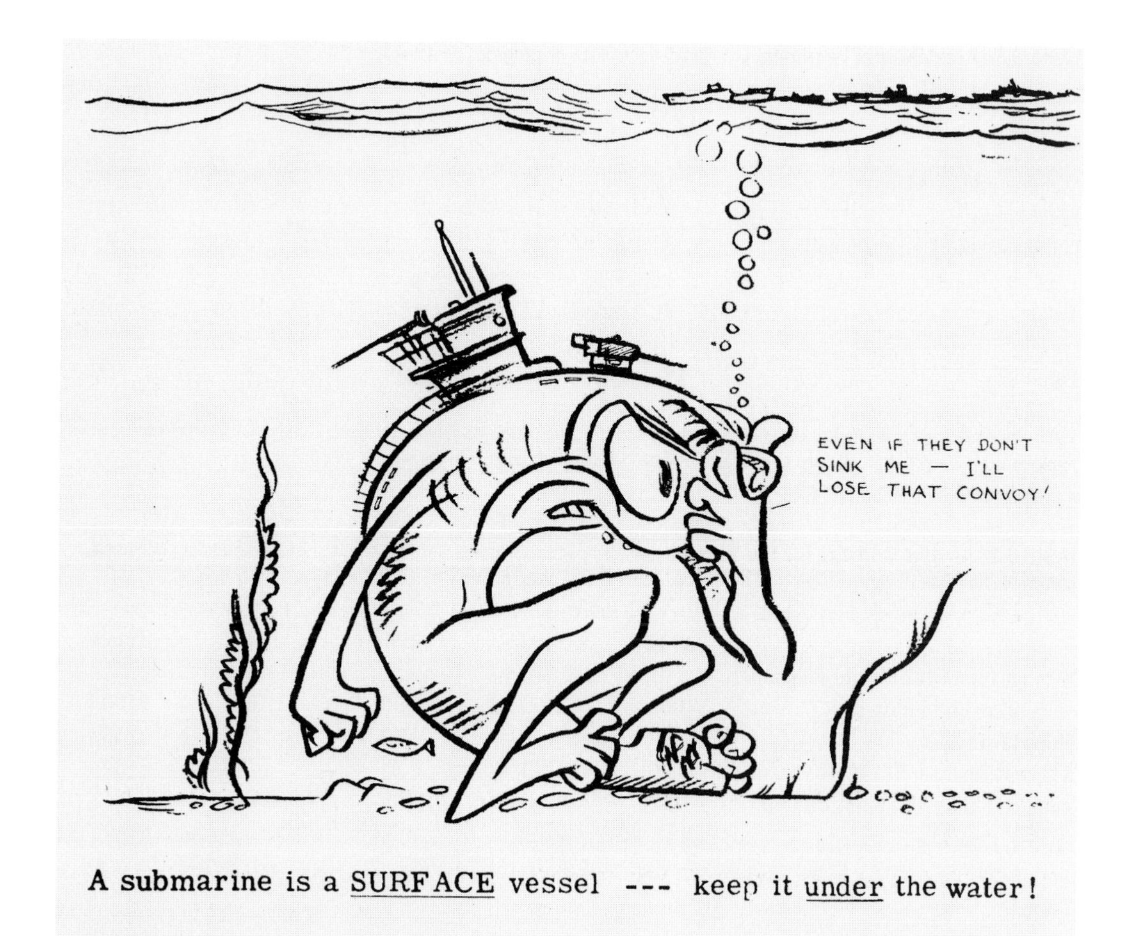

capacity, personnel, aircraft, bases, and special facilities—resources better applied elsewhere, perhaps?[19] The metric is invidious, according to Rosendahl: "The U-boat strategy of retreating from the coastal waters to the high seas areas beyond blimp range precludes the evaluation of a blimp score by the number of subs sunk."

For many, there was—and remains—an honest conviction that the airship was unreliable, that its utility was marginal, and there that were always other needs to which funds could have been applied with quicker and more certain results. "Look at the spring of 1943," Norman Polmar opines, "and the impact of a few RAF Liberators and Sunderlands in the Battle of the Atlantic. What would have been the impact if those blimp resources were devoted to more RAF/USN Liberators or escort ships. Those 7,000 Navy personnel could have manned about 25 destroyers."

Talent and resources dedicated to one purpose are diverted from another. "Their contribution was small [Polmar adds] when one considers the massive investment to build and operate them, and the cost and handling of the helium that kept them aloft, in comparison to their accomplishments."[20] Although modest relative to HTA, naval lighter-than-air was no cheap system of ships and air stations. (From the outset of serious discussions, Ottawa had held concerns as to the cost of a

TABLE 8.1 **Accident and Fatalities,** U.S. Navy lighter-than-air-program, 1942–45.

	1942	1943	1944	1945	Totals
Personnel Error	0	11	18	10	39
Weather and/or Material	1	4	5	0	10
Enemy Action	0	1	0	0	1
Unknown and Undetermined	3	3	0	0	6
Totals	4	19	23	10	56[1]
Fatalities	14	21	34	8	77[2]

1 Airships of all types, attached to both fleet and shore units. Broken down: 48 K-type, 5 L-type, 2 G-type, 1 free balloon accident. Totals do not include K-ships lost due to destruction of NAS Richmond hangars in September 1945.
2 Excludes fatal accidents to ground handlers.

TABLE 8.2 **Airship Statistics for the War,** aircraft and personnel losses were the result of ground handling accidents, material failure, pilot error, weather and from other causes. One ship, possibly two, was lost to enemy action.

	1942	1943	1944	1945	Totals
Average Number of Flight Personnel (Officer and Enlisted)	700	2300	4000	2500	9500
Ships Lost	3	10	12	13	38
Major Casualties	2	11	14	7	34
Average Number of Ships on Line	15	63	109	68	255

Canadian airship program.) Expenditures for 168 airships (K-, L-, G-, and M-types): $60,226,858. For continental bases: $131,183,032.[21]

Denied acceptance and legitimacy, the actual impact of LTA on the campaign's larger history is unappreciated. Enabled by pioneering work with airships, then adopted as standard gear, Loran and ASW sensors and systems had conferred a decisive air advantage. Yet, invariably, these contributions are missed. "I believe that we were the first aircraft ever to get PPI scopes—Planned Position Indicators." Captain Kane continued, "We also had advanced radio direction finders—the loop antenna was a thirty-foot diameter woven-into-the-bag antenna. That was good gear. . . . There were a lot of—I must say—inventions and adaptations that went into airships before anybody else had them."

The mere presence of aircraft—HTA and LTA—had obliged the enemy to submerge; underwater, diminished mobility deterred torpedo attack. "The most effective way to defeat the submarine is to capitalize on the weaknesses of the submarine itself, principally the batteries and air supply, by keeping it submerged."[22]

In September 1942, forced down three times in less than three hours by an escorting ZNP, the *U-69* recorded this entry: "The amusement at first caused by the appearance of airships has given place to a certain amount of respect." Kills, in other words, may not be the best measure of efficacy. Better (but far more difficult to estimate) is the number of merchantmen

TABLE 8.3 **Antisubmarine attacks by patrol airship** (ZNP) and official Navy Department assessments, 1942–45. Now declassified, Tenth Fleet archives betray further damage to the enemy by LTA, including a probable U-boat "kill" in April 1945. (National Archives)

Number of Attacks	Assessment
3	Probably Slightly Damaged
5	Insufficient Evidence of Damage
8	No Damage
53	Insufficient Evidence of the Presence of a Submarine
18	Target Attacked Not a Submarine
4	Insufficient Information to Assess the Attack

unmolested, seamen made safe, cargoes discharged. In the airborne antisubmarine world according to Morison, the *airplane* had proven itself: "The score of kills . . . far from exhausts the usefulness of planes in anti-submarine warfare. Their sightings, signaled ashore or to ships, resulted in numerous attacks by surface craft. Moreover, in 1942, German submarines were under orders to dive when they sighted a plane. Consequently air patrol over frontier waters or a convoy route was a constant embarrassment to the U-boats and indirectly protected shipping."[23]

The word "aircraft" applies here, surely. And there is this, written in August 1943—deep wartime:

> It is not considered that the "score" in submarines sunk or damaged is, alone, a proper gauge of the blimp's effectiveness. In general, its effectiveness in attacking submerged submarines lies between that of airplanes and surface types with QC gear. . . . [Effectiveness] should be measured by the numbers of ships lost out of blimp-escorted convoys, the hours per month underway . . . and their patrol and escort effectiveness in low visibilities. It is believed that the type is becoming increasingly effective in these respects, particularly in night and low-visibility missions.[24]

Convinced of a contact, pilots had orders to call in supporting forces, to bring surface ships in contact. That was doctrine. ("When we had [sensor] indications, we let the world know.") How incalculable the contribution, when a blimp could pinpoint a spot in the ocean and radio, "There's a U-boat there." By this one measure alone, U.S. Navy lighter-than-air—its dedicated officers and enlisted personnel, its civilian support and its casualties—deserve a respectable measure of credit.

Success in war is a weave of interrelated variables: training and experience, contingency and coincidence, politics, priorities, personalities. Much of warfare depends on chance—a factor in any profession. When opportunities were ripe, airships were few—and their sensors quirky laboratory prototypes.[25] When sufficient strength was deployed with personnel adapted to the latest systems and tactics, few U-boats were raiding coastwise shipping.

U.S. NAVY

Epilogue

The Battle of the Atlantic, as Churchill named the struggle against the U-boats, was the most complicated and technical form of warfare the world had ever seen. From relatively quiet beginnings it grew to a raging crescendo both in violence and cunning until Dönitz's defeat in 1943, yet continued thereafter for two years. It was a technical battle, but no less cruel for that.[1]

The Battle of the Atlantic—five momentous years—was the one campaign that lasted from the first day of the war to the last. The U-boat threat held ever present.

On VE Day, U.S. Navy airships were operational in North, Central, and South America—and in southern Europe and northwestern Africa. Operating facilities ranged from complex bases with hangars and repair capabilities to expeditionary masts in jungle clearings. War-honed and immeasurably more potent than they had been at the war's beginning, airships attached to fifteen squadrons--organized under five wings—had patrolled to seaward of four continents. Stateside, three continental sea frontiers had helped protect U.S. ports and Anglo-American maritime commerce.

Shipping is the heart of global trade. Seaborne commerce again uncontested, all five fleet airship wings were decommissioned; by the close of 1946, fifteen fleet airship squadrons stood trimmed to two, two detachments supporting. As well, force reductions brought an end to fleet squadron activity on the West Coast.[2]

Airship wings and squadrons had turned in a commendable, if somewhat stumbling, performance. Notwithstanding, skepticism persisted within the naval hierarchy, every constituency of navy air seeing in airships only what it wanted to see. In short, lighter-than-air would experience little substantive change in status. Investing their postwar resources, naval commands tended (still) to dismiss the platform, almost by definition, as an anachronism useless to naval warfare. Mere weeks before Germany capitulated, Commander in Chief, Atlantic Fleet, was moved to remark, "I see no practical use for the retention in the Atlantic Fleet of lighter-than-air, either during war or peace, other than to provide at-sea rescue and utility services. Aside from air-sea rescue, one squadron of blimps appears ample for these purposes."[3] The force of such professional opinion would, at the last, prevail.

[Opposite] The navy's first Airborne Early Warning (AEW) airship, the ZPG-2W, November 1956. Note the height finder radar in a radome atop the envelope. Five of these aircraft were procured between 1955 and 1957. Naval airships survived the competition between systems to 1961, when all LTA squadrons were decommissioned. The last United States Navy airship landed at Lakehurst on 31 August 1962.

In 1941, the United States had had no *rigid* airships. As Commander in Chief, U.S. Fleet, Admiral E. J. King supported intensive use of blimps as an antisubmarine weapon system (and for mine spotting). But no ZRs were authorized.[4] By 1945, probably earlier, King saw no future for the *military* type.[5] In a report that January on the rigid airship for naval transport, the General Board recommended that the Navy Department take no action toward construction for naval or commercial purposes. In August, conferring with Adm. "Tex" Settle, King remarked that ZRs were "out" for the postwar navy. Still, he favored the large airship for commercial applications—assuming sponsorship from a nonmilitary organ of the government, the navy cooperating in terms of facilities, design assistance, and personnel.[6] Indeed, conferences on LTA for commercial use were then under way in the Department of Commerce.

Various proposals would be put forth; each come to nothing. The airplane had advanced too far for the lumbering airship to catch up and compete. In 1947, the U.S. Navy divested itself of any official interest in the rigid type. Still, advanced postwar designs would operate blimps whose capabilities far outclassed those of 1945 for ASW (a core mission) and for airborne early warning (AEW) in a nuclear navy.

The United States emerged from World War II preponderant in the world. Its maritime position stood preeminent, its navy reigned supreme. Now, though, the world stood divided, between a major land power and a major sea power. A new kind of war, a "cold" war, had begun.

The 1939–45 campaign had required the marshaling of great technical and managerial skills to defeat the commerce-raiding submarine. Washington's federally funded research and development enterprise had proven robust—and remarkably innovative. A military-industry-university partnership stood forged: war had realized a permanent program of scientific research in the interests of national security. The U.S. Navy, indeed, had taken the lead in funding basic research. The consequences were to prove far-reaching.[7]

Among the senior LTA officers, George H. Mills—deft in judgment—had proven himself a superbly able team leader. His steadiness had bonded him to his subordinate commanders; as well, respect from higher command had been his (as would be the Legion of Merit). Commander, Air Force, Atlantic Fleet, noted that Mills had "contributed immeasurably to the successful completion of the war in the Atlantic."

In the realm of politics, Mills's partner in collaboration had helped nurture war-winning R&D. Impossibly energetic, Charles E. Rosendahl deserves the strongest measure of intellectual credit: preserving, protecting, promoting. Amid the gathering chaos of 1940–42, lighter-than-air had broken new ground.

> We at Columbia owe the LTA services quite a debt. I doubt if many are fully cognizant of the part the LTA played in enabling our group to turn out the ERSB [expendable radio-sonobuoy] which had such an encouraging success. . . . The ESBR was started by your Admiral Rosendahl. He saw the need for some such aid to MAD and started the ball rolling at a conference held on February 21, 1942 at Admiral Furer's office in Washington. [He] outlined the problem and stated the performance requirements. It is quite interesting, in retrospect, in looking over my notes of that meeting to see how well he visualized the requirements, for those he stated have proven to be remarkably well

> founded. Foresight is much better than hindsight, especially in war research. . . . The development of the ERSB was probably one of, if not the fastest bits of war development on record. In about three months the device had been developed to a stage where limited commercial production was warranted. . . . All of this pioneering ERSB work was done by LTA.[8]

The war record for LTA had not ratified the absolute faith of believers: Rosendahl, Mills, Settle, Zimmerman, Sullivan, Watson, Cope, Tyler, others.[9] The U.S. Navy had been unready for war; yet, belatedly, antisubmarine commands secured brilliant records. Chance favors the prepared. The attack by *K-74* on *U-134,* caught on the surface, had failed to realize the validating triumph that might, just might, have secured political weight for a postwar program. Reflexively in opposition, the navy's senior ranks saw no compelling claim in LTA to serious attention in a demobilized, contracting service. In the joint battle space of the Atlantic campaign, conventional operating forces—destroyers, carriers, HTA fleet units—had proven more consequential.

Its standing low, its voice tiny within naval aeronautics, LTA saw its wartime welcome withdrawn. Its needs subordinated, U.S. Navy lighter-than-air persisted: "The U.S. Navy is retaining a small number of airships as part of the Fleet organization. Lakehurst . . . is the chief experimental and training station. Mooring experiments, picking up ballast, and trials with bow elevators are continuing, and new designs are on the drawing board. The 725,000 c.f. XM.1, largest non-rigid airship in the world, has been making endurance flights."[10]

A veteran of the World War II office of the CNO saw scant prospect of change in the years to come: "I feel LTA has an important place in the new guided missile field as well as in AEW. But the opposition is terrible and of high caliber—naturally they can always design a new answer for the need while at the same time letting our personnel and experience slowly die out."[11]

Abbreviations

A&R	assembly and repair
AA	antiaircraft
AEW	airborne early warning
AIL	Airborne Instruments Laboratory
AMM2/c	Aviation Machinists Mate 2nd class
APD	attack transport
ARM3c	Aviation Rigger's Mate 3rd class
A/S	antisubmarine
Asdic	British acronym for shipborne sound-ranging device (sonar)
ASG	aircraft-ship-ground (radar)
ASV	air-to-surface vessel (radar)
ASW	antisubmarine warfare
ASWORG	Antisubmarine Warfare Operations Research Group
BlimpASTraLant	Airship Anti-Submarine Training Detachment, Atlantic Fleet
Blimpron	blimp (or airship) squadron
BuAer	Bureau of Aeronautics
BuOrd	Bureau of Ordnance
BuPers	Bureau of Personnel
BuShips	Bureau of Ships
CAC	combat air crew
CER	Charles E. Rosendahl
CESF	Commander, Eastern Sea Frontier
CGC	Coast Guard cutter
CGSF	Commander, Gulf Sea Frontier
C-in-C	commander in chief
CincLant	Commander in Chief, Atlantic
CincLantFlt	Commander in Chief, Atlantic Fleet
CincMed	Commander in Chief, Mediterranean
CincPac	Commander in Chief, Pacific
CincUS	Commander in Chief, U.S. Fleet
CincWA	Commander in Chief, Western Approaches

CNATE	Chief of Naval Airship Training and Experimentation
CNO	Chief of Naval Operations
CO	commanding officer
ComAirLant	Commander, Air Forces Atlantic
ComAirWingsLant	Commander, Air Wings Atlantic
ComEastSeaFron	Commander, Eastern Sea Frontier
ComFairShipLant	Commander, Fleet Airships Atlantic
ComFairShipWing	Commander, Fleet Airship Wing
ComFairWing	Commander, Fleet Air Wing
ComFour [etc.]	Commander, Fourth [etc.] Naval District
ComFourthFlt	Commander, Fourth Fleet
ComGulfSeaFron	Commander, Gulf Sea Frontier
Cominch	Commander in Chief, U.S. Fleet
ComMorSeaFron	Commander, Moroccan Sea Frontier
ComNavEU	Commander, U.S. Naval Forces Europe
ComNavNAW	Commander, U.S. Naval Forces North African Waters
ComNavZor	Commander, U.S. Naval Forces Azores
ComPaSeaFron	Commander, Panamanian Sea Frontier
CVE	escort aircraft carrier
DCNO	Deputy Chief of Naval Operations
DD	destroyer
DE	destroyer escort
Det	detachment
DF (or D/F)	direction finding
ERSB	expendable radio-sonobuoy
ESF	Eastern Sea Frontier
FairShipsLant	Fleet Airships, Atlantic
FAPTU	Fleet Airships Pacific Tactical Unit (counterpart to BlimpASTraLant)
FIDO	air-dropped A/S acoustic homing torpedo (Mark XXIV "mine")
FM	frequency modulation
FY	fiscal year
GFC	Garland Fulton Collection
GFE	government-furnished equipment
GHMC	George H. Mills Collection
HedRon	headquarters squadron
HF/DF	high-frequency/direction finding ("Huff-Duff")
HQ	headquarters
HTA	heavier-than-air
INA	Inspector of Naval Aircraft
LRN	long-range pulse navigational system (Loran)
LTA	lighter-than-air
MAAF	Mediterranean Army Air Forces

MAD	magnetic airborne (or anomaly) detection
MIT	Massachusetts Institute of Technology
NAAF	Naval Air Auxiliary Facility
NACA	National Advisory Committee of Aeronautics
NAEC	Naval Air Engineering Center
NAF	naval air facility
NARA	National Archives and Records Administration
NAS	naval air station
NASM	National Air and Space Museum
NDRC	National Defense Research Committee
NMCS	Naval Member Canadian Staff (Washington)
NOB	naval operating base
NRL	Naval Research Laboratory
O-in-C	officer in charge
ONI	Office of Naval Intelligence
OSRD	Office of Scientific Research and Development
PAO	Public Affairs Office(r)
PBY	multiengine patrol seaplane
PF	patrol frigate (U.S. Coast Guard)
PLE	prudent limit of endurance
PPI	plan position indicator
PROCTOR	later code name for FIDO (Mark XXIV "mine")
R&D	research and development
RCAF	Royal Canadian Air Force
RCN	Royal Canadian Navy
RDF	radio direction finding (a British cover name for radar)
RG	record group
rpm	revolutions per minute
SecNav	secretary of the navy
SecWar	secretary of war
USL	Underwater Sound Laboratory
USNR	U.S. Naval Reserve
VCNO	Vice Chief of Naval Operations
Z	U.S. Navy's designation for all lighter-than-air craft
ZJ	utility airship (or utility squadron), nonrigid
ZNN	training airship, nonrigid
ZNP	patrol (A/S) airship, nonrigid
ZP	airship squadron
ZR	rigid airship
ZRCV	very large rigid capable of lofting a striking force of dive bombers
ZRS	rigid airship scout [USS *Akron* (ZRS 4), USS *Macon* (ZRS 5)]
ZTF	free balloon (for training)

Appendix A
Airship Deliveries to the U.S. Navy September 1941–April 1944

On December 1941, the Navy and Goodyear had 16 airships of all types on hand, six of which were capable operationally of long-range patrol. By the end of 1944, a total of 133 K-ships, 10 L-ships, 7-G ships, and 4 M-type were delivered to the Navy from the contractor via the operational and overhaul centers at NAS Lakehurst or NAS Moffett Field. Most, in turn, were assigned to other lighter-than-air stations and to expeditionary bases. Eleven new ships reached the operator in both May and July 1943—the largest monthly totals of the war. In January 1945 the Navy had 141 blimps on hand—the high-water mark of naval LTA and the largest airship fleet ever manufactured, organized, and deployed.

Type	On Hand at Lakehurst (7 Dec 1941)	1941	1942	1943	1944	1945
K	(4)	4	20	92	17	—
L	(3)	2	9[1]	10	—	—
G	(1)	—	—	6	1	—
M	—	—	—	1	3	—
TC	(2)	—	—	—	—	—

1. L-4 to L-8 ex-Goodyear Fleet; L-9 to L-12 built by the navy.

Appendix B
Pilots Check-Off List
Blimp Squadron Twelve (ZP-12)

A. Before Flight

1. Attend weather conference 45 minutes before scheduled flight time.
   a. Obtain weather code and forecast.
   b. Check sequences and coast guard station reports particularly in the area of your flight. Check upper air charts for winds aloft and approaching weather.
2. Attend briefing conference in the Group Operations Room.
   a. Obtain directive and any special instructions.
   b. Examine carefully any pictures of ship(s) in your mission.
   c. Read CESF Form Zed for any recent information on contacts.
3. Obtain and sign for navigation and communication gear.
   a. Check folder to ensure that you have the correct calls and recognition signals.
   b. Check navigation kit to ensure that all gear is present and in good condition.
   c. Obtain camera, confidential chart, handheld pelorus, navigator's and communication notebook.

B. Manning Ship

1. Man ship fifteen minutes prior to undocking time.
2. CHECK PRESSURE—MINIMUM 1 ¼ INCHES GAS PRESSURE.
3. Ascertain amount of fuel on board and that the slip tanks are filled.
4. See that the Lawrance unit is running and properly warmed up, and relay cut in.
5. See that mechanic is running of #5 and #6 tanks and that there is at least 60 gallons of fuel in each one.
6. Have the auxiliary blower started. (Have a full tank of fuel.)
7. Check all lifesaving equipment aboard and that there are sufficient life-jackets for all hands, including any extra passengers.

8. Check pigeons aboard.
9. Check food and emergency rations aboard.
10. Ascertain hangar weighoff of the ship.
11. Estimate weight of crew and gear and heaviness of ship after manning ship. About 175 lbs. apiece is a good average for each man.
12. Check with the crew captain and see that all of the crew is aboard.
13. Set altimeter and record the setting (in inches of Hg) in the log.
14. Supply radioman with correct calls and the communication plan for the day. Man all interphone stations and test out.
15. Check and see that IFF is turned on.
16. Personally see that wheel is correctly locked for taxing.
17. See that the bomb safety wires are removed and that the bomb bay doors are closed.
18. Test tensions of major controls and adjust as necessary.
19. Test major controls by having a member of the ground crew SIGHT check the control surfaces to ensure that the control surfaces respond correctly to the controls.
20. Notify the ground handling officer of any casualty that may delay takeoff.
21. Check with the mechanic to ensure that engines are properly warmed up.
22. Have GHO check trim. Pump air so as to have ship slightly tail heavy for unmasting.
23. Check compass heading with hangar axis, (297°T., variation 10° West).
24. Request permission from the tower to undock when directed by GHO.
25. When in all respects ready, signal the GHO that you are ready to undock.

C. Undocking

1. CHECK PRESSURE AND KEEP IT ABOVE 1 ¼ INCHES.
2. Watch the GHO at all times and be ready to execute his signals concerning the use of rudder and elevator.
3. When clear of the hangar door, request clearance from the tower to the take-off area.
4. Never run engines above idling speed while the ship is on the mast and the mast is moving. The pilot should keep his hand on his throttle controls to prevent the mechanic from running up the engines while the mast is moving. Keep engines at idling speed until signaled by the GHO to warm up, after the mast is stopped.
5. Keep the auxiliary blower running to maintain pressure. Make sure blower intake port is open. Trim ship as directed by GHO.
6. Open the port scoop to facilitate trimming the ship on the field.
7. See that qualified pilots are in the elevator seat and rudder seat at all times and alert for orders from GHO. Keep windows open.
8. With one engine idling the maximum safe speed (above which the ship may override the mast) is 1400 RPM.

D. Unmasting

1. CHECK PRESSURE—HAVE AT LEAST 1 ¼ INCHES.
2. After mast is stopped and GHO signals, warm engines thoroughly, then idle back.
3. Request GHO check trim; if in trim or nose heavy pump air as directed by GHO. Be sure scoop is wide open while pumping.
4. Request clearance for takeoff from the tower when directed by the GHO.
5. See that bomb release lever safety locking collar is turned to ready position.
6. Clear both engines by running them up to 1200 RPM one at a time.
7. Signal the GHO that you are in all respects ready to unmast and takeoff and have received tower clearance.
8. Be alert to obey the GHO's signals as the ship is unmasted.
9. Assist the ground party by flying the ship on the field if the wind is gusty. (Do not use engine speed that will move the ship forward while the mast is directly in front of the ship.) However, NEVER let the ship drift astern.
10. Be prepared to trim the ship if the mast weighoff was in error.
11. DO NOT TAKE OFF WITH A NOSE HEAVY SHIP.
12. Be sure that an officer or competent enlisted man is stationed in the bombardier's seat to drop bombs on your orders if the engines fail during takeoff.
13. Based on the final static condition of the ship, make your decision as to what ballast willl be jettisoned in case of engine failure during takeoff.

a. Slip Tanks	#1 626 lbs.	#2 497 lbs.
b. Sand	Depends on the amount	
c. Bombs	325 lbs. apiece (1300 lbs total). Use outside two first.	
d. Dump tanks	12 lbs. per sec. (use as last resort)	

E. Takeoff

1. CHECK PRESSURE—HAVE AT LEAST 1 ¼ INCHES.
2. Advance the throttles slowly and steadily when signaled by the GHO. Use full throttle. "Don't be throttle timid on takeoff."
3. Maintain 1-2 degrees bow-up inclination (NEVER DOWN) during takeoff. Do not increase angle of attack until at least 35 knots speed is attained, and then only enough to pull off slowly, unless obstructions are in the way. Do not be too anxious to get off the ground.
4. Maintain straight flight until the ship has reached an altitude of 400 ft. unless it is necessary to turn to avoid obstructions. If necessary to turn, make LEFT hand turns.
5. When the ship has reached about 400 altitude, ease back to throttles. By this time, the ship will have accelerated to cruising speed, and further use of excessive engine power is unnecessary. When throttling back be careful of inversion conditions.

6. When flying altitude is reached circle the field to the left making at least a half circle of the field. When you are satisfied that engines are in proper working order, set course for destination.
7. When flying altitude is reached, set scoop to correct opening to maintain at least 1 ¼ inches gas pressure (depending upon the airspeed that you are using) an open the appropriate damper.
8. Adjust engines to desired cruising speed—1400 RPG for Wright Engines, 1300 RPM for P&W engines.
9. Make departure report to the tower.

F. In Flight

1. CHECK PRESSURE–HAVE AT LEAST 1 ¼ INCHES.
2. Fly at not less than 500 feet terrain clearance while over land unless otherwise directed.
3. Lock bombs until over water. Do not pass over cities or towns.
4. Set the watch.
5. Retract the landing wheel.
6. Check out of the control area with the tower prior to shifting frequencies.
7. Assign battle stations. See that each man is fully instructed in his duties.
8. Instruct the lookouts in their duties and see that the mechanic and radioman understand that they are also lookouts.
9. Explain the mission of the flight to the radarman early in the flight and clearly explain what results are desired of the equipment, during the days operations.
10. Post the recognition signals and the calls of any missions that are to be contacted, and the voice calls of your own and other airships.
11. Put on the lifejackets prior to flying over water.
12. Load the machine gun after crossing the coast.
13. Check your directive to make sure you are carrying out your mission correctly.
14. Darken ship over water unless weather conditions are such that lights are necessary for the safety of the airship with other aircraft in the vicinity.
15. Maintain flight records, log time position, altitude, ground speed and true course when crossing coast.
16. Navigate carefully and accurately at all times even though you are with a mission which is supposed to be on a certain course and speed. Have confidence in your own navigation; the other fellow may be wrong.
17. Solve wind hourly. Take drift sights every fifteen minutes, and if using a "directional gyro", check and reset every 20 minutes. It is wise to always think of those two things as one (drift sight and directional gyro).
18. Check Dead Reckoning navigation with radio beams, radar, and radio direction finder. Record at least 2 RDF fixes on the training forms for training.

19. Fly your ship in proper trim at all times. A heavy ship much be flown tail heavy and with down elevator. Under no circumstances allow the ship to become bow heavy. Pump air aft when descending from a higher altitude.
20. If engines fails:
    Heavy ship—Pull bow up. Jettison ballast to put the ship in equilibrium.
    Light ship—Valve manually before the ship forces itself above pressure height.
21. Maintain a close check on fuel consumption at all times. Know the static condition of the ship at all times. In rain, take into consideration the weight of water on the bag. In heavy rain, the envelope may carry 2000 lbs of moisture. Rain load increases as speed decreases.
22. Lean best power gives best economy even at high speeds (1600-1800 RPM) but temperatures have to be watched. Lean out the engines as soon as the engines are slowed from takeoff speed to cruising speed.
23. See that engines have the proper preheat—very little for the Wright, 35-40 degrees for the P&W. Do not apply too much preheat to the P&W engines. Damage may result to the engine. With RPM over 1400 in P&W engines, use not over 30 degrees preheat.
24. See that the mech uses the fuel from the correct tanks. Tanks 5 and 6 should not fall below an absolute minimum of 40 gallons each. Two tanks should be cut in at all times except when transferring fuel. After takeoff a satisfactory procedure is to hold #6 tank in reserve with 80 to 100 gallons and cut in tanks 7 or 8 along with number 5.
25. Maintain a watch on the radar at all times when it is capable of efficient operation.
26. Whenever the radar is operating poorly, give the radar man an opportunity to repair it.
27. Notify the radarman before the power supply is cut off in order to give him an opportunity to secure the equipment and avoid extensive damage to the radar.
28. Have the radar-mad operators relieved by the radio operator, if qualified, for rest periods. Also use any mechanic or rigger qualified as mad-rad operator.
29. See that the MAD watch has a slick ready, out of the box and placed near the rear door, or in the automatic chute if installed.
30. Instruct the mad operator to throw the slick before notifying the pilot other than by ringing the bell. Other slicks and smoke floats to be thrown only on orders from the pilot.
31. The radarman and the radioman are responsible for the distribution of power from the Lawrence while in flight.
32. Anytime the Lawrence fails in flight it will be secured and the control relay switch turned off PRIOR to turning on the DC switches (on the mechanics panel) for the outboard generator supply which furnishes the only DC power then available.
33. The mechanical maintenance of the Lawrance in flight in regards to fuel, lubrication, etc., is the responsibility of the flight mechanic.
34. CHECK PRESSURE—HAVE AT LEAST 1 ¼ INCHES.
35. Make hourly position reports if communication plan permits. The first position report over water should include the weather report. Make subsequent weather reports whenever the weather changes.

36. If the opportunity is available, once during the flight go to pressure height and record the data (altitude, temperature, superheat, CORRECT altimeter setting). Gas pressure must be 1 ¼ inches.
37. VOICE AND RADIO PROCEDURE: Only the pilot or co-pilot will use the voice equipment on action frequency or tower frequency. Radioman will listen in and copy as much as possible of voice transmission against time.

G. Returning to Base

1. CHECK PRESSURE–HAVE AT LEAST 1 ¼ INCHES.
2. After departing mission and when 50 miles from it, make your departure report, when and where you left it, where you are and when you will get home. Remember your mission is usually moving in the opposite direction, when figuring the 50 miles. The Base is anxious to hear from you.
3. Cruise at assigned altitude and speed. At night or in low visibility fly befow 750 feet.
4. Check altimeter by dropping a miniature bomb (do not drop it near any surface craft). A slick will be very nearly as accurate.
5. Unload machine gun prior to crossing the coast.
6. Set bomb release level safety locking collar on safe prior to crossing the coast.
7. Shift to the Lakehurst tower frequency when within 15 miles of Lakehurst. Check in with the tower, give your position and ETA. Receive landing instructions and weather. If the tower does not answer call up, broadcast the information. They may be receiving you.
8. Except under emergency conditions do not fly under 500 feet terrain clearance while over land.
9. Secure radar when it is no longer of service and retract the radar hat.
10. See that the wheel is down and check personally to see that the yoke is in proper position and locked.
11. Circle to the left (counterclockwise) around the field unless otherwise instructed by the tower, which may order you to hold in defite area. If assigned a sector by the tower, stay in it. Be sure of your position.
12. Check the neon weather lights at the field prior to landing:

General service roof	West to East	#1 pressure in hundredths of inch.
		#2 Temperature in degrees F.
Pay office façade	West to East	#1 Wind direction in tens of degrees.
		#2 Wind velocity in knots.

13. Notify the GHO of the condition of your ship.
14. If the mat temperature is not given, request it. It gives you a warning of falling through conditions or inversion.
15. Check radioman that he has his radio antenna reeled in.
16. Detail someone to standby drag-rope.
17. Clear long lines for dropping by toggle in pilots compartment.

H. Landing

1. CHECK PRESSURE–HAVE AT LEAST 1 ¼ INCHES.
2. Weigh off at 300 to 400 feet altitude by corrected altimeter (never below the height of #1 hangar).
3. Start blower before commencing approach and keep it running.
4. When ready to start approach, open the port scoop wide and use to maintain pressure and to shift large quantities of air in a hurry. Do not leave dampers on while engines are idling. Check valves may stick open allowing air to escape and pressure to drop.
5. Use landing light if desired but turn it off when over the landing area, clear of obstructions. This light drains as much current from the battery as the starter. It also blinds the ground party.
6. In light variable or no wind approaches, NEVER get under 30 feet ground or obstruction clearance.
7. Make strong, gusty, wind approaches with the accent on speed of masting, especially with more than one ground crew. The sunset lull may only last a few minutes. All the training ships and squadron ships may have to be landed during the lull. Keep close to landing area.
8. Do not try to put a light ship on the wheel. Do not put a heavy ship on the wheel in gusty conditions, but lighten ship until it is in equilibrium.
9. In making a high landing in light airs, do not release long lines or drag rope unless sure ground party can reach them–the lines may foul in obstructions on your second approach. Haul drag rope in if landing is missed.
10. Be sure long lines are lowered from the gunners window prior to arriving over the landing area.
11. Do not dump gasoline in the vicinity of open lights on the ground.
12. Before dumping gasoline, head into the wind and STOP ALL AUXILIARIES. Run engines at constant speed while dumping.
13. USE THE STERN DRAG ROPE for light wind landings. Station a man aft to drop the line and instruct him to be the shepherd's crock to shake it out if it falls in a fouled condition. You will not lose face by dropping the drag rope, but will be respected for using your head.
14. If the landing party is improperly stationed and you feel that it is unsafe to land to the present location of the party, notify the GHO and request that he move the party in the direction or to the location that you desire. The winds aloft are often different from those on the ground, but remember that you are landing into the wind on the ground and not the wind aloft.
15. GHO assumes responsibility for the safety of the ship after the lines are WELL-IN-HAND. The pilot then becomes responsible to the GHO and will keep alert for his signals.
16. Watch the GHO carefully for signals to use engine or to cut the engine.
17. If the ship is light, use UP ELEVATOR to spring the ship down toward the ground. Use engines as directed by GHO. Be careful to keep the ship from coming down too fast. If ship is nose heavy, pump air aft to trim it up for masting as soon as lines are well in hand.

18. Open the windows for the pilots compartment and listen for orders as you near the party.
19. Fly the ship after it is on the ground and in the hands of the ground party. Do not let it get off wind and use engine to keep it from drifting backward.

I. Masting

1. CHECK PRESSURE—HAVE AT LEAST 1 ¼ INCHES.
2. In a light ship as soon as the lines are well in hand and you are using the engines to work the ship down, pump air aft. Get the ship in trim as soon as possible to go on the mast.
3. Fly the ship by using rudder, elevator, and engines as necessary when ordered by the GHO. Use controls smartly.
4. Do not gun the engines while the ship is being masted. Be sure the mech does not rev up the engines while the ship is going on the mast.
5. When ordered by the GHO have the mechanic lean out and cut the engines. After the engines are cut, the pilot must turn off the toggle switches on the instrument board. Otherwise someone may be hurt by a prop turning over.
6. Align the props to give maximum ground clearance.
7. Secure radio with permission of the tower.
8. Align RDF loop on a 90-270 bearing.
9. Retract the landing light.

J. Docking

1. CHECK PRESSURE—HAVE AT LEAST 1 ¼ INCHES.
2. Watch the GHO for signals. A qualified pilot will man the elevator and rudder controls until the ship is docked and the GHO gives the word to disembark.
3. Keep the crew at their stations until the lines are secured in the hangar; do not let the crew mass aft and make the ship tail heavy for unmasting.
4. Be alert to use the elevator promptly and correctly to counteract kiting while docking.
5. Trim the ship while entering the hangar in an endeavor to have it in trim for unmasting.
6. Sign the pink sheet and record the defects noted during the flight. The S&R representative is not to enter the ship until it is in the hangar; or, if the masting out until the ship is masted. Explain any defects in detail to assist the night check crew in their repairs.

K. Checking In

1. Check in with the Squadron Operations Duty Officer. If the Squadron or the Group Commander is on the hangar deck, report to him also.
2. Report to the Group Operations for interrogation. Take your radio log, navigator work book, and track chart.
3. Check the ship duty pilot's board for your duty.

Appendix C
Emergency Bills in Flight
Fleet Airship Wing One (1944)

A. General

1. All positions having ICS outlets will maintain a continuous watch on the system. (ICS is the primary method of intra-ship communication. Shouting through the car is discouraged as it leads to confusion and excitement.)
2. All positions, in addition to other duties, act as lookouts and report all sightings to the pilot.
3. The forward lookout should normally be stationed at the machine gun.
4. Combat air crews will conduct emergency drill exercises at least once a week in each emergency bill herein outlined.

B. General Quarters

1. Command Pilot—In charge, take over rudder control. Receive reports over ICS.
2. Co-Pilot—Elevator. Maintain safe altitude. Go to bombing altitude on attack run. Use throttles as necessary.
3. Co-Pilot—Rudder. When relieved by command pilot take bombardier's position. Arm bombs.
4. Co-Pilot—Navigator. Prepare complete contact report for radioman. Record attack data. Take pictures of approach, attack, and results of attack.
5. Radioman—Open bomb-bay doors. Report when opened. Transmit contact report to base. Carry out communication plan for attack.
6. Radarman—Conn pilot in making radar approach. Release smoke float on first peak of MAD contact.
7. Mechanic—At engine panel. Mixture controls on full rich, report same. Be alert for mechanical emergencies.

8. Rigger—Open both scoops full. Start auxiliary blower. Break out hand fire extinguisher. Stand-by air to helium tie off.
9. Assistant Mechanic—Man BAR.
10. Gunner–At machine gun.

Note: ALL hands proceed to assigned stations promptly and quietly. Report to command pilot over ICS when on station and ready.

C. Engine Failure

1. Command Pilot—Order release of ballast in follow sequence:
   a. Bombs (unarmed).
   b. Slip tanks.
   c. Dump tanks (Note: Auxiliaries are running).
   d. Other equipment if necessary to save ship. Send report to base.
2. Co-Pilot—Elevator. Gain altitude but stay below pressure height.
3. Co-Pilot—Rudder. Bring ship into the wind slowly so altitude will not be lost.
4. Co-Pilot—Navigator. Give ship's position to radioman. Gather confidential equipment.
5. Radioman—On order from command pilot, transmit a plain language report of the engine failure and ship's position on operational frequency to the base and all ships.
6. Radarman—Check position, especially if near target. Prepare to destroy and jettison special equipment.

Appendix D
Memorandum (28 December 1944) from LTA Design Branch Cost of Nonrigid Airships, 1942–45

The initial costs of nonrigid airships acquired by the Navy since 1941 have been determined from the actual contracts plus an estimate of the costs of Government Furnished Equipment. The costs of changes by contract amendments are still be negotiated, and not included herein.

Model ZNP-K Airships

	4	Ships at $262,614	$1,050,456
	2	Ships at $250,034	500,068
	42	Ships at $318,328	13, 369,776
	86	Ships at $292,866	25,186,476
Total	134	40,106,776	
		Estimated G.F.E.	6,700,000
Total cost of	134	ships	$46,806,776

Model ZNN-L Airships

	2	Ships at $91,582	$183,164
	5	Used ships and misc. equipment	430,323
	4	Ships by Project Order at Moffett	330,000
	10	Ships at $91,497	$914,970
Total	21	$1,858,457	
		Estimated G.F.E.	100,000
Total cost of	21	ships	$1,958,457

Model ZNN-G Airships

	7	Ships at $157,478	$1,102,346
		Estimated G.F.E.	105,000
Total cost of	7	ships	$1,207,346

Model ZNP-M Airships

	1	Ship	$942,660
	3	Ships at $629,199	1,887,597
Total	4		2,830,257
		Estimated G.F.E.	200,000
Total cost of	4	ships	$3,030,257

Summary

	134	ZNP-K Airships	$46,806,776
	21	ZNN-L Airships	1,958,457
	7	ZNN-G Airships	1,207,346
	4	ZNP-M Airships	3,030,257
Total	166		$53,002,836
Spares approx.	10%		5,000,000
			$58,002,836

Appropriations

1941	8	ships	$2,350,000
1942	43	ships	18,481,380
1943	96	ships	36,330,000
Total	147	ships	$57,161,380

Appendix E
Statistical Summary
U.S. Fleet Airship Operations, 1942–45

Yearly Flight Totals

Flights	**1942**	**1943**	**1944**	**1945**	**Total**
Atlantic[1]	1,544	12,233	19,447	4,330	37,554
Pacific	1,073	5,313	8,112	5,658	20,156
Combined	2,617	17,546	27,559	9,988	57,710

Yearly Hour Totals

Flight Hours	**1942**	**1943**	**1944**	**1945**	**Total**
Atlantic	20,088.2	135,997.1	183,731.8	38,420.5	378,237.6
Pacific	6,763.7	43,991.4	69,089.3	47,446.6	167,291.1
Combined	26,851.9	179,988.5	252,821.6	85,867.1	545,529.1

Ships Escorted, Yearly

Ships Escorted	**1942**	**1943**	**1944**	**1945**	**Total[2]**
Atlantic	—	26,966	36,485	6,857	70,308
Pacific	14	3,023	4,574	2,119	9,730
Combined	14	29,989	41,059	8,976	80,038

Summary

	Operational Flights	Operational Flight Hours	Average Lenght of Operation Flight
Atlantic	22,155	279,211.7	12.6
Pacific	13,800	133,258.1	9.7
Total	35,955	412,469.8	

Airships Assigned Atlantic

1942	ZP11	ZP12	ZP14	ZP15	ZP21	ZP22	ZP23	ZP24	ZP41	ZP42	ZP51	Total
January	—	4.0	—	—	—	—	—	—	—	—	—	4.0
February	—	4.0	—	—	—	—	—	—	—	—	—	4.0
March	—	4.0	—	—	—	—	—	—	—	—	—	4.0
April	—	4.0	—	—	—	—	—	—	—	—	—	4.0
May	—	5.0	—	—	—	—	—	—	—	—	—	5.0
June	1.0	5.6	1.0	—	—	—	—	—	—	—	—	7.6
July	1.0	6.0	1.0	—	—	—	—	—	—	—	—	8.0
August	2.0	7.0	1.0	—	—	—	—	—	—	—	—	10.0
September	2.5	8.6	1.0	—	—	—	—	—	—	—	—	12.1
October	3.0	8.0	2.0	—	—	—	—	—	—	—	—	13.0
November	3.0	7.0	3.0	—	2.0	—	—	—	—	—	—	15.0
December	4.0	6.0	3.0	—	2.0	—	—	—	—	—	—	15.0
1943												
January	4.0	7.0	5.0	—	2.5	—	—	—	—	—	—	18.5
February	4.0	7.0	5.0	1.0	4.0	—	—	—	—	—	—	21.0
March	5.0	7.4	6.0	2.6	4.8	—	—	—	—	—	3.0	28.8
April	6.3	6.0	6.0	3.3	7.3	—	—	—	—	—	3.2	32.1
May	7.0	4.3	6.0	4.0	8.0	3.0	—	—	—	—	4.0	36.3
June	6.4	8.0	6.0	5.0	8.8	3.0	2.0	—	—	—	4.3	43.5
July	7.0	8.3	6.8	6.0	10.8	3.0	2.5	—	—	—	5.0	49.4
August	6.0	8.0	6.8	6.0	10.5	3.0	3.0	—	—	—	4.8	48.1
September	6.2	8.4	7.6	6.0	10.8	3.0	3.0	—	—	—	3.8	48.8
October	6.0	9.0	7.3	5.3	11.0	3.0	3.0	—	3.0	—	4.3	51.9
November	6.0	7.4	7.0	6.0	11.0	3.0	3.0	—	3.4	3.0	4.2	54.0
December	6.0	7.8	7.8	6.8	11.8	3.0	3.0	—	4.8	4.5	5.0	605.0

1944												
January	6.8	8.0	8.8	6.5	11.0	3.3	3.0	—	5.0	5.0	5.3	62.7
February	8.8	8.0	7.4	7.0	9.5	4.0	4.0	1.0	6.0	5.8	8.0	69.5
March	8.0	8.0	7.3	6.3	11.3	3.3	2.0	3.8	9.0	7.5	9.0	75.5
April	8.3	8.3	8.0	8.0	11.5	3.0	2.5	3.5	8.0	7.7	8.8	77.6
May	5.6	8.2	7.7	7.8	10.0	2.8	5.6	2.6	8.6	7.6	8.5	75.0
June	7.0	7.3	6.0	8.0	10.8	4.0	3.5	7.3	8.8	7.0	8.0	77.7
July	7.3	8.0	6.0	8.0	9.8	3.3	3.8	8.0	8.3	7.3	5.3	75.1
August	7.0	8.2	6.0	7.2	9.6	3.6	4.0	8.2	8.0	7.8	5.6	75.2
September	7.5	8.0	6.0	7.5	11.0	2.0	4.3	7.8	7.3	7.8	7.0	76.2
October	7.2	7.8	6.0	8.0	12.4	—	5.2	8.0	6.6	7.0	7.0	75.2
November	7.0	7.5	6.0	7.5	13.3	—	3.0	8.3	6.0	7.5	6.3	73.2
December	8.4	5.2	6.0	6.0	12.0	—	—	5.2	6.0	4.8	1.0	54.6
1945												
January	7.2	6.0	6.0	7.0	11.6	—	—	5.6	6.5	4.0	—	59.3
February	7.2	7.1	6.0	6.2	8.5	—	—	7.2	5.7	3.0	—	50.9
March	8.0	8.0	6.0	6.0	8.0	—	—	8.0	5.0	3.0	—	52.0
April	8.0	8.5	5.0	5.5	8.0	—	—	8.0	4.5	.08	—	48.3
May	8.0	8.4	6.0	5.4	8.0	—	—	8.0	4.4	—	—	48.2
June	—	—	—	—	—	—	—	—	—	—	—	—
July	—	—	—	—	—	—	—	—	—	—	—	—
August	—	—	—	—	—	—	—	—	—	—	—	—
September	—	—	—	—	—	—	—	—	—	—	—	—
October	—	—	—	—	—	—	—	—	—	—	—	—
November	—	—	—	—	—	—	—	—	—	—	—	—
December	—	—	—	—	—	—	—	—	—	—	—	—

Airships Assigned Pacific

1942	ZP31	ZP32	ZP33	Totals
January	—	—		—
February	—	1.8		1.8
March	—	4.3		4.3
April	—	4.3		4.3
May	—	4.7		4.7
June	—	4.1		4.1
July	—	3.0		3.0
August	—	2.5		2.5
September	—	3.0		3.0
October	—	3.0		3.0
November	—	2.5		2.5
December	2.0	3.1		5.1
1943				
January	3.0	2.7	—	5.7
February	3.0	2.5	1.0	6.5
March	3.0	3.0	1.6	7.6
April	3.0	2.7	1.0	6.7
May	4.0	3.4	2.0	9.4
June	5.0	4.6	3.0	12.6
July	6.0	6.0	3.4	15.4
August	6.0	6.8	4.0	16.8
September	6.0	7.2	5.8	19.0
October	6.0	8.0	6.0	20.0
November	8.0	8.0	5.7	21.7
December	9.0	9.7	6.0	24.7
1944				
January	11.0	10.0	5.5	26.5
February	11.0	9.0	6.0	26.0
March	11.0	9.0	6.0	26.0
April	9.0	8.4	7.1	24.5
May	9.0	8.0	8.0	25.0
June	9.0	7.7	5.4	22.1
July	8.0	7.0	5.0	20.0
August	8.0	7.3	5.4	20.7
September	9.0	8.0	4.7	21.7
October	8.0	7.0	4.5	19.5
November	8.0	8.3	4.0	20.3
December	8.0	10.1	4.6	22.7

1945				
January	12.6	12.0	5.5	30.1
February	12.6	12.0	5.5	30.1
March	12.3	11.0	5.6	28.9
April	12.0	10.1	5.0	27.1
May	10.4	10.0	5.0	25.4
June	12.3	10.5	5.9	28.7
July	12.6	10.5	7.5	30.6
August	11.9	10.8	6.9	29.6

Grand Totals

	Atlantic Fleet	Pacific Fleet	Combined Total
Escort Flights	3765	—	—
Hours	48680.4	—	—
Patrol Flights	11674	—	—
Hours	140454.1	—	—
Other Flights	3762*	2868	6630
Hours	27830.1*	20181.4	24011.5
Patrol and Escort Flights	2465	1224	3689
Hours	33223.6	13592.5	46816.1
Experimental Flights	825	215	1040
Hours	7926.2	436.0	8362.2
Ferry Flights	2995	1110	4105
Hours	20710.1	4447.3	25157.4
Training Flights	781.7	2163	9980
Hours	45559.5	8968.7	54528.2
Night Escort Flights	746	7	753
Hours	7501.3	90.9	9592.2
Night Patrol Flights	3252	47	3299
Hours	43565.2	250.0	44085.2
Night Escort and Patrol Flights	253	38	291
Hours	3787.1	543.2	4330.3
Total Flights	37554	20156	57710
Total Hours	378237.6	167291.5	545529.1
Ships Escorted	70308	9730	80038

Atlantic Fleet includes: ZP11, ZP12, ZP14, ZP15, ZP21, ZP22, ZP23, ZP24, ZP41, ZP42, ZP51, ZJ1.
Pacific Fleet includes: ZP31, ZP32, and ZP33.
*Includes 177 minespotting flights (1332.2 hours) flown by ZP 14 overseas.

Appendix F
Commanding Officers
Fleet Airships Atlantic, 1942–45

Blimp Squadron Eleven	USNAS South Weymouth, Massachusetts

Commissioned	2 June 1942
Decommissioned	8 June 1945

Lieut. Cmdr. Samuel M. BAILEY, USN	(2 June 1942–24 September 1943)
Lieut. Cmdr. John SHANNON, USN	(24 September 1943–29 March 1944)
Lieut. Cecil A. BOLAM, USN	(29 March 1944–31 October 1944)
Lieut. Cmdr. John F. PEAR, USNR	(31 October–8 June 1945)

Blimp Squadron Twelve	USNAS Lakehurst, New Jersey

Commissioned	2 January 1942
Decommissioned	—

Lieut. Cmdr. Raymond F. TYLER, USN	(2 January 1942–1 December 1942)
Lieut. Cmdr. Charles H. KENDALL, USN	(13 November 1942–17 July 1945)
Lieut. Cmdr. Franklin S. RIXEY, USN	(1 February 1944–3 October 1944)
Lieut. Cmdr. Herbert S. GRAVES, USN	(3 October 1944–23 June 1945)
Lieut. Cmdr. Harold B. VAN GORDER, USNR	(23 June 1945 ------------)

Blimp Squadron Fourteen	USNAS (LTA) Weeksville Elizabeth City, North Carolina

Commissioned	1 June 1942
Transferred overseas	22 May 1944, NAS Port Lyautey French Morocco
Decommissioned	17 January 1946

Lieut. Cmdr. Daniel J. WEINTRAUB, USN	(1 June 1942–13 November 1942)
Lieut. Cmdr. William A. COCKELL, USN	(13 November 1942–17 July 1943)
Lieut. Cmdr. Michael F. D. FLAHERTY, USN	(17 July 1943–15 April 1944)
Lieut. Cmdr. Harold B. VAN GORDER, USNR	(15 April 1944–22 May 1944)

Overseas

Cmdr. Emmet J. SULLIVAN, USN	(22 May 1944–19 October 1944)
Lieut. Cmdr. Franklin S. RIXEY, USN	(19 October 1944–17 October 1945)
Lieut. Cmdr. Robert B. BRETLAND, USNR	(17 October 1945–17 January 1946)

Blimp Squadron Fifteen — USNAS Glynco, Georgia

Commissioned	1 February 1943
Decommissioned	9 June 1945

Cmdr. John D. REPPY, USN	(1 February 1943–27 July 1943)
Lieut. Cmdr. Richard S. ANDREWS, USN	(27 July 1943–16 February 1944)
Lieut. Cmdr. Raymond C. GOSSOM, USNR	(16 February 1944–31 October 1944)
Lieut. Cmdr. Robert B. BRETLAND, USNR	(31 October 1944–9 June 1945)

Blimp Squadron Twenty-One — USNAS Richmond, Florida

Commissioned	1 November 1942
Decommissioned	14 November 1945

Cmdr. Gerald D. ZURMUEHLEN, USN	(1November 1942–1 February 1943)
Lieut. Cmdr. Alfred L. COPE, USN	(1 February 1943–15 April 1944)
Lieut. Cmdr. Henry C. SPICER, USN	(15 April 1944–6 February 1945)
Cmdr. Jack H. NAHIGIAN, USNR	(6 February 1945–5 October 1945)
Lieut. Cmdr. Donald W. DEFAY, USNR	(5 October 1945–14 November 1945)

Blimp Squadron Twenty-Two — USNAS Houma, Louisiana

Commissioned	15 May 1943
Decommissioned	12 September 1944

Lieut. Cmdr. J. J. MCCORMICK, USN	(15 May 1943–4 October 1943)
Lieut. Cmdr. R. C. GOSSOM, USNR	(4 October 1943–7 February 1944)
Lieut. Cmdr. H. M. HARRIS, USNR	(7 February 1944–8 May 1944)
Lieut. Cmdr. Herbert S. GRAVES, USN	(20 June 1944–12 September 1944)

Blimp Squadron Twenty-Three

Commissioned 1 June 1943
Decommissioned 2 December 1944

Lieut. Cmdr. Michael F. D. FLAHERTY, USN (1 June 1943–12 July 1943)
Lieut. Robert L. JACKSON, USN (12 July 1943–30 July 1943)
Lieut. Cmdr. Marion H. EPPES, USN (30 July 1943–16 November 1943)
Lieut. Cmdr. Louis M. AYERS, USNR (16 November 1943–18 February 1944)
Lieut. Cmdr. James H. CRUSE, USN (18 February 1944–11 May 1944)
Lieut. Cmdr. Herman K. ROCK, USN (11 May 1944–11 November 1944)
Lieut. Cmdr. Orville W. MELLICK, USNR (11 November 1944–2 December 1944)

Blimp Squadron Twenty-Four USNAS Hitchcock, Texas

Commissioned 9 February 1944
Decommissioned 9 June 1945

Lieut. Cmdr. Louis M. AYERS, USNR (9 February 1944–10 June 1944)
Lieut. Cmdr. Harold B. VAN GORDER, USNR (10 June 1944–25 April 1945)
Lieut. Cmdr. William A. J. LEWI, USN (25 April 1945–9 June 1945)

Blimp Squadron Forty-One

Commissioned 15 June 1943
Decommissioned 31 January 1946

Lieut. Cmdr. Daniel M. ENTLER, JR., USN (15 June 1943–1 May 1944)
Lieut. Cmdr. John J. MCLENDON, USNR (1 May 1944–28 December 1945)
Lieut. Cmdr. J. NOLEN, USNR (28 December–31 January 1946)

Blimp Squadron Forty-Two

Commissioned 1 September 1943
Decommissioned 9 June 1945

Cmdr. Charles L. WERTS, USN (1 September 1943–10 September 1944)
Lieut. Cmdr. Robert F. SMITH, USNR (10 September 1944–27 April 1945)
Lieut. Cmdr. Harold B. VAN GORDER (27 April 1945–9 June 1945)

Blimp Squadron Fifty-One

Commissioned 10 February 1943
Decommissioned 20 December 1944

Cmdr. Gerald D. ZURMUEHLEN, USN (10 February 1943–10 June 1943)
Lieut. Cmdr. John B. RIEKER, USNR (10 June 1943–1 August 1943)
Cmdr. John D. REPPY, USN (1 August 1943–2 October 1943)
Cmdr. Samuel BAILEY, USN (2 October 1943–26 October 1943)
Lieut. Cmdr. Robert J. WILLIAMS, USN (26 October 1943–4 February 1944)
Lieut. Cmdr. John NAHIGIAN, USNR (4 February 1944–20 December 1944)

Blimp Headquarters Squadron One

Commissioned 15 July 1943
Decommissioned 13 December 1945
Lieut. Cmdr. George R. LEE, USN (15 July 1943–6 May 1944)
Lieut. Cmdr. Arthur T. SEWELL, USN (6 May 1944–11 August 1945)
Lieut. Cmdr. Dudley B. W. BROWN (11 August 1945–8 September 1945)
Lieut. Cmdr. Norman V. SCURRIA, USNR (8 September 1945–13 December 1945)

Blimp Headquarters Squadron Two

Commissioned 15 July 1943
Decommissioned 13 December 1945

Lieut. Saxe P. GANTZ, USN (15 July 1943–5 August 1943)
Lieut. Robert L. JACKSON, USN (5 August 1943–20 November 1943)
Lieut. Cmdr. John B. RIEKER, USNR (20 November 1943–8 February 1945)
Lieut. Cmdr. Roland J. BLAIR, USNR (8 February 1945–25 April 1945)
Lieut. Cmdr. Robert D. MCNAULL, USNR (25 April 1945–16 June 1945)

Blimp Headquarters Squadron Four

Commissioned 15 July 1943
Decommissioned 15 July 1945

Cmdr. Gerald D. ZURMEUHLEN, USN (15 July 1943–20 January 1944)
Lieut. Roland J. BLAIR, USNR (20 January 1943–15 February 1944)
Lieut. Cmdr. Harold W. SPALDING, USNR (15 February 1944–15 July 1945)

Blimp Headquarters Squadron Five

Commissioned	2 August 1943
Decommissioned	7 December 1944

Lieut. Cmdr. John B. RIEKER, USNR	(2 August 1943–12 November 1943)
Lieut. Cmdr. John C. LAUTARET, USNR	(12 November 1943–15 February 1944)
Lieut. David R. GRACE, USNR	(15 February 1944–22 February 1944)
Lieut. Dudley B. W. BROWN, USNR	(22 February 1944–27 November 1944)
Lieut. Cmdr. Arthur T. HIGGINS, USNR	(27 November 1944–7 December 1944)

Fleet Airship Wing One

Commissioned	15 July 1943 (Redesignated from Fleet Airship Group One) 5 July 1945 (The commands of Fleet Airships, Atlantic and Fleet Airship Wing One were combined)

Captain Raymond F. TYLER, USN	(15 July 1943– ——)

Fleet Airship Wing Two

Commissioned	15 July 1943 (Redesignated from Fleet Airship Group TWO–Commissioned 1 May 1943)
Decommissioned	16 June 1945

Captain Walter E. ZIMMERMAN, USN	(15 July 1943–15 July 1943)
Cmdr. Alfred L. COPE, USN	(15 July 1943–6 August 1943)
Captain Maurice M. BRADLEY, USN	(6 August 1943–1 May 1944)
Cmdr. Michael F. D. FLAHERTY, USN	(1 May 1944–12 February 1945)
Cmdr. Alfred L. COPE, USN	(12 February 1945–16 June 1945)

Fleet Airship Wing Four

Commissioned	2 August 1943
Decommissioned	15 July 1945

Captain Walter E. ZIMMERMAN, USN	(2 August 1943–19 June 1945)
Lieut. Cmdr. Harold W. SPALDING, USNR	(19 June 1945–15 July 1945)

Fleet Airship Wing Five

Commissioned	2 August 1943
Decommissioned	11 December 1944

Cmdr. John D. REPPY, USN	(2 August 1943–6 October 1943)
Cmdr. Samuel M. BAILEY, USN	(6 October 1943–6 September 1944)
Cmdr. Charles L. WERTS, USN	(6 September 1944–11 December 1944)

Appendix G
MAD and Sonobuoy Training Exercises
Fleet Airships Pacific

MAD Exercises

Object of the Exercise

(a) To obtain a magnetic contact on a submarine by use of a trapping circle after visual contact has been made.

Tactical Situation

(a) Submarine has been seen to submerge. Distance to point of submergence is over 2 miles.

Procedure

(a) Upon contact proceed to scene at best speed.
(b) Deliver attack if submarine has been submerged less than 30 seconds. (This may be extended at the pilot's discretion).
(c) If submarine has been submerged too long for attack, drop a flare 1000 yards before arriving at point of submergence.
(d) Drop both a flare and a dye marker at point of submergence.
(e) Set throttles to make good 60 knots air speed. (In accordance with F.T.P. 223, paragraph 2942, maximum speed shall be used when trapping an enemy submarine).
(f) Use minimum safe altitude under 200 feet.
(g) Proceed along same course for 1000 yards (30 seconds at 60 knots) and drop another flare.
(h) Fly a circle of 1000 yards radius with point of submergence at the center and drop flares every 45° of arc.
(i) Continue flying the circular pattern thus described until contact is obtained or for a period of at least 30 minutes.
(j) If contact is obtained, commence tracking.
(k) If contact is not obtained within 30 minutes expand radio of trapping circle and continue "hunt".

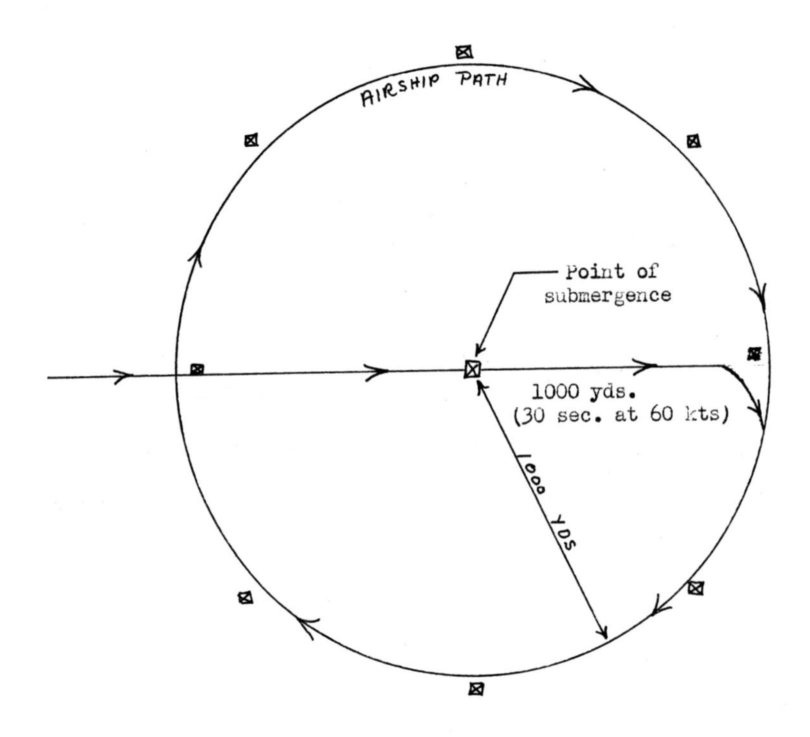

NOTE: *This exercise is in accordance with F.T.P. 223, paragraph 2942.*

MAD Exercise II

Object of the Exercise

(a) To establish appropriate course and speed of a submerged submarine by use of MAD tracking.

Tactical Situation

(a) Definite MAD indication has given approximate position of a submerged submarine.

Procedure

(a) Use "clover leaf" pattern, making 270° right turns.
(b) Use throttles and rudder to give maximum maneuverability.
(c) Use minimum safe altitude under 200 feet.
(d) In order for the clover leaf to be effective, each leaf of the pattern must be negotiate in less than one minute.
(e) After MAD contact has been made start flying "lazy eights" across the indicated track of the submarine.
(f) When approximate track is established, make 270° turns, alternating right and left.
(g) A marker is dropped upon receipt of each contact (automatically or manually depending upon tactical circumstances).

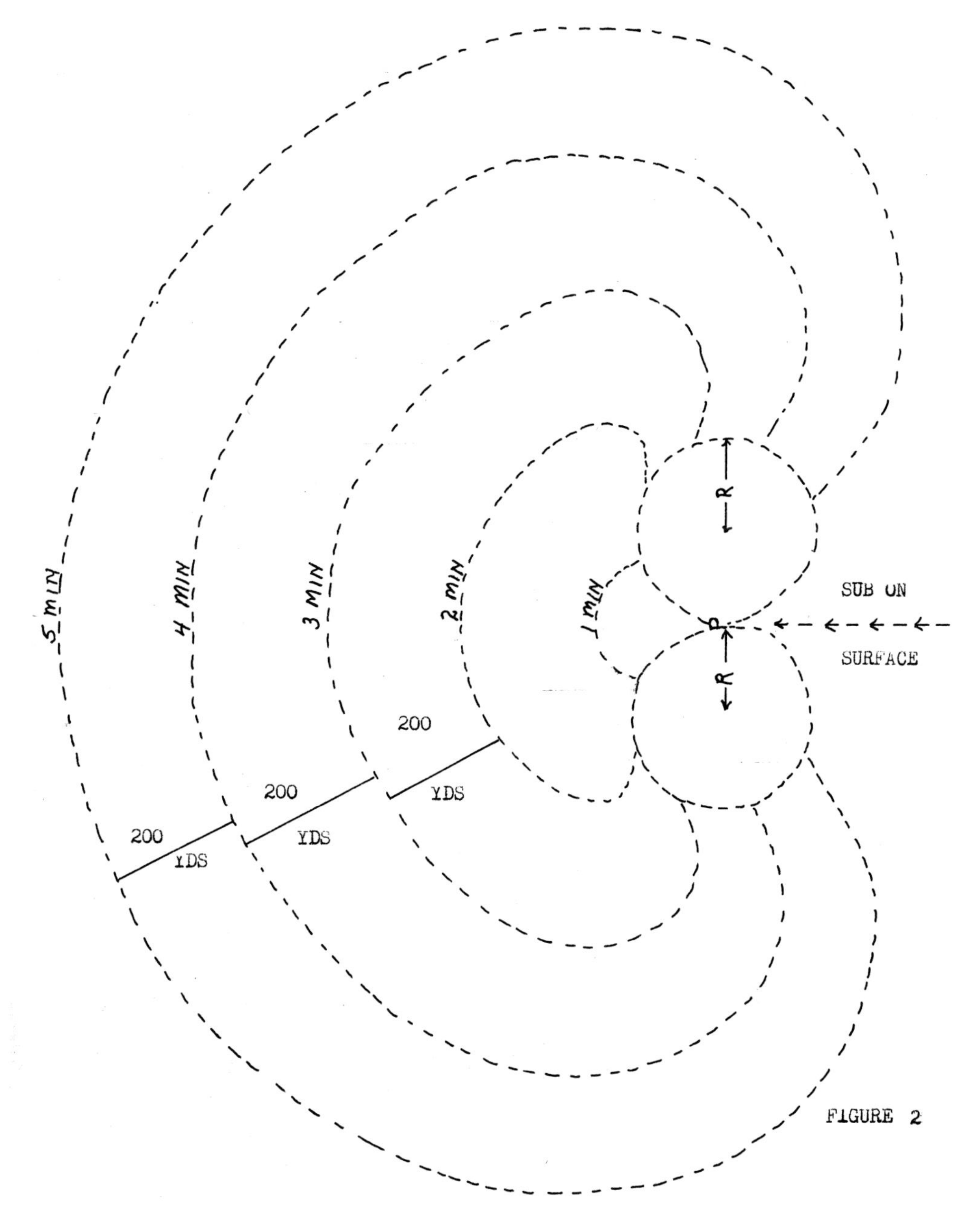

FIGURE 2

Diagram of underwater travel of a submarine

At 6 knots

P is point of submergence

R is turning radius - 135 yards

(h) Accurate plot of marker positions must be maintained throughout the exercise.

(i) After the approximate location and the direction of motion of the submarine has been determined, start a bombing run.

NOTE: This exercise is in accordance with F.T.P. 223, paragraph 2943, with the exception that all turns will be right turns taking into consideration the inherent advantages of an airship making right turns.

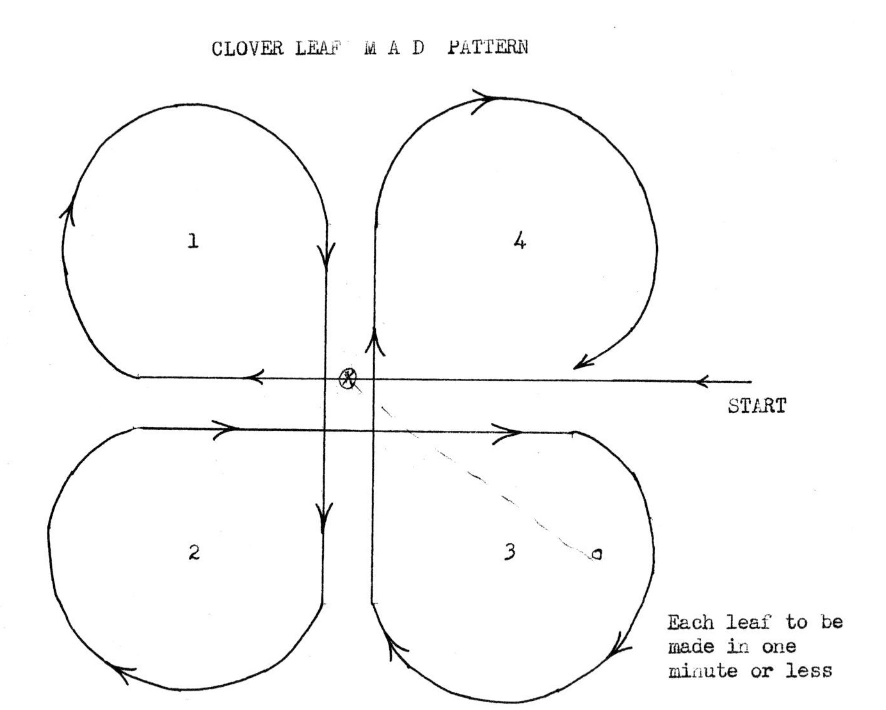

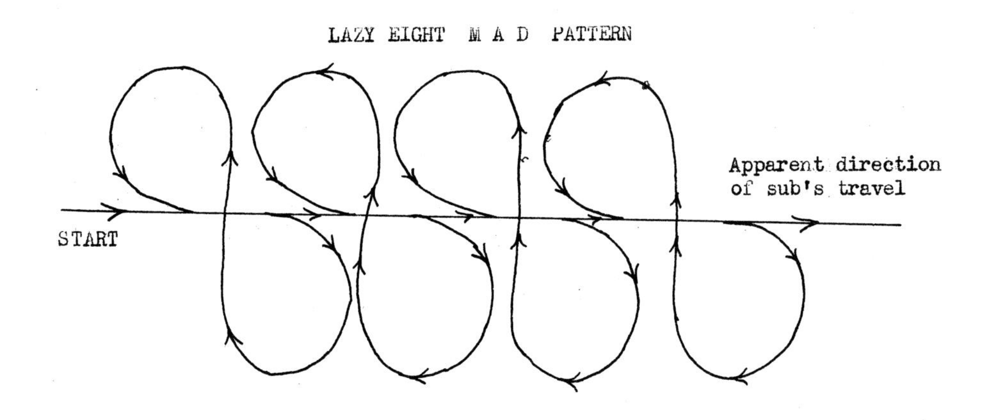

Object of the Exercise

(a) To train combat crews in the use of Sono-Buoy.

Tactical Situation

(a) Submarine has been seen to submerge. The airship arrives at the point of submergence too late for effective employment of the MAD trapping circle.
(b) 1500 yards prior to reaching the point of submergence, drop 1st sono-buoy.
(c) Continue on course and drop 2nd sono-buoy at point of submergence.
(d) Continue on course for 1500 yards and drop 3rd buoy.
(e) Commence 270° turn to the right. Hold turn and straighten out on heading of 270°.
(f) Drop 4th sono-buoy at estimated 1500 yards short of 2nd buoy.
(g) Continue on course of 270° and note time of passing over 2nd sono-buoy.

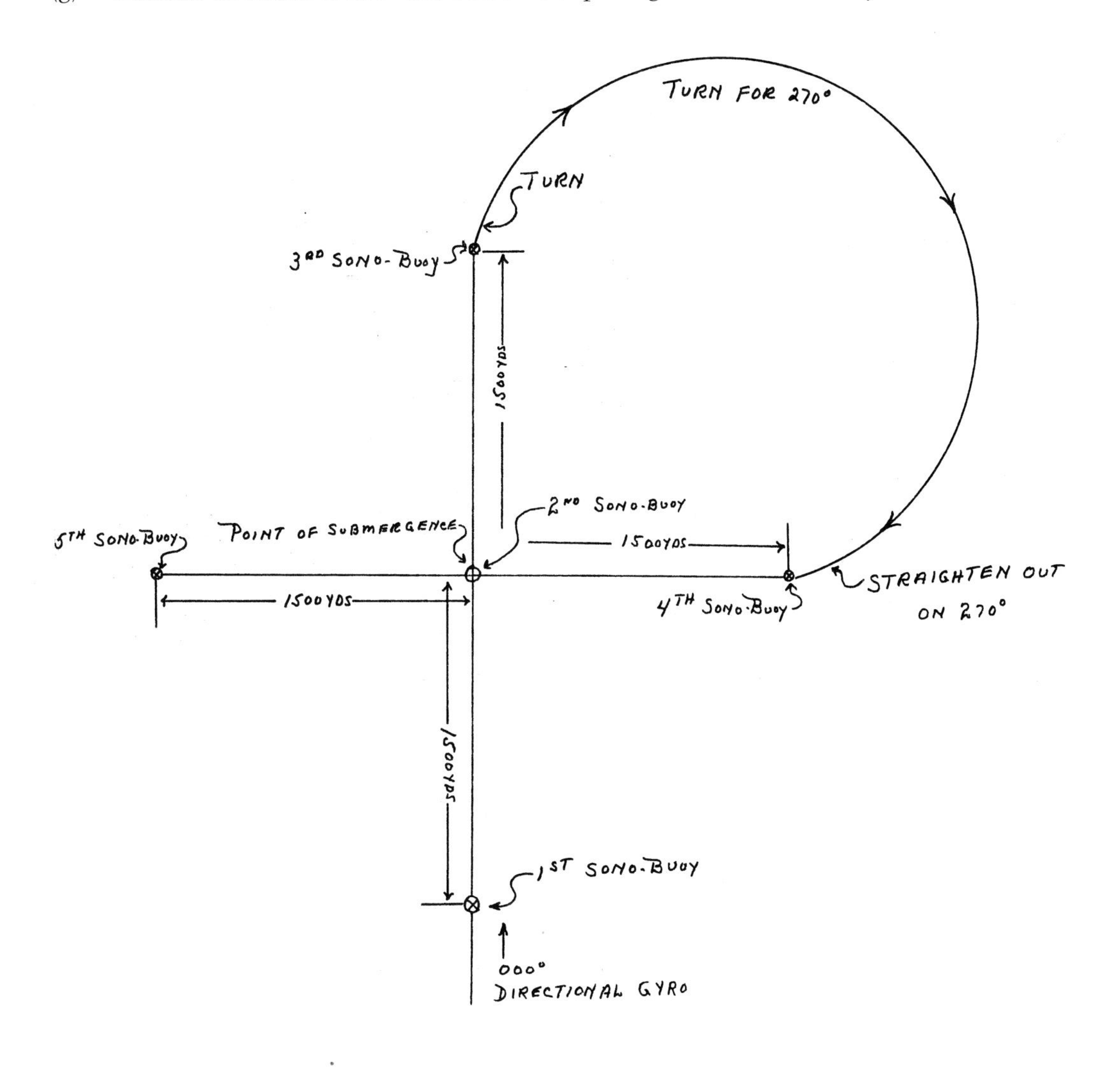

(h) Drop 5th sono-buoy 1500 yard from 2nd sono-buoy on course 270°.

(i) Continue to circle sono-buoy pattern at an altitude of 1000 feet.

(j) Upon localizing submarine, proceed to localized sono-buoy and make a MAD trapping circle 500 yards radius.

(k) Upon MAD signal, adopt MAD tracking procedures.

Exercise

(a) Following rendezvous with submarine, proceed to a point four (4) miles from submarine.

(b) When ready to commence exercise, signal "XRAY" by flashing light to submarine.

(c) Carry out above procedure.

NOTE: This exercise is in accordance with F.T.P., paragraph 2717, with the exception that all turns will be right turns taking into consideration the inherent advantages of an airship making right turns.

Appendix H
Legion of Merit Citation
Commodore George Henry Mills, USN

THE SECRETARY OF THE NAVY
WASHINGTON

The President of the United States takes pleasure in presenting the LEGION OF MERIT to

COMMODORE GEORGE HENRY MILLS
UNITED STATES NAVY

for service as set forth in the following

CITATION:

"For exceptionally meritorious conduct in the performance of outstanding services to the Government of the United States as Commander Fleet Airship Wing THIRTY from November 1942, to July 1943; and as Commander Fleet Airships, Atlantic, from July 1943, to July 1945. Consistently displaying sound judgment, initiative and leadership, Commodore Mills planned and directed the establishment, organization and training of lighter-than-air squadrons and directed their operations until assigned to operational commands. By his broad experience and unusual executive ability, he aided substantially in developing and improving tactics which utilized to the greatest extent the peculiar capabilities of airships. His sound recommendations regarding the need for and the use of facilities, equipment and personnel for the lighter-than-air organization in the Atlantic contributed directly to the successful operation of Atlantic Fleet lighter-than-air craft. His devotion to duty throughout this long period reflects the highest credit upon Commodore Mills and the United States Naval Service."

For the President,

John L. Sullivan

Secretary of the Navy

Notes

Introduction: End and Beginning

1. Rear Adm. Harold B. Miller, USN (Ret.), letter to author, 2 February 1972. In June 1932, Lieutenant (junior grade) Miller had reported for duty with *Akron*'s Heavier-than-Air Unit and, with *Macon*, was senior aviator of her hook-on pilots.
2. Richard K. Smith, *The Airships* Akron *and* Macon: *Flying Aircraft Carriers of the United States Navy* (Annapolis, Md.: Naval Institute Press, 1965), 171. A naval rigid airship or ZR, one notes, was commissioned as a ship, with its own captain, executive officer, and crew organization.
3. The U.S. Navy consisted of six major operating bureaus: Aeronautics, Ordnance, Ships, Supplies and Accounts, Yards and Docks, and Medicine and Surgery. Each carried out the day-to-day work of procurement and production, designed equipment for which it was responsible, and scheduled production of its items within the overall navy schedule.
4. Smith, Akron *and* Macon, 107; Holloway H. Frost, *The Battle of Jutland* (Annapolis, Md.: Naval Institute Press, 1936), 514–18, 521.
5. Lighter-than-air craft are divided into three classes. The rigid type (ZR) had a metal framework of girders within which were installed separate cells for the lifting gas. The semirigid had a fabric envelope, or "bag," strengthened by a metal keel. The nonrigid, or blimp, maintains its shape by the pressure of the gas inside the envelope.
6. With respect to the ZR, Admiral Cook was like-minded. In 1938, King's Bureau of Aeronautics (BuAer) successor told the House Committee on Appropriations: "I can frankly say that from the standpoint of the usefulness of rigid airships for scouting duty, I would not give you two cents for such a ship." Smith, Akron *and* Macon, 173.
7. Ibid., 7. "Clearly, when King was in the driver's seat, *all* LTA decisions were filtered through my dad. And my dad's duties during that period, in BuAer, were by no means limited to LTA. He remained in close contact with the HTA industry including his close friend, Donald Douglas, and many others. I honestly don't think he held out any viable future for the rigid airship." Langdon H. Fulton, letter to author, 19 March 2000.
8. Memorandum for Adm. John W. Greenslade, 20 October 1936, George H. Mills Collection [hereafter GHMC], series I, box 2, folder 5, Smithsonian. In a prescient remark, Fulton also wrote, "The thought occurs to me that recent developments in sound detection of submarines could be applied to airships as well as to surface vessels, through, perhaps, the provision of a trailing fish which the airship tows through the water. The use of infrared detectors would also enhance the value of airships for spotting not only submarines, but surface craft." Ibid.
9. SecNav, letter to the president, 21 July 1933.
10. A group of senior naval officers, the General Board by 1939 was a deliberative body that acted in an advisory capacity for the secretary on any problem put before it.

11. The *N* designates a training aircraft. Cubic volume is an airship's basic specification. The sister ships *Akron* and *Macon* each had a nominal gas volume of 6,500,000 cu. ft. (cells 95 percent full); *Graf Zeppelin* (LZ 127), 2,700,000; *Hindenburg* (LZ 129), 7,000,000 cu. ft.
12. Fulton, memorandum to Cook, 12 October 1938, Garland Fulton Collection [hereafter GFC], Smithsonian.
13. *J-4* (200,000-cu.-ft. envelope); *ZMC-2* (200,000); *G-1* (180,000); *L-1* (180,000); and *K-1* (360,000). *Los Angeles,* decommissioned in June 1932, was grounded and consigned to mooring-out tests and experimental projects.
14. Fulton to Cook. Lakehurst "should have been down around Weeksville [North Carolina] where the Fleet was. And Sunnyvale was another mistake. It should have been down around San Diego, where Miramar is now." Cdr. R. W. Widdicombe, USN (Ret.), interview by author, 31 May 1998.
15. Absent an acquisition strategy, "we can not expect to have an airship industry that will serve our needs in war unless we feed it orders during peace." Fulton to Brockholst Livingston, 21 July 1939, box 3, GHMC, Smithsonian.
16. In June 1939, Rear Adm. John H. Towers relieved Cook as chief of the bureau. In his report for FY 1940, expansion of the shore-station establishment, Towers was to assert, "was one of the most pressing needs of naval aviation."
17. *Statement of Commander C. E. Rosendahl before Senate Naval Affairs Committee—Tuesday 12 April 1938* (copy), GHMC, Smithsonian.
18. Fulton, memorandum to Chief, BuAer, 16 January 1937, box 4008, GFC, Smithsonian. "Blimps should be developed. The Army has 'shown us up' shamefully," an officer remarked, ruefully. T. G. W. Settle to Commanding Officer [CO], NAS Lakehurst, 20 April 1934, series I, box 2, folder 40, GHMC, Smithsonian. Largely because of weak congressional and high-command support, the army discontinued all LTA activities as of 30 June 1937—a further complication for the navy, since it had a combined procurement plan with the army. The army's offer to turn over its blimps and related materials was accepted.
19. Memorandum for Rear Adm. A. W. Johnson, 10 February 1937, series I, box 2, folder 7, GHMC, Smithsonian.
20. F. W. von Meister, letter to Fulton, 15 April 1939, GFC, Smithsonian.
21. "The *Akron* loss brought him [Roosevelt] face to face with what was to be done about future big airships—Navy and/or commercial. Appropriations were tight and pressures from airplane interests were strong. Helium shortages affected the situation." Fulton, letter to Charles L. Keller, 25 October 1959, courtesy Keller. Commissioned vessels, each ZR required specific authorization and appropriation. Each was treated as a surface ship.
22. Roosevelt to Representative John D. Dingell (D-Mich.), 25 April 1938, box 4008, GFC, Smithsonian. Dingell was on the Ways and Means Committee. In his reply, he deplored the navy's "so-called airship policy" and "stall position." "In a very real sense," Dingell argued, "lighter-than-air craft which have been useful in past wars and will be needed in future wars, is being starved to death." Dingell to Roosevelt, 30 April 1938.
23. *Aircraft Yearbook 1941* (New York: Aeronautical Chamber of Commerce of America, Inc., 1941), chap. 4, 58.
24. Langdon H. Fulton, letter to author, 20 January 2000.
25. Fulton to King, 4 October 1938, box 4008, GFC, Smithsonian. To help press the case, Fulton had enlisted like-minded officers. For instance, he had written Lt. Cdr. F. W. Reichelderfer, USN (Lakehurst LTA Class IV), then serving aboard USS *Lexington.* "There are some indications of interest in having blimps go out to the West Coast to help with target practice topography, chasing torpedoes, etc. If some of you people with lighter-than-air experience can help plant the conviction in the minds of Fleet command that blimps can be of service, it would help the situation." Letter, 7 February 1938. "Reich" left the service to become chief (1938–63) of the U.S. Weather Bureau.

26. "Essay by Gross Admiral Dönitz on the War at Sea," series III, box 17, folder 13, 7–8, GHMC, Smithsonian.
27. The half-million allocated in "Appropriations, Navy" for 1939 for the ZRN had been knifed. "We can place 'educational orders' for every conceivable type of war apparatus," Fulton fumed, "but apparently are unwilling to do anything to keep the airship art and airship industry alive against the time when it may be needed." Fulton to Col. R. G. Elbert, box 4008, GFC, Smithsonian. The law had been changed, however, so as to allow qualification of "naval aviators (airship)" on the basis of nonrigid experience.
28. "Lighter-than-Air Situation," *Army and Navy Register,* 24 February 1940. "Fulton and King, of course, were in virtual agreement on all aspects of Naval LTA." Langdon H. Fulton, e-mail to author, 20 January 2000.
29. Sunnyvale—renamed NAS Moffett Field—had been turned over to the Army Air Corps in fall 1935. The base was returned to the navy and re-commissioned in April 1942.
30. Ernest K. Gann, *Fate Is the Hunter* (London: Hodder and Stoughton, 1961), 148.
31. Fulton to Mills, 2 May 1940, series II, box 8, folder 18, GHMC, Smithsonian; Fulton to Dr. William F. Durand (Stanford University), 19 February 1940, box 4008, GFC, Smithsonian. Cdr. George H. Mills, USN, had just assumed command (January) of the naval air station at Lakehurst.
32. The press did its duty, e.g., "Navy Board Urges New Big Dirigible" *(Philadelphia Inquirer).* As well, magazine articles appeared—one by a young reservist who became wartime aide to Rosendahl: J. Gordon Vaeth. "If war comes to the United States [he wrote], our blimps, operating from bases along out coasts, should keep American coastal waters free from mines and submarines. If this fleet is augmented by Zeppelins, serving as airplane carriers and tactical scouts, the United States will have an arm of defense probably possessed by no other nation." "Blimps for Defense," *Current History,* 13 February 1941, 32.
33. Rosendahl, letter to Mills, 20 January 1940, series III, box 15, folder 4, GHMC, Smithsonian. "They were two entirely different personalities. People liked Mills, they respected him." Rosendahl, in contrast, "was somewhat like [Douglas] MacArthur." Mills's chief staff officer recalled "a negative, egotistical personality among the wheels of aviation in the Navy Department." J. Gordon Vaeth, interview by author, 19 May 1999; Capt. Douglas Cordiner, USN (Ret.), letter to author, 23 December 1977. Vaeth was air intelligence officer to Mills.
34. Much of this was personal: Rosendahl's zeal, energy, and passion had bred intense resentment within the Navy Department.
35. "I feel, retrospectively, that if around 1936–37, we [airship people] had said 'OK, rigids are out—give us blimps' a blimp program would have gotten started earlier." Fulton to Rosendahl, 20 August 1960, box 4008, GFC, Smithsonian. Concentrating on blimps was "probably the best strategy," Mills wrote, "but I hope we will not lose sight of the fact that large airships . . . are the ultimate Naval goal (except for coastal work)." Mills to Brockholst Livingston, 21 July 1939, series II, box 8, folder 21, GHMC, Smithsonian.
36. Dönitz, "Essay," 16.
37. Samuel Eliot Morison, *History of United States Naval Operations in World War II,* vol. 1, *The Battle of the Atlantic September 1939–May 1943* (Boston: Little, Brown, 1975), xii.
38. Charles M. Sternhell and Alan M. Thorndike, *Antisubmarine Warfare in World War II,* Report No. 51 of the Operations Evaluation Group, Office of CNO (Washington, D.C.: Navy Department, 1946), 6–7.
39. Francis L. Loewenheim, Harold D. Langley, and Manfred Jonas, eds., *Roosevelt and Churchill: Their Secret Wartime Correspondence* (New York: Saturday Review Press/E. P. Dutton, 1975), 107. The excerpt is from Churchill's letter of 31 July 1940. Within hours of the announcement, the first flotilla of destroyers sailed for Halifax, where British crews waited to take them over.

40. Dönitz, "Essay." U-Boat Command operated without long-range air support. The main instrument of the undersea battle, the U-boat platform, was a miserable platform for reconnaissance. Save for the England–Gibraltar run, "the main shipping routes in the North Atlantic had to be reconnoitered by the U-boats alone." Ibid., 20.
41. Lowenheim et al., 122–23. The excerpt is from the Churchill's letter of 7 December 1940.
42. Langdon H. Fulton e-mail; Smith, *Akron and* Macon, 170.

Chapter 1. Technical Decisions of High Consequence

1. Cdr. Gerald E. Wheeler, USN (Ret.), interview by author, 27 June 1999. Naval aviator, scholar, and professor, Wheeler was a student of naval warfare.
2. Sternhell and Thorndike, *Antisubmarine Warfare in World War II*, 2.
3. Ibid. Sir Archibald Hurd, *Official History of the Great War,* vol. 3, *The Merchant Navy* (New York, Longmans, Green, 1929), 35. Early phones yielded a rough bearing only, so attack with any degree of precision was impossible.
4. Alfred Price, *Aircraft versus Submarine* (Annapolis, Md.: Naval Institute Press, 1973), 28–29. As well, some experiments were made with hydrophonic listening gear *towed* from airships—a notion subsequently revived. "Underwater listening technology in WW I achieved remarkable capability, considering the lack of electronic amplification. . . . The WW-I experience set the stage for WW II to continue the struggle into which science and technology became vital to combat the threat of the submarine." Marvin Lasky, "A Review of World War I Acoustic Technology," *U.S. Navy Journal of Underwater Acoustics* 24, no. 3 (July 1973): 385.
5. *Notes on the Operation of Nonrigid Airships* (Washington, D.C.: Government Printing Office, 1920); reprinted NAS Lakehurst, 5 September 1939, 10. The document's reproduction is emblematic of unpreparedness for renewed antisubmarine warfare.
6. Starr Truscott, undated memorandum (1917) to Joint Army and Navy Airship Board, Jerome Clarke Hunsaker Papers, box 1, folder 1, Smithsonian. This folder also holds reports of encounters between Zeppelins and submarines in which the latter escaped.
7. Robin Higham, *The British Rigid Airship, 1908–1931* (London: G. T. Foulis, 1961), 121.
8. R. H. Gibson and Maurice Prendergast, *The German Submarine War, 1914–1918* (London: Constable, 1931), app. I, 339.
9. Vannevar Bush, *Pieces of the Action* (New York: William Morrow, 1970), 71–74. "The essence of a sound military organization is that it should be tight. But a tight organization does not lend itself to innovations in the technology of warfare." Ibid., 28.
10. As of 1940–41, the accumulated interwar experiences "brought out clearly the great disturbances made by the conditions of the water on the range and usefulness of the detector." The basic physics of the problem, in other words, had yet to be studied. Naval Research Advisory Committee of National Academy of Sciences, memorandum to Technical Aide to Secretary of the Navy, 28 January 1941, RG 298, box 96, National Archives and Records Administration [hereafter NARA].
11. Norman Friedman, *Naval Institute Guide to World Naval Weapon Systems* (London: Conway Maritime, 1983), 101.
12. Bush, *Pieces,* 33.
13. P. H. Schweitzer to Cdr. E. C. Rogers, USN, Fourth Naval District, 11 March 1939, RG 298, box 47, NARA. A professor of engineering research, Schweitzer, along with a group of army and navy reserve officers at Pennsylvania State College, sought to assist on technical and scientific problems. One suggestion: aircraft and submarine detection.
14. Richard Rhodes, *The Making of the Atomic Bomb* (New York: Simon & Schuster, 1988), 337–38.
15. Ibid., 358.

16. Conant letter, 1 July 1940, quoted in James B. Hershberg, *Conant* (New York: Alfred A. Knopf, 1993), 122.
17. Henry L. Stimson and McGeorge Bundy, *On Active Service in Peace and War* (New York: Harper and Bros., 1948), 465.
18. Bush, *Pieces,* 37; Stewart, *Organizing,* 151. Stimson's choice to smooth the path of new weapons into the army: General Stephen Henry. "There are several strong reasons why it is essential that a civilian organization be in a position to innovate. Military men are altogether too busy during wartime to think deeply about technical matters. The most flexibly minded officers are likely to be at the front, if they can get there, instead of at home base. Temporary government personnel can take chances that permanent personnel cannot." Bush, *Pieces,* foreword to paperback ed.; James Phinney Baxter, *Scientists against Time* (Cambridge, Mass.: MIT Press, 1968), ix.
19. S. W. Roskill, *The Navy at War* (London: Collins, 1960), 194; Furer, *Administration of the Navy Department,* 797. Conant went to England in February 1941. "I was hailed as a messenger of hope by the inhabitants of a beleaguered nation. I saw a stouthearted population under bombardment; I saw an unflinching government with its back against the wall. Almost every hour I saw or heard something that made me proud to be a member of the human race." James B. Conant, *My Several Lives: Memoirs of a Social Inventor* (New York: Harper & Row, 1979), 248.
20. M. Lasky, "A Review of World War I Acoustic Technology," *U.S. Navy Journal of Underwater Acoustics Technology* 24, no. 3 (July 1973): 368.
21. Ernest J. King, *U.S. Navy at War, 1841–1945: Official Reports to the Secretary of the Navy* (Washington, D.C.: U.S. Navy Department, 1946), 225.
22. Hershberg, *Conant,* 128–29; Conant, *My Several Lives,* 236. Until Pearl Harbor, latent isolationist hostility to the defense effort persisted in some universities. For a peacetime year and a half, NDRC worked under "a certain psychological handicap." Conant, *My Several Lives,* 243.
23. Both the Academy and the National Research Council, which held mandates similar to that of NDRC, were subsumed. "At its first meeting [2 July 1940], NDRC passed a resolution requesting the cooperation of the Academy and Council, especially through the physics, chemistry and engineering divisions." Ibid., 242.
24. Asdic—initials for the Anti-Submarine Division International Committee—was in the experimental stage when World War I ended. Effective underwater sound-ranging equipment was developed in the thirties; in 1939, this proved to be "quite a surprise" to the Germans. Sternhell and Thorndike, *Antisubmarine Warfare in World War II,* 2.
25. The blind zone was a function of the sonar beam projecting down at an angle. The eventual answer: tilting sonar. Vertical temperature and salinity largely define water density, which in turn is directly translatable into buoyancy and the operational characteristics of submersibles.
26. Since October 1940, the Woods Hole Oceanographic Institution had engaged in a broad survey of temperature gradients and other oceanographic conditions likely to affect the transmission of sound in seawater.
27. *Report of Subcommittee on the Submarine Problem,* and memorandum of transmittal, 28 January 1941, RG 298, box 96, NARA. Dr. F. B. Jewett, president of the Academy, had asked the committee "to examine critically all existing data on submarine detection methods now being used by the Navy or which have been proposed for the purpose." He noted also that "the object of this examination is to determine the extent to which the methods now employed are adequate; whether the experimental work for improvements is along promising lines, and what other lines, if any, should be followed up." Ibid.
28. Ernest J. King and Walter Muir Whitehill, *Fleet Admiral King: A Naval Record* (New York: W. W. Norton, 1952), 319, 325–26.
29. Hershberg, *Conant,* 147–48.

30. Though intended to disrupt and destroy merchant shipping, the German pocket battleships permitted by the Treaty of Versailles were unable to sustain their role as commerce raiders.
31. Baxter, *Scientists against Time*, 37.
32. Friedman, *Naval Weapons*, 100; Bush, *Pieces*, 75. Surprisingly, in the light of events, British naval war plans had regarded surface raiders as more dangerous than the submarine. Roskill, *The War at Sea, 1939–1945*, 34–35.
33. Winston S. Churchill, *The Gathering Storm* (Boston: Houghton Mifflin, 1948), 147. "The British felt, with reason, that they knew a lot more about hunting submarines than we did." Bush, *Pieces*, 85.
34. Prior to Robinson's invitation, NDRC's work in the antisubmarine (A/S) field had been confined to a contract with Gulf Research and Development Co.: for MAD (magnetic detection), the development of airborne microwave search radar, and a contract with Woods Hole Oceanographic Institution. Baxter, *Scientists against Time*, 173–74.
35. The organizing committee and laboratory directors found it "exceedingly difficult" to obtain first-rate scientists and technical staff because of other defense projects under way. "Fortunately, because of the public spirit manifested by many colleges, universities and industrial laboratories in their willingness to grant leaves of absence in these difficult times, it has been possible to assemble enthusiastic and capable staffs in a relatively short time." Tate, undated memorandum to Van Keuren, RG 298, box 96, NARA. Admiral Robinson had asked Rear Adm. A. H. Van Keuren, BuShips, to follow the program and take charge of naval cooperation. To ensure full cooperation, Van Keuren in turn suggested regular meetings with his staff and bimonthly progress reports. Ibid.
36. Baxter, *Scientists against Time,* 177.
37. The 12 July order also transferred NRL from the Office of the Secretary to BuShips, where it remained until the Office of Research and Inventions was established in 1945—the precursor of Office of Naval Research. NDRC, plainly, cost the navy full control over its own scientific research. "Almost inevitably this would lead to conflict with NDRC, to serious questioning of Navy scientific policy, and to a difficult sorting out of institutional roles." Initial relations between NDRC and the navy would be one reason that the atomic bomb project was placed with the army. See David Kite Allison, *New Eye for the Navy: The Origin of Radar at the Naval Research Laboratory* (Washington, D.C.: Naval Research Laboratory, 29 September 1981), 161–74.
38. Bush, *Pieces,* 50.
39. Forrestal to Senator H. M. Kilgore, 19 April 1943, Office of Naval Research/Coordinator of Research and Development, General Correspondence, 1941–45, RG 298, box 8, NARA. Complete secrecy was adopted at the outset. To ward off unwelcome leaks, confidential and secret information was transmitted only on a need-to-know basis. Conant, *My Several Lives,* 245.
40. "This matter was handed to N.D.R.C. by the Navy after special consideration by the General Board at which scientists were consulted." Bush, letter to Hunsaker, 24 March 1942, Jerome Clarke Hunsaker Papers, box 23, folder 6, Smithsonian.
41. Furer, *Administration of the Navy Department,* 785. The contractors for MAD: Columbia University (to equip staff and operate the New London laboratory), Harvard University, University of California, the Western Electric Co., the General Electric Co., the Gulf Research and Development Co., and the RCA Manufacturing Co.
42. Baxter, *Scientists against Time,* 405–6.
43. Tate, NDRC, undated memorandum to Van Keuren, RG 298, box 96, NARA.
44. Ibid.
45. Winfield E. Fromm, "The Magnetic Airborne Detector," in *Advances in Electronics* (New York: Academic, 1952), vol. 4, 267.
46. Fromm, "Personal Reminiscences of the Development of the Magnetic Airborne Detector," five-page statement prepared for author, November 1987.

47. Slichter to Hunsaker, 23 October 1941, RG 298, box 98, NARA.
48. Letter (handwritten), Rosendahl to Mills, 14 November 1941, series II, box 9, folder 15, GHMC, Smithsonian. "I believe we've *got* something worth while." Ibid.
49. Ibid.
50. Rosendahl held a near-theocratic belief in airships. Though he pushed full ahead for procurements, missions, and every scrap of publicity for the naval nonrigid, at heart he remained a creature of the rigid (ZR) type.
51. Baxter, *Scientists against Time,* 181.
52. Tate to Cdr. E. W. Sylvester, Office of SecNav, 26 December 1941, RG 298, box 98, NARA.
53. Fromm, "The Magnetic Airborne Detector," 268.
54. Office of the Coordinator, memorandum, 7 November 1941, RG 298, box 98, NARA. Some development work had been done on a towed "fish," or "bird," to carry the detector. Now it was ready for flight tests. Ibid.
55. Tate to Hunsaker, 4 November 1941, RG 298, box 98, NARA.
56. See Robert Morris Page, *The Origin of Radar* (Garden City, N.Y.: Doubleday, 1962), for a full account.
57. Churchill, *The Gathering Storm,* 157–58.
58. "This decision to pool research information, supplemented by a later decision to divide research effort, was the starting point for Allied supremacy in new weapons, notably radar and subsurface warfare devices." Irvin Stewart, *Organizing Scientific Research for War: The Administrative History of the Office of Scientific Research and Development* (Boston: Little, Brown, 1948), 168.
59. David Kite Allison, *New Eye for the Navy: The Origin of Radar at the Naval Research Laboratory* (Washington, D.C.: Naval Research Laboratory, 1981), 148–51. The mission convinced the military that radar was an operational tool that it had to have. "In general, the meetings resulted in a virtually complete exchange of ideas and information. All indications are that nothing in the field of radar was withheld." Ibid., 151.
60. "The enormous success attributed to the Tizard Mission rests almost entirely on microwaves, which changed warfare during the next few years more than any single weapon. . . . [It] opened up liaison with scientists in more fields than just radar, but it will be remembered more for radar than for any other matters. It was an overwhelming success for both sides." Louis Brown, *A Radar History of World War II: Technical and Military Imperatives* (Bristol, U.K., and Philadelphia: Institute of Physics, 1999), 162, 165.
61. Ibid., 159. "These [operational] tubes are strictly confidential," the Navy advised. "Store them in a safe place. When defective destroy them by melting or by throwing them overboard in deep water. In port they may be turned over to a R.M.O. for destruction. *Keep a record of what is done with each tube.*" *Air Force Atlantic Fleet Technical Bulletin 2CTB-43,* encl. B, 11 February 1943, RG 313, box 9091, NARA. In November 1943, for example, a defective magnetron was delivered to the command pilot of a ZNP patrol flight to be "dropped overboard in the deepest water available, not less than 15 fathoms. . . . [A]t least two officers must witness this action." RG 313, box 9094, NARA.
62. Indeed, the Rad Lab became the largest civilian research and engineering agency created during the war. In 1945, representatives from sixty-nine different academic institutions were on staff. This powerhouse was intentionally misnamed. On 18 November, the CNO had authorized use of the abbreviation "RADAR" in unclassified correspondence and conversation and directed that, in lieu of prevailing terms, "Radio Detection and Ranging Equipment" be used.
63. Dönitz, "Essay."
64. R. D. Hill, "The Origins of Radar," *Eos* 71, no. 27 (3 July 1990): 781–82. "[Dönitz] claimed to have pressed before the war for radar development to be taken up as a priority by the State, but as he was only a *Kapitan zur See* at the time he was ignored." Ibid.

65. Churchill, *The Gathering Storm,* 156. Experimental sets for the location of ships from the air had proven too bulky and were passed to the Admiralty for possible use on shipboard. Its lukewarm reaction to RDF progress at that moment baffled the prime minister. Ibid., 157–58.
66. OSRD memorandum to members of the Advisory Council, 25 February 1942, box 23, folder 6, Jerome Clarke Hunsaker Papers, Smithsonian. "Shared hatred of a common enemy, a more or less common language, generally similar liberal political principles, shared intelligence, combined military staffs, summitry, and the industrial prowess of the United States was to make the Anglo-American alliance perhaps more effective than any other in history." Karl Walling, review of *From World War to Cold War: Churchill, Roosevelt, and the International History of the 1940s, Naval War College Review* 60, no. 2 (Spring 2007): 160.
67. Page, *The Origin of Radar,* 175.
68. Rosendahl memorandum, series I, box 2, folder 17, GHMC, Smithsonian.
69. "Aspects of Antisubmarine Warfare," undated memorandum received in Office of Coordinator, 10 March 1943, RG 298, box 97, NARA. By that phase, nearly half of the attacks by aircraft were on *surfaced* submarines. "It would be useful to increase this proportion." Ibid.
70. "The doctrine during the last war was to attack. Of course our communications were unreliable. Also we had orders that when in doubt as to the identity of sub—friend or foe, to attack and ask questions afterward." Peck, memorandum to Mills, 15 January 1942, series II, box 8, folder 46, GHMC, Smithsonian.
71. Peter Padfield, *Dönitz: The Last Führer* (New York: Harper & Row, 1984), 248. The ASV Mark II (like its Mark I predecessor) was a metric-wavelength (long-wave) radar, but with a more powerful transmitter and a more sensitive receiver.
72. A nasty disappointment, this. Night patrols with Mark II–searchlight aircraft in the bay—a major U-boat transit area—had been "rendered almost entirely useless." Winston S. Churchill, *The Hinge of Fate* (Boston: Houghton Mifflin, 1950), 284. The boats' search receiver, however, covered a narrow field; a change in wavelength cancelled effectiveness.
73. Bush, *Pieces,* 81.
74. Karl T. Compton (Chairman Division D, NDRC) to Furer, 30 January 1942, RG 298, box 77, NARA; Bush, *Pieces,* 81–82.
75. Loewenheim, et al., *Roosevelt and Churchill,* 54–55; Douglas M. Norton, "The Open Secret: The U.S. Navy in the Battle of the Atlantic, April–December 1941," *Naval War College Review* 26, no. 4 (January–February 1974): 74–75. Ships and planes both were part of these operations, with U.S. vessels alternating with Canadian and British groups.
76. Headquarters of the Commander in Chief, U.S. Fleet, memorandum, "The Submarine Warfare along the Atlantic Coast," RG 38, box 49, NARA; Sternhell and Thorndike, *Antisubmarine Warfare in World War II,* 2.
77. CNO, confidential memorandum to C-in-C, U.S. Pacific Fleet; C-in-C, U.S. Atlantic Fleet; C-in-C, U.S. Asiatic Fleet, 6 November 1941, RG 298, box 96, NARA. Entitled "A Preliminary Study of Anti-Submarine Warfare," the enclosures were advance copies.
78. Stimson and Bundy, *On Active Service,* 510, 516. It was the conviction of the Navy (King) that "escort is not the *one* way of handling the submarine menace; it is the *only* way that gives any promise of success." King, letter to Marshall, 21 June 1942, quoted in Morison, *Battle of the Atlantic,* 310. The value of convoy for this new form of naval warfare was hardly novel. "The success of the convoy system proved the undoing of the [Great War submarine] enemy." Hurd, *History of the Great War,* vol. 3, 372.
79. Bush, *Pieces,* 87.
80. Evolving doctrine/training notwithstanding, not all airmen understood the limitations inherent to surface craft. On board the escorts, some did not understand the limits of aircraft.

81. Eliot A. Cohen and John Gooch, *Military Misfortunes: The Anatomy of Failure in War* (New York: Vintage Books, 1991), 79. Chapter 4 of this work is a brilliant historical analysis of the subject.

Chapter 2. Preparations

1. Padfield, *Dönitz*, 237–38.
2. Capt. Maurice M. Bradley, USN (Ret.), interview by author, 24 October 1977. That April, a navy patrol passenger reported that "the general area off Cape Hatteras was simply littered with wrecks and oil from wrecks; quite an impressive sight." Lt. Cdr. A. B. Vosseler, memorandum, to CO, Atlantic Fleet ASW Unit, 13 April 1942, RG 38, box 24, NARA.
3. Once the war started, it was too late to develop another shipbuilder; that lighter-than-air had even one manufacturer was fortuitous. Ponderous administrative procedures along with a relatively low priority exacerbated the ship-production rate—indeed, every aspect of the LTA program.
4. Development of the mobile mooring mast represented a huge leap in the safe handling of nonrigid airships during docking, undocking, and handling on the field.
5. Capt. M. H. Eppes, USN (Ret.), interview by author, 26 November 1978; Chief of Staff, Eastern Sea Frontier, memorandum to Rear Admiral Edwards, 16 February 1942, RG 38, box 24, NARA. "The present campaign is just a taste of what will probably come," warned a captain visiting from the Royal Navy. Ibid.
6. The Canadian experience with U-boats is largely ignored in the literature on the Atlantic war. The Canadian northwestern Atlantic was under the operational control of a *Canadian* admiral. To seaward, much of the Royal Canadian Navy was devoted to protecting the main North Atlantic trade convoys. "There is no gainsaying that the U.S. was the focal point of transatlantic shipping. But much of that shipping had to pass through Canadian waters to get there." Marc Milner, "Squaring Some of the Corners: The Royal Canadian Navy and the Pattern of the Atlantic War," in *To Die Gallantly: The Battle of the Atlantic,* ed. Timothy J. Runyan and Jan M. Copes (Boulder, Colo.: Westview, 1994), 121–36.
7. Cominch, memorandum for Rear Adm. W. A. Lee (Atlantic Fleet staff), 18 March 1942, RG 38, box 48, NARA.
8. "General Information," Navy Day handout, NAS Lakehurst (1939).
9. CO, NAS Lakehurst, memorandum to Chief, BuAer, 30 March 1939, series I, box 2, folder 8, GHMC, Smithsonian. Adm. C. C. Bloch, Commander in Chief, U.S. Fleet, was having none of it. "The services of the non-rigid airships [at NAS San Diego] are not desired. Their presence would decrease the efficiency of the operations of important units of the Fleet." C-in-C, U.S. Fleet to CNO, 1 March 1939, ibid.
10. Capt. Charles E. Rosendahl, USN, Boston radio talk, 15 September 1941, series VI, box 8, folder 33, GHMC, Smithsonian.
11. Naval Airship Training and Experimental Command, *War History of U.S. Naval Air Station, Lakehurst, New Jersey*, app. D., CO, NAS Lakehurst, to CNO via ComFour, 19 June 1940, author papers. Fulton, one up on the future, had suggested such tests three years earlier, remarking that "profitable lessons might be learned if Lakehurst and New London were to collaborate in certain airship-submarine exercises designed to show what airships can do in anti-submarine work." Memorandum for Admiral Greenslade, 20 October 1936, series I, box 2, folder 5, GHMC, Smithsonian.
12. Mills to Fulton, 9 May 1940, series II, box 8, folder 21, GHMC, Smithsonian.
13. *Fleet Airships Atlantic Semi-Monthly News Letter* 1-44, 1 January 1944, series I, box 3, folder 9, GHMC, Smithsonian.
14. Eppes interview; Capt. John C. Kane, USN (Ret.), interview by author, 19 September 1997.
15. Rosendahl to Mills, 20 January 1940, series II, box 9, folder 13, GHMC, Smithsonian.

16. "He goes to duty in Secnav's office and hell has popped loose in the department. Fulton is being blamed for engineering it. That will be a grand place for CER and he can do LTA more good there than anywhere else." Mills, letter to Kenworthy, 22 April 1940, series II, box 8, folder 33, GHMC, Smithsonian.
17. Mills to Fulton, 9 May 1940, series II, box 8, folder 21, GHMC, Smithsonian. T. G. W. Settle, on duty at the Naval War College, also wrote. Highly regarded, "Tex" was a veteran airman (Lakehurst Class II, 1924–25). "Am doing all possible at the War College here, but am greatly handicapped by our *record*—so much bad record to explain away and so little good to counteract the bad. We *know* what airships can do, but we have 'muffed' our opportunities in past years to *demonstrate* what they can do. All power to you, Shorty on your present program of demonstration." Settle, letter to Mills, 29 October 1940, series II, box 9, folder 26, GHMC, Smithsonian.
18. By fall 1941, such restrictions seemed highly imprudent. Submitting his proposals to Congress, Roosevelt declared, "It is the American policy to defend ourselves wherever such defense becomes necessary under the complex conditions of modern warfare. . . . We will not let Hitler proscribe the waters of the world on which our ships may travel. The American flag is not going to be driven from the seas either by his submarines, his airplanes, or his threats." Quoted in Loewenheim, et al., *Roosevelt and Churchill,* 159.
19. By 1940, the CNO had ranked port areas in order of importance: (1) The approaches to New York; (2) the Florida Straits; (3) the vicinity of Cape Hatteras; (4) the approaches to the capes of the Chesapeake; (5) the approaches to the Delaware River; (6) the approaches to Boston; (7) the approaches to San Francisco Bay; (8) Puget Sound and its approaches; and (9) the approaches to Los Angeles. CNO, memorandum to Chief, BuAer, 3 August 1940, series I, box 2, folder 11, GHMC, Smithsonian.
20. Mills, letter to Rosendahl, 29 April 1940, GHMC, series II, box 9, folder 13. Memorandum for Capt. Fulton (Mills), 16 October 1940; Operations Officer (Tyler), NAS Lakehurst, to all pilots, 11 September 1939; series I, box 2, folder 16, GHMC, Smithsonian.
21. Memorandum to All Pilots, NAS Lakehurst, 25 August 1941, series I, box 2, folder 15, GHMC, Smithsonian.
22. Blimps must maintain their shape for aerodynamic reasons and to ensure proper distribution of the loads imposed by the control car. The latter are transferred to the envelope via an internal system of cables. The envelope, in other words, is a structural element of the aircraft.
23. Excerpts from U-boat logs made by Lt. J. Gordon Vaeth, USNR, from captured German navy archives, Admiralty, London, series IV, box 17, folder 14, GHMC, Smithsonian.
24. The presence of impurities, notably air, increases the density of the inflating gas and decreases its lift.
25. Rigid airships had had water-ballast bags and gasoline-dump and slip tanks spaced along the keel corridor. "Word was sent up into the keel by at least two officers," Rosendahl wrote in his official report of *Shenandoah*'s destruction over Ohio, in 1925, "to stand by to slip fuel tanks as our only salvation lay in checking the ship's descent by such ballast."
26. A maximum was achieved in the Cold War–era ZPG-3W (1959–61): its operating instructions included normal "flight ops" at 10,500 pounds "heavy." Meantime, at Lakehurst, the average heaviness at takeoff was about 2,100 pounds for an eighteen-hour patrol.
27. An aerostatics problem for enlisted men at Lakehurst's LTA School, 1942, illustrates: "An airship with a capacity of 400,000 cubic feet has 75,000 cubic feet of air in its ballonets. The atmospheric pressure is 31.5 inches and the temperature 40° F. If the gas in the envelope is superheated 10° F before the airship takes off, how much lift will the ship pick up?"
28. Rear Adm. Richard S. Andrews, USN (Ret.), narrative prepared for author, 20 December 1976.
29. Bradley interview. In 1942, "Mike" Bradley held duty in the LTA Section, BuAer.
30. "We are reviving the 600,000 cubic foot ship project and will undoubtedly build a prototype very soon. However, we are of course going to be stuck with a full program of K-type so we certainly must

do something to help *their* performance." Rosendahl, letter to Mills, 27 February 1943, series II, box 9, folder 18, GHMC, Smithsonian.

31. "An angle which is not generally appreciated is that when you have extracted your helium content from natural gas you have only met about half the expense and half the problems an end-user must find solutions for." Fulton, letter to Charles L. Keller, 3 June 1960, courtesy Keller.
32. Charles Kauffman, interview by author, 15 July 1997.
33. Henry J. Tucker, interview by author, 13 October 1977. Mr. Tucker was associated with the air station's helium plant from 1932 to his retirement in 1965.
34. U.S. Department of the Interior, Bureau of Mines, "Helium Symposium," 14–15 October 1958, Amarillo, Texas; "Enclosure on Helium Plant U.S. Naval Air Station, Lakehurst, New Jersey," 1966; *New York Times,* 17 January 1946.
35. Clark G. Reynolds, *Admiral John H. Towers: The Struggle for Naval Air Supremacy* (Annapolis, Md.: Naval Institute Press, 1991), 309.
36. Bradley interview.
37. Rosendahl, letter to Knox, 19 August 1941, series II, box 9, folder 15, GHMC, Smithsonian. Commander C. V. S. "Connie" Knox had entered the Great War as a reserve officer and transferred to the regular navy as a Naval Constructor, later placed in the line for aeronautical engineering duty only. A graduate of Lakehurst LTA Class IX (1934–35), he was BuAer's representative at Goodyear Aircraft, focusing largely on production. In concert with the operators, he helped develop many of the design improvements worked into the wartime nonrigid.
38. *War History of U.S. Naval Air Station, Lakehurst, New Jersey,* 21–25.
39. David Brinkley, *Washington Goes to War* (New York: Alfred A. Knopf, 1988), 196. "The real cause of [Congress'] anger was a fact that they first denied but eventually had to accept—they were being stripped of their power because they could not run the war. Only a small, agile, centralized authority could run the war. Only the president could run the war." Ibid. Also *Congressional Record* 87, no. 116, 20 June 1941, 5518–31.
40. Peck to Mills, 15 April 1941, series II, box 8, folder 46, GHMC, Smithsonian; Roosevelt to Knox, 22 April 1941. Antipathy toward Rosendahl pervaded certain commands. Rear Adm. Arthur B. Cook, bureau chief 1937–39, was no ally. Nor was Capt. Marc A. Mitscher—in 1941, assistant chief of BuAer to Rear Adm. John H. Towers. "[Mitscher] said for the past 22 yrs L.T.A. craft have served as a vehicle for large and unwarranted quantities of personal publicity. Said we should go about our business in a quiet way and perhaps in time, if there is no new outcropping of personal publicity our sins along this line might be forgotten and forgiven." Rosie went to Stark when told of this, offering to "step out altogether" if such would advance the program. "My personal opinion," Peck continues, "is that the personal publicity angle accounts for ninety percent of our opposition."
41. A Halifax air station (pushed by Peck, opposed by Mills and Departmental higher-ups), versus the Florida area, was decided by Admiral King. "He says he wants blimps in Florida so that's that unless the President steps in to the picture." Peck to Mills, 6 February 1942, series II, box 8, folder 46, GHMC, Smithsonian.
42. An Airship Facilities Board was engaged to inspect and then select suitable locations for additional facilities in the southeastern Atlantic and Gulf areas. Eight sites, for example, were inspected in the Miami area. Mills was a member, Rosendahl its senior member.
43. To Mills, Rosendahl discussed a proposed thousand-foot hangar—"if we are ever to operate a 900 foot [rigid] airship from Lakehurst."
44. Fulton, letter to Rosendahl, 20 August 1960, unmarked file, box 4008, GFC, Smithsonian.
45. Rosendahl memorandum, 1 August 1941, series I, box 2, folder 17, GHMC, Smithsonian.
46. Anti-Submarine Development Detachment, Air Force, Atlantic Fleet, *Instructor's Training Manual for Aircraft Anti-Submarine Warfare,* 1st ed., 1 September 1943, RG 313, box 9093, NARA. LTA

squadron personnel were divided into combat air crews of four officers and six enlisted men each and one navigator, who was also a pilot.

47. Memorandum for Chief of Bureau, 16 January 1937, GFC, Smithsonian.
48. Rear Adm. George E. Pierce, USN (Ret.), interview by author, 2 July 1977.
49. Capt. W. E. Delong, USN (Ret.), interview by author, 26 June 1999.
50. "By plotting radius of action with wartime loading I wrote a thesis enthusiastically recommending an expanded non-rigid building program concurrently with building bases in the vicinity of Weymouth, Mass., Elizabeth City, NC, Brunswick, GA, Key West, FL, Houma, LA, Isle of Pines, Guantánamo, and Trinidad. These plans were approved by George Mills and adopted by the Navy Department." Capt. Douglas Cordiner, USN (Ret.), letter to author, 23 December 1977.
51. About five applications were received for each place. The men reporting were, in Rosendahl's view, "excellent material." For its part, the Lakehurst command had concluded that the officers and cadets who applied specifically for lighter-than-air "would be better for our purpose" than cadets destined for HTA or for general schools.
52. Minutes, Conference of Anti-Submarine Warfare, United States Fleet, 15 December 1942, RG 38, box 47, NARA. Approximately 30 percent of the Woman's Reserve (WAVES) would be assigned to shoreside naval aviation—for instance, repairing planes, packing parachutes, collecting weather data, and directing air traffic from control towers.
53. Mills, memorandum for Captain Mullinix, USN, 21 April 1942, series 11, box 10, folder 2, GHMC, Smithsonian.
54. Cdr. Robert Shannon, USN (Ret.), interview by author, 26 June 1999.
55. Lt. Cdr. R.W. Widdicombe, USN (Ret.), memorandum to Capt. Norman L. Beal, USNR, CND, Office of Naval Warfare, 1 November 1985, with report dated 1 July 1985, courtesy Widdicombe. "When I joined LTA, all the people within it—they dated back to the twenties. And they *really* knew their airships. So we really learned under people who knew the ropes thoroughly." Widdecombe interview, 30 May 1998.
56. In mid-1941, Commander Submarines, Atlantic Fleet had advised CNO, "With the limited supply of replacement torpedoes now available, every possible precaution must be taken against losses during practice approaches."
57. Kathleen Broome Williams, *Secret Weapon: U.S. High Frequency Direction Finding in the Battle of the Atlantic* (Annapolis, Md.: Naval Institute Press, 1996), 170–71.
58. Meigs, *Slide Rules*, 217–18.
59. Headquarters of the Commander in Chief, memorandum, "The Submarine Warfare along the Atlantic Coast," 8 December 1942, RG 38, box 49, NARA.
60. HQ Commander Eastern Sea Frontier to Masters of All Merchant Ships, bulletin 39, 3 April 1943, RG 38, box 49, NARA.
61. Commander in Chief, Atlantic Fleet (CincLant); Commander, Air Forces Atlantic (ComAirLant); and Commander, Fourth Naval District (ComFour).
62. Log, NAS Lakehurst, 1200–1600, 7 December 1941, NARA. Concern was such that foundations for antiaircraft mounts were discussed and machine-gun nests rigged at vital points on station. A bill was even drawn up for ship dispersal in the event of attack. Notes from Lakehurst staff conferences, 8, 15, and 24 December 1941, series I, box 1, folder 28; Mills to Peck, 7 December 1941, series II, box 8, folder 46, GHMC, Smithsonian.
63. Rosendahl to Mills, 8 December 1941. "I tell you right now, Captain," Mills lamented, "we are the only striking force in these two [naval] districts." Phone conversation (transcript), 24 December 1941, series II, box 1, folder 27, GHMC, Smithsonian.
64. Rosendahl to Mills, 8 December 1941, series II, box 9, folder 14, GHMC, Smithsonian. "This is terribly disconnected but my mental state today is anything but composed. I can't tell you anything, but the general situation is dark indeed." Marginalia, ibid.

65. "After *Macon* there was hesitation as to naval *need* for big airships, but Navy generally lent support to a 'Merchant Marine' of the air. Dept. of Commerce staged hearings and several bills were introduced." Fulton, letter to Keller, 10 March 1962, courtesy Keller.
66. Design Memorandum 345, "Progress in Rigid Airships, 1927 to 1942," by C. P. Burgess: "It is shown in this memorandum that a modernized version of the MACON could have about 74% more range than her predecessor due to improved propulsive efficiency and reduced weight of power plant and structure" (1). Burgess's "superior analytic powers and sheer ability won him a position of great respect throughout the whole Navy Department. He later came to be consulted frequently by the airplane people on their problems." Fulton, letter to Keller, 17 June 1960, courtesy Keller.
67. Memorandum, Resume of Correspondence on ZRs, 24 May 1944, LTA Class–ZR file, box LTA subject file (C–E), Naval Historical Center. Goodyear Aircraft had been subcontracted by the Martin Company to build the tail section for its B-26 *Marauder*; the firm soon earned more contracts—for example, designing control surfaces for Consolidated's PB2Y-3 flying boat. In 1942, the firm was building a complete airplane: Chance-Vought's *Corsair*, of which Goodyear produced more than four thousand.
68. For a review of these years and denouement, see Richard K. Smith, "The ZRCV: Fascinating Might-Have-Been of Aeronautics," *Aerospace Historian* 12, no. 4 (October 1965): 115–21, and Smith, *Akron and* Macon, chap. 11.
69. Mills to staff, box 1, folder 28, GHMC, Smithsonian.
70. Conference summary, 10 December 1941, RG 298, box 96, NARA.
71. Ibid.
72. *Instructor's Training Manual for Aircraft Anti-Submarine Warfare;* H.Q. Coastal Command, *Submarine and Anti-Submarine,* October 1942, reproduced May 1945, RG 38, box 44, NARA.
73. Churchill, *The Hinge of Fate,* 108.
74. The CO of USS *West Virginia* would recall his then–first lieutenant: "He [Rosendahl] was the only naval officer I have ever had to tell that he was working too hard." Series II, box 8, folder 12, GHMC, Smithsonian.
75. Rosendahl to Mills, 13 December 1941, series II, box 9, folder 14, GHMC, Smithsonian. Mill's reaction to a "rigid threat" is unrecorded. As for at-sea survival, he advised Tyler: "Please see this as done." Marginalia, ibid.
76. Notes of Lakehurst conference, 15 December 1941, series I, box 1, folder 28, GHMC, Smithsonian.
77. Meigs, *Slide Rules,* 44, 46.
78. Capt. L. Russell Ulrich, USN (Ret.), interview by author, 26 June 1999.
79. Brinkley, *Washington Goes to War,* 103–4.
80. All but Andrews declined. From King's flag lieutenant, this extract: "Regrets that he will be unable to attend due to pressure of duties. He has keen interest on development of these squadrons." From Stark: "Best of luck to the blimps. As Rosendahl will have told you, I believe in this program and hope it will be helpful." Commander, ZNP Group One, memorandum to Commander, ZNP Squadron Twelve, 5 January 1942, series I, box 2, folder 1, GHMC, Smithsonian.
81. "Once Admiral Andrews got his clutches on a destroyer, she ceased for practical purposes to belong to the Atlantic Fleet; only Admiral King could take her away." Morison, *Battle of the Atlantic,* 207.
82. "In speaking of Groups, let me say again that it is a damn shame that we had to change from Wing to Group. No where in the Navy is a Group recognized as an administrative unit, and I am having trouble getting correspondence sent to me. Instead, lots of mail (confidential and secret matter) which should come to me, goes to the Station and sometimes to Squadron 12." Mills to Rosendahl, 8 April 1942, series II, box 9, folder 17, GHMC, Smithsonian.
83. Andrews, address, series I, box 2, folder 1, GHMC, Smithsonian. The admiral's naval air arm at this moment comprised a few squadrons (mostly *Catalina* flying boats), whereas the army controlled most

military land-based planes. "In its dire need, the Navy called for help from the Army Air Force. The Army responded generously to the best of its ability." Morison, *Battle of the Atlantic,* 240–41.

84. Belke, "Roll of Drums," 60.
85. Various acoustic sensors were towed, using cable reels to raise and lower the hydrophone equipment. "The system towed to 25 knots with a minimum of water noise. With good sound transmission, freighters could be heard to ranges up to 15 miles while towing at speeds up to 25 knots." Still, the towed system for ZNPs was dropped in favor of sonobuoys. Marvin Lasky, "Historical Review of Underwater Acoustic Technology: 1939–1945 with Emphasis on Undersea Warfare," *U.S. Navy Journal of Underwater Acoustic Technology,* no. 25 (1975): 567–84.
86. BuOrd was sought, since "special types of anti-submarine barrages" for use with the detector were already wanted. One weapon: retro-rockets. Slichter, letter to Hunsaker, 23 October 1941, RG 298, box 98, NARA.
87. Key West is a geologically quiet area compared to Quonset–Long Island; tactical problems involved in the use of MAD would be worked out in Florida.
88. Tate to Sylvester, 3 January 1942, RG 298, box 98, NARA.
89. Fromm, "Personal Reminiscences."
90. Charles W. Long, letter to author, 8 May 2006. IBM was then the only supplier of automated data-processing equipment. "Punch card machines had initially gained recognition as *statistical machines* used to compile the U.S. census. These machines were never sold—always rented, installed and maintained scrupulously by IBM *systems engineers.* From the day and hour that any IBM machine went on rental it was carefully monitored and maintained by IBM. As preventive maintenance schedule was strictly adhered to and no one but an IBM system engineer . . . was allowed to fix or alter anything mechanical. However, the user (renter) was taught and encouraged to do his own wiring and rewiring of the flexible (plug board) control panels." Ibid. [emphasis original]. Long served with the Signal Intelligence Service, U.S. Army.
91. Furer to Vice Adm. R. S. Edwards, 10 November 1943, RG 298, box 97, NARA. One blockage: laboratories, naturally enough, wanted to continue to improve upon when the decision should have been made that the device—whatever it was—was good enough to be placed in production.
92. Speed had sponsored D/F assistance in the previous campaign. "In 1915 it was recognized that airships would be unlikely to sink a U-boat owing to their relatively slow speed in any breeze. Approval was, therefore, given to the establishment of a string of D/F stations along the coasts through which accurate positions of airships making sightings could be obtained and destroyers sent to the location as killers." Higham, *British Rigid Airship,* 120.
93. *Cominch U-Boat Trends,* biweekly no. 33, 1 January 1944, RG 38, box 49, NARA.
94. Williams, *Secret Weapon,* XIII.
95. *Cominch U-Boat Trends,* biweekly no. 24, 14 August 1943, and 32, 16 December 1943, RG 38, box no. 49, NARA.
96. C-in-C, United States Fleet Memorandum, "Submarine Warfare, Notes on," to distribution list, 21 February 1942, RG 38, box 24, NARA, 1.
97. Williams, *Secret Weapon,* 240.
98. Compton to Furer, 30 January 1942, RG 298, box 77, NARA.
99. Report of Conference, 14 February 1942, RG 298, box 77, NARA.
100. Long Range Navigation Project Priority Application, 11 April 1942, RG 298, box 77, NARA. "They have told us that it is urgent that the equipment be installed and working as soon as possible." Ibid.
101. John G. Trump (technical aide, Division D, NDRC) to Priorities Division, Army and Navy Munitions Board, 13 April 1942, box 77, RG 298, NARA. On 15 May, the board in turn requested special priority assistance from the War Production Board.
102. Report of Conference, 17 April 1942, RG 298, box 77, NARA.
103. Krause to Coordinator, 9 May 1942, RG 298, box 77, NARA.

104. Chief, BuAer, to CO, NAS Lakehurst, 22 May 1942, RG 298, box 77, NARA.
105. Chief, BuAer, memorandum to CNO, 22 May 1942, RG 298, box 77, NARA.
106. Eastham to Furer, 23 June 1942 (enclosing Pierce report, dated 13 June), box 77, RG 298, NARA. "This procedure seemed entirely satisfactory," Pierce cautioned, "although it is difficult to prove that the pilots were not actually flying by known landmarks, as the visibility was excellent." Ibid.
107. Navy Liaison Officer for Loran System, Radiation Laboratory, memorandum to VCNO, 24 August 1942, RG 298, box 77, NARA.
108. VCNO to Chief, BuShips, 20 January 1943, RG 298, box 78, NARA. In the Atlantic, destroyer and destroyer escort missions were devoted wholly to ASW. This was in contrast to the Pacific, where a fraction of destroyer attention, equipment, and training were so applied.
109. "Navy wants entire control," a comment continues, "but is conservative. Army . . . pushing for other locations for LRN, is impatient and NDRC is going ahead with their request regardless of Navy ok." Routing slip notation, 14 December 1942, Loran file, RG 298, box 77, NARA.
110. Coordinator of Research and Development, Report of Conference, 3 July 1943, RG 38, box 97, NARA. The British, assisted by the U.S. Coast Guard, had completed the survey of stations for extension of Loran to the *eastern* Atlantic. Transmitters were being installed—supplied by the Rad Lab. "By the end of the war 70 Loran stations and 75000 receivers were providing navigational information for 30% of the Earth's surface." Brown, *Radar History,* 431.
111. Furer, memorandum to Commander Conrad, 29 March 1944, RG 298, box 97, NARA.
112. This robbed the weapon of any "morale" effect derived from near misses.
113. High sink rates were attained by streaming, careful weighting, and a spin imparted by fins.
114. Fleet Airships, *Atlantic Semimonthly News Letter* 2-43 (1 August 1943), 13, series I, box 3, folder 8, GHMC, Smithsonian.
115. *Naval Aviation Confidential Bulletin* 4-44, 45, RG 313, box 9094, NARA.
116. Rosendahl, memorandum to CNO, 1st endorsement, 10 July 1944, series II, box 9, folder 19, GHMC, Smithsonian.
117. "Aspects of Antisubmarine Warfare," undated memorandum (received by Office of Coordinator 10 March 1943), box 97, RG 298, NARA.
118. A sampling for January 1944: aircraft searchlights and new underwater detection systems. The British, who had their own A/S developmental laboratories or establishments, tended to produce less complicated equipment.
119. Mills to Peck, 1 April 1941, series II, box 8, folder 46, GHMC, Smithsonian; A&R Officer, memorandum to CO, NAS Lakehurst, 28 March 1941, series I, box 2, folder 12, ibid.
120. *Fleet Airships Atlantic Semi-Monthly News Letter* 2-44, 15 January 1944, series I, box 3, folder 9, GHMC, Smithsonian.
121. Conference of Anti-Submarine Warfare, 15 December 1942, RG 38, box 47, NARA.
122. Louis A. Gibhard, *Evolution of Naval Radio-Electronics and Contributions of the Naval Research Laboratory* (Washington, D.C.: Naval Research Laboratory, 1979), 203.
123. Stimson and Bundy, *On Active Service,* 509–10.
124. Mills, memorandum to Rosendahl, 16 April 1942, series II, box 9, folder 17, GHMC, Smithsonian.

Chapter 3. Bitter Spring

1. Dönitz, *Memoirs,* 228. This remark was penned on 15 April 1942. The merchant marine remains underappreciated. So-called Liberty ships—2,708 of which were launched during 1941–45—conveyed two-thirds of all the cargo shipped from the United States during the war. More than 200,000 men served—about 6,800 of whom were lost at sea.
2. Stimson and Bundy, *On Active Service,* 508. In Washington, Independence Day 1942 proved emblematic of the crisis. The traditional fireworks display at the Washington Monument was cancelled, as

was the usual patriotic parade. The president, at his desk that holiday, called on government workers to be on the job. In addition, "needless travel" was to be avoided.

3. Roosevelt to Churchill, 18 March 1942, in Loewenheim, et al., *Roosevelt and Churchill,* 196.
4. A continuing analysis of U-boat force dispositions served to indicate the best routing, especially for merchantmen sailing independently.
5. Why BuShips? Its participation with the further work of development—whatever the device—would facilitate and expedite final standardization.
6. By shielding them from flow noise, streamlined domes around the sonar transducers increased the effective sound range. This permitted initial detection up to speeds of twenty to twenty-four knots for both echo ranging and listening. Without domes, it was difficult to listen effectively on any bearing when the escort was steaming above fifteen knots. Further, they rendered hurried attacks—retaining sound contact—more accurate.
7. NDRC was empowered to make contracts with university and industrial laboratories. R&D work was carried only to the point where regular production of promising devices could be undertaken by the navy.
8. Coordinator, enclosure for memorandum, to CNO, 22 January 1942, RG 298, box 96, NARA.
9. Chief, BuShips, confidential memorandum to Chief, BuAer, 25 February 1942; Cdr. E. W. Sylvester (office of SecNav), confidential memorandum for files, 7 February 1942, RG 298, box 98, NARA. The British Central Scientific Committee requested NDRC to furnish two MAD units, to which the president readily assented.
10. ONR/NDRC Coordinator, General Correspondence, 1941–46, RG 298, box 21, NARA.
11. With U-boats devoting most of their attention to merchant vessels, urgency spawned consideration of such defensive measures as ship camouflage, increases in speed via antifouling paints, and anti-torpedo nets.
12. "Unfortunately Coastal Command crews had received no training at all in anti-submarine warfare; and the belief that to destroy a U-boat from the air was a comparatively easy matter was all too widely held." Further, its antisubmarine bombs were "completely useless." Roskill, *The War at Sea, 1935–1945* (Her Majesty's Stationary Office, London, 1956), 45.
13. Ladislas Farago, *The Tenth Fleet* (New York: Ivan Obolensky, 1962), 66.
14. The magnetic intensity (signal) of known wrecks was usually larger than that of a U-boat. Pilots exploited wrecks as checks on their MAD gear.
15. Though wanting for the detection of U-boats (which were small targets), the Mark I equipment assisted navigation courtesy of significant returns from, say, assigned convoys and fog-shrouded coastlines.
16. A large building program had been ordered; still, the shortage of U-boats persisted. "I did my utmost," Dönitz records, "to get more boats for the American operations." Naval High Command had insisted on strong U-boat forces in the Mediterranean and west of Gibraltar. In January, seven were diverted to the Nova Scotia–Newfoundland area. Karl Dönitz, *Memoirs,* 197–202.
17. Ibid., 202.
18. Gannon, *Drumbeat,* 414. Dönitz was to characterize the American operational area as "exceptionally favourable." *Memoirs,* 202.
19. CO, NAS Lakehurst, memorandum to CNO via ComFour and Chief, BuAer, 31 March 1939, series I, box 2, folder 9, GHMC, Smithsonian.
20. Also that December, Lakehurst's supplier of ice cream notified the station that rationing was necessary. The Officer's Club supply was cut by more than half as a result. "Members are requested not to ask for ice cream as a desert unless it is on the regular menue [*sic*] for that meal."
21. *History of Blimp Squadron Twelve,* box 153, History of Aviation Collection, University of Texas, Richardson, Texas [hereafter HOAC]; Gannon, *Operation Drumbeat,* 215–21; *New York Times,* 15 January 1942.

22. On surface passage, a submarine is near maximum buoyancy; it therefore takes near-maximum time to dive. The standard of efficiency with a well-trained crew (according to one British report) was to reach fifty feet in fifty seconds from the instant of alarm. "Great Britain—Tactics—Miscellaneous Notes," series I, box 2, folder 16, GHMC, Smithsonian.
23. Oil slicks and air bubbles were frequently mistaken for indications of damage following an attack, particularly early on. Correct assessments were exceedingly difficult; further, aircrews had a marked tendency to overestimate the accuracy of their antisubmarine attacks.
24. Summary of projects discussed at conference, USL, New London, 12 March 1942, RG 298, box 96, NARA. The practical difficulties of gyroscopic stabilization led to using the earth's magnetic field to control stabilization.
25. Lt. Harris F. Smith, USNR (Ret.), interview by author, 5 August 1997.
26. Daily War Diary, 30 May 1942, LTA ZP-12 War Diaries, May–August 1942, Naval Historical Center, Washington Navy Yard, Washington, D.C.
27. Naval Operating Base Guantánamo, naval message to Cominch, 1 April 1943, RG 38, box 47, NARA.
28. *K-3* would log 2,531.8 total hours in 1942 following installation of its MAD. Of this total, 1,745.9 hours—68.9 percent—were MAD hours. Though its total exceeded that of any sister to *K-16* that year, percentages climbed as the year progressed. For instance, *K-9* logged 89.2 percent. CO, ZP-12, memorandum to ComFairShipWing 30, 22 January 1943, RG 298, box 98, NARA.
29. Army A/S aircraft were likewise afflicted. When, for example, a Trinidad-based B-18 delivered a three-run attack on a diving U-boat, "No bombs dropped due DC [depth charge] release mechanism failure each time though checked prior flight." Naval message, 8 December 1942, RG 38, box 44, NARA.
30. Peck to Sachse, 20 January 1942, series II, box 8, folder 46, GHMC, Smithsonian. Peck advised Mills that date: "As I see it, LTA now has a great opportunity to prove what it has claimed over a period of years. Now that it has that opportunity it's no time to try to prove our case in the public press. . . . Our branch of the service is much discussed right now and everyone hoping that you sink a sub but these fairy stories in the papers make life difficult." Peck to Mills, 20 January 1942, ibid.
31. Farago, *Tenth Fleet,* 251.
32. Mills to Peck, 18 January 1942, series II, box 8, folder 46, GHMC, Smithsonian. Mills "required firm substantiation of contact reports by his airships, particularly in view of the early rash of nonsensical and often ridiculous reports of submarine sightings by other ASW craft." Vice Adm. Charles E. Rosendahl, "How Soon We Forget: A History of United States Navy Airships in World War Two," unpublished manuscript, chap. IX, 11, courtesy Evelyn (Eppes) Azzaretto.
33. "Tactical Use of Radar in Aircraft," U.S. Fleet, Headquarters of C-in-C (undated), 25–26, RG 313, box 9091, NARA.
34. T. E. Van Metre, memorandum to Rear Adm. Edwards, 16 February 1942, RG 38, box 24, NARA.
35. Excerpts from U-boat logs prepared by Lt. J. Gordon Vaeth, USNR, from captured German archives, Admiralty, London, series IV, box 17, folder 14, GHMC, Smithsonian. What depths the expression "A-20" refers to is unknown.
36. Coastal Command's experience had been similar. In mid-1941, wanting more from his radar gear, Air Officer Commanding-in-Chief Sir Philip Joubert launched an investigation. This "quickly revealed numerous problems impeding the best use of the available equipment. Quick design and manufacture under wartime pressures had produced sets that were neither very robust nor very reliable. They required a high level of maintenance and highly skilled operators. Coastal Command units were poorly equipped to provide either, and personnel seldom knew enough about the equipment to be able to get the best out of it." Max Schoenfeld, *Stalking the U-Boat: USAAF Operations in World War II* (Washington, D.C.: Smithsonian Inst. Press, 1995), 11.
37. Summary of Projects Discussed at Conference, 12 March 1942, RG 298, box 96, NARA. One attack weakness: depth settings absent knowledge of the target's depth. Better suited to sonar was the

forward thrower, first deployed by British forces. "Hedgehog" threw a large number of small, streamlined charges, giving a greater probability of success per unit weight of explosive. Ibid.

38. Roskill, *The War at Sea, 1939–1945*, 194.
39. Memorandum for president, 10 April 1942, series I, box 2, folder 22, GHMC, Smithsonian.
40. Why 1,000 feet? "Also, if *rigid* airships are to enter the picture at any time, it should be much cheaper to construct our present ZNP hangar facilities initially of such characteristics as to permit their use by either rigids or nonrigids. For this purpose, the South Weymouth–Elizabeth City design is of adequate cross-section but the length should be increased from 600 to 1000 feet, such increase also permitting accommodation for an increased number of ZNPs." Memorandum, Rosendahl to CNO, 23 March 1942, box 9, folder 17, GHMC, Smithsonian.
41. Mills to Rosendahl, 16 April and 28 December 1942, series II, box 9, folder 17, GHMC, Smithsonian. "No suitable hangar for a modern ZR is available here," Mills added.
42. Pierce interview. CO of ZP-14: Lt. Cdr. William A. Cockell, USN. Pierce was his executive officer.
43. The functions of naval air stations, as they relate to the squadrons, were to provide bases for the operation, repair, and overhaul of ZNP squadrons.
44. Address of Rear Adm. Manley H. Simons, 1 April 1942, box 2, folder 4, GHMC, Smithsonian. The ceremonies were closed to the public. "All guards, sentries and station personnel are to keep the station security uppermost in their minds throughout the ceremonies and until the station is cleared of all visitors and guests. A thorough inspection should be made of any suspicious automobiles and a challenge should be made of any person whose actions or intentions appear unusual." Ibid.
45. Pierce interview.
46. Cdr. James A. Hotham, USN (Ret.), interview by author, 20 September 1997. In May 1944, when ZP-14 was assigned to North Africa, Hotham was part of the advance party that sailed from Norfolk. (See chapter 6.)
47. Mills, series VI, box 21, folder 17, GHMC, Smithsonian.
48. Memorandum for Capt. Rosendahl (Mills), "Allocation of ZNPs," 16 April 1942, series II, box 9, folder 17, GHMC, Smithsonian.
49. "I am definitely of the opinion that we should continue mooring out experiments. I feel that one of the greatest mistakes we ever made was in not mooring the Los Angeles out and leaving her out during a complete year's cycle. We have not solved the problem of snow and ice formation and disposition and it is extremely important one. Never again . . . shall we ever have a modern full scale model for such tests as the L.A. represented. The next best thing is to run them with blimps. . . ." Memorandum, Rosendahl to Mills, 20 January 1940, series II, box 9, folder 13, GHMC, Smithsonian.
50. Dönitz, *Memoirs*, 242.
51. Most of the ships lost on the eastern seaboard that half-year were sunk within about 20 to 25 miles of the coast. Many hulks lay in shipping lanes, rendering it inadvisable to buoy them. And so "wreck charts" were published.
52. Dönitz, *Memoirs*, 216. "This was a phenomenal and unprecedented episode in the whole history of warfare—a major and potentially decisive victory being scored by a tiny force of submarines. It showed how even formidable oceanic barriers will crumble if a skilled and determined onslaught on them is not matched by defenses comparable in skill and determination." Farago, *Tenth Fleet,* 61.
53. Rosendahl to Mills, 31 January 1942, series II, box 9, folder 16, GHMC, Smithsonian.
54. The October 1942–June 1943 period was the first in which aircraft led in U-boat kills, sinking seventy-six alone (45 percent of the total) plus another ten in cooperation with surface craft. Sternhell and Thorndike, *Antisubmarine Warfare in World War II,* 41.
55. Memorandum for Cominch, Assist. Chief of Staff (Readiness), 2 February 1942, series II, box 9, folder 16, GHMC, Smithsonian. Among those copied: Coordinator of Research.
56. In any tideway or when wind was strong, flares and bronze slicks drifted, giving the impression that an underwater object was moving.

57. Morison, *Battle of the Atlantic,* 308.
58. Memorandum to Rosendahl, 23 June 1942, series II, box 9, folder 17, GHMC, Smithsonian.
59. "Lighter-than-Air Activities in Anti-Submarine Warfare Operations," 15 December 1942, series I, box 2, folder 49, GHMC, Smithsonian.
60. Ibid. "Scientists quickly found much of their time consumed as engineering troubleshooters and trainers who conducted remedial seminars in the field on basic functions and maintenance of the equipment." Meigs, *Slide Rules,* 83. The reverse was no less useful, that is, comments from operating personnel on how newly introduced A/S devices were performing in service.
61. "Memorandum of [NDRC] Conference at 172 Fulton Street, New York City," 9 June 1942, RG 298, box 98, NARA. Maintenance training courses were established at Corpus Christi and at Lakehurst.
62. Friedman, *Naval Weapons,* 138.
63. Sonobuoys lost their usefulness in the presence of other surface vessels and, therefore, were of questionable assistance in convoy-escort tactics.
64. Tentative requirements were a radio range of five miles and a continuous life of two hours. The two expendable buoys at the laboratory were not designed to withstand much shock, "but it was felt that the method could be checked by placing the available buoys in the water by boat." Summary of projects discussed at conference, USL, 12 March 1942, RG 298, box 96, NARA.
65. Installed in May 1941, *Seemes* boasted the first microwave radar with plan-position-indicator presentation to be used shipboard. A true advance, PPI followed introduction of the rotating antenna.
66. The antenna for the receiver in *K-5* was a twelve-foot wire mounted outside the car. "While this temporary antenna worked very well it was far from an ideal installation; future work should utilize a properly mounted vertically polarized dipole." Summary of Reports (reference E), RG 298, box 96, NARA.
67. The AN/CRT-1 sonobuoy, ordered by the army in June, was operational that August. Cylindrical in shape, the buoy was three feet, nine inches in length, four inches in diameter, and weighed fourteen pounds. A parachute slowed its fall; upon impact, the hydrophone released itself from the base of the buoy and sank to the limit of a connecting cable.
68. Summary of Reports plus references C and E, 7–11 March 1942, RG 298, box 96, NARA. Sylvester was disapproving of Rounds's dismissal of the device unmodified. "Useful as is—more useful with directional characteristics." Ibid. NDRC was confident that a directional sonobuoy was practicable. (British directional phones, indeed, were in service late in 1917.) The army formally requested one in February 1943. This became AN/CRT-4, first tested in January–February 1945. Friedman, *Naval Weapons,* 139.
69. *Fleet Airship Wing Thirty Intelligence Bulletin* 13, n.d., series I, box 3, folder 6, GHMC, Smithsonian. Rounds died that June, one of a dozen casualties in a midair collision between *G-1* and *L-2*.
70. Lt. J. H. Cruse, USN, pilot, *K-5,* report submitted, reference C attached to "Summary of Reports of Airship-Submarine MAD, Sono-Radio Buoy, and Dummy Bombing Tests Held March 7, 1942, and Recommendations as to Future Development," RG 298, box 96, NARA.
71. Magnetic "noise" was much reduced by locating the MAD head in the wingtip, aft in the tail structure, or by towing it in a nonmagnetic streamlined housing well behind or below the aircraft. Eventually, the hydrophone project for ZNPs was dropped.
72. Chief, BuAer, to Coordinator, 17 December 1942, RG 298, box 98, NARA. BuShips was now handling the procurement of a thousand sonobuoys and a hundred receivers. Of the initial deliveries, seventy-five and six, respectively, were slated to the Commander, Caribbean Sea Frontier. Ibid.
73. *Naval Aviation Confidential Bulletin* 33-36, April 1944, RG 313, box 9094, NARA.
74. Memorandum for FX-01, FX-30, FX-40, 19 April 1944, RG 38, box 26, NARA.
75. For the first eleven months of 1943, the United States would produce 85 percent of all oceangoing merchant vessels built by the Allies.

76. ComGulfSeaFron, naval message to ComSeven, ComEight, 4 May 1943, RG 38, box 46, NARA. The number of German submarines almost doubled during 1942.
77. Director of Anti-Submarine Warfare (Great Britain), *Periodic Summary of the Anti-U-Boat Campaign 19,* to Naval Staff, 2 June 1942, RG 298, box 98, NARA.
78. VCNO, memorandum to distribution list, "Monthly Summary of Merchant Ship Losses and Trends in the Battle of the Sea Lanes (1–30 September 1942)," 27 January 1943, RG 38, box 43, NARA.
79. *Cominch U-Boat Trends,* biweekly no. 37, 2 March 1944, RG 38, box 49, NARA.
80. *Cominch U-Boat Trends,* biweekly no. 54, 15 November 1944, RG 38, box 49, NARA.
81. Mills, letter to Rosendahl, 28 December 1942, series II, box 9, folder 17, GHMC, Smithsonian. "We may not be able to operate many days during the winter, but we certainly can operate a few days and should be able to do much good. I would have these four stations operate sections of one squadron, locating the Squadron Commander near the Halifax area." Ibid.
82. See Jeff Noakes, "The Thirteenth Recommendation: Blimps for Canada," *Canadian Military History Since the 17th Century*, A-JS-007-DHH/AF-001 (2000); also Kent O'Grady "The Americans Are Coming! But Should We Let Them Land?" (part 1), *Noon Balloon,* no. 45 (February 1997).
83. A simple method of intercommunication between ships of a convoy was needed. It had to be secure—to foreclose decoding by the enemy—as well as short in range, so that the enemy could not use it to "home" on the convoy.
84. Minutes of St. Lawrence Operations Conference Held in Ottawa, 22–24 February 1943, National Archives of Canada (hereafter NAC), Department of National Defence, Directorate of History and Heritage, Naval Historian's files, 1650-239/16B, vol. 2.
85. Commander, Caribbean Sea Frontier, memorandum (with attachment) to All Aircraft Activities and Units, 28 October 1942, RG 38, box 48, folder 33, NARA.
86. Morison, *Battle of the Atlantic,* 307. "Yet, over and above all these difficulties, the want of a definite anti-submarine doctrine for escort vessels was the greatest fault, which explains more than any other factor this lack of success in killing U-boats." Ibid.
87. W. B. Lodge, memorandum to D. G. C. Hare, 26 May 1942; Edward L. Bowles, memorandum to SecWar, 1 June 1942, RG 298, box 99, NARA. In the months prior, Lodge had seen "at least" thirty Mark 17 depth bombs dropped from aircraft; fourteen failed to detonate, although dropped in water deeper than the fuse setting. Unless the percentage of duds could be reduced, air-arm effectiveness against submarines "must necessarily remain at a low level." Ibid. (draft memorandum).
88. Henry L. Stimson diary, Sterling Library, Yale University, entry for 23 July 1942, quoted in Meigs, *Slide Rules*, 69. "Some of the Army-Navy troubles, in Stimson's view, grew mainly from the peculiar psychology of the Navy Department, which frequently seemed to retire from the realm of logic into a dim religious world in which Neptune was God, Mahan his prophet, and the United States Navy the only true Church." Stimson and Bundy, *On Active Service,* 506.
89. King and Whitehill, *Fleet Admiral King,* 455–59.
90. Commander Eastern Sea Frontier, memorandum to C-in-C, U.S. Fleet, 10 September 1942, RG 38, box 47, NARA.
91. Morison, *Battle of the Atlantic,* 241.
92. Mills, memorandum to Captain Mullinix, 26 May 1942, series I, box 2, folder 23, GHMC, Smithsonian. Beginning with *K-9,* cost sharply increased because of accelerated deliveries from the rate of one ship per month to a maximum of eleven per month. Ibid., folder 40.
93. Meigs, *Slide Rules,* 77–78.
94. ComEastSeaFron to CNO, 25 May 1942, quoted in "Lighter-than-Air Activities in Anti-Submarine Warfare Operations," 15 December 1942, 9–10, series I, box 2, folder 50, GHMC, Smithsonian.
95. Bradley interview.
96. Dönitz, *Memoirs,* 223; Roskill, *The War at Sea, 1939–1945,* 195.

97. Dönitz, *Memoirs*, 231, 265–66.
98. "As this relation continues to remain approximately constant it may be assumed that, up to date, the U-boats have adopted no new effective anti-aircraft detecting devices or tactics." *Periodic Summary of the Anti-U-Boat Campaign 19.*
99. Dönitz, *Memoirs*, 234–35.
100. Lothar-Günther Buchheim, *U-Boat War*, trans. Gudie Lawaetz, (Toronto, New York, London: Bantam Books, 1979). That June, Dönitz began to push for a new type of boat, one that could operate submerged almost continuously. Though its production was delayed, German engineers realized a number of innovations during 1942. Meigs, *Slide Rules,* 78–81.
101. Dönitz, *Memoirs*, 232, 234.
102. Meigs, *Slide Rules,* 87. Biscay ports were the shortest departure points for U-boats deployed to the western North Atlantic.
103. "It is not easy to picture the difficulties which our escort ships must have had to face," ONI reported of the North Russia run, "but the descriptions of depth-charges frozen to the traps and the throwers, the mistaking of small 'growlers' for U-boat conning towers and other such incidents reported give some idea of conditions." *Periodic Summary of the Anti-U-Boat Campaign 19.*
104. Navy Department, Office of CNO, Director of Naval Intelligence, "Axis Submarine Manual," 1942, n.p. Gun batteries and ramming were a merchant captain's sole direct means for inflicting damage.
105. Befehlshaber der Unterseeboote (BdU)—log of 12 April 1942, excerpts of U-boat logs made by Lt. J. Gordon Vaeth, USNR, from captured German navy archives, Admiralty, London, series IV, box 17, folder 14, GHMC, Smithsonian. The abbreviation "BdU" denoted Dönitz and was also a shorthand for the admiral's staff or headquarters.
106. Army and navy representatives had agreed to pool their equipments and distribute to whichever service could put them to best use, have only one procurement agency, and, with NDRC cooperation, hammer out common standards.
107. "Memorandum of Conference at 172 Fulton Street, New York City," 9 June 1942, RG 298, box 98, NARA. "With any new form of equipment for naval use, the organization of shake-down testing work is of first-order importance. Experience has shown that, one the performance limitations that can be disclosed by laboratory tests are removed, there is no other way to find out probable service troubles than by cumulative experience under known conditions of operation." Ibid.
108. Confidential memorandum for files, BuAer, 7 July 1942, RG 298, box 98, NARA.
109. Memorandum of conference, 13 July 1942, RG 298, box 98, NARA. "In order to keep the commanding officer of a given blimp informed as to possibility of the emergence of additional submarines while concentrating on a given MAD contact, it was agreed that either the pilot or co-pilot or possibly the radio operator would continue to observe the radar screen while a local MAD contact was being developed." Ibid.
110. Senior Escort, Escort Group Fox (CO, USS *Decatur*) to ComFive, 4 July 1942, series I, box 2, folder 24, GHMC, Smithsonian.
111. Memorandum for files, BuAer, 10 August 1942, RG 298, box 98, NARA.
112. Commander, Airship Patrol Group One to Airship Patrol Group One, 22 August 1942, series 1, box 2, folder 24, GHMC, Smithsonian.
113. Fromm, "Personal Reminiscences."
114. OSRD, Bi-weekly Report Covering Period October 11–21, 1942, 28 October 1942, RG 38, box 24, NARA. An instruction manual for the MAD gear was released early in 1943.
115. In addition, NDRC had completed about twenty units in their model production plant at La Guardia.
116. As of 10 December, tests were in planning in which the detector (with alterations) would be towed from a ZNP. Flight tests persisted into 1942, at Quonset.
117. Confidential memorandum for file, BuAer, 15 June 1942, RG 298, box 98, NARA.

118. "Contacts and Attacks in Atlantic Area," Rosendahl Collection, HOAC, box 161, F4, 85.

119. Memorandum of 10 July conference at office of CO, ZP-12, 13 July 1942, RG 298, box 98, NARA. In another decision, the ships' generator would be reserved for the radar equipment.

120. Dönitz, *Memoirs,* 250; Churchill, *Hinge of Fate,* 123.

121. The airplane was cleaned up magnetically, the rudder removed and inspected, the control cables replaced. Also, brackets for mounting the MAD apparatus were installed.

122. Memorandum for files, BuAer, 10 August 1942, RG 298, box 98, NARA.

123. Farago, *Tenth Fleet,* 213; King and Whitehill, *Fleet Admiral King,* 471–74.

124. Code breaking was indispensable to the campaign. Still, Ultra was no panacea: at best, decryptions gave the course and destination of oncoming boats—not enough information to grant contact to A/S forces or even to assure suppression. HF/DF networks granted accurate positions. Less well known are the parallel efforts by the German navy to break Allied naval codes. See Jak P. Mallmann Showell, *German Naval Codebreakers* (Annapolis, Md.: Naval Institute Press, 2003).

125. "While a few mathematical geniuses might 'break' a new code (i.e. encryption technique) the sheer volume of such 'traffic' was overwhelming. Thousands of people were thus employed at Bletchley Park in England. The possibility of using IBM electro-mechanical machines to help ferret out crypt-analytic keys and manipulate huge volumes of data was very seriously considered." Charles W. Long, letter to author, 8 May 2006.

126. The report on its radio equipment gives its frequency spectrum and general capabilities along with complete specifications, including wiring diagrams and photographs of its high-frequency transceiver. (A separate report discussed *U-570*'s DF gear.) Possible use of these data for confusing U-boat communications is mentioned. On the NDRC copy, "No radar apparatus was on board." is underlined. ONI (Naval Attaché) Intelligence Report, 9 July 1942, RG 298, box 98, NARA.

127. Lts. J. T. Burwell and J. F. Parker, memorandum to Coordinator, 2 December 1942; memorandum, 24 September 1942, RG 298, box 97, NARA.

128. Furer, *Administration of the Navy Department,* 781.

129. Naval Intelligence Translation 565, 13 October 1942, "Some Questions on Submarine Warfare Answered by the Commander of Submarines Admiral Karl Donitz," *Voelkischer Beobachter,* 4 August 1942, series IV, box 17, folder 17, GHMC, Smithsonian.

130. Dönitz, *Memoirs,* 253, 261.

131. Series I, box 2, folder 23, GHMC, Smithsonian.

132. Jewett to Chief, BuShips, 26 January; Jewett to Coordinator, 30 July 1942, RG 298, box 96, NARA. Testing alone did not end the matter. For permanent shipboard use, new devices had to be simple and rugged, and require a minimum of training for operating personnel.

133. Drs. Varney and Rack, memorandum to Dr. Elmer Hutchisson, 11 June 1942, RG 298, box 96, NARA.

134. Rosendahl, letter to Mills, 10 June 1942, series II, box 9, folder 17, GHMC, Smithsonian.

135. Sternhell and Thorndike, *Antisubmarine Warfare in World War II,* 33.

136. Naval air stations had nothing to do with fleet/squadron operations. They were logistics, overhaul (for stations with A&R departments), and support commands providing communications and weather facilities, fuel, ordnance, "berthing, and beans." Capt. Fred N. Klein, USN (Ret.), undated note to author.

137. Naval message 6 November 1942, RG 38, box 44, NARA.

138. Chief, BuAer, memorandum to Coordinator, 17 December 1942, RG 298, box 98, NARA. Progress was indicated also on the development of the lightweight Mark VI unit and auxiliary apparatus to exploit MAD gear as a bombsight. Ibid.

139. Mills to Peck, 25 November 1942, series II, box 8, folder 46, GHMC, Smithsonian.

140. Auxiliary sites were capable of mooring out two ZNPs and supply helium, fuel, oil, and ammunition. "Now we make [120-hour] engine checks at the masts," Mills advised a midmonth briefing. "The

K-19 has been at Richmond since November 12th without entering a hangar." Minutes, conference of Anti-Submarine Warfare (no. 5), 15 December 1942, RG 38, box 47, NARA.

141. The earliest K type had had an envelope volume of 424,000 cubic feet. From *K-14* on, an extra panel realized a volume of 454,000 cubic feet, granting more lift. Range: about 1,900 miles at forty knots.
142. "Lighter-than-Air Activities in Anti-Submarine Warfare Operations," 15 December 1942, 7–8, series I, box 2, folder 50, GHMC, Smithsonian. Rosendahl totaled thirty attacks by ZP-12 on sighted or indicted contacts. "They participated in many others made by planes and surface craft, sometimes directing the action, frequently making underwater observations with MAD." Rosendahl, "How Soon We Forget," 12.
143. Cominch, memorandum to Commander Fleet Air Wings, Atlantic Fleet, 11 December 1942, RG 38, box 5, NARA.
144. Dönitz "Essay," "I am extremely anxious about shipping situation," Churchill wrote that March—the apogee of German U-boat success in the North Atlantic battleground. Loewenheim, et al., *Roosevelt and Churchill,* 322.

Chapter 4. Turning Tide

1. "We need to import 27,000,000 tons for our food and war effort in 1943. Our stocks are running down with dangerous rapidity. These Islands are the assembly base for the war against Hitler." Churchill, letter to Roosevelt, 31 October 1942, in Loewenheim, et al., *Roosevelt and Churchill,* 263.
2. Office CNO, Intelligence Division, 3 June 1943 Intelligence Report, RG 38, box 43, NARA. Convoy stragglers continued, in most cases, to fall victim to shadowing submarines. CVE operations emphasized daytime aircraft searches, so as to deny the surface to U-boats during daylight in areas beyond the operating range of shore-based aircraft.
3. The comfort conferred by accurate long-range navigation (Loran) to air and surface forces well to sea should be appreciated.
4. Aspects of Submarine Warfare, n.d. (received by Office of Coordinator 19 March 1943), RG 298, box 97, NARA. Further development of both retro-bombing and MAD equipment then installation in the TBF-type airplane led to TBF deployment for ASW aboard escort carriers.
5. Capt. T. G. W. Settle, USN, letter to Gayer G. Dominick, 16 April 1943, courtesy Langdon H. Fulton.
6. Memorandum 25 July 1943, series I, box 2, folder 30, GHMC, Smithsonian.
7. *Fleet Airship Wing Thirty Semi-Monthly News Letter* 2-43, series I, box 3, folder 7, GHMC, Smithsonian; *Airship,* 7 July 1943, 1.
8. According to an official history, VP-63 "Mad Cat" *Catalinas* logged the first MAD detection of a submerged U-boat while flying a magnetic barrier across the Strait of Gibraltar. With the assistance of surface forces, the *U-761* was attacked and sunk on 24 February 1944 (see chap. 6). Yet, in fact, numerous anomalies were recorded during operations off the East Coast during 1942–43.
9. (Preceding three paragraphs) Conference on Anti-Submarine Warfare, 23 March 1943, R38, box 47, NARA.
10. Meigs, *Slide Rules,* 124.
11. Brown, *Radar History,* 218.
12. Ulrich interview.
13. Weintraub, handwritten letter to Mills, 2 August 1942, series II, box 9, folder 7, GHMC, Smithsonian. "The pilots are becoming more efficient and I don't mind telling you that I've had to keep on their tails to keep them off their tails." Weintraub, letter to Mills, 4 November, ibid.
14. "Lighter-than-Air Activities in Anti-Submarine Warfare Operations," 15 December 1942, series I, box 2, folder 50, GHMC, Smithsonian, 18.

15. Cdr. Charles A. Mills, USN (Ret.), letter to author, 18 May 1988.
16. *Naval Aviation Confidential Bulletin* 1-44, January 1944, RG 313, box 9094, NARA, 35.
17. *Instructor's Training Manual for Anti-submarine Warfare.* The periscope feather was almost never spotted; in a moderate sea it was all but invisible. The wake of a surfaced boat was tell-tale. "A white streak a long way off is the thing to look for. Every appearance of a white thread or ribbon just below the horizon should be immediately investigated." Ibid.
18. Dönitz, *Memoirs,* 343.
19. Letters dated 4 and 24 March 1943, in Loewenheim, et al., *Roosevelt and Churchill,* 320, 322.
20. M. L. Shettle Jr., *United States Naval Air Stations of World War II,* 2nd ed. (Bowersville, Ga.: Schaertel, 1995), vol. 1, 89. Each major U.S. station had one or more auxiliary bases supporting. For Glynco, it was NAS Charleston. *K-34* (ZP-15) was the first fleet airship to land and moor at Charleston, on 24 March 1943.
21. *Fleet Airships Atlantic Intelligence Bulletin* 7, n.d., 2, series I, box 4, folder 5, GHMC, Smithsonian.
22. Dönitz, "Essay," 29.
23. Dönitz, *Memoirs,* 330, 332.
24. Jürgen Rohwer, *The Critical Convoy Battle of March 1943: The Battle for HX.229/SC122* (Annapolis, Md.: Naval Institute Press, 1977), 47.
25. Mills to Rear Adm. John S. McCain—first DCNO (Air), though not yet in March—20 March 1943, series I, box 2, folder 26, GHMC, Smithsonian. "Under no circumstances do I recommend the abolishment of an LTA section in the Bureau of Aeronautics." Ibid.
26. Memorandum to Under Secretary James Forrestal, 29 April 1943, series I, box 2, folder 27, GHMC, Smithsonian.
27. Lakehurst: *K-54, K-56, K-57, K-58, K-60, K-61, K-62;* Moffett Field: *K-39, K-43, K-47, K-51.* That July, again, eleven K-ships reached the navy, as did *L-16, L-18* (to Moffett), and *L-19.*
28. Memorandum for Forrestal.
29. *Fleet Airship Wing Thirty Intelligence Bulletin* 8, n.d., series I, box 3, folder 6, GHMC, Smithsonian. "An outstanding feature of NAS Houma is the speed with which construction has progressed. Every attempt has been made to get essential things accomplished first. The hangar is well along although the lean-tos have not been begun as of May first. The radio towers are up. The two officers' quarters have been occupied. All the barracks are about complete. Two of the first buildings completed were storehouses. Unessential structures have just been started." Ibid.
30. *Fleet Airship Wing Thirty Intelligence Bulletin* 12, n.d., 1, series I, box 3, folder 6, GHMC, Smithsonian.
31. *Fleet Airship Wing Thirty Intelligence Bulletins* 11 and 12, n.d., series I, box 3, folder 6, GHMC, Smithsonian.
32. M. H. Eppes, personal letter, 8 August 1943, courtesy Evelyn (Eppes) Azzaretto.
33. *Fleet Airships Atlantic Semi-Monthly News Letter* 11-43, 16-17, 15 December 1943, series I, box 3, folder 8, GHMC, Smithsonian.
34. Meigs, *Slide Rules,* 98.
35. Farago, *Tenth Fleet,* 174.
36. The statistics analyzed in one ASWORG study, for example, underscored the effectiveness of coordinated operations. A joint attack—aircraft and surface ships—was four times as likely to realize success as an attack by either alone. Another study showed that four vessels had an 80 percent probability of finding a submarine once located and submerged if they got to the spot within thirty minutes after location, whereas three vessels had only a 40 percent chance.
37. Cominch naval message, 21 June 1943, RG 38, box 44, NARA.
38. "Instructions for ASWORG Members," 1 December 1942, RG 38, box 47, 1, 5.
39. Meigs, *Slide Rules,* 120–25, NARA, Dönitz "Essay," 34.
40. Ibid. Dönitz, *Memoirs,* 339; Churchill, *Closing the Ring,* 8 and 13.

41. Dönitz, *Memoirs,* 341.
42. Establishment of the Training Command placed the Naval Airship Training Center at Moffett Field under CNATE authority.
43. ASW projects were specifically exempted, left under the jurisdiction of Commander, Tenth Fleet.
44. *Airship,* 24 November 1943, 1.
45. Reserved for experiments, *M-1* became *XM-1.* In March 1944, a modified Piper NE-1 was mounted beneath and released from a trapeze in flight. The intent: depth charge equipped, the drone would be steered into a surfaced U-boat. Footage of *XM-1* and *K-76* appears in the MGM film *This Man's Navy,* with Wallace Beery.
46. VCNO, memorandum to distribution list, 4 October 1943, LTA subject file (C–E), Naval Historical Center, Washington Navy Yard, Washington, D.C. The Mineola Laboratory acted as a test and acceptance center for MAD equipment received from manufacturers.
47. *Fleet Airship Wing Thirty Semi-Monthly News Letter* 6-43, 1 June 1943, series I, box 3, folder 7, GHMC, Smithsonian.
48. Mills, letter to Settle, 19 May 1943, series II, box 9, folder 28, GHMC, Smithsonian.
49. USNAS (Lakehurst) Training Department order 7-43 to all flight instructors, 31 August 1943, box 151, file F7, HOAC. That March, the Chief of Naval Personnel had been obliged to direct that no "Qualified LTA" enlisted men be ordered to other than LTA activities.
50. "Personnel," box 151, file F-9, HOAC, 10. In April 1945, anticipating acquisition of K-ships for air/sea rescue after demobilization, the U.S. Coast Guard dispatched nine officers and thirty enlisted ratings to Lakehurst for training. But the helicopter displaced the airship for rescue missions.
51. "History of BAR Akron," box "LTA/B.A.R. Akron," Naval Historical Center, Washington Navy Yard, Washington, D.C.
52. Project Sail—established to carry out technical and operational tests of antisubmarine devices for aircraft—remained concerned primarily with MAD, only secondarily with sonobuoys.
53. Together, the navy and army had 750 MAD units on order in late 1942, to be divided according to requirements. Scarcity of critical materials had introduced "production troubles"; still, tactical use of the MAD equipment had become central. "We believe it is worth carrying on rather than dropping it," an army colonel remarked. "The M.A.D. gave us some information we didn't have before." Conference on Anti-Submarine Warfare, 20 October and 1 December 1942, RG 38, box 47, NARA.
54. Fromm, "Personal Reminiscences."
55. Watson, Headquarters Cominch (Tenth Fleet), letter to Rosendahl, 3 October 1943, series II, box 9, folder 18, GHMC, Smithsonian.
56. All had been cleared by ONI for work on navy classified material.
57. C-in-C W.A., naval message to action and info addressees, 27 May 1943, RG 38, box 45, NARA.
58. Brown, *Radar History,* 343–44.
59. DCNO (Air), confidential memorandum to Vice Chief of Naval Operations, 27 August 1943, box 161, file F-8, HOAC. The subject was a survey of the LTA program as directed by the VCNO, accompanied by recommendations concerning the advisability of reductions.
60. Gannon, *Black May,* 385.
61. Baxter, *Scientists against Time,* 161–62; Conrad, memorandum to Coordinator, 6 December 1943, RG 298, box 97, ONR/NDRC, Coordinator, General Correspondence, 1941–46, box 7, NARA. The army wanted to use MAD to detect land objects, such as armored columns and gun emplacements.
62. *Fleet Airship Wing Thirty Intelligence Bulletin* 13, n.d. [mid-1943], series I, box 3, folder 6, GHMC, Smithsonian.
63. *Fleet Airships Atlantic Semi-Monthly News Letter* 7-44 (1 April 1944), series I, box 3, folder 10, GHMC, Smithsonian. The quote mimics "Notes on the Operation of Nonrigid Airships," published

in 1920. "Successful antisubmarine work by aircraft depends usually on the bright lookout kept and the patience and endurance displayed in watching an area in which a submarine has recently been reported."

64. "It was no use sending a crew in a noisy, open conveyance on interminable patrols, for they soon ceased to be vigilant enough to spot a U-boat, though their presence might be sufficient to deter it from action." Hingham, *The British Rigid Airship, 1908–1931*, 82. See chapter 7 for an analysis of the nonrigid airship in the Great War. "The usefulness of the blimps was well recognized by the end of the war," 117.
65. Hotham interview.
66. Cdr. Gerald E. Wheeler, USN (Ret.), letter to author, 10 June 1999. "During my time in LTA, I had 161.9 hours of primary training in L-ships, 77.9 hours of advanced training in K-ships, and 660.4 hours in the K-ships of ZP-12. All officers were assigned collateral duties." Ibid. Pigeons? Carrier pigeons were routinely aboard, as a secure means of communications to base. Releases back to the air-station loft were for training.
67. Mills, letter to Cdr. Robert G. Payne, USNR (headquarters Eastern Sea Frontier), 5 May 1943, series II, box 8, folder 45, GHMC, Smithsonian; Morison, *Battle of the Atlantic,* xvi; Bradley interview.
68. Bolam, letter to Mills, 27 April 1944, series II, box 8, folder 6, GHMC, Smithsonian.
69. Not all flights were operational in nature. "To maintain itself, its officers and men in a proper state of operational readiness, each squadron has a carefully planned training program which necessitates the making of frequent training flights. These . . . are concerned with gunnery practice, navigational training, practice landings, and the like." *Fleet Airships Atlantic Intelligence Bulletin* 2-44, 1 July 1944, series I, box 4, folder 5, GHMC, Smithsonian.
70. Daily War Diary, ZP-12, 29 August 1942, Naval Historical Center, Washington Navy Yard, Washington, D.C.
71. Ibid., 136.
72. Commander Eastern Sea Frontier, memorandum to Cominch, 24 October 1943, RG 38, box 47, NARA.
73. "Contacts and Attacks," box 161, file F4, HOAC. 85, in Atlantic Area.
74. As doctrine evolved, the trend was to discredit oil slicks that produced no MAD contacts or other evidence substantiating a genuine target.
75. "Contacts and Attacks," 87.
76. "Digest of Minutes," Conference of Anti-Submarine Warfare, 12 January 1943, no. 7, 26, RG 38, box 47, NARA. Two big problems were its installation in aircraft and the training of operating and maintenance personnel.
77. "Digest of Minutes."
78. "The carriers used the buoys in many attacks and the buoys are now considered well-nigh indispensable as carrier equipment. They have verified the presence of enemy submarines many times." Ibid.
79. Ibid.
80. Bradley to Mills, 15 June 1943, series II, box 8, folder 7, GHMC, Smithsonian.
81. Loewenheim, et al., *Roosevelt and Churchill,* 354–55. The quote is from Roosevelt's message of 15 July 1943. A new system of monthly statements on the anti-U-boat war had begun. After receiving this message, Churchill referred to destroyed submarines as "canaries." Ibid.
82. Planning Directive 10-ZZ-43, from Director Planning Division to distribution list, 24 July 1943, file—LTA WW-I, Naval Historical Center, Washington Navy Yard, Washington, D.C. The hedron idea was sound; however, it introduced internal competition that made the system somewhat counterproductive.
83. Mills, letter to Rosendahl, 22 June 1943, series II, box 9, folder 18, GHMC, Smithsonian.
84. *Fleet Airships Atlantic Intelligence Bulletin* 4, 8 August 1943, 5–7, series I, box 4, folder 5, GHMC, Smithsonian.

85. Meigs, *Slide Rules,* 181.
86. Bradley to Mills, 29 August 1943, series II, box 8, folder 7, GHMC, Smithsonian.
87. Tyler to Mills, 26 July 1943; "Rixey Comments" (handwritten), n.d., series I, box 2, folder 30, GHMC, Smithsonian.
88. Tyler to Mills, ibid. "Outline of Reasons for Three (3) Crews per Airship," 28 August 1943, ibid. Flight duration during April–September tended to be several hours longer than in winter months.
89. *Fleet Airship Atlantic News Letter* 9-43, September 1943, 3, series I, box 3, folder 8, GHMC, Smithsonian.
90. ARM 3/c J. J. Turek, on duty as radioman in *K-32,* received fragments of this transmission and deduced its source. He immediately relayed the information to base, stating he believed it to be from *K-74.*
91. Brosin radioed U-Boat Command immediately after the exchange. Nothing was said of casualties, though he did report damage to his quick-dive tanks by machine-gun fire. Vaeth, *Blimps and U-Boats,* 79–80. On 31 July, a monitored broadcast from Berlin commented on the action, stating that the airship's entire bomb load had been dropped and, further, that blimps were being used extensively in A/S warfare.
92. May sighted Grills *after* his airship had passed. "Conditions of the sea, sun and small size of the object made sighting most difficult," read May's commendation. Bourne and Turek received wing commendations as well.
93. Not only for helping keep a U-boat's deck clear. "Besides, the rattle of bullets on the hull is not a pleasant sound to those inside the boat, and a burst will certainly relieve the feelings of the aircraft crew." "Submarine and Anti-Submarine," Coastal Command, October 1942, RG 38, box 44, NARA.
94. Widdicombe interview.
95. "Report of *K-74* in Combat with Enemy Submarine," *Fleet Airships Atlantic Intelligence Bulletin* 1, 8 August 1943, series I, box 4, folder 4, GHMC, Smithsonian. "Each pilot should study the report and become fully acquainted with the facts of the case and the lessons to be learned from it." *Fleet Airships Atlantic Semi-Monthly News Letter* 3-43, 15 August 1943, 9, series I, box 3, folder 8, GHMC, Smithsonian.
96. Rosendahl, "How Soon We Forget," chap. 8, 6; *Fleet Airships Atlantic Semi-Monthly News Letter* 3-43, 7. The mechanism had a record of malfunctions. "Had it done so? Had Stessel worked it properly? He was dead, and no one could answer for him," Vaeth, *Blimps and U-Boats,* 81. The failure to drop was due, apparently, to the bombardier not pulling the releases more than halfway. In any event, lethal damage was "not considered probable" had the charges let go, given their fifty-foot settings.
97. Series I, box 1, folder 26, GHMC, Smithsonian. "Should an enemy ship or sub shoot down one of our ships at sea following the present build up," Peck had worried, "I hate to think of the consequences. Without the build up such a circumstance would pass unnoticed as a necessary part of naval warfare." Peck to Mills, 20 January 1942, series II, box 8, folder 46, GHMC, Smithsonian.
98. *Fleet Airships Atlantic Intelligence Bulletin* 1, 8 August 1943, 6–7, series I, box 4, folder 4, GHMC, Smithsonian.
99. Sample comments: "A royal cockup"; the CAC "was not at General Quarters"; "It was a mistake in tactics, there's no question about that"; "No match. So he disobeyed orders by engaging"; "If Grills had sunk that submarine, there'd be an everlasting monument to him at Lakehurst."
100. Cdr. Edward R. McMillan, USN (Ret.), interview by author, 18 May 1999. Assigned to several squadrons, McMillan would fly ZNPs from four continents.
101. Excerpts from U-boat logs made by Lt. J. Gordon Vaeth, USNR, from captured Germany Navy archives at Admiralty, London, series IV, box 17, folder 14, GHMC, Smithsonian. Two purported photographs of the *K-74* derelict, taken presumably from the conning tower of *U-134,* were published in 1958 in the U.S. Naval Institute *Proceedings.* The images (one assumes) had been transferred to a tanker submarine.

102. *Fleet Airships Atlantic Semi-Monthly News Letter* 4-43, 1 September 1943, series I, box 3, folder 8, GHMC, Smithsonian, 2.
103. Mills to Bradley (ComFairWing 2), 23 August 1943, series II, box 8, folder 7, Smithsonian. Bradley, in his turn, sent Grills to NAS Hitchcock and to NAS Houma. "Until his arrival here," Mills remarked, "I was firmly convinced that he identified his target as a submarine on his first approach. He told me that he really did not identify his target as a submarine until it opened fire on him. . . . In talking to Grills I became firmly convinced that Squadron 21 has not been getting sufficient gunnery practice. Grills told me that he had never seen a live bomb dropped." Ibid.
104. *Fleet Airships Atlantic Intelligence Bulletin* 1, 7.
105. Joint Canadian-American Board on Non-Rigid Airship Operations, memorandum to VCNO (U.S.) and the Chiefs of Staff Committee (Canada), 10 July 1943, NAC, RG 24 E1, vol. 5202, courtesy Barry Jan Countryman.
106. NSHQ (Naval Staff Headquarters), Ottawa, naval message to NMCS, 21 July 1943, NAC, RG 24 E1, vol. 5202.
107. "Use of Non-Rigid Airships in Eastern Canadian Waters," memorandum, 27 August 1943, NAC, RG 24 E1, vol. 5202.
108. VCNO, memorandum (planning directive) to Chief, BuAer, 15 September 1943, Naval Historical Center, Washington Navy Yard, Washington, D.C.
109. King and Whitehill, *Fleet Admiral King,* 465–71.
110. Mills to Bradley, 22 November 1943, series II, box 8, folder 7, GHMC, Smithsonian.
111. Mills to Bradley, 2 October 1943, series II, box 8, folder 7, GHMC, Smithsonian.
112. Bowen to Bush, 13 August 1945, RG 298, box 97, NARA. Bowen's letter contained a translation of Dönitz's own top-secret letter.

Chapter 5. Southern Squadrons

1. Morison, *Battle of the Atlantic,* 135–36.
2. Ibid., 142.
3. Naval Airship Training and Experimental Command, NAS Lakehurst, N.J., *Statistical Summary of United States Fleet Airship Operations in World War Two,* 15 February 1946, courtesy Cdr. James M. Punderson, USN (Ret.).
4. Air-ferry traffic and congestion had eliminated the army-navy air base at Natal, on the "bulge," as a main base site in northeastern Brazil. The board's search of the Belem–São Luiz area had found no site reasonably near the coast having acceptable transportation. The second dock diverted from the Gulf coast, together with necessary ancillary facilities, was therefore erected on Trinidad.
5. Cominch, memorandum to SecNav, 26 February 1943, LTA subject file(W), Naval Historical Center, Washington Navy Yard, Washington, D.C.
6. Airship Base Facilities and Organization Board to VCNO via Commander Fourth Fleet, 9 April 1943, LTA subject file(W), Naval Historical Center, Washington Navy Yard, Washington, D.C.
7. Delong interview.
8. Naval message, ComPaSeaFron, 13 July 1942, RG 38, box 46, NARA.
9. "Happily, the Canadian authorities had anticipated just such a development and had organized A/S air patrols and convoy escorts in readiness. This organization was put into effect and this particular development of the U-boat campaign has, so far, been short-lived." *Periodic Summary of the Anti-U-Boat Campaign 19.*
10. Grossnick, Roy A., ed. *Kite Balloons to Airships . . . The Navy's Lighter-than-Air Experience.* Washington, D.C.: Government Printing Office, for Deputy Chief of Naval Operations (Air Warfare) and Commander, Naval Air Systems Command, 1987. Some sea frontier commanders were not particularly interested in airships. In November 1942, the "only real mission" the commander of the

Gulf Sea Frontier had assigned to ZP-21 was night patrol of the Yucatan Channel, basing at the Isle of Pines, Cuba.

11. Dönitz, *Memoirs,* 212–13.
12. ONI, Intelligence Report, 9 June 1942, RG 298, box 98, NARA.
13. "There never was any shortage of gasoline. There was only a shortage of tankers to transport it. Deliveries elsewhere—by train, truck, pipeline and tankers up the Pacific coast—were normal." Brinkley, *Washington Goes to War*, 128.
14. Samuel Eliot Morison, *History of United States Naval Operations in World War II,* vol. 10, *The Atlantic Battle Won May 1943–May 1945* (Boston: Little, Brown, 1975), 8.
15. VCNO to distribution list, 27 January 1943, RG 38, box 43, NARA.
16. Dönitz, *Memoirs,* 221, 238, 251, 252, 290.
17. Dönitz, *Memoirs,* 290. Lt. (jg) T. J. Bellke, USN, discusses the onslaught in his "Roll of Drums," U.S. Naval Institute *Proceedings* 109/4/962 (April 1983): 58–64; also, Churchill, *Hinge of Fate,* 122–23.
18. Note the following remark as to summer temperatures at Hitchcock, Texas: "Right now, our biggest problem is trying to get off with any sort of a load on the ships. It is so hot that the pressure height remains just slightly above sea-level readings." No working ceiling, in other words. Eppes, personal letter. The term "pressure height" originated in the operation of rigid airships. For ZNPs, this is the height at which the ballonets become completely emptied of air and the envelope completely filled with helium.
19. The officers solicited: Bailey, May, Mills, Reppy, Tyler, and Whittle—seasoned aviators all.
20. CO, NAS Lakehurst, memorandum to Cdrs. Mills and Whittle and to Lt. Cdrs. Tyler, Reppy, May, and Bailey, 28 February 1942; CO, NAS Lakehurst to Peck, 28 February 1942, series III, box 15, folder 1, GHMC, Smithsonian. Mills wrote Towers directly. For an account of how ZNPK-21 was upgraded/modernized into a postwar type before 1945, see Richard Van Treuren, "Airships v. Submarines in WW II," *Airshipworld,* no. 48 (June 2001): 23–26.
21. *Naval Aviation Confidential Bulletin* 2-44, February 1944, RG 313, box 9094, NARA. For the M type, dynamic lift provided three to five thousand pounds of additional lift and useful load. A dynamic lift of about four thousand pounds was conservative for take-off at forty knots air speed. *United States Navy M-Type Airships: Pilot's Manual,* August 1944.
22. "Memorandum to Mr. Forrestal, Under Secretary of the Navy," 29 April 1943, box 2, folder 28, GHMC, Smithsonian. The Hawaii–Somoa mention suggests that senior civilian or military officials had considered ZNPs accompanying fleet units into the island-dotted Pacific. See chapter 7.
23. On 14 April 1944, Cope was awarded the Distinguished Flying Cross—the war's first LTA pilot to receive the DFC. Citation (in part): "For heroism and extraordinary achievement in aerial flight as Commanding Officer of Blimp Squadron Twenty-One in salvaging a wrecked non-rigid airship from the Bay of Biscayne, October 30, 1943." *K-17* had flown into the water. Cope, with the assistance of a volunteer crew, free-ballooned the badly damaged ship off the surface and returned it to base.
24. Mills, letter to Bradley, 8 February 1944, series II, box 8, folder 7, GHMC, Smithsonian.
25. "The M ship sported the most creature comforts of any of the Navy airships," an airman (ZP-12, ZP-21) recalls. "You could sit in the lower blister and hear nothing but the hum of the engines and the bubbling of the air on the faring." Also, reversible props eased many a landing. T. C. Watters, "The Mike Series"; *Buoyant Flight: Bulletin of the Lighter-than-Air Society* 24, no. 1 (November–December 1976): 6.
26. *Cominch U-Boat Trends,* biweekly no. 15, 2 April 1943, RG 38, box 49, NARA.
27. Gann, *Fate is the Hunter*, 135. Also based at Paramaribo, for a time: a unit of P-40 fighters installed to guard the mine. 135–36
28. "The crews of the bauxite shuttle ships between Trinidad and the Guianas, a route for which no surface escorts could at first be spared, are said to have threatened mutiny unless they were given

protection; they were afforded blimp cover all the way and the men were satisfied." Morison, *Battle of the Atlantic,* 251.

29. Commander Task Force Three, memorandum to CNO via C-in-C, U.S. Atlantic Fleet and C-in-C, U.S. Fleet, 26 February 1942, RG 298, box 96, NARA. "The issue facing us may well be the deciding factor of the war." Ibid.
30. On the U.K.–Gibraltar run, northeast of the Azores: "Constant attacks by our CVEs with intermittent support from the night flying Wellingtons from Azores have kept these U-boats mostly on the defensive." *Cominch U-Boat Trends,* biweekly no. 33, 1 January 1944, RG 38, box 49, NARA. The notion of hunter-killer groups was hardly new: "It is my belief that the use of dirigibles in co-operation with chaser flotillas will make an operating unit some 50 per cent stronger than if the two worked separately." Scientific Attaché, Report 51, London to Research Information Committee, Washington, D.C., 22 April 1918. series IV, box 17, folder 9, GHMC, Smithsonian.
31. ONI, Intelligence Report, to distribution, 9 June 1942, RG 298, box 98, NARA.
32. Ibid.
33. This raised the question of the proper lean-out mixture during prolonged operations, for economy of fuel and to prevent sticking due to fouled plugs or accumulation of lead on valve stems and guides. Leaning out engines to "lean best power" or "best economy" plus slightly higher engine temperature eased but did not banish the problem.
34. *Fleet Airship Wing Thirty Semi-Monthly News Letter,* 1 April 1943, series I, box 3, folder 7, GHMC, Smithsonian.
35. Morison, *Atlantic Battle Won,* 190.
36. Memorandum to Mr. Forrestal.
37. Commander Gulf Sea Frontier, memorandum to VCNO via Commander Air Force Atlantic Fleet, 23 December 1943, RG 313, box 67, NARA.
38. "Fleet Airship Wing 2, Ferry Pilot Instructions between N.A.S. Richmond and N.A.S. Hitchcock," 1, undated, RG 313, box 9091, NARA. "All classified documents and equipment must be burned, sunk, or destroyed in any case where they would be considered open to capture or compromise by the enemy." Ibid., 3.
39. McMillan interview.
40. Ibid.
41. *Fleet Airships Atlantic Semi-Monthly News Letter 6-43,* October 1943, GHMC, series I, box 3, folder 8, GHMC, Smithsonian. Thunderstorms afflicted northern squadrons as well. In May 1945, *K-76* (ZP-12) was driven to within feet of the water upon entering a squall line. Only by instantly dropping his bomb load was the pilot able to stay in the air.
42. The distances between European ports and the Far East eliminated unrefueled air freight as a practical means of transporting war commodities. Reliant as it was on Soviet meteorological assistance, the Arctic Ocean route to Norwegian ports was impracticable as well.
43. Leo A. Borah and Wellman Chamberlain, "New Map of the Atlantic Ocean," *National Geographic* 80, no. 3 (September 1941): 408. See Martin Brice, *Axis Blockade Runners of World War II* (Annapolis, Md.: Naval Institute Press, 1981), for a full account.
44. Quoted in Mills to All Wing Squadron Commanders, 10 June 1944, series II, box 8, folder 18, GHMC, Smithsonian. Articles and editorials appeared during the war endorsing ZR development for strategic scouting or for peacetime production, for commerce. Example: "The value of the rigid airship in the present conflict would seem to deserve thorough investigation." *New York Times,* 15 November 1943.
45. Harold G. Dick and Douglas H. Robinson, *Graf Zeppelin and Hindenburg* (Washington, D.C.: Smithsonian Institution Press, 1985), 183.
46. Office of CNO, Intelligence Report, 2 December 1942, RG 38, box 47, NARA.
47. *Cominch U-Boat Trends,* biweekly no. 35, 2 February 1944, RG 38, box 49, NARA. In late

December–early January 1943, five merchant runners were in the South Atlantic heading north. One made port, badly damaged. "This was the last attempt the enemy made to run the blockade with merchant vessels, but U-boats continued to make occasional trips between Germany and Japan." Sternhell and Thorndike, *Antisubmarine Warfare in World War II,* 49.

48. *Cominch U-Boat Trends,* biweekly no. 59, 1 February 1945, RG 38, box 49, NARA.
49. *Cominch U-Boat Trends,* biweekly no. 61, 1 March 1945, RG 38, box 49, NARA.
50. See Vaeth, *Blimps and U-Boats,* 116–18. Two ships from Forty-two took part in the recovery of bales of rubber from the sunken enemy, by finding the cargo then directing surface craft to the scene. In one instance, instructions were written on a marker buoy and dropped, no other means of communication being available.
51. *Fleet Airships Atlantic Semi-Monthly News Letter* 6-44, 15 March 1944, 6, series I, box 3, folder 9, GHMC, Smithsonian.
52. FX-40, F42(1), "Radar, Aircraft—General," 1943, RG 38, box 6, NARA.
53. One outbound runner carrying mercury for the Japanese munitions industry now threatens the coastal environment of Norway. Torpedoed by a British submarine in February 1945 at the start of its clandestine voyage, *U-864* carried an estimated sixty-five tons of mercury in canisters stowed along its keel. See "Nazi U-Boat Imperils Norwegians Decades after the War," *New York Times,* 11 January 2007.
54. Dönitz, *Memoirs,* 239.
55. Morison, *Battle of the Atlantic,* 376–77.
56. Furthering its efforts to analyze all data and prepare operational advice, effective June 1943 the Cominch unit analyzed all contact and action reports against enemy submarines made by U.S. air and surface forces, worldwide.
57. *Cominch U-Boat Trends,* biweekly no. 1, 1 September 1942, RG 38, box 49, NARA. "IN ORDER TO PROTECTSOURCES,INFORMATIONCONTAINEDHEREINSHOULDBELIMITEDTOTHOSEWHONEEDTOKNOWX." Ibid.
58. *Cominch U-Boat Trends,* biweekly no. 2, 15 September 1942, RG 38, box 49, NARA.
59. *Cominch U-Boat Trends,* biweekly no. 21, 30 June 1943, RG 38, box 49, NARA.
60. *Cominch U-boat Trends,* biweekly no.19, 1 June 1943, RG 38, box 49, NARA.
61. Commander Fourth Fleet, memorandum via Commander Atlantic Fleet to CincUS, 23 August 1943, RG 38, box 43, NARA. Although ZP units soon were sharing Brazilian bases with VP (patrol) squadrons, no mention whatever is made of lighter-than-air in the document.
62. Excerpts from U-boat logs made by Lt. J. Gordon Vaeth, USNR, from captured German navy archives, Admiralty, London, series IV, box 17, folder 14, GHMC, Smithsonian. The Aphrodite was a German radar decoy balloon made of aluminum foil streamed from a hydrogen-filled India-rubber balloon. The device simulated the radar signature of a conning tower.
63. *Fleet Airship Wing Thirty Intelligence Bulletin* 15, n.d., series I, box 3, folder 6, GHMC, Smithsonian. Entler, a career-conscious officer of the regular navy, considered LTA duty a dead end and transferred to HTA. Vaeth, *Blimps and U-Boats,* 50. A number of senior LTA officers from early in the war requested orders for transfer into HTA or surface billets—career insurance.
64. So as to conserve materials and avoid unnecessary construction, existing facilities were exploited at base sites wherever possible.
65. Zimmerman, letter to Mills, 24 August 1943, series II, box 9, folder 11, GHMC, Smithsonian. Zimmerman was fresh from command of Wing Two at Richmond; there, on 28 July, during final squadron inspection (ZP-21), he had commended three of the downed aircrew from *K-74.* Conditions prevailing at advance bases in South America must be understood. The ninety-mile road connecting the port city of Belem to Igarape, for example, required five hours by car, five days for heavy equipment.
66. Total decrease in dead weight: 157 pounds "[This] may not be impressive taken alone, but this saving coupled with the weight of one less crew member will enable our ships to carry an additional bomb."

Fleet Airships Atlantic News Letter 9-43, 15 November 1943, series I, box 3, folder 8, GHMC, Smithsonian.

67. Grossnick, *Kite Balloons to Airships,* 50.
68. Both ferry flights had included layovers. *K-84* logged nine days of operational flying under the command of Fleet Airship Wing Five (Trinidad); *K-88* loitered in Amapa one day, to provide flight training for base personnel.
69. *Fleet Airship Wing Thirty Intelligence Bulletin* 15, n.d., series I, box 3, folder 6, GHMC, Smithsonian.
70. Morison, *Atlantic Battle Won,* 223.
71. Unidentified confidential document, 1 August 1944, series I, box 3, folder 3, GHMC, Smithsonian.
72. Vaeth, *Blimps and U-Boats,* 153.
73. On 3 May 1945, *K-51* took fire while on approach at NAS Santa Ana, California. Gasoline vapors still noticeable in the car, the Lawrance APU (auxiliary power unit) was ordered restarted in order to use the blower. A flash of flame inside the car promptly enveloped the ship. It crashed short of the mat—a total loss. The eight crew members were the only fatalities that year on either U.S. coast.
74. "Due to shortage of airship spares [ZP-23], no material that is salvageable should be discarded. All material, the salvage of which is beyond the capacity of the local facilities, should be sent to the nearest overhaul station." *Fleet Airships Atlantic Semi-Monthly News Letter* 5-43, 15 September 1943, series I, box 3, folder 8, GHMC, Smithsonian.
75. *Fleet Airships Atlantic Semi-Monthly News Letter* 9-43, 15 November 1943, 14, series I, box 3, folder 8, GHMC, Smithsonian. *K-128,* one might note, was delivered to Lakehurst in February 1944. That April, its ferry crew arrived in the steaming jungle (BlimpHedRon Four, Recife) with a complete set of *winter* flight gear.
76. "You could set your watch" by the afternoon cumulus, gathering moisture, expanding with the heat. Farther south, a one-ship detachment occupied Caravelas. "Caravelas," Zimmerman wrote, "is getting to be such a horrible place to live, with malarial mosquitoes and now with high winds blowing black dust into everything and alternating with heavy rains to make it black mud." Letter (handwritten), Zimmerman to Mills, 15 November 1944, series II, box 9, folder 11, GHMC, Smithsonian.
77. Delong interview.
78. *Fleet Airships Atlantic News Letters* 1-44, 1 January 1944, 28; and 6-44, 15 March 1944, 25; both series I, box 3, folder 9, GHMC, Smithsonian.
79. *K-68* had been investigating a combat action: HTA attacking a surfaced U-boat. One plane had circled, warning against too close an approach because of effective fire from the raider's deck gun. *Fleet Airship Atlantic Intelligence Bulletin* 5, 15 September 1943, series I, box 4, folder 5, GHMC, Smithsonian.
80. Parts of *K-68*'s "special equipment" were flown out: a blimp had lowered a line. The salvage crew was under former Goodyear barnstormer Lt. Cdr. John B. Rieker, USNR. "We didn't really suffer too much—on the job every day a blimp would lower a milk can full of ice and beer." Letter to author, 13 August 1977.
81. *Fleet Airships Atlantic Semi-Monthly News Letter* 1-44, 1 January 1944, 28, series I, box 3, folder 9, GHMC, Smithsonian. The humidity was such that "we had to put a light in our closet to keep our clothes from mildewing." McMillan interview.
82. For hangar-based ZNPs, a maintenance crew was divided into day and night sections. A 120-hour check required two days of hangar availability, an interim overhaul about two weeks in non-operational status.
83. Fleet Airships Atlantic, *Fabric Maintenance Manual for Non-Rigid Airships,* 18 December 1944, 17. Frequent visual inspections by ZP-14 overseas, in the Mediterranean (see chapter 7), disclosed no appreciable deterioration of envelope fabric or finish. Unless specially authorized, every ship underwent an interim overhaul prior to a thousand hours' operating time or six months' operation for hangar-based airships, or four months' operation if mast based, whichever was earlier.

84. Goodyear, *United States Navy Handbook for Fabric Repair and Maintenance of Airship Envelopes,* 1. Major overhauls were required after approximately 3,840 flight hours and consumed four to six weeks. It was necessary, however, to deflate ships based south of North Carolina more often than those assigned to midlatitude squadrons.
85. Mills, letter to P. W. Litchfield (Chairman of the Board, Goodyear Tire and Rubber Co.), 25 November 1943, series II, box 10, folder 22, GHMC, Smithsonian.
86. *Fleet Airships Atlantic Intelligence Bulletin* 7 [c. January–February 1944], 28, series I, box 4, folder 5, GHMC, Smithsonian.
87. *Fleet Airships Atlantic Semi-Monthly News Letter* 3-45, 1 February 1945, series I, box 4, folder 1, 1, GHMC, Smithsonian. In all, 3,712 ship-handling operations had been carried out by ZP-12 during 1944 without major mishap despite emergencies—a record worthy of commendation. *News Letter* 2-45, 15 January 1945, 12.
88. Squadron statistics: 17,771 patrol hours (7,343 in 1943, 10,428 in 1944) on 1,612 patrol flights, 158 escort flights for 1,810 hours, 281 ferry flights, 503 sorties for training, 402 night-escort flights (4,353 hours). Total flights: 3,132; total hours 33,554; number ships escorted, 3,012. Naval Airship Training and Experimental Command, *Statistical Summary.*
89. *Fleet Airships Atlantic News Letter* 6-44, 15 March 1944, 22, series I, box 33, folder 9, GHMC, Smithsonian.
90. Zimmerman, letter to Mills, 30 April 1944, series II, box 9, folder 11, GHMC, Smithsonian. Basing at Caravelas, for example, ceased in January 1945, when ComFourthFlt authorized discontinuance of air coverage in that sector.
91. Mills, memorandum to All Wing and Squadron Commanders, 6 May 1944, series II, box 33, folder 18, GHMC, Smithsonian.
92. Mills, memorandum to All Wing and Squadron Commanders, 10 June 1944, series II, box 33, folder 18, GHMC, Smithsonian.
93. King and Whitehill, *Fleet Admiral King,* 340–41; ComSouthGroup to ComEastSeaFron, 12 October 1943, series I, box 2, folder 31, GHMC, Smithsonian.
94. Headquarters Cominch, memoranda, 27 August 1943, RG 38, box 49, NARA. Attacks by blimps: two, probably slightly damaged; four, insufficient evidence of damage; six, no damage; forty-two, insufficient evidence of presence of submarine; nine, target not submarine; three, insufficient evidence to assess. A "doubtful" rating is assigned to 50 of 112 contacts.
95. ComBlimpRon 51 to O-in-C, BlimpRon 51, Detachments One, Two, and Three, 17 April 1944, series I, box 2, folder 55, GHMC, Smithsonian.
96. Admiral Rosendahl, in making the awards, remarked: "You cannot imagine how gratifying it is to those of us who carried LTA along in the lean years to see examples like this of how today's young Americans are adding laurels to the cause of lighter-than-air." *Airship,* 25 October 1944, 2.
97. "Air-Sea Rescue Show Thrills Spectators," *Airship,* 4 October 1944, 5.
98. Eppes interview. Eppes was commanding officer of ZJ-1, with additional duty as CO, Airship Anti-Submarine Training Detachment, NAS Key West.
99. The tight turning circle and better hovering ability of the G-type made it preferable to the "K". No special equipment was needed. "A G-ship with its normal complement of gear and personnel plus a convenient place to base it when it is not flying is all that is required." *Fleet Airships Atlantic Intelligence Bulletin* 2-45, [c. March 1945], 7, series I, box 4, folder 5, GHMC, Smithsonian.
100. Ibid., 1.
101. Mills, letter to Cope (NAS Richmond), 13 March 1945, series II, box 8, folder 12, GHMC, Smithsonian.
102. Commander Fleet Air, West Coast, memorandum to Commander Aircraft, Southern California Sector, Western Sea Frontier, 19 August 1945, series I, box 2, folder 38, GHMC, Smithsonian. The first sea-to-ZNP rescue was logged by *K-59* on 3 March 1944. Command pilot: Ens. Lowell E. Buys, USNR.

103. O-in-C, Blimp Squadron Forty-one, Det 1, to Commander, Blimp Squadron Forty-one, undated (February 1944?), GHMC, Smithsonian.
104. Bradley, letter to Mills, 29 August 1943, series II, box 8, folder 7, GHMC, Smithsonian.
105. Capt. Fred N. Klein, USN (Ret.), interview by author, 5 January 1983. A graduate of LTA Class 19, Lieutenant Commander Klein was (among other assignments) third skipper of ZP-33, at Tillamook, and commander of the first carrier-supported long-endurance flight by a nonrigid airship. He would serve continuously in LTA to 1962.
106. Klein interview. Surface units were likewise afflicted. "Destroyers and other anti-submarine vessels can become proficient only through far more work with actual submarines. Such results as eight or ten of our submarines might accomplish in Atlantic or Pacific waters seem to be of less importance in the war effort than increased skill of our anti-submarine units in combating the enemy submarine." Commander Destroyers, U.S. Atlantic Fleet, memorandum to C-in-C, U.S. Atlantic Fleet, 12 February 1943, box 3, RG 38, NARA.
107. Memorandum to Rosendahl, 23 June 1943 (copy to Mills and six senior LTA officers, e.g., George Watson and "Scotty" Peck).
108. Settle, memorandum to Rosendahl, 24 December 1943, series II, box 9, folder 18, GHMC, Smithsonian.
109. Naval aviators were aboard the target boats. "During training at the school I was assigned to an old . . . R type boat to observe the action taken by our submarine commanders to avoid attacks during training exercises. Nothing was required of me submerged, but to follow closely all the maneuvers ordered by the submarine captain to elude detection and bombing by the forces above." John A. Fahey (Cdr., USN, Ret.), *Wasn't I the Lucky One* (Virginia Beach, Va.: B and J Books, 2000), 42.
110. Mills, letter to Settle, 11 January 1944, series II, box 9, folder 29, GHMC, Smithsonian.
111. Wheeler interview.
112. *Fleet Airships Atlantic Intelligence Bulletin* 2-44 [c. March 1944]; *History of Atlantic Fleet Airship Operations,* 1 July 1944, series I, box 4, folder 5, GHMC, Smithsonian. The school wanted crews to have read a certain amount of relevant material before arriving at Key West.
113. "Airship A/S training has been so long neglected that it is felt no further time should be lost in providing for it such essential items as the magnetic attack trainer." CNATE to Coordinator Research and Development, 25 October 1943, RG 298, box 99, NARA. In January 1945, Rosendahl requested transfer of certain personnel and equipment at AIL so as to establish a "MAD Laboratory" under CNATE.
114. *Fleet Airships Atlantic Semi-Monthly News Letter* 20-44, 15 October 1944, 25, series I, box 3, folder 12, GHMC, Smithsonian.
115. Klein interview.
116. Eppes to Mills, 19 May 1944, series II, box 8, folder 18, GHMC, Smithsonian.
117. Letter report, Mills to Eppes, 22 May 1944, series II, box 8, folder 18, GHMC, Smithsonian.
118. Mills to Bradley, 10 January 1944, series II, box 8, folder 7, GHMC, Smithsonian.
119. *Cominch U-Boat Trends,* biweekly no. 32, 16 December 1943, RG 38, box 49, NARA.
120. Mills to Bradley.
121. "Lou" Ayers was awarded the Air Medal for piloting *K-65* to a wheel-landing rescue of two downed airmen in the Bahamas. "It was a type of rescue that would be repeated a number of times in jungle clearings, in mainland and island areas, on sandy beaches—indeed, wherever a low, flat, slow approach to survivors could be made. Often these rescue landings followed preliminary runs to test the firmness of the landing surface and to drop off a crew member who would instruct the survivors about how to handle the lines and board the airship." Vaeth, *Blimps and U-Boats,* 94–95.
122. "This is a bad day!" Bradley wrote the commodore. "Up to this time today two ships have tried to knock down hangars. Looks like hangars are an expensive luxury or that brains are not necessarily

an inherent quality of ground handling officers." Bradley to Mills, 17 February 1944, series II, box 8, folder 7, GHMC, Smithsonian.

123. *Fleet Airship Atlantic Semi-Monthly News Letter* 8-44, 15 April 1944, 3, series I, box 3, folder 10, GHMC, Smithsonian.
124. *Fleet Airships Atlantic Semi-Monthly News Letter* 11-44, 1 June 1944, 2, series I, box 3, folder 10, GHMC, Smithsonian.
125. Shannon interview.
126. "Consider special equipment. Fully three quarters of out time on the job is spent over a surfaced or submerged sub. The pilots take great pride in tracking down the sub and being right over it when it surfaces or periscopes." *Fleet Airships Atlantic Semi-Monthly News Letter* 20-44, 15 October 1944, 20, series I, box 3, folder 12, GHMC, Smithsonian.

Chapter 6. Mediterranean Squadron

1. Simmering army-navy "air problems" were settled in 1943: Army Air Forces resources assigned to service in the Atlantic were withdrawn from A/S operations by 1 October.
2. Loewenheim, et al., *Roosevelt and Churchill,* 121–22. This extract is from a 23 November 1940 message.
3. HQ Cominch, memorandum, 11 February 1943, RG 38, box 45, NARA.
4. Dönitz, *Memoirs,* 365–67.
5. "Factors Pertaining to the Use of MAD in the Straits of Gibraltar," with appendix "Effect of Changes in U/B Tactics," 11 January 1944, RG 298, box 99, NARA. An extension of a preliminary (December) study, the plan is an enclosure to an unknown document. "ASV" is air-to-surface vessel.
6. The difficulty of effective night air attacks largely explains this.
7. The magnetic disturbance (signal) decreases with increasing altitude. As for background noise, natural anomalies inherent to the strait were deemed unlikely, given the distances to possible magnetic material. Also, different current velocities at different depths would not interfere with MAD tracking techniques.
8. Sternhell and Thorndike, *Antisubmarine Warfare in World War II,* 50. That March–April, the status of work on surface MAD (either on board or towed) was assessed with a view to its possible application in the strait. "If this project is successful it might readily have general application, and would have immediate application in the Straits of Gibraltar possibly sooner than blimps could be made available." HQ Cominch, memorandum, 29 March 1944, RG 38, box 26, NARA.
9. Antiaircraft fire from shore batteries had become an "almost daily occurrence" for patrol aircraft outside of territorial waters, including airships. "Blimp has been instructed to remain 3 miles outside of Spanish Moroccan waters and to approach Tangier coast only when necessary." And, "Spanish government is requested to issue special instructions to all antiaircraft and coastal batteries strait area to insure that no unfortunate incidents occur." Naval message (extracts), 24 May 1944, Commander, Moroccan Sea Frontier, to Commander, Naval Forces North African Waters, RG 38, box 26, NARA.
10. "Use of MAD in the Straits of Gibraltar." (See endnote 5.)
11. Fleet Airship Wing Twenty, Instructions, 1942, series III, box 13, folder 7, GHMC, Smithsonian. Ships as much as a thousand pounds light were flown into the ground attempting to lose altitude in turns when trim was down by the bow. On 7 November 1943, ZNP *K-78* suffered major damage by approaching the mat at Lakehurst too low and then attempting a turn. "K-ship was not a paragon of virtue as far as aerodynamics is concerned." Rear Adm. Carl J. Seiberlich, USN (Ret.), undated conversation with author.
12. "Use of MAD in the Straits of Gibraltar" [emphasis added].

13. *Fleet Airships Atlantic Semi-Monthly News Letter* 2-44, 15 January 1944, series I, box 3, folder 9, GHMC, Smithsonian.
14. That April, Commander Patrol Wing Fifteen suggested that additional MAD-equipped planes would enable him to fly a double daylight fence on the strait. "A second and separate barrier, also maintained during daylight hours only, would so overlap as to assist in preventing night runs through the Straits. This would be helpful regardless of the decision as to blimps." Low, memorandum for the Admiral, 11 April 1944, RG 38, box 26, NARA.
15. MAD was highly classified; hence, use of the term "magnetic anomaly detector" was discouraged, because "the name revealed its nature and principal of operation. German submariners were apparently unaware it was being used against them!" J. Gordon Vaeth, letter in *Buoyant Flight: Bulletin of the Lighter-than-Air Society* 41, no. 5 (July–August 1994): 8.
16. CO, VP-63, secret report to Commander, Moroccan Sea Frontier, n.d., enclosure to ComMorSeaFron, memorandum to Cominch, 1 March 1944, RG 298, box 99, NARA. Routing slip remarks include, "Suggest routing around the office." The first service installation of retro-rockets (a Project Sail device) had gone to VP-63 in 1942.
17. *Cominch U-Boat Trends,* biweekly no. 37, 2 March 1944, RG 38, box 49, NARA.
18. A ZNP-K carried twenty-four float lights (2.2 pounds each) as disposable equipment.
19. *Cominch U-Boat Trends,* biweekly no. 37, 2 March 1944, RG 38, box 49, NARA.
20. CincMed, secret naval message to Admiralty, 25 April 1944, RG 38, box 26, NARA.
21. Dönitz, *Memoirs,* 367.
22. S. W. Roskill, *The War at Sea, 1939–1945*, 356. Between September 1941 and May 1944, Dönitz ordered ninety-five boats into the Mediterranean, sixty-two of which gained the basin. Ibid.
23. Naval Member Canadian Staff (Washington), message to Naval Service Headquarters, Ottawa, 22 February 1943, NAC, RG 24, vol. 11975. "British have also made request for squadron to be sent to Africa, but shortage of helium bottles may prevent this." As well, discussions were under way as to the question of operating U.S. blimps from bases in the Gulf of St. Lawrence or on the Atlantic coast of Canada.
24. ComNavNAW, naval message to Cominch and CNO, 24 March 1944, RG 38, box 26, NARA.
25. Memorandum for the Admiral, 27 March 1944, RG 38, box 26, NARA.
26. Memorandum, 28 March 1944, RG 38, box 26, NARA.
27. Letter to author, 23 December 1977.
28. ComNavNAW to Cominch, 6 May 1944, RG 38, box 26, NARA.
29. MAAF Algiers to Air Ministry, 6 May 1944, RG 38, box 26, NARA. "The great contention between the American and British Chiefs of Staff was, of course, over the Mediterranean campaign and its impact on Overlord." Noel Annan, "How Wrong Was Churchill?" *New York Review of Books,* 8 April 1993, 38.
30. Memorandum for FX-01, 7 May 1944, RG 38, box 26, NARA. "As result of earlier requests there is actually a Blimpron and all of its material standing by ready for immediate movement." Ibid.
31. Cominch to CincLant, 9 May 1944, RG 38, box 26, NARA.
32. A plan to furnish a maintenance hangar at Port Lyautey had been based on availability within four months. When it developed that one could not be made available in less than six months without special arrangements—too late to be useful—a revised plan assumed at least four months' operations without a hangar, perhaps six months.
33. Flight crews for the transatlantic run were changed at each stop. Six crews flew the ferrying operation; two took the ships from South Weymouth to Argentia and then returned to Massachusetts for the next pair. Similarly, two crews were assigned the middle leg to the Azores, another two from there to North Africa. "History of Blimp Squadron Overseas," undated, NASM Archives, file A3U-601500-02, Smithsonian, 4.

34. One portable helium purification unit was furnished to each advanced base. These were small, however, having a capacity of about 6,000 cu. ft. per hour—insufficient to act as a purging unit and measurably increase the purity of a low-purity ship. At Port Lyautey, two units would support its ZNP contingent.
35. Without maintenance crews, no pilot gets in the air. Port Lyautey had hosted HTA units. Of necessity, then, maintenance personnel, 128 men, were transferred as part of the LTA squadron. These included ground handlers as well as riggers, mechanics, and electronics specialists.
36. Kane interview.
37. Cdr. Ben B. Levitt, USN (Ret.), interview by author, 19 September 1997.
38. Forecasts for the benefit of airmen along the seaboard and over the North Atlantic had commenced in 1921, from Arlington; the U.S. broadcasts had full access to the regular Canadian observations as well as their own sources.
39. Kane interview.
40. *Fleet Airships Atlantic Intelligence Bulletin* 5-44, [c. June 1944)], series I, box 4, folder 5, GHMC, Smithsonian.
41. Roy D. Schickendanz, "Squadron Fourteen and the Transoceanic Crossing," *Buoyant Flight: Bulletin of the Lighter-than-Air Society* 18, no. 2 (January–February 1971): 5.
42. "History of Blimp Squadron Overseas," 8.
43. The third pair would be the fastest to cross. Average ground speed for its 3,145 nautical miles: 60.1 knots.
44. ComFairShipLant, secret naval message to ComNavZor and ComFairWing 15, 28 June 1944, RG 38, box 26, NARA.
45. Letter to Sullivan, 3 July 1944, series II, box 8, folder 56, GHMC, Smithsonian.
46. Vaeth, *Blimps and U-Boats,* 130.
47. *Fleet Airships Atlantic Intelligence Bulletin* 5-44, 15 August 1944, 4, series I, box 4, folder 5, GHMC, Smithsonian. Night vision—the ability to see well in very dim light—was integral to these missions. All nonessential lights within the aircraft were turned off; to assist dark adaptation all essential lights dimmed as much as possible.
48. Naval Airship Training and Experimental Command, *Statistical Summary.* Ferry and training flights added another 405 hours.
49. Hotham interview. The code word "Scram" was used for sightings of German aircraft. One night, so notified by his radioman, a ZP-14 pilot hit the throttles—when nose down, presumably. The airship hit the water. On port engine only, it returned to base, all hands mustered for emergency landing. "I remember the floodlights as he came into view, and there was a bomb still dangling out of the bomb bay. We radioed him to go back out to the ocean and kick out that bomb. And they did, and he landed safely." Ibid.
50. Naval Member Chiefs of Staff, naval message to Naval Service Headquarters, 22 February 1943, NARA of Canada, RG 24, vol. 11975.
51. See, for example, Roger Sarty, "Ultra, Air Power, and the Second Battle of the St. Lawrence, 1944," *To Die Gallantly,* ed. Runyan and Copes, part 3, chap. 12. Airships receive no mention. This second concentrated wave of U-boats in Canadian waters achieved little.
52. *Joint Report on Net Defence Policy of the First Sea Lord of the Admiralty and the Minister of War Transport,* 3 January 1945, RG 38, box 44, NARA.
53. *Cominch U-Boat Trends,* biweekly no. 51, 1 October 1944, RG 38, box 49, NARA.
54. Richard Boyle and Waldo Lyon, "Arctic ASW: Have We Lost?" U.S. Naval Institute *Proceedings* 124/6/1,144 (June 1998): 32.
55. "The test carried out with H.M. submarine 'VIKING' demonstrated the value of an intensive air patrol in producing an exhausted surfaced boat." RCN, Operational Research Report 24, NAC, Department of National Defence, Directorate of History and Heritage, Naval Historian's Files, 1650-239/16B, vol. 2.

56. Monthly Anti-Submarine Report C.B. 04050/44(9), quoted in "Minutes of 37th Meeting held at 1500 hours Thursday, 28th December, 1944," NAC, RG 24, vol. 5273.
57. Noakes, 204.
58. Mills to Bradley, 13 March 1944, series II, box 8, folder 7; Bolam to Mills, 27 April 1944, series II, box 8, folder 6; Bradley to Mills, 22 June 1944, series II, box 8, folder 7, GHMC, Smithsonian. Bolam doubted the airmanship of his equatorial colleagues. "I have found from hard experience," he wrote from South Weymouth, "that a majority of the pilots from the South are very poor airmen. They haven't had much to worry about. Long missions, heavy weather, and tough landing conditions are things they never heard of. Nearly every one has to have a near accident in order to get down to earth." At that time, ZP-11 had a reduced allowance of six ZNPs and ten combat crews. Ibid.
59. Rosendahl, letter to Capt. W. E. Zimmerman (Commander Fleet Airship Wing Four), 29 November 1944; Mills, letter to Zimmerman, 1 December 1944, series II, box 9, folder 11, GHMC, Smithsonian.
60. Julius Augustus Furer, *Administration of the Navy Department in World War II* (Washington, D.C.: Government Printing Office, 1979, 380–81.
61. That September, its first days of operations from France would have *K-112* riding out severe mistral weather—steady winds to forty knots, with gusts to sixty. Full preparations at the mast realized no damage.
62. Van Treuren, "Airships v. Submarines in WWII," *Airshipworld,* no. 50 (December 2001): 28; e-mail to author, 17 December 2006.
63. Sullivan to Mills, 13 August 1944, series II, box 8, folder 56, GHMC, Smithsonian.
64. Mills to Sullivan, 21 August 1944, series II, box 8, folder 56, GHMC, Smithsonian.
65. *Cominch U-Boat Trends,* biweekly no. 62, 16 March 1945, and no. 65, 2 May 1945, RG 38, box 49, NARA.
66. *Notes on the Operation of Nonrigid Airships* (Washington, D.C.: Government Printing Office, 1920; repr. NAS Lakehurst, 5 September 1939), 10.
67. Higham, *British Rigid Airship,* 121.
68. COW 6, naval message, to ComEastSeaFron, 11 August 1942, RG 38, box 46, NARA.
69. The port of New York was closed once, on 13–14 November 1942, upon discovery of mines some two miles southeast of Ambrose Light. Ten mines had been laid by *U-608*. Joseph F. Meany Jr., "Port of New York in World War II," in *To Die Gallantly,* ed. Runyan and Copes, 286. "With an absolute minimum expenditure of material, *U-608* closed the world's largest port to shipping for two days while sweepers cleared the channel of five mines." Arnold S. Lott, *Most Dangerous Sea* (Annapolis, Md.: Naval Institute Press, 1959), 48.
70. Rosendahl, letter (handwritten) to Mills, 6 April 1941, series II, box 9, folder 14, GHMC, Smithsonian. That same week, President Roosevelt had approved the first year's increment of the Navy Department's LTA program.
71. Mills to Sullivan, 7 September 1944, series II, box 9, folder 14, GHMC, Smithsonian. The increasing importance of air/sea rescue operations (see chapter 7) conferred useful practice in hovering, slow, low-altitude flying—and long, low approaches to targets.
72. Preparations to abandon ship for ZNPs: urgent message radioed to base and surface craft, life rafts broken out, exits cleared, emergency gear collected. Frequent drills ensured that every crew member knew his job.
73. *Fleet Airships Atlantic Semi-Monthly News Letter* 8-43, 1 November 1943, 4–5, series 1, box 3, folder 8, GHMC, Smithsonian.
74. "Whether the finding of the Court of Inquiry was directed by higher authority I shall never know. But it was obvious that the court wanted no record of any sub attack in those waters. At the hearing they admitted no evidence except that obtained from interrogating the survivors. . . . It would not even accept in evidence the written statement of the technicians that they found many bullet holes

in the fabric, presumably 40-millimeter. When the bag was spread out on the field they were able to determine that the bullets entered the bag aft of the car and exited at the top amidships." Alexander W. Moffat, *A Navy Maverick Comes of Age* (Middletown, Conn.: Wesleyan University Press, 1977), 95. During 1942–44, Moffat was Commander, Northern Sea Lane Patrol, Northern Group, Eastern Sea Frontier.

75. "The pilot on the elevator at the time of the accident was a command pilot with a great deal of experience. This type of accident can be attributed only to carelessness and very sloppy flying." *Fleet Airships Atlantic Semi-Monthly News Letter,* 1 October 1944, 22, series I, box 3, folder 12, GHMC, Smithsonian.
76. "Considering how often airships were handled on the ground in gusty winds, on small mats, with tricky hangar spillovers, by tired men who had to keep their footing in water, in mud, or on ice, it is remarkable that there were not more accidents involving members of the ground crews. There were the ever present dangers of spinning propellers and dangling handling lines to watch out for." Vaeth, *Blimps and U-Boats,* 157.
77. Letter to author, 20 July 1993.
78. *Fleet Airships Atlantic Intelligence Bulletin* 8-44, 25 November 1944, 2, series 1, box 4, folder 5, GHMC, Smithsonian. "Radar contact was made on Minorca thus giving an accurate check at the half-way mark across the Mediterranean." Ibid.
79. Vaeth, *Blimps and U-Boats,* 138.
80. *Fleet Airships Atlantic Intelligence Bulletin* 8-44, 25 November 1944, series 1, box 4, folder 5, GHMC, Smithsonian. "After some weeks, we successfully located all the mines, and then proceeded to guide the French minesweepers by radio and loud-hailer out of the stern of the cabin of the blimp." McMillan, letter to author, 20 July 1993.
81. Lott, *Most Dangerous Sea,* 205.
82. Ibid.
83. Joining the escort, ZNP *K-101* swept ahead of the task force conveying President Franklin Roosevelt (in February 1945) to Yalta, to confer with Prime Minister Churchill and Premier Stalin. *K-109* acted as escort on the return.
84. Vaeth, *Blimps and U-Boats,* 141, 143.
85. *Fleet Airships Atlantic Intelligence Bulletin* 3-45, March 1945, 3, series I, box 4, folder 5, GHMC, Smithsonian.
86. Naval Airship Training and Experimental Command, *Statistical Summary.*
87. CincMed, naval message to Admiralty and ComNavNAW, 7 November 1945, series I, box 2, folder 39, GHMC, Smithsonian.
88. ComNavNAW, naval message to ComNavEU, and to CNO, COMMORGE, ComNavNAW (ADM) and ComNavNAW (Naples), 7 November 1945, series I, box 2, folder 39, GHMC, Smithsonian.
89. Hewitt to SecNav, 1 April 1947, series I, box 2, folder 39, GHMC, Smithsonian.

Chapter 7. Pacific Coast Operations and Atlantic Finale

1. Grahame F. Shrader, *The Phantom War in the Northwest: And an Account of Japanese Submarine Operations on the West Coast 1941–1942* (1969), 34; Rosendahl, "How Soon We Forget," 3.
2. HQ, Northwest Sea Frontier, operational order, 12 December 1941, in Shrader, *Phantom War in the Northwest.*
3. Rosendahl, "How Soon We Forget," chap. 9, 6. The discussion of I-boat operations in 1941–42 is from this source, 1–6.
4. Marvin Lasky, "Review of Scientific Effort for Undersea Warfare: 1939–1945," *U.S. Navy Journal of Underwater Acoustic Technology* 25 (July 1975): 574. For an extended discussion, Mark R. Peattie,

"Japanese Strategy and Campaigns in the Pacific War, 1941–1945," in *World War II in Asia and the Pacific and War's Aftermath, with General Themes: A Handbook of Literature and Research,* ed. Loyd E. Lee (Westport, Conn.: Greenwood, 1998).

5. *Periodic Summary of the Anti-U-Boat Campaign 19.* Japan, for its part, had little exact knowledge about U.S. submarines.
6. Interview by author, 27 June 1999. "The Japanese Navy's cavalier attitude toward the U.S. undersea force also arose from misunderstanding the vital role merchant shipping played in winning a war. They credited their potential enemies with the same mentality." Gordon W. Prange, with Donald M. Goldstein and Katherine V. Dillon, *Pearl Harbor: The Verdict of History* (New York: McGraw-Hill, 1986), 510.
7. Widdicombe interview.
8. Baxter, *Scientists against Time,* 49. By 1922, one should note, Japan had created the world's third-largest navy.
9. Cominch and CNO, memorandum to All Ships and Stations, 7 June 1943, RG 298, box 97, NARA.
10. Fromm, "Magnetic Airborne Detector," 267–68.
11. Charles Kittel, SORG, memorandum to Capt. C. C. Smith, F-4253, 21 February 1945, RG 298, box 99, NARA.
12. Lasky, "Review of Scientific Effort for Undersea Warfare, 1939–1945," 575.
13. Bradley interview.
14. Memorandum for Admiral King, 26 December 1941, series I, box 2, folder 13, GHMC, Smithsonian. "We hate to see the ships go," Mills remarked, "because we certainly need them here, but if they need them worse out there that is up to the Navy Department."
15. Greenslade to Rosendahl, 17 December; Rosendahl, memorandum to King, 26 December; Rosendahl to Greenslade, 26 December 1941, series II, box 8, folder 46, GHMC, Smithsonian.
16. CNO, memorandum to Chief BuNav and Chief BuAer, 29 December 1941, series II, box 10, folder 2, GHMC, Smithsonian.
17. Ulrich interview; McMillan interview.
18. A survey was conducted for establishing expeditionary bases to support transcontinental delivery of K-ships. As well, a Ferry Command was set up for acceptance and test of airships delivered from Akron to Lakehurst and then the ferrying of ships assigned to the continental squadrons. Officer in charge: Cdr. E. J. Sullivan, USN. Capt. Emmett J. Sullivan, USN (Ret.), letter to author, 12 December 1975.
19. McMillan interview. Lakehurst's weather was far from ideal; the station's war diary records fourteen flying days in October 1944, for example. Training flights that month: thirty-seven.
20. That April, *L-8* was ordered to drop three hundred pounds of air freight onto the deck of USS *Hornet* (CV 8)—parts for Lt. Col. J. H. Doolittle's bombers used in attacking the Japanese homeland.
21. Charles M. Bowen, letter to author, n.d.
22. Greenslade, letter to Rosendahl, 23 May 1942, series II, box 9, folder 17, GHMC, Smithsonian.
23. Kane interview.
24. R. F. Tyler, memorandum to Commander, Airship Group One (Mills), 16 April 1942, series II, box 9, folder 17, GHMC, Smithsonian.
25. Cdr. Harold W. Johnston, USN (Ret.), letter to author, 20 August 1999. Johnston's official statement adds this: "A guard was immediately placed on the ship and the radioman was placed in charge of the confidential gear armed with a pistol borrowed from the army."
26. Ibid.
27. *Wall Street Journal,* 21 June 2000.
28. Interview by author, 1 August 2004, Whitehouse Station, New Jersey.
29. Mills, letter to Watson, 8 August 1942, series II, box 9, folder 6, GHMC, Smithsonian.

30. M. L. Shettle Jr., *United States Naval Air Stations of World War II,* 2nd ed. (Brownsville, Ga.: Schaertel, 1997), vol. 2, 213. In May–June 1943, two auxiliary sites were established: at Lompoc, northwest of Los Angeles, and at Del Mar, just north of San Diego. Ibid.
31. Transition from the Mark II to Mark IV-B design had occurred in June, when the latter went into limited production. The navy—procuring agency for all MAD equipment for the armed services—had ordered 218, the army 260, the British 4. Improvements in weight and performance incorporated into the Type VI and Type X rendered the Mark IV-B obsolescent by spring 1943.
32. Series II, box 8, folder 46, GHMC, Smithsonian.
33. Sullivan, letter to author.
34. Grossnick, *Kite Balloons to Airships,* 39–40.
35. Fleet Airships Atlantic, *Confidential Intelligence Bulletin 2,* 8 August 1943, series I, box 4, folder 5, GHMC, Smithsonian.
36. Commander Battle Force, memorandum to C-in-C, U.S. Fleet (CincUS), 29 April 1939, GFC, Smithsonian. Noting their "enormous improvements" since 1918 and the relative effectiveness of airplanes, CincUS reiterated nonetheless that assignment of blimps to the fleet was "not desired and is again not recommended." CincUS to SecNav, 11 May 1939, ibid. E. J. King, then a vice admiral, was Commander Aircraft, Battle Force.
37. Shrader, *Phantom War in the Northwest,* 58.
38. Rosendahl (CNATE), letter to Settle (Moffett Field), 30 November 1943, series II, box 10, folder 2, GHMC, Smithsonian.
39. The U.S. Navy conducted coordinated mine warfare against Japan, including its home waters. In contrast, "no Japanese mines were laid off any West Coast port, although during the last year of the war, drifters from Empire waters began to arrive on the Japan Current." Lott, *Most Dangerous Sea,* 58.
40. Norman Polmar, e-mail to author, 24 September 2006. The archival record was not examined in depth for a definitive analysis. The author is nonetheless confident that no senior Pacific command had advocated deployment.
41. Grossnick, *Kite Balloons to Airships,* 64.
42. Rosendahl, letter to C. J. Maguire (Navy Department), 9 October 1943, series II, box 9, folder 18, GHMC, Smithsonian. "Consequently, it is my feeling that we should be definitely planning on giving him as many ships here in the Atlantic as we possibly can." Ibid.
43. Planning Directive 3-ZZ-44, CNO to ComAirPac, ComAirLant, and Chief, BuAer, 10 November 1944, Washington Navy Yard, Washington, D.C.
44. OP-31, memorandum to OP-03, undated (1944—September?), "LTA Deployment upon the Defeat of Germany," HOAC, box 161, F8; memorandum, CNATE to Cominch and CNO, "Employment of Airships after Defeat of Germany," 27 October 1944, ibid.
45. A/S Measures Conference no. 32, 25 July 1944, RG 38, box 49, NARA.
46. *Cominch U-Boat Trends,* biweekly no. 35, 2 February 1944, RG 38, box 49, NARA.
47. Meigs, *Slide Rules,* 196.
48. *Cominch U-Boat Trends,* biweekly no. 60, 15 February 1945, RG 38, box 49, NARA.
49. "Joint Report of Net Defence Policy by the First Sea Lord of the Admiralty and the Minister of War Transport," 3 January 1945, RG 38, box 44, NARA.
50. Office of War Information, press release, 9 July 1944, RG 38, box 48, NARA.
51. Pre-*schnorkel,* boats had to surface when charging. (The batteries were quickly exhausted during high-speed surface runs.) The diesel engine revolved the motor armature on the main shaft. The motor then became a dynamo and supplied electricity to the batteries. On patrol, the necessity of surfacing to charge batteries was an ever-present source of anxiety, in periods of long daylight and bright moonlight particularly.
52. Brown, *Radar History,* 347.

53. Karl Heinz Kurzak, "German U-Boat Construction," U.S. Naval Institute *Proceedings* 81, no. 4 (April 1955): 384.
54. *Cominch U-Boat Trends,* biweekly no. 51, 1 October 1944, RG 38, box 49, NARA.
55. *Cominch U-Boat Trends* biweekly no. 57, 2 January 1945, RG 38, box 49, NARA.
56. Buchheim, *U-Boat War.*
57. In general, areas having sandy or gravel-type lithology and (early in the war) depth of less than about three hundred feet were suitable for submarines to bottom.
58. Designated "AAA," the project was overriding—of highest priority—and urgently needed. "It must be prosecuted with utmost vigor with a view to placing in service in the shortest possible time." Commander, Tenth Fleet, memorandum to Commander, Anti-Submarine Development Detachment (ASDevLant), 22 April 1945, RG 38, box 17, NARA. Urgently needed as well: an attack procedure for use against submarines capable of diving to eight hundred feet and submerged speeds up to fifteen knots—that is, the Type XXI.
59. RG 38, box 97, NARA.
60. CNO, naval message, 6 March 1945, RG 38, box 44, NARA. Tests of the effectiveness of then-operational radars against *schnorkels* were ordered—a comparison of maximum ranges under various sea conditions having "particular interest."
61. *Cominch U-Boat Trends*, biweekly no. 46, 15 July 1944, RG 38, box 49, NARA.
62. *Cominch U-Boat Trends,* biweekly no. 53, 1 November 1944, RG 38, box 49, NARA. "The advent of these new U-boats would have revolutionized submarine warfare." Morison, *Battle of the Atlantic,* 86.
63. Albert Speer, *Inside the Third Reich* (New York: Macmillan, 1970), 273.
64. Ibid., 274. Facilities at French ports were such that, home waters astern, U-boats seldom returned to Germany.
65. David Muller and John Jordan, *Modern Submarine Warfare* (New York: Military, 1987), 37. "So advanced was the XXI design that it became the template for all immediate postwar submarines commissioned in the U.S., British, and Soviet Union navies. But it never got into the war at hand." Gannon, *Black May,* 387–88.
66. *Cominch U-Boat Trends*, biweekly no. 64, 15 April 1945, RG 38, box 49, NARA.
67. Canada was contributing in both the eastern and western Atlantic. In May 1944, the total hours flown by RCAF squadrons attached to Coastal Command in the United Kingdom was 1,337 hours, sixteen minutes. Canadian Joint Staff (Washington), letter to Tenth Fleet, 1 July 1944, box 45, RG 38, NARA.
68. Air Chief Marshal Douglas, letter to Secretary, the Admiralty, 6 April 1945. Blimp escorts over a convoy, the wing opined, would not aid the enemy in detecting inshore traffic, because the convoy lanes there were doubtless known. The wing was eager to apply the blimp's "great deterrent effect."
69. The CNO had ordered two ZNPs ferried to Port Lyautey. Caught by freak local cyclone, *K-109* had been lost there on 26 March when it (and *K-130*) had kited violently to the vertical. Breaking free from its mast, which overturned, *K-109* crashed and burned to destruction. *K-130* withstood the kiting and subsequent impact without major damage. (The pressure watches had jumped clear.) *K-89* and *K-114* reached Africa on 1 May, having established a world record for long-distance flight for its type: 1,900 miles nonstop (the longest leg of the ferry route) in twenty-nine hours, thirty-eight minutes.
70. This despite its RCN members being "extremely worried about the forecasted German underwater offensive." Air Member for Air Staff, memorandum to Chief of Air Staff, 12 March 1945, NAC, RG 24, vol. 5273.
71. Mills to Zimmerman, 20 April 1945, series II, box 9, folder 11, GHMC, Smithsonian.
72. "With the situation developing in Europe as it is, it begins to look as though we had better start our plans for the next personnel reduction based on having to cut back the Atlantic units as per the latest

existing directive, and not contemplating any further expansion into the Pacific, or elsewhere. . . . Accordingly, I wish you would quietly begin the study of personnel to be released when European hostilities fold up and we are required to cut back East Coast activities and LTA personnel in general." Rosendahl, letter to Coulter, 27 March 1945, series II, box 9, folder 19, GHMC, Smithsonian. Capt. Howard Coulter, USN, was then Commander, Fleet Airships, Pacific.

73. U.S. Atlantic Fleet, Air Force, Fleet Air Wing Seven, "Summary of Discussions on the Practicability of Using Lighter than Air Craft Based in the British Isles," 16 April 1945.
74. *Cominch U-Boat Trends*, biweekly no. 46, 15 July 1944, RG 38, box 49, NARA.
75. Wheeler interview.
76. In all, 9,300 V-1s were fired against England alone, about six thousand of which reached the English coast. The first V-2 fell on London (from Holland) that September. Walter Dornberger, *V-2*, trans. James Cleugh and Geoffrey Halliday [New York: Viking, 1958], 267–68. Major General Walter Dornberger was the commanding officer of the Rocket Research Institute at Peenemünde, on Germany's Baltic coast.
77. (London) Journal no. 360 (W-4044), 4 September 1943, RG 38, box 44, NARA.
78. Fromm, "Personal Reminiscences." In September 1944, the V-2 rocket debuted. To counter the radio-command guidance used in early models, AIL built a ground-based jammer (the AN/ARQ-11), of which eleven were delivered in 1944–45.
79. Dornberger, *V-2*, 246.
80. Ibid., 246–47. One reference claims "at least" twelve towable devices were actually built at the end of the war. Marvin Lasky, "Historical Review of Undersea Warfare Planning and Organization 1945–1960 with Emphasis on the Role of the Office of Naval Research," *U.S. Navy Journal of Underwater Acoustics* 26, no. 2 (April 1976): 329.
81. Wheeler interview.
82. Commander Task Group 02.8, confidential letter to Commander, Eastern Sea Frontier (enclosure A), 1 September 1944, box 155, file F1, HOAC.
83. Rosendahl (CNATE) to C-in-C, United States Fleet and CNO, 27 October 1944, HOAC, box 161, F8.
84. Admiralty, naval message to A.G.M. Home and Abroad (A or R), 28 September 1943, RG 38, box 44, NARA.
85. "Commander C. R. Todd's Visit to NDRC Conference, Dec. 10, 1941," RG 38, box 24, NARA. See Gannon, *Black May*, 340–46, for development and first operational use.
86. "The Bell Telephone Laboratories engineers have continued using the New London Laboratory facilities, and the complete time of one engineer for this project." *OSRD Bi-Weekly Report*, 24 August–5 September 1942, RG 38, box 24, NARA.
87. Conference on Anti-Submarine Warfare, 20 October 1942, RG 38, box 24, NARA; Gannon, *Black May*, 342.
88. Watson (Tenth Fleet), letter to Rosendahl, 3 October 1943, series II, box 9, folder 18, GHMC, Smithsonian.
89. CNATE to CNO, 10 July 1944, RG 38, box 44, NARA. CNATE had cognizance over airship experimentation and development with the exception of ASW projects, which were under the jurisdiction of Commander, Tenth Fleet.
90. Vaeth interview.
91. Vaeth, *Blimps and U-Boats*, 63; Gannon, *Black May*, 341–42. "Even the aircrews employing the weapon were not to be told anything about its operation other than the drill required for maintaining, arming, and releasing it." Gannon, *Black May*, 344.
92. Norman Polmar, e-mail to author, 18 October 2007.
93. Rosendahl, "How Soon We Forget," chap. 8, 9.

94. ABCM George W. Roberts, USN (Ret.), letter to author (with enclosures), 28 September 2005. "We did have a lot of training on the use of sonobuoys." James H. Hughes, letter to author, 8 December 2005.
95. The frigate was unfamiliar with the blimp's attack procedure, its equipment, its ordnance. "Subsequent favorable indications as a result of the airship's attack were not informative to the surface craft." Commander Eastern Sea Frontier, memorandum to Cominch, 1 May 1945, courtesy James H. Hughes.
96. Roberts letter. As in the Navy's sound schools, training of LTA combat crews for weapon deployment had included recordings of cavitation created by the rotating blades of U-boat propellers.
97. Ibid.
98. Once it was marked with a buoyed line, a diver from Navy salvage descended to the boat (127 feet) to confirm. He reported massive damage to the hull and bodies strewn about inside. Today, scuba divers routinely dive to the hulk of *U-853*. Clay Blair, *Hitler's U-Boat War: The Hunters 1939–1942* (New York: Random House, 1996). *U-879* has yet to be located—and dived on. Stern damage would confirm a Mark XXIV "kill" for LTA.
99. *Fleet Airships Atlantic Semi-Monthly News Letter* 5-45, 1 March 1945, 12–13, series I, box 4, folder 1, GHMC, Smithsonian.
100. *U-1228* was snorkel equipped. *U-234* (a minelayer) held a cargo of war materials: mercury and uranium—and blueprints for production in Japan of the V-1 and V-2 rockets and of the Messerschmitt 262. See Moffat, *Navy Maverick,* chap. 15.
101. Record Group 38, box 97, NARA.
102. Zimmerman, letter to Mills, 31 January 1945, series II, box 9, folder 11, GHMC, Smithsonian. The detachment at Fernando de Noronha was being eliminated, leaving its equipment. Also, the squadron had ceased to base a ZNP at Caravelas: ComFourthFlt had authorized discontinuance of air coverage in that area.
103. Rosendahl, letter to Zimmerman, 29 November 1944, series II, box 9, folder 11, GHMC, Smithsonian. "For some reason," Mills wrote, "it appears the officers are not catching on." Personal letter, Mills to Zimmerman, 1 December 1944.
104. Zimmerman, personal letter to Rosendahl, 17 May 1945, series II, box 9, folder 11, GHMC, Smithsonian.
105. "My most optimistic estimate is that the Atlantic LTA organization will consist of two ZPs, one airship utility squadron, plus the Lakehurst training and experimental ships. Lakehurst and Richmond would be the only NAS (LTA) remaining open." Rosendahl, letter to Zimmerman, 29 November 1944, series II, box 9, folder 11, GHMC, Smithsonian.
106. Mills was to recommend an award as well for Zimmerman's "outstanding courage and tenacity of purpose" in establishing operations in a new area. "By his superb leadership [as Commander Airship Group Two], sound judgment and personal example in unusually long hours of work he brought his unit to a high degree of efficiency and so indoctrinated them that not one day of flight was missed in areas then infested with enemy submarines." Mills to SecNav, 7 June 1946, series II, box 9, folder 11, GHMC, Smithsonian.
107. Personal letter, series II, box 9, folder 11, GHMC, Smithsonian.
108. Zimmerman, personal letter (handwritten) to Mills, 27 August 1945; letter, Mills to Zimmerman, 19 September 1945, series II, box 9, folder 11, GHMC, Smithsonian.

Chapter 8. The Performance

1. Commander Task Force Three, memorandum U.S. Atlantic Fleet (Jonas H. Ingram) to CNO, 26 February 1942, RG 298, box 96, NARA.

2. Capt. George P. Sotos, USN, "Comment and Discussion: A Future for the Destroyer?" U.S. Naval Institute *Proceedings* 98, no. 1/827 (January 1972): 86.
3. Eppes interview; Widdicombe interview.
4. Smith, *The Airships* Akron *and* Macon, 171.
5. Kane interview. An HTA officer concurs. "Briefly, the reason for the failure of the [rigid] airship to continue in the Navy was that there simply was not enough money available. The Heavier-than-Air people were livid when money was taken from their development programs . . . and rightly so. They did not have enough period." Rear Adm. D. Ward Harrigan, USN (Ret.), letter to author, 29 February 1972. Then, Lieutenant Harrigan was a primary figure in hook-on development for ZRs and was senior aviator of the HTA unit attached to USS *Akron.*
6. Pierce interview.
7. Klein interview. The loss of three U.S.-built rigid airships (1925–35), one notes, resulted primarily from *operational* rather than design or construction failures.
8. Ulrich interview; memorandum, Tyler to Mills, 25 May 1943, series II, box 10, folder 2, GHMC, Smithsonian; Pierce interview; Delong interview.
9. "In general, there seems to be something lacking in the basic training program, particularly in regard to the officers. Most of our woes have been directly attributable to a failure on the part of a great number of the officer students to exercise intelligence, initiative, or a sense of responsibility." Eppes, letter to Mills, 19 May 1944, series II, box 8, folder 18, GHMC, Smithsonian.
10. "Personnel," box 151, F-9, HOAC, F-8.
11. John McCormick (CO, ZP-22), letter to Mills, 26 May 1943; Mills, letter to Zimmerman, 18 February 1946. "The average line officer," Rosendahl observed, "gets into his own rut and seldom makes any effort to learn anything else than his own particular endeavor." Rosendahl, letter to Mills, 26 August 1940, series II, box 9, folder 13, GHMC, Smithsonian.
12. Watson, letter to Rosendahl, 3 October 1943, series II, box 9, folder 18, GHMC, Smithsonian.
13. Settle, memorandum to distribution list, 15 August 1947, author files. Mills shared this concern. "An organization is only as good as the personnel who compose it. In this respect practically all of our accidents can be attributed to personal errors." Address to Class 3-44, 2 March 1944, series VI, box 22, folder 8, GHMC, Smithsonian.
14. Vaeth, *Blimps and U-Boats,* 172. This is from Dönitz's letter to Vaeth. Douglas H. Robinson was preeminent among historians of German airships. His sources notwithstanding, "I have been unable to obtain any German comments on the effectiveness of the American pressure airships in anti-submarine warfare." Douglas H. Robinson, "The Effectiveness of the Dirigible in Military Operations." American Aviation Historical Society *Journal* 19, no. 4 (4th Quarter 1974): 284.
15. ComEastSeaFron, naval message to ComBlimpRons 15, 24, and 11, 16 May 1945, series I, box 1, folder 12, GHMC, Smithsonian.
16. Morison, *Battle of the Atlantic,* 251. He adds: "The writer has spent a good deal of time talking with lighter-than-air advocates in the Navy, and even went on one patrol out of South Weymouth to find out how they operated; his somewhat gloomy conclusions as to their usefulness were reluctantly reached after much cogitation." As for sighting an airship, efforts to eliminate the glint from the aluminized envelopes proved inconclusive.
17. Vaeth, *Blimps and U-Boats,* 172.
18. Archival burrowing has found support for this hoary assessment. See Van Treuren, "U.S. Navy Airships v. Submarines in World War II," *Airshipworld,* series (March 2001–December 2003). Confirmed ZNP/U-boat contacts are obscured by faulty record keeping (particularly in the early months), insufficient evidence, and fallible assessments—conducted, often, well after the contact. Misleading translations ("flying boat" for "airship") further blur an accurate tally. Tenth Fleet files comprise millions of pages. Also, neither the U.S. nor the German U-boat archive has proven infallible. See for

example Gary Gentile, *Shadow Divers Exposed: The Real Saga of U-869* (Philadelphia: Bellerophon Bookworks, 2006), 40.

19. MAD reveals the presence of *any* large, submerged metallic body. Playing it safe, ZNPs often attacked on signal, including night and poor-visibility actions. This helps to explain the large number of "Insufficient Evidence" and "Target Not Submarine" assessments.
20. E-mail to author, 13 September 2004; (Polmar) "Historic Aircraft," *Naval History* (October 2005): 14.
21. Series I, box 2, folder 40, GHMC, Smithsonian. Naval air stations and their squadrons had absorbed a great deal of manpower. An operating base for coverage in the western Gulf, NAS Hitchcock was placed in commission (May 1943) with twenty officers, thirty-three Marines, and 107 enlisted men. Its squadron, ZP-23, was commissioned with thirty-one officers and 119 enlisted men.
22. Brief for the Defense of the Gulf of Mexico—Caribbean Area (Summary), War Department, Military Intelligence Service, 2 July 1942, RG 38, box 23, NARA.
23. Morison, *Battle of the Atlantic,* 249.
24. DCNO (Air) (J. S. McCain), memorandum to VCNO, 27 August 1943, box 161, file F-8, HOAC.
25. More than 500 were incorporated into the workhorse K-type ZNP patrol platform.

Epilogue

1. Brown, *Radar History,* 335.
2. As of 30 June 1945, thirty K-ships were assigned to fleet airship (patrol) squadrons, thirty-eight to utility and air-sea rescue, seven to training; thirty-two were in storage. Three "Mike" ships were operating with patrol squadrons, one consigned to training. The L-ships: two for training, nineteen in storage. G-ships: four assigned to utility and air-sea rescue, one for training, two in storage. Airships in inventory: 139. HOAC, box 150, F11.
3. Commander in Chief, U.S. Atlantic Fleet (Jonas H. Ingram), memorandum to CNO, 13 April 1945. In 1946, proposal was made for dual LTA-HTA training. Objective: to better integrate lighter-than-air into the naval service.
4. In 1944, Goodyear had proposed a ten-million-cubit-foot troop transport or hospital airship. After the war, this became a passenger and freight airship proposal.
5. If Admiral King, as Cominch, had thought the ZRCV airship practicable in the circumstances prevailing early in 1942, he could probably have forced the issue.
6. Mills, letter to Zimmerman, 14 August 1945, series II, box 9, folder 11, GHMC, Smithsonian; box LTA subject file (C–E), Naval Historical Center, Washington Navy Yard, Washington, D.C.
7. See, for example, Stuart W. Leslie, "Profit and Loss: The Military and MIT in the Postwar Era," *Historical Studies in the Physical and Biological Sciences* (Berkeley: University of California Press for the Office for History of Science and Technology, 1990), vol. 21, part 1, 60, 62–63; and "Global Warming, Cold War, and the Evolution of Research Plans," in ibid., vol. 27, part 2, 332.
8. Russell I. Mason, Columbia University, Division of War Research, USN Underwater Sound Laboratory, New London, letter to Cdr. S. W. Townsend, USN, NATEC, 14 May 1945, series II, box 8, folder 59, GHMC, Smithsonian.
9. K-ships engaged in at least two dozen combats with U-boats, research has revealed, inflicting damage in at least eight attacks. See Van Treuren, "Airships v. Submarines in WW II," *Airshipworld,* no. 58 (December 2003): 19. "Its disappointing, of course, that no airship scored a one-on-one U-boat kill—but what can you expect when doctrine called for it to stay upwind and away from surfaced targets?" J. Gordon Vaeth, letter to author, 12 July 2007.
10. *Airship* (Autumn 1947): 9, courtesy Lt. Harris F. Smith, USN (Ret.).
11. Cdr. Henry Spicer, letter to Capt. George H. Mills, 11 June 1946, series I, box 8, folder 51, GHMC, Smithsonian. Spicer was then in the office of CNO.

Bibliography

THE WRITER HAS RELIED primarily on original archival sources. Particularly useful were the navy records held by the National Archives and Records Administration (cited as NARA) and the personal papers (collections) donated to, and now organized by, the Smithsonian Institution. The Operational Archives at the Naval Historical Center, in Washington, D.C., hold a wealth of material; for this project, records pertaining to the establishment of lighter-than-air operations in South America were particularly useful.

Decades of oral-history research (audio-recorded) with surviving principals inform this work, as does an extensive, wide-ranging correspondence.

These sources are supplemented with published works: primary and selected secondary sources essential to establish context, corroborate background information, and support with factual description. Additional miscellaneous (but invaluable) materials from a host of individuals were useful in rounding out the narrative.

Primary Unpublished Sources

National Archives and Records Administration

Record Group [hereafter RG] 38, Records of the Office of the Chief of Naval Operations, NARA.

RG 72, Bureau of Aeronautics, Formerly Confidential Correspondence (1922–1944), NARA.

RG 80, General Records of the Department of the Navy (1798–1947), NARA.

RG 227, Records of the Office of Scientific Research and Development, NARA.

RG 298, Records of Office of Naval Research/National Defense Research Committee, General Correspondence, 1941–1946, NARA.

RG 313, Records of Naval Operating Forces, NARA.

Smithsonian Institution (National Air and Space Museum)

Fulton [Cdr. Garland, USN (Ret.)] Collection, National Air and Space Museum [hereafter NASM] Archives, Smithsonian Institution (Garber facility, Suitland, Maryland).

Hunsaker [Dr. and Cdr. Jerome C.] Collection (partial), NASM Archives, Smithsonian Institution (Garber).

Mills [Commo. George H., USN (Ret.)] Collection, NASM Archives, Smithsonian Institution (Garber).

National Archives of Canada

Department of National Defence, RG 24 E1, vol. 5202.

Department of National Defence, Directorate of History and Heritage, Naval Historian's files, 193.009 D21/C.S.C. Misc. Memoranda July 43/vol. 20.

Naval Historical Center, Washington, D.C.

Lighter-than-Air Collection, Operational Archives Branch, Naval Historical Center, Washington Navy Yard, Washington, D.C.

University of Texas at Dallas (Richardson, Texas)

Rosendahl [Vice Adm. Charles E., USN (Ret.)] Collection, History of Aviation Collection [hereafter HOAC], University of Texas at Dallas.

Correspondence (Letters, E-mails, Letter-Statements)

Mr. Charles M. Bowen.

Capt. Douglas L. Cordiner, USN (Ret.).

Capt. J. H. Cruse, USN (Ret.).

Capt. M. H. Eppes, USN (Ret.). Courtesy Evelyn Eppes Azzaretto.

Mr. Winfield E. Fromm (with attachments).

Mr. Langdon H. Fulton (with attachments).

Rear Adm. D. Ward Harrigan, USN (Ret.).

Lt. (jg) James H. Hughes, USN (Ret.) (with attachments).

Cdr. Harold W. Johnston, USN (Ret.).

Mr. Charles W. Long.

Cdr. Charles A. Mills, USN (Ret.).

Mr. Jeff Noakes.

Mr. Norman Polmar.

ACBM George W. Roberts, USN (Ret).

Lt. Cdr. James W. Spencer, USNR (Ret.).

Capt. Emmett J. Sullivan, USN (Ret.).

Lt. J. Gordon Vaeth, USN (Ret.).

Cdr. Gerald E. Wheeler, USN (Ret.).

Published Sources

Books

Allison, David Kite. *New Eye for the Navy: The Origin of Radar at the Naval Research Laboratory.* Washington, D.C.: Naval Research Laboratory, 29 September 1981.

Althoff, William F. *Sky Ships: A History of the Airship in the United States Navy.* New York: Orion Books, 1990.
Baxter, James Phinney, 3rd. *Scientists against Time.* Cambridge, Mass.: MIT Press, 1968.
Blair, Clay, Jr. *Hitler's U-Boat War: The Hunted, 1942–1945.* New York: Random House, 1998.
Brinkley, David. *Washington Goes to War.* New York: Alfred A. Knopf, 1988.
Brown, Lois. *A Radar History of World War Two: Political and Technical Imperatives.* Bristol, U.K. and Philadelphia: Institute of Physics, 1999.
Buchanan, A. R., ed. *The Navy's Air War: A Mission Completed.* New York: Harper & Bros., 1946.
Buchheim, Lothar-Günther. *U-Boat War.* Translated by Gudie Lawaetz. New York: Bantam Books, 1979.
Bush, Vannevar. *Pieces of the Action.* New York: William Morrow, 1970.
Central Office of Information *The Battle of the Atlantic: The Official Account of the Fight against the U-Boats 1939–1945.* London: His Majesty's Stationery Office, 1946.
Churchill, Winston S. *The Gathering Storm.* Boston: Houghton Mifflin, 1948.
——. *The Hinge of Fate.* Boston: Houghton Mifflin, 1950.
Cohen, Eliot A., and John Gooch. *Military Misfortunes: The Anatomy of Failure in War.* New York: Vintage Books, 1991.
Conant, James B. *My Several Lives: Memoirs of a Social Inventor.* New York: Harper & Row, 1970.
Dick, Harold G., and Douglas H. Robinson. *Graf Zeppelin and Hindenburg.* Washington, D.C.: Smithsonian Institution Press, 1985.
Dornberger, Walter. *V-2.* Translated by James Cleugh and Geoffrey Halliday. New York: Viking, 1958.
Fahey, John A. *Wasn't I the Lucky One.* Virginia Beach, Va.: B and J Books, 2000.
Farago, Ladislas. *The Tenth Fleet.* New York: Ivan Obolensky, 1962.
Friedman, Norman. *Naval Institute Guide to World Naval Weapon Systems.* London: Conway Maritime, 1983.
Frost, Holloway H. *The Battle of Jutland.* Annapolis: Naval Institute Press, 1936.
Furer, James Augustus. *Administration of the Navy Department in World War II.* Washington, D.C.: Government Printing Office, 1959.
Gannon, Michael. *Black May.* New York: HarperCollins, 1998.
——. *Operation Drumbeat.* New York: Harper & Row, 1990.
Gentile, Gary. *Shadow Divers Exposed: The Real Saga of U-869.* Philadelphia: Bellerophon Bookworks, 2006.
Gibhard, Louis A. *Evolution of Naval Radio-Electronics and Contributions of the Naval Research Laboratory.* Washington, D.C.: Naval Research Laboratory, 1979.
Gibson, R. H., and Maurice Prendergast. *The German Submarine War, 1914–1918.* London: Constable, 1931.
Hershberg, James. *James B. Conant: Harvard to Hiroshima and the Making of the Nuclear Age.* New York: Alfred A. Knopf, 1993.

Higham, Robin. *The British Rigid Airship, 1908–1931. Study in Weapons Policy*. London: G. T. Foulis, 1961.

The History of NAS Tillamook and Its Role in World War II. Gresham, Ore.: M&A Tour Books, for Tillamook Naval Air Station Museum, 1995.

Hurd, Sir Archibald. *Official History of the Great War.* Vol. 1, *The Merchant Navy.* New York: Longmans, Green, 1929.

King, Ernest J. *U.S. Navy at War 1941–1945: Official Reports to the Secretary of the Navy.* Washington, D.C.: Navy Department, 1946.

King, Ernest J., and Walter Muir Whitehall. *Fleet Admiral King: A Naval Record.* New York: W. W. Norton, 1952.

Langer, William L., and S. Everett Gleason. *The Undeclared War 1940–1941*. Gloucester, Mass.: Peter Smith, 1968.

Loewenheim, Francis L., Harold D. Langley, and Manfred Jonas, eds. *Roosevelt and Churchill: Their Secret Wartime Correspondence.* New York: Saturday Review Press/E. P. Dutton, 1975.

Lott, Arnold S. *Most Dangerous Sea.* Annapolis, Md.: Naval Institute Press, 1959.

Meigs, Montgomery C. *Slide Rules and Submarines: American Scientists and Subsurface Warfare in World War II*. Washington, D.C.: National Defense University Press, 1990.

Moffat, Alexander W. *A Navy Maverick Comes of Age*. Middletown, Conn.: Wesleyan University Press, 1977.

Morison, Samuel E. *The History of United States Naval Operations in World War II*. Vol. 1, *The Battle of the Atlantic September 1939–May 1943*. Boston: Little, Brown, 1975.

——. *The History of United States Naval Operations in World War II*. Vol. 10, *The Atlantic Battle Won May 1943–May 1945*. Boston: Little, Brown, 1975

Naval Airship Training and Experimental Command. *They Were Dependable: Airship Operation in World War Two*. 2nd ed. Lakehurst, N.J.: U.S. Naval Air Station, July 1946.

——. *War History of U.S. Naval Air Station, Lakehurst, New Jersey.* Lakehurst, N.J.: U.S. Naval Air Station, July 1946.

Padfield, Peter. *Dönitz: The Last Fuhrer.* New York: Harper & Row, 1984.

Page, Robert Morris. *The Origin of Radar.* Garden City, N.Y.: Doubleday, 1962.

Peattie, Mark R. "Japanese Strategy and Campaigns in the Pacific War, 1941–1945." In *World War II in Asia and the Pacific and War's Aftermath, with General Themes: A Handbook of Literature and Research,* edited by Lloyd E. Lee. Westport, Conn.: Greenwood, 1998.

Price, Alfred. *Aircraft versus Submarine: The Evolution of the Anti-Submarine Aircraft, 1912–1972*. Annapolis, Md.: Naval Institute Press, 1973.

Reynolds, Clarke G. *Admiral John H. Towers: The Struggle for Naval Air Supremacy.* Annapolis, Md.: Naval Institute Press, 1991.

Rhodes, Richard. *The Making of the Atomic Bomb*. New York: Simon & Schuster, 1988.

Rohwer, Jürgen. *The Critical Convoy Battles of March 1943: The Battle for HX. 229/SC122*. Annapolis, Md.: Naval Institute Press, 1977.

Roskill, S. W. *The War at Sea, 1939–1945*. London: Collins, 1960.

Runyan, Timothy J., and Jan M. Copes, eds. *To Die Gallantly: The Battle of the Atlantic.* Boulder, Colo.: Westview, 1994.

Schoenfeld, Max. *Stalking the U-Boat: USAAF Operations in World War II.* Washington, D.C.: Smithsonian Institution Press, 1995.

Shettle, M. L., Jr. *United States Naval Air Stations of World War II.* Vol. 1, *Eastern States.* Bowersville, Ga. Schaertel, 1995.

——. *United States Naval Air Stations of World War II.* Vol. 2 *Western States.* Bowersville, Ga.: Schaertel, 1995.

Shrader, Grahame F. *The Phantom War in the Northwest: And an Account of Japanese Submarine Operations on the West Coast 1941–1942,* n.p. 1969.

Smith, Richard K. *The Airships* Akron *and* Macon: *Flying Aircraft Carriers of the United States Navy.* Annapolis, Md.: Naval Institute Press, 1965.

Sternhell, Charles M., and Alan M. Thorndike. *Antisubmarine Warfare in World War II.* Report No. 51 of the Operations Evaluation Group, Office of CNO. Washington, D.C.: Navy Department, 1946.

Stewart, Irvin. *Organizing Scientific Research for War: The Administrative History of the Office of Scientific Research and Development.* New York: Arno, 1980.

Stimson, Henry L., and McGeorge Bundy. *On Active Service in Peace and War.* New York: Harper & Bros., 1947, 1948.

Terraine, John. *The U-Boat Wars, 1916–1945.* New York: G. P. Putnam's Sons, 1989.

Vaeth, J. Gordon. *Blimps and U-Boats: U.S. Navy Airships in the Battle of the Atlantic.* Annapolis, Md.: Naval Institute Press, 1997.

Williams Kathleen Broome. *Secret Weapon: U.S. High Frequency Direction Finding in the Battle of the Atlantic.* Annapolis, Md.: Naval Institute Press, 1996.

Articles in Periodicals and Essay Collections

Althoff, William F. "Airships." U.S. Naval Institute *Proceedings* 114/1/1019 (January 1988): 57–64.

——. "NAS Lakehurst: The War Years (A Photographic History)." American Aviation Historical Society *Journal* 30, no. 2 (Summer 1985): 140–51.

Belke, T. J. "Roll of Drums." U.S. Naval Institute *Proceedings* 109/962 (April 1983): 58–64.

Boyle, Richard, and Waldo Lyon. "Arctic ASW: Have We Lost?" U.S. Naval Institute *Proceedings* 124/6/1,144 (June 1998): 31–35.

Buckley, Franklin D. "Let's Try a New Weapon." U.S. Naval Institute *Proceedings* 67, no. 459 (May 1941).

Fromm, Winfield E. "The Magnetic Airborne Detector." In *Advances in Electronics* (New York: Academic, 1952), 257–99.

Furer, Julius A. "Civilian Science in the War Effort." *Army Navy Journal,* special issue (December 1945); 111, 138.

Gladwell, Malcolm. "The Talent Myth." *New Yorker,* 22 July 2002, 28–33.

Goodman, John B. "Blimp Bloodhounds." *U.S. Air Services* 28, no. 7 (July 1943).

Grosvenor, Melville Bell. "Cruise on an Escort Carrier." *National Geographic* 84, no. 5 (November 1943): 513–46.

Heinz, Karl. "German U-Boat Construction." U.S. Naval Institute *Proceedings* 81, no. 4 (April 1955): 375–90.

Hill, R. D. "The Origins of Radar." *Eos* 71, no. 27 (3 July 1990): 781–82.

Hunt, Doris S. "Blimps Will Attempt to Clear Tropic Seas of Submarine Menace." *U.S. Air Services*. 27, no. 7 (July 1942).

Knox, C. V. S. "Design Details of the Goodyear Model K Airship." *Aeronautical Digest,* Part 1, 50, no.1 (1 July 1945), 64–71, 150, 154, 156; Part 2, 50, no. 3 (1 August 1945), 64–70, 150–51; Part 3, 50, no. 5 (1 September 1945), 70–75, 180.

Lasky, Marvin. "Historical Review of Undersea Warfare Planning and Organization 1945–1960 with Emphasis on the Role of the Office of Naval Research," *U.S. Navy Journal of Underwater Acoustics* 26, no. 2 (April 1976): 329.

——. "A Historical Review of Underwater Acoustic Technology 1916–1939 with Emphasis on Undersea Warfare." *U.S. Navy Journal of Underwater Acoustic Technology* 24, no. 4 (October 1974): 597–624.

——. "Review of Scientific Effort for Undersea Warfare: 1939–1945." *U.S. Navy Journal of Underwater Acoustic Technology* 25 (July 1975): 567–84.

——. "Review of World War I Acoustic Technology." *U.S. Navy Journal of Underwater Acoustic Technology* 24, no. 3 (July 1973): 363–85.

Leary, H. F. "Eastern Sea Frontier vs. U-Boats." *Army Navy Journal*, special issue, December 1945, 59, 200.

"LTA: Vitalized Lighter-than-Air Service Shares the Task of Clearing Sea Lanes of Underwater Menace." *Naval Aviation News,* 15 September 1943, 1–7.

Milner, Marc. "Squaring Some of the Corners: The Royal Canadian Navy and the Pattern of the Atlantic War." In *To Die Gallantly: The Battle of the Atlantic,* edited by Timothy J. Runyan and Jan M. Copes. Boulder, Colo.: Westview, 1994.

Norton, Douglas M. "The Open Secret: The U.S. Navy in the Battle of the Atlantic April–December 1941." *Naval War College Review* 26, no. 4 (January–February 1974): 63–83.

O'Grady, Kent. "The Americans Are Coming! But Should We Let Them Land?" Part 1. *Noon Balloon,* no. 45 (February 1997).

Picinich, R. G., Jr. "Blimps Blast Subs." U.S. Naval Institute *Proceedings* 69, no. 488 (October 1943): 1324–34.

Robinson, Douglas H. "The Effectiveness of the Dirigible in Military Operations." American Aviation Historical Society *Journal* 19, no. 4 (4th Quarter 1974): 276–85.

——. "Zeppelins in the German Navy, 1914–1945." U.S. Naval Institute *Proceedings* 82, no. 7 (July 1956): 742–61.

Rounds, Clinton S. "Teaching an Old Dog New Tricks." U.S. Naval Institute *Proceedings* 66, no. 450 (August 1940): 1153–66.

Sarty, Roger. "Ultra, Air Power, and the Second Battle of the St. Lawrence, 1944." In *To Die Gallantly: The Battle of the Atlantic,* edited by Timothy J. Runyan and Jan M. Copes. Boulder, Colo.: Westview, 1994.

Schickendanz, Roy D. "Squadron Fourteen and the Transoceanic Crossing." *Buoyant Flight: Bulletin of the Lighter-than-Air Society* (January–February 1971).

Settle, T. G. W. "Why No Blimps?" U.S. Naval Institute *Proceedings* 65, no. 432 (February 1939): 238–40.

Smith, Richard K. "The ZRCV: Fascinating Might-Have-Been of Aeronautics." *Aerospace Historian* 12, no. 4 (October 1965): 115–21.

Sutherland, Mason. "Aboard a Blimp Hunting U-Boats." *National Geographic* 84, no. 1 (July 1943): 79–96.

Vaeth, J. Gordon. "Blimpron 14: The Africa Squadron." Naval Aviation Museum *Foundation* 2, no. 1 (January 1981): 53–59.

——. "Utility Uses for Airships." U.S. Naval Institute *Proceedings* 14, no. 3 (March 1948): 297–99.

Van Treuren, Richard. "Airships v. Submarines in WW II." Series. *Airshipworld* (March 2001, June 2001, December 2001, March 2002, September 2002, December 2002, March 2003, June 2003, September 2003, December 2003).

——. "An Effective Umbrella." *Naval History* 12, no. 3 (May/June 1998): 41–44.

——. "Georgia Draw: A Rare Duel between Air and Sea." Naval Aviation Museum *Foundation* 21, no. 2 (Fall 2000): 65–69.

——. "Making It Happen: Captain C. V. S. Knox and Aeronautical Evolution." Naval Aviation Museum *Foundation* 28, no. 1 (Spring 2007): 89–97.

Technical and Miscellaneous Documents

Aircraft Yearbook 1941. New York: Aeronautical Chamber of Commerce of America, 1941.

Airship Accidents: World War II. NAS Moffett Field, 17 September 1945. Source and author unknown. Courtesy Richard G. Van Treuren.

Airship Squadron Twelve, U.S. Naval Air Station Lakehurst ,N.J. Squadron Order No. 29-43, Pilot's check-off list [C. H. Kendall, Lt. Cdr., USN], 1943.

Fleet Airship Wing [Two] *Pilot's Manual.* Approved [Capt. M. M. Bradley, USN], n.d. [1944?].

Fleet Airships Atlantic. *Fabric Maintenance Manual for Non-Rigid Airships,* 18 December 1944.

Fleet Airships, Atlantic. *MAD Instructions.* 1944[?].

Fleet Airships, Atlantic. *Navigator's Manual.* 1943[?].

Fleet Airships, Atlantic. "Operational Flight," ZP-24 [photographic essay with text], 1944.

Fleet Airships Pacific Tactical Unit, NAAF Del Mar. *Fight Training Exercises.* Approved [Capt. H. N. Coulter, USN], 24 August 1944. Courtesy Capt. Frederick N. Klein, Jr., USN (Ret.).

Fromm, Winfield E. "Personal Reminiscences of the Magnetic Airborne Detector," November 1987. Five-page statement prepared for author.

Goodyear Aircraft Corporation, Akron, Ohio. *United States Navy Handbook for Fabric Repair and Maintenance of Airship Envelopes,* 1 July 1945.

——. *United States Navy G-type Airships: Descriptive Specifications,* January 1944.

——. *United States Navy K-type Airships: Control Car Assemblies,* November 1943.

——. *United States Navy K-type Airships: Descriptive Specifications,* September 1942.

——. *United States Navy K-type Airships: Pilot's Manual,* September 1942.

——. *United States Navy M-type Airships: Pilot's Manual,* August 1944.

Grossnick, Roy A., ed. *Kite Balloons to Airships . . . The Navy's Lighter-than-Air Experience.* Washington, D.C.: Government Printing Office, for Deputy Chief of Naval Operations (Air Warfare) and Commander, Naval Air Systems Command, 1987.

Kane, Capt. John C., USN (Ret.), personal papers. Courtesy Captain Kane.
Klein, Capt. Frederick N., Jr., USN (Ret.), notebook, Officers Ground School (Class L-19), Naval Training School (LTA), June–October 1942, NAS Lakehurst, New Jersey. Courtesy Captain Klein.
"Major Accidents: Pacific Coast L.T.A." NAS Moffett Field, 28 March 1944. Source and author unknown. Courtesy Richard G. Van Treuren.
National Advisory Committee for Aeronautics [hereafter NACA]. *Annual Reports:* Twenty-fifth (1939), Twenty-sixth (1940), Twenty-seventh (1941), Twenty-eighth (1942), Twenty-ninth (1943), Thirtieth (1944), and Thirty-first (1945).
Naval Airship Training and Experimental Command, NAS Lakehurst, N.J. *Statistical Summary of United States Fleet Airship Operations in World War Two.* 15 February 1946. Courtesy Cdr. James M. Punderson, USN (Ret.).
Noakes, Jeff. "The Thirteenth Recommendation: Blimps for Canada." In *Canadian Military History since the 17th Century,* A-JS-007-DHH/AF-001, Canadian Military History Conference, 2000, 195–204. Courtesy Mr. Noakes.
Notes on the Operation of Nonrigid Airships. Washington, D.C.: Government Printing Office, 1920. Reprinted NAS Lakehurst, 5 September 1939.
Office of Scientific Research and Development, National Defense Research Committee, Division 6—Section 6.1, "Signal Recognition Manual, M.A.D. Type IV-B2 in Airships," December 1943.
Rosendahl, Charles E. "How Soon We Forget: A History of United States Navy Airships in World War II." Unpublished manuscript. Courtesy Captain Marion H. Eppes, USN (Ret.).
Shock, James R., comp. "A History of U.S. Navy Airships (Non-Rigids, Semi-Rigid and Metalclad), 1915 through 1962, by Individual Airship." Courtesy Mr. Shock.
Ulrich, Capt. L. Russell, USN (Ret.), notebook, Officers Training School (Class 15), 1941, NAS Lakehurst, New Jersey. Courtesy Captain Ulrich.
United States Department of the Interior, Bureau of Mines. "Helium Symposium," 14–15 October 1958, Amarillo, Texas.
U.S. Naval Air Station Lakehurst, N.J. "Lighter-than-Air Ordnance and Gunnery" [Lt. J. C. Carew, USNR, Gunnery Officer], December 1942.
Van Treuren, Richard G., comp. *Attacks by U.S. Navy Airships during World War II.* Courtesy Mr. Van Treuren.
Widdecombe, Lt. Cdr. R. W., USN (Ret.), selected papers, notably "Operational Experience with Large Navy Patrol Airships, 1940–1961," to Capt. Norman L. Beal, USNR, Memorandum-Report, 1 November 1985. Courtesy Lieutenant Commander Widdecombe.

Interviews (Audio-Recorded)

Andrews, Rear Adm. Richard S., self-recorded remarks prepared for author, 1977.
Bradley, Capt. Michael M., USN (Ret.), interview by author, Springfield, Virginia, 24 October 1977.
Delong, Capt. W. E., interview by author, Fairfield, California, 26 June 1999.

Eppes, Capt. Marion H., USN (Ret.), interviews by author, Bethesda, Maryland, 23–24 October 1977, 26 November 1978, and 2 December 1983.
Hotham, Cdr. James A., USN (Ret.), interview by author, Akron, Ohio, 20 September 1997.
Kane, Capt. John C., Jr., USN (Ret.), interview by author, Akron, Ohio, 19 September 1997.
Kauffman, Charles, interview by author, Lakewood, New Jersey, 15 July 1977.
Klein, Capt. Frederick N., Jr., USN (Ret.), interview by author, Toms River, New Jersey, 5 January 1983.
Levitt, Cdr. Ben B., USN (Ret.), interview by author, Akron, Ohio, 19 September 1997.
Mayer, Roland E., interview by author, Alexandria, Virginia, 30 January 2001.
McMillan, Cdr. Edward R., USN (Ret.), interview by author, Silverdale, Washington, 18 May 1999.
Pierce, Rear Adm. George E., USN (Ret.), interviews by author, Bethesda, Maryland, 2 July and 27 November 1977.
Rieker, Cdr. John B., USN (Ret.), self-recorded remarks prepared for author, 11 November 1977.
Shannon, Cdr. Robert USN (Ret.), interview by author, Alameda, California, 26 June 1999.
Smith, Lt. Harris F., USNR (Ret.), interview by author, Califon, New Jersey, 5 August 1977.
Ulrich, Capt. L. Russell, USN (Ret.), interview by author, Fairfield, California, 26 June 1999.
Vaeth, Lt. J. Gordon, USNR (Ret.), interview by author, Olympia, Washington, 19 May 1999.
Wheeler, Cdr. Gerald E., USN (Ret.), interview by author, Los Gatos, California, 27 June 1999.
Widdecombe, Cdr. Richard W., USN (Ret.), interviews by author, Knoxville, Tennessee, 30–31 May 1999.

Newspapers

The Airship (NAS Lakehurst, New Jersey), various volumes/issues, 1941–45.
New York Times. 1939–45.

Index

About the Author

WILLIAM F. ALTHOFF is the author of *USS* Los Angeles*: The Navy's Venerable Airship* and *Aviation Technology*. A former Ramsey Fellow in naval aviation history at the Smithsonian National Air & Space Museum, he has conducted research on polar aeronautics during several visits to the Arctic. This is his fifth book of history. He resides in New Jersey.

THE NAVAL INSTITUTE PRESS is the book-publishing arm of the U.S. Naval Institute, a private, nonprofit, membership society for sea service professionals and others who share an interest in naval and maritime affairs. Established in 1873 at the U.S. Naval Academy in Annapolis, Maryland, where its offices remain today, the Naval Institute has members worldwide.

Members of the Naval Institute support the education programs of the society and receive the influential monthly magazine *Proceedings* or the colorful bimonthly magazine *Naval History* and discounts on fine nautical prints and on ship and aircraft photos. They also have access to the transcripts of the Institute's Oral History Program and get discounted admission to any of the Institute-sponsored seminars offered around the country.

The Naval Institute's book-publishing program, begun in 1898 with basic guides to naval practices, has broadened its scope to include books of more general interest. Now the Naval Institute Press publishes about seventy titles each year, ranging from how-to books on boating and navigation to battle histories, biographies, ship and aircraft guides, and novels. Institute members receive significant discounts on the Press's more than eight hundred books in print.

Full-time students are eligible for special half-price membership rates. Life memberships are also available.

For a free catalog describing Naval Institute Press books currently available, and for further information about joining the U.S. Naval Institute, please write to:

Member Services
U.S. NAVAL INSTITUTE
291 Wood Road
Annapolis, MD 21402-5034
Telephone: 800.233.8764
Fax: 410.571.1703
Web address: *www.usni.org*